ORDER FORM

LexisNexis® Butterworths
Sale of a Business, 5th Edition

YES! I would like to order _____ copies of the Sale of a Business, 5th Edition at $90 + GST (ISBN 0 433 44461-4)
I understand that I will be placed on standing order to receive future editions on a 30-day examination basis.
New editions are published regularly as required.

Number of Copies	Per Copy Price (plus GST)	You Save
1 to 9	$90	n/a
10 to 24	$86	5%
25 to 49	$81	10%
50 to 99	$77	15%
100 or more	$72	20%

Order in quantity and save!

SUB TOTAL $ _____

Add 7% G.S.T. $ _____

GRAND TOTAL $ _____

Price & other details are subject to change without notice.
We pay shipping & handling if payment accompanies order.

CUSTOMER INFORMATION

Firm/Organization _____

Name _____

Dept/Title _____

Address _____

City/Town _____

Phone # _____

Fax # _____

Email _____

BILLING INFORMATION

Butterworths Acct. # _____

P.O. # _____

Charge my: ❑ Mastercard ❑ VISA ❑ AMEX

Card # _____

❑ Personal Card ❑ Company Card ❑ Cheque Enclosed

Cardholder's Name _____

Expiry Date _____

Signature _____

5 WAYS TO ORDER

Phone:	1.800.668.6481 • 905.479.2665
Fax:	1.800.461.3275 • 905.479.2826
Email:	orders@lexisnexis.ca
Online:	www.lexisnexis.ca
Contact:	your Account Executive

 LexisNexis®

LexisNexis Canada Inc. 123 Commerce Valley Drive East, Suite 700, Markham, Ontario, L3T 7W8

Sale of a Business, 5th Edition
© LexisNexis Canada 2004
November 2004

Members of the LexisNexis Group worldwide

Canada	LexisNexis Canada Inc, 123 Commerce Valley Drive East, MARKHAM, Ontario
Argentina	Abeledo Perrot, Jurisprudencia Argentina and Depalma, BUENOS AIRES
Australia	Butterworths, a Division of Reed International Books Australia Pty Ltd, CHATSWOOD, New South Wales
Austria	ARD Betriebsdienst and Verlag Orac, VIENNA
Chile	Publitecsa and Conosur Ltda, SANTIAGO DE CHILE
Czech Republic	Orac sro, PRAGUE
France	Éditions du Juris-Classeur SA, PARIS
Hong Kong	Butterworths Asia (Hong Kong), HONG KONG
Hungary	Hvg Orac, BUDAPEST
India	Butterworths India, NEW DELHI
Ireland	Butterworths (Ireland) Ltd, DUBLIN
Italy	Giuffré, MILAN
Malaysia	Malayan Law Journal Sdn Bhd, KUALA LUMPUR
New Zealand	Butterworths of New Zealand, WELLINGTON
Poland	Wydawnictwa Prawnicze PWN, WARSAW
Singapore	Butterworths Asia, SINGAPORE
South Africa	Butterworth Publishers (Pty) Ltd, DURBAN
Switzerland	Stämpfli Verlag AG, BERNE
United Kingdom	Butterworths Tolley, a Division of Reed Elsevier (UK), LONDON, WC2A
USA	LexisNexis, DAYTON, Ohio

Library and Archives Canada Cataloguing in Publication

Babe, Jennifer E., 1953-
    Sale of a business : reproduction of Title 9 of Canadian forms & precedents : commercial transactions / Jennifer E. Babe. — 5th ed.

Includes index.
ISBN 0-433-44461-4

    1. Sale of business enterprises--Law and legislation--Canada.
2. Sale of business enterprises—Law and legislation—Canada—Forms. I. Title. II. Title: Canadian forms & precedents : commercial transactions.

KE1345.B32 2004	346.71'065	C2004-906274-3
KF1355.B32 2004		

Printed and Bound in Canada.

SALE OF A BUSINESS

5TH EDITION

JENNIFER E. BABE, B.A., LL.B., LL.M.

Member of the Law Society of Upper Canada

Reproduction of "Title 9" of
Canadian Forms & Precedents: Commercial Transactions

Miller Thomson LLP

LexisNexis®
Butterworths

ABOUT THE AUTHOR

Jennifer E. Babe, LL.B., LL.M., a partner at Miller Thomson LLP, practices commercial law, with a focus on secured transactions, the securing of sales and leases of significant products and the purchases of businesses, assets and shares. Ms. Babe is the Chair of the Commercial Law Strategy of the Uniform Law Conference of Canada, and is listed in "Women in the Lead" – Ivey Women in Management Newsletter Directory.

For E.W.T., V.B., J.G. and A.H.
who put up with this and me during the writing

ACKNOWLEDGEMENTS

There are many people to thank for their ongoing patience and assistance in the completion of this book. Any purchase and sale transaction is made so much simpler when there is a team of people to assist you and the client.

The team of solicitors at Miller Thomson who assisted me in writing portions of this text in their areas of expertise are as follows:

Bulk Sales Act	John J. Chapman, Jeff Carhart, Arthi Sambasivan
Employment and Labour Relations	Hugh R. Dyer and Fred Heerema*
Business Valuations and Motor Vehicles	Mark J. Fuller*
Taxation	Susan M. Manwaring and Douglas Han
Realty, Estate Conveyancing	F. Max E. Maréchaux
Realty and Powers of Sale	Douglas J.R. Moodie, Peter Prattas
Securities	Brent H. Moore*, Robert Stewart
Estates	Sara J. Plant*
Commercial	James A Proskurniak, Gerry Hollyer, Robert Stewart
Corporate paralegal, corporate records	Dianne Singer*, Elizabeth Gillis, Brenda Taylor
Environmental Concerns	A. Catherina Spoel and Norman S. Rankin
Pensions	Greg Callahan, Brent K. Duguid, Robert J. Fuller, Q.C. and Dona L. Campbell
Privacy, Franchising	Paul Jones

* formerly of this firm

DISCLAIMER

While every effort has been made to ensure the completeness and utility of the material contained in this book, there is no warranty, express or implied, that the user will achieve the desired end. The publisher and author disclaim any liability for loss, whether direct or consequential, flowing from the use of the precedents and other materials contained in the work.

CD-ROM INFORMATION

© LexisNexis Canada Ltd. 2004

Notice: This disc contains copyrighted material and may be copied only by a registered subscriber for the purpose of creating working files. Unlimited copying is not permitted. Network users will require a multi-user licence. Any other use is prohibited. Please contact LexisNexis Canada Inc. with copyright inquiries.

Introduction

The enclosed CD-ROM contains the checklists and forms included in *Canadian Forms & Precedents: Commercial Transactions*, "Title 9 – Sale of a Business" and is designed to be used in conjunction with *Sale of a Business*, 5th edition.

The checklists and forms are in Word 97 format. Once the selection of the appropriate form or precedent is made, a lawyer need only provide the information to be inserted and an assistant can then easily locate and complete the form on a computer.

Please note that although most of the forms and precedents included in *Canadian Forms & Precedents: Commercial Transactions*, "Title 9 – Sale of a Business" have been successfully used, there is no warranty, express or implied, that these documents are appropriate for the reader. Liability for the use, or misuse, of any documents is hereby waived.

System Requirements

The files on the enclosed CD-ROM have been designed for use on a personal computer with the following capabilities and configuration:

> IBM or IBM-compatible with a hard drive and CD-ROM drive
> Windows 95 or higher operating system
> Microsoft Word for Windows 97 or higher software
> At least 4.5 MB of hard disk space

Copying Files to Hard Drive

Before they can be used, files must be copied from the CD-ROM to a local hard drive or network drive. Create a folder (e.g., Sale of a Business 5) on the drive into which you wish to copy the files. Open Windows Explorer. Click on your CD-ROM drive. Select the Word files and copy to the Sale of a Business 5 folder.

USING THE CHECKLISTS AND FORMS

What's on the CD-ROM?
File names on the CD-ROM correspond to the form names in the book. The Table of Contents lists all forms by form number and form name.

The checklists and forms are set out in a way that makes them easy to use and, wherever possible, a standard and consistent style has been adopted.

Numbering
Recitals are not numbered
Sections are numbered 1, 2, 3, etc.
Subsections are numbered 1(a), 1(b), 1(c), etc.
Paragraphs in subsections are numbered 1(1)(a), 1(1)(b), 1(1)(c), etc. 1(a)(i), (ii), (iii), etc.

Round Brackets
Round brackets are used in the following instances:

a) to indicate pieces of information known only to the end user of the form, such as names, addresses, dates, descriptions of fixtures, etc. For example, Whereas (*principal*) has entered into a contract with you dated (*date*) for the supply of (*specify goods or as the case may be*);

b) to give the user specific instructions. For example, (*State clearly the name of the franchise or area franchise in the form in which the offer will be made to the public*);

c) to enclose explanatory notes/text provided by the contributor and which directly relate to a specific form or precedent. These notes appear in roman type within round brackets directly underneath the title of the form and preceding the form itself.

Square Brackets

Some precedents contain alternative or optional wordings. If the alternative or optional word or phrase is singular, it will appear in italics within square brackets directly following the existing word or phrase as follows:

> head office [*principal place of business*]

If an entire optional clause or paragraph is presented, it will appear in italics within square brackets following the existing clause or paragraph, with the word "OR" in between as follows:

> The Licensor shall install the Computer program on the Designated Hardware at the Designated Location.

> OR

> [*The Licensee shall be responsible for the installation of the Computer Program and the Licensor shall perform the installation services specified in the service specification.*]

If several optional words or phrases are offered, they all appear in italics within square brackets with the word "or" in between each option as follows:

> We the undersigned authorize and request you to open an account or accounts in our joint names as [*either* or *anyone* or *both* or *all*] of us shall direct.

Completing the Forms

Retrieving a Form

Forms are accessed in the same way as any other Word file. Within Microsoft Word, select Open from the File menu, choose the drive and folder into which the files were copied, and then select the file you wish to complete.

Using a Form

We have created the files using certain defaults, such as line margins, tabs, spacing, and justification, but you are free to change the page layout, edit the forms, add or delete information, or make other client-specific modifications, just as you would with documents you create from scratch.

Saving a Form

Once the form has been completed for a specific client matter, it is ready to save or print. Save the form under a new file name to preserve the text of the original file.

Printing a Form

Depending on the application you are using, you may have different print options available to you. The type of printer you use will also have an effect on the final appearance of the form. Any style changes you elect to use may require adjustment or realignment to achieve desired page lengths or page layout.

SALE OF A BUSINESS

TABLE OF CONTENTS

TABLE OF CONTENTS

TABLE OF CONTENTS

TABLE OF CONTENTS

TABLE OF CONTENTS

Page

1. PRELIMINARY NOTES

9.001—Discussed in this title is structuring and documenting purchases and sales of businesses. There are some references to case-law, but by and large the title refers only to statutory authority. The goal is to direct the solicitor to legal issues but not discuss those issues in a detailed legal analysis. The focus is on the practical concerns in effecting the sale.

Much of this title is written from the perspective of a solicitor representing the purchaser, as it is the purchaser's solicitor who bears the largest burden of conducting appropriate due diligence to determine that the client is actually getting what it is paying for without also acquiring unwanted problems. This title also assumes that the vendor and purchaser are at arm's length and the solicitor is representing only one side. If the user is asked to represent two parties, such as the purchaser and its financiers, due regard needs to be had to the *Rules of Conduct* of the Law Society of Upper Canada and such Rules observed.

Able assistance may be available from other solicitors within the firm who are specialized in various areas of the law and who can handle legal issues concerned with such matters as employees, pension plans, taxation implications, realty conveyancing, securities laws issues, the avoidance of environmental liability, and pension plan concerns, let alone the remaining paperwork and organization. If such a team is not available this title is designed to assist in the key aspects of these areas of the law with sample precedents that may be used as the starting point for appropriate modification and tailoring to each client's unique circumstances and instructions.

This title does not explore the areas of computer contracts, franchises and other topics for which there are separate titles in Butterworth's Canadian Forms and Precedents. For such unique topics, please refer to those titles for study and precedents.

As a starting point for each file, one must clearly determine the nature of the business being purchased or sold, such that peculiar problems unique to that industry or trade become apparent. A picture is indeed worth a thousand words. If at all possible, endeavour to attend at the facility or locations the client is endeavouring to sell or purchase. An inspection and guided tour of the operation will make clear in the drafter's mind many more details and issues that will need to be addressed properly to ensure the client's interests are preserved. Given the widespread use of trade jargon, it may be that the visual inspection raises questions that the clients had assumed were understood by use of their industry phrases and names.

Such due diligence is of concern whether the client is buying assets or shares. It is possible that the purchasing client has leapt to the conclusion that it wishes to purchase assets but certain statutory concerns may not have crossed its mind. It may only be after full discussion with the solicitor as to relevant income tax, Bulk Sales Act, land transfer tax and other issues, that the deal may need to be restructured to a share transaction (or vice versa) to avoid unpleasant income tax consequences or statutory liabilities.

It will also be necessary to effect a number of searches of public records to ensure that the assets or shares of the target company may be purchased free and clear of third parties' lien claims and encumbrances. In addition, there are such matters as arranging for employees to be hired or fired, accounting for pension plan obligations and surpluses, assets leased from third parties and numerous matters to investigate.

Once the due diligence is complete, there are all the necessary documents to record the agreement of purchase and sale, convey title to the assets or record transfer of the share ownership, and possibly create and organize a purchasing entity. It is also necessary to organize all of the events to come together for a particular closing day, with a closing agenda that will be changing up to the time of the start of the closing and throughout the closing as documents are waived, varied or created. This is of course somewhat complicated if the purchaser also has to conclude a borrowing to do a "leveraged buy-out" to use the target assets or shares as a source of collateral for the loan needed to make payment of part of the price. Alternately, there could be vendor take-back security or both vendor take-back and third party financing.

Post-closing, there will be transfer documents to record, income and other taxation remittances to make or file, reporting letters to lenders, reporting letters to clients, creation of closing books and following up on undertakings. In short, there is much to do and organization is of the essence.

The balance of this title outlines the legal implications of the foregoing topics and tries to provide helpful precedents where possible.

2. PRELIMINARY ISSUES

General

9.010—The fundamental question in structuring a transaction is whether the client should be buying specific assets to the exclusion of certain liabilities or acquiring all or the majority of the shares in a target company. Many statutory and practical concerns must be considered to assist the client in making the decision to acquire or sell assets versus shares.

Tax Planning and Consequences

9.020—The tax consequences of the sale will directly impact on the vendor and the purchaser. It is of utmost importance that this issue be considered by the parties in the preliminary stages. Generally, from a taxation perspective, a vendor prefers to sell shares and a purchaser prefers to buy assets. Proper analysis of the tax characteristics of the underlying assets of the business will be required to assess the costs or benefits of the agreed form of the transaction. It is critical that this analysis be completed prior to the final negotiation of the purchase price for both parties. In fact, the sale of shares by the vendor instead of assets may be significantly less expensive from a tax perspective, with the result that the vendor may be able to lower the asking price significantly enough that it will be cost effective for the purchaser to agree to purchase shares instead of assets.

The general preferences of both parties are summarized below, followed by a discussion of further issues which should be considered, the allocation of the purchase price among assets on an asset sale, and finally, a few negotiating tips to assist the parties in reaching an agreement.

Vendor

9.021—The sale of capital property gives rise to a capital gain, 50 per cent of which is included in income for federal tax purposes. Generally, this inclusion rate is the same for provincial income tax. The capital gain is the difference between the vendor's adjusted cost base of the capital property sold and the purchase price. Shares (unless the vendor is a trader or dealer in securities) are generally considered to be capital property and therefore only 50 per cent of the appreciation is subject to tax. Further, the Income Tax Act[1] (the "ITA"), exempts from tax $500,000 of capital gains realized on the disposition of qualified small business corporation shares (generally shares of a Canadian–controlled private corporation substantially all the assets of which are used to carry on an active business in Canada). This factor creates a strong bias in favour of the sale of shares of a Canadian-controlled private corporation by a vendor.

If assets are sold, the quantum tax cost to the vendor will be dependent upon the underlying tax characteristics of the assets of the business. For example, the tax cost may be reduced if the vendor corporation has non-capital or net capital losses available to offset any income inclusion or gain. Capital property (other than depreciable property, for example, land) sold gives rise to capital gain; depreciable capital property to recapture to original cost (100 per cent taxable) and capital gain above original cost; inventory gives rise to income gains; eligible capital property gives rise to income treatment but only 50 per cent of the proceeds received in excess of cumulative eligible capital is taxable, therefore the treatment is analogous to capital gain treatment.

On an asset sale, a further consideration for the vendor is the tax cost of distributing the proceeds from the corporation subsequent to the sale which is a second level of taxation resulting from the asset sale. The non-taxable portion of the capital gain realized is added to the corporation's capital dividend account and can be distributed to the shareholders as a tax-free dividend provided the appropriate election is filed by the corporation using Form T2054 prior to the dividend being declared. Also relevant to the cost of distribution of the proceeds to the vendor is whether the corporation is a Canadian-controlled private corporation. If so, the tax paid on the proceeds will be added to the corporation's Refundable Dividend Tax On Hand account, and the corporation will receive $1 refund for every $3 of dividend declared, reducing the overall tax cost by refunding to the corporation a portion of the tax it paid on the sale at the time the corporation declares a taxable dividend to its shareholders. If the vendor intends to utilize the proceeds in the corporation after the sale, the second level of the taxation issue can generally be ignored.

---

1. R.S.C. 1985, c. 1 (5th Supp.), as amended.

Purchaser

9.022—The purchaser is generally concerned with the post-transaction tax characteristics of the business; in particular, those which will enable it to shelter tax on income earned in carrying on the business after the transaction is completed. If a purchaser agrees to buy shares, the assets of the corporation bought generally retain the tax characteristics held before the transaction was completed. The purchase price is not reflected in the cost base of the assets of the corporation which form the basis upon which tax depreciation can be claimed. If the assets in the corporation are relatively recent purchases, their undepreciated capital cost may be high and therefore this will not be a significant concern to the purchaser when negotiating the structure. If, however, the undepreciated capital costs of assets are relatively low, future tax shelter will be minimal and dispositions after the transaction is completed could give rise to recapture and capital gains, the tax on which the purchaser will be required to pay.

If the purchase is being financed, the purchaser will be interested in how best to utilize the deduction for interest on the money borrowed. If the transaction is structured as an asset sale, the interest will be deductible against the profit realized in carrying on the business. If shares are bought the interest will have to be deducted by the shareholder. Whether this will be as beneficial will depend on the circumstances of the shareholder.

A high cost base in the shares purchased is a benefit that will not be realized by the purchaser until disposition, at which time the capital gain realized will be less. In certain circumstances, it may be possible to increase the cost of the assets in the corporation to equal the cost of shares purchased by winding-up the purchased corporation into a parent corporation. If available, this tax structure will further minimize the purchaser's concern about structuring the transaction as a share sale.

Other Relevant Considerations

9.023—Losses: A purchase of shares gives rise to an acquisition of control and loss restrictions. (See **Para. 9.052** for further discussion of the tax impact of an acquisition of control and these losses carry forward restrictions). If the purchaser intends to carry on the same or similar business, the non-capital losses will be available to shelter future income earned. On a purchase of assets, losses cannot be utilized and therefore to the extent the business has losses that can be used subsequent to the acquisition of control, the purchaser will prefer to acquire shares.

9.024—Tax History: If the transaction is a share sale, a purchaser will want the vendor to represent and warrant that there are no undisclosed tax liabilities of the corporation. If there are Notices of Reassessment issued against the corporation or waivers filed and therefore years for which the tax liability has not been accurately determined the vendor will be required to indemnify the purchaser for unknown/undisclosed liability before the purchaser will agree to a share purchase. **[See Para. 9.401]**

9.025—Replacement Property Rules: If the vendor intends to carry on additional or new business, it may be able to take advantage of the replacement property rules found in section 44 of the ITA,[1] which generally defer the tax payable on disposition of a former business property (capital or depreciable) if the taxpayer acquires a "replacement" property, to the time that the "replacement" property is sold. If the vendor is eligible to take advantage of these rules, the cost of selling assets will be reduced.

---

1. R.S.C. 1985, c. 1 (5th Supp.), as amended.

9.026—Accounts Receivable: Generally the sale of accounts receivable, a capital asset, gives rise to capital gains or losses. In some cases, accounts receivable are eligible for income treatment. The impact of the different rules can be problematic for a vendor on the sale of accounts receivable, resulting in an income inclusion for previous reserves claimed for doubtful accounts together with capital loss treatment on the sale, which capital loss will not fully offset. If the parties agree to an asset sale and all or substantially all of the assets of a business that is carried on in Canada is sold, the parties can jointly elect under section 22 of the ITA[1] (using Form T2022) regarding the tax treatment of the receivables sold. To be eligible for this election the purchaser must propose to continue to carry on the same business.

If a Form T2022 is filed, the vendor will be able to deduct on income account, the difference between the face amount of the receivables and the proceeds received, and the purchaser is required to include the same amount in income. Subsequent to the transaction, the purchaser is able to treat the receivables as its own, claiming an allowance for doubtful accounts and bad debt expense. This issue is not a concern if the vendor sells shares.

---

1. R.S.C. 1985, c. 1 (5th Supp.), as amended.

9.027— Capital Cost Allowance: Classes and Rates—Certain capital cost allowance classes which carry favourable rates of depreciation are no longer available to taxpayers. Thus, if the assets are purchased, they will be added to new classes with a lower rate of depreciation. If shares are purchased, the class will not change and the high rate of depreciation will continue to be available.

Another consideration is the half-year rule. In the year of acquisition of an asset a taxpayer is deemed to have owned the asset for half of the year. The net effect is that the taxpayer is only permitted to deduct one-half of the depreciation which can otherwise be claimed for such an asset in the year of acquisition. If shares are purchased, ownership of the assets does not change and the half-year rule does not apply.

9.028—Small Business Rates: If the vendor qualifies for the small business deduction, the effective tax rate on gains realized on the disposition of assets will be lower than on the disposition of shares (Note: Ontario government clawback of small business rate if company earns income over a certain threshold which is $400,000 in 2004. As well, the small business rate is not available to companies with taxable capital in excess of $15 million and is circumscribed for companies with $10-15 million of taxable capital.

9.029—Land Transfer Tax: If the corporation owns land and building, land transfer tax is payable by the purchaser on acquisition of the property. A share sale does not normally give rise to this concern. [**See Paras. 9.075–9.078 for further information on this tax.**]

9.030—Retail Sales Tax: Generally, retail sales tax is exigible on the sale of tangible personal property or goods and therefore the purchaser of assets of a business will be required to pay it notwithstanding that the goods are "used". The retail sales tax legislation in each province should be reviewed to calculate the retail sales tax cost of the asset purchase.

In certain provinces, exemptions will be available which are applicable to certain goods purchased such as real property, finished goods, and inventories available for resale. Further, the sale of shares is exempt from retail sales tax and if the sales tax cost is expected to be high consideration should be given to a share sale.

If the purchaser does not wish to purchase the shares of the existing corporation because of unknown liabilities or other reasons, it may be possible to structure the transaction to minimize retail sales tax payable. This is accomplished by negotiating that the vendor will transfer the assets to be sold with the purchase to a newly incorporated subsidiary and have the purchaser acquire the shares of that subsidiary. In certain provinces, the transfer of assets from a parent to a subsidiary is exempt from retail sales tax and therefore this reorganization enables the transaction to be completed without payment of the retail sales tax. Particular provinces have rules which require the vendor to remain a subsidiary for a minimum period of time.[1] Parties should be cautious when implementing such a plan and the retail sales tax office in the province of the vendor should be contacted to confirm that this reorganization would be effective and would not be considered to be an offensive avoidance of retail sales tax.

Retail sales tax will not be an issue in participating provinces[2] for which the Harmonized Sales Tax (the "HST") applies. Although it has a provincial "component", the HST operates under substantially the same rules as the federal Goods and Services Tax. Thus, a vendor and purchaser may be eligible to make an election under section 167 of the Excise Tax Act for an exemption. [See Paras. 9.1040-9.1043 for further information on the GST and HST].

---

1. Including B.C. and Sask. In 2004, Ontario has released draft regulations to provide for such a hold period.

2. As of April 1, 1997, when the HST came into effect, the participating provinces were Nova Scotia, New Brunswick and Newfoundland.

Allocation of Purchase Price—Asset Sale

9.031—If the parties agree on a sale of assets, they should allocate the purchase price to the specific assets sold. To those assets which are expensive to sell, the vendor will want to allocate the least costs and vice versa. On the other hand, the purchaser generally will want to allocate the largest portion of the price to those assets which give rise to current immediate deductions (*i.e. those which are the most expensive for the vendor to sell*).

Section 68 of the ITA[1] permits the Canada Revenue Agency to reallocate the purchase price amongst the assets bought if the allocation is unreasonable and notwithstanding the parties have agreed otherwise. It is generally the case that Revenue Canada will not interfere with the parties' agreed allocation if hard bargaining of that allocation can be demonstrated. In any event, the parties should attach a schedule to the purchase and sale agreement setting out the allocation agreed upon and should covenant and agree to file future tax returns using the agreed figures.

---

1. R.S.C. 1985, c. 1 (5th Supp.), as amended.

Negotiating Tips

9.032—Vendor: When acting on behalf of the vendor, estimate the tax cost of selling shares vs. assets to ascertain how much more tax, if any, will be paid if assets are sold and the proceeds are distributed to the shareholder, as compared to that paid on a sale of shares. Determine whether the vendor wants the proceeds paid to the shareholders or whether the proceeds are to be used to carry on another business or the same business elsewhere. Analyze from the purchaser's perspective, the aspects of a purchase of assets (*i.e. losses cannot be carried forward, shifting capital cost allowance classes, ability to bump assets with the windup provisions*) to help in negotiation.

9.033—Purchaser: When acting on behalf of the purchaser, counsel should obtain disclosure of information which will enable the purchaser to determine the cost of the purchase of shares over the purchase of assets. Disclosure should also be made of all tax liabilities and careful consideration should be given to the potential for future tax assessments against prior years.

Goods and Services Tax ("GST")

9.040—The sale of a business enterprise by sale of shares or assets raises specific GST problems which must be addressed.

Generally, the GST is imposed by section 165 of the Excise Tax Act[1] at a rate equal to 7 per cent of the consideration paid for the taxable supply. A "supply" for GST purposes is defined to include any provision of a property or service and includes any sale, transfer, lease or disposition of property. Any such disposition made in the course of a commercial activity attracts GST.

The federal government and certain participating provinces[2] have implemented the Harmonized Sales Tax (the "HST"). The HST is a value-added tax which operates at the rate of 15 per cent and is composed of a federal component (7 per cent like the GST) and a provincial component (8 per cent). The HST is administered by the Canada Revenue Agency under essentially the same rules as the GST and applies to the same goods and services.

Whether a supply is made in a participating province and subject to the 15 per cent HST rate or in a non-participating province at the 7 per cent GST rate will depend on the "place of supply rules". The following commentary relating to GST applies to HST for the sale of a business in the participating provinces. The potential tax costs or cash flow issues related to the GST on the sale of a business will be magnified in participating provinces which have the higher 15% HST rate.

The province of Quebec has a sales tax ("TPS") which is substantially the same as the GST. If a particular transaction involves a supply of shares or assets in Quebec, consideration must be given to the application of TPS as well as GST. Quebec advisors should be consulted.

---

1. R.S.C. 1985, c. E-15 (en. S.C. 1990, c. 45, s. 12, adds new s. 165; am. 1993, c. 27, s. 31).

2. As at April 1, 1997, when the HST came into effect, the participating provinces were Nova Scotia, New Brunswick and Newfoundland.

Purchase and Sale of Shares of a Corporation

9.041—Equity securities are specifically included in the definition of "financial instrument" under the Excise Tax Act[1] and the transfer of ownership of a financial instrument is further defined to be a "financial service". The provision of supplies which are financial services are exempt from the application of the GST pursuant to Part VII of Schedule V to the Excise Tax Act. As a result, the purchase and sale of shares will not attract GST.

Ancillary costs to the making of an exempt supply (*i.e. the professional fees and other costs incurred in connection with the share sale*) are not exempt from GST and do not generate input tax credits for either party to the exempt transaction. Depending on the size of the transaction, the payment of GST on such ancillary costs (*without a corresponding input tax credit*) could be a strong incentive to structuring the transaction as an asset sale since an asset sale is not considered to be an exempt supply (*see further discussion in (b) below*). To counteract this bias in favour of asset transactions, specific legislative authority provides some relief from these rules.

Subsection 186(2) of the Excise Tax Act[2] provides purchasers with access to input tax credits for ancillary costs incurred in a "takeover" transaction. The input tax credits are only available after the shares have been acquired or the proposed acquisition was completely abandoned, regardless of when the GST was actually paid. It is the Canada Revenue Agency's administrative position that taxpayers can take advantage of this provision if the transaction contemplates the purchase of 90 per cent of all of the shares of a corporation that the purchaser does not currently own. It is therefore not restricted to transactions where a purchaser does not currently own any shares or owns less than 10 per cent of the shares of the corporation bought. This administrative position significantly broadens the application of this relieving provision.

---

1. R.S.C. 1985, c. E-15.

2. *Ibid.*, (en. S.C. 1990, c. 45, s. 12, adds new s. 186(2) (am. 1993, c. 27, s. 49)).

Purchase and Sale of Business Assets

9.042—The sale of assets used in a business operation is a taxable supply of property for GST purposes. Because the transaction is a taxable supply, there is no restriction on claims for input tax credits for GST incurred on ancillary costs which creates a bias in favour of an asset sale in certain situations. As such, the general rule is that GST must be collected by the vendor on the purchase price paid for the assets (including the price paid for intangible property) at the earlier of the time that payment is made or when payment becomes due, whether or not payment has actually been made.

Except where the supplier is a registrant and the recipient is not a registrant, section 167 of the Excise Tax Act[1] provides relief from GST on the sale in circumstances where a supplier has made a supply to a recipient of a business or part of a business that was established or carried on by the supplier or that was established or carried on by another person and acquired by the supplier, and the recipient is acquiring ownership, possession or use of all or substantially all of the property that can reasonably be regarded as being necessary for the recipient to be capable of carrying on the business or part of a business.[2] In these circumstances, the vendor and the purchaser may file a joint election (Form GST-44) with the Canada Revenue agency and, upon the election being made, no GST is payable in respect of the supply of business assets. The election must be filed by the purchaser with its GST return filed for the purchaser's reporting period in which the supply of business assets is made. **[See form 9F46:1]**

Until the purchaser files the election, the vendor remains responsible and liable for collecting and remitting GST on the transaction. As a result, it would be wise for the vendor to include an appropriate indemnity clause in the agreement of purchase and sale. In the alternative, one of the conditions of closing could be that the purchaser covenant that the election will be filed at the time of closing by registered mail. In any event, assurances should be obtained from the purchaser concerning the timely filing of the election in order to protect the vendor from liability.

The rule was designed in this manner to ensure that the sale of a business as a going concern will not attract GST if both parties so agree. The provision will apply equally to the sale of all of the business or a recognizable part of it, such as a division. The broadening of the section permits parties to avail themselves of the election where there are redundant assets which the purchaser does not want to acquire.

Coincident with these amendments was the addition of section 167.1[3] to the Excise Tax Act which provides that the supply of goodwill will be exempt from GST where there is a supply of a business or part of a business.

The amendments further clarified that, notwithstanding the filing of the Form GST-44 election on an asset sale, GST will be payable on the following:

(a)   a taxable supply of a service to be rendered by the vendor (e.g. consulting fees)

(b)   a taxable supply of property by way of lease or licence

(c)   a taxable supply by way of sale of real property to an unregistered purchaser.

---

1. R.S.C. 1985, c. E-15 (new S.C. 1990, c. 45, s. 12; am. 1993, c. 27, s. 32).

2. This provision may be different for TPS purposes. Please consult Quebec counsel.

3. R.S.C. 1985, c. E-15 (new S.C. 1990, c. 45, s. 12).

Sale of Business Assets between Closely Related Corporations

9.043—A sale of a business may first require a reorganization of assets by a vendor, to be completed prior to the arm's length sale. For example, a vendor corporation may find it necessary to cause some assets to be transferred to a subsidiary, or between subsidiaries, before the sale of that subsidiary.

If the transferor corporation is a registrant, the transaction is a taxable supply and would attract GST. As well, if the transfer did not take place at the fair market value of the property being transferred, subsection 155 of the Excise Tax Act[1] would deem the transfer to take place at the fair market value.

If the corporations are related they could elect by completing a Form GST-25 joint election and retaining it in their files. If completed, the supplies between them will be deemed to have been made for nil consideration and will not attract GST. Subsection 156(1)[2] of the Excise Tax Act governs the election between "specified members" of closely related corporate groups.

A closely related group for these purposes is any group of corporations, each member of which is closely related to every other member of the group.

Generally, in order for corporations to be closely related, one corporation (or its qualifying subsidiaries) must own shares of the other, representing not less than 90 per cent of the value and full voting rights of that other corporation. Subsidiaries of a corporation will be members of a related group where the parent corporation satisfies the "votes and value" test in respect of each subsidiary. A corporation can only take advantage of this election if its supplies are all or substantially all taxable. The Excise Tax Act has similar rules for qualifying closely related Canadian partnerships.

---

1.   R.S.C. 1985, c. E-15, new S.C. 1990, c. 45, s. 12.

2.   En. 1990, c. 45, s. 12; am. 1993, c. 27, s. 26.

Other Tax Issues

Effect of Delaying Payment of the Price

Reserves

9.050—The parties will agree to a purchase price and then negotiate how that price is to be paid. If the transaction is an asset sale, it is not unusual for the purchase price to be satisfied by cash, assumption of liabilities and/or promissory note for the balance. If a share sale is to be completed the price will generally be satisfied by cash and a promissory note for the balance.

The Income Tax Act[1] permits taxpayers to defer the inclusion in income of proceeds not payable until a year after the year the transaction is completed, by claiming a reserve. This common sense approach means that taxpayers do not have to pay tax on proceeds realized on the sale that are not received until a later date. Reserves are not available to defer tax payable on all types of property sold. Generally, a reserve cannot be claimed for proceeds paid for eligible capital property or the recaptured income inclusion required on the disposition of depreciable property.

To be eligible to claim a reserve, it is not sufficient that the purchase price has not been paid; it must not be *due* until a later date. For example, if a demand promissory note is issued for a portion of the proceeds, it is the Canada Revenue Agency's position that a reserve cannot be claimed because the amount would be *due* at the moment of demand. A reserve will be available if the demand cannot be made until some date in a future year or if it is not a demand note.

The reserve provisions of the Income Tax Act apply differently to different property. Capital gain reserves are governed by subsection 40(1) of the Income Tax Act[2] and inventory reserves by paragraph 20(1)(*n*) and subsection 20(8) of the Income Tax Act.[3]

(i)   capital gains reserves—The amount of capital gain which can be reserved in each year is generally the lesser of:

    (A)   that portion of the proceeds which is allocated to the capital property and that is not due until after the year in which the transaction is completed; and

    (B)   one-fifth of the capital gain realized on the disposition of the capital property sold, multiplied by four, minus the number of years which have ended after the year of disposition.

In other words, the vendor is required to report a minimum of 20 per cent of the capital gain in each year. The proceeds should not therefore be payable over a term longer than four years because the remainder of the proceeds will be taxable in the fifth year after sale.

(ii)   inventory reserves—This reserve is available on proceeds received for property (other than land) sold in the course of the business and where the proceeds are not due, until more than two years after the day on which the property is sold. The reserve is not available if the sale occurred more than 36 months before the end of the year in which the reserve is claimed.

As indicated, reserve is unavailable for the proceeds allocated to goodwill or other eligible capital property sold. Also, a reserve cannot be claimed in respect of an amount of recapture on depreciable property sold. The cash portion of the purchase price should be allocated to the payment for the goodwill or other non-reservable profit, and the portion of the proceeds in respect of which a note or shares are issued should be allocated to inventory or capital property in respect of which the reserve can be claimed.

---

1. R.S.C. 1985, c. 1 (5th Supp.), as amended.

2. *Ibid.*

3. *Ibid.*

Earnouts

9.051—It is common for a portion of the purchase price to be dependent on the future profits realized by the business. Such clauses are commonly referred to as "earnout" clauses. It is also possible to have "reverse earnouts" (*i.e. a portion of the earnout price paid is returned*), although these are less common.

Paragraph 12(1)(g) of the Income Tax Act[1] requires that amounts paid on the sale of property which are dependent upon use of or production from property (whether or not the amount is an instalment of a sale price) be included as income for tax purposes and fully taxed. In other words, capital gain treatment will not apply to amounts paid pursuant to an earnout clause. Carefully structured payment clauses will minimize the effect of this provision and should preserve capital gain treatment for a large percentage of the purchase price paid. Interpretation Bulletin IT-462 sets out the Canada Revenue Agency's administrative position with respect to earnouts.

---

1. R.S.C. 1985, c. 1 (5th Supp.), as amended.

Acquisition of Control

9.052—An acquisition of shares of a corporation may result in an acquisition of control. If an acquisition of control takes place, subsection 249(4) of the Income Tax Act[1] deems the taxation year of a corporation sold to have ended immediately before the acquisition of control, thereby, potentially resulting in a short taxation year. The tax impact of an acquisition of control can be costly and parties may reconsider the timing of the transaction after reviewing the tax costs of a short taxation year. The implications which must be considered are the following:

Short Taxation Year: A new taxation year commences at the time of acquisition of control. The implications of the short year are numerous and should be carefully considered. Some of the more common ones are listed below:

> (i) acceleration of the use of loss carry forwards;[2] acceleration of taxation of gains previously reserved;[3] acceleration of charitable donation claiims[4]

> (ii) shareholder loans may have to be repaid sooner;[5] accrued salary or bonus must be paid within 180 days of the year end and payment will be accelerated;[6]

> (iii) capital cost allowance must be claimed on a *pro rata basis for the short year*.[7]

Restrictions on Loss Carry Forwards:[8] Losses from a business which is to be sold may be valuable to the purchaser and result in an upward adjustment to the purchase price in favour of the vendor. Before such an adjustment is made consideration should be given by the purchaser to whether it can utilize the losses after the transaction is completed. Generally, non-capital losses can be carried forward for ten years and back three in a taxation year that ends after March 22, 2004 (and carried forward seven years and back three for taxation years ending before that date); net capital losses can be carried back three years and forward indefinitely. On acquisition of control these carry-forward provisions are strictly limited. These limitations are summarized below:

> (i) Non-capital losses: Generally, non-capital losses of the target corporation can be carried forward to be deducted from income in years after the

acquisition of control, only if the same or a similar business in which the non-capital loss was sustained is carried on after the acquisition of control with a reasonable expectation of profit. The ability to carry forward non-capital losses to a same or similar business is further restricted to income, substantially all of which is derived from the sale, leasing, rental or development of similar properties or the rendering of similar services. Similar restrictions apply to the carry back of losses of a target corporation.

(ii) Net Capital Losses: Net capital losses and allowable business investment losses cannot be carried forward and therefore are lost. The carry back of such losses to a taxation year prior to the acquisition of control is also prohibited.

(iii) Write-downs for Built in Losses: The Income Tax Act contains rules which may result in the further recognition of a loss (business or capital) prior to the acquisition of control. The carry forward of these losses so realized will be restricted by the rules described above. As an example, the Income Tax Act requires a write down and deduction to the extent the undepreciated capital cost of depreciable property exceeds its fair market value in the taxation year immediately before the acquisition of control. A similar write down is required for capital property in circumstances where the target corporation's cost of that property is greater than its fair market value.

(iv) Election to Realize Capital Gains—The rule which requires a write down of basis of capital property immediately prior to the acquisition of control outlined above, is particularly onerous because capital losses cannot be carried forward have an acquisition of control. To provide relief, a taxpayer may elect to be deemed to have disposed of capital property that has appreciated immediately before the acquisition of control, the gains from which can be sheltered with the losses realized in the year ending immediately prior to the acquisition of control. This election is also available in respect of depreciable property and any non-capital losses realized can be used to offset the amount recaptured up to original cost. The purchaser of the target corporation will be eligible to take advantage of this step up in cost after acquisition.

---

1. R.S.C. 1985, c. 1 (5th Supp.), as amended.

2. *Ibid.*, s. 111 (am. 1993, c. 24, s. 49).

3. *Ibid.*, ss. 28, 44.

4. *Ibid.*, ss. 110.1(1).

5. *Ibid.*, s. 15(2).

6. *Ibid.*, s. 78.

7. Regulation 1100.

8. *Supra*, note 2.

Statutory Concerns

Competition Act

9.060—The provisions of the Competition Act[1] may apply to the acquisition of either shares or assets in one of two ways. The transaction may be subject to:

    (a)   review by the Competition Tribunal under Part VIII of the Competition Act and specifically section 91; or

    (b)   may be a notifiable transaction under Part IX of the Competition Act.

---

1. R.S.C. 1985, c. C-34.

Reviewable Transactions

9.061—The acquisition of shares or assets of a corporation may constitute a "merger" as defined in the Competition Act[1] and thus may be potentially reviewable by the Competition Tribunal.

Section 91 of the Competition Act[2] defines merger to mean "the acquisition or establishment, direct or indirect, by one or more persons, whether by purchase or lease of shares or assets, by amalgamation or by combination or otherwise, of control over or significant interest in the whole or a part of a business of a competitor, supplier, customer or other person." Section 92 of the Competition Act[3] provides certain criteria under which the Competition Tribunal is entitled to make an order concerning the proposed merger. Part IX of the Competition Act[4] requires that the Commissioner of Competition (the "Commissioner") be notified concerning certain proposed mergers prior to transaction proceeding. Section 97 of the Competition Act[5] provides a three-year limitation period from the date of completion of the merger, after which the merger cannot be reviewed by the Competition Tribunal.

The Competition Bureau has issued guidelines under which it proposes to seek reviews of mergers and proposed mergers. The Federal Court of Appeal, in the Superior Propane case [2001] FCA 104, has stated that the guidelines are not a binding statement and to the extent that they are inconsistent with the Competition Act, should be ignored.

Section 92(1) of the Competition Act[6] provides that upon the application from the Commissioner, where the Competition Tribunal finds that a merger or proposed merger prevents or lessens or is likely to prevent or lessen, competition substantially:

— in a trade, industry or profession;

— among the sources from which a trade, industry or profession obtains its products;

— among the outlets through which a trade, industry or profession disposes of a product; or

— otherwise than described above,

the Competition Tribunal may order the dissolution of the merger, order the disposal of assets or shares by the merged entity, order that the merger not be proceeded with, or any other order to which the Commissioner and the parties involved consent.

Section 92(2) of the Competition Act[7] specifically provides that the Competition Tribunal may not make a determination that a merger sub-stantially prevents or lessens competition solely on the basis of evidence of concentration or market share. The Competition Act does not define the term "substantially" with respect to the lessening of competition.

It is important to note that in the case of two merging corporations it is not essential that the corporations compete in every area of business. In the case of corporations with diverse business investments it is sufficient if the corporations are in competition in one type of business, for such transaction to be reviewable by the Competition Tribunal.

Section 93 of the Competition Act[8] sets out factors that the Competition Tribunal is to consider in determining whether a proposed merger would prevent or lessen competition. Among the factors to be considered are:

— the extent to which foreign products or competitors will provide effective competition to the business;

— whether the business or part of the business has failed or is likely to fail prior to the merger;

— the extent to which acceptable substitutes for products supplied by the parties are available;

— barriers to entry into the market, including tariff and non-tariff barriers to international trade, interprovincial barriers to trade and regulatory control over the entity;

— the extent to which effective competition remains in the market;

— the likelihood that the merger would result in the removal of a vigorous and effective competitor;

— the nature and extent of change and innovation in a relevant market; and

— any other factor relevant to the affected market.

The Competition Tribunal is also empowered to consider such other factors as it considers relevant to the market and the effect on the market by the proposed merger.

Section 96[9] provides that the Competition Tribunal is not to make an order respecting a merger if it is determined that such merger has brought about, or is likely to bring about, gains in efficiency that will be greater than, and will offset, the effects of any prevention or lessening of competition resulting from the merger, if the gains in efficiency would not be obtained if an order preventing the merger were made. The section provides that the Competition Tribunal should consider whether there will be a significant increase in the real value of exports or a significant substitution of domestic products for imported products in determining whether there have been gains in efficiency.

Section 102[10] permits the parties to a proposed merger to apply to the Commissioner for a certificate that the Commissioner will not take the proposed transaction to the Competition Tribunal under section 92. This application is to be considered "as expeditiously as possible"; there is no time limit for a reply. The Competition Act provides for binding advanced rulings by the Commissioner, because section 103 prevents the Commissioner, where it has issued a certificate under section 102, from making an application for review by the Competition Tribunal concerning a transaction to which the certificate relates (and which is substantially completed within one year after the certificate is issued) where such application would be based solely on information that is the same or substantially the same as the information on which the certificate was issued.

It is important to note that mergers that are not subject to the notification requirements of Part IX may still be reviewed by the Competition Tribunal under Part VIII.

---

1. R.S.C. 1985, c. C-34.

2. *Ibid.*, am. R.S.C. 1985, c. 19 (2nd Supp.), s. 45.

3. *Ibid.*

4. *Ibid.*

5. *Ibid.*

6. *Ibid.*

7. *Ibid.*

8. *Ibid.*

9. Competition Act, R.S.C. 1985, c. C-34, am. R.S.C. 1985, c. 19 (2nd Supp.), s. 96.

10. *Ibid.*

Notifiable Transactions

9.062—Part IX[1] of the Competition Act creates a dual threshold test for notifiable transactions. The first threshold which must be met before a transaction will be notifiable is provided for in section 109 of the Competition Act.[2] Section 109 provides that the notification sections do not apply in respect of a proposed transaction unless the parties thereto, together with their affiliates:

— have assets in Canada exceeding $400,000,000 in aggregate value; or

— have gross revenue from sales in, from or into Canada which exceed $400,000,000.

Only if this $400,000,000 threshold is met is it necessary to review the second threshold test. The second threshold test is provided for in section 110 of the Competition Act.[3] These thresholds are:

— the acquisition of assets in Canada of an operating business or gross revenues from sales in or from Canada generated from such assets which exceed $35,000,000;

— the acquisition of voting shares of a corporation carrying on an operating business where the aggregate value of the assets in Canada of the corporation or the gross revenues from sales in or from Canada generated by the corporation exceed $35,000,000; and

where the result of the proposed acquisition of voting shares would result in the acquiror, together with its affiliates owing voting shares in:

A. a publicly traded corporation of greater than 20 per cent, or if such entity already owns more than 20 per cent before the proposed acquisition 50 per cent, of the votes attached to all outstanding voting shares of the corporation are acquired; or

B. in a non-publicly traded corporation of greater than 35 per cent, or if such entity already owns more than 35 per cent before the proposed transaction 50 per cent, of the votes attached to all outstanding voting shares of the corporation are acquired;

— in the case of an unincorporated entity where the assets or gross revenues of such unincorporated entity exceed $35,000,000; and

— in the case of a proposed amalgamation where one of the corporations carries on an operating business and where the aggregate value of assets in Canada of the amalgamated corporation would exceed $70,000,000 or the gross revenue from sales in or from

Canada generated from the assets of the amalgamated corporation would exceed $70,000,000.

---

1. R.S.C. 1985, c. C-34, am. R.S.C. 1985, c. 19 (2nd Supp).

2. *Ibid.*

3. *Ibid.*

EXEMPT TRANSACTIONS

9.063—Section 111 provides for certain exemptions from the pre-notification requirements under the Competition Act.[1] The following types of transactions will not require pre-notification of the Competition Director even if both the $400,000,000 and $35,000,000 thresholds are met:

— the acquisition of real property or goods in the ordinary course of business, if as a result of the acquisition the acquiror would not hold all or substantially all of the assets of a business or of any operating segment of a business;

— the acquisition of voting shares solely for the purpose of underwriting the shares;

— the acquisition of voting shares or assets that would result from a gift, intestate succession or testamentary disposition;

— the acquisition of collateral or receivables, or an acquisition resulting from a foreclosure or default or forming part of a debt work-out, made by a creditor in or pursuant to a credit transaction entered into in good faith in the ordinary course of business; or

— the acquisition of a Canadian resource property or acquisition of shares pursuant to a written agreement by a person who incurs expenses for the exploration or development activities relating to such property or relating to the acquisition of shares of a holding corporation holding such Canadian resource property.

Section 113 of the Competition Act[2] also exempts from the pre-notification requirements a number of classes of transactions; including the following:

(a) transactions between affiliated entities;

(b) transactions pursuant to which the Commissioner has issued a certificate under section 102; and

(c) transactions prescribed by the regulations (asset securitizations).

Section 114[3] provides that parties proposing to enter into transactions listed in section 110, for which no exemption applies, must, prior to completing the transaction, notify the Commissioner of the proposed transaction and provide the Commissioner with the information prescribed by the Competition Act.

The parties can opt to provide the prescribed information to the Commissioner via the prescribed short form as the prescribed long form. If the parties use the short form, the Commissioner may still require the submission of a long form (section 114(2)[4]).

Section 123[5] sets out the time deadlines within which a Commissioner must act. The time requirements on the Commissioner depend on whether the short-form notice (section 121) or the long-form notice (section 122) has been utilized. These sections are augmented by the regulations to the Act and the forms can be obtained from the Competition Bureau's website.

---

1. R.S.C. 1985, c. C-34 (am. R.S.C. 1985, c. 19 (2nd Supp.)).

2. *Ibid.*, s. 113 (en. R.S.C. 1985, c. 19 (2nd Supp.), s. 45; am. 1991, c. 45, s. 550; 1991, c. 46, s. 594; 1991, c. 47, s. 717).

3. *Supra*, note 1.

4. *Supra*, note 1.

5. *Supra*, note 1.

Investment Canada Act

9.064—In any transaction involving a non-Canadian acquiring an interest in a Canadian business the provisions of the Investment Canada Act,[1] must be complied with.

The purpose of the Investment Canada Act, as stated in section 2 is ". . . to encourage investment in Canada by Canadians and non-Canadians that contributes to economic growth and employment opportunities and to provide for the review of significant investments in Canada by non-Canadians in order to ensure such benefit to Canada".[2]

For the purpose of the Investment Canada Act a "Canadian" is defined to mean:

(a) a Canadian citizen,

(b) a permanent resident within the meaning of the *Immigration Act* who has been ordinarily resident in Canada for not more than one year after the time at which he first became eligible to apply for Canadian citizenship,

(c) a Canadian government, whether federal, provincial or local, or any agency thereof, or

(d) an entity that is Canadian-controlled, as determined pursuant to section 26.

"Canadian business" is defined to mean:

> a business carried on in Canada that has:
>
> (a) a place of business in Canada,
>
> (b) an individual or individuals in Canada who are employed or self-employed in connection with the business, and
>
> (c) assets in Canada used in carrying on the business.

"Non-Canadian" is defined to mean "an individual, ", a government or an agency thereof or an entity that is not a Canadian".

Section 11 of the Investment Canada Act[3] provides that the following types of investments by non-Canadians are subject to notification under the Act:

> (a) an investment to establish a new Canadian business; and
>
> (b) an investment to acquire control of a Canadian business, directly or indirectly, unless the transaction is a reviewable transaction.

---

1. R.S.C. 1985, c. 28 (1st Supp.).

2. *Ibid.*

3. *Ibid.*

Exempt Transactions

9.065—The provisions of the Investment Canada Act[1] do not apply to acquisitions by non-Canadians where such acquisition is:

— an involuntary acquisition of control of the Canadian business;

— by security dealers, traders or venture capitalists in the normal course of the business of such persons;

— to facilitate the financing of the Canadian business, where such control position is ultimately divested;

— by inheritance;

— through the acquisition of control of the Canadian business by the realization of security granted for a loan or other financial assistance;

— in the case of the acquisition of control of a Canadian business by reason of an amalgamation, merger, consolidation or corporate reorganization where the ultimate control of the business remains unchanged;

— the acquisition of control of the business of a crown corporation or of a provincial or municipal corporation;

— investments regulated under the Bank Act;[2]

— the acquisition of control of farms; and

— investments by life insurance companies for the benefit of their Canadian policyholders.

---

1. R.S.C. 1985, c. 28 (1st Supp.).

2. R.S.C. 1985, c. B-1, as am. S.C. 1991, c. 46.

Notifiable Transactions

9.066—In any other type of transaction involving the acquisition by a non-Canadian of control of a Canadian business, either establishing a new business or acquisition of an established business, there must be compliance with the provisions of the Investment Canada Act.[1] At a minimum the acquiring party will be required to notify Investment Canada. The transaction may also be reviewable if it fits the criteria established by the Investment Canada Act.

Section 12 of the Investment Canada Act[2] requires that where a transaction is a notifiable investment, the non-Canadian making the investment shall, at any time prior to the implementation of the investment or within 30 days after the completion of the investment provide notice in the prescribed form to the Director of Investments. Section 13 of the Investment Canada Act[3] provides that the Director of Investments shall forthwith send a receipt to the non-Canadian that provided the prescribed notification. Such receipt shall:

(a) certify the date on which the complete notice required under Section 12 was received or the further information required to complete the notice was received by the Director of Investments; and

(b) advise the non-Canadian that:
  (i) the investment is not reviewable; or

  (ii) unless the Director of Investments sends the non-Canadian notice of review pursuant to Section 15 of the Investment Canada Act within 21 days after the certified date referred to above the investment is not reviewable.

Section 15 of the Investment Canada Act[4] permits investment which would otherwise only be notifiable under the Act to be reviewable if:

(a) the investment is within a prescribed specific type of business activity that, in the opinion of the Governor in Council, is related to Canada's cultural heritage or national identity; and

(b) within 21 days after the certification date referred to in the receipt from the Director of Investments:
  (i) the Governor in Council issues an order for review of the investment; and

(ii)   the Director of Investments sends the non-Canadian making the investment a notice for review.

---

1. R.S.C. 1985, c. 28 (1st Supp.).

2. *Ibid.*

3. *Ibid.*

4. *Ibid.*

Reviewable Transaction

9.067—Section 14 prescribes the types of transactions which will be subject to review under the Investment Canada Act.[1] Notice of any reviewable transaction must be provided prior to the completion of the transaction in the prescribed form. The nature of the reviewable transactions essentially falls into four categories. These are:

—   the direct acquisition of a Canadian business, either through the acquisition of shares, voting control or assets, where the assets of the Canadian business are $5 million or greater;

—   the indirect acquisition of a Canadian business through the acquisition of control of a foreign entity, where 50 per cent or more of the value of such foreign entity is attributable to the Canadian business, and where the assets of the Canadian business are $5 million or more;

—   the indirect acquisition of a Canadian business through the acquisition of control of a foreign entity, where less than 50 per cent of the value of the foreign entity is attributable to the Canadian business and where the assets of the entity carrying on the Canadian business and of all other entities in Canada, the control of which is acquired directly or indirectly, is $50 million or more; and

—   certain acquisitions which would normally only be notifiable where pursuant to the orders of the Governor in Council are reviewable due to the nature of the Canadian cultural, national identity or heritage designation.

The limits of $5 million is varied with respect to an acquisition or sale of a Canadian business by a person or entity from a country that is a member of the World Trade Organization ("WTO"). The limits placed on the review of transactions involving persons or entities from WTO member countries ratchet up each year based on a formula set out in the Investment Canada Act. The notification requirements remain the same.

For investors from WTO member countries, any direct investment in excess of $218 million in 2002 is reviewable.

An indirect acquisition subject to the $50 million limit is not reviewable if the purchaser or vendor is a person or entity from a country that is a WTO member.

---

1. R.S.C. 1985, c. 28 (2nd Supp.).

Non-resident Vendors

Section 116 of the Income Tax Act[1]

9.068—Dispositions of taxable Canadian property by non-residents give rise to special tax concerns. Taxable Canadian property, other than depreciable property or excluded property, is defined to include real property situated in Canada, shares of private corporations and interests in trusts resident in Canada. The gain realized on the disposition of taxable Canadian property by the non-resident is subject to tax in Canada. Section 116[2] specifically requires a non-resident vendor to obtain a "clearance" certificate from the Canada Revenue Agency prior to sale. Such a certificate will only be issued by the Canada Revenue Agency if the tax payable on the sale (if any) has been paid or acceptable security for the tax has been delivered to the Canada Revenue Agency. Section 116 further requires that a purchaser of taxable Canadian property from a non-resident vendor require delivery of the section 116 certificate on closing. If the vendor does not produce the certificate, the purchaser is liable to withhold 25 per cent of the purchase price and remit it to the Canada Revenue Agency on account of the vendor's tax. If the disposition by the non-resident involves a life insurance policy in Canada, a Canadian resource property, real property that is inventory, a timber resource or depreciable property, the rate of withholding by the purchaser is 50 per cent. Failure to do so will cause the purchaser (often in such circumstances a Canadian resident) to be jointly and severally liable with the vendor for any tax owing.

It is common practice in such transactions for the parties to agree that the vendor will deliver a section 116 certificate on closing, otherwise the purchaser will withhold the applicable portion of the purchase price. The purchaser is not required to forward the tax to the Canada Revenue Agency until the 30th day of the month following the month in which the transaction was completed. Therefore, if the vendor has not received the section 116 certificate at the time of closing, the parties generally agree that the purchaser will withhold the amount and hold it in trust for the vendor pending delivery of the section 116 certificate. If the vendor has failed to deliver the section 116 certificate by the 30th day of the month following the month of the transaction, the purchaser will forward the funds to the Canada Revenue Agency.

Section 1098 of the Québec Taxation Act

Section 1098 of the Québec Taxation Act is a parallel regime to section 116 of the federal Income Tax Act.[3] Again it applies to dispositions of taxable Canadian property by non-residents which requires the withholding of 18 per cent of the purchase price for remittance to the Québec Ministry of Revenue, unless the requisite exemption certificate has been obtained from the Québec government and delivered to the purchaser for closing.

---

1. R.S.C. 1985, c. 1 (5th Supp.).

2. *Ibid.*

3. *Ibid.*

Securities Act

Application of the Act

9.069—The provisions of the Securities Act[1] (the "Act") are applicable to transactions involving a trade in securities. Consequently, in any transaction involving the sale of shares, or the issuance of securities for financing purposes, the provisions of the Securities Act should be reviewed in order to ensure compliance. In the case of a sale of assets, other than an interest in assets, the provisions of the Securities Act are unlikely to apply.

The definitions of "security", "trade" and "distribution" contained in the Securities Act are very broad in scope. In simplified terms:

"security" means any document evidencing an interest or participation in the assets, property, profits, earnings or royalties of any person or company and specifically includes any document commonly known as a security, any document evidencing an option, subscription or other interest in a security, any bond, debenture, note or other evidence of indebtedness, share, stock or unit;

"trade" includes any sale or disposition of a security for valuable consideration, and includes any act, advertisement, solicitation, conduct or negotiation directly or indirectly in furtherance of an trade, but does not include a purchase of a security or a transfer, pledge or encumbrance of securities for the purpose of giving collateral for a debt made in good faith;

"distribution" means a trade in securities of an issuer that have not been previously issued or which have been re-issued after having been redeemed or donated to the issuer, or a trade from the holdings of any person, company or combination of person or companies which hold a sufficient number of such securities to affect materially the control of the issuer (i.e., a control block), with any person or company or combination thereof holding more than 20% of the outstanding voting securities of an issuer, in the absence of evidence to the contrary, being deemed to hold a sufficient number of shares to affect materially the control of such issuer. In addition, as summarized below, certain other provisions of the Securities Act and its rules and regulations deem certain other trades to be a "distribution".

Consequently, in any transaction that involves the issuance of a security, or the sale of a previously issued security, including shares of a corporation, there must be a review of the provisions of the Securities Act. If a determination is made that the interest involved in a transaction is not a security, for example, where specific assets are being sold outright, then the Securities Act will not apply. However, if the interest being sold is a security and the transaction would be a distribution of securities, then there must be compliance with the provisions of the Securities Act.

It should also be noted that while the Securities Act was updated and renumbered with the Revised Statutes of Ontario, the section references in the Regulation have not been amended in concordance with the Securities Act. As well, Canadian securities authorities have in recent years been implementing the Policy Reformulation Project, pursuant to which the existing regulatory framework is being reorganized and substantially changed. Consequently, care must be taken to ensure that those recent changes are considered when reviewing a transaction.

---

1. R.S.O. 1990, c. S-5, as amended.

Dealer Registration

9.070—Section 25 of the Securities Act[1] provides that no person or company shall trade in a security or act as an underwriter unless the person or company is registered as a dealer, or act as an advisor unless the person or company is registered as an advisor. Such registration must be made with the securities commission in the jurisdiction of the trading activity. In Ontario that is the Ontario Securities Commission, or OSC.

Alternatively, a person can trade in a security pursuant to one of the exemptions from the registration requirement contained in the Securities Act. Those registration exemptions are typically found in Section 35 of the Act and in OSC Rule 45-501 – Exempt Distributions under the Act. Note also that certain of the exemptions contained in Section 35 are expressly removed under Part 3 of OSC Rule 45-501. Certain additional registration exemptions and restrictions on existing exemptions are also contained in the regulation (the "Regulation")[2] and other rules under the Act including OSC Rule 45-503 – Trades to Employees, Executives and Consultants which replaces and enhances the exemption previously contained under Paragraph 19 of Subsection 35(1).

It is important to note that, in addition to the foregoing, both the Regulation[3] and OSC Rule 45-501[4] provide that a significant number of specific registration exemptions do not apply to trades carried out by market intermediaries. A "market intermediary" is a person or company that engages or holds itself out as engaging in the business of trading in securities as principal or agent, other than trading in securities purchased by the person for its own account for investment only and not with a view to resale or distribution.[5] A person registered as a "limited market dealer" may act as a market intermediary in respect of those registration exemptions which would otherwise be unavailable to a market intermediary.[6] The registration requirements for a "limited market dealer" are less onerous than those applicable to other categories of registration (e.g., international dealer, foreign dealer, broker, investment dealer, securities dealer) but ensures universal registration of all market intermediaries. The universal registration requirements are set out in Part X of the regulations to the Securities Act. A careful review of the universal registration requirements should be made prior to any distribution taking place.

---

1. R.S.O. 1990, c. S-5, as amended.

2. Ontario Regulation 1015 made under the Securities Act (Ontario).

3. Section 206 of Ont. Reg.1015.

4. Section 3 of Rule 45-501.

5. Section 204(1) of Ont. Reg. 1015.

6. Rule 31-503 and Subsection 3.4(2) of Rule 45-501.

Distribution of Securities

9.071—Section 53 of the Securities Act[1] provides that no person or company shall trade in a security where such trade would be a distribution of such security, unless a preliminary prospectus and a (final) prospectus have been filed and receipts therefor obtained from the Director of the OSC.

Alternatively, a person or company can distribute securities pursuant to one of the exemptions from the prospectus requirements contained in the Securities Act. Such prospectus exemptions are typically found in Section 72(1) of the Act and in OSC Rule 45-501 – Exempt Distributions under the Act. In many cases, these exemptions are identical to those applicable to the registration requirement under the Act (see above). Note also that certain of the exemptions contained in Section 72 are expressly removed under Part 3 of OSC Rule 45-501. Certain additional prospectus exemptions and restrictions on existing exemptions are contained in the Regulation and other rules under the Act, including OSC Rule 45-503 – Trades to Employees, Executives and Consultants which replaces and enhances the exemption previously contained under Section 72(1)(n).

Hence, an issuer can only distribute securities in one of two ways:

- pursuant to a (final) prospectus; or
- pursuant to an exemption from the prospectus requirements contained in the Securities Act.

---

1. R.S.O. 1990, c. S-5, as amended.

Prospectus

9.072—The Securities Act[1] provides that an issuer can distribute securities pursuant to a prospectus. A prospectus shall provide full, true and plain disclosure of all material facts relating to the securities issued or proposed to be distributed and shall comply as to form and content with Ontario securities laws. OSC Form 41-501F1 outlines the information generally required in a prospectus. This form consolidates and replaces old Forms 12, 13 and 14 under the Regulation, and restates the prospectus disclosure requirements from the Regulation and former OSC Policies 5.1 and 5.7. Guidelines for the form and substantive content of a prospectus are also provided for in National Instrument 45-101 – Prospectus Disclosure Requirements and OSC Rule 41-501 – General Prospectus Requirements. A substantial portion of the latter rule addresses financial statement disclosure for the issuer, credit supporters, and significant acquisitions that are proposed or have been recently completed by the issuer.

The Securities Act requires that the chief executive officer, the chief financial officer and, on behalf of the board of directors, any two directors of the issuer other than the foregoing, sign a certificate confirming that the contents of the prospectus constitutes full, true and plain disclosure of all material facts related to the issuer. The underwriter of the distribution is required to execute and deliver with the prospectus a similar certificate based on its best knowledge, information and belief.

Once prepared, a prospectus must be filed with the securities commissions for review and approval in the provinces where the securities are to be distributed. Only after review and approval and the issuance of a final receipt can the securities being issued in conjunction with the prospectus be distributed. In the case of a cross-Canada distribution the provisions of National Policy 43-201 – Mutual Reliance Review System for Prospectuses and Annual Information Forms has established a mutual reliance review system (MRRS) pursuant to which prospectuses and annual information forms (AIFs) are subject to review and receipting by the issuer's "principal regulator". The principal regulator for a particular issuer is determined generally on the basis of head office location. The principal regulator is responsible for issuing and resolving comments on the filed material and issuing the MRRS decision document (i.e., in the case of a prospectus, the final receipt) on behalf of itself and the other applicable, "non-principal" regulators. While the non-principal regulators may review the materials and advise the principal regulator of any concerns that, if left unresolved, would cause the regulator to opt out of the MRRS in respect of the filing, the issuer will generally deal solely with the principal regulator.

---

1. R.S.O. 1990, c. S-5, as amended.

Exemptions from Prospectus and Registration Requirements

9.073—With effect as of November 30, 2001, significant changes were made to Ontario securities laws with respect to the available exemptions from the prospectus and registration requirements contained in the Securities Act.[1]

Prior to that date, the most popular of the exemptions included:

(a) the "exempt purchaser" exemption — the issuance of securities to one of about eight different listed exempt purchasers (generally a bank, loan or trust corporation, insurance company, a subsidiary of any of the foregoing, a registered dealer, either the federal or provincial government or any municipal government or public board or commission in Canada (Sections 35(1)(3) and 72(1)(a)) of the Securities Act;

(b) the "private placement" exemption — where the purchaser purchased as principal and the aggregate acquisition cost for the securities acquired by it under the trade was not less than $150,000 (Sections 35(1)(5) and 72(1)(d)):

(c) the "seed capital" exemption — a distribution of securities where solicitations were made to not more than 50 prospective purchasers resulting in sales to not more than 25 purchasers (Sections 35(1)(21) and 72(1)(p)). This exemption was subject to a number of requirements, including:

(i) that each purchaser have access to substantially the same information concerning the issuer that a prospectus would provide;

(ii) that each purchaser be a sophisticated purchaser by virtue of its net worth, investment experience or consultation with a qualified advisors; and

(iii) that the distribution be completed within a six month period; and

(d) the "private company" exemption — where the issuer was a "private company" as defined under the Securities Act and the securities distributed were not offered for sale to the public (Sections 35(2)(10) and 73(1)(a)). In 1999, this exemption had been supplemented by the original OSC Rule 45-501 to include "private issuers" i.e., entities other than corporations.

On November 30, 2001, a revised OSC Rule 45-501 – Exempt Distributions came into effect. That rule now provides that a number of previously available exemptions, including the exempt purchaser, private placement, seed capital and private issuer exemptions described above, are no longer available for trades of securities in Ontario. The foregoing exemptions have been replaced by two new exemptions, known as the "closely-held issuer" exemption and the "accredited investor" exemption.

The "Closely-Held Issuer" Exemption

The "closely-held issuer" exemption[2] replaces the private issuer exemption and permits issuers to raise a total of $3 million, through any number of financings, regardless of an investor's relationship to the issuer, financial status, sophistication, or ability to withstand the loss, provided that following any such trade the issuer qualifies as a closely-held issuer. There is no limit on the number of investors who can be approached under this exemption.

A "closely-held issuer" means an issuer whose: (a) shares are subject to restrictions on transfer requiring the approval of either the board of directors or the shareholders of the issuer (or the equivalent in a non-corporate issuer) contained in the constating documents of the issuer or one or more shareholders agreements; and (b) outstanding securities are beneficially owned, directly or indirectly, by not more than 35 persons or companies. Current and former directors, officers or employees, of the issuer, or an affiliated entity of the issuer, current or former consultants, who beneficially own securities of the issuer that were issued as compensation by or under an incentive plan, of the issuer or an affiliate of the issuer and "accredited investors" are excluded from the 35 security-holder limit.

To rely on the "closely-held issuer" exemption:

- The constating documents or shareholders' agreement of a "closely-held" issuer must require directors' or shareholders' approval for share transfer;
- No selling or promotional expenses can be paid in connection with the trade (except for services performed by a registered dealer);
- A promoter of the issuer cannot act as a promoter of any other issuer that has relied on this exemption in the last 12 months;

- The issuer must provide a purchaser with a prescribed "don't buy" statement (OSC Form 45-501F3) at least four days prior to the trade unless the issuer will not have more than five beneficial security holders following the trade;

- The issuer must "share" the $3 million dollar cap with all other issuers engaged in a common enterprise; and

- The issuer cannot be a mutual fund or a non-redeemable investment fund.

The "Accredited Investor" Exemption

The "accredited investor" exemption[3] permits issuers to raise any amount at any time from any person or company defined as an "accredited investor". These investors are considered to have the capacity to obtain and analyze the information needed to assess an investment opportunity without the assistance provided by a prospectus and to have the financial ability to withstand the loss of the investment.

The "accredited investor" list includes: financial institutions; registered advisors and dealers (other than limited market dealers); governments and governmental agencies; pension funds; registered charities; persons or companies that meet certain net worth criteria or other qualifications; persons or companies recognized by the OSC as an accredited investor (to replace the exempt purchaser exemption); promoters of the issuer; affiliates of the issuer; holders of control blocks; a spouse, parent, grandparent or child of an officer, director or promoter of the issuer and "managed accounts".

To rely on the "accredited investor" exemption:

- The investor must be an "accredited investor" as defined in OSC Rule 45-501;

- The "accredited investor" must purchase as principal: and

- Most trades to an "accredited investor" require that an OSC Form 45-501F1 together with the applicable form, be filed with the OSC within 10 days of the trade together with the applicable fee.

Offering Memorandum Requirements

The new exemptions do not require an issuer to provide an offering memorandum to purchasers. However, if a document which constitutes an "offering memorandum" is provided, a copy must be filed with the OSC within 10 days of the trade and the statutory right of action as provided by the Securities Act must be described in the offering memorandum.

---

1. R.S.O. 1990, c. S-5, as amended.

2. Section 2.1 of OSC Rule 45-501.

3. Section 2.3 of OSC Rule 45-501.

Resale Requirements

9.073.1—OSC Rule 45-501 adopts the new resale provisions of Multilateral Instrument 45-102 effective November 30, 2001. Under this instrument the traditional six, twelve and eighteen month hold periods contained in Subsection 72(4) are replaced by restricted periods of twelve months for issuers that are not "qualifying issuers" on the date of the placement and four months for issuers that are "qualifying issuers" on the date of the placement. In addition, the traditional twelve month seasoning period (being the period in which the issuer has been a reporting issuer in Ontario) contained in Subsection 72(5) is replaced by a period of twelve months for issuers that are not "qualifying issuers" and four months for issuers that are "qualifying issuers" on the date of the trade.

After November 30, 2001, the new resale rules apply to resales of securities issued on an exempt basis before that date.

The Ontario securities system operates on the "closed system" approach. Consequently, a trade of securities issued pursuant to a prospectus exemption will be deemed to be a distribution under the Securities Act and can only be made:

- pursuant to a (final) prospectus;
- pursuant to another exemption from the prospectus requirements provided for under Ontario securities law; or
- following the expiry of the applicable hold or seasoning period specified under Multilateral Instrument 45-102.

The length of the applicable hold and seasoning period is contingent upon the exemption utilized. In order to become a reporting issuer, the issuer must have filed a prospectus and complied with the continuous reporting requirement provided for in the Securities Act.[1] Unless the hold period requirements are complied with, or an exemption order is obtained from the Ontario Securities Commission, a purchaser of securities may only trade such securities if another prospectus exemption can be utilized.

---

1. R.S.O. 1990, c. S-5, as amended.

Change of Control

9.073.2—While the definition of "distribution" includes securities which have not been previously issued and securities which had been redeemed by the issuer and were to be reissued, the definition also includes a trade from a control block.

The Securities Act requires that where there is any sale from the holdings of a control block, not just the entire block, then such a trade would be a distribution within the meaning of the Act. Consequently, a prospectus or prospectus exemption must be relied upon, or the distribution must be made in compliance with Section 2.8 of Multilateral Instrument 45-102.

Under Subsection 2.8(2) of multilateral instrument 45-102, if the issuer of the securities is a "qualifying issuer" then the control block distribution is subject to the following conditions: (a) the issuer has been a reporting issuer for four months; (b) the selling security holder has held the securities for at least four months; (c) no unusual effort is made to prepare the market or to create a demand for the securities; (d) no extraordinary commission is paid to a person or company in respect of the trade; and (e) the selling security holder has no reasonable grounds to believe that the issuer is in default of securities legislation.

If the issuer of the securities is not a "qualifying issuer" then Subsection 2.8(3) of the multilateral instrument imposes the following conditions: (a) the issuer has been a reporting issuer for twelve months; (b) no unusual effort is made to prepare the market or to create a demand for the securities; (c) no extraordinary commission or consideration is paid to a person or company in respect of the trade; (d) the selling security holder has no reasonable grounds to believe that the issuer is in default of securities legislation; and (e) the selling security holder has held the securities for a period of either twelve months or six months depending upon the exemption, if any, under which the securities were originally acquired.

The multilateral instrument also provides for the filing of insider trading reports within three days after the completion of any trade and the filing of a Form 45-102F3 at least seven days and not more than fourteen days before the first trade, on the sixtieth day after the first form is filed, and thereafter at the end of each twenty-eight period during which the distribution is carried out.

The control block seller is also required to file an insider trading report within 3 days of the completion of such trade. No unusual effort can be made to prepare the market or create a demand for the securities and no extraordinary commission or other consideration can be paid in respect of such trade.

Consequently, any change in control of an issuer through the trade of securities would constitute a distribution for the purposes of the Securities Act. Consequently, in order to complete such a transaction, there must be either compliance with Section 2.8 of Multilateral Instrument 45-102 or a further exemption of the prospectus requirements of the Securities Act.

Bulk Sales Act

9.074—Compliance with the Bulk Sales Act[1] will be of utmost concern to the purchaser in an asset transaction. Failure to comply with this Act may enable the unpaid creditors of the vendor to set the transaction aside or cause the purchaser to make further payments to them as a result of the purchaser's failure to require compliance.

If the vendor cannot comply with the Bulk Sales Act, the purchaser may choose to restructure the transaction as a share purchase or, if the vendor is in serious financial trouble, purchase the assets from the secured creditors of the vendor or its bankruptcy trustee, as such sales of assets are exempt from the application of the Act by section 2 thereof. (See also §9.074.1 on exemption orders for insolvent vendors.)

If the purchaser in an asset transaction chooses not to require compliance with the Bulk Sales Act, it may be doing so based on a business decision that the remaining assets of the vendor are so significant and the vendor is so creditworthy that there is no risk of the action being attacked by any unpaid creditors. However, in such a situation, the purchaser may require, as additional comfort, an indemnity from the vendor and possibly also from some of its related corporations, indemnifying the purchaser in the event that the sale is indeed attacked. Of concern in accepting an indemnity is whether the party providing the indemnity is creditworthy enough to be able to pay should the indemnity be called upon. If there is such a concern, security may be required for the indemnity, such as a letter of credit issued by a financial institution acceptable to the purchaser.

It is important to explain the perils of non-compliance with the Act to the purchaser client, before the decision is made by the client to accept a waiver.

If the purchaser client instructs compliance with the Bulk Sales Act, the initial concern is to determine that such Act does apply to the assets transaction at hand. The statute was created to assist creditors of the vendor when such vendor effects a sale of "stock in bulk" out of the ordinary course of business or trade of the seller. "Stock" is further defined in section 1 of the Act[2] as essentially all of the goods, wares, merchandise and chattels with which a person carries on a trade or business. "Stock" can include intangible assets as well.[3]

There is no provision in the Act to specify when a transaction is so large as to constitute a "sale of stock in bulk". Generally, compliance with the Act is recommended if the client is purchasing all of the goods of a vendor who is ceasing to carry on business or an entire division of a large corporation, such that the sale is one out of the ordinary course of the vendor's business. However, the sale of three or four pieces of machinery of a sole proprietor may in fact be a sale out of the ordinary course of the sole proprietor's business when it is known that the vendor is retiring from operations. The price tag may not be large nor the number of assets significant but in such a situation compliance with the statute may still be required.

A purchaser complies with the Bulk Sales Act in one of the following three ways:

— obtaining a section 3 exemption order[4] issued by the court where on evidence it is shown that the vendor has remaining assets sufficient to ensure that all of its creditors will be paid in full. **[See Para. 9.074.1 and Form 9F62]**

— obtaining the vendor' affidavit of creditors pursuant to sub-sections 4 and 8(1)[5] of the Act. The vendor is required to provide its sworn statement giving particulars of the amounts owing by it to both its secured and unsecured creditors. Ideally, this affidavit will produce a "nil" result and the purchaser may pay the vendor in full. If such is not the case, the purchaser must either ensure that the purchase price is paid to such parties, or obtain written waivers from the creditors in which they agree that the purchaser may proceed with the sale, all in accordance with the provisions of sections 8 and 9 of the Act,[6] using the required forms to the Act. **[See 9F60 for a copy of the vendor's section 4 disclosure affidavit]** or

— payment of the purchase price to a trustee pursuant to subsection 8(2) of the Bulk Sales Act.[7] This final procedure rarely happens and is difficult to administer.

Note with regard to section 3 of the Bulk Sales Act, that if one obtains an exemption order in a transaction where there is an absolute assignment (sale) of accounts and chattel paper, that the Personal Property Security Act[8] will continue to apply to the transaction and will require registration. Subsection 4(1)(g) of the PPSA[9] provides that such statute does not apply to a sale of accounts or chattel papers as part of a transaction to which the Bulk Sales Act applies. However, if an exemption order has been obtained pursuant to the Bulk Sales Act, such an exemption deems the Bulk Sales Act not to apply. Consequently, the PPSA will again apply to the transaction and the registration of a financing statement will be necessary.

If there is to be a deposit paid toward the purchase price, note section 6 of the Bulk Sales Act[10] which limits such deposit to 10 per cent before the buyer receives the vendor's affidavit of disclosure pursuant to section 4. Such deposit is to be held by the vendor in trust for disposition as required by section 6.[11] **[See Paras. 9.560–9.561]**

For deals closing in several provinces, note that bulk sales legislation has been repealed across Canada, except in Ontario and Newfoundland and

Labrador. Other provinces have taken the view that trade creditors should take PPSA security or otherwise protect themselves to ensure payment.

---

1. R.S.O. 1990, c. B.14.

2. *Ibid.*

3. *Re Excelsior Brand Limited and Italfina Inc. et al* (1995), 24 O.R. (3d) 801. Held a sale of a trademark with artwork, goodwill, packaging, inventory and customer appreciation was part of a sale of "stock in bulk".

4. *Ibid.*

5. *Ibid.*

6. *Ibid.*

7. *Ibid.*

8. R.S.O. 1990, c. P.10.

9. *Ibid.*

10. *Supra*, note 1.

11. *Ibid.*

Bulk Sales by Insolvent Vendors —

Some Recent Jurisprudence from the Canadian Red Cross Society CCA Proceeding

Article by Jeffrey Carhart of Miller Thomson, Toronto, reprinted from *Commercial Insolvency Reporter* (Butterworths, June 1999, Vol. 11, No. 5)

§9.074.1 — The *Companies' Creditors Arrangement Act* (R.S.C. 1985, c. C-36; hereinafter the "CCAA") has been back in the news lately with Livent, SkyDome and, most recently, Royal Oak Mines, having sought protection under what is sometimes referred to as Canada's version of the U.S. Chapter 11. The way in which the courts will allow companies to conduct their CCAA reorganizations is a process of steady evaluation. Almost every major case — such as *Eaton's* or *Dylex* — establishes some new benchmark in terms of what is an "acceptable procedure" in using the CCAA.

Another ongoing CCAA proceeding which has contributed to that process is that of The Canadian Red Cross Society (the "Red Cross"). Early last year, the Red Cross was under siege by victims of the tainted blood tragedy. Lawsuits claming in excess of $8 billion had been filed against the Red Cross and the pure task of managing all of this litigation had become simply impossible for the Red Cross. In addition, the Red Cross had agreed with the position of the Canadian government that it should get out of the blood supply business. However, the Red Cross had significant other businesses — such as disaster relief, humanitarian services, etc. — which it wished to preserve through a corporate reorganization.

On July 10, 1998 the Red Cross entered into an agreement of purchase and sale (the "Acquisition Agreement") whereby it agreed to sell its "blood program assets" for fair market value plus a premium to the two new governmental agencies which had been established (The Canadian Blood Services and Héma-Québec) conditional on, among other things, the obtaining of a court order providing for:

(1)   the "vesting" of title to the assets in the purchasers; and

(2)   the exemption of the transaction from the application of the *Bulk Sales Act* (R.S.O. 1990, c. B.14).

Shortly thereafter, on July 20, 1998 the Red Cross sought — and received — a court order granting protection under the CCAA. As referred to below, one of the terms of that "Initial Order" was a provision prohibiting the Red Cross from disposing of assets valued at more than $1 million without court approval.

On August 18, 1998 the Acquisition Agreement came before Mr. Justice Blair for both approval and the necessary vesting order. In a careful decision *Re Canadian Red Cross Society* (1998), 5 CBR (4th) 299, Mr. Justice Blair gave his approval to the sale and granted the vesting order. However, as reflected in the decision, lawyers for a number of the creditors (and in particular various groups of victims of tainted blood transfusions) sought to attack Mr. Justice Blair's jurisdiction to approve the agreement and grant the vesting order and his decision is noteworthy for the consideration which he gave to those arguments.

VESTING ORDERS ALLOWING THE SALE OF ASSETS BEFORE A REORGANIZATIONAL PLAN UNDER THE CCAA HAS BEEN FILED

First, some of the creditors' counsel argued that the court did not have jurisdiction to approve the sale at such an early stage in the proceedings — before the creditors had voted on anything or had much input into the process.

In this regard, a practice certainly had developed of companies under CCAA protection selling assets with court approval and pursuant to companion vesting orders before the company had filed a reorganizational plan. For example, Eaton's sold certain large pieces of real estate and some of their "non-core businesses" (such as a home security monitoring business) before they had even filed a reorganizational plan, subject to court approval and vesting order.

These vesting orders are typically styled as having been granted pursuant to both the CCAA and the *Courts of Justice Act* (R.S.0. 1990, c. C.43). In this regard, s. 100 of the *Courts of Justice Act* provides as follows:

> **100.** A court may by order vest in any person an interest in real or personal property that the court has authority to order be disposed of, encumbered or conveyed.

In the *Red Cross* case, Mr. Justice Blair made a careful evaluation of the court's jurisdiction in this regard. First he considered the Initial Order. Under s. 11(4) of the CCAA, such "stay orders" may be made "on such terms as [the court] may impose". In this regard Mr. Justice Blair commented:

> ... Paragraph 20 of the Initial Order granted in these proceedings on July 20, 1998, makes it a condition of the protection and stay given to the Red Cross that it not be permitted to [sell] or dispose of assets valued at more than $1 million without the approval of the Court. Clearly this is a condition which the Court has the jurisdiction to impose under section 11 of the [CCAA]. It is a necessary conjunction to such a condition that the debtor be entitled to come back to the Court and seek approval of a sale of such assets, if it can show it is in the best interests of the Company and its creditors as a whole that such approval be given. That is what it has done.

Thus, with reference to the terms of s. 101 of the *Courts of Justice Act*, the court had "authority to order" that the assets be disposed of by virtue of the terms of the Initial Order of July 20, 1998 — and which order was final and unappealed by the date of the approval hearing.

Mr. Justice Blair went on to consider the more general jurisdictional issues.

> It has been well established that the purpose of the CCAA is to facilitate compromises and arrangements between companies and their creditors, in order to assist insolvent companies to continue to carry on all or part of their business and to avoid bankruptcy, if that is economically feasible. In turn, a number of decisions have held that the court has a broad inherent jurisdiction to supplement the (relatively sparse) statutory provisions of the CCAA when it is just and equitable to do so: see, for example, *Re Lehndorff General Partner Ltd.* (1993), 17 C.B.R. (3d) 24; *Re Westar Mining* (1992), 14 C.B.R. (3d) 88 and *Re Dylex Ltd.* (1995) 31 C.B.R. (3d) 106.

In the *Re Dylex* case, Mr. Justice Farley referred (at pate 110) to the inherent jurisdiction of the Court and specifically discussed the availability of this inherent jurisdiction to the Court during the period prior to the preparation and submission of a plan pursuant to the CCAA in the following terms:

> [T]he court has the inherent jurisdiction to fill in gaps in legislation so as to give effect to the objects of the CCAA, including the survival program of a debtor until it can present a plan.

In his decision in the *Red Cross* case, Mr. Justice Blair commented:

> It is very common in CCAA restructurings for the Court to approve the sale and disposition of assets during the process and before the Plan [is] formally tendered and voted upon. ... The CCAA is designated to be a flexible instrument, and it is that very flexibility which gives it its efficacy. As Farley J. said in *Dylex, supra* (p. 111), "the history of CCAA law has been an evolution of judicial inter-pretation". ... [T]he orders are made, if the circumstances are appropriate and the orders can be made within the framework and in the spirit of the CCAA legislation. Mr. Justice Farley has well summarized this approach in the following passage from his decision in *Re Lehndorff General Partner* (1993) 17 C.B.R. (3d) 24, at p. 31, which I adopt:

> The CCAA is intended to facilitate compromises and arrangements between companies and their creditors as an alternative to bankruptcy and, as such, is remedial legislation entitled to a liberal interpretation. It seems to me that the purpose of the statute is to enable insolvent companies to carry on business in the ordinary course or *otherwise deal with their assets* so as to enable [a] plan of compromise or arrangement to be prepared, filed and considered by their creditors for the proposed compromise or arrangement which will be to the benefit of both the company and its creditors. See the preamble to and section 4, 5, 7, 8 and 11 of the CCAA (a lengthy list of authorities cited here is omitted).

> The CCAA is intended to provide a structured environment for the negotiation of compromises between a debtor company and its creditors for the benefit of both.

> Where a debtor company realistically plans to continue operating *or to otherwise deal with its assets* but it requires the protection of the court in order to do so and it is otherwise too early for the court to determine whether the debtor company will succeed, relief should be granted under the CCAA (citations omitted) (emphasis added)

> In the spirit of that approach, and having regard to the circumstances of this case, I am satisfied not only that the Court has the jurisdiction to make the approval and related orders sought, but also that it should do so. There is no realistic alternative to the sale and transfer that is proposed, and the alternative is a liquidation/ bankruptcy scenario which, on the evidence would yield an average of about 44% of the purchase price which the two agencies will pay. To forego that purchase price — supported as it is by reliable expert evidence — would in the circumstances be folly, not only for the ordinary creditors but also for the Transfusion Claimants, in my view.

> ... [A]s to exactly what considerations a court should have in mind in approving a transaction such as this, ... [the authorities] are scarce, ... [A]n appropriate analogy may be found in cases dealing with the approval of a sale by a court-appointed receiver. In those circumstances, as the Ontario Court of Appeal has indicated in *Royal Bank v Soundair Corp.* (1991), 7 C.B.R. (3d) 1, at p. 6, the Court's duties are,

> (i) to consider whether the receiver has made a sufficient effort to get the best price and has not acted improvidently;

> (ii) to consider the interest of the parties;

(iii) to consider the efficacy and integrity of the process by which offers are obtained; and

(iv) to consider whether there has been unfairness in the working out of the process.

I am satisfied on all such counts in the circumstances of this case.

Bulk sales act (ontario) exemption orders

As noted above, the terms of the Acquisition Agreement also required the Red Cross to obtain an order exempting the transaction from the application of Ontario's *Bulk Sales Act*.

The *Bulk Sales Act* focuses on "sale[s] of stock in bulk out of the usual course of business or trade of the seller" (s. 1). Although the term "stock" is generally defined as tangible personal property, the term "stock in bulk" is defined as "stock or part thereof that is the subject of a sale in bulk *and all other property, real or personal, that together with stock* is the subject of a sale in bulk" (s. 1) (emphasis added). As such, sales which involve largely intangible property — such as customer lists, etc. — may well be within the ambit of the Act.

Compliance with the *Bulk Sales Act* is often achieved through the following procedure. The seller provides an affidavit listing all of the seller's "trade creditors", classified as secured or unsecured. In this regard — as discussed below — it may be noted that the definitions of "secured trade creditors" and "unsecured trade creditors" in s. 1 focus on people who have supplied "stock, money or services... for the purpose of enabling the seller to carry on a business ...". In other words, the definitions do not speak of creditors with purely contingent claims, such as a damages claim, against the seller.

If the affidavit shows that the secured and unsecured trade creditors are not owed more than $2,500 for each category then, absent any knowledge to the contrary, the buyer may proceed to complete the transaction. However, if the amounts shown in the affidavit exceed $2,500 the purchaser comes under an onus to obtain verification that these creditors are being provided for as part of the terms of the sale.

Of course, the tension comes when an insolvent company tries to sell all or substantially all of its assets. In those circumstances, even if the amount of the purchase price fairly represents the market value of the assets (or, as sometimes is the case, even exceeds that market value) the money will not be enough to allow for treatment of all of the trade creditors. In this regard, the *Bulk Sales Act* contains a specific exemption for sales of assets of companies which have formally lapsed into bankruptcy or which have come under the legitimate exercise of the rights of a secured creditor or other properly authorized officials. In those cases, the vendor is not the company itself.

Specifically, s. 2 (as am., S.O. 1992, c. 32, s. 2) of the *Bulk Sales Act* provides as follows:

> **2.** This Act applies to every sale in bulk except a sale in bulk by an executor, an administrator, a guardian of property under the *Substitute Decisions Act*, 1992, a creditor realizing upon security, a receiver, an assignee or trustee for the benefit of creditors, a trustee under the *Bankruptcy Act* (Canada), a liquidator or official receiver or a public, or a public official acting under judicial process.

At the other end of the spectrum from insolvent companies are companies who are so demonstrably solvent (and sometimes also so large) that complying with the *Bulk Sales Act* through the preparation of the detailed affidavit of "trade debt" is really not appropriate.

For example, suppose that Chrysler Corporation wants to sell the assets of a small production facility for $2 million. Technically the *Bulk Sales Act* would require Chrysler to provide affidavit evidence of *all* its trade debt. In practice, vendors under such transactions routinely go to Court for Orders allowing them to complete such sales without complying with the *Bulk Sales Act*. Section 3(1) of the *Bulk Sales Act* provides specific jurisdiction for the seeking of such Orders in the following terms:

> **3.** (1) A seller may apply to a judge for an order exempting a sale in bulk from the application of this Act, and the judge, if satisfied, on the affidavit of the seller and any other evidence, that the sale is advantageous to the seller and will not impair the seller's ability to pay creditors in full, may make the order, and thereafter this Act, except section 7, does not apply to the sale.

The use of the expression "pay creditors in full" in s. 3 seems to connote that these court orders are only available to solvent companies. Interestingly, however, a number of unreported decisions have accepted the argument that *insolvent* companies — *i.e.* companies which have admitted that they cannot pay their creditors "in full" — may also seek Orders under s. 3 of the *Bulk Sales Act*.

Of course, where an insolvent company — such as the Red Cross — has filed for protection under the CCAA and wishes to sell assets, none of the classic exemptions provided for in s. 2 of the *Bulk Sales Act* are available because it is *the company itself* that wants to sell the assets — and not, say, a trustee in bankruptcy or a receiver. In fact, the company is trying to *avoid* bankruptcy or receivership by restructuring its affairs through, among other things, selling certain assets out of the ordinary course.

In the approval hearing before Mr. Justice Blair with respect to the sale of the blood program assets, counsel for some of the Red Cross's creditors questioned his jurisdiction to make an order under s. 3 of the *Bulk Sales Act*, exempting the sale form the *Bulk Sales Act*.

In considering this aspect of the attack on his jurisdiction to approve and authorize the sale, Mr. Justice Blair commented as follows:

> Some argument was directed towards the matter of an order under the *Bulk Sales Act*. Because of the nature and extent of the Red Cross assets being disposed of, the provisions of that Act must either be complied with, or an exemption from compliance obtained under s. 3 thereof. The circumstances warrant the granting of such an exemption in my view. While there were submissions about whether or not the sale would impair the Society's ability to pay its creditors in full, I do not believe that the sale will *impair* that ability. In fact, it may well enhance it. Even if one accepts the argument that the emphasis should be placed upon the language regarding payment "in full" rather than on "impair", the case qualifies for an exemption. It is conceded that the Transfusion claimants do not qualify as "creditors" as that term is defined under the *Bulk Sales Act*, and if the claims of the Transfusion Claimants are removed from the equation, it seems evident that other creditors could be paid from the proceeds in full.

Accordingly, Mr. Justice Blair specifically made clear that in interpreting the phrase "the sale ... will not impair the seller's ability to pay creditors in full ..." in section 3 of the *Bulk Sales Act*, the emphasis belongs on the word "impair" as opposed to the words "in full". As such, the section is available to demonstrably insolvent companies who can otherwise show that the sale is advantageous in the overall circumstances. Clearly, in the Red Cross situation, that was the case.

Mr. Justice Blair's decision also makes it clear that the only creditors whose claims should be counted in terms of evaluating whether the creditors are being provided for through the sale and in evaluating which creditors have jurisdiction to speak to the issue of whether an exemption order should be given, are "trade creditors" within the narrow definitions in s. 1 of the *Bulk Sales Act* and not creditors with damage claims.

INTER-PROVINCIAL RECOGNITION OF CCAA ORDERS

Companies seeking to reorganize obviously initiate the proceedings in a Court in a particular province. For example, a company headquartered in Toronto will make their court filing in Ontario. However, large companies usually have operations throughout the country.

In this regard, ss. 16 and 17 of the CCAA provide as follows:

> **16.** Every order made by the court in any province in the exercise of jurisdiction conferred by this Act in respect of any compromise or arrangement shall have full force and effect in all the other provinces and shall be enforced in the court of each of the other provinces in the same manner in all respects as if the order had been made by the court enforcing it

> **17.** All courts that have jurisdiction under this Act and the officers of those courts shall act in aid of and be auxiliary to each other in all matters provided

for in this Act, and an order of a court seeking aid with a request to another court shall be deemed sufficient to enable the latter court to exercise in regard to the matters directed by the order such jurisdiction as either the court that made the request or the court to which the request is made could exercise in regard to similar matters within their respective jurisdictions

It has been the practice that when the court orders have been made in CCAA proceedings — such as the Sale Approval Order which Mr. Justice Blair made with respect to the sale of the Red Cross blood program assets — a provision has been included requesting the assistance of courts in other provinces in giving effect to the Order. In turn, as a matter of practice, usually the company under protection has then gone to the courts in the various other relevant provinces and obtained "corresponding orders" recognizing the original Order. Thus, for example, if real estate properties located in both Toronto and Winnipeg are being sold, pursuant to a vesting order made in Ontario, the vendor would obtain a "corresponding order" in the Manitoba court and it would be that Manitoba Order which would be registered on the title to the Manitoba real estate in the Winnipeg registry office on the "closing date".

The *Red Cross* case routinely sought such orders in all other provinces after the granting of Mr. Justice Blair's order. The companion orders were given routinely in all of the provinces except British Columbia where counsel for one of the creditor groups opposed the granting of such a "companion order" by the British Columbia Supreme Court. In a very thorough decision Mr. Justice Fraser of the British Columbia Supreme Court held that, as a result of the terms of s. 16 of the CCAA, these "companion orders" are really not necessary and orders made in CCAA proceedings in one province are essentially "automatically enforceable" in the other provinces in which the debtor company is carrying on business.

In this regard, Mr. Justice Fraser commented, in part, as follows:

> Section 16 [of the CCAA] has no counterpart in other federal legislation, so far as counsel and I are aware. In particular, s. 188 of the *Bankruptcy and Insolvency Act* contains only the second branch of s. 16:
>
>> 188.(1) An order made by the court under this Act shall be enforced in the courts having jurisdiction in bankruptcy elsewhere in Canada in the same manner in all respects as if the order had been made by the court hereby required to enforce it.
>
> Section 188(1) links the extra-provincial effect of an order made in one province to an enforcement proceeding taken in the court of the other province, that is, it implies the commencement of proceedings in that other court. By contrast, the statement in s. 16 is freestanding, with enforcement proceedings made subordinate.

...

Those for whom legislative language is a working tool can recognize s. 16 as having been nicely conceived and cleanly rendered.

I conclude that the meaning of s. 16 is clear; and that it is never necessary to apply for an order such as the one sought here. In a situation of need, such as the refusal of an official to recognize an order made in another province, the enforcement component of s. 16 can be invoked by an application to court.

In particular, I reject the contention of the petitioners and the Red Cross that the words "shall be enforced" in s. 16 mean that proceedings like this one *must* be commenced, that the parties are required automatically to go to the courts of all the other provinces. That interpretation would negate the principal thrust of the section; and make cumbersome what is now efficiently realized.

Although it might seem a relatively technical point, this decision should prove to be quite important in minimizing the costs associated with reorganizing a "multi-provincial" company under the CCAA.

Leave to appeal the decision of Mr. Justice Blair in the *Red Cross* proceedings was sought from, and denied by, the Ontario Court of Appeal and Mr. Justice Fraser's decision was not appealed. As such, these two decisions represent important benchmarks in terms of the questions which they considered. In particular, these decisions seem to put to rest the issue of whether or not the insolvent companies can avail themselves of s. 3 of the Ontario Bulk Sales Act, whether or not companies which have obtained an Initial Order of "protection" under the CCAA can sell assets (with court approval) before they have filed a reorganizational plan and the extent to which CCAA Orders made in the court of any particular province are automatically enforceable in any other provinces.

[Editor's note: Jeffrey Carhart, B.A., L.L.B., practises corporate and commercial law with the firm of Miller Thomson, Toronto. He is the author of the book *The Business Owner's Guide to Bankruptcy and Insolvency Law in Canada* (John Wiley & Sons Canada Ltd.) and has written articles on commercial insolvency published in the Canadian Bankruptcy Reports, The National Creditor/Debtor Review and other publications. Mr. Carhart is also an instructor in the Debtor/Creditor Law section of the Bar Administrations Course. A portion of this article — dealing with the Bulk Sales Act issues — appeared earlier in slightly different form in Vol. 14, No. 3, May 1999 *Insolvency News* published by the Canadian Bar Association - Ontario.]

BULK SALES ACT — RECENT CASES

9.074.2—Most provinces have repealed their Bulk Sales legislation, with the view that there is sufficient fraudulent conveyance law to protect creditors, and that Bulk Sales legislation is in practice, commercially disruptive. However, Ontario continues to preserve its Bulk Sales Act[1] (the "Act").

The purpose of the Act is to protect creditors of the seller by ensuring that the proceeds of the sale are used to pay the seller's debts. That said, the legislation is for the benefit of the trade creditors and the Act places the responsibility on the purchaser to comply with certain mechanisms in the Act to ensure that this purpose is fulfilled. If the purchaser fails to comply with the Act, and the sale proceeds are not used to pay the seller's creditors, the purchaser becomes personally liable to account to the creditors for the value of what the seller should have paid them.

Recent case law in Ontario suggests that those in commercial transactions which involve a sale of assets in bulk should pay close attention to the compliance mechanisms within the Act.

The following discussion provides an overview of the recent jurisprudence which addresses various issues arising under the Act.

1. What Constitutes a "Sale in Bulk"?

Generally, the Act, is directed to a sale of stock in bulk out of the usual course of business or trade of the seller (section 1). The term "stock in bulk" is also defined in section 1 as "stock or part thereof that is the subject of a sale in bulk and all other property, real or personal, that together with the stock is the subject of the sale. Therefore, a sale which involves in part intangible property, such as licenses, trademarks, and customer lists in addition to tangible property would likely be considered to be within the scope of Act.

In *Toronto (Overseas) Freight Services Inc. v. Grover*[2] one of Toronto Freight's customers, SNG, had defaulted in payment on a number of invoices in the amount of $30,000. Subsequently, SNG entered into an agreement of purchase of sale with the respondent, Grover, pursuant to which SNG agreed to sell all of its assets to Grover for a purchase price of $45,000. SNG refused to provide an affidavit to Grover listing details of its secured and unsecured trade creditors as required under section 4 of the Act. SNG alleged that the sale was not a "sale in bulk" as it would continue to carry on business elsewhere and further alleged that the assets being sold were not a "substantial part" of the business. As such, Grover did not comply with the Act by paying the sale price before obtaining the affidavit from SNG. Subsequently, Grover went out of business, and one of its creditors seized all the assets on the premises, including the assets purchased from SNG.

The court found that the sale of the assets was in fact a sale in bulk as the sale was a sale "out of the ordinary course of the usual business or trade of the seller". Justice Molloy stated the following at page 143:

> The test for whether a sale of assets is covered by the Act is found in sections 1 and 2 of the Act. This sale was a sale of the seller's "stock", and was a sale "out of the ordinary course of the usual business of or trade of the seller". This was

not an isolated sale of one or two individual items, out of the ordinary course. It was a sale of numerous items of the seller's stock, designed to enable the purchaser to carry on business previously engaged in by the seller at a particular location. It was clearly a "sale in bulk". Therefore the Act applies.

The court emphasized that a sale in bulk does not require the sale of the assets to wipe out the entire operation of the seller or prevent the seller from continuing to carry on its business. Further, Justice Molloy held that a sale in bulk does not require that there be a sale of "substantially all" of the assets of a company. Specifically, the court noted that if there was a sale of substantially all of the assets of a company, the sale would obviously be a sale in bulk. However, the reverse was not necessarily true.

2. The Effect of Non-compliance with the Act

Generally, the compliance mechanisms are as follows:

- The purchaser is to demand from the seller before paying or delivering to the seller any part of the proceeds of the sale, a statement verified by affidavit of the seller. The statement is to list all of the "trade" creditors, (secured and unsecured) and the amount of indebtedness owing to each of these creditors (section 4).

- If the affidavit shows that the secured creditors and unsecured trade creditors are not owed more than $2,500 for each category, the purchaser can proceed to complete the transaction. However, if the amounts for each category exceed $2,500, then the purchaser is under an onerous obligation to ensure that the seller provides verification that the trade creditors are being provided for pursuant to the terms of the sale (section 8(1)).

- Within five days after the completion of a sale in bulk, a purchaser is required to file with the court an affidavit setting out the particulars of the sale, and is also required to attach as an exhibit the seller's affidavit as provided under section 4 of the Act (section 11).

- If the purchaser does not comply with the Act, the sale is voidable. If the sale in bulk is set aside or declared void, and the purchaser has already taken possession of the stock in bulk, the purchaser is personally responsible to account to all the creditors of the seller for the value of the stock in bulk (section 16(2)).

- A creditor of the seller, or a trustee of the seller (if the seller is an adjudged bankrupt) can apply to have the sale set aside or declared void (section 17(1)).

Sidaplex-Plastic Inc. v. Elta Group Inc.[3] involved corporate parties who were all engaged in the production and sale of equipment in the graphic arts industry. Sidaplex was a judgment creditor of the defendant Elta Group. The terms of the judgment were secured by an irrevocable letter of credit in favour of Sidaplex further to which Sidaplex could not call on the letter of credit until there was a resolution of another action commenced by Elta Group against Sidaplex. In the meantime, Elta Group entered into an asset purchase agreement with the other defendant in the action, Kimoto Canada Inc. The proceeds of the sale were used to eliminate some of Elta Group's debts, with the exception of its debt owed to Sidaplex. The sale did not comply with the Act, in that neither Elta Group nor Kimoto filed affidavits with the court, nor did they obtain an order exempting the application of the Act. The Court of Appeal made the following conclusions at page 165:

> …..Sidaplex was not a "trade creditor" for whom provision would have to made under s. 8(1)(c) of the Act, if Kimoto and Elta had complied with s. 4, since the debt to Sidaplex did not become "due and payable upon completion of the sale". However, resort to either method under s. 8 depends upon the buyer having received the s. 4 statement. That was not done in this case. In my view, the fact that had Kimoto complied with s. 4, it could have completed the sale under s. 8(1) without making provision for Sidaplex does not deprive Sidaplex of a remedy. Under s. 17 (1) of the Act, an action or proceeding to set aside or have declared void a sale in bulk may be brought or taken by " a creditor". *Thus, even though Sidaplex was not a person for whom provision needed to be made under s. 8, it is entitled to apply to set aside the sale. As there was no doubt that Sidaplex was a creditor of Elta, it was entitled to apply under s. 17 to have the sale set aside.* [Emphasis added]

Further, the court held that section 16(2) of the Act, which makes the buyer personally liable to account "to creditors" of the seller for the value of stock taken into possession under the sale, was not limited only to trade creditors, but was also available to Sidaplex, who was in fact a judgment creditor.

The court commented on two additional issues which are worth consideration:

i)   Whether the court has discretion to refuse to set aside a bulk sale under an application under section 17; and

ii)   Whether a creditor can waive its right to relief under section 16(2) of the Act.

On the issue of discretion, the court held that since an application to set aside a bulk sale is in fact a representative action for the benefit of all the creditors of the seller, *except where there has been some technical non-compliance, the court does not have the discretion to refuse to declare a sale void. It should be noted that this strict interpretation of section 16(2) is later rejected by the Supreme Court of Canada, in a case discussed below.*

On the issue of the waiver, the purchaser argued that Sidaplex waived compliance with the Act through its conduct. Sidaplex argued that the waiver must be in compliance with section 8 of the Act, by delivering a Form 2, which was never done in this case. The court held that since Sidaplex was not a trade creditor under section 8, the written waiver Form 2 requirement would not have any application. *However, the court did recognize that just because the Act allows for a written waiver in certain circumstances, this did not preclude the buyer from asserting that the creditor waved its right to relief in view of its conduct.*

In *National Trust Co. v. H&R Block Canada Inc.,*[4] the defendant, H&R Block, purchased stock in bulk from Tax Time Services ("Tax Time"), a company in serious financial difficulty. All of the sale proceeds ($800,000) were used to pay off Tax Time's most heavily secured creditors. The other secured creditors were not all paid in full and the unsecured creditors were paid nothing. The Appellant, National Trust Company, was an unsecured creditor. H&R Block did not comply with the Act, by failing to demand affidavits, or by obtaining a court order to dispense with the application of the Act pursuant to section 3. National Trust moved under the Act to have the sale declared void, and further required H&R Block to account to it for the value of the bulk goods pursuant to section 16(2) of the Act.

3. Court of Appeal

The majority of the Ontario Court of Appeal endorsed the conclusions of the Applications Judge stating that purpose of the Act was to protect unsecured as well as secured creditors. In the majority's view, *the fact that no party acted dishonestly or with any fraudulent intent to defeat the creditors of Tax Time, and the fact that Tax Time did not pocket any proceeds of the sale but rather paid its secured creditors in priority to their claims, was still not sufficient in light of purpose the Act.* The court further stated that H&R Block's calculated unilateral decision not to comply with the Act meant that all unsecured creditors, including National Trust, were deprived of their statutory right to contest the sale. In light of H&R Block's conduct, the court held H&R Block liable to National Trust for the debt owed to them, plus interest on that amount.

In a strong dissent, Justice Borins held that even if H&R Block complied with the Act (i.e. pursuant to section 8 of the Act), National Trust, as an unsecured creditor, would not have been entitled to anything from the sale regardless of compliance. Justice Borins was of the view that it was not the legislature's intention that section 16(2) of the Act be applied to enable a creditor, where there has been no compliance with the Act, to be in a better position than it would have been if there had been compliance. In sum, Justice Borins held that since no party was unjustly enriched at the expense of National Trust and since there was no misuse of the sale proceeds, the application by National Trust to have the sale declared void for non-compliance and for an accounting to it in respect of the value of the bulk sale should be denied.

4. Supreme Court of Canada

In a majority decision by the Supreme Court of Canada, the court agreed with Justice Borins' reasoning, as National Trust was not deprived of any money it would have received on a rateable distribution of the proceeds of the bulk sale. In other words, Tax Time's payments to its two highest ranking creditors did not place National Trust at a disadvantage. To now require H&R Block to pay National Trust the value of the proceeds of the sale would be an unfair result. The court ultimately held that National Trust was not entitled to damages under the section 16(2) duty to account.

Upon an extensive and thorough overview of the history of bulk sales legislation, the court outlined two significant purposes of the Act at paragraph 6:

> The Bulk Sales Act has at least two significant objectives or purposes: (i) to protect the interest of all creditors whose debtors have disposed of all or substantially all of their assets; and (ii) to ensure the fair distribution of the proceeds of a sale in bulk among the sellers' creditors, based on their priority ranking. The clear legislative intent is to deter fraud and to ensure that creditors are properly paid. This said, I am of the view that the Bulk Sales Act is not intended to be punitive in nature and that this should be taken into account in its interpretation. A purposive approach to the accounting required under s. 16(2) directs us to look to the substance and not merely the form of the payment to the seller's creditors from the proceeds of the sale. The court retains the discretion to consider all of the facts of the case to determine whether liability to account under s. 16(2) has been fulfilled.[5]

The court also comments on Justice Rosenberg's reasons in the *Sidaplex* case (*supra*). The court in essence rejects Justice Rosenberg's proposition that once the buyer has failed to comply with the provisions of the Act, the necessary result is that the buyer be penalized by paying to creditors what the vendor was required to pay them. The court reasoned that had the Applications Judge (Justice Spence) not been required to follow the Court of Appeal in *Sidaplex*, he should have, based on the proper interpretation of section 16(2), have simply refused to set aside the bulk sale.

On issues of policy, the court emphasized that there are strong policy reasons for facilitating efficient business transactions while protecting creditors. The court states at paragraph 43:

> As a matter of policy, a strong argument for a "strict liability" reading of the duty to account is one focused on certainty. A strict accounting is a bright-line rule: if you do not comply, then you pay twice. Indeed … the wording of s. 16(2) could be seen to support such view. It is my opinion, however, that a purposive approach to s. 16(2) precludes such an interpretation. With great respect for my colleague's dissenting reasons, it seems unreasonable that an unsecured creditor who would not have recovered any payment *even* if the

buyer had complied with the Act, should now be in a position to benefit from the buyer's non-compliance with the Act.[6]

Goldhar v. J.M. Publications Inc.[7] presented an interesting dilemma to the court where the parties to the sale transaction waived compliance with the Act and further agreed that the vendor indemnify any liability of the purchaser. This term was part of the transfer documents. The court held that while such practice may be a common commercial practice where the sale is between non-arm's length related companies, *it is not technically possible to waive compliance with the Act, as far as creditors are concerned. As such, the court held that the creditors continued to have protection under the Act, and could seek payment from the purchaser.*

5. Effect of a Stay under the Bankruptcy and Insolvency Act on a Bulk Sales Act Application

Mondetta Telecommunications Inc. Re[8] involved a motion brought by a secured creditor of the debtor, Mondetta, to prohibit an unsecured creditor from proceeding with its application under the Act.

Mondetta entered into a transaction with Symphony Telecom Inc. ("Telecom"), whereby Telecom acquired Mondetta's customer base, goodwill, trade name, accounts receivables and some of its liabilities in exchange for shares in Telecom's parent company. Pepper Plus was an unsecured creditor of Mondetta and had an outstanding judgment against it. Pepper Plus commenced an application under the Act seeking a declaration that the action was void and seeking damages from Telecom in the amount of the full value of its judgment ($307,382.62) pursuant to section 16(2) of the Act. The hearing of the application was adjourned but with a further order prohibiting the parties from actually transferring the assets pending determination of the Bulk Sales Act application. As a result, the shares which were to be transferred to Mondetta remained in the hands of Telecom. Subsequently, Mondetta made an assignment in bankruptcy.

One of the issues to be determined was whether, Pepper Plus had standing to proceed, given the bankruptcy, because of the effect of section 17(1) of the Act. Under this section, either a "creditor of the seller" or a trustee of the seller's estate if the seller is bankrupt, are the only parties who can apply to set aside a bulk sale. Justice Swinton was of the view that a stay is not read into section 17(1) of the Act when a bankruptcy occurs, as the language of the section seems to confer a right on the trustee to bring an application, in addition to creditors. As such, Justice Swinton held that "standing is not lost under the Act by a creditor on bankruptcy".

The second issue to be determined was whether the stay imposed under section 69.3 of the Bankruptcy and Insolvency Act[9] (the "BIA"), operates to preclude Pepper Plus from continuing with its Bulk Sales Act application. Justice Swinton held that the application of the stay provision in the BIA would necessitate a stay of the Bulk Sales Act proceeding against Telecom and Mondetta, as the application by Pepper Plus would have an effect against the debtor's property. Specifically, the court noted that should the application proceed and Pepper Plus obtain an order that would void the sale, the shares to be transferred to Mondetta under the sale agreement would not likely turn over since the bankrupt's proprietary interest in the shares would terminate. Justice Swinton further held that since the trustee in bankruptcy had a duty to act in the best interest of all the creditors, and was in the best position to determine whether to pursue the Bulk Sales Act application, it was not appropriate to lift the stay at this time.

6. Application of the Exemption

Section 2 of the Act provides for a specific exemption for a sale of assets of a person who has gone into bankruptcy or has come under the exercise of the rights of a secured creditor or other authorized persons, (i.e. a sale in bulk by an executor, an administrator, a creditor realizing upon its security, a receiver, or a trustee would be exempt from the Act).

Section 3 of the Act provides an exception for a seller, whereby a seller can apply to a judge for an order exempting them from the application of the Act, if the judge is satisfied that, on the affidavit of the seller, the sale is advantageous and will not impair the ability of the seller to pay its creditors in full.

While this section appears to apply to only solvent entities, there has been case law that suggests that even an insolvent seller can apply for the exemption, in circumstances where the seller is restructuring its operations through selling some of its assets in an effort to avoid bankruptcy. In such a situation, the section 2 exemption would not apply, since it is the seller itself who wishes to sell its assets and not one of the authorized persons as listed in this section. Hence, in order to dispense with the application of the Act, the seller would have to move under section 3 of the Act.

In *Canadian Red Cross Society Re*[10] the Society obtained protection under the Companies' Creditors Arrangement Act, and put forward a proposal to transfer its blood supply assets to two new agencies. This proposal was a result of a massive number of lawsuits in excess of $8 billion that had been filed against the Society in relation to the tainted blood tragedy. The plan proposed that the proceeds of the sale would be used to satisfy the claims of the victims. The Society sought among other things, an exemption from the application of the Act. A cross-motion was brought on behalf of one of the groups of the Transfusion Claimants for an order that the court consider its counter proposal that the Society continue to operate its blood supply system long enough to generate enough revenue to create a compensation fund for the victims.

The motion was granted and the cross-motion was dismissed. Justice Blair delineated the scope of section 3 of the Act at page 317 of his decision:

Some argument was directed to the matter of the order under the Bulk Sales Act. Because of the nature and extent of the Red Cross assets being disposed of, the provisions of that Act must either be complied with, or an exemption from compliance obtained under s. 3 thereof. The circumstances warrant the granting of such an exemption in my view. While there were submissions about whether or not the sale would impair the Society's ability to pay its creditors in full, I do not believe that the sale will impair that ability. In fact, it may well enhance it. Even if one accepts the argument that the emphasis should be placed upon the language regarding payment "in full" rather than on "impair", the case qualifies for an exemption. It is conceded that the Transfusion Claimants do not qualify as "creditors" as that is defined under the Bulk Sales Act; and if the claims of the Transfusion Claimants are removed from the equation, it seems evident that other creditors could be paid from the proceeds in full".

Based on the foregoing, it would seem therefore that section 3 is available to an insolvent seller who can show that the sale is otherwise advantageous in light of the overall circumstances of the sale. Further, it would seem that creditors with damage claims, such as the Transfusion Claimants, are not to be included when determining whether or not the creditors will be provided for under the sale pursuant to the section 3 and the creditors who are to be accounted for are "trade creditors" as defined in section 1 of the Act.

7. Definition of a Trade Creditor

Section 1 of the Act defines a "creditor" as "any creditor, including an unsecured trade creditor and a secured trade creditor". While certain sections of the Act apply only to "trade creditors", it would appear that section 17(1) of the Act, includes "any creditor" as defined in section 1.

In *Devry v. Atwood's Furniture Showrooms Ltd.,*[11] the court seemingly and incorrectly narrowed the definition of a "creditor" in section 17(1). In this case, a judgment creditor (Devry) obtained damages for wrongful dismissal from her former employer. Subsequent to Devry's claim, the company's assets were sold and the affidavit did not list Devry as an "unsecured trade creditor". Devry moved to have the sale declared void pursuant to section 16(1) and 17(1) of the Act. Justice Swinton was of the view that since Devry was not an unsecured trade creditor for which the seller was required to list to the buyer pursuant to section 4(1) of the Act, she could not apply under section 17(1) as a "creditor of the seller" to have the sale declared void, since Devry's debt arose from the breach of an employment contract which did not "arise as a result of services provided to enable the seller to carry on its business within section 1 of the Bulk Sales Act".

It is worthwhile to note that Justice Swinton's decision does not coincide with the Court of Appeal in *Sidaplex* discussed above. Recall, that in that case, the Court of Appeal interpreted "creditor" in section 17(1) to include *any creditor* of the seller, including judgment creditors.

8. Conclusion

In summary, the following considerations should be made when acting for a purchaser or a seller who is engaged in a transaction involving a sale of assets:

- Whether the seller is selling stock which consists of one or two items, or whether the sale involves a sufficient amount of stock out of the ordinary course of business or trade of the seller. A sale of "substantially all of the assets" is not a prerequisite to have a "sale in bulk".

- Whether or not a creditor is a "trade creditor", and ensuring compliance with those sections which refer to "trade creditors" as well as a consideration of whether the unsecured creditors, including judgment creditors can be accounted for from the proceeds.

- Whether a stay under the BIA may impact a creditor's application to set aside the sale under the Act.

- Whether the exemption under section 3 of the Act is also available to an insolvent seller, where the sale could be proven to be advantageous in the overall circumstances.

- Whether a waiver of compliance with the Act by conduct may be asserted by an applicant in certain circumstances (i.e. buyers are not necessarily limited to asserting the written waiver provision in section 8(1)(c) of the Act).

- Whether non-compliance of the Act, in circumstances where there has been proper and fair distribution of proceeds to creditors in accordance with the priority scheme, will, nevertheless, enable a creditor to invoke the remedy available in section 16(2) of the Act, notwithstanding the fact that there has been no dishonesty or fraud by the parties involved in the sale.

[*Editor's note*: Arthi Sambasivan is an associate in Miller Thomson's Litigation Department. Her practice includes a wide range of commercial litigation matters with a focus on insolvency, restructuring and collection-related issues.]

---

1. R.S.O. 1990, c. B-14

2. (2001), 16 B.L.R. (3d) 140, [2001] O.J. No. 2857 (S.C.J.).

3. (1998) 43 B.L.R. (2d) 155, [1998] O.J. No. 2910 (C.A.).

4. (2001) 18 B.L.R (3d) 172, [2001] O.J. No. 4127 (C.A.); rev'd, [2003] 3 S.C.R. 160, [2003] S.C.J. No. 70.

5. *Ibid.*, at p. 166, para 6.

6. *Ibid.*, at p. 189.

7. (2000) 13 B.L.R. (3d) 181, [2000] O.J. No. 843 (S.C.J.).

8. (2001) 24 C.B.R. (4th) 222 (Ont. S.C.J.).

9. R.S.C. 1985, c. B-3.

10. (1998) 5 C.B.R. (4th) 299 (Ont. Gen. Div.) (leave to appeal on the issue refused).

11. (2000) 11 B.L.R. (3d) 227, [2000] O.J. No. 4283 (S.C.J.).

Land Transfer Tax

9.075—In any transaction involving "land", as defined in section 1(1) of the Land Transfer Tax Act[1] (the "Act"), land transfer tax may be payable. Generally speaking, whenever a conveyance of land is tendered for registration[2] or where there is a disposition of a beneficial interest,[3] land transfer tax will be payable based on the "value of the consideration"[4] unless the transaction qualifies for an exemption or a deferral. Prior to the enactment of the Land Transfer Tax Amendment Act,[5] registration was a requirement before land transfer tax was payable. The effect of the amendment is to require payment of land transfer tax on certain dispositions of a beneficial interest *whether or not* registration in fact occurs.

The following is only intended to be a brief overview of those provisions of the Act that may apply on the sale of a business. The Act and the regulations thereunder contain many of the required forms along with additional information which have not been duplicated here.

1. R.S.O. 1990, c. L.6, s. 1, am. 1994, c. 18, s. 4, 1996, c. 18, s. 7, 1996, c. 29, s. 16, 1997, c. 10, s. 8, 1998, c. 5, s. 29, 1999, c. 6, s. 32.

2. *Ibid.*, s. 2, am. 1994, c. 18, s. 4.

3. *Ibid.*, s. 3, am. 1994, c. 18, s. 4.

4. As defined in s. 1(1).

5. S.O. 1989, c. 77 [now R.S.O. 1990, c. L.6].

PRELIMINARY CONSIDERATIONS

9.076—**Residency:** The Act was amended effective May 7, 1997[1] to delete any distinction between "resident" and "non-resident".

Value of the Consideration: The definition is extremely broad and is defined to *include* seven distinct subclauses. In most cases it will be the agreed purchase price where that purchase price is with respect to "land". However, in many commercial transactions, the purchase price includes many other elements such as equipment, goodwill, inventory, shares, etc. In those situations, it is necessary for the parties to direct their minds to an appropriate allocation of the purchase price. In the case of a conveyance of land to a corporation where any part of the consideration consists of the allotment and issuance of the corporation's shares, or in the case of a conveyance of land from a corporation to any of its shareholders, "the value of the consideration" is the fair market value, ascertained at the time of the tender for registration, of the land to which the conveyance extends[2].

Land: The definition of land is very broad and is defined to include "lands, tenements and hereditaments and any estate, right or interest therein, a structure to be constructed on land as part of an arrangement relating to a conveyance of land, a leasehold interest or estate, the interest of an optionee, the interest of an optionee, the interest of a purchaser under an arrangement to sell land, or good will attributable to the location of land or to the existence thereon of any building or fixture, and fixtures".[3]

Rate:

(a) .5 per cent of the value of the consideration for the conveyance up to and including $55,000 ($275);

(b) 1 per cent of the value of the consideration which exceeds $55,000 up to and including $250,000; and

(c) 1.5 per cent of the value of the consideration which exceeds $250,000.

There is one further notch provision dealing with single family dwellings (as defined) where the value of the consideration is in excess of $400,000.

---

1. Land Transfer Tax Act, R.S.O. 1990, c. L.6, am. 1997, C. 10, s. 22.

2. *Ibid.*, s. 1(1).

3. *Ibid.*, s. 1, am. 1994, c. 18, s. 4.

COMMON EXEMPTIONS

9.077—Although certain transactions may be included in the definition of "conveyance" under the Land Transfer Tax Act,[1] the following is a list of the more common exemptions:

Certain inter-spousal transfers: Where there is a separation agreement, court order or natural love and affection where the only consideration is the assumption of existing encumbrances, no land transfer tax is payable.[2]

Natural love and affection: Where the whole of the value of the consideration is natural love and affection, no tax is payable. However, if part of the value of the consideration is the assumption of any encumbrance on the land, tax is payable on the amount assumed.[3]

Contributions of capital to corporations: Where a conveyance of land that is a contribution of capital to a corporation is tendered for registration and no consideration is given by the corporation for the land, no tax is payable.[4]

Change in legal tenure: Simple changes in the form of legal tenure of land between the same parties from tenancy in common to joint tenancy or vice versa are not taxable. However, where the interest of a transferee is increased in land, land transfer tax will be payable on the amount of the increase.[5]

Statutory amalgamation: Where by virtue of a statutory amalgamation, the land or lands of two or more companies become vested in the company resulting from the amalgamation, no land transfer tax is payable.[6] (See Bulletin LTT-4 issued under the Act).

Family farm or family business: Where the conveyance involves a family farm corporation or family business corporation the transaction may qualify for an exemption.[7]

Certain mineral lands: Certain conveyances involving only mineral rights, or the grant, sale, transfer or assignment of a surface rights option (but not the exercise thereof) or any combination of the two is exempt subject to the requirements under Regulation 703 of the Act.[8]

Oil or gas pipe line easements: This exemption is of interest only to those corporations whose principal business is the construction or operation of pipe lines for the transportation of oil, gas or other liquid and gaseous hydro-carbons and products thereof.[9]

Leases: Where at the time the instrument is tendered for registration the lease is for an unexpired term which, including renewals or extensions of the terms, cannot exceed fifty years, no land transfer tax is payable. A recent amendment[10] includes a separate option to lease or other document entered into as part of the arrangement relating to the lease (whether or not the lessee and the optionee or person named in the document are the same persons). If the term including renewals and extensions does exceed 50 years, land transfer tax is payable on the fair market value.[11]

Conveyances to the Crown: Where the only transferee is the Crown or Crown agency, no land transfer tax is payable.[12]

Testacy and intestacy: Where a conveyance of land from the personal representative of a deceased person to a transferee, who is receiving the property in satisfaction of all or part of his beneficial interest in the estate of a deceased person, no land transfer tax is payable.[13]

---

1. R.S.O. 1990, c. L.6.

2. Refer to R.R.O. 1990, Reg. 696 under the Land Transfer Tax Act.

3. See Bulletin LTT-8 issued under the Act.

4. See Bulletin LTT-3 (2000) issued under the Act.

5. See Bulletin LTT-10 (2000) issued under the Act and the definition of "transferee", section 1 of the Act.

6. See Bulletin LTT-3 (2000) issued under the Act.

7. See R.R.O. 1990, Reg. 697 and O. Reg. 87/04 under the Act.

8. R.R.O. 1990.

9. R.R.O. 1990, Reg. 695.

10. S.O. 1994, c. 18, s. 4(4) deemed in force November 29, 1993.

11. R.S.O. 1990, c. L.6, s. 1(6).

12. R.S.O. 1990, c. L.6, s. 2(8).

13. See Bulletin LTT-10 (2000) issued under the Act.

Reduction or Deferral of Tax

9.078—Certain conveyances between trustees and between trustees and beneficial owners: Where no monies or value of the consideration of any kind passes between trustees or between trustees and beneficial owners and provided all other requirements are met, the value of the consideration is deemed to be nil and therefore no land transfer tax is payable. In order to qualify, the strict requirements of not only Bulletins LTT-1 and LTT-2 issued under the Act but also the corresponding guide issued under the Act must be followed. So long as a transferor, transferee or the solicitor for either is able to swear an affidavit with respect to all of the requirements, the value of the consideration will be deemed to be nil.[1] This procedure was used quite frequently to avoid payment of land transfer tax. The transferor, transferee or the solicitor for either was able to swear the appropriate affidavit, transfer the title to the trustee and avoid payment of land transfer tax. After registration, an unregistered change in beneficial ownership with respect to the trustee (usually a corporation) was effected. This procedure, however, is no longer available since the passing of the Land Transfer

Tax Amendment Act,[1] as unregistered dispositions of beneficial interests of this nature are now subject to land transfer tax.

---

1. S.O. 1989, c. 77 [now R.S.O. 1990, c. L.6].

International Sale of Goods Convention

9.079—Effective May 1, 1992, Canada became a signatory to the United Nations Convention on Contracts for the International Sale of Goods,[1] more popularly known as the Vienna Sales Convention (the "Convention"). Most of the jurisdictions within Canada have already passed their enabling legislation codifying the Convention into their own statute. In Ontario, this is the Inter-national Sale of Goods Act,[2] which statute also came into effect on May 1, 1992.

The goal of the Convention is to bring uniformity of terms to international sales of goods. This is much the same as the application of implied terms and conditions found in various sale of goods statutes in Canada. With certain exceptions (for sales of household goods, electricity, aircraft and ships), the Convention provides that the terms and conditions set out in the Convention will apply to an international sale unless the parties specifically except application of the Convention. A sale will include goods to be manufactured or produced unless the purchaser supplies the majority of materials necessary for the production. In addition, the Convention sets forth certain rules considering the respective obligations of the buyer and the seller, formation of the contract, passage of title and risk, and remedies for breach of the contract. The Convention applies whether or not there is a written agreement.

Consequently, if the asset transaction for the client includes goods both within and without Canada, it may be necessary to include in the agreement of purchase and sale, a specific provision respecting the Convention. The parties may wish to have the implied terms and conditions of the Convention regulate their transaction or conversely, they may choose a law of a specified jurisdiction to interpret their agreement.

It is essential to exclude the application of the Convention in writing if that is what the parties wish. A clause such as the following should be used:

> The parties hereto agree that the Convention on Contracts for the International Sale of Goods shall not apply to this agreement. The parties choose to have the laws of the province of * to apply to the interpretation and enforcement of this agreement, and the parties attorn to the law and the Courts of such jurisdiction.

As of May 1, 1992, the contracting states to the Convention include the United States, France, Italy, Germany, China, Mexico, the Scandinavian countries and about 20 others. Japan and the United Kingdom have not signed the Convention as of that date.

---

1. R.S.O. 1990, c. I.10, Schedule.

2. R.S.O. 1990, c. I.10.

Privacy Legislation—General Information

9.079.1 – On January 1, 2001 the federal Personal Information Protection and Electronic Documents Act[1] ("PIPEDA") came into force. The legislation was adopted both to strengthen e-commerce in Canada and to ensure that Canada complied with the E.U. Data Directive[2] to permit the free flow of personal information between the European Union and Canada.

PIPEDA prohibits the collection, use or disclosure of personal information without the informed consent of the individual concerned, except where specifically permitted in PIPEDA. It requires organizations to appoint compliance officers, prepare privacy policies, and to make this information available to individuals. Personal information is to be retained for a limited time, to be held in reasonable security, and provided to the individual concerned in a timely fashion upon request. Organizations are also required to develop data retention policies, compliance and complaint procedures, and contractual means for providing a comparable level of protection when personal information is provided to a third party for processing on behalf of the organization.

For organizations to which PIPEDA applies, the consent of the individuals concerned will now be required for the transfer of items such as customer lists, mailing lists, and employee records, whether in electronic or paper form. While the primary remedy for a breach is a complaint to the federal Privacy Commissioner, whose findings are not binding on the parties, matters not resolved may lead to an action in Federal Court.[3]

In the United States, the failure of organizations to comply with the requirements of their own privacy policies has led to interventions that have effectively halted the transfer of the data,[4] or have required that consent be obtained from each individual. If the individual refuses to consent to the transfer, then that person's name and information must be deleted, reducing the value of the list.[5]

The provisions of PIPEDA apply to personal information collected by organizations before it came into effect.[6]

The federal government relied on the trade and commerce power[7] as interpreted by the Supreme Court in *General Motors v. City National Leasing*[8] as the authority for PIPEDA. Accordingly it applies only to commercial activities and to employees of federal works, undertakings or businesses.[9] Further until January 1, 2004 it does not apply to personal information collected, used, or disclosed entirely within a province, "… unless the activity is carried out in connection with the operation of a federal work, undertaking or business, or the organization discloses the information outside the province for consideration."[10] Care should be taken in relying on a narrow interpretation of "discloses" or "consideration" to fall within the exemption. There is no policy rationale in privacy for this exemption, and there is concern that a court may thus choose a broad interpretation. Finally after January 1, 2004 if a province passes substantially similar legislation, the federal government may exempt from PIPEDA organizations in respect of the collection, use or disclosure of personal information within a province.[11]

Four provinces have passed health sector specific legislation. And prior to the development of PIPEDA four provinces had passed short pieces of legislation declaring an invasion of privacy a fact, without defining precisely what constitutes an "invasion of privacy". These statutes have not been often used as the basis for an action.[12]

---

1. S.C. 2000, c. 5 [Sections 60-71 not in force at date of publication], as am. S.C. 2000 c. 17, s. 97(1); 2001, c. 41, ss. 81, 82, 103.

2. Directive 95/46/EC of the European Parliament and of the Council of 24 October, 1995.

3. *Supra*, note 1, s. 14(1).

4. See *In re Toysmart.com, LLC*, Case No. 00-13995-CJK (Bankr. E.D. Mass.) where the Federal Trade Commission and several states intervened.

5. See *In re Egghead.com, Inc.*, Case No. 01-32125-SFC-11 (Bankr. N.D. Calif.); *In re Living.com, Inc.*, Case No. 00-12522 FRM (Bankr. W.D. Texas); and *In re eToys, Inc.*, Case Nos. 01-706 through 709 (MFW) (Bankr. D. Del.).

6. *Thomas v. Robinson*, 2001 Carswell Ont 3986, 34 C.C.L.1. (3d) 75 (Ont. S.C.J.) October 16, 2001.

7. Constitution Act, 1867 (U.K.), 30 & 31 Vict., c. 3, s. 91(2), reprinted in R.S.C. 1985, App. II, No. 5.

8. [1989] 1 S.C.R. 641.

9. *Supra*, note 1, s. 4(1).

10. *Ibid*, s. 30(1).

11. *Ibid*, s. 26(2)(b).

12. As of July, 2004 the other provincial private sector privacy legislation consisted of:

Newfoundland	– Privacy Act, R.S.N. 1990, c. P-22
Manitoba	– The Privacy Act, R.S.M. 1970, c. 74
	– The Personal Health Information Act, S.M. 1997, c. 51
Saskatchewan	– The Privacy Act, R.S.S. 1978, c. P.24
	– The Health Information Protection Act, 1999, c. H-0.021 – sections 17(1), 18(2), 18(4) and 69 not yet proclaimed in force
Alberta	– Health Information Act, R.S.A. 2000, c. H-5
British Columbia	– Privacy Act, R.S.B.C. 1979, c. 336
Ontario	– Personal Health Information Protection Act, 2004, S.O. 2004, c. 3

Privacy Legislation—Compliance

9.079.1.1—The purpose of this section is to highlight the steps that your organization must complete in order to comply with the Federal Personal Information Protection and Electronic Documents Act ("PIPEDA") and certain provincial statutes with respect to protection of personal information across Canada.

1. What legislation applies?

As of January 1, 2004, the following legislation is in effect to regulate the collection, use and disclosure of personal information:

(a)   The Quebec Act in respect of the Protection of Information in the Private Sector (the "Quebec Act") which has been in force since 1994 and applies to organizations operating inside the Province of Quebec.

(b)   The British Columbia Personal Information Protection Act came into force on January 1, 2004. This applies to organizations operating inside the Province of British Columbia.

(c)   The Alberta Personal Information Protection Act came into force on January 1, 2004. This applies to organizations operating inside the Province of Alberta.

(d)   The federal PIPEDA applies to organizations operating entirely within a province that has not passed its own privacy legislation that is "substantially similar" to PIPEDA and for organizations that deal with personal information that is transferred intra-provincially or internationally.

There is a constitutional issue as to whether PIDEDA applies in a province which has enacted its own statute, whether it is "substantially similar" or not. Quebec has taken a constitutional challenge on this point which is now before the courts in Quebec and will likely go to the Supreme Court of Canada.

There are other statutes now in effect that govern health and medical records. These are not discussed in this section.

2. What is "Personal Information"?

This is information that identifies a human being. PIPEDA excludes a person's business contact information. BC has created a regulation excluding public sources of personal information, like phone books.

The various privacy statutes extend protection to personal information and regulate the collection, use and disclosure of personal information. Many organizations will have employee information, retail customer information and/or information about persons involved as directors, officers, shareholders or guarantors of themselves, or of wholesale customers. Your organization needs to identify all of the information it obtains about people.

3. What do you have to do to comply?

PIPEDA has ten (10) guiding principles. While the requirements of the provincial legislation vary, generally speaking, observing the ten (10) principles under PIPEDA will help you comply with all statutes:

(a)   Principle 1—Accountability

All organizations in Canada are responsible for personal information under their control and must designate a privacy compliance officer who is responsible to ensure compliance.

(b)   Principle 2—Identifying Purposes

Your organization should effect an internal audit to determine the purposes for which it collects personal information; in the Quebec Act this is referred to as "the object of the file". Your organization needs to do an audit of the personal information it obtains and document the purpose for which the information is collected. For example, the purpose may be to collect information to recruit new employees and this means that the personal information collected may include resumes, job application forms, employment histories and reference checks.

(c)   Principle 3—Consent

The focus of the legislation is informed consent of an individual as to the collection, use, and disclosure of personal information about him or her. Your organization may need to consider whether there has been implied consent (deemed consent in BC), such as an employee choosing to give information about his or her family for purposes of the company benefit plan. Alternatively, you may require a specific consent such as a signed customer consent about the purposes, uses and permissions to disclose to third parties information about him or her. Such specific consent is now being obtained by many organizations in their retail consumer credit application form.

(d)   Principle 4—Limiting Collection

You need to ensure that your organization is collecting personal information only as is necessary to achieve the purposes identified by your audit.

(e)   Principle 5—Limiting Use, Disclosure and Retention

Your organization may not use or disclose information for purposes other than those for which it was collected unless the individual has consented, or as required by statute or other legal requirements. Then you may keep the personal information only as long as is necessary for the fulfillment of the stated purposes. Among other things, this means you should have a policy on record destruction so that files containing information about individuals are kept only so long as necessary (for example, tax audits of payroll information), and then destroyed in a secure method.

(f)   Principle 6—Accuracy

Your organization has a duty to ensure that the information it keeps about people is accurate, complete and up to date for the purposes for which it is required.

(g)   Principle 7—Safeguards

Your organization has a duty to protect personal information within its control as appropriate to the sensitivity of the information. You need an internal audit on your security methods such as locked fireproof cabinets, software firewalls to stop hackers, restricting access to personal information to only those employees who have a need to know, confidentiality covenants from third party service providers such as a payroll service or an insurance or benefit plan provider or provider of safe storage or backup off site for electronic data.

(h)   Principle 8—Openness

Your organization has a duty to make readily available to individuals information about its privacy policy and practices related to personal information. This means you may want to post your organization's privacy policy on your website or within human resources booklets.

(i)   Principle 9—Individual Access

Your organization has a requirement to comply with the request of individuals as to the existence, use and disclosure of information about him or her and allow them to challenge the accuracy and completeness of the information and have it amended if necessary. For example, would your reception and customer call centre know the identity of your privacy compliance officer and direct calls as necessary to that person? The compliance officer should track follow-up to ensure that all complaints or inquiries have been fairly and completely addressed.

The legislation has certain statutory exceptions to provide the person access to his or her file for such matters as documents prepared for litigation and documents that contain proprietary business information, such as credit scores, which can be reverse engineered to reveal a lender's credit scoring formulas.

All file entries should be prepared with an expectation that the subject person may ask, and be entitled, to see the contents of his or her file.

(j)   Principle 10—Challenging Compliance

Your organization has a duty to be ready to address challenges to its compliance regimes through the compliance officer and satisfaction of the foregoing 9 principles.

There is no one solution for privacy compliance that will apply equally to all organizations. Each organization needs to effect its own internal audit and determine both from the perspective of an employer and in relation to third parties outside the organization, how the organization will comply with PIPEDA and the applicable provincial requirements.

Privacy Statutes and Due Diligence

9.079.1.2—In buying and selling shares or assets, or financing a deal, the solicitors for the vendor, buyer and lender engage in due diligence, to ensure among other things, the risks and liabilities being undertaken by their clients, and consequent price adjustments as necessary. Obviously personal information will be produced and reviewed dealing with *inter alia*, current employees, pensioners, officers, directors, shareholders, customer marketing lists, customer warranty programs, customer contracts and receivables, and collection efforts.

In addition the solicitors for each side may need third party expertise to assist their due diligence review, such as actuaries for pension plans and accountants.

We are all acutely aware that the federal Personal Information Protection and Electronic Documents Act, S.C. 2000, c. 5 ("PIPEDA") requires the informed consent by the individual to the collection, use and disclosure of his or her information, absent a valid basis for implied consent or a statutory exemption. There is no statutory exemption in PIPEDA permitting the disclosure of personal information for the purpose of due diligence by prospective purchasers and lenders or transfers of personal information in share and asset transactions. It is a glaring omission.

There are statutory exemptions for business transactions in the British Columbia and Alberta privacy legislation and these sections are found in Schedules "A" and "B" to this paper. Note that Alberta and British Columbia at least have 'rules for the road' to assist us, but their respective rules are not identical.

The federal Privacy Commissioner's Office ("PCO") has informally noted this omission in PIPEDA and indicated it will be resolved in the statutory revisions to the Act likely to occur several years from now. In the meantime, the PCO feels the public expects business sales and financings to continue and there is consequent implied consent to the disclosure and transfer of personal information to effect such deals.

In speaking with Quebec counsel, it is found that the Quebec privacy regulators, under the Quebec Act in respect of the Protection of Information in the Private Sector, have taken the same informal policy position, given the Quebec Act does not have rules to deal with business deals and financings.

This informal policy of the PCO and the Quebec regulator has no force of law. So what does the Ontario lawyer do to protect his or her client required to produce personal information as part of a pending sale or financing?

After advising the client as to the lack of statutory authority under PIPEDA to make disclosures in business deals without consent:

(i) consider the likelihood of success in asking for and obtaining the needed specific consents. For example, some receivers and bankruptcy trustees are seeking specific consent from employees of the debtor corporation, before disclosing their employment records to prospective buyers. Apparently few employees fail to give consent; or

(ii) discuss the risks of not obtaining such consent and whether a complaint to the PCO would be held to be well founded.

Where the client determines to proceed without seeking specific consent, following the guidelines set out in Alberta and British Columbia legislation may go to lessen the likelihood of a complaint to the PCO being held to be well founded.

The solicitor should at least ensure:

(i) a confidentiality and non-disclosure agreement is signed by the prospective purchaser or financier and its advisers;

(ii) the client produces copies of only the personal information the purchaser or lender needs to see;

(iii) the copies given are either kept in a secure 'documents room' for third party review or given as marked copies and the recipient per copy recorded;

(iv) the marked copies are returned or certified to be destroyed by unsuccessful parties or by all parties, if the deal fails to close;

(v) the vendor, purchaser and lender enter into an agreement to restrict the use of the transferred personal information to the purposes for which it was given and carrying out the objects for which the transaction took place; and

(vi) note in British Columbia the additional need to give the employees, customers, officers, directors and shareholders notice that the deal has occurred and that their personal information has been disclosed to the other party to the deal.

Attached as Schedule "C" is an extract from the initial stay order pursuant to the Companies' Creditors Arrangement Act granted by Justice Farley and dated January 29, 2004 in the Stelco restructuring. At paragraph 28 of this Order, Justice Farley sets out the rules for disclosure of personal information in the possession of Stelco to parties involved in its restructuring.

With this gap in PIPEDA for business deals, clients have to make informed business decisions. The materials in Schedules "A", "B" and "C" may assist the client who cannot obtain specific consents, to proceed cautiously inside the guidelines of the British Columbia and Alberta legislation and Justice Farley's rules. **[See Form 9F3:1]**

SCHEDULE "A"
PERSONAL INFORMATION PROTECTION ACT

Statutes of Alberta, 2003
Chapter P-6.5

Division 6
Business Transactions

Disclosure respecting acquisition of a business, etc.

22(1)   In this section,

    (a)   "business transaction" means a transaction consisting of the purchase, sale, lease, merger or amalgamation or any other type of acquisition or disposal of, or the taking of a security interest in respect of, an organization or a portion of an organization or any business or activity or business asset of an organization and includes a prospective transaction of such a nature;

    (b)   "party" includes a prospective party.

(2)   Notwithstanding anything in this Act other than this section, an organization may, for the purposes of a business transaction between itself and one or more other organizations, collect, use and disclose personal information in accordance with this section.

(3)   Organizations that are parties to a business transaction may,

    (a)   during the period leading up to and including the completion, if any, of the business transaction, collect, use and disclose personal information about individuals without the consent of the individuals if

        (i)   the parties have entered into an agreement under which the collection, use and disclosure of the information is restricted to those purposes that relate to the business transaction, and

        (ii)   the information is necessary

            (A)   for the parties to determine whether to proceed with the business transaction, and

(B)   if the determination is to proceed with the business transaction, for the parties to carry out and complete the business transaction,

and

(b)   where the business transaction is completed, collect, use and disclose personal information about individuals without the consent of the individuals if

(i)   the parties have entered into an agreement under which the parties undertake to use and disclose the information only for those purposes for which the information was initially collected from or in respect of the individuals, and

(ii)   the information relates solely to the carrying on of the business or activity or the carrying out of the objects for which the business transaction took place.

(4)   If a business transaction does not proceed or is not completed, the party to whom the personal information was disclosed must, if the information is still in the custody of or under the control of that party, either destroy the information or turn it over to the party that disclosed the information.

(5)   Nothing in this section is to be construed so as to restrict a party to a business transaction from obtaining consent of an individual to the collection, use or disclosure of personal information about the individual for purposes that are beyond the purposes for which the party obtained the information under this section.

(6)   This section does not apply to a business transaction where the primary purpose, objective or result of the transaction is the purchase, sale, lease, transfer, disposal or disclosure of personal information.

SCHEDULE "B"
PERSONAL INFORMATION PROTECTION ACT

Statutes of British Columbia, 2003
Chapter 63

Transfer of personal information in the sale of an organization or its business assets

20(1)   In this section:

"business transaction" means the purchase, sale, lease, merger or amalgamation or any other type of acquisition, disposal or financing of an organization or a portion of an organization or of any of the business or assets of an organization;

"party" means a person or another organization that proceeds with the business transaction.

(2)　An organization may disclose personal information about its employees, customers, directors, officers or shareholders without their consent, to a prospective party, if

(a)　the personal information is necessary for the prospective party to determine whether to proceed with the business transaction, and

(b)　the organization and prospective party have entered into an agreement that requires the prospective party to use or disclose the personal information solely for purposes related to the prospective business transaction.

(3)　If an organization proceeds with a business transaction, the organization may disclose, without consent, personal information of employees, customers, directors, officers and shareholders of the organization to a party on condition that

(a)　the party must only use or disclose the personal information for the same purposes for which it was collected, used or disclosed by the organization,

(b)　the disclosure is only of personal information that relates directly to the part of the organization or its business assets that is covered by the business transaction, and

(c)　the employees, customers, directors, officers and shareholders whose personal information is disclosed are notified that

(i)　the business transaction has taken place, and

(ii)　the personal information about them has been disclosed to the party.

(4)　A prospective party may collect and use personal information without the consent of the employees, customers, directors, officers and shareholders of the organization in the circumstances described in subsection (2) if the prospective party complies with the conditions applicable to that prospective party under that subsection.

(5)　A party may collect, use and disclose personal information without the consent of the employees, customers, directors, officers and shareholders of the organization in the circumstances described in subsection (3) if the party complies with the conditions applicable to that party under that subsection.

(6)   If a business transaction does not proceed or is not completed, a prospective party must destroy or return to the organization any personal information the prospective party collected under subsection (2) about the employees, customers, directors, officers and shareholders of the organization.

(7)   This section does not authorize an organization to disclose personal information to a party or prospective party for purposes of a business transaction that does not involve substantial assets of the organization other than this personal information.

(8)   A party or prospective party is not authorized by this section to collect, use or disclose personal information that an organization disclosed to it in contravention of subsection (7).

SCHEDULE "C"

Court File No. 04-CL-5306

Ontario
Superior Court of Justice
(Commercial List)

The Honourable   Thursday, the 29th day
Mr. Justice Farley   of January, 2004

"Paragraph 28: THIS COURT ORDERS that, pursuant to clause 7(3)(c) of the *Personal Information Protection and Electronic Documents Act*, S.C. 2000, c. 5, the Applicants are permitted in the course of these proceedings to disclose personal information of identifiable individuals in their possession   or control to stakeholders or prospective investors, financiers, buyers or strategic partners and to their advisers (individually, a "Third Party"), to the extent desirable or required to negotiate and complete the Restructuring or the preparation and implementation of the Plan or a transaction in furtherance thereof, provided that the Persons to whom such personal information is disclosed enter into confidentiality agreements with the Applicants binding them to maintain and protect the privacy of such information and to limit the use of such information to the extent necessary to complete the transaction or Restructuring then under negotiation. Upon the completion of the uses of personal information for the limited purpose set out herein, the personal information shall be returned to the Applicants or destroyed. In the event that a Third Party acquires personal information as part of the Restructuring or the preparation and implementation of the Plan or a transaction in furtherance thereof, such Third Party shall be entitled to continue to use the personal information in a manner which is in all material respects identical to the prior use of such personal information by the Applicants."

Franchise Disclosure Legislation

9.079.2—There are two franchise specific laws in Canada[1] that require pre-contractual disclosure to effect the sale of a franchise business in some circumstances. As well the Code civil du Québec[2] requires that parties act in good faith in the creation of the contract.[3] This is interpreted as requiring pre-contractual disclosure in Québec.[4] Generally the remedies are recission and/or an action for damages.[5] **[For a more extensive discussion of these statutes see Edward Levitt's Title #5 on franchising (Distribution of Goods and Services) in Volume 1 of Canadian Forms & Precedents—Commercial Transactions.]**

If the business to be acquired is caught within the definition of a "franchise" it will be necessary to either find an exemption to the disclosure requirement or prepare a disclosure document that complies with the applicable law and regulations. It is not possible for the purchaser to waive its rights under the relevant law.[6] Generally speaking a "franchise" is defined in the legislation as being:

- a right to engage in a business;
- where the franchisee is required to make a payment or continuing payments, whether direct or indirect, to the franchisor;
- in which goods or services are sold, offered for sale or are distributed that are substantially associated with the franchisor's trade-mark;
- and in which the franchisor exercises significant control over, or offers significant assistance, in the franchisee's method of operation.

Whether or not the business to be acquired considers itself to be a franchise is irrelevant. There is a substantial body of caselaw on the meaning of these elements of the definition in the United States,[7] but no known cases in Canada. As the definitions were in some cases borrowed almost word for word from American law, these cases are likely to be relevant in Canada.

Some of the commercial arrangements that may, unknown to the participants, fit with such definitions include:

1.   Trade-mark Licences

2.   Joint ventures, corporate partnership and strategic alliances

3.   Distribution agreements

4.   Sweat equity programs

5.   Dealer relationships

6.   Sales agent relationships

7.   Software and computer licences

8.   Subcontractor agreements

9.   Business referral networks

Even in the United States, where franchise laws have been in force for almost 30 years, prospective purchasers of a business sometimes currently find that the proposed acquisition is a "franchisor" but that it has never complied with the franchise laws.

In Ontario there is an additional list[8] of continuing commercial relationships to which the legislation does not apply even if the business fits within the definition. In Alberta there is not a similar list although there is an exemption for leased or licensed premises in another retailer. The Ontario exceptions are:

- employer-employee relationships;
- partnerships;
- membership in a co-operative association;
- licensing of a certification mark;
- single licence, where it is the only one of its general nature and type;
- licence or leased space in other retailers;
- unwritten arrangements;
- an arrangement with the Crown.

If the business is caught by the definition, and does not fit within an exemption, then it is obligated to disclose to the purchaser at least 14 days before the signing of any agreement or the payment of any funds,[9] all material facts, including material facts as prescribed in the regulations.[10] Alternatively the proposed transaction may fall within one of the exemption to the disclosure requirements.[11] The exemptions in Ontario and Alberta, although very similar, differ in numerous places and must be read with care. Because of the difficulty of determining, for example, on the sale of an additional franchise to an existing franchisee that "… there has been no material change since the existing franchise agreement or latest renewal of a franchise agreement was entered into; …" many franchisors automatically make disclosure in such circumstances.

In both provinces there is an exemption from the disclosure requirement where the transaction is between two franchisees and is not effected by or through the franchisor. This also applies to a master franchise where the entire franchise is sold.[12] The other types of exemptions are:

- a sale to an officer or director of the franchisor;
- a sale of additional franchise to an existing franchise;
- a renewal or extension of an existing agreement;
- a sale by an executor, trustee in bankruptcy or other like person;
- a sale of a fractional franchise;
- franchises having a total annual investment of less than $5,000.00, a term of less than a year, or that are governed by the multi-level marketing provisions of the Competition Act (Ontario only);
- franchises where the total annual investment exceeds $5,000,000.00. (Ontario only).

---

1. In Alberta – Franchises Act, R.S.A. 2000, c. F-23 in force November 1, 1995 (the "Alberta Act"); and in Ontario – Arthur Wishart Act (Franchise Disclosure) 2000, S.O. 2000, c. 3, as amended by 2001, c. 9, Sched. D, s. 1, in force January 31, 2000 (the "Ontario Act").

2. L.Q. [1991], c. 64.

3. See Art. 6, 7 and 1375.

4. See Art. 1401, Bruno Floriani and Anne-Marie Gauthier, "Franchising and the Civil Code of Québec" (1995), 15(2) *Franchise L.J.* 51, and Markus Cohen, Paul Jones, G. Lee Muirhead, "Franchising in Canada/La Franchise au Canada" in American Bar Association Forum on Franchising, *Gateway to the Future of Franchising – October 10-12, 2001, San Francisco* (Chicago: American Bar Association, 2001).

5. See sections 6 and 7 of the Ontario Act, and sections 9, 10, 13 and 14 of the Alberta Act.

6. See section 11 of the Ontario Act and section 18 of the Alberta Act.

7. For a discussion of these cases see Rochelle B. Spandorf and Mark A. Kirsch, "The Accidental Franchise" in *Gateway to the Future of Franchising, October 10-12, 2001 San Francisco, supra* note 4; James R. Sims III and Mary Beth Trice, "The Inadvertent Franchise and How to Safeguard Against It" (1998), 18(2) *Franchise L.J. 54;* and James R. Sims III and Mary Beth Trice, "Hidden Franchises", in American Bar Association Forum on Franchising, *Franchising: The Next Generation, October 22-24, 1997, Colorado Springs* (Chicago: American Bar Association, 1997).

8. Ontario Act, section 2(3).

9. Alberta has exceptions for fully refundable deposits and confidentiality agreements, see section 4(7). Ontario does not have such exceptions.

10. Ontario Act, section 5(4). Alberta Act, section 4(3), together with section 2(1) of Alberta Regulation 240/95 and Schedule 1 to such regulation.

11. Ontario Act, section 5(7) (c).

12. Ontario Act, section 5(7)(a). Alberta Act, section 5(1)(a).

The Ontario Limitations Act, 2002

9.079.3—This Act came into effect on January 1st, 2004. It changes fundamentally how arm's-length, business parties may negotiate the allocation of risk and cost in commercial deals in Ontario.

Until the enactment of this statute, the limitation period for breach of contract and tort was six years from discovery of the claim for most tort claims and from the date of breach for most contract claims. With a six-year period, most breaches of representations, warranties and covenants were naturally found during the life of an asset or share deal, or a loan agreement, as most problems or financings issues were found during a six year period.

The new limitation period is now two years from discovery of the claim, with some transition rules found at section 24. Section 5 makes this two years more troublesome, by providing that a claim is discoverable upon the earlier of certain events happening, or the day a reasonable person ought to have known of such breaches or events giving rise to the claim. The outside limitation date is 15 years from the happening of the event, down from the prior outside date of 30 years. If the claim is discovered in the 14th year, the remaining limitation expires not in two years from that discovery, but on the 15th anniversary of the event giving rise to the claim.

Up to January first, 2004, commercial parties created agreements allocating risk and cost by having such things as survival clauses, and agreeing to the time period during which a claim might be made for a breach of a representation, warranty or covenant. Vendors traditionally want very short survival periods for their representations, warranties and covenants. Buyers wanted longer ones. Usually the parties would pick a year or two from closing for survival of most representations, warranties and covenants, and selected ones, like taxes, would survive for at least six years to deal with audits by taxing authorities post closing. Price might alter or indemnities be provided, depending on the risks being assumed by either side.

Subsection 22(1) of the Act now provides that "the limitation period under this Act applies despite any agreement to alter or exclude it." Note this applies to attempts to either shorten or lengthen the two year limitation from discoverability. Ontario stands alone with this provision and we are unaware of any other common law jurisdiction with such a statutory provision.

In December, 2003, a number of bodies, including the Law Society of Upper Canada, the Ontario Bar Association, the Advocates Society and members of private firms wrote the Attorney General and asked that section 22 be suspended from proclamation pending further study. This request was denied and the Act came into effect on January first, 2004. It may be reviewed by the Attorney General several years after it has been in effect.

Consequently, firms have been working hard considering how the Act impacts on survival of representations, warranties, and covenants, defaults that are triggered by these breaches, indemnities and remedies triggered by events and how those events are 'discovered', etc. Obviously lenders and purchasers want longer periods than two years from discovery or discoverability (which might in some circumstances mean two years from signing the agreement), to cover breach of representation for such matters as lack of good title, tax reassessments, environmental claims and fraudulent representations. Vendors and borrowers usually want finite periods for liability to end.

One solution is to pick the law of a jurisdiction other than Ontario to govern the agreement, where there is a logical nexus to another jurisdiction for the parties and the subject matter. One then has to watch for conflicts of law and possible application of *renvoi* back to Ontario law. Anecdotal information among Toronto firms is that they are using the law of other jurisdictions, where possible, taking business deals out of the province. The parties need to understand that a court may find the selection of the law other than Ontario, is unenforceable and Ontario law is held to apply.

Another solution is to have the representations, warranties and covenants survive closing—in short, a survival clause which has no time period in it. The net effect is that the Limitations Act, 2002 will apply to cap survival at two years from discovery.

The second part of the solution is to cap the parties' liability for the breach. For example, the parties might agree that for any action commenced more than 18 months from closing, the vendor's liability is capped at $100.

The net effect is a limitation of liability clause such that the purchaser may sue for as long as Ontario law allows an action to be commenced, but the vendor only becomes liable for the fixed amount agreed for damages if the action is started after the set time period.

A third solution being discussed, is whether to have the parties agree that all disputes will go to arbitration and then in the arbitration provisions, the parties agree that the Ontario Limitations Act, 2002 shall not apply. Section 52 of the Ontario Arbitration Act, 1991 has the limitation legislation apply to arbitrations, but this is not a mandatory provision; the parties may agree to exclude section 52. This is a possible mechanism but not one with which many solicitors are comfortable.

The Act also impacts demand notes and demand guarantees, which may have a two-year limitation from the time they are signed. Lenders are considering annual bring down certificates reaffirming the debt to start the two year limitation clock again, or replacing the paper before its second anniversary. Some argue that a payment of principal or interest is in itself an affirmation of the debt, again restarting the clock.

Until we either have case law interpreting the Act to give us some comfort, or the legislation is amended to delete these provisions, solicitors need to be very careful to ensure their client's rights are protected or the clients are aware of the new exposure.

The Ontario Limitations Act, 2002—Opinion Qualifications

9.079.4—Most opinion letters contain an enforceability opinion. The Limitations Act, 2002, in effect on January first, 2004, has created uncertainty in agreements governed by Ontario law with the new provisions of these enforceability opinions which need to be qualified. The following are three alternative sample clauses to deal with this new Act. These alternatives are repeated below as samples only, and the reader is warned that thought is of course needed to draft for the circumstances of each transaction.

1. We express no opinion as to whether the provisions of (*sections* ___ *and* ___) of the (___) Agreement that purport to stipulate the time within which a party must bring a claim thereunder would be unenforceable by reason of subsection 22(1) of the Limitations Act, 2002 (Ontario), which provides that a limitation period under such Act applies despite any agreement to vary or exclude it.

OR

2. Enforceability of the (*agreement/documents*) will be subject to the limitations contained in the Limitations Act, 2002, and if a court determined that any of the provisions of the (*agreement/documents*) constituted an attempt to vary or exclude the limitation periods set out in the Act, the time periods set out in the Act would apply notwithstanding any agreement to the contrary.

OR

3. Enforceability of the (*agreement/documents*) will be subject to the limitations contained in the Limitations Act, 2002 and we express no opinion as to whether a court may find any provision of the (*agreement/documents*) to be unenforceable on the basis that any such provision is an attempt to vary or exclude a limitation period under that Act.

Privacy Statutes—Opinion Qualification

Many opinions contain an opinion to the effect that the company is in compliance with all laws. Given the vague drafting of the PIPEDA 10 guiding principals, it is very unlikely that counsel will be able to give this compliance with laws opinion for privacy compliance. Consider how you might determine whether all necessary consents to collection, use and disclosure of personal information had been made by your client. It is just too vague, and as a consequence, among downtown Toronto firms, there is a growing practice neither to ask for nor give a privacy law compliance opinion.

Consequently, it is considered appropriate to qualify an opinion on compliance with all laws by providing:

> We express no opinion on whether the Company is in compliance with PIPEDA or any other privacy laws.

[See Forms 9F153:1 and 9F154]

Setting the Price

9.080—The negotiation and determination of the purchase price is usually carried on directly between the principals of the purchaser and vendor. Typically, that process is complete or substantially complete before lawyers become involved in the transaction, whether at the letter of intent or agreement stage. In those cases, the function of the lawyer is to properly document the agreement the parties have reached. The majority of this section relates to the primary alternative methods of price determination and issues relating to documenting those arrangements.

In certain cases, however, a client will seek counsel's advice with respect to price. In other cases, it may become apparent to counsel that the client needs assistance in setting a price whether the client is a prospective purchaser or vendor. Price setting is a very complex process which requires planning, an analysis of the subject business, identification of possible purchasers, analysis of the economic benefits which might flow to particular purchasers as a result of the acquisition of the subject business recently purchased and sold. Lawyers are not competent to provide advice with respect to business valuation. In those cases, it may be appropriate to refer the client to an experienced and qualified business valuator. Indeed, it would be sound practice to recommend it. The Canadian Institute of Chartered Business Valuators has developed a course of study leading to the designation of Chartered Business Valuator. In order to be eligible for the designation, candidates must successfully complete the course of study and have considerable practical experience in business valuation. A Chartered Business Valuator can assist a prospective purchaser in assessing the appropriate price of a target business. For example, a Chartered Business Valuator may be able to: (a) help to identify the value in a business and thereby help the vendor to negotiate a higher price; (b) assist the vendor by identifying possible special purchasers that may be prepared to pay a higher price than other possible special purchasers; or (c) assist a purchaser by identifying the net economic benefits that might accrue to the purchaser through the acquisition and thereby assist the purchaser in negotiating an appropriate price.

9.081—While lawyers should not engage in business valuation, it is essential that they thoroughly understand the basis for the price agreed to in each transaction. This is the case whether they represent the vendor or the purchaser. In order to properly understand the basis for the agreed upon price, lawyers should have a general understanding of valuation theory and practice. A discussion of valuation theory and practice is beyond the scope of this section. However, there is a great deal of literature in the area.[1]

There are several reasons why lawyers must understand the basis for the price. The primary reason is that the lawyer is charged with documenting the transaction and ensuring that the documents reflect the parties' agreement. It is impossible to do this properly without an understanding of the principal bases for the price to which the parties have agreed. Both value and price factor into every aspect of a share or asset purchase agreement. A few examples will serve to illustrate. Assume that a lawyer acting for a purchaser is negotiating the terms of a share purchase agreement in which the primary value to the purchaser is the vendor's customer list and, in the purchaser's view, the bulk of the price is for that list. The lawyer must understand this in order to negotiate appropriate covenants, representations and warranties. In the assumed transaction, the non-competition covenant of the vendor will merit special attention as will the representations and warranties with respect to customer contracts and the status of customer relationships. On the other hand, the representations and warranties with respect to the status of fixed assets might not merit particular attention. In negotiating terms, counsel to the purchaser might well negotiate toward weak representations and warranties with respect to the latter in return for strong representations and warranties with respect to the former. Counsel cannot work toward that desirable result without a full understanding of the bases for the price.

In the second example, assume a lawyer is acting for a purchaser who has identified substantial economic benefit that it might gain by combining the vendor's business with its own. The economic benefit, sometimes referred to as synergy, is expected to be generated in part by operating the combined business with the purchaser's existing employees. The transaction is a share purchase and the purchaser intends to terminate the vendor's employees after closing. The purchaser will therefore bear the cost of the termination and it will be critical that the purchaser accurately predict the cost of terminating the vendor's employees. Detailed and accurate information with respect to those employees will be required in order to do so and the purchaser will rely on that information in determining the price it is prepared to pay. The purchaser's lawyer must ensure that the information on which the purchaser relied in calculating the cost of termination if fully represented and warranted by the vendor. In summary, a failure on the part of the purchaser's counsel to fully appreciate the bases for the price might well result in counsel failing to adequately protect the client's interests.

---

1. For examples see Campbell, Ian R., *The Principles and Practice of Business Valuation* (Toronto: Richard De Boo Ltd., 1975); Campbell, Ian R., *Business Valuation for Business People* (Toronto: Richmond House Publishing Limited, 1981); Horvath, James L., *Valuing a Business, in Buying and Selling a Business* (Toronto: The Canadian Institute, 1989). This is recommended reading for every commercial lawyer who is not otherwise familiar with business valuation.

Pricing Methods

9.090—The price which a vendor is prepared to accept and which a purchaser is prepared to pay will always be affected by the form of transaction. In general, a purchaser would be prepared to pay a higher price to purchase assets than shares. Conversely, a vendor will usually demand a higher price on a sale of a business through an asset sale than through a share sale. There are two primary reasons for this. From the vendor's perspective, except for claims by the purchaser, a share sale relieves the vendor from any further exposure to liability with respect to the business. On the other hand, an asset sale leaves the vendor with a corporate shell which may or may not have assets and liabilities. At the very least, the corporate shell is an administrative nuisance to the vendor. Conversely, a purchaser wishes to avoid a share purchase because all of the unwanted assets and the undisclosed, unknown and contingent liabilities remain with the corporation in which the shares are purchased. In an asset purchase, with certain exceptions, the purchaser may effectively choose the assets it wishes to purchase and the liabilities that it wishes to assume.

The pricing methods used in an asset purchase are very different from those used in a share purchase. Some of those methods are outlined below.

Asset Purchases

9.091—In asset purchases the purchase price will usually be the aggregate of separate prices for the fixed assets, the goodwill, inventory, work-in-progress, supplies and accounts receivable, if included, all as at closing. Typically, the value of the fixed assets and the goodwill will remain the same between the signing of the agreement and closing. The terms of the agreement will require that no material diminution in value in those as-sets has occurred prior to closing. Therefore, the price of those assets will usually be established firmly in the agreement. The value of inventory, work-in-progress, supplies and accounts receivable will fluctuate between the signing of the agreement and closing. As a result, special provisions are required to determine the price of those assets.

Inventory, Work-in-progress and Supplies

9.092—There are two issues in pricing inventory. The first is the formula for valuing the inventory. Usually inventory will be valued on the basis that only full merchantable and current inventory is included and that included inventory is valued at the lower of cost and realizable value. Since the cost of inventory may change, it is usually provided that cost is determined on a first-in first-out basis.

If the business is small, the agreement may provide for an inventory audit to be conducted as of the close of business the day before closing. In that event, the inventory price can be fixed on closing. In larger businesses, an inventory count or audit will take longer to complete and a final price will not be finalized in time for closing. In those cases the inventory price is often estimated at the time of the signing of the agreement or, in any event, prior to closing. The estimate might be based on an inventory count conducted by the parties or on an extrapolation of the figures in the most recent financial statements of the vendor. The promissory note or cash paid on closing would be based on that estimate. The agreement will contain a provision for an inventory count or audit to be conducted jointly by the parties as at closing, to be completed within a certain number of days after closing and for an adjustment of the purchase price in accordance with the final inventory price so determined.

Work-in-progress may be priced on the basis of the aggregate of the cost of the component raw materials or on the basis of the component costs plus some factor for added value. Typically, the former method is used because the assessment of the value added is extremely difficult. Otherwise the procedure for finalizing the price of work-in-progress is the same as that used for inventory. Good quality supplies are usually valued at cost and, again, the procedure for finalizing the price is the same as that used for inventory. The quality of the supplies would be determined by an inspection.

Accounts Receivable

9.093—There is usually a two step process for fixing the price of accounts receivable when they are included in the purchased assets. First, an estimated price is established as at closing. Generally, the formula for the estimate is the aggregate face value of all good quality accounts receivable. The definition of a "good quality accounts receivable" can vary depending on the industry collection norms. However, the standard is all accounts receivable under 90-days-old, unless there is a specific reason to believe that an account receivable under 90 days is not collectable. An adjustment is provided for some time after closing. The adjustment will result in a decrease of the price in an amount equal to the purchase price of the accounts receivable that were included in the estimated price but remain uncollected. In some cases those outstanding accounts receivable will be reassigned, in effect sold back, to the vendor so that it can pursue collection on its own behalf.

One of the vendor's obvious concerns if such a method is used relates to the fact that the business sold is ongoing and continues to generate accounts receivable from the same customers after closing. As a result, the purchaser will have accounts receivable with the same customer that arose after closing as well as those which arose prior to closing and were assigned to it by the vendor. The vendor will wish to include a provision requiring the purchaser to apply all monies received from such a customer to the earlier accounts receivable until those earlier accounts receivable of that customer are paid in full. This will prevent a purchaser from simply collecting the newest accounts receivable and ignoring the collection of the assigned accounts receivable. The purchaser should attempt to qualify the obligation to apply funds received in that manner. The qualification should provide that the obligation does not operate if:

A.   the customer expressly designates the account receivable to which the payment is to be applied; or

B.   a customer is disputing a particular assigned account receivable.

If the purchaser is both making the effort and incurring the expense to collect significant accounts receivable, an argument can be made that the purchaser should pay a discount from face value for the accounts receivable.

Share Purchases

9.094—In share purchases the component assets are not usually separately priced since the nature of a share purchase results in all of the assets and liabilities of the target business passing, indirectly, to the purchaser. Rather, an *en bloc* price is usually set in the share purchase agreement. The price is based on the assets, liabilities and profit or loss reflected in the financial statements of the target business' most recently completed fiscal year and several prior years. There are exceptions, but most share purchase agreements do not contain provisions which contemplate adjustments on or after closing as a result of a change in any line item in the financial statements. Rather, the covenants, representations and warranties are generally designed to ensure that the purchaser receives a business of substantially equal value to what it agreed to purchase. A particular concern in share purchases is undisclosed liabilities on closing. A material undisclosed liability which is revealed after closing may substantially decrease the actual value of the business. Therefore, in a share purchase, detailed representations and warranties regarding the liabilities of the business are critical, as are the provisions for indemnification of the purchaser for material undisclosed liabilities which are revealed after closing. The vendor will want to ensure that it is liable only for inaccuracies in its representations and warranties which result in a material loss to the purchaser. Often the agreement will contain a provision which sets a threshold in dollars which must be exceeded before the vendor will be liable for any undisclosed liability or breach of any other representation or warranty. In effect, those provisions define materiality.

Deferral of Payment of the Purchase Price

9.095—The parties often agree to a price of a business without contem-plating or taking into account the manner in which the price is to be paid. The payment of the purchase may be deferred or may be made in full on closing. The deferral of payment will almost always result in a value to the vendor which is lower than that of the face value of the purchase price. This is so for several reasons. First, if the vendor receives the price in full on closing it can invest the funds received and receive a return on that investment. Therefore, unless the deferred portion of the purchase price bears interest at a rate equivalent to that which the vendor could achieve by investing the funds elsewhere, the value of the deferred portion to the vendor will be lower than its face value. The second reason is that the purchaser may become insolvent prior to paying the deferred portion in full. Therefore, unless the vendor receives excellent security for the payment of the deferred portion, the risk of non-payment as a result of insolvency will be significant. The final reason is that purchasers are frequently not completely satisfied that the business purchased meets their pre-closing expectations. Disgruntled purchasers frequently seek to avoid payment of some or all of the deferred portion on the basis that the vendor breached a covenant, or representation and warranty resulting in damages to the purchaser. Even if the vendor has received excellent security it will be at risk of a loss of some part of the deferred portion.

It will be obvious that, conversely, a purchaser will wish to have payment of a meaningful portion of the purchase deferred for a significant period of time after closing. If the purchaser pays the full price on closing it will have no recourse for a breached covenant or representation and warranty except an action for damages against the vendor. The cost of litigation, the uncertainty of the result and the difficulty of obtaining payment of a judgment make that a very unsatisfactory result for a purchaser who may have suffered a substantial loss as a result of the breach. The arrangements for the payment of the purchase price will be negotiated in each transaction. The main point here is that those arrangements have a marked effect on the effective price otherwise agreed to by the parties and the effect of payment arrangements should be forefront in counsel's mind in every transaction.

The foregoing is a very brief discussion of the major pricing issues and concerns that a lawyer will face in acting for a vendor or a purchaser in the purchase and sale of a business. It should be clear from the discussion that every aspect of an asset or share purchase agreement relates in some way to price. While lawyers generally do not, and should not, become involved in advising as to the appropriate price, they play a critical role in ensuring that the purchaser receives what it has agreed to purchase at the price agreed upon and that the vendor receives the price it has agreed upon for the business it has agreed to sell.

Letters of Intent

9.100—In many situations, the parties may, without benefit of counsel, have entered into a short letter agreement or letter of intent to demonstrate their agreement to certain key terms for the transaction.

The basic principles of contract law come into play to determine whether a binding agreement has been entered. Many letters of intent are expressed as an invitation to treat, expressing an interest in a transaction but not binding a party to go forward. The document merely extends the purchaser's or the vendor's interest to enter into further negotiations. Conversely, a vendor may require a binding letter agreement before it will take the transaction off the market, and cease to negotiate with other third party bidders. Great care needs to be taken to distinguish clearly between entering into an expression of interest, made subject to the creation of formal documentation after further negotiation, as opposed to a binding contract based on fixed terms. **[See Form 9F1]**

Options to Purchase

General

9.110—It may be that the client is not prepared to enter into an acquisition at this time but is prepared to pay a fee for the rught to acquire assets or shares upon the happening of certain events or within a certain time period.

Options to purchase are frequently seen in equipment financings where expensive machinery and equipment is acquired pursuant to a conditional sale agreement or lease containing an option to purchase for either a nominal amount or at fair market value at the end of the given time period. In essence, many of these documents may be a means of allowing the purchaser to acquire title to the assets by financing them over time. These acquisition documents may require registration pursuant to the Ontario Personal Property Security Act[1] and the taking of appropriate steps to enable the vendor to claim a purchase-money security interest or "PMSI". If acting for the vendor/secured party in such situation, great care is needed to comply with section 33 of the PPSA.[2]

Alternatively, the option to purchase may be for more than just specific items of equipment and may be for the entire business or for the purchase of a block of shares at a future date. In the event of an option to purchase on shares, note the requisite Securities Act[3] requirements regarding an appropriate exemption within which to make an application of securities. **[See Paras. 9.069–9.073 and Form 9F2]**

---

1. R.S.O. 1990, c. P.10.

2. *Ibid.*

3. R.S.O. 1990, c. S.5.

Real Estate

9.120—In certain cases, an option to purchase real property can be a viable alternative to a conditional agreement of purchase and sale. It is especially worth considering when the period of time required to satisfy a particular condition is a lengthy one. For example, a developer wishing to rezone a particular piece of property or bring an application for a severance under the Planning Act,[1] or indeed the same developer wishing to assemble a number of parcels of real property, may have more flexibility by holding an option to purchase rather than being constrained by various requirements under a conditional agreement of purchase and sale. The landowner has the benefit of receiving consideration for an option at the time the option is granted. Usually, the sum paid for the option is forfeited in the event the option is not exercised and if the option is exercised, the sum is credited against the purchase price. Normally, an option agreement contains two basic parts. The first part is the option setting out the terms of the option and how and when the option is to be exercised. The second part sets out the terms of the agreement of purchase and sale which take effect if and when the option is exercised.

---

1. R.S.O. 1990, c. P.13.

9.121—When preparing the option, consider the following points:

1. *Property* : Obtain a proper legal description of the lands and preferably obtain a copy of an up-to-date building location survey showing all the boundaries and all buildings and structures located within the boundaries.

2. *Option Price* : It should be expressly stated what price is being paid for the option and how and when this sum is to be paid.

3. *Purchase Price* : The actual amount to be paid by the purchaser if and when the option is exercised is in most cases a fixed amount. It is unlikely that the vendor will agree to a formula based on the then appraised value because this leaves the vendor without control over the ultimate

purchase price. Furthermore, the activities that the purchaser may initiate with respect to the property while the option is outstanding could have a direct effect on the purchase price.

4.   *Option Period*: The period of time during which the option may be exercised should be clearly set out and considered in light of the notice provisions which prescribe how notice is to be given and when such notice is to be effective.

5.   *Addresses* : The addresses of each of the parties should be clearly specified so there is no confusion where notice is to be given. In the event of corporate parties, the rank of the officer should be specified (rather than an individual who may be replaced.) Service by telefax is risky and not recommended especially where particular individuals or particular corporate officers are the ones to be served.

6.   *Inspection Rights* : In order to allow the purchaser to conduct inspections, soil tests, environmental studies and other searches that require access to the property, inspection rights should be clearly spelled out.

7.   *Authorizations* : In order to permit the purchaser to act on behalf of the vendor in any applications for rezoning, severances, minor variances, building and demolition permits, draft plan approvals or any other matters where the owner's authorization is required, authorizations should be clearly spelled out. It is at this point that the vendor/owner will be made aware what the purchaser intends to do during the option period. It will be up to the vendor/owner to decide whether such activities during the option period are desirable with respect to the property in the event the option is not exercised.

8.   *Right to Assign*: Most purchasers require the right to assign to a third party for a variety of reasons. The main question to be addressed is the ongoing liability of the purchaser in the event of such assignment. However, before this issue is addressed, the financial solvency and viability of the original purchaser must be established.

9.   *Financing* : Because of the nature of the option, it is unusual for the resulting agreement of purchase and sale to be conditional upon financing or in the alternative to provide for a vendor take back mortgage or other loan between vendor and purchaser. Generally, the purchaser is expected to use the option period to arrange financing in the event the option is exercised.

10.   *Closing* : The closing date cannot be determined until the option has been exercised. Normally this is accomplished by prescribing a period of time (60 days for example) after the exercise of the option. It is normal to have a short period because of the presumption that once the option has been exercised by the purchaser, the purchaser has satisfied

itself with respect to those matters undertaken during the option period.

11. *Planning Act:*[1] Where the vendor owns abutting lands, it is important to stipulate not only in the agreement of purchase and sale (which only becomes effective upon the exercise of the option) but also in the option that it is subject to compliance with the subdivision control provisions of the Planning Act. **[See Form 9F3 for a sample realty option agreement.]**

---

1. R.S.O. 1990, c. P.13.

The Broker

9.130—The business broker most often encountered is the real estate agent acting as the agent for the purchaser or the vendor in advertising for sale and obtaining and concluding offers for purchase and sale for the property. There are also business brokers seeking purchasers or endeavouring to obtain target businesses for their respective clients. All such brokers need to be properly registered pursuant to the Real Estate and Business Brokers Act,[1] if the broker is engaged in a "trade" in "real estate", as defined in section 1 of that Act. "Real estate" includes not only freehold and leasehold lands, but also businesses, fixtures and goods. "Trade" includes purchases, sales, exchanges, leases, options, offers, listings, advertising, negotiation and other acts relative to the "real estate", direct or indirect.

Section 5 of the Act indicates that certain persons need not be registered as brokers, such as solicitors in Ontario, where the trade is made in the course of the solicitor's practice, and persons acting on their own behalf. If the services of a broker have been used, provision needs to be made for payment of the appropriate fees and ascertaining the liability for such payment by either the vendor or the purchaser, or as shared by both.

It may be that the vendor's broker is holding a deposit towards the purchase price and arrangements need to be made for attributing such deposit towards the broker's fees, or arranging for the broker to make payment of the deposit on closing of the sale, or return of the deposit if the transaction aborts. If a deposit is being made in a transaction to which the Bulk Sales Act[2] applies, note the restriction in section 6 limiting such deposit to 10 per cent.

If the broker has acted for the vendor, there may be additional concerns as to representations and warranties expressed by such agent of the vendor and possibly subsequently denied by the vendor. The scope of au-thority of the broker may become an item of contention and key repre-sentations and warranties to the purchaser may need to be confirmed in the agreement of purchase and sale to ensure that the principal does not subsequently deny liability for such statements.

---

1. R.S.O. 1990, c. R.4.

2. R.S.O. 1990, c. B.14.

Documents to Obtain

9.140—In effecting either the purchase of shares or of assets, the following documents should be obtained to thoroughly investigate the affairs of the vendor and to assist in determining whether to purchase assets or shares and in preparing to conduct due diligence investigations and searches discussed in Part 3. If acting for the vendor it should be anticipated that the purchaser will ask for such documents and the production of the same should be organized with the client to expedite negotiations and closing.

In either an asset or a share purchase, the same due diligence should be effected to the following purposes:

(a) in an asset transaction, it will be necessary to determine if there are any liabilities or burdens which the client does not wish to assume so the same may be properly recorded as excluded assets; and

(b) in a share purchase, the client needs to be fully informed of all liabilities, burdens and problems of the business, since on becoming the owner of the shares, it will be assuming these obligations.

Depending on what is uncovered, the deal may need to be restructured as an asset purchase or share purchase, to avoid tax and other statutory and practical problems. Therefore, it is necessary to obtain complete disclosure about the target business, including the following:

(i) Description of the Business — Documents to describe the business being acquired including past histories, present and past annual reports, financial statements, corporate organizational charts, office and director's manuals, etc.

(ii) Tangible Assets — Lists describing all tangible assets owned by the corporation including the following:

— equipment complete with all operating manuals, manufacturer's warranties, service agreements;

— listings of inventories from most recent count or records concerning same, including supply agreements and production agreements;

— real property documentation including all deeds, mortgages, surveys, tax assessment numbers; and

— valuations regarding any of the same.

(iii)   Intangible property — Lists of all tangible property such as: —

all intellectual property such as patents, trade-marks, industrial property of all kinds, including particulars of all documents registered to prove ownership and registered user arrangements; — information concerning any know-how borrowed or obtained from third parties and any royalties paid; and — information concerning key employees who are possessed of such know-how and operation processes.

(iv)   Leased Properties — Lists of all leased goods and realty including: — copies of all leases of equipment and motor vehicles together with telephone numbers and contact parties of such lessors so that assignments may be arranged; and

— leases of real property including copies of all such leases with information regarding registration of notice of the same against title, documents relevant to leases such as tax bills and name and contact party for the landlord;

(v)   Employees — All employment records including:

— detailed list of all employees by departments such as management, sales and labour and details of salaries, commissions, bonuses or other remuneration, length of service, age, sex and fringe benefits;

— copies of all employee benefit plans, pension plans, drug and health care insurance;

— copies of any employment agreements; and

— copies of any consulting agreements with agents or other independent contractors providing specific services.

(vi)   Services — Copies of all supply and service agreements such as snow removal, landscaping, waste removal, railway siding, freight for materials and goods, etc.

(vii)   Utilities — Copies of all utilities arrangements such as agreements with Hydro, waste sampling portals for the City, etc.;

(viii) Licensing and Permits — Copies of all necessary licences to operate the business, including elevator licences, GST and PST numbers and all other government filings;

(ix)   Insurance — Copies of all insurance policies necessary for operation of the business and copies of premiums to determine the adequacy and expense of coverage;

(x)   Litigation — Information concerning all outstanding or pending claims or actions against the company;

(xi) — Records, including copies of or access to:

    A.   audited annual financial statements and management prepared monthly or quarterly statements for past years and projections for the future;

    B.   information regarding pre-paid expenses and contingent liabili-ties for such matters as intercorporate or shareholder guarantees;

    C.   information regarding taxes and copies of returns, assessments, etc.;

    D.   information regarding any outstanding obligations such as trust indentures and banking operations;

    E.   customer lists, customer supply agreements, advertising and public relations;

    F.   listing of accounts receivable aged by 30, 60, 90 and over 90 days, including information on all bad debts; and

    G.   environmental and occupational health and safety records. **[See Checklist 9C9]**

If the transaction includes a purchase of shares, you will also require access to the minute books, share ledgers, and other corporate records to ensure that the target corporation has been properly incorporated and is duly organized with all requisite proceedings in all necessary jurisdictions effected. These corporate records will need to be made available so that any deficiencies can be noted and corrected as soon as possible.

3. DUE DILIGENCE AND INVESTIGATIONS

Real Estate

Freehold

9.150—In business transactions involving assets that are freehold lands, whether the transaction is by way of a sale and purchase of assets or a sale and purchase of shares, title and title related searches must be con-ducted as soon as possible in order to allow sufficient time to resolve any problems that may be uncovered by such searches. Checklist 9C1 sets out the many searches involving title and title-related matters but the list need not be carried out in every transaction. Certain searches may not be appropriate to the particular transaction at hand. Obviously it is up to the solicitor to exercise judgment with respect to matters of this nature. It is also important that the client be informed and that instructions be obtained and subsequently confirmed in writing with respect to those searches that should be done but for one reason or another have been dispensed with. For example, if instructed by a client to proceed without a building location survey and the client is made aware of the ramifications, then these instructions should be confirmed in writing with the client before the completion of the transaction. **[See Checklist 9C1]**

Leasehold

9.160—With respect to leasehold lands, the searches involved begin with the same as those on freehold lands. This is particularly the case if the leasehold interest being assigned is a net lease where the tenant is responsible for some or all of the obligations with respect to the property such as utilities, work orders, by-law compliance and similar matters. In addition, it is necessary to determine whether the leasehold interest being assigned to the purchaser is valid. The starting point for determining whether the leasehold interest is valid lies in determining who the landlord is. The landlord's interest can only be properly determined by carrying out a search of title. As previously indicated, the extent of the title-related searches depends on the nature of the tenant's obligations under the lease and of course, on the client's instructions and solicitor's judgment.

In addition to title and title related searches, the following additional matters must be considered in a leasehold situation and, if appropriate, acted upon in each case:

1. Lease Review
    As early as possible, the lease should be reviewed in detail and a commentary prepared for the client listing all the important points in the lease and pointing out any deficiencies. **[See Checklist 9C6]**

2. Estoppel Certificate
    A certificate from the landlord confirming the status of the lease being assigned is essential. Without it, the new tenant would be liable for any arrears of rent or other defaults under the lease. **[See Form 9F41]**

3. Landlord's Consent
    Most leases require the consent of the landlord to any assignment or sublease. Normally the matter of the landlord's consent is made a condition of closing of the transaction. **[See Form 9F42]**

4. Mortgagees
    With respect to outstanding mortgages revealed by the title search, the matter of non-disturbance or postponement agreements must be considered. The provisions of the lease must first be consulted to ascertain the rights of the tenant with respect to mortgagees' interests. A non-disturbance agreement basically protects a tenant's possession so long as the tenant is not in default under the lease. On the other hand, the postponement agreement deems the tenant's leasehold interest to have priority over the mortgagee's interest. **[See Forms 9F44 and 9F45]**

5. Sublease

In the event the leasehold interest being assigned is a sublease, the matter of the head lease has to be addressed, and in context to the status of the head lease, the consent of both the head landlord and the sublandlord should be considered. Outstanding mortgages have to be addressed in the same manner. [**See generally Checklist 9C6 and Forms 9F40–9F45**]

Owned Personalty

General

9.170—There is no title registry system for personal property in the province of Ontario. Consequently, one may only make enquiries of public records to determine if liens or encumbrances have been recorded against a particular debtor. One cannot say that a person owns a particular item of personalty based only on public records.

In properly effecting personal property searches, certain initial information is required before searches may be commenced. This basic information is as follows:

Who and Where to Search

9.171—With respect to corporations, all past and present corporate names (in both official languages when so adopted), and all business styles, registered or not;

- Partnerships — the partnership name as stated in the partnership agreement as well as the name as recorded in partnership registration legislation and all partners' names; and
- Individuals — first name, middle initial (if any) and surname, date of birth, and business styles for sole proprietors.

Verification of the foregoing information is effected by conducting searches of corporate records filed with provincial or federal corporate records offices, partnership registrations and business style registrations and obtaining copies of birth certificates, and passport or Canadian citizenship papers for individuals.

Searches of corporate, partnership and business style records filed in Ontario are effected in person, by mail, on the internet or by faxed request at the following address:

> Ministry of Consumer and Business Services
> Companies and Personal Property Securities Branch
> 375 University Ave, 2nd Floor (in person)

393 University Ave, Suite 200 (by mail)
Toronto, ON M5G 2M2
Tel: (800) 361-3223
        (416) 314-8880
TTY: (416) 212-1476
Fax: (416) 314-4852
www.cbs.gov.on.ca/mcbs (only forms can be downloaded)

The search may also be conducted for a fee by two primary service providers who are under contract with the Ministry. These are, as of June 2, 2004:

1.   Oncorp Direct Inc.
       www.Oncorp.com
       Tel: (800) 461-7772
              (416) 964-2677

2.   Cyberbahn Inc.
       www.Cyberbahn.ca
       Tel: (800) 806-0003
              (416) 595-9522

Ministry personnel will not take search requests by telephone. The same office is the place to order certificate of status for corporations incorporated in Ontario or registered to carry on business in Ontario.

Fees for the usual searches and registrations are as follows, as of June 2, 2004:

Corporate Microfiche — $10
Copy of business name registration — $12
Corporate business name search — $12
Registration of corporate business name — $80 in person or by mail/ primary server provider for a fee
Registration of general partnership — $80 in person or by mail / primary service provider for a fee
Registration of limited partnership — $210
Certificate of Status — $30 (no longer a fee for search)

Searches for federal non-profit corporations are conducted in person at:

Industry Canada
Corporations Canada
151 Yonge Street
4th Floor
Toronto, ON M5C 2W7
Tel.: (416) 954-2714
http://corporationscanada.ic.gc.ca

Federal certificates of compliance for federal corporations may be ordered there at a cost of $10 each, as of June 2, 2004.

Searches for federal for-profit corporations are conducted in person at the same place. Searches can be performed at http://corporationscanada.ic.gc.ca free of cost.

With respect to individuals, social insurance number or provincial drivers' licence papers are not adequate proof of a person's name, as these offices merely recite the name given by the person. If in any doubt, search against the individual by both the name revealed on the birth certificate, passport or Canadian citizenship papers, as well as the name by which the person is usually known. For example, searches against "William A. Jones" may be augmented by searches against "Bill Jones".

If the individual has recently married, divorced or separated, it is advisable to check to see if he or she has filed a declaration pursuant to the Change of Name Act,[1] adopting the other spouse's surname, reverting to their surname or adopting a combined name. **[See Form 9F8 for sample enquiry letter.]** If in any doubt, search all combinations. For example, Susan A. Smythe, Susan A. Brown, Susan A. Smythe-Brown and Susan A. Brown-Smythe. For individuals who are of cultures that have unique name customs, be sure to make thorough investigations about names and search all combinations.

If the vendor has acquired the assets or shares from a third party, that third party vendor should also be searched. It is necessary to know not only the provinces in which assets of the vendor are located, but also in which counties or judicial districts within those provinces, as some searches are done by county or judicial district, as opposed to province-wide registration systems.

Failure to search against the correct name or in the correct location will provide inaccurate search results, making your due diligence inquiries irrelevant. Consequently, great care needs to be used to determine exact names and locations to ensure that all proper searches are done as accurately as possible.

---

1. R.S.O. 1990, c. C-7.

Status of the Vendor

Corporate filings

9.172—For corporate vendors it is necessary to determine that the entity is subsisting and that it is duly organized and properly registered to conduct its business in all requisite jurisdictions. To this end, the following should be ordered or obtained from the vendor's counsel:

— a certificate of status from the provincial government or certificate of compliance from the federal government for the jurisdiction, pursuant to which the corporation was incorporated, and a provincial certificate of status for each province in which the corporation carries on business, to show it has been properly recorded to conduct business in that jurisdiction;

— certified or notarial copies of its constating documents, being the letters patent, supplementary letters patent, articles of incorporation, articles of amendment, articles of amalgamation, articles of continuance, or other chartered documents that created the entity, as amended; and

— copies of any unanimous shareholders' agreements.

Copies of these records may be ordered for the Ontario and federal governments at the addresses noted in **Para. 9.171**, on "who to search".

A review of the constating documents and any unanimous shareholders' agreements will show if any special steps or restrictions exist regarding the ability of the corporation to carry on or sell its business or a portion of its shares. In a share purchase transaction, obviously there should be a thorough review of the minute books, share ledgers and all other corporate records to determine that the entity being acquired is duly organized and up-to-date in all proceedings and filing.

It may take some time to effect a complete corporate search to determine all correct names, as the vendor entity may be as a result of a series of amalgamations. Each of the predecessor corporations should be searched for any further changes of name or further prior amalgamations.

Bankruptcy

9.173—It is essential to search bankruptcy records to determine that the vendor has the capacity to be able to deal in its assets and that such have not been vested in a bankruptcy trustee.

Voluntary assignments into bankruptcy and failed proposals to creditors (resulting in a deemed assignment into bankruptcy) are searched through the records of the Official Receiver for the bankruptcy registration district in which the individual resides or the corporation has its head office. Such federal records are usually two and three weeks in arrears of real time. These searches are conducted through the local offices of the Official Receiver or by contacting the office of the Official Receiver in Ottawa.

Separately, petitions by creditors pushing the debtor involuntarily into bankruptcy may be searched with the office of the Official Receiver and also with more current records found in the local office of the Superior Courts of Justice, sitting in bankruptcy for the judicial district or county in which the individual resides or the corporation has its head office. Such a search is typically done by a law clerk or paralegal by using microfiche in the court offices. Note that the court issues a certificate only when the microfiche reveals a recorded entry showing the issuance of the petition.

The most up-to-date bankruptcy records are kept by the main office of the Official Receiver in Hull. These records may be serviced by faxed request at the following address:

> Office of Superintendent of Bankruptcy, Search Services
> 365 Laurier Avenue West
> Jean Edmonds Tower South, 8th Floor
> Ottawa ON K1A 0C9
> Tel: (613) 941-2863
> Fax: (613) 941-6176

Searches of bankruptcy records can also be conducted through Industry Canada's corporations database, accessed on the Internet at www.strategis.gc.ca.

The local office must be searched or other local offices of the Superior Court of Justice throughout Ontario, for the bankruptcy division

As of June 2, 2004, bankruptcy search certificates cost $8.

Citizenship

9.174—The citizenship of the vendor should be confirmed. As noted in subsection 2.1.4(c), section 116 of the Income Tax Act[1] requires withholding of a certain portion of the purchase price in the event the funds are being paid to a non-resident vendor. Consequently, it must be determined whether such vendor is indeed a non-resident of Canada for purposes of the Income Tax Act. This is usually satisfied by obtaining the vendor's statutory declaration as one of the closing documents or by obtaining such representation or warranty within the agreement of purchase and sale, and having such representation survive closing.

---

1. R.S.C. 1985, c. 1 (5th Supp.).

Marriage

9.175—In acquiring assets from an individual sole proprietor or from individuals engaged in a partnership, it should be determined whether any of the assets involved are in fact matrimonial assets. Declarations as to the status of the person as a spouse and consents from the spouse may be necessary to ensure that the spouse is acting with the consent and approval of the other spouse. In addition, if the person has gone through a form of separation or divorce and there are any outstanding support or custody orders, the Crown has the ability to file claims against title to land in order to enforce payment of the support order. Regard should be had to the Support and Custody Orders Enforcement Act.[1]

Searches for outstanding support and custody orders are done in person at the Court offices where the orders were issued. Files are requisitioned from the Court staff by court file number. In Toronto, this is done with the Ontario Court (Provincial Division), Records Office at 311 Jarvis Street, Toronto, Ontario, M5B 2C4, Tel.: (416) 327-6868.

In Ontario, the Family Responsibility Office may be contacted at the following address:

Family Responsibility Office

(a)   24-Hour Automated Information Line
         Tel: (416) 326-1818 (from within the 416 & 905 area)
         Toll Free: 1-800-267-7263
         Client Services Call Centre
         Tel: (416) 326-1817 or toll free 1-800-267-4330
         TTY: (416) 240-2414
         Fax: (416) 240-2401

(b)   Field Office Addresses
         All offices have been closed. One central office located at:
         Family Responsibility Office
         P.O. Box 220
         Downsview, ON M3M 3A3
         Fax No. for Correspondence (416) 240-2401

If the spouse is consenting to the disposition of any matrimonial property or stating that such asset is not matrimonial property, it is advisable to obtain a certificate of independent legal advice for that spouse before such consent or declaration is signed.

---

1. R.S.O. 1990, c. S.28.

Registered Personalty Encumbrances

9.176—Unlike real estate, there is no title registry system in Canada for the registration of ownership to personal property, with the exception of ownership to ships under the Canada Shipping Act[1] and intellectual property under other various federal legislation discussed in Para. 9.190.

In Ontario there are two systems for obtaining information concerning registered consensual encumbrances against title to the vendor's personalty. These are notices of intention filed pursuant to section 427 of the Bank Act[2] and filings made pursuant to the Personal Property Security Act.[3]

---

1. R.S.C. 1985, c. S-9.

2. S.C. 1991, c. 46; as am. 1992, c. 27, s. 90; 1993, c. 6, s. 6; 1993, c. 28, s. 78, Sch. III, item 5; 1998, c. 36, s. 21.

3. R.S.O. 1990, c. P.10.

Section 427 Bank Act Security

9.177—Canadian banks are entitled to take security against specified inventories and other specific assets owned by certain borrowers as listed in section 427 of the Bank Act.[1] For example, the cattle and machinery of farmers, the boats of fishermen, and the inventories of manufacturers and retailers. Evidence that such security has been taken is found by conducting a search for registered notices of intention with the appropriate agency of the Bank of Canada. Subsection 427(4)(b) of the Bank Act[2] requires that the notice of intention be filed with the "appropriate agency" for the jurisdiction in which the Borrower is conducting its business (if there is only one place of business), or in the jurisdiction where the head office of the borrower is located (where the borrower has more than one location).

For example, a business operating with offices in Ontario, Manitoba and British Columbia and having its main place of business in Winnipeg, would require a search of the Winnipeg agency of the Bank of Canada. The bank need not file in any location other than the Winnipeg agency to have its security cover the assets of the borrower throughout all three provinces. Consequently, it is necessary to ensure that the correct agency of the Bank of Canada is searched.

As of December 15, 1997, the Bank of Canada chose to "out source" all of the work of the agencies of the Bank of Canada. Canadian Securities Regulation Systems ("CSRS") won the bid from Industry Canada to take over the registration and searching pursuant to section 427 of the Bank Act.[3] Searches and registration will be done in person until the database is live for remote work.

The Bank Act has not been amended to change to a national database. Consequently, you still need to read section 427 of the Bank Act[4] to determine the correct "Agency" of the Bank of Canada in which to register a notice of intention to take such security in the correction location.

Searches will still be conducted by "Agency" district, but once remote access is available to the database, searchers will be able to search the database of each Agency (e.g., Vancouver or Halifax) from their own offices. Each Agency location is as of June 2, 2004, a CSRS office or the office of an agent of CSRS.

For further information from CSRS on setting up an account for remote service, CSRS can be contacted at:

> Central Processing Facility
> Canadian Securities Registration Systems
> Suite 200, 4126 Norland Avenue
> Burnaby, BC V5G 3S8
> Tel: (604) 637-4014
> Fax: (604) 637-4015
> Toll Free: 1-888-278-2116

Searches in Ontario for the Bank of Canada are conducted at the following address in person, by mail, or by fax:

> Canadian Securities Registration Systems
> 2605 – 180 Dundas Street West
> Toronto, ON M5G 1Z8
> Tel: (416) 204-3000
> Fax: (416) 204-3003
> Toll Free: 1-800-254-3094

Searches in other areas of Canada are done in person, by mail or by fax at the following locations:

Canadian Securities Registration Systems
Suite M23, 10060 Jasper Avenue NW
Edmonton, AB T5J 3R8
Tel: (780) 429-0411
Fax: (780) 424-3725
Toll Free: 1-800-387-9568

L.C. Taylor & Associates
Suite 702, 310 Broadway
Winnipeg, MB R3C 0S6
Tel: (204) 925-6400
Fax: (204) 956-2335

Marshall Trustee Services
Suite 400, 53 King Street
Saint John, NB E2L 1G5
Tel: (506) 634-7850

Deloitte & Touche LLP
Fort William Building
10 Factory Lane
St. John's, NL A1C 6H5
Tel: (709) 576-8480
Fax: (709) 758-5238

Deloitte & Touche LLP
900 Bank of Montreal Building
2103 – 11th Avenue
Regina, SK S4P 3B3
Tel: (306) 525-1600
Fax: (306) 757-4753

CRAC-CSRF
1080 Beaver Hall Hill, Suite 1717
Montreal, QC H2Z 1S8
Tel: (514) 861-2722
Fax: (877) 851-7855
Charles Wackett & Associates
1675 Bedford Row, Suite 100
Halifax, NS B3J 1T1
Tel: (902) 482-2000
Fax: (902) 482-2005

Arsenault, Best, Cameron, Ellis, Chartered Accountants
80 Water Street
Charlottetown, PE C1A 1A6
Tel: (902) 368-3100
Fax: (902) 566-5074

Searches for the Yukon and the Northwest Territories are effected through the Clerk of the local Superior Courts in Whitehorse and Yellowknife, respectively.

---

1. S.C. 1991, c. 46, am. 1992, c. 27, s. 90, 1993, c. 6, s. 6, c. 28, Sch. III, item 5, 1998, c. 36, s. 21.

2. *Ibid.*

3. *Ibid.*

4. *Ibid.*

PPSA

9.178—In the PPSA system it is essential to be as accurate as possible with names to ensure that all possible registrations in the system are found. Searches pursuant to the Personal Property Security Act[1] in Ontario may reveal encumbrances governed by the following schemes:

— security interest governed pursuant to the Personal Property Security Act;

— registered liens pursuant to the Repair and Storage Liens Act;[2]
— trust deeds, bonds and debentures issued by a corporation pursuant to the Corporation Securities Registration Act[3] (since repealed) and now brought forward into the PPSA database; and
— seizures of security interest by the sheriff pursuant to the Execution Act[4]

When conducting PPSA searches, either manually or electronically,[5] you may choose to obtain any of the following types of searches:

— an individual debtor specific search, which requires you to provide the exact first name, middle initial, if any, surname, and birth date of the individual;
— an individual non-specific search, by using the first name and last name of the debtor. This search printout provides a broader source of information. For example, a search against "Charles Brown" will reveal all entries for "Charles Brown" "Charles A. Brown" "Charles B. Brown", etc., whereas an individual debtor specific search will reveal only searches filed against "Charles A. Brown" born on a specified date;
— business debtor searches, against debtors other than individuals, such as corporations, partnerships, estates of deceased persons, churches, unions, and other unincorporated associations. When conducting searches against corporations with bilingual names, be sure to request searches against both the English and French names separately and against the joint English/French and French/English names, to ensure all possible ways that a secured party may have selected to enter their data (whether or not in conformance with the PPSA Regulations); are found and
— searches against individual vehicle identification numbers. Note that for purposes of the PPSA, a "vehicle identification number" or "VIN" is defined as being the number affixed to a "motor vehicle" (as defined in the Regulations) by the manufacturer of that motor vehicle. For example, a North American built automobile will have a 17-digit alphanumeric VIN, but a motorized golf cart or battery powered forklift truck will have the manufacturer's serial number as its "VIN".

To ensure as many entries as possible are found, also search business styles and nicknames, in addition to the current corporation or individual name. It is preferable to locate and have discharged all registrations, whether or not correctly entered by the third party.

The PPSA system will allow the choice of an uncertified or a certified search. Presumably one would select a certified search so that one could rely upon the insurance fund maintained by the Ministry, for errors caused by the

Ministry which causes harm after one has relied upon such a defective certified search.

It is also essential that all prior names of a corporation are searched. The database from the old Corporation Security Registration Act[6] ("CSRA") was entered by the ministry personnel using the name of the debtor as it appeared on the corporate debenture, trust deed or bond. Secured parties had until October 10, 1991 to enter any changes of name of that debtor to bring the database current. However, trustees under trust deeds have no such obligation and consequently, there may be valid registrations sitting in the database under a prior name. Further search information is available in the Registration and Search Guide published by the Ontario Ministry of Consumer and Corporate Relations.

If the PPSA search results reveal a CSRA registration, it is necessary to obtain a copy of the underlying instrument (trust deed, bond, debenture, etc.) from the Ministry, as only the old CSRA registration number and the debtor name as it appears on that instrument were entered in the PPSA database.

Searches in Ontario are effected in person at a local office or by mail or by telephone at the following address and prices, as of June 2, 2004.[7] **[See Checklist 9C18]**

Companies and Personal Property Security Branch

In Person:

375 University Avenue
2nd Floor
Toronto, ON M5G 2G1
Tel: (416) 325-8847

Mailing Address:

393 University Ave, 3rd Floor
Toronto, ON M5G 2M2

Costs:
PPSA search — verbal/certificate: $8 online/$10 in person
Initial registration for period of 25 years or less: $8/year + $5 administration fee
Amendment registration: $12 + $5 administration fee
Discharge registration: $5/administration fee
Copy of CSRA debenture: $12 fee for up to 12 pages and $1/page for each page of particulars after 12 pages.
Copies of Documents: $14
Certified/Registered copies of document: $15

---

1. R.S.O. 1990, c. P.10.

2. R.S.O. 1990, c. R.25.

3. Repealed S.O. 1989, c. 16, s. 84(1).

4. R.S.O. 1990, c. E.24.

5. Electronic Registration Act, S.O. 1991, c. 44.

6. *Supra*, note 3.

7. Regulation under the Personal Property Security Act, O. Reg. 547/94.

Executions

9.179—Searches should be conducted with the sheriff in each judicial district or county in which the vendor has assets that the purchaser is acquiring, to determine if there are any writs of executions outstanding. Note section 10 of the Execution Act,[1] with regard to the peril of a purchaser who acquires chattels with knowledge of a writ of execution. The safest course of action is to have the execution satisfied from the purchase proceeds if possible, or discharged, or lifted if even for the day, before concluding the transaction.

Execution certificates cost $11 per name searched as of June 2, 2004. Searches may be conducted in person at self-serve computer search facilities at the following 54 land registry offices throughout Ontario. Searches may also be conducted at self-serve computers at the sheriff's office for Ontario counties.

Land Registry Offices and Services Offered:

Hours: 8:30 – 5:00
Services Provided:
Registry – REG
Land Titles – LT
Personal Property Security Registration – PPSR
Company Incorporation – CO
Registrar General – ORG
Ontario Business Connects – OBC
Automated land registration data base – POLARIS

Algoma
Land Registry Office – REG, LT,
PPSR, CO, OBC, ORG (Bilingual)
420 Queen St E PO Box 550
Sault Ste. Marie ON P6A 5M8
Tel: (705) 253-8887
Fax: (705) 253-9245

Brant
Land Registry Office – LT, REG,
PPSR, POLARIS
Court House
80 Wellington Street
Brantford ON N3T 2L9
Tel: (519) 752-8321
Tel: (519) 752-5571– PPSR
Fax: (519) 752-0273

Bruce
Land Registry Office – REG, LT,
PPSR, OBC
203 Cayley Street
PO Box 1690
Walkerton ON N0G 2V0
Tel: (519) 881-2259
Fax: (519) 881-2322

Cochrane
Land Registry Office – REG, LT,
PPSR (Bilingual)
149 4th Avenue
Court House
PO Box 580
Cochrane ON P0L 1C0
Tel: (705) 272-5791
Fax: (705) 272-2951

Dufferin
Land Registry Office – REG, LT,
PPSR, POLARIS, OBC
10 Louisa St
Orangeville ON L9W 3P9
Tel: (519) 941-1481
Fax: (519) 941-6444

Dundas
Land Registry Office – REG
(Bilingual)
8 - 5th St PO Box 645
Morrisburg ON K0C 1X0
Tel: (613) 543-2583
Fax: (613) 543-4541

Durham
Land Registry Office – REG, LT,
PPSR, ORG, CO, OBC, POLARIS
590 Rossland Road E
Whitby ON L1N 9G5
Tel: (905) 665-4007
Fax: (905) 665-5247

Elgin
Land Registry Office – REG, LT,
PPSR
Court House Block
4 Wellington ST
St. Thomas ON N5R 2P2
Tel: (519) 631-3015
Tel: (519) 633-4471 – PPSR
Fax: (519) 631-8182

Essex
Land Registry Office – ORG, REG,
LT, PPSR, CO, POLARIS (Bilingual)
949 McDougall St, Suite 100
Windsor ON N9A 1L9
Tel: (519) 971-9980
Tel: (519) 971-9976 – PPSR
Fax: (519) 971-9937

Frontenac
Land Registry Office – LT, REG,
PPSR, CO, OBC, POLARIS
1 Court Street
Kingston ON K7L 2N4
Tel: (613) 548-6767
Fax: (613) 548-6766

Glengarry
Land Registry Office – REG
(Bilingual)
PO Box 668
63 Kenyon Street West
Alexandria ON K0C 1A0
Tel: (613) 525-1315
Fax: (613) 525-0509

Grenville
Land Registry Office – REG
(Bilingual)
499 Centre Street
P.O. Box 1660
Prescott ON K0E 1T0
Tel: (613) 925-3177
Fax: (613) 925-0302

Grey
Land Registry Office – REG, PPSR,
OBC
1555 16th St E, Suites 1 and 2
Owen Sound ON N4K 5N3
Tel: (519) 376-1637
Fax: (519) 376 1639

Haldimand
Land Registry Office – REG, PPSR
10 Echo St.
PO Box 310
Cayuga ON N0A 1E0
Tel: (905) 772-3531
Fax: (905) 772-0105

Haliburton
Land Registry Office – REG
Newcastle Street Box 270
Minden ON K0M 2K0
Tel: (705) 286-1391
Fax: (705) 286-4324

Halton
Land Registry Office – REG, LT,
PPSR, POLARIS
491 Steeles Ave E
Milton ON L9T 1Y7
Tel: (905) 878-7287
Fax: (905) 876-8806

Hastings
Land Registry Office – REG, LT,
PPSR, ORG
15 Victoria Ave
Belleville ON K8N 1Z5
Tel: (613) 968-4597 – General
Inquiry
Fax: (613) 968-3606

Huron
Land Registry Office – REG, PPSR,
OBC, LT, POLARIS
38 North Street
Goderich ON N7A 2T4
Tel: (519) 524-9562
Fax: (519) 524-2482

Kenora (Bilingual)
REG, LT, PPSR, OBC
220 Main St S
Kenora ON P9N 1T2
Tel: (807) 468-2794
Fax: (807) 468-2796

Kent
Land Registry Office – REG, PPSR,
LT, POLARIS (Bilingual)
40 William Street North
Chatham ON N7M 4L2
Tel: (519) 352-5520
Fax: (519) 352-3222

Lambton
Land Registry Office – REG, PPSR,
CO, OBC
Court House
700 Christina Street North, Suite
102
P.O. Box 3021
Sarnia ON N7V 3C2
Tel: (519) 337-2393
Fax: (519) 337-8371

Lanark
Land Registry Office – REG, OBC,
PPSR
2 Industrial Dr
P.O. Box 1180
Almonte ON K0A 1A0
Tel: (613) 256-1577
Fax: (613) 256-0940

Leeds
Land Registry Office – REG, PPSR,
OBC
7 King St West
Box 633
Brockville ON K6V 3P7
Tel: (613) 345-5751
Fax: (613) 345-7390

Lennox
Land Registry Office – REG, PPSR
2 Dairy Ave, Unit 10
Murphy's Business Centre
Napanee ON K7R 3T1
Tel: (613) 354-3751
Fax: (613) 354-1474

Manitoulin
Land Registry Office – REG, LT,
PPSR
27 Phipps St
Gore Bay ON P0P 1H0
Tel: (705) 282-2442
Fax: (705) 282-3245

Middlesex
Land Registry Office – REG, PPSR,
ORG, CO, LT, POLARIS (Bilingual)
Provincial Court Bldg
80 Dundas St Ground Floor J
London ON N6A 6A7
Tel: (519) 675-7600
Tel: (519) 675-7612 – PPSR
Fax: (519) 675-7611

Muskoka
Land Registry Office – REG, LT,
PPSR, OBC
15 Dominion Street North
Bracebridge ON P1L 2E7
Tel: (705) 645-4415
Fax: (715) 645-7826

Niagara North
Land Registry Office – REG, LT,
PPSR, POLARIS, OBC
59 Church St
St. Catharines ON L2R 3C3
Tel: (905) 684-6351
Fax: (905) 684-5874

Niagara South
Land Registry Office – CO, REG,
LT, PPSR, OBC, POLARIS
(Bilingual)
200 Division St
Welland ON L3B 4A2
Tel: (905) 735-4011/13
Fax: (905) 735-2430

Nipissing
Land Registry Office – REG, LT,
PPSR, ORG (Bilingual)
360 Plouffe Street, Court House
North Bay ON P1B 9L5
Tel: (705) 474-2270
Fax: (705) 495-8511

Norfolk
Land Registry Office – REG, LT,
PPSR
530 Queensway W., 2nd Fl
Court House
Simcoe ON N3Y 4K8
Tel: (519) 426-2216
Fax: (519) 426-9627

Northumberland
Land Registry Office – LT, REG,
PPSR
1005 William St Suite 105
Cobourg ON K9A 5J4
Tel: (905) 372-3813
Fax: (905) 372-4758

Ottawa-Carleton
Land Registry Office – LT, REG,
PPSR, CO, OBC, ORG, POLARIS
(Bilingual)
Court House
161 Elgin Street 4th Floor
Ottawa ON K2P 2K1
Tel: (613) 239-1230
Fax: (613) 239-1422

Oxford
Land Registry Office – REG, LT
PPSR, OBC, POLARIS
75 Graham Street
Woodstock ON N4S 6J8
Tel: (519) 537-6287
Fax: (519) 537-3107

Parry Sound
Land Registry Office – REG, LT,
PPSR
28 Miller Street
Parry Sound ON P2A 1T1
Tel: (705) 746-5816
Fax: (705) 746-6517

Peel
Land Registry Office – REG, LT,
PPSR, OBC, POLARIS, ORG
(Bilingual)
7765 Hurontario St
Brampton ON L6V 2L8
Tel: (905) 874-4008
Fax: (905) 874-4012

Perth
Land Registry Office – REG, LT,
PPSR, POLARIS
5 Huron St
Stratford ON N5A 5S4
Tel: (519) 271-3343
Fax: (519) 271-2550

Peterborough
Land Registry Office – REG, LT,
PPSR, CO, OBC, POLARIS
300 Water St, 2nd Floor
P.O. Box 7000
Peterborough ON K9J 8M5
Tel: (705) 755-1342
Fax: (705) 755 1343

Prescott
Land Registry Office – REG, LT,
PPSR (Bilingual)
179 Main St E
Hawkesbury ON K6A 1A1
Tel: (613) 636-0314
Fax: (613) 636-0772

Prince Edward
Land Registry Office – REG, PPSR
1 Pitt Street
PO Box 1310
Picton ON K0K 2T0
Tel: (613) 476-3219
Fax: (613) 476-7908

Rainy River
Land Registry Office – REG, LT,
PPSR
353 Church Street
Fort Frances ON P9A 1C9
Tel: (807) 274-5451
Fax: (807) 274-1704

Renfrew
Land Registry Office – REG, PPSR,
OBC, LT (Bilingual)
400 Pembroke St E
Pembroke ON K8A 3K8
Tel: (613) 732-8331
Fax: (613) 732-0297

Russell
Land Registry Office – REG, LT
(Bilingual)
1122 Concession St.
PO Box 10
Russell ON K4R 1C8
Tel: (613) 445-2138
Fax: (613) 445-0614

Simcoe
Land Registry Office – REG, LT,
PPSR, CO, OBC, POLARIS, ORG
(Bilingual)
Court House
114 Worsley Street
Barrie ON L4M 1M1
Tel: (705) 725-7232
Fax: (705) 725-7246

Stormont
Land Registry Office – REG, PPSR,
OBC (Bilingual)
127 Sydney Street
Cornwall ON K6H 3H1
Tel: (613) 932-4522
Fax: (613) 932-4524

Sudbury
Land Registry Office – REG, PPSR,
LT, CO, ORG, POLARIS, OBC
(Bilingual)
199 Larch St, Suite 301
Sudbury ON P3E 5P9
Tel: (705) 564-4300
Fax: (705) 564-4148

Thunder Bay
Land Registry Office – REG, PPSR,
LT, CO, OBC, ORG (Bilingual)
189 Red River Rd, Suite 201
Thunder Bay ON P7B 1A2
Tel: (807) 343-7436
Fax: (807) 343-7439

Timiskaming
Land Registry Office – REG, LT,
PPSR, OBC (Bilingual)
375 Main St PO Box 159
Haileybury ON P0J 1K0
Tel: (705) 672-3332
Fax: (705) 672-3906

Toronto Registry
Land Registry Office – REG,
POLARIS, LT (Bilingual)
20 Dundas St W, Suite 321
Box 108
Toronto ON M5G 2C2
Tel: (416) 314-4430
Fax: (416) 314-4453

Victoria
Land Registry Office – REG, LT,
PPSR
Provincial Court Building
440 Kent St W
Lindsay ON K9V 6G8
Tel: (705) 324-4912
Fax: (705) 324-6290

Waterloo
Land Registry Office – ORG, REG,
PPSR, CO, OBC, LT, POLARIS
200 Frederick St, 3rd Floor
Kitchener ON N2H 6H9
Tel: (519) 571-6043
Fax: (519) 571-6067

Wellington
Land Registry Office – LT, REG,
PPSR, POLARIS
1 Stone Rd W
Guelph ON N1G 4Y2
Tel: (519) 826-3372
Fax: (519) 826-3373

Wentworth
Land Registry Office – REG, LT.
PPSR, CO, ORG, POLARIS
(Bilingual)
119 King Street West, 4th Floor
PO Box 2112
Hamilton ON L8P 4Y7
Tel: (905) 521-7561
Fax: (905) 521-7505

York Region
Land Registry Office – REG, LT,
PPSR, ORG, OBC, POLARIS
50 Eagle Street W, 1st Floor
Newmarket ON L3Y 6B1
Tel: (905) 895-1561
Fax: (905) 895-6517

Bulk Sales Act[1]

9.180—It is advisable to conduct a bulk sales search against the vendor to determine whether it has already sold some or all of the assets which the client wishes to purchase. Such searches are conducted in person in the Court records in the matters book in each county or judicial district in which the vendor has assets. In Toronto, this is located at Ontario Court (General Division) at 393 University Avenue, 10th Floor, Toronto, Ontario, M5G 2M2.

In particular, if it is known that the client is purchasing assets from a vendor that recently acquired its assets from a third party, it may be necessary to conduct searches against such third party to ensure that the vendor obtains compliance with the Bulk Sales Act, otherwise, that the sale between the third party and the vendor is liable to being attacked or set aside.

These searches will only reveal filings made by the buyer within five days of the closing of the sale or exemption orders. If the parties failed to comply, or waived compliance, no records will be available and additional representations and indemnities may be required. **[See Paras. 9.560–9.561]**

---

1. R.S.O. 1990, c. B.14.

Bills of Sale

9.181—The Ontario Bills of Sale Act was repealed on October 10, 1989.[1] This ended the obligation of a purchaser to file a bill of sale in a public office where there was not a transfer of possession of the collateral upon the happening of a sale. However, the bills of sale registrations records still exist and it may be advisable to check the same to ensure that the vendor has not previously sold any of the assets to a third party or entered into any sale and lease back transactions. Such a search is done by reviewing the records found in the PPSA offices in Ontario, by each county or jurisdiction in which the vendor maintained its assets. In Toronto, this would be done at 375 University Avenue, 2nd floor, Toronto, Ontario, M5G 1E6.

---

1. Repealed S.O. 1989, c. 16, s. 84(1).

Other Jurisdictions

9.182—If the vendors own assets or carry on business outside the Province of Ontario, it will be necessary to consult counsel in other jurisdictions to determine which searches need to be conducted against the vendor and its assets located in that jurisdiction. For example, there are conditional sales debt, conditional sales, chattel mortgages, assignment of book debt, transfer of property and stock, corporate security registration,

It may be most cost-effective to conduct searches in Ontario first, and to send copies of the results with full corporate histories, to the agents in order to expedite their work. **[See Forms 9F9–9F11]**

Deemed Trusts and Possessory and Statutory Liens

9.183—Apart from consensual transactions registered as personal property encumbrances, additional encumbrances may arise by operation of common law or statute. These are usually referred to as deemed trusts and possessory and statutory liens. Such matters arise in favour of the Crown with respect to unremitted withholdings for employees under the Income Tax Act,[1] the Canada Pension Plan[2] and Unemployment Insurance Commission, and such deemed trusts for vacation pay and pension benefit amounts under the Employment Standards Act[3] and the Pension Benefits Act.[4] In addition, unpaid repairmen and storers may have registered or unregistered possessory liens pursuant to the Repair and Storage Lien Act,[5] unpaid solicitors may hold legal documents in accordance with a solicitor's lien, unpaid brokers may hold share certificates with respect to unpaid broker's fees, etc.

Only some of the foregoing may be found by searches of public records. Others may be uncovered by contacting government departments. Some of these government department searches are indicated in the real property, employee, pension and taxation sections of Part 3 of this title. **[See Forms 9F4–9F7 for sample letters to effect such searches and consents of the vendor where necessary.]**

However, not all of these statutory trust liens and common law possessory liens may be found by searching. Legal opinions are usually qualified to reflect that they are not providing an opinion with respect to liens and trusts for which there is no public filing or recording.

---

1. R.S.C. 1985, c. 1 (5th Supp.).

2. R.S.C. 1985, c. C-8.

3. R.S.O. 1990, c. E.14.

4. R.S.O. 1990, c. P.8.

5. R.S.O. 1990, c. R.25.

Intellectual Property

9.190—If the business being acquired has or uses rights to intellectual property, one should be sure to obtain from the vendor a listing of all patents; copyrights; trade-marks; industrial designs; trade secrets; plant breeders' rights; integrated circuit topographies or other "know-how"; and any licences to use the same, including copies of all registrations of any of the foregoing both inside Canada and in any other jurisdiction.

In addition, it is advisable to conduct searches to ensure none of the foregoing intellectual property has been assigned or encumbered in favour of a third party. Such intellectual property rights constitute intangibles and choses in action that may be subject to a security interest under a security agreement; recorded under the Personal Property Security Act[1] of Ontario or of any other PPSA jurisdiction. It may also be advisable to determine that such intellectual property has been recorded with the necessary federal offices to record the vendor's rights as owner or licensee thereof under one or more of the following statutes:

    (i)   Patent Act;[2]
    (ii)   Copyright Act;[3]
    (iii)   Industrial Design Act;[4]
    (iv)   Trade-mark Act;[5]
    (v)   Plant Breeders' Rights Act;[6] or
    (vi)   Integrated Circuit Topography Act.[7]

In addition to recording rights of ownership and use, some of the foregoing statutes enable a secured party or assignee the right to record their interest. Consequently, additional searches may be required under the Patent Act, Copyright Act, and Plant Breeders' Rights Act to ensure that no third party has an encumbrance recorded against such intellectual property.

As a separate matter, the vendor may have some provincial business style registrations to record uses of business styles, in addition to either its corporate name or as a sole proprietorship. Consequently, the purchaser may wish copies of these business style filings in order to prepare the necessary forms to facilitate the vendor's "deregistration" of it name, thus allowing the purchaser to purchase and assume such names pursuant to its own filings. **[See Para. 9.520 and Checklist 9C7]**

---

1. R.S.O. 1990, c. P.10.

2. R.S.C. 1985, c. P-4.

3. R.S.C. 1985, c. C-42.

4. R.S.C. 1985, c. I-9.

5. R.S.C. 1985, c. T-13.

6. R.S.C. 1985, c. T-13.

7. R.S.C. 1985, c. T-13.

Specialty Chattels

Ships

9.200—The Canada Shipping Act,[1] creates a title registration and encumbrance system for "ships" as defined in that Act. Section 2 of that Act[2] defines a "ship" as a vessel of any description used in navigation not propelled by oars. This will include hovercraft lighters, barges and drilling platforms. Subsection 7(3)[3] requires a ship that is owned by a majority of Canadian residents to be registered in Canada unless already registered elsewhere. By section 8, "pleasure yachts" of up to 20 registered tons and "ships" of less than 15 registered tons are exempted from compulsory registration. Smaller vessels may voluntarily be registered.

Ownership of a ship is recorded in a registry system maintained in the port of registry of that vessel. Such registry records the ownership of up to 64 shares of that ship, as well as the mortgages registered against her. The forms of bills of sale and mortgages for a British ship are specified in the Canada Shipping Act. For vessels that are not "ships" and have not been registered pursuant to the Canada Shipping Act either compulsorily or voluntarily, the forms of bill of sale or mortgages are recorded and taken pursuant to provincial law.

To determine where in Canada a Canadian ship has its port of registry, call Transport Canada — Registry of Ships and Small Vessel Licensing office at 1-877-242-8770 and follow the instructions to access the regional offices in Canada. A search for a ship's registration may also be conducted on Transport Canada's website (www.tc.gc.ca/shipregistry) by entering a ship's official number or name. The List of Ships, Volumes I and II, may also be purchased from Canadian Government Publishing through their website at http://publications.gc.ca/control/simplePublicSearchCriteria.

To contact the Canadian port of registry write or call the following Transport Canada Marine Safety Centres:

Transport Canada-Marine Safety
National Headquaters
Mailstop: AMS 330 Sparks Street
Ottawa, ON K1A ON5
Tel: 1-888-242-8770

Centres/Offices of Atlantic Region

New Brunswick

Moncton
95 Foundry Street
PO Box 42
Moncton NB E1C 8K6
Ph: (506) 851-7314

Bathurst
275 Main Street
PO Box 1207
Bathurst NB E2A 4J1
Ph: (506) 548-7491

Saint John
Peter's Wharf,
CCG Bldg., 4th Floor
PO Box 7730, Stn. A
Saint John NB E2L 4X6
Ph: (506) 636-4748

Nova Scotia

Dartmouth
45 Alderney Drive
PO Box 1013
Dartmouth NS B2Y 4K2
Ph: (902) 426-7795
-and-
50 Goudy Drive
Enfield NS B2T 1K3
Ph: (902) 873-1376

Port Hawkesbury
811 Reeves Street
Shediac Plaza
PO Box 2012
Port Hawkesbury NS
B0E 2V0
Ph: (902) 625-0803

Sydney
196 George Street
Federal Arts Bldg. 2nd Floor
Sydney NS B1P 1J3
Ph: (902) 564-7002

Yarmouth
248 Pleasant Street
PO Box 850
Yarmouth NS B5A 4K5
Ph: (902) 742-6860

Newfoundland & Labrador

Corner Brook
4 Harold Avenue, Fortis Tower
PO Box 22
Corner Brook NL A2H 6C3
Ph: (709) 637-4390

Goose Bay
110 Dow Street
Goose Bay Airport
PO Box 189, Stn. A
Goose Bay NL A0P 1S0
Ph: (709) 896-6190

Lewisporte
396 Main Street
Chipman Complex
PO Box 237
Lewisporte NL A0G 3A0
Ph: (709) 535-2503

Marystown
Ville Marie Drive
PO Box 1143
Marystown NL A0E 2M0
Ph: (709) 279-2201

St. John's
10 Barter's Hill
PO Box 1300, John Cabot Bldg.
St. John's NL A1C 6H8
Ph: (709) 772-6197

Prince Edward Island

Charlottetown
97 Queen Street
PO Box 1270
Charlottetown PE C1A 7M8
Ph: (902) 566-7987

Centres/Offices of Ontario Region:

Regional Office
4900 Yonge Street, Suite 300
North York ON M2N 6A5
Tel: (416) 973-8142 (Port of Toronto)
　　(416) 973-8145 (All other Ontario Ports and Manitoba)

Centres/Office of the Pacific Region

TCC-Civil Aviation and Marine Safety
620-800 Burrard Street
Vancouver BC V6Z 2J8
Tel: (604) 666-5300

TCC-Marine Safety
501-1230 Government Street
Victoria BC V8W 3M4
Tel: (250) 363-0394

Centres/Offices of Prairie and Northern Region

Prairie and Northern Region
Regional Office
344 Edmonton Street
Winnipeg MB R3C 0P6
Tel: (204) 983-3152/1-888-463-0521
Fax: (204) 983 -7339

Branch Office
MacDonald Building, 4th Floor
344 Edmonton Street
Winnipeg MB R3C 0P6
Tel: (204) 983-7498 (General Information)

Branch Office
Canada Place
1100, 9700 Jasper Avenue
Edmonton AB T5J 4E6
Tel: (780) 495-4023

Centres/Offices of Quebec Region

Transport Canada – Marine Transport
Regional Office
700 Leigh Capreol, 3rd Floor
Dorval QC H4Y 1G7

To determine the port of registry of a non-Canadian registered ship, contact one of the recognized listings. For Canadians, the closest location is Lloyd's Register in Montreal, P.Q.

Pleasure craft under 20 registered tons and "ships" of under 15 registered tons must be licenced by a custom officer pursuant to the Small Vessels Regulations[4] under the Canada Shipping Act.

---

1. R.S.C. 1985, c. S-9, as am.

2. *Ibid.*, am. R.S.C. 1985, c. 40 (4th Supp.), s. 2(1).

3. *Ibid.*

4. Small Vessel Regulations, C.R.C., c. 1487.

Rolling Stock

9.201—Subsection 105(1) of the Canada Transportation Act[1] provides that an instrument evidencing a lease, sale, mortgage, conditional sale, or bailment of rolling stock running on lines in Canada, may be deposited with the Registrar General of Canada. Thereafter, by subsection 105(3)[2] no such instrument need be recorded under any other statute regarding registration of instruments affecting realty or personality, and such instrument is valid against all persons. Subsection 105(4)[3] requires notice of the deposit to be published in the *Canada Gazette*. Subsection 104(1) of the Act[4] creates separate requirements for charges contained in deeds of trust securing railway company issuances of its securities.

If the charge against the railway cars or rolling stock is not registered pursuant to section 105[5], the law of various provincial registries governing the perfection of security interests or chattel mortgages in rolling stock located in that province, will apply to the transaction.

Searches for Canada Transportation Act registrations are conducted in person at the following office:

Registrar General of Canada
c/o Corporations Canada, Industry Canada
365 Laurier Avenue West
Jean Edmonds Tower South
10th Floor
Ottawa ON K1A 0C8
Attn: Jacqueline Gravelle, Deputy Registrar General of Canada
Tel: (613) 941-9053, (613) 941-4550
Fax: (613) 941-9047

As of June 4, 2004, there is no charge for a search.

---

1. S.C. 1996, c. 10.

2. *Ibid.*

3. *Ibid.*

4. *Supra,* note 1.

5. *Supra,* note 1.

Aircraft

9.202—The use and operation of aircraft is governed in Canada pursuant to the Aeronautics Act[1] and the Canadian Aviation Regulations[2] passed pursuant thereto. Section 202.13(2) of the Canadian Aviation Regulations[3] requires registration of aircraft by its "owner" for it to be flown in Canada.

"Ownership" is defined in section 101.01(1) of the Regulations[4] to mean the party in possession or control of the aircraft and does not mean the owner of legal title. For example, the aircraft may be owned by a third party which leases it to an international carrier, but the international carrier will be recorded as the "owner" of such aircraft.

As of June 3, 2004, searches with Transport Canada are effected free of charge on the internet at www.tc.gc.ca/CivilAviation/general under the "aircraft registration and leasing" link. The following regional offices can provide further information.

Main Office
Canada Civil Aviation
Civil Aviation Program
  Communications (AARC)
Tower C, Place de Ville
29th Floor, 330 Sparks Street
Ottawa ON K1A 0N5
Tel: (613) 990-2309
Fax: (613) 990-6215 or
    (613) 990-1007
TTY: 1-888-675-6863

Quebec Region – Air Transport
700 Leigh Capreol Place, Zone 3A
Dorval QC H4Y 1G7
Tel: (514) 633-2717
Fax: (514) 633-2751

REGIONAL OFFICES

Transport Canada, Civil Aviation
Atlantic Region–Air Transport
Street Address:
Heritage Court, 6th Floor
95 Foundry Street
Moncton NB E1C 5H7
Mailing Address:
95 Foundry Street, P.O. Box 42
Moncton NB E1C 8K6
Tel.: (506) 851-7131
Fax: (506) 851-2563
1-800-387-4999

Transport Canada, Civil Aviation
Calgary Transport Canada Centre
800, 1601 Airport Road NE
Calgary AB T2E 6Z8
Tel.: (403) 292-5227
Fax: (403) 292-5030

Transport Canada, Civil Aviation
Ontario Region
300-4900 Yonge Street
North York ON M2N 6A5
Tel.: (416) 952-0230
Fax: (416) 952-0196

Transport Canada, Civil Aviation
Pacific Region
620-800 Burrard Street
Vancouver BC V6Z 2J8
Tel.: (604) 666-3518
Fax: (604) 666-7255

Transport Canada, Civil Aviation
Prairie and Northern Region
1100-9700 Jasper Avenue
Edmonton AB T5J 4E6
Tel.: (204) 983-3152
Fax: (780) 495-7449
1-888-463-0521

Transport Canada, Civil Aviation
Prairie and Northern Region
Street Address:
344 Edmonton Street, 2nd Floor
Winnipeg MB R3B 2L4
Mailing Address:
P.O. Box 8550
Winnipeg, MB R3C 0P6
Tel.: (204) 983-4341
Fax: (204) 984-2069

Transport Canada, Civil Aviation **Quebec Region** Regional Office 700 Leigh Capreol, Zone 3A Dorval QC H4Y 1G7 Tel.: (514) 633-2714 Fax: (514) 633-2751	Transport Canada, Civil Aviation **Saskatoon Transport Canada** **Centre** 2625 Airport Road Saskatoon SK S7L 7L1 Tel.: (306) 975-8941 Fax: (306) 975-5926

Security interests in aircraft are taken and perfected in accordance with provincial law. Hence it is necessary to search in each province or registration district within that province where the aircraft is or may be located.

Note for purposes of searching under various Personal Property Security Acts and other statutes, that an aircraft may be a "motor vehicle" under definitions in some provinces and not in others, requiring registration and searches be conducted by serial number or "VIN".

By contrast, the United States has one central aircraft registry, located in Oklahoma City, to record both ownership and security interests in aircraft. Canada has contemplated one central aircraft registry but to date has made no progress towards a central system.

---

1. R.S.C. 1985, c. A-2.

2. SOR96-433 in force Oct. 10, 1996; Regulations Respecting Aviation and Activities Relating to Aeronautics.

3. *Ibid.*

4. *Supra,* note 2.

Privacy and Personalty Rights

9.202.1—If the business being acquired collects, uses or discloses personal information, such as in customer lists, direct marketing lists, employee records or on a web site, a determination will have to be made as to the applicability of the federal Personal Information Protection and Electronic Documents Act[1] ("PIPEDA") to such activities, and/or the relevance of other provincial legislation.[2] Further the web site itself, and the location of the other parties in any transactions or enquiries originating from the web site should be reviewed in order to determine if there are sufficient connections to other jurisdictions to make the business liable in those jurisdictions.

Finally any privacy policies or statements used should be reviewed to determine the promises made to individuals when the information was collected. The failure to comply with such policies has resulted in findings of unfair trade practices in the United States and have the potential to be grounds an action for misleading advertising in Canada.[3]

In addition marketing campaigns may be reviewed to determine whether or not the images of identifiable individuals are used, and if so the nature of the consent obtained for such use.

Where the transaction is a sale of shares, this is currently not considered to result in a "disclosure" within the meaning of PIPEDA. Accordingly the primary concern of the due diligence process is whether verifiable consent has been obtained for the purposes for which the purchaser intends to use the information. Care should be taken when dealing with subsidiaries of foreign corporations. In many cases employment services are provided by the parent, and personal information is collected directly from the employees of the subsidiary. In a share purchase the vendor is required to transfer such information to the purchaser, arguably resulting in a "disclosure" to which PIPEDA applies.

Where the transaction is a sale of assets, the transfer of the personal information from vendor to purchaser results in a disclosure. There are no exemptions in PIPEDA for such transactions, and the normal rules of Schedule 1[4] to PIPEDA will apply. Principle 5 provides that personal information shall not be used or disclosed for purposes other than those for which it was collected, except with the consent of the individual or as required by law. Accordingly the original consent given must authorize a sale in bulk of the information, or consent must be obtained from the individual concerned prior to the transfer.

In addition to determining whether or not there is consent for the transfer of the personal information, the following items should be obtained to determine the conditions under which the personal information has been maintained, and whether or not they are in compliance with PIPEDA:

1. All privacy policies, statements, procedures manuals.
2. Any records retention policies, or actual practices.
3. Any security policies, or actual practices.
4. Copies of all agreements with third-party contractors who collect, use, process, or disclose the personal information on behalf of the vendor.
5. Any access policies, or practices, together with descriptions of any ongoing access requests.
6. A description of the procedures used to receive and respond to complaints or enquiries, and descriptions of any ongoing complaints.
7. Copies of all correspondence with the relevant privacy commissioners.

8. Copies of any requests made for the disclosure of personal information to third parties, together with the vendor's response.

With respect to the last item, it is important to note that with respect to disclosures to government, the federal Privacy Commissioner has indicated that he will expect a high degree of due diligence from the holders of personal information.[5]

---

1. S.C. 2000, c.5 [Sections 60-71 not in force at date of publication], as am S.C. 2000, c.17, s. 97(1); 2001, c.41, ss. 81, 82, 103.

2. As of September, 2002 the other provincial private sector privacy legislation consisted of:

    Newfoundland and Labrador – Privacy Act, R.S.N.L. 1990, c. P-22

Québec	– Code civil du Québec, L.Q. 1991, c.64, art. 35 et seq.
	– Loi sur la protection des renseignements personnels dans le secteur privée, L.R.Q., c. P-39.1
Manitoba	– The Privacy Act, R.S.M. 1970, c. 74
	– The Personal Health Information Act, S.M. 1997, c. 51
Saskatchewan	– The Privacy Act, R.S.S. 1978, c. P.24
	– The Health Information Protection Act, 1999, c. H-0.021 – sections 17(1), 18(2), 18(4) and 69 not yet proclaimed in force
Alberta	– Health Information Act, R.S.A. 2000, c. H-5
British Columbia	– Privacy Act, R.S.B.C. 1979, c. 336

3. See for example the Competition Act, R.S.C. 1985, c. C-34, as amended, sections 52, and 74.01.

4. Schedule 1 – Principles Set Out in The National Standard of Canada Entitled Model Code for The Protection of Personal Information CAN/CSA-Q-830-96.

5. Privacy Commissioner of Canada, *Airline accused of improper disclosure of travel information to government department*, released July 22, 2002.

Motor Vehicles

9.203—If motor vehicles are included in the transaction, additional searches may be required to ensure that they are acquired free and clear of any lien, claim, or encumbrance.

In addition to determining that there are no unregistered possessory liens of unpaid repairmen or storers or registered liens pursuant to the Repair and Storage Lien Act[1] filed under the Personal Property Security Act[2] database, it is advisable to conduct a PPSA search in Ontario to determine that there are no other security interests against such motor vehicles.

Take due note of section 1 of Reg. 912[3], passed pursuant to the PPSA, which defines "motor vehicle" as follows:

> "motor vehicle" means an automobile, motorcycle, motorized snow vehicle, or any other vehicle that is self-propelled, but does not include,
>
> (a) a street car or other vehicle running only upon rails,
> (b) a farm tractor,
> (c) an implement of husbandry,
> (d) a machine required for use or used as road building machinery, or
> (e) a craft intended primarily for use in the air or in or upon the water.

According to the foregoing definition, such items as forklift trucks, all terrain vehicles, motorized golf carts, riding lawn mowers, and electric wheelchairs are "motor vehicles" for purposes of the Ontario PPSA. They may be searched by their "vehicle identification number", i.e. the serial number affixed thereto by the manufacturer of the vehicle.

Also note that in other jurisdictions, a "motor vehicle" may include different machines such as aircraft. Hence if the transaction includes motor vehicles used in more than one jurisdiction, it may be necessary to obtain the assistance of local counsel to verify which additional searches are necessary to investigate encumbrances against those motor vehicles in the other jurisdictions.

Unlike the United States, which has "pink slips" to record title to motor vehicles, no such system exists in Canada. Hence the Ontario provincial green "ownership papers" record only the party in possession and control of the motor vehicle (as defined under the Ontario Highway Traffic Act[4]) and not the owner of legal title. For example, many long-term leasing companies require that the ownership papers be issued in the name of the lessee to ensure that the lessor does not receive the parking tickets or statements of claim relative to automobile accidents.

In conducting searches against motor vehicles in Ontario, it is possible to search the PPSA database not only by the vendor' name, but also by the vehicle identification number for each motor vehicle. If a large number of motor vehicles are included in a transaction, instructions may be obtained by the purchaser to only search the debtor's name instead of the numerous vehicle identification numbers. However, such a decision should be made by the client after receiving advice with respect to the availability and scope of such searches and possible encumbrances that may be missed. **[See Paras. 9.540–9.544]**

---

1. R.S.O. 1990, c. R.25.

2. R.S.O. 1990, c. P.10.

3. R.R.O. 1990, Reg. 912.

4. R.S.O. 1990, c. H.8.

Fixtures

9.204—A significant number of pieces of equipment may cease to be personal property upon affixation to real property. Such items include dishwashers and other kitchen equipment, shelving, lighting, satellite dishes, computers connected by coaxial cable and other telecommunications devices, weigh scales, automobile hoists and other garage maintenance equipment, large production machines requiring heavy plumbing, and electrical connections or embedding and special foundations to prevent vibration, and elevators, etc.

To determine whether there is an encumbrance recorded against "fixtures", it is necessary to search both the Personal Property Security Act[1] for financing statements filed to record a security interest, and to search against title to the lands to which the personalty was affixed, to determine whether a fixtures notice has been filed by way of a Form 4—Document General against title to that property giving notice of such interests.

Note that the PPSA does not define the word "fixture". The case law on fixtures was reviewed in *Cormier v. Federal Business Development Bank.*[2] In that case, there was a discussion of two classes of fixtures as being those that were not removable and those that were referred to as "trade fixtures" or "tenant fixtures", which were removable. In this case, the court held that regardless of the characterization of a fixture in the "primary sense", i.e., one that may not be severed from the freehold, or a fixture in the "secondary sense", i.e., one which may be severed if it is either for the purposes of carrying on a trade or is a domestic convenience or ornament, the use of the word "fixture" in the PPSA is intended to cover all fixtures. Consequently, regardless of whether the item in question may or may not be easily removed from the realty, it is prudent to search for notices filed in accordance with section 54 of the PPSA[3] against title to land and to review subsection 34 of that Act[4] regarding the rules of priority relative to fixtures.

---

1. R.S.O. 1990, c. P.10.

2. (1983), 25 B.L.R. 194 (Ont. Co. Ct.), additional reasons at (1983), 25 B.L.R. 207 (Ont. Co. Ct.).

3. *Supra,* note 1.

4. *Supra,* note 1.

Leased Personalty

Assignability

9.210—It is necessary to act quickly on an asset transaction to determine which, if any, leased assets being acquired in the transaction, are leased by the vendor from third parties. Copies will be needed of each lease and any related documents such as service and maintenance warranties and agreements. Each lease will need to be reviewed to determine whether the lease is assignable by the vendor as lessee. Some leases will not be assignable and arrangements will have to be entered into between the vendor as lessee and the third party lessor concerning early termination and any penalties or forfeitures associated with early termination. If the lease is assignable, the purchaser as sublessee will need to ensure that the terms and conditions of the lease itself are acceptable. Such obvious provisions as quantum of rent, insurance covenants, maintenance requirements, etc. will need to be reviewed with the client to ensure it is prepared to accept such obligations. If the lease is to be assigned, a general conveyancing document will be required to convey to the purchaser the vendor's interests as lessee. In addition, the third party lessor may require that its form of assignment documents be executed to record the assignment for its purposes. Such assignment may be with or without recourse to the vendor as lessee and such recourse may have to be negotiated.

It is also advisable to obtain a Personal Property Security Act[1] search against the vendor as lessee, to determine whether or not there have been any registrations against the vendor for such leased personalty. It may be a courtesy to inform the lessor of any assignments for which consent was not required, or if consent was required, it may be a courtesy to again remind them, that financing change statements may be recorded to show a transfer of collateral by debtor. **[See Form 9F48]**

---

1. R.S.O. 1990, c. P.10.

Termination

9.211—If lease obligations are not to be assumed by the purchaser then the vendor no longer has a need for the equipment. Termination of the lease may be in order. Early termination may result in certain penalties being payable by the vendor as lessee to its third party lessor and the vendor may require that the purchaser assume or indemnify the vendor for such cost.

From Personal Property Security Act[1] searches against the vendor it should be determined whether there are any PPSA filings for leases to be terminated and such documents should be discharged to ensure there is no confusion with respect to any future registrations that might shelter under this registration as permitted by subsection 45(4) of the PPSA.[2]

---

1. R.S.O. 1990, c. P.10.

2. *Ibid.*

Employees

9.220—There are many significant employment and labour relations concerns that require thorough investigation by a purchaser contemplating the purchase of the shares or assets of a business. A purchaser will need full disclosure from the vendor of all matters related to the vendor's employees and any trade union that may represent the employees. The Agreement of Purchase and Sale should contain appropriate vendor representations and warranties with respect to the disclosure of all matters involving the vendor's employees, any trade union, and other employment related issues. The Agreement of Purchase and Sale should also contain appropriate indemnifications from the vendor for contingent liabilities which a purchaser may incur arising from the period prior to the sale, and a general indemnification for any liabilities that a purchaser may incur arising from any employment or labour related matter which the vendor failed to disclose to the purchaser. [**See Paras. 9.470–9.490 and 9.620** for appropriate vendor' representations and warranties that should be included in an Agreement of Purchase and Sale related to each particular area of concern. A general clause respecting indemnification for liabilities arising out of any matter not disclosed can also be found in these sections.]

In order to be as fully informed as possible, the purchaser should, at a minimum, seek disclosure concerning all items contained on the disclosure checklist. [**See Checklist 9C8**]

The distinction between a share purchase and an asset purchase is significant in terms of the obligations and liabilities which the purchaser would be assuming in each case. Generally speaking, the result of a share purchase is that the business which employs the employees continues to exist and the purchaser assumes all obligations and liabilities attaching to the business, unless specific provisions to the contrary are made in the Agreement of Purchase and Sale. On the other hand, an asset purchase is more complex. The issues that arise will depend on the nature of the asset purchased, the number of assets purchased, the employment significance of the assets purchased, and relevant provisions of any governing labour legislation. For example, if a purchaser purchased the real estate and machinery of a functioning unionized business and carried on similar operations without interruption after such a purchase, the purchaser would likely be a successor employer under the relevant labour relations legislation and would thus be bound to the collective agreement between the vendor and the union representing the vendor's employees. On the other hand, if a purchaser purchases an insignificant asset from another ongoing business, such purchase may not give rise to any labour and employment consequences.

Counsel for a purchaser should be aware that whether an acquisition is by way of share purchase or asset purchase, the purchaser may assume particular employment-related obligations of the vendor. These could include union certifications, collective agreements, and obligations set forth in relevant employment standards legislation. There are also certain employment-related obligations which a purchaser would not likely assume in an asset purchase. For example, a written employment contract between the vendor and an individual employee of the vendor would not be assumed by the purchaser in an asset purchase transaction, although the purchaser may nevertheless choose to enter into a new employment contract with any such employee that the purchaser wishes to hire. **[See Checklist 9C8]**

Federally and Provincially Regulated Employers

9.230—It is important at the outset for the purchaser to determine whether the business which is being purchased is one over which the province or the federal government exercises jurisdiction with respect to matters of employment and labour relations. As a rule, provincial governments have legislative jurisdiction over matters of employment and labour relations. However, the federal government may assert exclusive jurisdiction over employment and labour relations matters if it is shown that such jurisdiction is an integral part of its primary competence over some other single federal subject. The question of whether an undertaking, service or business is a federal one depends on the nature of its operation and not the identity of the employer. In order to determine the nature of the operation one must look at the normal or habitual activities of the business.

Businesses which are subject to federal jurisdiction concerning employment and labour relations matters include banking, aeronautics, shipping, and transportation and communications enterprises connecting provinces or extending beyond the limits of a province. If a business is determined to be under federal employment and labour jurisdiction, then the Canada Labour Code[1] will govern its labour relations, its occupational health and safety obligations, and employment standards obligations in areas like vacation pay, holidays, severance pay and termination pay. Appropriate searches will need to be made with the Canada Industrial Relations Board concerning labour relations and with the Labour Program of Human Resources

Development Canada concerning employment standards and occupational health and safety. [**See Paras. 9.240–9.253 and 9.290–9.291** which comment upon these areas of concern from a provincial perspective.] While the provisions of applicable federal legislation may not be the same as parallel provincial legislation, the areas of concern addressed are often similar. [**See Forms 9F12 and 9F13**]

If the purchaser is purchasing a federal business, the Canadian Human Rights Act[2] would also be applicable to that business. If there are complaints or orders outstanding against the vendor, the purchaser may become liable for such complaints or orders. The Canadian Human Rights Commission will generally pursue the vendor in such cases, although the Commission takes the position that liability may pass to the purchaser. There are no decided cases dealing with federal legislation.[3] For this reason, the purchaser should know whether there are any outstanding complaints or orders against the vendor. [**See Forms 9F14 and 9F15**]

If a federal business is being purchased, that business may also be governed by the federal Employment Equity Act,[4] under which federal private sector employers who employ 100 or more employees and federal public sector employers must attempt to eliminate employment barriers affecting women, aboriginal peoples, disabled persons and visible minorities, prepare an employment equity plan and file a report concerning compliance with the requirements of that Act. [**See Form 9F16**]

Businesses operating in Ontario that are normally subject to federal labour jurisdiction will also have to comply with provincial workers' compensation legislation and Ontario's employers' health tax legislation. [**See Paras. 9.260–9.263 and 9.330**]

If the vendor's business is not subject to any federal employment or labour legislation, then it will in all respects be governed by Ontario legislation. [**See Paras. 9.240–9.330**]

An employer who is subject to provincial labour and employment legislation may occasionally obtain contracts from the federal government. Such employers may, by contract, be bound to federal fair wage, hours of work, and employment equity requirements. A purchaser should ascertain from the vendor whether there are any outstanding federal contracts that have to be completed or whether there are any current bids for federal contracts.

The provisions of the Canada Labour Code[5] that deal with labour relations include provisions pertaining to successor rights and the transfer of obligations upon the sale of a business. The statute also specifies that the person to whom the business is sold becomes a party to any pending proceeding taken under Part I of the Code, that affects the employees employed in the business or their bargaining agent. Although there is presently no jurisprudence with respect to this section of the Canada Labour Code,[6] it implies that the purchaser of a business could assume the liabilities of the vendor under proceedings relating to unfair labour practices. The purchaser should carefully ascertain from the vendor and the Canada Industrial Relations Board whether there are any proceedings pending under Part I of the Canada Labour Code[7] on the date on which the business is sold.

---

1. R.S.C. 1985, c. L-2

2. R.S.C. 1985, c. H-6

3. See also *Great Atlantic & Pacific Co. of Canada v. Ontario* (1983), 18 C.H.R.R. D/97 (Ont. Gen. Div.) where the Ontario Human Rights Code was considered. The court concluded that a purchaser of assets was not a party to a human rights complaint filed against the vendor.

4. S.C. 1995, c. 44

5. *Supra*, note 1.

6. *Ibid.*

7. *Ibid.*

LABOUR CANADA REGIONAL TERRITORY AND CONTACT LIST

REGION	TERRITORY	TELEPHONE NUMBERS
New Brunswick **By mail:** Carmen Comeau-Anderson Director HRSDC Labour Program 1045 Main St, 1st Floor P.O. Box 1166 Moncton NB E1C 8P9	New Brunswick	Office hours: (506) 851-6640 (Info); (506) 851-6648 Fax: (506) 851-6645
P.E.I. Jeannine Ettinger Regional Manager HRSDC Labour Program P.O. Box 8000 85 Fitzroy Street Charlottetown PE C1A 8K1	Prince Edward Island	Office hours: (902) 566-7171 Fax: (902) 566-7580

Nova Scotia Michael Grace Regional Manager HRSDC Labour Program 99 Wyse Road, 8th Floor P.O. Box 1350 Dartmouth NS B3Y 4B9	Nova Scotia	Office hours: (902) 426-9072 Fax: (902) 426-1390
Newfoundland and Labrador Brendan Kenny Regional Manager HRSDC Labour Program Prince Charles Building 120 Torbay Road, Suite E 110B P.O. Box 8548 St. John's NL A1B 3P3	Newfoundland and Labrador	Office hours: (709) 772-5022 (Info); (709) 772-3928 Fax: (709) 772-5985
Quebec Jean Pierre Laporte Director HRSDC Labour Program Complexe Guy Favreau 200 Blvd René Levesque West 4th Floor, West Tower Montreal QC H2Z 1X4	Quebec	Office hours: (514) 982-2384 ext 2096 Fax: (514) 283-6737
Ontario Trevor Mills Regional Director HRSDC Labour Program 4900 Yonge Street Penthouse North York ON M2N 6A5	Ontario	Office hours: (416) 954-5900 1-800-463-2493 (Info) Fax: (416) 954-6178
Manitoba Diane Kocela Director HRSDC Labour Program 750-266 Graham Ave Winnipeg MB R3C 0K3	Manitoba	(204) 983-7249 Fax: (204) 983-2117

Saskatchewan Garry Enmark Director HRSDC Labour Program 2045 Broad Street, Main Floor Regina SK S4P 2N6	Saskatchewan	(306) 780-5409 Fax: (306) 780-5415
B.C./Yukon Mary Huitson Director HRSDC Labour Program 125-10th Avenue East Vancouver BC V5T 1Z3	British Columbia and Yukon	Office hours: English- (604) 872-4384 local 650 Fax: (604) 666-3166
Alberta/N.W.T. G.G. Thompson Director HRSDC Labour Program Canada Place 280-220 4th Avenue SE Calgary AB T2G 4X3	Alberta and Northwest Territories	(403) 292-4020 Fax: (403) 292-5153

CANADIAN HUMAN RIGHTS COMMISSION

NATIONAL OFFICE

Canadian Human Rights Commission
8th Floor, 344 Slater Street
Ottawa ON K1A 1E1
Tel: (613) 995-1151
TTY: (888) 214-1090
Fax: (613) 996-9661
Toll Free: (888) 214-1090
Email: info.com@chrc-ccdp.ca

REGIONAL OFFICES

ATLANTIC
Office Address:
5475 Spring Garden Road
Suite 504
Halifax NS B3J 3T2
Tel: (902) 426-8380
TTY: (888) 643-3304
Fax: (902) 426-2685
Toll Free: (800) 999-6899

ONTARIO
1002-175 Bloor Street East
South Tower
Toronto ON M4W 3R8
Tel: (416) 973-5527
TTY: (888) 643-3304
Fax: (416) 973-6184
Toll Free: (800) 999-6899

QUEBEC
470-1253 McGill
College Avenue
Montreal QC H3B 2Y5
Tel: (514) 283-5218
TTY: (888) 643-3304
Fax: (514) 283-5084
Toll Free: (800) 999-6899

PRAIRIES & NUNAVUT
Room 750
175 Hargrave Street
Winnipeg MB R3C 3R8
Tel: (204) 983-2189
TTY: (888) 643-3304
Fax: (204) 983-6132
Toll Free: (800) 999-6899

BC & YUKON
301-1095 West Pender St
Vancouver BC V6E 2M6
Tel: (604) 666-2251
TTY: (888) 643-3304
Fax: (604) 666-2386
Toll Free: (800) 999-6899

**ALBERTA AND
NORTHWEST
TERRITORIES**
308-10010 -106th Street
Edmonton AB T5J 3L8
Tel: (780) 495-4040
TTY: (888) 643-3304
Fax: (780) 495-4044
Toll Free: (800) 999-6899

Labour Relations (Ontario)

Sale of a Business

9.240—Section 69 of Ontario's Labour Relations Act, 1995[1] is of particular concern to a purchaser contemplating the purchase of the shares or assets of a business. In general terms, the effect of section 69 is that when a business or part thereof is sold or transferred, the transferee will be bound by any subsisting collective agreement to which the vendor was a party or any pending applications for certification. A purchaser who is a successor employer within the meaning of section 69 may also be found liable for unsatisfied monetary obligations such as retroactive wages arising from the terms of the collective agreement. A successor employer may not become a party to or be bound by any unfair labour practice proceedings commenced against the predecessor if the successor is a bona fide purchaser for value who did not have notice of the outstanding proceedings or orders.

It is not uncommon that some employees may be terminated or laid off prior to a sale of a business. Most collective agreements contain provisions which protect employees against termination without just cause and guarantee laid off employees certain rights to recall, usually for a predetermined period. The question therefore arises as to whether employees who have protection against termination without just cause and who retain recall rights under a collective agreement, also retain their employment status with the new operator of the business. The Ontario Labour Relations Board has ruled that section 69(2) continues the effect of a collective agreement over a sales transaction and the purchaser stands literally in the shoes of its predecessor with respect to any rights or obligations under that Agreement. In other words, the purchaser is given neither an opportunity to weed out undesirable employees contrary to the provisions of the collective agreement, nor an opportunity to decline to recognize any of the seniority or other rights accrued by employees under the collective agreement during their employment with the predecessor employer.

---

1. S.O. 1995, c. 1, Sched. A.

Union Bargaining Rights with Respect to Vendor

9.241—Ontario's Labour Relations Act, 1995[1] provides for the right of employees to be represented by a trade union and for that trade union to seek certification on behalf of a group of employees of an employer. The provisions of section 69[2] outline the consequences of such a certification in the context of a sale of a business. Given the significance of union certification in the system of industrial relations established in Ontario, it is important that a purchaser know whether any certificates have been issued by the Ontario Labour Relations Board to any union for the employees of the vendor or any predecessor to the vendor. The purchaser should seek appropriate disclosure from the vendor with respect to any certifications that may have been issued by the Ontario Labour Relations Board. The purchaser should also write to the Ontario Labour Relations Board and ask the Board to conduct a search of its records pertaining to any certifications of the vendor's business or any predecessors thereof. A purchaser should communicate with the Ontario Labour Relations Board at least four weeks in advance of the closing date of the transaction in order to give the Ontario Labour Relations Board ample time to respond.

A purchaser should inquire as to whether the vendor has any knowledge of union organizing campaigns in progress or applications which have been filed with the Ontario Labour Relations Board. If a certification application has been filed against the vendor but the vendor has not yet been certified, the provisions of section 69 stipulate that the purchaser will be treated as the respondent employer in the certification procedings.

Just as trade unions can be certified, in a parallel fashion, certain employers in the construction industry can be the subject of an accreditation order which operates in a manner similar to certification. The purchaser of a construction business should seek full disclosure from the vendor as to whether the vendor is bound by any accreditation orders issued by the Ontario Labour Relations Board. An employer may also voluntarily recognize a union as representing a group of employees and negotiate a collective agreement with that union. Section 69 of the Labour Relations Act would operate so as to make such a collective agreement binding upon any purchaser. **[See Forms 9F17 and 9F18]**

---

1. S.O. 1995, c. 1, Sched. A.

2. S.O. 1995, c. 1, Sched. A.

Collective Agreements

9.242—There is a statutory obligation upon each party to a collective agreement, once it is concluded, to file a copy of the collective agreement with the Minister of Labour. A purchaser may consider writing the Collective Agreements Library in order to obtain verification of whether any collective agreements are on file to which the vendor may be bound. Purchasers are cautioned that many parties to collective agreements do not fulfil their statutory obligation and hence little reliance can be placed on whatever response the purchaser may receive from the Collective Agreements Library.

The purchaser will want to seek disclosure from the vendor as to any collective agreements which may be binding upon the vendor and any pending or ongoing negotiations in which the vendor may be involved. If the vendor is involved in ongoing negotiations, the purchaser will wish to know whether strike action may be pending or in progress as well.

The purchaser should obtain copies of any collective agreements which may be binding upon the vendor. These could include province-wide collective agreements in the construction industry, collective agreements held in the name of any employer's organization or, most commonly, collective agreements to which the vendor is a party. The purchaser will want to examine these collective agreements for restrictions which may be contained in the collective agreement concerning the manner in which the vendor (and subsequently the purchaser) can conduct business. **[See Form 9F18]**

Other O.L.R.B. Proceedings Against the Vendor

9.243—There are a number of Ontario Labour Relations Board proceedings which have significant implications for the purchaser of a business. As a result, the purchaser will want to be fully informed of the vendor's involvement with any of these proceedings.

The purchaser should enquire as to whether there are any pending unfair labour practice complaints under section 96 of the Labour Relations Act, 1995[1] against the vendor or any predecessor of the vendor. While the Ontario Labour Relations Board has ruled that a bona fide purchaser for value may be indicative of an underlying problem which may continue to affect the operations after the purchase. The Ontario Labour Relations Board may also conclude that the purchaser violated the Labour Relations Act, if the bargaining rights of the union and the attendant rights of employees under the Act have not been honoured (for example, where certain employees were not hired by the new operator of the business due to the fact that such employees were union supporters).

Section 99 of the Ontario Labour Relations Act[2] provides a procedure whereby the Board can inquire into a complaint that an employer is assigning particular work to persons in a particular trade union to the detriment of another trade union. Such complaints are more common for construction businesses than those in other sectors. The Board has the power to direct what action, if any, the employer shall take, or refrain from taking, with respect to the assignment of work and may, in its discretion, alter the bargaining unit determined in a certificate or defined in a collective agreement as it considers proper. Given the repercussions which such decisions could have for the manner in which a purchaser may wish to carry on business, a purchaser would want to be fully aware of any such jurisdictional dispute complaints which may be in progress.

The Ontario Labour Relations Board also has the authority to deal with unlawful strike proceedings, complaints under the Occupational Health & Safety Act[3] for reprisals against employees, related employer declarations, and grievance arbitrations in the construction industry. The purchaser should require full disclosure from the vendor as to whether the vendor is directly or indirectly involved in any such proceedings and whether there are any Labour Relations Board orders in relation to such proceedings which remain unfulfilled. Since the purchaser may bear liability if it acquires the vendor's business, the purchaser should make diligent inquiries with the vendor and with the Ontario Labour Relations Board concerning the status of any such matters. **[See Form 9F17]**

---

1. S.O. 1995, c. 1, Sched. A.

2. S.O. 1995, c. 1, Sched. A.

3. R.S.O. 1990, c. O.1.

Grievances and Arbitrations

9.244—The purchaser will need disclosure of any outstanding grievances against the vendor or any predecessor of the vendor and of any labour arbitration proceedings involving the vendor which may be in progress.

Of particular importance, the vendor will need assurance that any arbitration awards have been fully complied with by the vendor. Section 69 of the Labour Relations Act, 1995[1] makes the purchaser party to any collective agreement to which the vendor was bound.

---

1. S.O. 1995, c. 1, Sched. A.

Conflicting Bargaining Rights

9.245—Where the purchaser intermingles the unionized employees in the acquired business with his/her other employees in another business, the Labour Relations Board may define the appropriate bargaining structure, may decide whether in fact the union bargaining rights should be continued, may declare which trade union, if any, shall be the bargaining agent for the employees, and may amend, to such extent as the Board considers necessary, any certificate issued to any trade union or any bargaining unit defined in any collective agreement. This can have the effect of unionizing a previously non-union operation and, therefore, the risks arising from intermingling union and non-union employees must be carefully considered.

Employment Standards (Ontario)

9.250—The Ontario Employment Standards Act[1] establishes a number of minimum employment rights for most of Ontario's employees. An employer cannot contract out of or waive an employment standard. There is also a provision in the statute stipulating that greater benefits conferred under any contract or other statute shall prevail over a statutory employment standard. The Employment Standards Act specifies minimum requirements with respect to hours of work, overtime, wages, public holidays, vacations with pay, pregnancy leave, parental leave, notice of termination (or pay in lieu thereof) and severance pay.

Section 9 of the Employment Standards Act will be a significant consideration for any purchaser. It reads as follows:

> 9(1) If an employer sells a business or a part of a business and the purchaser employs an employee of the seller, the employment of the employee shall be deemed not to have been terminated or severed for the purposes of this Act and his or her employment with the seller shall be deemed to have been employment with the purchaser for the purpose of any subsequent calculation of the employee's length or period of employment. [2000, c. 41, s. 9(1)]
>
> *Exception*
>
> (2) Subsection (1) does not apply if the day on which the purchaser hires the employee is more than 13 weeks after the earlier of his or her last day of employment with the seller and the day of the sale. [2000, c. 41, s. 9(2)]

Definitions

(3) In this section,

"sells" includes leases, transfers or disposes of in any other manner, and "sale" has a corresponding meaning. [2000, c. 41, s. 9(3)]

Predecessor Acts

(4) For the purposes of subsection (1), employment with the seller includes any employment attributed to the seller under this section or a provision of a predecessor Act dealing with sales of businesses. [2000, c. 41, s. 9(4)]

---

1. S.O. 2000, c. 41.

2. S.O. 2000, c. 41, s. 9.

9.251—In the case of a share purchase, the status of the corporation would not be affected, there would be no break in the continuity of the existence of the employer corporation, and the purchaser would step into the shoes of the vendor.

In the case of an asset purchase, the purchaser's position as regards section 9 will depend on a number of factors. Some of the key factors in determining whether there was a sale of the business include: the value of the assets sold as a percentage of the value of the business as a going concern before the sale; whether the purchaser continues the same type of operation as the vendor; whether the purchaser continues at the same location as the vendor; whether the purchaser retains the same employees as the vendor; whether there is a transfer of an operating licence or similar concessions; whether the accounts payable or receivable are transferred; whether the good will of the vendor is transferred to the purchaser; and whether there is some measure of continuity between the vendor and the purchaser of the assets. The majority of cases look to whether the assets sold are transferred as a going concern and are operated in the same manner by the vendor. If the objective observer could say that the current business is essentially the same as the predecessor business in the manner in which it operates, then it is likely that a sale of business would be established. The purchaser should be aware that many purchasers purchasing assets of a business that require persons to operate them that are sold as going concerns have been construed as successors to the vendor under section 9.

9.252—In *Ontario (Employment Standards Officer) v. Equitable Management Ltd.,*[1] the Divisional Court resolved the question of the applicability of section 9 in situations where the vendor of the business gives notice of termination to an employee effective on the date of sale and the purchaser of the business then hires that employee immediately thereafter. The court held that the termination by the previous employer is irrelevant to a consideration of the applicability of section 9. The court reasoned:

Section 9, when broken into its constituent elements, sets up two preconditions to the operation of the section and then provides two results which flow from those preconditions being met. The preconditions are:

(1) that an employee sells his business to a purchaser; and

(2) that the purchaser employs an employee of the employer.

The two results which flow when these preconditions are met are that:

(1) the employment of the employee is not terminated by the sale; and

(2) the period of employment of the employee with the employer is deemed to have been employment with the purchaser for the purposes of Parts VII (public holidays), VIII (vacations), XI (pregnancy leave), and XII (notice of termination) of the Act. As long as these two preconditions are met the deeming provision is operative and the employee's total period of employment is deemed to have been employment with the purchaser for the purposes set out.[2]

The court further reasoned that if the protection of section 9 could be avoided merely by the vendor giving written notice of termination at the time of the sale, the purpose of section 9 would be completely thwarted.

While this decision serves to clarify, to some degree, the issues relating to the applicability of section 9, it does leave open the question of whether the decision would have been the same had there been a gap in the employment of the employee in question.

Section 9 effectively creates a contingent financial liability for the purchaser arising from an employee's period of employment with the vendor, since a purchaser could acquire employees with lengthy periods of service who in turn may be entitled to lengthier notices of termination (or pay in lieu thereof) in the future and, perhaps also entitled to severance pay by virtue of their total length of employment. This is a subject area which the purchaser may wish to address specifically in the Agreement of Purchase and Sale.

---

1. (1990), 75 O.R. (2d) 506 (Div. Ct.).

2. (1990), 75 O.R. (2d) 506 at p. 509 (Div. Ct.).

9.253—The purchaser will want to obtain appropriate vendor representations that there are no unpaid wages, vacation pay or other unmet statutory requirements by the vendor. The purchaser will also benefit from an inquiry with the Employment Standards Branch of the Ministry of Labour to determine whether there are any outstanding complaints, orders, claims, or prosecutions against the vendor and/or a predecessor of the vendor. This is a subject area which should be addressed with appropriate clauses and indemnifications in the Agreement of Purchase and Sale. The purchaser may also want to make appropriate inquiries with the vendor as to whether the hours of work provisions of Part VII of the Employment Standards Act[1] have been varied by agreement. Similarly, there may be special arrangements in place between an employer and his employees or their agent respecting vacation. Such arrangements are subject to the approval of the director and a purchaser may wish to satisfy itself whether there are any such arrangements in place and whether the director has given approval to them.

Section 4 of the Employment Standards Act provides that associated or related activities, or businesses carried on by or through more than one corporation, individual, firm, syndicate or association may be treated as one employer for the purposes of this Act, if the intent or effect of the arrangement is to defeat either directly or indirectly the true intent and purpose of the Act. The purchaser will want to be aware of whether the vendor was related in any significant way to another business activity in a way that might impact upon liabilities which the vendor (or subsequently the purchaser) might have with respect to particular employees. For instance, if the vendor was related to another business and one employee had worked various periods of time for each of these two businesses, the employee's total period of employment might be considered to be one period of employment, if the intent or effect of the arrangement of having the employee work in the two businesses was to defeat particular entitlements which the employee might acquire under the Employment Standards Act. **[See Form 9F4]**

---

1. S.O. 2000, c. 41.

Workers' Compensation (Ontario)

9.260—Most businesses that employ workers are subject to the obligations imposed by the Workplace Safety and Insurance Act, 1997.[1] The Act classifies employers as Schedule 1 or Schedule 2 employers. Schedule 1 employers are liable to contribute to the accident fund maintained by the Workplace Safety and Insurance Board but are not liable individually to pay compensation to injured workers. Schedule 2 employers are directly liable to pay compensation and health care benefits to injured workers.

The Workplace Safety and Insurance Act, 1997[1] became effective on January 1, 1998. It replaced the Workers' Compensation Act[2] and clarifies the workers' compensation obligations of purchasers of assets. The purchaser of the shares of a corporation operating a business has always assumed the workers' compensation liability of the corporation. However, under the previous legislation, the liability of a purchaser of assets for the workers' compensation liabilities of the predecessor was not always perfectly clear. The Workplace Safety and Insurance Act, 1997 provides that a purchaser who purchases all or part of a business is liable to pay any amount owed, pursuant to the Act by the predecessor employer. This does not apply in certain insolvency situations such as when the assets are transferred to a bankruptcy trustee, a receiver or a purchaser of assets pursuant to an arrangement under the Companies Creditors Arrangement Act.

The Act permits the Workplace Safety and Insurance Board to develop binding policies with respect to the implementation of various provisions of the Act including the sale of business provisions. Pursuant to that authority, the Board has developed operational policies concerning the sale of business issue. The Board's operational policies state, in part, that:

> A purchaser is liable for all outstanding amounts owing by the employer disposing of all or part of the business. Amounts owing to the Board up to the time of disposition which are not paid by the employer are issued against and collected from the purchaser, the vendor or both at the discretion of the Board.
>
> To determine whether Section 146 [i.e., the sale of business provision] applies to the disposition of all or part of a business, the Board considers what part of the business was sold and the relative value the transferred assets represent to the original business.
>
> An employer disposes of "part of a business" when it disposes of a distinct division, branch, plant, store, outlet, cost centre or an asset that is used to carry on the business and has a significant relationship to the business. An asset has a significant relationship to the business when selling the asset impairs the ability of the original business to carry on as before; meet its financial obligation to the Board or impacts the board's ability to collect premiums due.

Later in the same document, the Board states that it may hold a purchaser liable for any unpaid amounts including payroll premiums, non-compliance charges and experience rating surcharges.

The Board's operational policies require an employer to notify the Board of any change in ownership, including the sale or purchase of a business or assets, within ten days of its occurrence. If requested, the Board will issue a purchase certificate to confirm that, as of the date of the disposition, there are no outstanding amounts owed to the Board by the Vendor. If the Board does not issue a purchase certificate, the Board advises that a purchaser is responsible for resolving any outstanding debts to the Board before closing the deal. Otherwise, responsibility for the debts may transfer to the purchaser. When a business is sold, all amounts billed to the vendor become due immediately.

Any amounts which were billed at the time of disposition or are later reconciled up to the date of disposition potentially become the responsibility of the purchaser.

The Board's policy, prior to January 1, 1998, provided that, upon the sale of a business, the Board would determine whether to close a vendor's account or to continue the existing account for the purchaser. The Board has advised that, upon the transfer of a business, the vendor's account will be now closed and a new account will be opened for the purchaser.

---

1. S.O. 1997, c. 16.

2. R.S.O. 1990, c. W.11.

9.261—Based on the above, a purchaser should seek full disclosure from the vendor regarding the status of the vendor's accounts with the Workplace Safety and Insurance Board and other potential claims which may be of concern to the purchaser. The purchaser should also obtain the Board's purchase certificate and a written statement from the Board concerning the vendor's history of claims for experience-rating and penalty purposes, since the vendor's experience-rating will have a direct impact on the amount of additional surcharges or penalties, if any, which the successor purchaser may be required to pay to the Board in the future. The Board has authority to penalize an employer by significantly increasing the amount of any contributions which the employer must make, if the Board is of the opinion that sufficient precautions have not been taken for the prevention of accidents to workers, working conditions are not safe for workers, the employer has not complied with the Board's regulations respecting first aid, or the work injury frequency and the accident costs of the employer are consistently higher than that of the average in the industry in which the employer is engaged.

9.262—If the vendor is in default in payment of any assessment or special assessment, the Board may file a certificate stating such default with the Ontario Superior Court of Justice or the Ontario Small Claims Court. A certificate so filed becomes an order of that court and may be enforced as a judgment of that court. In addition, the Board may also file such a certificate with the Clerk of the Municipality in which the defaulting employer is situated. In such a case, the amount remaining unpaid is entered upon the collector's roll as if it were taxes due by the defaulting employer in respect of such establishment. Hence, a purchaser will want to ensure that there are no outstanding Workplace Safety and Insurance Board assessments that have been added to the municipal tax roll for the vendor and that no certificates have been filed with any court for default in payment.

In view of the possibility that there may be as yet unidentified claims, assessments or penalties arising out of the period prior to the closing of the purchase transaction, the purchaser should also seek indemnification from the vendor for all workers' compensation costs attributable to the period prior to closing.

9.263—A purchaser should also be aware that section 41 of the Workplace Safety and Insurance Act, 1997[1] creates an obligation upon an employer to re-employ a worker who, as a result of an injury has been unable to work and who, on the date of the injury, had been employed continuously for at least one year. This obligation to re-employ crystallizes only after the Board has determined that the worker is able to perform the essential duties of the worker's pre-injury employment or is medically able to perform suitable work, as the case may be. This obligation to re-employ also entails the duty of accommodation of the work or the workplace to the needs of the worker who is impaired as a result of the injury, to the extent that the accommodation does not cause the employer undue hardship. Under the provisions of this section, an employer has an obligation to re-employ until the day that is the earliest of: two years after the date of the injury to the worker; one year after the date the Board notifies the employer that the worker is medically able to perform the essential duties of the worker's pre-injury employment; and the date the worker reaches 65 years of age. This obligation to re-employ does not apply to employers who regularly employ fewer than 20 workers and to certain other particular classes or subclasses of employers and workers as may be exempted by the regulations. A purchaser could be requested to re-employ injured workers of the vendor. Accordingly, a purchaser should carefully review section 41 in order to be fully aware of the extent of its potential obligations under this section and to make the appropriate inquiry of the vendor.

---

1. S.O. 1997, c. 16.

Human Rights (Ontario)

9.270—The Ontario Human Rights Code[1] provides that every person has the right to equal treatment with respect to employment without discrimination because of race, ancestry, place of origin, colour, ethnic origin, citizenship, creed, sex, sexual orientation, age, record of offences, marital status, family status or handicap.

A purchaser who acquires a business by way of a share purchase would stand in the shoes of the vendor with respect to any outstanding complaints, orders, investigations, Boards of Inquiry, or prosecutions under the Human Rights Code. A purchaser who purchases the assets of the vendor's business would generally take the assets free of any liability for matters arising under the Code during the period when the vendor was the employer.[2] Nevertheless, a purchaser who is purchasing significant assets of the vendor, including a plant and equipment, and who acquires the services of the same employees, will want to obtain full disclosure from the vendor as to whether there are any outstanding human rights complaints, investigations, or orders so that the purchaser does not find itself in a positon where there may be conditions or circumstances that would generate human rights complaints against it.

In the case of employees who may have a handicap, the Code now provides that the Commission, a Board of Inquiry, or a court shall not find a person incapable of performing or fulfilling the essential duties or requirements attending the exercise of his or her employment rights, unless it is satisfied that the needs of the person cannot be accommodated without undue hardship on the person responsible for accommodating those needs. The Ontario Human Rights Commission has published guidelines with respect to the accommodation of persons with disabilities and its guidelines include the establishment of phased-in accommodation plans or the establishment of reserve funds to fulfil the obligation to accommodate. A purchaser of significant assets of the vendor's business will need to obtain specific disclosure from the vendor as to any accommodation plans that may be currently operative with respect to employees who may be incapable of performing or fulfilling the essential duties of their job because of handicap. The purchaser may also wish to have specific indemnification from the vendor concerning the costs of any accommodation that is imminent or ongoing.

A purchaser is also cautioned that if it retains some but not all of the employees of the vendor, the purchaser may be held accountable by the Human Rights Commission upon the complaint of any person who considers him or herself to be discriminated against by the purchaser's failure to hire him or her in the new business. In such a situation, the purchaser would need a credible non-discriminatory explanation as to why it had not hired the employee in question if it had hired other former employees of the vendor. **[See Forms 9F22 and 9F23]**

---

1. R.S.O. 1990, c. H.19.

2. *Great Atlantic & Pacific Co. of Canada v. Ontario* (1993), 18 C.H.R.R. D/97 (Ont. Gen. Div.).

Pay Equity (Ontario)

9.280—The purpose of the Ontario Pay Equity Act[1] is to redress systemic gender discrimination in compensation for work performed by employees in female job classes. Systemic gender discrimination in compensation is to be identified by undertaking comparisons between female job classes and male job classes in terms of compensation and the value of the work performed. For the purposes of this Act, the criteria to be applied in determining value of work shall be a composite of the skill, effort, and responsibility normally required in the performance of the work and the conditions under which the work is normally performed. The Act establishes the groups for which a pay equity plan is to be established and a timetable for the implementation of pay equity. A purchaser contemplating the purchase of a business by way of share purchase or asset purchase would need to obtain full disclosure from the vendor with respect to the status of any pay equity plan and its implementation. The purchaser should also inquire with the vendor and the

Pay Equity Commission to determine whether there are any outstanding complaints, investigations, orders of review officers, tribunal proceedings or orders, or prosecutions involving the vendor.

Section 13.1 of the Pay Equity Act provides that the purchaser of all or part of a business is bound to make the adjustments to compensation required under the vendor's pay equity plan or plans. If either the vendor's or purchaser's pay equity plans are no longer appropriate because of the sale, the employer may have to prepare a new plan. In the case of unionized employees, the new plan must be negotiated, with the employees' bargaining agent.

Obviously, a purchaser's concern over the above matters would vary, depending upon whether the purchaser is acquiring the business by way of share purchase or asset purchase. In the case of a share purchase, the purchaser would take over the vendor's obligations under the Pay Equity Act.[2] In the case of an asset purchase, s. 13.1 must be considered. A purchaser who will effectively be operating a new business in Ontario (for example where the purchaser is a shell corporation set up to purchase assets) must immediately establish and maintain compensation practices that provide for pay equity in every establishment it operates. **[See Form 9F24]**

---

1. R.S.O. 1990, c. P.7.

2. R.S.O. 1990, c. P.7.

Health and Safety (Ontario)

9.290—An employer's statutory obligations with respect to health and safety have become increasingly more stringent under Ontario's Occupational Health & Safety Act.[1]

If the purchaser is acquiring a business by way of a share purchase, it will stand in the shoes of the vendor with respect to all considerations related to health and safety. The same result would apply if two corporations were to be amalgamated to become one new corporation. In the case of an asset purchase, consideration should be given to whether the purchaser is continuing the same type of operation as the vendor, whether the purchaser will continue at the same location as the vendor, whether the purchaser will retain the same employees as the vendor, and whether there is some measure of continuity between the business operated by the vendor and the purchaser of the assets. If the assets are transferred as a going concern and are operated in the same manner by the purchaser as by the vendor, it is likely that any outstanding orders or directives from the Ministry of Labour would remain applicable to the purchaser. In any event, the concern which prompted such order or directive may remain intact and hence the Ministry of Labour could issue similar orders or directives to the purchaser.

In any share purchase or major asset purchase where the purchaser is essentially acquiring the vendor's business as an ongoing concern, the purchaser should obtain an up-to-date inspection from a Ministry of Labour inspector. In this way, the purchaser can ensure that the present state of the vendor's operations are in compliance with the requirements of the Act.

In addition, the purchaser should obtain from the vendor and the Ministry of Labour copies of all previous inspection reports, testing results, and health and safety audits pertaining to the vendor's business. These will enable the purchaser to be aware of issues or concerns that have arisen during past years in the areas of health and safety. The Ministry of Labour levies a fee for such a search. The purchaser should make appropriate arrangements with the vendor for the vendor to pay these search fees.

---

1. R.S.O. 1990, c. O-1.

9.290.1—In March 2004, the Criminal Code[1] was amended to allow criminal prosecutions against officers, directors and organizations for workplace accidents that result in "bodily harm". As "bodily harm" is defined as "...any hurt or injury to a person that interferes with the health or comfort of the person and that is more than merely transient or trifling in nature", only serious workplace accidents will result in prosecution. The Criminal Code amendments,[2] often called Bill C-45 or colloquially referred to as the "Westray Bill", obviously have important implications for occupational health and safety law and the criminal liability of every individual who directs how others perform work, and every organization in Canada. One of the most important aspects of the amendments was to create a broader spectrum of associations, groups and bodies that have a positive duty to create a safe workplace. Where a safe workplace is not provided that results in "bodily harm", or where corporate officials show wanton or reckless disregard for the lives of persons in the workplace, both the organization[3] and its officials could face criminal prosecution.

Where an asset purchase is contemplated, one need not be concerned, simply by virtue of the asset purchase, about vicarious or continuing liability for the vendor's misconduct. In the case of a share purchase of an incorporated entity, however, one should engage in the appropriate due diligence to ensure that criminal, in addition to regulatory, prosecutions for occupational health and safety violations are not ongoing.

While individual liability of an officer or director would not extend to the purchaser, the newly acquired corporation would continue to be responsible for fines and/or penalties incurred or imposed on the corporation, regardless of the change in beneficial ownership. For example, if ABC Ltd. engages in conduct that is criminal, charges can be brought against ABC Ltd., notwithstanding that, between the time of the conduct in question and the laying of the Information and/or the trial, there has been a change in the beneficial ownership of that company.

If an officer or director engages in conduct that is criminal, he or she can be prosecuted for that conduct, notwithstanding that at the time of the Information and/or trial, he or she no longer holds the position of officer or director. Finally, no criminal liability would attach to an officer or director of a corporation, in his or her personal capacity, for the conduct of others that took place before he or she was an officer or director.

With no maximum fines for an organization convicted of an indictable offence (the more serious means of prosecuting a criminal offence) under the Criminal Code, and a $100,000 limit for summary conviction offences (the less serious means of prosecuting a criminal offence), there is a significant incentive to engage in the appropriate inquiries or obtain relevant indemnities.

---

1. R.S.C. 1985, c. C-46.
2. An Act to Amend the Criminal Code (Criminal Liability of Organizations), 2nd Sess. 37th Parl., 2003 (1st reading 12 June 2003). The bill received Royal Assent on 7 November 2003 as 2003, c. 21.
3. "Organization" is defined to include various forms of organization regardless of how they choose to structure their affairs. Now public bodies, trade unions, municipalities, and associations of persons, whether incorporated or not, have the same potential criminal liability as corporations.

9.291—The purchaser should also seek written assurances from the vendor and the Ministry of Labour's Occupational Health & Safety Branch that the vendor has been in compliance with the requirements of the Occupational Health & Safety Act,[1] including the provisions applicable to the Workplace Hazardous Materials Information System, and that there are no outstanding orders or directives against the vendor. The purchaser should also determine whether there are any contemplated or ongoing prosecutions under the Occupational Health & Safety Act although the purchaser would not appear to be liable for any prosecutions carried out against the vendor.

In view of the special provisions of the Act pertaining to toxic substances and designated substances which may be hazardous to employees, a purchaser should seek to be fully apprised by the vendor with respect to all matters pertaining to the present use, control, and storage of such substances.

If a joint health and safety committee is or was in existence for the vendor's business, the purchaser should obtain from the vendor for its review, copies of the minutes of the meetings of the joint health and safety committee for prior years.

In view of the liabilities that can arise with respect to health and safety concerns for the period in which the vendor operated the business, the purchaser should seek indemnification from the vendor for any claims from employees of the vendor (or their family members) which are directly or indirectly attributable to that time period. **[See Forms 9F25–9F27]**

---

1. R.S.O. 1990, c. O.1.

Main Office

Employment Practices Branch	Tel: (416) 326-7160
400 University Avenue, 9th Floor	Toll Free: (800) 531-5551
TORONTO M7A 1T7	Fax: (416) 326-7599

Employment Practices Branch
400 University Avenue, 9th Floor
TORONTO M7A 1T7

Tel: (416) 326-7160
Toll Free: (800) 531-5551
Fax: (416) 326-7599

Publications
655 Bay Street, 14th Floor
TORONTO M7A 1T7

Tel: (416) 326-7731
Toll Free: (800) 268-8013
(ext 6-7731)
Fax: (416) 326-7745

Regional Offices

Employment Standards Inquiries
Tel: (416) 326-7160
Toll Free: 1-800-531-5551 (Canada-wide)

Occupational Health and Safety Inquiries
1-800-268-8013 (Province-wide)

Many of the 1-800 or toll-free numbers listed below are accessible only within the area code of the relevant office.

Northern Region
Sudbury, Timmins, Thunder Bay, Sault Ste. Marie

Sudbury East
Sudbury West
159 Cedar Street, Suite 301
Sudbury ON P3E 6A5
705-564-7400
1-800-461-6325
Sudbury East Fax: 705-564-7076
Sudbury West Fax: 705-564-7437

Timmins
Ontario Government Complex
P. O. Bag 3050 "D" Wing
Highway 101 East
South Porcupine ON P0N 1H0
705-235-1900
1-800-461-9847
Fax: 705-235-1925

Thunder Bay
435 James Street South, Ste. 222
Thunder Bay ON P7E 6S7
807-475-1691
1-800-465-5016
Fax: 807-475-1646

Sault Ste. Marie
70 Foster Dr, Ste. 480
Sault Ste. Marie ON P6A 6V4
705-945-6600
1-800-461-7268
Fax: 705-949-9796

Western Region
Hamilton, Halton, Brant, Niagara, London, Windsor, Kitchener

Hamilton
1 Jarvis Street, Main Floor
Hamilton ON L8R 3J2
905-577-6221
1-800-263-6906
Fax: 905-577-1200

Halton
1 Jarvis Street, Main Floor
Hamilton ON L8R 3J2
905-577-6221
1-800-263-6906
Fax: 905-577-1324

Brant
1 Jarvis Street, Main Floor
Hamilton ON L8R 3J2
905-577-6221
1-800-263-6906
Fax: 905-577-1324
Niagara

301 St. Paul St, 8th Floor
St. Catharines ON L2R 7R4
905-704-3994
1-800-263-7260
Fax: 905-704-3011

London North
London South
217 York St., 5th Floor
London ON N6A 5P9
519-439-2210
1-800-265-1676
Fax: 519-672-0268

Windsor
4510 Rhodes Drive, Suite 610
Windsor ON N8W 5K5
519-256-8277
1-800-265-5140
Fax: 519-258-1321

Kitchener
155 Frobisher Drive, Unit G213
Waterloo ON N2V 2E1
519-885-3378
1-800-265-2468
Fax: 519-883-5694

Central Region
Toronto East, Durham, Toronto North, Toronto West, Peel, York, Barrie

Toronto East
2275 Midland Avenue
Unit #1, Main Floor
Scarborough ON M1P 3E7
416-314-5300
Fax: 416-314-5410

Durham
67 Thornton Road South
Oshawa ON L1J 5Y1
905-433-9416
1-800-263-1195
Fax: 905-433-9843

Toronto North
1201 Wilson Avenue
Building E, 2nd Floor
Downsview ON M3M 1J8
416- 235-5330
Fax: 416- 235-5080

Toronto West
1201 Wilson Avenue, Building E,
2nd Floor, West Building
Downsview ON M3M 1J8
416-235-5330
Fax: 416-235-5090

Peel North
Peel South
1290 Central Parkway West, Main
Floor
Mississauga ON L5C 4R3
905-273-7800
Fax: 905-615-7098

York
1110 Stellar Drive, Unit 102
Newmarket ON L3Y 7B7
905-715-7020
1-888-299-3138
Fax: 905-715-7140

Barrie
114 Worsley Street, Suite 201
Barrie ON L4M 1M1
705-722-6642
1-800-461-4383
Fax: 705-726-3101

Eastern Region
Ottawa, Kingston, Peterborough

Ottawa West
Ottawa East
1111 Prince of Wales Drive
Suite 200
Ottawa ON K2C 3T2
613-228-8050
1-800-267-1916
Fax: 613-727-2900

Peterborough
300 Water Street North
3rd Floor, South Tower
Peterborough ON K9J 8M5
705-755-4700
Fax: 705-755-4724

Kingston
Beechgrove Complex
51 Heakes Lane
Kingston ON K7M 9B1
613-545-0989
Fax: 613-545-9831

Other Employment Perqs and Benefits

9.300—A purchaser should seek disclosure from the vendor with respect to any and all employment benefits which may pertain to the employees of the vendor. These could include insurance benefits, pension plans, bonus plans, stock option plans, profit sharing plans, car allowances, and travel allowances. The purchaser will want to know the precise obligations it may be assuming, and in many cases will wish to obtain appropriate representations that the vendor has fulfilled all of its obligations with respect to these matters. If the vendor were to terminate the employment of his employees immediately prior to closing, the vendor would bear liability for any claims arising from these matters prior to closing and the purchaser should seek appropriate indemnifications from the vendor with respect to this. If the purchaser will be acquiring any of the employees of the vendor upon closing of the purchase transaction, it will also want to know whether any insurance claims may have been filed recently by these employees for short-term disability, long-term disability, or any other form of disability benefit program. The impact of such claims upon experience-rating would be a concern.

One of the purchaser's reasons for wishing to know about all of the employment benefits that have been provided by the vendor, is to ensure that the purchaser is able to obtain the services of the employees that it wishes to retain in the new business, by providing them with wages and benefits and other conditions of employment that are at least comparable to those which the employees enjoyed with the vendor.

Vacation Pay Trust

9.301—Many jurisdictions in Canada have passed legislation requiring employers to make certain salary and wage payments to employees for employee vacation periods. Under the terms of many collective bargaining agreements the employer may be required to make contributions on account of vacation pay credits earned by individuals to a trust established for that purpose. The trust property is managed by the trustees in accordance with the terms of trust deed and payments out of the trust to employees are made at the times and levels as specified in the trust deed. The trust is not taxed on its income for a taxation year if no part of its property is payable (after 1980) to any person (other than a tax exempt labour organization under section 149(1)(k) of the Income Tax Act[1]) other than a consequence of being an employee or an heir or legal representative of an employee.[2] If a vacation pay trust does not meet these requirements, the tax consequence for the trust, employer, and employee will be the same as if the vacation pay trust were an employee benefit plan. To ensure this tax treatment is continued after the purchase of a business, the terms of the trust should be reviewed to ensure the trust complies with the requirements of subsection 149(1)(y) of the Income Tax Act.

---

1. R.S.C. 1985, c. 1 (5th Supp.).
2. R.S.C. 1985, c. 1 (5th Supp.), subs. 149(1)(y).

Health and Welfare Trusts

9.302—There are numerous ways for employers to provide health and welfare benefits for their employees. One method is for the employee health and benefit program to be administered by an employer through a trust arrangement, under which the trust receives contributions from the employer (and possibly employees) to provide the health and welfare benefits that have otherwise been agreed to by the employer and employees.

If the health and welfare benefits administered are restricted to:

    (i)   a group sickness or accident insurance plan,

    (ii) a private health services plan,

    (iii) a group term life insurance policy, or

    (iv) any combination of (i) to (iii)

and certain other restrictions are met, the arrangement is referred to as a "health and welfare trust". With the exception of a private health services plan, two or more employees must be covered by the plan and the trust funds cannot revert to the employer or be used for any purpose other than providing health and welfare benefits for which the contributions are made. The employer must also ensure that the contributions made to the trust do not exceed the amount required to provide the benefits being offered. Finally, the payments by the employer must be enforceable under the trust deed, rather than merely voluntary or gratuitous.

From the employer's point of view, contributions to the trust are deductible in the taxation year in which the legal obligation to make the contribution arose, to the extent that the contribution is reasonable and is made to earn income from a business or property.

Revenue Canada, Taxation has not established a formal registration procedure for establishing a trust and Revenue Canada, Taxation's agreement is not needed on the form of the trust deed prior to the implementation of the plan. It is possible, however, to request the advice of the District Taxation Office of the employer, where there is any doubt as to the acceptability of the trust arrangement as a health and welfare trust. As such, any health and welfare trust that a vendor may have in place should be reviewed by the purchaser prior to the closing of the transaction to ensure that it meets the requirements of Revenue Canada, Taxation.[1]

---

1. Interpretation Bulletin, IT-85R2 – Health and Welfare Trusts for Employees.

Employment Contracts

9.310—A purchaser should ascertain from the vendor whether the vendor has any written employment contracts with any of its employees. If so, a decision will have to be made whether the purchaser will assume these employees and their employment contracts. This issue is particularly pertinent if the purchaser acquires assets of the vendor. If the purchase is by way of share purchase, the purchaser would automatically assume the place of the vendor with respect to any employment contracts that exist between the vendor and any of its employees.

In an asset purchase, an employee's employment is deemed, at common law, to be terminated upon the sale of the business, and a purchaser would not be liable under any employment contract applicable to such an employee nor would it be required to assume the services of such employee. The purchaser can decide prior to the acquisition that it will not employ certain employees of the vendor. The purchaser would thus have no liability pertaining to the terminated employees and they would have to look to the vendor for compensation. The purchaser should not direct or request the vendor to dismiss any of the vendor's employees prior to the closing of the transaction, lest the purchaser become liable for inducing a breach of contract. The purchaser is also cautioned that some employees terminated by the vendor may name the purchaser as a defendant in a wrongful dismissal suit if, for example, the vendor has no remaining assets in Ontario and the employee is looking for a defendant with assets. To protect itself against such an eventuality, a purchaser may wish to seek an appropriate indemnification clause or reserve fund from the vendor.

If the purchaser does acquire certain employees from the vendor, an attempt should be made to secure an agreement that the vendor will contribute toward the redundancy costs associated with any such employees that it will not be able to retain after the purchase. Arguably, the vendor should contribute to such costs since a significant portion of such an employee's severance entitlements may arise from a period during which the employee was employed by the vendor, and the vendor would be obligated to make such termination payments if the purchaser had chosen not to acquire that employee.

In the event that the purchaser wishes to employ certain employees of the vendor on a speculative basis, employment contracts can be entered into with these employees at the commencement of their employment with the purchaser, limiting their right to claim for damages on termination, in the event they prove unsatisfactory in the future. Such arrangements would nevertheless be subject to the minimum employment standards stipulated by the Employment Standards Act.[1]

Even though a written employment contract will not be assumed unless the purchaser specifically assumes the same, a purchaser should be aware of section 9 of the Employment Standards Act.[2] This provides that where an employer sells its business to a purchaser who employs an employee of the former employer, the employment of the employee shall not be terminated by the sale, and the period of employment with the former employer shall be deemed to have been employment with the purchaser for the purposes of parts of the Employment Standards Act.[3] In particular, Part XV deals with the notice of termination and severance pay which must be provided by an employer terminating the services of an employee. In this instance, the purchaser would be obliged to provide such an employee with appropriate notice, based on the employee's combined period of employment with the purchaser and the vendor. Correspondingly, in any wrongful dismissal action brought by such an employee in a civil court, a court could also consider this combined period of employment. While this appears to be at odds with the normal common law position that an employee's employment is deemed to be terminated upon the sale of the business by the vendor, the law in this area is evolving [see, for example, *Addison v. M. Loeb Ltd.*[4]]. To protect itself, a purchaser may wish to seek an appropriate indemnification clause or reserve fund from the vendor. The purchaser's liabilities in these circumstances would need to be weighed against the positive benefits of obtaining experienced, qualified, and skilled employees from the vendor.

---

1. S.O. 2000, c. 41.
2. *Ibid.*, s. 9.
3. *Ibid.*, Parts X, XI, XIV, XV.
4. (1986), 53 O.R. (2d) 602 (C.A.).

Source Deductions—Canada Revenue Agency

9.320—The provisions of the Income Tax Act, the Employment Insurance Act and the Canada Pension Plan[1] respectively, require all employers to make appropriate source deductions, contributions and remittances to Canada Revenue Agency for Income Tax, Unemployment Insurance Premium contributions and Canada Pension Plan contributions. Canada Revenue Agency has the authority to reassess and penalize employers who do not meet their statutory obligations. If a sale transaction is by way of share purchase, the obligations and liabilities of the business would remain intact and the purchaser would normally assume responsibility for same. In an asset transaction, the vendor would remain liable to Canada Revenue Agency for unpaid taxes, unemployment insurance contributions and Canada Pension Plan contributions.

A purchaser should satisfy itself that the vendor has met these obligations by inquiring with Canada Revenue Agency. The Agreement of Purchase and Sale should also include appropriate vendor's representations and warranties. **[See Forms 9F28 and 9F29]**

---

1. S.C. 1996, c. 23.

Employer Health Tax

9.330—The Employer Health Tax Act[1] (the "Act") provides generally for the replacement of Ontario Health Insurance Premiums with a tax levy on employers. An employer means a person or a government who pays remuneration to an employee. The new tax is imposed on employers at different rates, depending upon the total value of remuneration paid by each employer. The tax is to be remitted to the provincial government on a monthly basis at the time prescribed under the Act, unless the employer is a "small employer", in which case quarterly instalments are to be made.

Those contemplating the purchase of a business by way of an acquisition of shares will find it necessary to obtain assurances that the vendor does not have any outstanding liabilities such as unpaid taxes, penalties, interest, garnishment orders, or other court orders under the Act. As a result of amendments made on June 23, 1994, any outstanding tax liability can, upon registration by the Minister in the appropriate registry, become a charge and lien on real property and/or a charge and lien on the personal property of the taxpayer. Searches of the appropriate registries should be made to ensure that no such registrations exist, as a purchaser of shares or of assets would take subject to those encumbrances. Agreements should take this into account with proper warranties and indemnifications.

The Act, unlike the Income Tax Act[2] does not provide generally for the issuance of clearance certificates with respect to outstanding liabilities. The Ministry is prepared to entertain requests for written verification that an employer does not have outstanding obligations or liabilities under the Act. This verification will be provided to any person (or his legal representative) who has a "legitimate need for same" and has provided a written consent from the employer. **[See Forms 9F30 and 9F31]**

Each request should contain a short description of the transaction. The employer's consent form must indicate that the employer's consent is being given pursuant to subsection 27(c) of the Act,[3] and should set out the type of information to be released and give the name of the person entitled to receive the information. The Ministry's response will normally follow within two weeks of its receipt of a request.

Subsection 11(5)[4] allows an Ontario court to make an order requiring the employer to make a payment as required by the Act. Lawyers involved in a purchase transaction may want to check court records to determine whether any such order is outstanding against the target corporation.

Section 18[5] provides that where the Minister suspects that a person is or will be, within one year, liable to make a payment to an employer who is liable to make a payment under the Act, he or she may garnish any monies otherwise payable to the employer on account of this liability. The power of garnishment also includes the garnishment of loans or other advances of monies made by financial institutions or other persons.

---

1. R.S.O. 1990, c. E.11.
2. R.S.C. 1985, c. 1 (5th Supp.).
3. R.S.O. 1990, c. E.11, s. 27(c) (am. 1994, c. 8, s. 25).
4. R.S.O. 1990, c. E.11, s. 11(5) (am. 1994, c. 8, s. 12(3)).
5. R.S.O. 1990, c. E.11, s. 18 (am. 1994, c. 8, s. 18).

Pension and Benefits Considerations

General

9.340—A vendor may sponsor a variety of retirement savings arrangements, including one or more registered pension plans, a deferred profit sharing plan, a group registered retirement savings plan[1] as well as a variety of supplemental retirement arrangements and deferred compensation agreements which may or may not be pre-funded. In addition, a wide variety of other benefit programs could be provided by the vendor for its employees, including stock purchase, option or bonus plans, a health and welfare plan, private health services plan, disability insurance or compensation plan, vacation pay plan, or a supplementary unemployment benefits plan. What the vendor and the purchaser agree to with respect to these arrangements will depend upon a number of considerations. **[See Checklists 9C2 and 9C3]** Many of the considerations discussed below in the context of registered pension plans will also be relevant to other benefit plans provided by a vendor for its employees, particularly if one or more of these other benefit plans are funded. Tax implications of a change of ownership should be considered where relevant. Furthermore, plan texts, in particular those relating to retirement arrangements, should be carefully reviewed to determine whether a change of control would trigger payment of enriched benefits.

A particular concern with respect to some types of benefit programs may be benefit coverage for transferring employees from the date of closing to either the date the purchaser can establish coverage for the employees or, if applicable, to the date the purchaser can finalize assumption of the vendor's plan. Also, care should be exercised by a purchaser when considering assumption of so-called "insured" plans (for example, plans covering health or dental care, disability and so forth). Such plans may be administered by an insurance company but may not, in fact, be fully insured. The details of the funding of these programs, including the possibility of future premium increases based on the experience rating of the plan, should be fully explored by the purchaser.

In dealing with a registered pension plan, a purchaser must be very cautious in agreeing to allocate a value to existing "surplus" in the vendor's plan. "Surplus" can be described as an excess of plan assets over liabilities at a stated time. If the plan in question provides defined benefits (i.e. where the amount of a participant's pension is determinable by reference to a specific formula set out in the plan), the plan actuary will estimate plan liabilities based on assumptions as to future salary increases, mortality rates, interest rates, and so forth. Different assumptions will have a significantly different impact on the value of estimated liabilities and, therefore, on the amount of "surplus". A purchaser should be aware of the assumptions used by the vendor's actuary and the possible impact of a different set of assumptions (which could possibly be more realistic in the circumstances). It would be prudent for a purchaser to engage its own actuary to review the analysis of the plan's financial status prepared by the vendor's actuary.

A purchaser should also be aware of possible restrictions as to access to or use of existing surplus in a vendor's pension plan. For pension plans registered in Ontario, surplus may only be withdrawn by an employer with regulatory approval. On an application for such approval, the employer must demonstrate not only that it has legal entitlement to the payment to it of surplus, but that it has also obtained the requisite consents from plan beneficiaries.[2] As well as the possibility of future provincial legislation regulating surplus use, a purchaser should not automatically anticipate accessing surplus through an application for withdrawal from an Ontario plan. It is also possible that surplus may not be available for a "contribution holiday".[3] Even in circumstances where a vendor has been utilizing surplus to fund its contribution obligations, a purchaser should not assume that it could continue the practice. Depending on the provisions of the plan text in question, it may be possible for prior contribution holidays to be successfully challenged.[4]

In the event the defined benefit pension plan of a vendor is underfunded, a purchaser will typically attempt to negotiate a reduction in the purchase price. To the extent the plan is in a deficit position on a going concern basis, Ontario pension legislation requires special payments to be made over a maximum period of 15 years to liquidate the liability. If there is a deficit on a solvency basis, special payments required to liquidate the solvency deficiency must be made over a period not to exceed 5 years.

---

1. The term "registered pension plan", "deferred profit sharing plan" and "registered retirement savings plan" are all defined under and regulated by the Income Tax Act, R.S.C. 1985, c. 1 (5th Supp.). However, only a "registered pension plan" is regulated by pension benefits legislation as well as by the Income Tax Act.
2. See section 10 with respect to ongoing plans and section 8 with respect to terminated plans of the Regulations to the Pension Benefits Act, R.S.O. 1990, c. P.8, as amended by O. Reg. 625/98. The Financial Services Commission of Ontario Act, R.S.O. 1997, c. 28 ("FSCO Act"), which was fully proclaimed on July 1, 1998, amends the Pension Benefits Act, R.S.O. 1990, c. P.8. The FSCO Act replaces the Pension Commission of Ontario with the Financial Services Commission of Ontario. The FSCO Act also establishes the Superintendent of Financial Services in place of the Superintendent of Pensions. Effective July 1, 1998, FSCO released Policy S900-508 which governs surplus withdrawal applications commenced after July 1, 1999.
3. A "contribution holiday" can be described as the practice of using surplus to offset a plan sponsor's contribution obligation for current service.
4. For examples of cases considering an employer's right to take contribution holidays, see *Schmidt v. Air Products of Canada Ltd.*, [1994] 2 S.C.R. 611, *Hockin v. Bank of British Columbia* (1995), 123 D.L.R. (4th) 538 (B.C. C.A.), *Maurer v. McMaster University* (1995), 23 O.R. (3d) 577 (C.A.) and *Askin v. Ontario Hospital Assn.* (1991), 2 O.R. (3d) 641 (C.A.).

Share Acquisition

9.341—In a share acquisition there is generally no change of plan sponsor.[1] No regulatory approval is required with respect to existing benefit plans. All of the assets and liabilities of benefit plans remain with the company whose shares are acquired, unless there is specific provision to the contrary in the purchase and sale agreement. It is therefore crucial that a purchaser obtain full disclosure relating to, and quantify the cost of maintaining, any existing benefit arrangements. An actuary should be retained to perform an assessment of the cost of benefits and the funded status of existing plans.

The purchaser should obtain full disclosure of all documentation relating to the plans maintained by the company to be acquired (including plan texts, funding or trust agreements, employee summaries, etc.). The purchaser should also inquire as to whether the vendor has made any promises relating to future plan improvements and the company's past practice in the administration of its benefit plans. For example, a purchaser should be informed as to whether the company has administered its plan in a manner more generous than required by the specific provisions of the plan text, or whether it has developed a practice of regular inflation adjustments to retirement pensions.

In order for a purchaser to protect themselves from financial responsibility for potential pre-purchase administration problems and the adequacy of funding of a vendor's pension and benefit plans, the onus is on a purchaser to uncover all of the relevant liability issues through effective due diligence. In addition, a purchaser should attempt to negotiate extensive representations and warranties and broad indemnification protection from the vendor in order to isolate itself from any prior administration or funding abnormalities that occurred during the vendor's administration of such pension and benefit plans.

A purchaser should also be wary of any previous partial wind ups that may have been implemented by a vendor in light of the recent Supreme Court of Canada decision in *Monsanto Canada Inc. v. Ontario (Superintendent of Financial Services)* ("Monsanto").[2] In the Monsanto decision, the Court held that the Ontario Pension Benefit's Act imposes an obligation on an employer who undertakes a partial wind up of a defined benefit pension plan to distribute a proportional share of actuarial surplus to affected plan members.

A purchaser should also take the precaution of inquiring about the existence, not only of documented pension arrangements, but also of other plans, such as supplemental pension arrangements, that may not be documented or funded.

The purchaser should ascertain the funded status of any benefit programs maintained by the company. Furthermore, the purchaser should ensure that an accurate valuation is made of the potential costs of future funding obligations and the cost of funding any existing liabilities of such benefit programs.

---

1. An exception to this general rule would occur if the acquired company is a participating employer in a parent or other related company's pension plan. In such circumstances, future participation is often precluded by the share purchase documents, giving rise to issues more common to an asset transaction.
2. [2004] S.C.J. No. 51, 2004 SCC 54.

Asset Acquisition

Preliminary Considerations

9.342—In an asset transaction, the vendor will retain responsibility for the provision of pension benefits accrued to closing for those employees affected by the sale, unless there is a specific provision to the contrary in the agreement of purchase and sale. A determination must be made by the purchaser as to whether or not the assets and/or liabilities of the vendor's pension plan are to be assumed.

From a purchaser's perspective, there are three possible scenarios:

(a)   the purchaser has no existing plan and does not intend to set up a plan;

(b)   the purchaser has its own plan and will permit employees transferring employment from the vendor to the purchaser to become members in its existing plan;

(c)   the purchaser will establish or assume from the vendor a separate plan for transferring employees.

If the vendor maintains a registered pension plan, the purchaser should determine whether federal or provincial pension benefits legislation governs the plan. A registered pension plan is subject to the federal Pension Benefits Standards Act, 1985[1] when the number of plan members in "included employment" (as defined in the statute) outnumber those not in included employment.[2]

Broadly speaking, "included employment" means employment within the legislative authority of the federal government including banking, broadcasting, inter-provincial and international transportation, as well as employment in the Yukon and the Northwest Territories.

If a pension plan is not subject to the federal statute, the plan will be registered in the province in which the largest number of its menbers is employed. If the plan covers members in more than one jurisdiction, the plan must comply with the requirements of the relevant jurisdiction with respect to plan members in that jurisdiction.[3] Required compliance with legislation of several jurisdictions may be complex and costly. A purchaser's decision as to whether or not to agree to assume the liabilities of the vendor's plan, or to establish a separate plan for the transferred employees, may be influenced by questions of jurisdiction, such as whether the vendor's plan covers members of several jurisdictions or is registered in a different jurisdiction to the purchaser's own pension plan.

From a vendor's perspective, a decision must also be made in the particular circumstances whether assets should be transferred to the purchaser. It is unclear as to whether the transfer of assets and liabilities to a purchaser will relieve the vendor of liability with respect to the provision of accrued pension benefits. This may be a consideration should the purchaser subsequently terminate the plan, and the pension assets held by the purchaser at that time are insufficient to meet liabilities for former employees of the vendor.[4]

---

1. Pension Benefit Standards Act, 1985, R.S.C. 1985, c. 32 (2nd Supp.), as amended.
2. Section 4(4) of the Pension Benefits Standards Act, 1985, *supra*, note 1, defines "included employment". Section 4(5) of the Pension Benefits Standards Act, 1985 and s. 4 and Schedule "I" of the Pension Benefits Standards Regulations, 1985, SOR/87-19 define "excepted employment".
3. Most provinces have executed reciprocal agreements to the effect that the province of registration will enforce the laws of the other jurisdiction in which plan members are located. See s. 95 of the Ontario Pension Benefits Act, R.S.O. 1990, c. P.8. Section 6 of the Pension Benefits Standards Act, 1985, *supra*, note 1, also authorizes reciprocal agreements with "designated" provinces; section 3 of the Pension Benefits Standards Regulations, 1985, as amended by SOR/93-109 and SOR/94-0384 prescribes Ontario, Quebec, New Brunswick, Nova Scotia, Manitoba, Saskatchewan, Alberta and British Columbia as designated provinces. See also s. 28 of the Regulations to the Pension Benefits Standards Act, 1985, SOR/87-19.
4. Micallef v. Gainers Inc. (1988), 63 O.R. (2d) 687 (H.C.J.) should be considered in this context. The vendor had transferred insufficient assets to the purchaser's plan to meet the pension liabilities. The purchaser subsequently made an assignment in bankruptcy. An application was brought by a trustee for the transferred employees to recover the shortfall from the vendor's pension plan. This case dealt only with an interim injunction granted to restrain the vendor from transferring its plan assets to another out of jurisdiction plan sponsored by it. The parties reached a settlement prior to the adjudication of the substantive issues.

No Successor Plan

9.343—If the purchaser has no pension plan and will not be establishing a plan for transferring employees, a partial or complete windup of the vendor's plan may be triggered by the sale pursuant to the provisions of applicable pension legislation.[1]

Windup of a pension plan involves significant costs to the plan sponsor:

(a) Members affected by the windup will be become fully vested in their benefits, regardless of whether or not they have met the vesting rules set out in the pension plan.[2]

(b) If the plan is registered in Ontario, special rights will be provided to any Ontario member affected by the windup whose age plus service (or whose age plus plan membership) equals at least 55.[3]

(c) If the plan in question is a contributory defined benefit plan, provisions of applicable pension legislation may set out additional benefits payable on plan termination to recognize the contributory nature of the plan.[4]

(d) A plan sponsor is required to pay interest on employee entitlements in the amount prescribed by applicable legislation[5] from the date of plan windup to the date of payment of the entitlement.

(e) Amounts required to meet the prescribed rules for solvency set out in applicable pension legislation must be paid into a plan upon windup. If a vendor's plan is in a deficit position, this may be a significant cost.[6]

(f) The windup itself involves special administrative costs, including the preparation of a windup report.

(g) The windup may crystallize an entitlement to surplus for members affected by the windup.

In addition, if the purchaser does not establish a plan with substantially similar provisions to that provided by the vendor, the vendor may be liable for claims of wrongful dismissal costs.

---

1. See section 69(1)(f) of the Pension Benefits Act, R.S.O. 1990, c. P.8 and s. 29(2) of the Pension Benefits Standards Act, 1985, R.S.C. 1985, c. 32 (2nd Supp.), as amended. If no plan members will remain with the vendor after the sale, the vendor may decide to voluntarily wind up its plan. See section 68 of the Pension Benefits Act or section 29(5) of the Pension Benefits Standards Act, 1985.

2. See section 73(1)(b) of the Pension Benefits Act, ibid., and section 29(7) of the Pension Benefits Standards Act, 1985, ibid.

3. See s. 74 of the Pension Benefits Act, supra, note 1. For discussion as to the application of s. 74, see Firestone Canada Inc. v. Ontario (Pension Commission) (1990), 78 D.L.R. (4th) 52 (Ont. C.A.).

4. If the plan is contributory, pension benefits legislation will require that 50 per cent of the value of benefits accrued after a date prescribed in the applicable legislation (post 1986 for Ontario and federal plans) be provided by employer contributions. This is the "50 per cent cost rule". If a member has contributed more than the maximum 50 per cent, the excess contributions must either be refunded to the member on plan

termination (under the Ontario Act) or used to provide an increased benefit to the member (under the federal Act) and the plan sponsor must pay the difference into the plan. See ss. 39(3) and (4) of the Pension Benefits Act, and s. 21(2) of the Pension Benefits Standards Act, 1985, supra, note 1. If the plan is registered under the Pension Benefits Standards Act, 1985 the 50 per cent rule will not apply if the plan provides for indexation in the prescribed amount (s. 21(5)). See also s. 39(1) of the Pension Benefits Act, and s. 21(1) of the Pension Benefits Standards Act, 1985 for the minimum requirements for pre-1987 accrued pension.

5. Section 24(12) (rep. & sub. 629/92, s. 2(2)) of the Regulations to the Pension Benefits Act, R.R.O. 1990, Reg. 909. Section 19 of the Pension Benefits Standards Act, 1985, supra, note 1.

6. Section 75 of the Pension Benefits Act, supra, note 1 and ss. 30 and 31, of the Regulations to the Pension Benefits Act, supra, note 5; section 29(6) of the Pension Benefits Standards Act, 1985. Amounts required by windup must be funded within 5 years; see ss. 30 and 31 of the Regulations to the Pension Benefits Act, supra, note 5 and s. 9(4) of the Regulations to the Pension Benefits Standards Act, 1985.

Successor Plan Established or Maintained by Purchaser

9.344—A purchaser may be willing to establish a pension plan for employees of the vendor to whom it will be offering employment or to permit transferring employees to join an existing plan sponsored by the purchaser. If the plan is registered in Ontario, in these circumstances, the employment of transferred employees will be deemed not to have terminated[1] and, therefore, the Superintendent cannot require a windup of the vendor's plan on this basis.[2]

Even if a purchaser provides a successor plan for transferring employees, a vendor may be still liable for claims for wrongful dismissal if an employee refuses the purchaser's offer of employment for the reason that the benefits provided by the purchaser's plan are not substantially similar to those provided by the vendor's plan. Furthermore, if the plan provided by the purchaser is terminated shortly after closing, a full or partial windup of the vendor's plan could be triggered, resulting in costs to the vendor as discussed in Para. 9.343. For this reason, a vendor should obtain a covenant from the purchaser that any plan provided for transferring employees will be maintained for an agreed period of time after closing.

If a plan is to be provided for transferring employees, the purchaser must determine whether or not to assume any of the vendor's benefit obligations to the transferring employees. If any part of the vendor's obligations are to be assumed by the purchaser, it will be necessary to transfer sufficient assets to fund the liability from the vendor's plan to the purchaser's own plan or to a new plan established for the employees. Alternatively, in certain circumstances a purchaser may be willing to undertake sponsorship of the vendor's plan; in this situation, any existing surplus or deficit in the vendor's plan will likely be recognized by an adjustment to the purchase price.

If the vendor is one of several employers participating in a large plan, it may not be possible for a purchaser to continue participation in the plan. A transfer of assets in these circumstances will be complex. Similarly, if the assets of the vendor's plan are pooled for investment purposes under a Master Trust with assets of other plans, an asset transfer will be somewhat more complicated.

---

1. Section 80(3) of Pension Benefits Act, R.S.O. 1990, c. P.8.
2. That is, pursuant to s. 69(1)(d) or (f) of the Pension Benefits Act, R.S.O. 1990, c. P.8.

NO OBLIGATIONS ASSUMED BY PURCHASER

9.345—The parties may agree that each will be responsible to provide benefits earned for service with the respective party. The vendor would be responsible for benefits accrued for service to closing and the purchaser for benefits earned for service thereafter.[1]

Pension benefits legislation sets out certain rights for transferring employees in these circumstances:[2]

(a) The employee will continue to be entitled to benefits accrued to closing in the vendor's plan.

(b) For purposes of determining the employee's eligibility for membership in the purchaser's plan or the vesting of benefits earned in the purchaser's plan, credit will be given for the period of the employee's membership in the vendor's plan.

(c) For purposes of determining the vesting of benefits in the vendor's plan, credit will be given for the employee's period of service with the purchaser.

On retirement the employee will receive a pension from the vendor's plan and one from the purchaser's plan. Unfortunately, if the plan is a defined benefit plan, the sum of the two pensions may be less than the pension a member would have received had the entire pension been earned from membership in one plan. This is especially true in a plan where benefits are based on a final average earnings formula. Where both vendor and purchaser are each responsible for a portion of service, the value of benefits payable from the vendor's plan will be "frozen" at the employee's earnings level as of closing. Any future salary increases will only be applied to the portion of the benefit earned in the purchaser's plan. To remedy this potential benefit loss, a purchaser may be willing to recognize service with the vendor for the purpose of calculation of benefits under the purchaser's plan. This is termed a "wrap around" provision. Benefits are calculated under the purchaser's plan using service with the vendor and the purchaser; a deduction is then made for benefits payable[3] from the vendor's plan. The purchaser's plan will pay the remainder. Obviously this is more costly to a purchaser than simply providing benefits based on service with the purchaser.

---

1. Although the relative simplicity of this strategy makes it one of the most common arrangements, the strategy does raise concerns from the prospective of both the purchaser and vendor. If the purchaser's plan is wound up in the future, that will trigger a concurrent partial windup of the vendor's plan. See Gencorp Canada Inc. v. Ontario (Superintendent of Pensions) (1998), 39 O.R. (3d) 38 (Ont. C.A.).
2. Section 80(1) of the Pension Benefits Act, R.S.O. 1990, c. P.8; s. 30 of the Pension Benefits Standards Act, 1985, R.S.C. 1985, c. 32 (2nd Supp.), as amended.
3. In designing a "wrap around" provision care should be taken that reference is made to benefits "payable" rather than "paid" from the vendor's plan. Otherwise, should the vendor's plan be unable to meet its benefit obligations to the member at retirement, the purchaser's plan could be obligated to fund a greater amount than anticipated.

Purchaser Assumes Vendor's Pension Liabilities

9.346—In certain circumstances, especially if a significant number of the members of a vendor's plan are being offered employment by a purchaser, the purchaser may be willing to assume some or all the assets and liabilities of the vendor's pension plan. An indemnity should be obtained by the vendor with respect to any liability assumed.

The relevant pension authority should be notified as soon as possible of a proposed transfer of assets in order to obtain necessary approval of the transfer.[1] The applicable pension commission will wish to review any amendment to the vendor's plan authorizing the transfer as well as documentation from the purchaser relating to the assumption of the liabilities. A cost certificate (or actuarial report, where necessary) should be filed setting out details of the value of the liabilities and assets transferred and the sufficiency of any assets retained to meet ongoing benefit obligations of the vendor.

Section 80(4) of the Ontario Pension Benefits Act[2] provides that any asset transfer affecting members in Ontario must comply with "prescribed terms and conditions". Although to date no terms and conditions have been included in the legislation, the Financial Services Commission of Ontario (formerly the Pension Commission of Ontario)[3] has set requirements for the transfer of pension assets resulting from the sale of a business in a Policy Statement.[4] The Policy Statement requires that reports relating to the funded status of the vendor's plan be filed with the Financial Services Commission of Ontario and that notice of the proposed transfer be given to plan members and, if the vendor's plan is subject to a collective agreement, to the union.

If the consent of the Superintendent of Financial Services is obtained and assets are transferred, a valuation report must be filed for the plan to which assets are transferred within 120 days of the date approval is obtained.

The Superintendent of Financial Services may waive some or all of the requirements set out in the Policy Statement if the liabilities being transferred do not represent a significant portion of the total liabilities of the vendor's or the purchaser's plan.

Where all the liabilities and assets of a vendor's plan are transferred to a purchaser and maintained by the purchaser in a plan separate from any other pension plan it sponsors, approval of the transfer will be relatively straightforward. There is no obligation to provide the reports relating to the funded status of the vendor's plan nor to file a valuation report otherwise required within 120 days of obtaining the consent.

It is more difficult to obtain approval for a partial transfer of assets and liabilities. A partial transfer may be requested where only some of the plan members are being offered employment by the purchaser. If the purchaser is willing to assume liability for benefits accrued prior to closing with respect to such members, it will be necessary to transfer sufficient assets to fund this liability from the vendor's plan to the purchaser's plan. If the vendor's plan is a defined benefit plan, a valuation of the liability must be obtained. The vendor's actuary will prepare the valuation. It would, however, be prudent for the purchaser to engage its own actuary to review the report. A summary of the methods and assumptions used to value the liability should be set out in the agreement, together with a method for resolving any dispute concerning the valuation. The agreement should also address the possibility that the regulatory authorities may impose conditions on the transfer not contemplated by the parties or may require calculation of the value of the assets to be transferred on a different basis to that agreed. The vendor should obtain an indemnity from the purchaser for any assets and liabilities transferred.

Each party should agree to use its best efforts to obtain approval of the transfer. The purchaser should also agree to amend its existing plan or to establish a new plan to accommodate the transferred assets. The vendor should agree to amend its plan to authorize the transfer of assets and to provide any information or documentation necessary to obtain the required approval.

There will be a significant time lag between the date of closing and, if approved, the date of transfer of assets. The agreement would normally provide a credit for interest on the value of transferred assets at a specified rate from closing to the date of transfer. Provision should also be made for the management of the assets post-closing and prior to transfer. Until the date of actual transfer of assets, a vendor could make any payments necessary on account of employees affected by the asset transfer (due, for example, to premature death, disability, termination from employment with the purchaser prior to the transfer of plan assets and so forth). Any payments made by the vendor during this period should be deducted from the value of assets to be transferred.

If the vendor's plan includes Ontario members and any part of surplus from the vendor's plan is to be included in the asset transfer, the requirements of the Policy Statement relating to permitted surplus transfer should be reviewed carefully. If surplus is to remain in the vendor's plan, the purchaser should obtain an indemnity from the vendor with respect to any claim of a transferred employee to an entitlement in excess of the liability transferred.

---

1. Section 80(4) of the Ontario Pension Benefits Act, R.S.O. 1990, c. P.8 specifically requires approval of the Superintendent of Pensions before pension assets can be transferred. Although the federal Pension Benefits Standards Act, 1985, R.S.C. 1985, c. 32 (2nd Supp.), as amended, does not include such provision, approval of the federal pension authority will be required for a transfer from a federally regulated plan. As a result of the Ontario Court of Appeal decision in *Aegon Canada Inc. and Transamerica Life Canada v. ING Canada Inc.*, [2003] O.J. No. 4755 (the "ING decision") (leave to appeal to the Supreme Court of Canada was subsequently denied), questions have been raised regarding the authority of plan sponsors to transfer assets between pension plans where one or more of the pension plans is subject to a trust, and the authority of the Superintendent of Financial Services to consent to such transfers. FSCO is reviewing the implications of this development.
2. R.S.O. 1990, c. P.8.
3. The Financial Commission of Ontario Act, R.S.O. 1997, c. 28 ("FSCO Act"), which was fully proclaimed on July 1, 1998, amends the Pension Benefits Act, R.S.O. 1990, c. P. 8. The FSCO Act replaces the Pension Commission of Ontario with the Financial Services Commission of Ontario. The FSCO Act also establishes the Superintendent of Financial Services in place of the Superintendent of Pensions.
4. Policy Statement No. 2 dated July 28, 1988 "Transfer of Assets Resulting from Sale of a Business". Policy Statements and Guidelines are updated from time to time and the reader should, therefore, ensure that the most current Policy Statement is utilized. See Part VIII.

Union Plans

9.347—Provisions of applicable labour relations legislation provide that a successor employer is bound by the terms of a vendor's collective agreement. A purchaser will therefore be required to continue any benefits that are part of, or incorporated by reference into the collective agreement. It is essential for the purchaser to obtain full disclosure as to the administration of any existing benefit plans established pursuant to the collective agreement. If a vendor has adopted a practice of administrating the plans in a more generous manner, than required by the collective agreement or plan documentation, a purchaser may not subsequently be able to rely on the specific provisions of the collective agreement or plan texts.

Typically, where the vendor participates in a multi-employer pension plan, the purchaser will continue to participate. For this reason, a purchaser should ensure a full investigation is undertaken concerning any such plan to which the vendor contributes, including a determination of the current funded status of the plan and information relating to liability for past service or obligations for future costs.

The Ontario Pension Benefits Act sets out special rules for unionized multi-employer pension plans.[1] Generally, where a bargaining agent ceases to represent a group of members of a multi-employer pension plan and such members become represented by another bargaining agent and in turn, become members of a different pension plan, the assets and liabilities of the first plan attributable to such members must be transferred to the second plan. This will not, however, be necessary if there is a reciprocal agreement in force relating to both plans or where the plan members elect to transfer their entitlements out of the first plan pursuant to the portability provisions set out in section 42 of the Ontario statute.[2]

---

1. Section 1 of the Pension Benefits Act, R.S.O. 1990, c. P.8 defines a "multi-employer pension plan" as a pension plan maintained for employees of two or more employers who are not affiliates within the meaning of the Ontario Business Corporations Act, R.S.O. 1990, c. B.16. Section 1 of the Pension Benefits Standards Act, 1985, R.S.C. 1985, c. 32 (2nd Supp.) defines a "multi-employer pension plan" as a pension plan organized for employees of two or more employees provided not more than 95 per cent of members are employed by affiliates within the meaning of the Canada Business Corporations Act, R.S.C. 1985, c. C-44.
2. Sections 80(8), (9) and (10) of the Pension Benefits Act, *ibid*.

Amalgamation or Merger

9.348—Assets and liabilities of amalgamating corporations continue in the amalgamated entity. It is not necessary to obtain any consent for pension plan purposes. However, continuing plans will be known by the name of the amalgamated corporation. Regulatory authorities must be informed of any resulting plan name change[1] and the plans should be amended to reflect any name change.

The merger or amalgamation of corporations will not automatically trigger merger of the assets and liabilities of the pension plans previously sponsored by the separate corporate entities.[2] Plans of amalgamating corporations will remain separate unless steps are taken to merge the plans by way of plan amendment. If the plans are not to be merged, provisions should be reviewed and amended, where necessary, to accurately describe the employees eligible for membership.

Furthermore, the amalgamation of different plans after the merger or amalgamation of separate corporate entities will not result in the termination of such plans or of the trust agreements, if any, pursuant to which the plans may be administered.[3]

If it is desirable to merge plans, consent of the appropriate regulatory authorities must be obtained.[4] The merged plan will continue to provide any member entitlements found in predecessor plan documentation, but only in respect to the particular plan member group to which the previous documentation specifically relates.

---

1. Section 147.1(7)(b) of the Income Tax Act, R.S.C. 1985, c. 1 (5th Supp.) provides that Canada Customs and Revenue Agency must be informed within 30 days of any change of name or address of the sponsor of a registered pension plan.
2. See *Heilig v. Dominion Securities Pitfield Ltd.* (1989), 67 O.R. (2d) 577 where the Court of Appeal confirmed the lower Court decision (1986), 55 O.R. (2d) 783 on this particular point.
3. *Heilig v. Dominion Securities Pitfield Ltd.*, Court of Appeal decision, *supra*, note 2, reversing the lower Court decision, on this particular point. See also *Schmidt v. Air Products of Canada Ltd.*, [1994] 2 S.C.R. 611 for a discussion of the implications of pension plan mergers.
4. The Superintendent of Financial Services has the discretion to refuse a plan merger under section 81 of the Pension Benefits Act, R.S.O. 1990, c. P.8, and may do so if there is any concern relating to protection of benefits, for example, where one plan is in deficit and another in surplus in circumstances where members have an entitlement to surplus. Although no requirements relating to mergers have yet been prescribed under the Ontario statute, the Financial Services Commission of Ontario has issued Policies A700-251 and A700-226, setting out guidelines for full and partial asset transfers. Also see footnote one under paragraph 9.346, regarding the implications of the ING decision.

Representations and Warranties

9.349—The following general representations and warranties should be included in the agreement of purchase and sale:

(a) that all benefit plans (whether funded or otherwise) and other related documents and employee summaries of the same have been disclosed. [A specific list of such plans should be attached as a schedule to the agreement.]

(b) that all information provided with respect to such plans, including member data, is accurate, current and complete.

(c)   that no amendments or improvements have been made to pension plans or will be made prior to closing, except as specifically disclosed.

(d)   that all plans listed in the schedule comply with applicable legislation and have been administered in accordance with the terms of the plan and applicable legislation and, where applicable, remain duly registered with each applicable regulatory authority.

(e)   that any registered pension plans are fully funded.[1]

(f)   that all required contributions or premiums have been paid and that there are no outstanding liabilities, except as specifically disclosed.

(g)   that all required filings and other documentation for the plans listed in the schedule are up-to-date.

(h)   that any previous transfers or withdrawals of assets from such plans, or affects of plan surplus against ongoing contribution obligations, were made in accordance with plan documentation and applicable legislation.

---

1.   There may be unfunded supplementary plans and, therefore, the wording of this representation should specifically relate to those plans listed in the schedule for which a fund has been established. Where a representation is being made with respect to a registered defined benefit pension plan, the actuaries acting for the vendor and purchaser should agree as to meaning of "fully funded", for example, whether or not funding of the plan has included an assumption for future salary increases and so forth.

Relevant Ontario Policy Statements

9.349.1—The following is an extract of the restatement of policy Statement No. 2 of the Pension Commission of Ontario (now the Financial services Commssion of Ontario)[1], reprinted with the permission of the Commission:

July 28, 1988

Transfer of Assets Resulting from Sale of a Business

(1)   This statement is applicable to transfers made pursuant to agreements signed and transactions implemented on or after October 1, 1988.

(2)   In this part,

(a)   "asset transfer ratio" shall mean the ratio of the market value of investments held by the employer's pension plan plus any cash balances and accrued or receivable income items to the sum of the transfer liabilities and the residual liabilities.

(b)   "asset transfer value" shall be the transfer liabilities multiplied by the lesser of

   (i)   the asset transfer ratio, or

   (ii)   1.00.

(c)   "residual asset value" shall be the residual liabilities multiplied by the lesser of

   (i)   the asset transfer ratio, or

   (ii)   1.00.

(d)   "residual liabilities" are the higher of the going concern liabilities or the solvency liabilities of the pension, deferred pensions, ancillary benefits or pension benefits for which the employer has retained responsibility.

(e)   "transfer liabilities" are the higher of the going concern liabilities or the solvency liabilities of the pension, deferred pensions, ancillary benefits or pension benefits for which the successor employer has assumed responsibility.

(f)   "transferred members" shall mean those members, former members and persons entitled to a payment from a pension fund that are affected by the transfer and for whose accrued benefits in whole or in part the successor employer has assumed responsibility.

(3)   The Superintendent shall not permit a transfer of assets from a pension plan of an employer to a pension plan of a successor employer unless the application for transfer by the employer is accompanied by,

(a)   those portions of the purchase and sale agreement and any subsequent revisions to that agreement which relate to the employer's pension plans and pension funds; and

(b)   a report prepared by a person authorized under the Regulations[2] containing the following information:

   (i)   the going concern liabilities, solvency liabilities and asset transfer value of the benefits for which the successor employer has assumed responsibility;

      (ii)   the going concern liabilities, solvency liabilities and residual asset value of the benefits for which the employer has retained responsibility;

      (iii)   where the plan is in a surplus position, the intended treatment of surplus and the basis for any allocation of the surplus; and

      (iv)   the amount of and the basis for the determination of the assets to be transferred to the successor employer's pension plan.

(4)   The review date of the report required under subsection (3) shall be the effective date of the sale.

(5)   Notwithstanding subsection (4), the Superintendent may permit a review date of the report required under subsection (3), other than the effective date of sale where the Superintendent is of the opinion that the other date is justified in the circumstances.

(6)   Prior to the proposed transfer of assets and liabilities from the employer's pension plan to the successor employer's pension plan, notice by the employer shall be transmitted to the transferred members. Where the transferred members are represented by a trade union that is a party to a collective agreement filed as a document that creates or supports the pension plan, notice shall also be transmitted to the trade union, and the notice shall contain, at least, the following information:

      (a)   the name of the employer's pension plan and its provincial registration number;

      (b)   the name of the successor employer's pension plan and its provincial registration number, if any;

      (c)   the review date of the report filed with the application;

      (d)   notice that copies of the report, filed with the Superintendent, in support of the transfer of asset request, excluding information as to the service, salary, pension benefits or other personal information related to any specific person without the person's prior consent, are available for review at the offices of either the employer or the successor employer and information on how copies of the report may be obtained; and

(e)   a description of the benefits of the transferred members for which the successor employer has assumed responsibility and a description of the benefits of the transferred members for which the employer has retained responsibility.

(7)   The Superintendent shall not permit a transfer of assets from a pension plan of an employer to a pension plan of a successor employer unless a certified copy of the notice referred to in subsection (6) has been filed with the superintendent together with a statement that subsection (6) has been complied with, and indicating the last date the notice was transmitted.

(8)   Where a transaction described in section 81 of the Act[3] occurs, and the successor employer assumes responsibility in whole or in part for the pension benefits under the employer's pension plan, then,

(a)   where, under the windup provisions of the plan, the employer has clear entitlement to surplus, subject to subsection (10), assets having a market value as at the review date of not less than the lower of the asset transfer value or the solvency liabilities reported under subsection (3)(b)(i) shall be transferred from the employer's pension plan to the pension plan of the successor employer;

(b)   where, under the windup provisions of the plan, the members and former members of the employer's pension plan have clear entitlement to the surplus of the employer's pension plan,

(i)   assets having a market value as at the review date of not less than the asset transfer value reported under subsection (3)(b)(i) shall be transferred from the employer's pension plan to the pension plan of the successor employer; and

(ii)   where a transfer of assets representing surplus is to be transferred from the employer's pension plan to the successor employer's pension plan, then,

(aa)   the successor employer shall maintain the transferred assets and liabilities as separate and distinct from any other pension plans which the successor employer may sponsor; or (bb)   prior to the transfer of assets and liabilities, the proposed transfer of surplus shall be allocated to improve the accrued benefits of the transferred members on a basis acceptable to the Superintendent; or

(c)   where, under the windup provisions of the plan, the entitlement to surplus under the employer's pension plan is unclear,

        (i)   without prejudicing future determination of entitlement to surplus under the employer's pension plan, the employer may follow the procedure as provided for in subsection (b);

        (ii)   without prejudicing future determination of entitlement to surplus under the employer's pension plan, the employer may apply to the Superintendent for a determination of whether the transfer shall be made according to the procedure as provided for in subsection (a) or (b); or

        (iii)   subject to the approval of the Superintendent, a partial transfer of assets from the employer's pension plan to the successor employer's pension plan may be made on an interim basis until the requirements of section (13), if applicable, are met.

(9)   Assets representing surplus attributable to the transferred members may remain in the employer's pension plan and the transferred members' entitlement to surplus in the employer's pension plan, if any, remains unaffected by the transfer.

(10)   The Superintendent shall refuse to consent to a transfer under subsection (8)(a) if after such a transfer the market value of the assets remaining in the employer's pension plan as at the review date would be less than the lower of the residual asset value or the solvency liabilities reported under subsection (3)(b)(ii).

(11)   The superintendent shall refuse to consent to a transfer under subsection (8)(b) if after such a transfer the market value of the assets remaining in the employer's pension plan as at the review date would be less than the residual asset value reported under subsection (3)(b)(ii).

(12)   Notwithstanding subsections (8), (10) and (11), the Superintendent may, under exceptional circumstances, require or permit a transfer of assets determined using some other equitable bases.

(13)   Where a transfer of assets representing surplus is to be made from the employer's pension plan to the successor employer's pension plan, and the ratio of the assets transferred to the successor employer's pension plan to the assets retained in the employer's pension plan is greater than the ratio of the transfer liabilities to the residual liabilities, then the transfer shall, for the purpose of this part, be treated as a surplus withdrawal and subject to the requirements of sections 78 and 79 of the Act.[4]

(14)   Subsections (3)(b), and (6)(c) and (d) shall not apply where the successor employer assumes all assets and liabilities of the employer's plan and maintains these assets and liabilities in a pension plan that is separate and distinct from any other pension plans that the successor employer may sponsor.

(15)   Where a member of the employer's pension plan is transferred to the pension plan of the successor employer, such member shall be deemed to be a person eligible to become a member of the successor employer's pension plan for the purpose of notification as required under section 25(1) of the Act.[5]

(16)   Where there is a transfer of assets and liabilities from the employer's pension plan to the successor employer's pension plan, the administrator of the successor employer's pension plan shall file a report required under the Regulations[6] within 120 days following the date the transfer is approved by the superintendent.

(17)   In the preparation of the reports required under subsection (16), the successor employer may include as past service unfunded actuarial liabilities, the net income in liabilities as a result of:

(a)   benefit improvements granted to the transferred employees on the date they become members of the successor employer's pension plan; and

(b)   the difference in going concern liabilities arising as a result of the differences in actuarial funding method or assumptions between the successor employer's pension plan and the employer's pension plan as reported in the last report filed under section 11 of the Regulations.[7]

(18) Subsections (16) and (17) shall not apply where the successor employer assumes all assets and liabilities of the employer's pension plan and maintains these assets and liabilities in a pension plan that is separate and distinct from any other pension plans that the successor employer may sponsor, and the successor employer shall make payments in accordance with the requirements of the most recent report filed under section 3, 10 or 11 of the Regulations[8] by the administrator of the employer's pension plan.

(19) The Superintendent may waive any or all of the requirements of subsections (3)(b) and (4) through (18) where the amount of liabilities to be transferred to the successor employer does not, in the opinion of the Super-intendent, represent a significant portion of the total liabilities of either the employer's pension plan or the successor employer's pension plan.

---

1. Various Policy Statements and Guidelines are under review by the Financial Services Commission of Ontario. The reader is, therefore, cautioned to ensure at any given time that the most current statement relating to transfer of assets after a sale is used.
2. That is, the Regulations to the Pension Benefits Act, R.R.O. 1990, Reg. 909.
3. Pension Benefits Act, R.S.O. 1990, c. P.8.
4. *Ibid.*
5. *Ibid.*
6. *Supra*, note 2.
7. *Ibid.*
8. *Ibid.*

Retirement and Other Allowances
Employee Profit Sharing Plans "EPSPs"

9.350—An employee's profit sharing plan is defined in subsection 144 of the Income Tax Act.[1] Profit sharing plans involve the contribution of profit by the employer to a trust for eventual allocation of all amounts the trust receives to some or all employees. An EPSP may also permit employee contributions. Contributions to any EPSP made by an employer during a taxation year or within 120 days after a taxation year are deductible expenses to the extent that they were not deductible in the preceeding year. The EPSP must provide that in each year the trustees will allocate all amounts received from the employer and all profits of the trust realized by the trust property to the beneficiaries of the trust. The beneficiaries will bring these amounts into their regular income when the amounts are allocated, subject to certain exceptions.

While there are no registration requirements for EPSP's, it is important that an EPSP continue to meet the requirements of eligibility for the plan set out in the definition of an EPSP under section 144[2] to ensure a continued deductibility of employer contributions. As such, the records of the trust should be reviewed along with the terms of the plan to ensure the plan meets statutory requirements. As well, the plan records should be reviewed to ensure the trustees have met all statutory reporting requirements in connection with the reporting of allocated income and the filing of trust returns.

---

1. R.S.C. 1985, c. 1 (5th Supp.).
2. Ibid.

Deferred Profit Sharing Plans "DPSPs"

9.351—Similar to the EPSP, DPSP's involve the contribution of profit by an employer to a trust for eventual allocation to some or all employees.

Subsection 147(2) of the Income Tax Act[1] sets out the conditions which must be complied with to ensure the registration of a profit sharing plan as a DPSP by the Minister of National Revenue. Acceptance of a plan as a DPSP may entitle employers and employees to advantageous tax treatment in terms of contribution deductibility to employers, the allocation of income to the DPSP beneficiaries, and the receipt of income by the plan's trust, as is the case with standard profit sharing plans. With a DPSP there is the added advantage of the possibility of employee retirement benefits being generated by tax deferred growth of investments from contributions. The details of these rules are complex and beyond the scope of this work; however, some issues arise that the parties to a purchase and sale of a business should take into consideration:

1. The trustees of the DPSP must file a Form T3D within 90 days of the year end of the trust. Trust records should be reviewed to ensure this has been done, and a representation and warranty should be obtained from the vendor to that effect.

2. All amendments or revisions to a DPSP must be filed, along with a copy of the authorizing resolution and by-law, if any, with Canada Customs and Revenue Agency, Taxation. Canada Customs and Revenue Agency, Taxation must also be advised of any change of trustee. Failure to do so

may prejudice the registration of the plan. The records of the DPSP should be reviewed to ensure all changes have been filed and if the purchase transaction mandates any changes, Canada Customs and Revenue Agency, Taxation must be advised.

3.   An employer may terminate a DPSP and is required to submit (*i*) a copy of the resolution of the board of directors terminating the plan, (*ii*) the effective date of such termination, and (*iii*) a trustee's statement setting out the date and manner of distribution of the assets of the fund. The employer is required to submit this information after all DPSP funds have been distributed. The trust records should be reviewed to ensure notice has been given, if required, or steps should be taken to ensure compliance if the DPSP is to be terminated after closing of the transaction.

---

1.   R.S.C. 1985, c. 1 (5th Supp.).

Private Health Services Plan "PHSP"

9.352—A contribution by an employee to a PHSP (or a deduction from pay by an employer in respect of a PHSP) will qualify as a medical expense for the purpose of calculating the employee's medical expense credit which is used in computing the employee's tax payable. To qualify, the amount so paid must be used for one or more of the employees, their spouses or any related member of the employee's household.[1]

A PHSP is a contract of insurance in respect of hospital or medical expenses (or a combination of both) or a hospital or medical insurance plan (or a combination of both). As it is a contract in the nature of insurance, the plan must contain (i) an undertaking by one person; (ii) to indemnify another person; (iii) for an agreed consideration; (iv) from a loss or liability in respect of an event; (v) the happening of which is uncertain.[2]

A contribution by an employer on behalf of an employee is excluded from the employee's income, but is generally deductible by the employer as a business outlay or expense. To ensure continued deductibility, the purchaser of a business should undertake a review of the PHSP's the vendor has in place at the time of sale to ensure they meet the standards set out above.

---

1.   Income Tax Act, S.C. 1970-71-72, c. 63, as am., s. 118.2(2)(*q*).
2.   IT-339R2.

Retirement Allowances

9.353—Amounts paid to employees on cessation of employment in recognition of long service or in respect of loss of office or employment, whether or not received on account of damages or pursuant to an order or a judgment of a competent tribunal will qualify as a "retiring allowance" for tax purposes.[1] A retiring allowance is taxable when received by the retiring or terminated employee under section 56 of the Income Tax Act.[2] Taxpayers may transfer a portion of such payments directly to an RRSP and defer the payment of tax. The amount that may be transferred to an RRSP under subsection 60(j.1) of the Income Tax Act[3] is limited to the aggregate of:

(i) $2,000 × the number of years of employment with the employer (or persons related to the employer) prior to 1996;

plus

(ii) $1,500 × the number of years before 1989 in which the employee was employed by the employer and in respect of which employer contributions under either a pension plan or a DPSP had not vested in the retiree.

Such amounts can be paid directly to an RRSP without being subject to the requisite statutory withholdings. In order to qualify for this treatment, a Form T2097 (a Form TD2 is often used and will be accepted by Canada Customs and Revenue Agency) must be completed by the employee, employer and the carriers of the RRSP and the funds must be paid directly to the RRSP by the employer.

Otherwise, retiring allowances are treated as lump-sum payments which are subject to withholding as follows:[4]

(i)   if the amount paid is less than $5,000—   10%

(ii) if the amount paid is more than $5,000 and less than $15,000—   20%

(iii) if the amount paid is more than $15,000— 30%

An employer is required to report the full amount of the retiring allowance paid to the employee (or to the RRSP on direction of the employee) on a Form T4A.

---

1. Income Tax Act, R.S.C. 1985, c. 1 (5th Supp.), s. 248(1).
2. *Ibid.*; am. 1993, c. 24, s. 17.

3. *Ibid.*; rep. & sub. 1996, c. 21.
4. Income Tax Regulations, s. 103(4).

Environmental Considerations
General

9.360—Until recently environmental considerations were not specifically addressed in agreements of purchase and sale of businesses. Today, however, the environment is a major public concern. There has been extensive action taken concerning the environment by (*i*) governments to pass new laws and regulations; (*ii*) regulators to ensure that the laws and regulations are understood and properly carried out; and (*iii*) enforcers to prosecute polluters and those who do not comply with the law. As a result property owners, tenants, lenders, trustees in bankruptcy, receivers, insurers and others are all very concerned. Consequently, environmental issues are very much part of the transaction due diligence process and environmental provisions are now being included in the documentation.

Because of the complexities that often are involved in the environmental area it is important to do the due diligence as early as possible, understand the requirements of all interested parties (including lenders and insurers) and then negotiate and conclude the contractual arrangements that are appropriate for the particular transaction. Often this can be done most effectively by using various experts in the environmental field, lawyers, engineers and other professionals, who understand not only the legal requirements but also the policies and practicalities that may be involved.

It is important to understand that in the environmental field the law is usually very broad and general. There is a great deal of discretion for the regulators at all government levels, federal, provincial and local, as to the precise meaning, scope and extent of liability. Since much of this legislation has only recently been passed, the Canadian courts or special environmental tribunals have not rendered decisions to clarify and make the law more certain. In the important area of understanding whether a property is "contaminated" or suitable for further development or land uses, governments are issuing guidelines to assist in determining "how clean is clean". However, they will not issue clearance certificates and the responsibility is on the owners and persons involved in a transaction and their professional environmental consultants to do the appropriate site assessment and restoration to meet the particular requirements. In the environmental area the trend is also moving towards the use of voluntary initiatives and compliance beyond the law. It is very important, therefore, to be familiar with the standards, practices and procedures that are in place generally regarding the type of business involved in a transaction. A careful review should be conducted in this regard of the due diligence systems, programs, policies and procedures that have been established and maintained by the business.

It is very important, therefore, that the parties to a transaction understand exactly what the possible areas of concern are and agree upon an allocation of risk as between themselves to appropriately deal with the potential environmental problems.

Types of Liability

9.361—Environmental concerns for a business today in Canada include being (*i*) prosecuted for environmental offences; (*ii*) subject to a wide range of regulatory orders; (*iii*) subject to licencing or other regulatory restrictions on their operations; or (*iv*) involved as a party in a civil action as a result of some sort of environmental damage.

Canadian environmental statutes create a wide range of environmental offences, the breach of which may result in substantial fines and penalties including a profit-stripping element and orders for environmental site cleanups and remediation for damage done as a result of the offences. The environmental statutes provide environmental officers with a very broad range of powers to carry out inspections and investigations to ensure the proper administration of the legislation and to direct that remedial action be taken in a spill, discharge or other environmental emergency or concern.

The environmental legislation contains numerous provisions whereby regulatory orders may be made by a court or by the regulators. Stop orders may be issued requiring cessation of certain operations or discharges. Continuing orders to manage or to require preventive measures may be imposed. In addition, direct action may be required, through orders to remediate contaminated lands, to clean up spills or to remove wastes. Governments even have the ability to carry out the necessary work upon default, to obtain an order for the costs incurred and to register liens against lands to try and secure the repayment of those costs.

There is great concern as to how extensive the group of people is against whom regulatory orders can be made. The persons responsible for the "source of contamination" (the "polluter pay" principle) have always been included. Similarly, the present owners, occupiers or persons in management or control at the site where pollution is now a problem can be the subject of orders whether the problem was due to current or past practices. Recently, however, there have been legislative developments so that the order making powers may be extended to former owners, former occupiers and persons who were in charge, management or control. These have not yet been tested or judicially interpreted in the courts or environmental tribunals to clarify the retrospective effect or what degree of knowledge or control of the pollution problem may be necessary before liability can be established against persons formerly connected with the property. Accordingly, on any asset sale the vendor may be liable in the future for cleanup costs unless it can establish that the contamination problem was not there at the time that it owned and operated the property. In a share transaction, on the other hand, the environmental liabilities will stay with the corporation. To date in Canada, mere shareholders have not been held liable in this environmental area so that the present or former shareholders would not have to worry about being subject to regulatory orders.

Lenders, insurers, trustees and receivers are also very concerned about liability that they may incur for environmental matters and are now addressing the environmental issues as part of their due diligence before a loan is advanced or renewed or an account is taken on, and as part of the security realization process.

Officers and directors of a corporation may attract personal liability under a prosecution or by being the subject of a regulatory order to the extent that they are viewed as having personal responsibility for the matter. Ontario legislation also imposes "take all reasonable care" to prevent a corporation from causing or permitting unlawful discharges or non-compliance with the environmental and occupational health and safety legislation.[1]

---

1. See Environmental Protection Act, R.S.O. 1990, c. E.19, s. 194; Ontario Water Resources Act, R.S.O. 1990, c. O.40, s. 116 and Occupational Health and Safety Act, R.S.O. 1990, c. O.1, s. 32.

Approvals and Licences

9.362—Environmental legislation often requires certain approvals, permits, or licences with respect to the construction and/or operation of equipment or processes that may have adverse environmental effects. Examples of this include air discharges into the atmosphere, noise, water discharges and treatment plants, dealing with waste, underground storage tanks and PCB waste disposal or storage sites.[1] Municipalities also have by-laws regulating environmental issues, eg. sewer use restrictions; noise and public safety or nuisance matters; public health requirements etc. The transportation of dangerous goods is also regulated in an extensive and detailed way under provincial and federal legislation.[2]

---

1. Environmental Protection Act, R.S.O. 1990, c.E.19; Ontario Water Resources Act, R.S.O. 1990, c.O.40; General Waste Management Regulation, R.R.O. 1990, Reg. 347; Waste Management PCB's Regulation, R.R.O. 1990, Reg. 362; Gasoline Handling Act, R.S.O.

1990, c.G.4; Gasoline Handling Code, O. Reg. 52193, s. 17; Energy Act, R.S.O. 1990, c.E.16; Fuel Oil Code, R.R.O. 1990, Reg. 329.
2. Transportation of Dangerous Goods Act, 1992, S.C. 1992, c.34; Dangerous Goods Transportation Act, R.S.O. 1990, c.D.1.

Transfer of Certificates, Permits, etc.

9.363—The issue of whether any environmentally related licences, permits or certificates of approval are transferable is always of concern. Reference needs to be made first to the documents themselves, as they will often dictate this condition, and also to the legislation under which they were issued. In Ontario, certificates of approval are clearly binding on successors and assigns. The legislation does not make it clear that the certificates are transferable and a purchaser needs to apply to have a new certificate issued in its name. The Ministry will sometimes take the opportunity to review the conditions and may update them at any time.

With respect to PCB waste disposal and storage sites, a person offering to sell, lease or otherwise give permission must notify the prospective purchaser, tenant or person taking possession, of the existence of the site and the requirements in law concerning the site and the Director must be notified within ten days after the sale, lease or change of possession. Similarly with respect to waste generally, where there is a change in information submitted in a waste generator registration report, a supplementary generator registration report must be submitted to the Director within fifteen days after the change including a change of name, address and telephone number.

Due Diligence

9.364—Generally, in dealing with land transactions the principle of *caveat emptor, i.e.* "let the buyer beware", applies and a vendor has no common law obligation to disclose a patent defect concerning the physical attributes and conditions of real property. However, a vendor has a legal obligation to disclose any known latent defect (one that cannot be discovered on inspection by a reasonably careful purchaser) that renders the premises unfit for habitation, dangerous, or in certain circumstances, even where there is a likelihood of danger.

There may be specific statutory requirements, however, to disclose. In Ontario, there are not very many examples. PCB waste storage sites must be disclosed; and any prohibition from dealing with property in any way contained in an order or decision by the Ministry of Environment and Energy must be disclosed (in the latter case the dealing transaction may be voidable by the person who was not given a copy of an order or decision as required before acquiring an interest in the property).

However it is in the interests of both vendors and purchasers to obtain and provide as much information as possible concerning the environmental status of a property or business that is being sold. If the vendor can establish that environmental issues are not an issue the vendor's bargaining position is much stronger and a better price should result. Having evidence of the status of the business at the time of the sale will assist a vendor in any subsequent claims made by the purchaser or third parties, including the government, with respect to future responsibility and liability for cleanup.

Getting all appropriate information from a vendor is a very important first step. However many vendors may not know everything about their property and potential environmental problems. Obtaining information from public bodies may be of assistance but it must be kept in mind that records have not been kept for very long nor have proper procedures and practices been established to ensure that the information that is publicly available is as complete and accurate as it could be [**See Form 9F7:14** for an environmental form of search letter to be sent to the Ontario Ministry of Environment and Energy and the local municipality.]

Depending on the circumstances, inquiries can be made of a wide range of public sources e.g. land registry or titles offices; media searches; court records for any lawsuits in process; fire departments; medical officers of health; conservation authorities; building use records, building permits, property use directories and fire insurance maps and records; aerial photographs; topographic maps; geological maps; historical archives; inventories of wells, waste disposal sites; waste generator records; PCB waste disposal sites; coal gasification plants (or the like); underground and aboveground storage tanks; and any other specific concerns.

One of the most cost effective and efficient ways of specifically defining any environmental problems that exist or may arise is to have an independent "environmental audit" or "property transfer site assessment" conducted by qualified environmental consultants. General issues that need to be addressed by the parties to a transaction include (i) the selection of the consultant; scope of work—terms of reference; time periods involved; form of report to be delivered and to whom; standards or approaches to be used to determine if remedial work is required; whether or how recommendations are to be made if the review reveals environmental problems; contact to be made with the regulators; and maintaining confidentiality during the investigation process. Usually environmental investigations are done in stages or phases. A Phase I Environmental Site Assessment ("ESA") involves the evaluation and reporting of information collected through a review of records, a site visit and interviews but does not involve the investigative procedures of sampling, analyzing and measuring which constitute a Phase II ESA which are undertaken by specialized environmental professionals. A

Phase II ESA involving soil and groundwater sampling and analysis is usually needed to establish a quantitative baseline for environmental conditions at a property. A remedial investigation and work program is sometimes described as Phase III with Phase IV being work done to confirm that the remedial action was taken and was effective. The scope of work that is needed in any particular case needs to be examined carefully and set out in some detail. [**See Checklist 9C9** for a checklist of information that should be considered relating to environmental issues.]

It is important to be aware that environmental regulators and enforcers in Canada as part of their aggressive conduct, in some cases will attempt to obtain environmental audit information in order to be successful in a prosecution for noncompliance. The use of confidentiality provisions and the special protection of solicitor-client privilege is therefore important to ensure that the results of investigations are not disclosed at a time when all the facts have not been analyzed completely and action plans have not been fully developed or implemented. The client-solicitor relationship must be clearly documented in the first place and then care must be taken to ensure that the contractual arrangements with the environmental consultant contain appropriate confidentiality provisions and procedures so that the environmental investigation information can be properly used by counsel to provide appropriate legal advice and thereby keep the material privileged. [**See Form 9F34** for a sample clause in a contract proposal from an environmental consultant that may be appropriate in this regard.]

Contractual Arrangements

9.365—As indicated above, it is important that the parties enter into clear contractual arrangements to address the environmental issues. [**See Checklist 9C9:1** for a Checklist overview of many of the key environmental contractual provisions and their importance in agreements of purchase and sale, leases and the procedures and documentation now being used by lenders.]

Because of the complexity of the issues, elaborate definition clauses are often used to make the drafting simpler and the agreement easier to read and understand. Special attention must be taken, however, to ensure that the definitions themselves are clear and appropriate in the circumstances. Because of the nature of environmental issues it also is important to use materiality provisions and qualifications such as "to the knowledge of the vendor". The length of time during which representations and warranties can be relied on or a claim made under an indemnity is often an area of intense negotiation. Environmental liabilities or concerns may arise in the future and may not have been discovered even with a baseline audit being done. Purchasers therefore usually require a period of time of two years or more following the closing to make further environmental investigations and claims if needed once they have a better understanding of the business and property involved.

Although it is possible to do so, "as is, where is" terms are not usually acceptable to purchasers unless there is a substantial reduction of the purchase price or it is a sale by a trustee or receiver. [**See Form 9F35:1** for a brief clause describing an "as is, where is" transaction; even more detail is often added to it to clarify all the environmental liabilities the purchaser is acquiring.]

With respect to environmental representations and warranties, they are now being demanded regularly from vendors, landlords and borrowers as key information sources in connection with purchase, lease and lending transactions. The level of detail and the nature of the rights that can flow if they are not true depend upon each particular deal. [**See Form 9F35** for both a general clause and more specific detailed clauses for representations and warranties.]

Often it is advisable to put in a specific provision to deal with environmental access and testing and for provisions dealing with an environmental audit or site assessment and the cleanup or remedial action that will take place in the event that adverse environmental conditions are discovered. [**See Form 9F35** for sample clauses] Needless to say there is a wide range of deals that can be made with respect to how environmental matters will be addressed. It is beyond the scope of this publication to discuss these in detail or to provide more elaborate precedent material.

Indemnity clauses also need to be looked at carefully and drafted clearly to deal with the environmental aspects of the transaction. Again, indemnities are often very complicated, i.e. conditions precedent, exclusions, threshold of deductible claim amounts, maximum claim amounts, cost sharing arrangements, notification and settlement procedures.

In situations that are particularly environmentally sensitive, often the parties are newly incorporated, special purpose legal entities. Therefore, a number of financial security arrangements should be kept in mind to ensure that the contractual arrangements really will be significant in the event of default, *i.e.* extended payment terms, escrow arrangements, third party guarantees, letters of credit, performance bonds or insurance coverage.

As indicated at the beginning of this section the environmental area is an emerging and developing area where changes in the laws and practice are commonplace. It is therefore advisable to seek expert assistance to ensure that all matters are properly considered and dealt with in a transaction.

Licensing

9.380—Many manufacturers of goods and providers of services require operating licences or permits in order to conduct their affairs. Examples of such operations include nursing and retirement homes, agricultural quotas, food handling and processing, chemical compounding, dealings in medical devices containing radiation sources, medical laboratories, maintenance standards for elevators and other specialized equipment.

Such licences may be readily attained or may be strictly issued in a controlled market. It may be essential to effect a share transfer, as opposed to an asset acquisition, to ensure that the appropriate licence is available for the purchaser's need. However, great care should be taken before effecting a share transfer to check whether the licence contains a term that specified persons remain the majority shareholders. In certain circumstances, licences may be lost if there is a change of control from those shareholders in effect when a licence was issued.

Copies of all appropriate licences should be obtained from the vendor together with appropriate names and phone numbers of contact parties at various Ministries for other licensing authorities. This is required to effect due diligence; i.e., to determine both from statute and from dealing with the licensing authorities directly, the materials required to obtain such licensing and that the licences may be obtained within the requisite time frame.

Many licences are not transferable. This is obviously an important fact to determine when initiating due diligence so that necessary applications may be tendered by the purchaser to obtain its own licence in its own right, or, if the licence is transferable, to ensure that the requisite licensing   authority forms are completed to record a transfer of the licence to the purchaser.

Service Contracts

Assignability

9.390—The vendor should disclose a list of all service contracts used by the business. Copies of these contracts need to be obtained to ensure that the purchaser is fully informed of the existing obligations. Service con-tracts may cover a wide spectrum of matters such as snow removal, landscaping, garbage removal, hazardous waste handling, maintenance of machinery and office equipment, security services, alarm systems with monitoring stations, etc. These all need to be carefully reviewed with the purchaser to establish which provisions it is prepared to accept.

Again, it is necessary to ensure, as with leased personalty, that such contracts are assignable with or without the service provider's consent. Where such agreements are assignable, they should be properly conveyed in the Agreements of Purchase and Sale, and any additional documents needed by the third party service provider should be executed, so that the latter is content to record the assignment or the creation of a new contract with the purchaser on its books and records.

Software Licences and Maintenance

9.391—Many machines come with software imbedded in them or supplied separately on floppy disks. The vendor should be required to produce all software licences to ensure that it has the authority to properly use such software. To ensure that the purchaser has proper authority to assume software licences, assignments may be required.

In addition, some software will come with maintenance contracts providing that upon payment of certain fees, updates of software will be provided and/or assistance with "bugs" will be given. These maintenance agreements should be reviewed for desirability and the possibility of assignment to the purchaser.

Tax Arrears

Income Taxes—Federal and Provincial

9.400—It is very important that the purchaser of a business determine the extent of the vendor's existing liabilities for taxes and ensure that those tax liabilities of the business that arose prior to the completion of the transaction will remain with the vendor. Due diligence investigation for income tax purposes is very important, as is the negotiation and drafting of appropriate tax indemnity clauses to protect the purchaser. These issues are especially critical on a share sale, although they are also relevant to an asset sale. The nature of both the questions to be asked and the investigations to be carried out are set out below:

Share Sale Investigations

9.401—In the course of performing due diligence the purchaser's representative should determine:

(i)   whether the vendor is the object of a tax assessment or reassessment in respect of a prior fiscal year, and the status of such assessment or reassessment and the objections or appeals filed in connection with it;

(ii)   whether all income tax returns for prior years, both federal and provincial, together with any other required tax filings, have been completed and filed on a timely basis;

(iii)   whether notices of assessment or reassessment have been issued by the appropriate taxation authority in respect of the returns filed and tax elections made;

(iv)   whether waivers have been filed by the vendor corporation in respect of any taxation year, which waivers would enable the Canada Revenue Agency to reassess the vendor corporation after the expiry of the normal limitation period (and the specific subject matter of such waivers);

(v)   whether all taxes owing and required tax instalments have been paid to the appropriate taxation authority, i.e. the Canada Revenue Agency or the Ministry of Finance in Ontario;

(vi)   whether all amounts to be deducted by a payer at source have been so deducted and remitted to the appropriate taxation authority as required under the applicable tax legislation, including any requirements to deduct and remit Part XIII Non-Resident withholding tax, source deductions on payroll, or deductions for Canada Pension Plan and Employment Insurance; and

(vii)   whether any tax elections have been filed in connection with pre-acquisition transactions and the nature of those elections.

Such investigation would review not only income taxes owing and instalments against such income tax owing, but also would confirm that all capital taxes, any old federal sales tax imposed under the Excise Tax Act,[1] goods and services tax ("GST"), provincial sales tax ("PST"), and any other form of tax collected by any level of government, have been paid and all accounts are up-to-date. (Further details of PST and GST due diligence are summarized below). Copies of all relevant returns, filings, assessments, and reassessments should be obtained.

If there are losses in the vendor corporation which the purchaser intends to use, the nature of those losses should be reviewed and it should be determined when they arose, in order to confirm that they could be utilized following an acquisition of control.

Canada Revenue Agency does not have a formal search procedure that would enable a purchaser to independently verify that all tax liabilities have been paid by the vendor. It is recommended that a purchaser obtain a letter of confirmation from the Canada Revenue Agency that the vendor's taxes for prior years have been paid; that there are no outstanding notices of reassessment, and that tax instalments are current. It appears that it is easier to obtain such information from some District Taxation Offices than from others. A purchaser should not be alarmed if this information is not forthcoming, and should still proceed with the acquisition relying solely on the vendor's representations and warranties. Such a letter obtained from the Canada Revenue Agency should be viewed only as further information of the vendor's representations and warranties.

Precedents of appropriate representations, warranties, covenants, and indemnities to be obtained from the vendor by a purchaser when purchasing the shares of a corporation are contained in **Forms 9F32 and 9F78.**

---

1. R.S.C. 1985, c. E-15.

Sale of Assets

9.402—On an acquisition of assets, the purchaser has fewer concerns than with a share sale regarding the vendor's prior outstanding tax liabilities.

Notwithstanding, it is important to ensure that there are no claims that may be made against the vendor's assets by the Canada Revenue Agency or the Ministry of Finance for income taxes due. Appropriate representations and warranties should be obtained from the vendor in connection with the title which is transferred to the purchaser, being free from all interest, including any that the Canada Revenue Agency or any other tax authority may have, and an indemnity should be obtained to ensure that if the Canada Revenue Agency attempts to claim rights to such assets, the vendor may be sued for losses suffered by the purchaser.

Precedents of the appropriate representations, warranties, covenants and indemnities which should be obtained from the vendor by a purchaser purchasing assets of a corporation are contained in **Forms 9F32 and 9F78.**

Retail Sales Taxes

9.410—The liability for the collection of retail sales tax rests with a vendor of goods, who will have registered under the Retail Sales Tax Act (Ontario)[1] and obtained a vendor permit number.

---

1. R.S.O. 1990, c. R.31.

Share Sale

9.411—On a share sale, a purchaser should require the vendor to represent and warrant that all retail sales tax due and payable has been collected and remitted to the appropriate taxation authority. The vendor should indemnify the purchaser for any claims made by the Ministry of Revenue after the date of acquisition for taxes not collected and remitted prior to completion of the sale.

A purchaser could require the vendor to produce a Retail Sales Tax Act[1] clearance certificate issued under section 6 of the Retail Sales Tax Act (Ontario)[2] (for further detail see the discussion below).

---

1. R.S.O. 1990, c. R.31.
2. *Ibid.*, s. 6, am. 1994, c. 13, s. 8.

Asset Sale

9.412—Section 6 of the Retail Sales Tax Act (Ontario)[1] provides that no person shall dispose of its stock through a sale in bulk to which the Bulk Sales Act[2] applies, without first obtaining from the Minister a certificate in duplicate that all taxes collectable and payable by such person have been paid, or that a satisfactory arrangement has been entered into with the Minister for the payment of those taxes.

Subsection 6(2) of the Retail Sales Tax Act (Ontario)[3] provides that the purchaser must request a copy of the certificate on the closing of the transaction, as failure to obtain the certificate renders the purchaser liable for any retail sales taxes that are owing by the vendor. Appropriate review should be made to determine whether the Bulk Sales Act[4] applies to the transaction and if so, a certificate should be obtained from the Retail Sales Tax branch. Attached are the current addresses of local retail sales tax branch offices in Ontario to which such requests should be directed. Note that the Bulk Sales Act does not apply to a sale of shares.

---

1. R.S.O. 1990, c. R.31.
2. R.S.O. 1990, c. B.14.
3. *Supra*, note 1, s. 6(2), am. 1994, c. 13, s. 8.
4. *Supra*, note 2.

ADDRESSES FOR DISTRICT RETAIL SALES TAX OFFICES

General Inquiries: Ministry Information Centre, Ministry of Finance
33 King Street West
P.O. Box 627
OSHAWA L1H 8H5
Toll Free: 1-800-263-7965 (English); 1-800-668-5821 (French)
TTY: 1-800-263-7776
www.rev.gov.on.ca

Durham
Retail Sales Tax Field Office
1600 Champlain Avenue, 2nd Floor
WHITBY L1N 9B2
Tel: (905) 432-3332
Toll Free: (800) 668-5810
Fax: (905) 435-3535
Refunds: (905) 432-3431

Hamilton
District Tax Office
119 King Street West, 15th Floor
HAMILTON L8P 4Y7
Tel: (905) 521-7504
Toll Free: (800) 263-9229 (Ontario)
Fax: (905) 521-7868

Kitchener
District Tax Office
305 King Street West, 9th Floor
KITCHENER N2G 1B9
Tel: (519) 576-8400
Toll Free: (800) 265-2303 (Canada/US)
Fax: (519) 571-6100

London
Regional Tax Office
Dufferin Corporate Centre
130 Dufferin Avenue, Suite 400
LONDON N6A 6G8
Tel: (519) 433-3901
Toll Free: (800) 265-1540 (Canada/US)
Fax: (519) 661-6618

Mississauga Regional Tax Office
77 City Centre Drive
Suite 200
MISSISSAUGA L5B 1M5
Tel: (905) 273-9490
Toll Free: 1-800-265-9969
(Ontario and Quebec)
Fax: (905) 949-3389

Oshawa
Ministry of Finance
33 King Street West
OSHAWA L1H 8P5
Toll Free: 1-800-265-9005
Fax: (905) 436-4474

Ottawa
Regional Office
1400 Blain Place, Suite 300
GLOUCESTER K1J 9B8
Tel: (613) 746-9200
Toll Free: (800) 461-4909 (Ontario and Quebec)
Fax: (613) 842-3593

Sudbury
Sudbury Tax Office
199 Larch Street, Suite 102
SUDBURY P3E 5P9
Tel: (705) 564-6118
Fax: (705) 564-4499

Thunder Bay
130 South Syndicate Avenue
3rd Floor
THUNDER BAY P7E 1C7
Tel: (807) 625-5840
Toll Free: (800) 465-6699
Fax: (807) 625-5848

Toronto
North York Regional Tax Office
5 Park Home Avenue
Suite 200
NORTH YORK M2N 6W8
Tel: (416) 222-3226
Toll Free: (888) 565-6433 (Ontario)
Fax: (416) 218-3738

Windsor
District Tax Office
215 Eugenie Street West, Unit 103
WINDSOR N8X 2X7
Tel: (519) 250-0066
Toll Free: 1-800-465-4021
(Ontario and Quebec)
Fax: (519) 972-2950

GST

9.420—GST is imposed under the Excise Tax Act.[1] It is important in most transactions for both the purchaser and the vendor to be "registrants" for GST purposes and agreements should include a representation of each party to that effect.

The following concerns should be addressed depending on whether the acquisition is a sale of assets or shares:

---

1. R.S.C. 1985, c. E-15.

Sale of Shares

9.421—When buying shares of a corporation, the purchaser takes on all prior liabilities of the vendor. Thus, the purchaser must inquire and confirm that the vendor is a registrant and that in the past it has collected and remitted GST as required. It would be prudent to review the GST returns on which the GST collected and the input tax credits have claimed are summarized, together with supporting documents for these numbers. Also, the vendor should be required to disclose whether any elections have been filed or agreements entered into with the Canada Revenue Agency or the Canada Border Services Agency (in situations where the corporation is an importer of goods) in connection with the collection and remittance of GST. The purchaser should review prior input tax credit claims and require the vendor to provide the information and documents on which these input tax credit claims are based, to protect it from subsequent notices of assessment in connection with invalid input tax credit claims.

Finally, the vendor should be required to disclose any notices of assessment which have been received to date and those that remain outstanding. Copies of these should be obtained. Appropriate tax indemnity clauses should be included in the acquisition agreement to cover any tax owing which is subsequently claimed by the Canada Revenue Agency or the Canada Border Services Agency.

Sale of Assets

9.422—Under section 321 of the Excise Tax Act,[1] if the Canada Revenue Agency has issued a notice of assessment, it is authorized to order the seizure and sale of the registrant's assets within 30 days of issuing the notice of seizure and sale to the defaulting registrant. There is no formal mechanism available for a purchaser to determine whether such an assessment has been issued. Notwithstanding, a purchaser should attempt to confirm with the Canada Revenue Agency that the vendor is a registrant for GST purposes, and that it is not subject to any outstanding notices of assessment.

The vendor should provide representations and warranties to that effect as well. Precedent GST representation and warranties are contained in **Forms 9F32 and 9F78.**

---

1.   R.S.C. 1985, c. E-15 (en. 1990, c. 45, s. 12).

Employer Health Taxes
9.430—See **[Para. 9.330]** for discussion of due diligence review of employer requirements to remit on account of Employer Health Tax.[1]

---

1.   R.S.O. 1990, c. E.11.

Litigation
9.440—The vendor should be required to disclose on a Schedule to the Agreement of Purchase and Sale all outstanding litigation and claims actual and pending against it. In addition, searches may be done against the vendor's name in each of the counties or judicial districts in which it maintains locations, to determine if any of the court records reveal that an action or matter has been commenced.

Outstanding litigation for a large claim may necessitate an asset acquisition be effected (assuming there can be compliance with the Bulk Sales Act), to avoid buying the shares of a company subject to such contingent liability. Be concerned with fraudulent preferences and conveyances in such event. In particular, the existence of, or lack of, such litigation and claims may disclose the standard of care exercised by the vendor in the provision of its goods or services. This in turn, informs the purchaser of difficulties it may have in obtaining cost effective insurance coverage and any requirements it may have to make to revamp systems or product design in order to avoid further claims.

If a share transaction is being completed while litigation is outstanding, care should be taken to ensure that insurance coverage is in place that will protect the company. A purchaser will need to know that if such coverage is called upon, future premiums may become expensive and detract from the overall profitability of the transaction. When insurance is not affordable, the consequences of self-insurance need to be understood by the client.

Inventories and Receivables

9.450—On or before closing, representatives of the vendor and purchaser may wish to attend at the vendor's premises to evaluate inventories as part of determining the outstanding purchase price owing. Time to conduct such an evaluation should be worked into the closing schedule, and mechanisms should be created to arrive at a price calculation formula. In addition, the vendor and purchaser may wish jointly to review the vendor's records regarding receivables outstanding, with decisions being made as to the value of receivables aged less than 90 days and over 90 days, and as between the parties, who may be prepared to effect collection of the doubtful accounts.

As part of determining the value of the inventories and receivables the following issues might be addressed:

— outstanding orders;

— pre-paid orders;

— security deposits;

— monies held in trust;

— notification to account customers to now pay the purchaser;

— accounting for sales made between a closing date and an effective period;

— accounting for receivables received after the effective date but attributable to sales made before the effective date;

— liability for products made by the vendor and sold by the purchaser after closing;

— returns to suppliers of out-of-date products for credit; and

— identifying goods held in bailment for customers for storage or services to be performed.

Equipment

9.460—Presumably the purchaser will attend at the vendor's premises to review all equipment to ensure that it is of a standard and in such workable condition as is acceptable. The vendor should be required to produce all records relevant to such equipment including the following:

— acquisition agreements;

— service and maintenance manuals;

— operating manuals;

— drawings and specifications;

— software licences and software maintenance agreements;

— servicing and maintenance agreements;

— conditional sale agreements, leases, or other equipment financing arrangements that might be assumed by the purchaser;

— operating licences that may be transferable;

— supply arrangements to provide goods that are used up in the operation of the machines; and

— parts and supplies, inventories and sources of the same.

The vendor will need to produce a detailed listing, to be included as a schedule to the Agreement of Purchase and Sale, describing as many of the items of equipment as possible, including vehicle identification numbers, manufacture serial numbers, or other identifying marks.

A quick source of a listing for many of these items is the last inventory done for the company or for insurance coverage. The parties may agree that to avoid undue paperwork, items under a certain dollar value will not be included on the list while significant and expensive items should be listed and specifically conveyed.

4. DOCUMENTING THE ASSET DEAL

The Agreement of Purchase and Sale

9.470—Once having gathered together lists of all the documents recorded and effected due diligence, it is time to create the agreement of purchase and sale accurately to reflect the business deal between the parties and to record the particular circumstances of that transaction. [**See Checklist 9C10, Forms 9F32–9F33 and 9F38–9F39**]

Representations, Warranties and Covenants

9.480—The essence of the agreement of purchase and sale is an accurate reflection of the assets being purchased, the assets being excluded, and the specific representations, warranties, and covenants upon which the vendor and the purchaser are relying in entering into this transaction. The law concerning representations, warranties, and covenants is not reiterated here but if in doubt, regard should be had to the textbooks concerning contractual law.

In going through the "boilerplate" found in most agreements of purchase and sale, there will be many standard representations, warranties, and covenants for both parties. However, care must be exercised to supplement these boilerplate representations and warranties, with statements designed to cover the specific facts of each client's situation. Care must also be taken to determine whether any of the representations and warranties should survive closing.

In addition, if certain representations, warranties, and covenants are fundamental to one of the parties, it may be essential to not only have such provisions survive closing, but to provide indemnities or means of compensation in the event of a breach or where such statement was made recklessly or misleadingly. Security for any breach may also be obtained through mortgages or charges on realty or personalty and by way of standby letters of credit or banker's guarantees. For example, if the vendor is to warrant that a production line is capable of producing a set number of units per hour, and profitability of the operation depends upon such minimum production quota, it may be essential to the purchaser to have recourse to the vendor for breach of such representation and warranty, both by having the same survive closing and by providing means of recompense (an abatement of the purchase price or recovery under a standby letter of credit to offset the purchaser's losses).

Non-Competition Clauses

9.490—There is considerable case-law concerning the ability of parties to contract for non-competition with one another. Usually the purchaser requires the vendor to covenant that it will not compete in the same kind of business operation, either directly or indirectly, in any other corporation, partnership, or arrangement, for a certain period of time and/or in a certain geographic area following closing of the transaction.

Courts have been reluctant to uphold agreements that deny a party from earning a livelihood. However, carefully considered competition clauses may be a fundamental part of the transaction to ensure that the purchaser has the opportunity of establishing itself. [**See Form 9F74**]

Conveyancing Documents for Assets
Land

OWNED

9.500—Each closing to convey title to freehold property requires preparation of the documentation to satisfy the individual requisitions against title to that property, in terms required either by the Registry system or the Land Titles system in Ontario.

LEASED REALTY

9.501—In addition to such matters as may be required to satisfy requisitions against title, insurance, keys, and other practical concerns regarding the purchaser's access to leased premises, it may be necessary to prepare any of the following documents to record a conveyance of a leasehold interest in favour of the purchaser:

Personalty

9.510—The vendor will likely be required to provide a bill of sale or a general conveyance to record a transfer of personalty in favour of the purchaser. While a bill of sale does not require registration in Ontario, since the October 10, 1989 repeal of the Bill of Sales Act it may be necessary to file the bill of sale in requisite form in other jurisdictions in which the vendor has assets. Such form and content should be checked with local counsel. In addition to the general conveyance or bill of sale, the purchaser may require specific documents separately to convey various items such as assignments of leased equipment, so that a specific lessor may join in consenting to such a transaction. [**See Forms 9F46–9F50**]

It will also be necessary to ensure that any encumbrances recorded against such personalty have been dealt with, by either having discharged or obtaining the warranty of the vendor that none of the search results affected the personalty conveyed, with or without additional security to support and indemnify the purchaser for such warranty.

Intellectual Property and Goodwill

9.520—These assets will probably be conveyed to the purchaser in a general conveyance. However, it may be necessary to prepare additional documentation to record with federal departments assignments of trademarks, patents, industrial designs, and registered user agreements. These forms need to be checked with the government of the country in which such registrations are being made to ensure that they are in the requisite form for conveyancing.

Separately, additional "goodwill" may be conveyed by causing the vendor to change its corporate name or de-list its business styles and thereby permit the purchaser to assume the same. Such documents need to be in appropriate form for the jurisdiction in which they were registered. [**See Forms 9F51–9F53 and Checklist 9C7**]

Employee Benefits and Agreements

9.530—The transfer of any specific service agreement of a particular employee should be consented to by that employee in writing. New employment agreements may need to be created with specific persons assuming unique positions with the purchaser. If any employee benefit plans, such as drug plans and long-term disability insurance coverage, are being transferred to the purchaser, the issuer and/or the regulatory authorities with which the plan is registered may require a record of the plan transfer from vendor to purchaser. This is accomplished by using the particular forms supplied by the provider of such policies and coverages.

Separately, new documentation may need to be filed with such parties to create plans for the purchaser.

Additional documentation will be required to assume existing pension plans or covenants may be needed to compel the purchaser to establish a new pension plan where the purchaser is not assuming the vendor's plan. [**See Paras. 9.340–9.349 and Forms 9F54–9F57**]

Motor Vehicles

9.540—This section addresses the issues that will arise with respect to transferring motor vehicles in connection with the purchase and sale of a business. Obviously, these issues will arise only in the context of an asset purchase and sale. It will be necessary to obtain a conveyance, usually a bill of sale, with respect to motor vehicles owned by the vendor that form part of the assets being purchased. The so-called "ownership" cards issued by the Ministry of Transportation in Ontario are, in fact, not title documents. Therefore, the endorsement for transfer of those cards, while necessary, is not sufficient to transfer the vendor's interest in the vehicles.

Permits

9.541—Section 7 of the *Highway Traffic Act*[1] (the "HTA") prohibits any person from driving a motor vehicle or drawing a trailer on a highway unless there exists a currently validated permit (the so-called "ownership") for the motor vehicle or trailer. Section 10 of the HTA[2] requires a person who becomes an owner of a used motor vehicle or trailer for which a permit has been issued, to apply to the Ministry of Transportation for a new permit within six days of becoming the owner. Therefore, having obtained a bill of sale, it is also necessary for the purchaser to address the requirements of the Ministry of Transportation with respect to permit transfers.

---

1. R.S.O. 1990, c. H.8, s. 7 (re-en. 1992, c. 20, s. 2; am. 1993, c. 31, s. 2).
2. R.S.O. 1990, c. H.8, s. 10.

Safety Inspection Certificates

MOTOR VEHICLES

9.542—In order to transfer the permit for motor vehicle, subsection 2(1) of the Regulations[1] passed pursuant to the HTA require the original permit together with a valid safety standards certificate to be presented to the Ministry of Transportation Licensing Assistance Section. The safety standards certificate must be with respect to an inspection of the vehicle that was conducted within the 36 days preceding the presentation of the transfer documentation. It is possible to transfer a permit without presenting a safety standards certificate. However, pursuant to subsection 2(3) of the Regulation[2] the permit issued on the transfer will be marked "unfit motor vehicle". Pursuant to section 7 of the HTA, an unfit motor vehicle may not be operated on a highway.

TRAILERS

There is no requirement that a safety standards certificate be submitted in connection with the transfer of a trailer permit. In a transaction in which a large number of motor vehicles or trailers are being transferred, the co-ordination of the safety standards certificates and permits by the vendor and purchaser, and the presentation to and processing of those documents by the Ministry will be very cumbersome. It may be impossible to complete the permit transfers and distribute the new permits to the vehicles within the six day period. In those circumstances the Ministry of Transportation may well be prepared to provide some administrative relief. For example, the Ministry may issue a bulletin to enforcement officers and police allowing the purchaser a longer period to comply with the transfer requirements. The officials in the Licensing Assistance Section of the Ministry are highly competent and very conversant with the logistical problems involved in the transfer of a large number of vehicles. A purchaser should anticipate these problems and approach the Ministry well before closing to make the appropriate arrangements. A great deal of labour goes into large volume transfers at the Ministry's end and its officials appreciate advance warning enabling them to make the appropriate internal arrangements.

---

1. R.R.O. 1990, Reg. 628.
2. Ibid.

Plates

9.543—Section 7 of the Highway Traffic Act[1] prohibits any person from driving a motor vehicle or drawing a trailer on a highway unless displayed on the motor vehicle or trailer, in the prescribed manner, is a number plate, showing the number of the permit issued for the motor vehicle or trailer. Plates are generally not transferred when a vehicle is transferred; they are personal to the owner of a vehicle. Therefore, in the normal course the vendor will remove the plates and the purchaser will have to obtain new plates for the subject motor vehicles and trailers. The Ministry may make special arrangements and allow plates to be transferred to a purchaser in a transaction in which a large number of vehicles are being transferred. Again, it is important that the purchaser directly contact the Officials at the Ministry as early as possible.

---

1. R.S.O. 1990, c. H.8, s. 7 (re-en. 1992, c. 20, s. 2; am. 1993, c. 31, s. 2).

Operating Authorities

9.544—Operating authorities are the licences administered by federal, provincial or municipal regulatory agencies granting the authority to an over-the-road transporter of goods or people to engage in the transportation activity. A copy of the operating authority must be carried in the motor vehicle that is operating under the licence granted in the operating authority. These operating authorities are issued to the person or corporation and are generally non-transferrable. The name of the holder of the operating authority must conform to the name of the owner or lessee of the motor vehicle. Therefore, a purchaser of a transportation undertaking must obtain an appropriate new operating authority prior to completing the transaction. This applies both to share and asset purchases since most of the governing statutes contain provisions that deem a change of control of a corporation holding an operating authority to be a transfer of the operating authority. A motor vehicle that is operating without the required operating authority may be pulled off the road and impounded. The owner of the vehicle so operating may also be charged. [**See Para. 9.203**]

Receivables

9.550—In order to record an assignment of receivables, in addition to a transfer of the same pursuant to either general conveyance or a specific assignment, additional documents will be needed to satisfy further statutory requirements.

A direction to the account debtor of the vendor will be required to ensure that the account debtor has the obligation to pay the purchaser. A written direction to such effect is required pursuant to subsection 53(1) of the Conveyancing and Law of Property Act.[1] Such notice is usually sent by the vendor, or the vendor in conjunction with the purchaser, as part of a general notice of the sale of a business conveying some positive information about the purchaser's abilities to continue to serve the customers and to ensure smooth supply to them. In addition, the Personal Property Security Act[2] applies to absolute assignments of accounts and chattel paper necessitating the filing of a Form 1C financing statement. The PPSA registration will be made showing the vendor as debtor and the purchaser as secured party and should be registered for a sufficient time period to allow the purchaser to collect the subject accounts or chattel paper. [**See Forms 9F58 and 9F59**]

---

1. R.S.O. 1990, c. C.43.
2. R.S.O. 1990, c. P.10.

Bulk Sales Act Compliance and Exemption Orders

9.560—It is incumbent upon the purchaser of assets to comply with the Bulk Sales Act,[1] or risk the creditors of the vendor either moving to set the sale aside or seeking further payment from the purchaser for the value of the stock in bulk acquired. An application may be brought pursuant to section 3 of the Bulk Sales Act[2] seeking an exemption order where the vendor is creditworthy and can satisfy a court that it has assets remaining after the sale sufficient to satisfy its creditors [**See Form 9F62**]: and the form of disclosure affidavit to be sworn by the vendor pursuant to section 4 of the Act[3] and to be attached to the affidavit of the purchaser to be filed in the Courts of Justice (General Division) in the judicial district in which the assets are located, within 5 days of the closing of the sale. [**See Para. 9.074 and Forms 9F60 and 9F61**]

With respect to the section 3 exemption order, it was formerly the case that the motion was brought before a County Court judge in the county where the assets were located. After the merger of the courts, the County Courts no longer exist. The vendor's counsel can bring the application, therefore, before any judge of the Ontario Court (General Division). The only restriction on the location return of the motion is that if it is proposed to serve any parties in the motion (*e.g.* if it is known that one particular creditor will be objecting), it may be necessary to make the motion returnable at the place where the objecting creditor's solicitor practises law. However, in virtually all cases, the vendor's counsel can simply set the matter down where he or she chooses.

Under the practice direction governing the Commercial Court, Bulk Sales Act applications are not specifically directed to be heard in the Commercial Court. However, in a sufficiently complex case, it may be appropriate to bring an application in the Commercial Court. This is particularly the case if there is ongoing litigation involving the company in the Commercial Court and it is therefore appropriate to have the judge who is seized with that litigation also hear the Bulk Sales Act claim.

---

1. R.S.O. 1990, c. B.14.
2. Ibid.
3. Supra, note 1.

9.561—In many instances, there is difficulty with respect to financial disclosure. For instance, the vendor securing the order may not want to file its financial statements in a public manner and leave may be sought of the Court to file affidavits in a confidential manner and to have those affidavits sealed under section 147 of the Courts of Justice Act.[1] Notwithstanding the fact that the jurisprudence under section 147 holds that a court is only to seal the record in the clearest of cases, where there is a probability of harm if the order is not granted, the practice on Bulk Sales Act[2] applications is usually to allow the sealing of financial statements. This may be the case because the application is usually heard without notice.

The Act provides that a judge has jurisdiction to grant an exemption order if the judge is satisfied that the "sale is advantageous to the seller and will not impair the seller's ability to pay creditors in full". The Act is only directed at the seller's abilities to pay creditors in full. It would follow that as a matter of statutory interpretation, any arrangement whereby the purchaser agrees to pay trade creditors is not particularly relevant. Notwithstanding this, it is common practice to point out to the Court in the affidavit material and in submissions that an arrangement is in place if, in fact, the sale agreements so provide. Counsel then attempts to convince the judge that trade creditors are doubly protected; they are protected as they have a claim against the seller and they are also protected in that the purchaser has agreed to assume the vendor's liability to the trade creditors. As a legal matter, as there is no contractual privity between the purchaser and the trade creditors, the trade creditors cannot sue a purchaser directly should the purchaser fail to live up to its assumption obligations to the vendor. However, such assumptions and indemnities do give a measure of business protection even if the legal protection is substantially less than ironclad.

It appears to be somewhat more difficult now to receive a Bulk Sales Act exemption order than it was a few years ago. This is probably because judges are more sensitive to insolvency questions generally and are not likely to take at face value the assertions in an affidavit that everything is going to be paid. There may, therefore, be a greater tendency for the Court to require that notice be given to particular trade creditors or to impose terms under subsection 3(2) with respect to the dispositions of proceeds for sale.[3] For instance, a judge may be reluctant to simply allow the seller to receive a large amount of cash. He or she might order instead that a certain amount of cash has to be held in trust to protect all or particular trade creditors. [**See Para. 9.074 and Forms 9F63 and 9F64**]

---

1. R.S.O. 1990, c. C.43.
2. R.S.O. 1990, c. B.14.
3. Ibid.

Additional Documents

Closing Agendas

9.570—A closing agenda is a programme for the financing transaction. It lists the time, place, parties involved, documents to be delivered and by whom, and how many copies of each, and what events are to occur. The first draft of the closing agenda can be prepared from a review of the first draft of the loan agreement or commitment letter.

A closing agenda has a variety of purposes. Some of these are as follows:

COMMUNICATION TOOL

The agenda functions as a communications tool for all parties. It tells the members inside the office who are preparing the agenda what documents and events must be prepared and organized within the firm. It tells the parties receiving the agenda what items are expected of them by the other side.

ORGANIZATION TOOL

A.   The agenda may serve as an index to the closing file, with the numbers on the file or on dividers corresponding to the numbers on the agenda. As a result, locating a document is easily done by locating the document on the closing agenda and reaching for the same numbered file folder.

B.   A copy of the closing agenda serves as a note page during the course of preparing for closing. As documents are completed, check them off on the agenda and place them in the closing file for storage. A look at the working copy of the agenda indicates which matters are completed and what work is left to be done.

C.   At closing, the agenda can also function as a checklist, with each document being checked off as it is received, so that at the end of the session, it is evident which documents were received, waived, or must be obtained after closing.

D.   After closing, the closing agenda may constitute the basis of the index to the closing book.

The agenda finally used will be a blend of the earlier drafts, reflecting the negotiated documents both sides have agreed to provide or accept.

The closing agenda will go through a series of drafts reflecting the transaction as it evolves. Frequently, the final draft taken into the closing, does not reflect the transaction as completed, as changes take place during the closing itself. The annotated agenda from closing becomes the closing book index and the source of the post-closing outstanding matters to be completed. [See Form 9F65]

Corporate Records

9.571—If an asset sale constitutes a sale of substantially all of the assets of the corporation, a "special resolution" may be required to be passed by shareholders of the corporation, in accordance with subsection 184(3) of the Ontario Business Corporations Act[1] or subsection 189(3) of the Canada

Business Corporations Act,[2] as such "special resolution" is defined in those statutes. In addition, it should be ascertained if there are any unanimous shareholder agreements that require any sale of assets of the corporation to be approved by the shareholders in order to satisfy such an agreement. **[See Form 9F66 and Forms 9F67–9F76 generally]**

---

1. R.S.O. 1990, c. B.16.
2. R.S.C. 1985, c. C-44.

Registrations and Filings
Realty

9.580—Registration in this context refers to registration under the Registry Act[1] or the Land Titles Act[2] as amended. The topic is briefly reviewed in light of the considerations that may be encountered in a transaction involving the sale of a business.

---

1. R.S.O. 1990, c. R.20.
2. R.S.O. 1990, c. L.5., am. 1991, c. 9, s.2.

General

9.581—Under the Registry Act,[1] there are two main reasons for registration: (a) to give notice of your interest to third parties; and (b) to establish priorities. Under the Land Titles Act,[2] registration is necessary in order to transfer ownership[3] and to create a valid charge.[4]

With respect to leasehold interests, section 44(1)4 of the Land Titles Act[5] provides that all land registered under the land titles system is subject to "[a]ny lease or agreement for a lease, for a period yet to run that does not exceed three years, where there is actual occupation under it." With respect to the registry system, section 70(2) of the Registry Act[6] provides that the protection under section 70(1) "does not extend to a lease for a term not exceeding seven years where the actual possession goes along with the lease, but it (the protection under section 70(1)) does extend to every lease for a longer term than seven years". As a general rule, if it is practical to do so, leases with terms longer than those referred to should be registered.

---

1. R.S.O. 1990, c. R.20.
2. R.S.O. 1990, c. L.5, am. 1991, c. 9, s. 2.
3. See *ibid.*, s. 86(2).
4. See *ibid.*, s. 93(3).

5. *Ibid.*, s. 2.
6. *Supra*, note 1.

Time for Registration

9.582—Ideally registration should take place at the time the transaction is completed and funds are released or advanced. This is not always possible. So long as documents are executed and acceptable for registration, they can be registered before closing. In that case, a subsearch of title and executions (as a bare minimum) should be completed at the time closing actually occurs to ensure that there were no intervening registrations that may claim priority over the funds being advanced. In those circumstances, it would be advisable to have a written undertaking from the part for whose benefit such registrations are made to release, discharge or quit claim such registrations in the event the transaction does not proceed for whatever reason.

Documents for Registration

FREEHOLD LANDS

9.583—Transfers: A conveyance of freehold land is completed by the completion and registration of the prescribed Form 1 entitled Transfer/Deed of Land. The same form is used whether the property is registered under the registry system or the land titles system or both. In order to register, the affidavit of residence and of value of the consideration must be completed and attached to the document together with the applicable land transfer tax (if any is payable) and registration fees.

Charges: Again, the form of mortgage is prescribed in this instance as Form 2, Charge/Mortgage of Land, which applies whether or not the land is registered under the registry system or the land titles system or both.

LEASEHOLD LANDS

9.584—Notice of Lease: Under the registry system, notice of the lease is effected by way of a notice under subsection 22(7) of the Registry Act.[1] This form of notice does not constitute notice of the entire lease but only of certain prescribed parts of the lease. It is important to include in the notice any provisions that may affect third parties such as restrictive covenants, renewal options, options to purchase, rights with respect to adjoining lands, etc. With respect to lands under the land titles system, until recently it was a requirement under subsection 111(1) of the Land Titles Act[2] that the entire lease be registered. In view of the fact that part of the lease document may contain sensitive business terms, it was the practice in many cases for the landlord and tenant to execute a short form of lease agreement that sets out all the important terms of which third parties should have notice, and that the document was registered rather than the entire lease. Effective December 18, 1998, it is acceptable to register a notice setting out particulars similar to those required under the Registry Act.

Leasehold Charge: The charge or mortgage of leasehold can be effected in two ways under both the registry and land titles systems.

Registry System

(a) A notice of mortgage of lease under subsection 22(7) of the Registry Act,[3] OR

(b) A Charge/Mortgage of Land (Form 2) so long as box (7) is amended to provide for a charge of leasehold rather than fee simple. In this case it is also important to determine which standard charge terms (if any) would be applicable to the leasehold mortgage. If such a form is not available, it is appropriate to attach one's own form of leasehold mortgage. The advantage to using the Form 2 Charge/Mortgage of Land is that the chargee would have the benefit of the implied covenants under the Land Registration Reform Act.[4]

Land Titles System

(a) The notice of an interest in a lease under subsection 111(6) of the Land Titles Act[5] may be registered and an executed copy of the mortgage or charge of lease must be attached, OR

(b) As in the registry system, a Charge/Mortgage of Land with the appropriate amendment to box (7) may be registered *provided that* an application for leasehold parcel under subsection 38(6) of the Land Titles Act[6] has been made and registered by the tenant.

---

1. R.S.O. 1990, c. R.20, am. 1994, c. 27, s. 99, 1998 c. 18, Sch. E.
2. R.S.O. 1990, c. L.5, am. 1991, c. 9, s. 2, 1998, c. 18, Sch. E.
3. *Supra*, note 1.
4. R.S.O. 1990, c. L.4, am. 1994, c. 27, s. 94, 1998, c. 18, Sch. E.
5. *Supra*, note 2.
6. *Supra*, note 2.

Electronic Registration

9.585—The implementation of electronic registration has already begun in many of the land registry offices. The Land Registration Reform Act[1] was amended in 1994 to allow for electronic registration of documents and the passing of regulations in connection therewith. By way of general observation, compliance of law statements made by solicitors will replace many of the affidavits, certificates and other supporting evidence that were previously registered. This does not mean that such affidavits, certificates, or other supporting evidence are no longer required as part of a transaction. Solicitors must continue to ensure that all required affidavits, certificates and other supporting documentary evidence are completed prior to making any compliance with law statements. Thereafter, it is important to retain all such documents in the event any compliance with law statements are questioned or challenged. Please note that electronic regulation only applies to lands registered under the Land Titles Act.[2] Ontario Regulation 19/99[3] made under the Land Registration Reform Act sets out the general and specific requirements for electronic registration.

---

1. R.S.O. 1990, c. L.4; am. S.O. 1994, c. 27; S.O. 1998, c, 18.
2. R.S.O. 1990, c. L.5.
3. O. Reg. 19/99

Personalty

9.590—Following closing of the transaction any of the following personal property registrations may be necessary to record the conveyance in favour of the purchaser:

Accounts Receivable and Chattel Paper

9.591—Section 2 of the Ontario Personal Property Security Act[1] provides that an absolute assignment of accounts and chattel paper constitutes a security interest. Hence, the Act applies to the assignment and registration is necessary. A Form 1C financing statement should be filed to record an absolute assignment of either of these classes of collateral, naming the vendor as debtor and the purchaser as secured party on the form. The registration should be effected for a period of time longer than is necessary to have collected the accounts or enforced the chattel paper.

Note subsection 4(1)(g) of the PPSA[2] provides that an assignment of chattel paper or accounts that is part of a sale in bulk is excluded from application of the PPSA. However, if a section 3 Bulk Sales exemption order was obtained, a catch-22 comes into play. The exemption order will deem the Bulk Sales Act[3] not to have applied to the transaction. Consequently the PPSA will apply, making registration of the financing statement again necessary properly to record the assignment to the purchaser. [**See Form 9F62**]

---

1. R.S.O. 1990, c. P.10.

2. *Ibid.*
3. R.S.O. 1990, B.14.

Intellectual Property

9.592—All absolute assignments and licences of intellectual property should be recorded in the appropriate registration office in Canada and in other countries, where registered by the vendor, to record the client's interest in the same.

Bills of Sale

9.593—On October 10, 1989, Ontario repealed its Bills of Sale Act.[1] Consequently, there is nowhere in Ontario to record a bill of sale. However, if any of the chattels included in the transaction are located in other jurisdictions, it may be necessary to complete and record a bill of sale in the appropriate form and in the appropriate time periods to comply with the legislation of that jurisdiction. [**See Form 9F46**]

Note that all affidavits for registration outside the province of Ontario need to be sworn before a notary public and not before a commissioner.

---

1. R.S.O. 1980, c. 43, repealed 1989, c. 16, s. 84(1).

Motor Vehicles

9.594—The provincial motor vehicle ownership papers will need to be completed by the vendor and filed by the purchaser with the Ontario Ministry of Transportation and Communications, together with transfers or surrenders of necessary vehicle plates as agreed to by the parties. [**See Para. 9.203**]

Other Assets

9.595—If some of the personal property of the vendor includes such matters as fixtures, ships or rolling stock, review the appropriate sections of the governing legislation to ensure that the requisite fixtures notice is filed against title to the land in the appropriate time periods as required in the Personal Property Security Act,[1] and Bills of Sale are filed as necessary under the Canada Shipping Act[2] at the port of registry. [**See Paras. 9.200–9.204**]

---

1. R.S.O. 1990, c. P.10.
2. R.S.C. 1985, c. S-9.

Income Taxes and GST

Income Tax

Form T2022—Election on Sale of Accounts Receivable

9.600—The Income Tax Act[1] does not contain a specific deadline for the filing of this form. Generally it should be filed with the tax returns filed by each of the purchaser and the vendor for the year in which the transaction occurred.

Form T2057—Election on Disposition of Property by a Taxpayer to a Taxable Canadian Corporation

If the transaction involves a section 85 transfer of assets,[2] the Form T2057 must be filed on or before the earlier of:

— the day the vendor must file its return for the year in which the transaction occurred, and

— the day the purchaser must file its tax return for the year in which the transaction occurred.

Section 116 Withholding

— If a non-resident vendor does not provide a section 116[3] certificate at closing, evidencing payment of the tax owing or posting of security therefor, a purchaser is required to withhold either 50 per cent or 25 per cent of the purchase price, depending on the nature of the property sold. If the certificate is not produced on or before the 30th day following the month in which the transaction was completed, the purchaser must remit the amount withheld to the Canada Revenue Agency. [**See Para. 9.068**]

GST

Form GST-44

— If the transaction involves a sale of all or substantially all of the assets of the business, the vendor and purchaser, except where the vendor is a registrant and the purchaser is not a registrant, can agree to execute a joint election which avoids the requirement to pay GST and claim a corresponding input tax credit. Where the purchaser is a registrant, the Form GST-44 must be filed with the purchaser's return for the period in which the transaction was completed. Until the purchaser files the election, the vendor remains responsible and liable for collecting and remitting GST on the transaction. The vendor should obtain adequate assurance from the purchaser concerning the timely filing of the election in order to protect the vendor from liability. Where the vendor and purchaser are both non-residents, the parties should keep a copy of the election with their records, but it does not need to be filed with the Canada Revenue Agency. [**See Paras. 9.420–9.422**]

---

1. R.S.C. 1985, c. 1 (5th Supp.).
2. *Ibid.*; am. 1993, c. 24, s. 35.
3. *Supra*, note 1.

Corporate Filings

9.610—If, as part of the transaction, the vendor has agreed to record a change of its name so that the purchaser may adopt the same, it will be necessary to ensure that the vendor follows through by filing its articles of amendment to record a change of its name to a name other than that sold to the purchaser, and that the purchaser files the requisite articles of amendment to adopt the purchased name from the vendor's business. In addition, the same is true for partnership or business style filings to be de-registered by the vendor and registered by the purchaser, so that the purchaser may continue to use the goodwill generated from that name. It may be advisable to send a letter to the telephone company providing it with the vendor's consent to the purchaser assuming the listing and numbers from the vendor's name.

5. DOCUMENTING THE SHARE DEAL

The Agreement of Purchase and Sale

9.620—Most of the comments made with regard to documenting the asset deal are true with respect to share transactions. Having organized the documents, reviewed all the minute books, and effected all due diligence, it is time to create the agreement of purchase and sale to record the transfer of the shares. The same comments with regard to representations, warranties and covenants and non-competition found in Part 4 for the asset deal hold true for the share transaction as well. [**See Forms 9F77–9F105 and Checklist 9C11**]

Section 116 Withholding

9.620.1—If a non-resident sells shares of a Canadian corporation, section 116 withholding tax will be required. If the non-resident does not provide a section 116 certificate at closing, evidencing payment of the tax owing or posting of security therefor, a purchaser is required to withhold 25 per cent of the purchase price. If the certificate is not produced on or be-fore the 30th day following the month in which the transaction was completed, the purchaser must remit the amount withheld to the Canada Revenue Agency. [See Para. 9.068]

6. THE SPECIAL VENDOR

Estates

General

9.621—The sale of a business from an estate poses unique issues and problems for the individual responsible for administering the estate and for those purchasing from an estate. This section is intended to assist the executor or estate representative in his or her duties in selling an active business from an estate. Suggestions will also be made as to how to prepare for the sale from the vendor's and purchaser's perspective, and examples of forms are provided that deal with issues particular to an estate sale transaction.

This section focuses on the sale of a family owned business to an arms-length purchaser. The deceased will either have wholly owned the business or will have been a controlling shareholder. The issues of estate taxation and valuating the business are not covered.

An estate representative is in a difficult position as he or she must expeditiously decide whether to provide for the continuation, sale, or liquidation of the business. At the same time, the representative must not only protect the estate, but in order to avoid personal liability, must also fulfil his or her fiduciary responsibilities. Consequently, it is critical to learn as much about the business as quickly as possible in order to make an accurate assessment of the appropriate course of action.

The Vendor's Perspective—the Information Gathering Process

9.622—The following steps should be taken to ensure the representative gains the maximum knowledge to satisfy his or her duties in administering the business:

> Review the Will—The executor must be aware of his or her powers and limitations to deal with the business provided for in the will. Such powers and directions will form the parameters within which the executor may act. For example, the executor must consider whether there are powers or directions to sell or convert the shares, powers to retain or postpone conversion, powers to renew or

extend guarantees, directions to employ or sell to specific people, or directions to maintain the business as an asset of the estate.

What If There is No Will?—If the individual died without a will, the estate representative must apply for letters of administration. The executor cannot take action on behalf of the estate until he or she receives the grant.

Review the Financial Statements—It is best to review the financial circumstances surrounding the business early in the information gathering process, as future decisions respecting the sale will often be based on financial realities. As well, the executor must be capable of demonstrating to other individuals involved with the company or the estate, his or her understanding of the financial implications. The financial analysis will provide an indication of the business's assets, and in some cases, of their value. The analysis may also provide some indication of the difficulties inherent in preserving the assets, as well as assist in valuating the business for tax and probate purposes.

Review the Business Records—If the business is incorporated, the executor should review records such as the shareholders' and directors' minutes, corporate share ledger, shareholder agreement, executive committee minutes, corporate charter and by-laws, and any other records which would provide an overview of the corporation's activities and abilities to sell shares. The same is true for partnerships where partnership agreements may provide for dealing with partnership interests of the deceased.

Contact Those Individuals Who Have Knowledge of the Company's Affairs—Having reviewed the will, the financial statements, and other corporate records, the executor will have a basis from which to determine where further information is available and where problems may exist. At this point, it is useful to approach the people who have been involved in the business's affairs, to obtain further information to assist in the process.

Meet with the Deceased's Family—The executor should determine the extent of family involvement in the business operations. The members of the family should be approached to assist in gaining further knowledge about the operations. Families will often add "emotional" elements to the decision-making process. This is a factor which cannot be ignored. The representative, however, must be sensitive not only to the sentiments of the family, but also to the financial and administrative realities inherent in the family business and economic results.

Interview the Business's Employees—The employees of the business provide an additional source of information to assist the executor in assessing the status of the operation. Discussions should focus on immediate problems and those that may occur in the near future, such as changes to the organizational structure. The employees may also offer valuable opinions about the business's functions in general.

Interview the Corporate Solicitors and Accountants—The professionals associated with the business after often a valuable source of information for the executor. The solicitors and accountants can provide an independent opinion, combined with a degree of knowledge concerning the business and its operations. The accountant or auditor will be able to supplement the executor's knowledge of the financial condition of the company and of the control of its assets.

Meet with the Bank Representatives—The bankers are important in the information gathering process. The executor should ascertain the bank's attitudes towards the business. Once again, prior analysis of the financial statements by the executor is important, as the executor should be able to demonstrate to the bank both a knowledge of the business and the ability to project an image of competence that will sustain the bank's confidence in the future transaction.

Instruct Professional Valuators—The executor may be required to instruct professional valuators respecting certain assets of the business, as these valuations will form an integral part of the valuation for probate and taxation purposes. The need for valuators will depend on the nature of the business assets. Real estate is a typical example of where a valuation is usually necessary.

Insure the Business Assets—The executor must confirm that the assets of the business are properly insured. If the sale will take some time to finalize, the representative should review existing insurance, along with an insurance agent or broker, to determine that the current valuation is appropriate and that all assets are adequately covered.

Consider the Needs of the Estate—The executor must consider the requirements of the estate. In this context, he or she will need to consider the estate as a whole, bearing in mind that the business may form a substantial portion of the assets. It is important that the executor address whether the disposal of the business is essential to meet estate liabilities and any pecuniary legacies.

THE PURCHASER'S PERSPECTIVE—THE INFORMATION GATHERING PROCESS
9.623—The following steps should be taken to ensure the representative gains the maximum knowledge required before purchasing the business:

> Review the Will—The purchaser's counsel should review the will to satisfy him or herself that the vendor has the authority under the will to sell the business. If the executor is acting beyond his or her jurisdiction, the purchaser could eventually suffer the consequences.

> Review the Financial Statements—The purchaser's counsel should review the financial statements of the business to confirm that the proceeds of the sale are sufficient to meet estate liabilities and legacies. If the proceeds are insufficient, the business may be at risk with respect to claims from estate creditors and beneficiaries.

> Check for Shareholder or Partnership Agreements—The purchaser must also address whether there are shareholder or partnership agreements in existence that may affect the purchase of the business. Although such agreements may not be mentioned in the will, they often govern how shares of partnerships interests are to be dealt with upon death.

Documents Particular to an Estate Sale Transaction

9.624—[See Forms 9F106–9F110 for sample forms particular to an estate sale transaction.]

Estate Conveyancing of Real Estate

9.625—Conveyances of real property of deceased owners require consideration of numerous matters. The following is not intended to be an exhaustive study of all aspects of estate conveyancing. Rather, it is intended to provide an overview and summary of the important considerations involved. References for the most part have been restricted to the relevant statutes.

Preliminary Concerns

Spousal Rights

9.626—Dower: If the deceased died prior to March 31, 1978, the widow may be entitled to a dower right in the lands, where the deceased husband during marriage owned the legal estate. There are, of course, numerous exceptions to the widow's dower right. For example, if lands were held in joint tenancy, in partnership, or to uses, no dower right would attach. Although The Family Law Reform Act, 1978[1] abolished the widow's common law right of dower and repealed The Dower Act[2], it did not abolish any dower rights that had vested prior to March 31, 1978. Under section 25 of the Real Property Limitations Act[3], no action of dower shall be brought but within ten years from the death of the husband of the doweress, despite any disability of the doweress or any person claiming under her. The only exception occurs where the doweress is in actual possession. In that case, the ten-year limitation begins when such possession ends.

A further aspect of dower is the widow's right to make an election under The Devolution of Estates Act[4] (repealed and replaced by the Estates Administration Act[5] effective March 31, 1978). Simply put, the personal representative of the deceased may require the widow to make an election within 6 months of service of a notice. If the widow fails to make any election, she will only be entitled to her dower right and a share of her husband's personalty. If she elects to take her distributive share, she would have received the first $50,000.00 (this sum was increased, from time to time, $50,000.00 being the sum at the time of repeal) of the deceased husband's estate, plus interest from the date of the deceased husband's death, together with her distributive share of the undisposed of real and personal property. Such an election must be made in the prescribed form and registered on title. If it has not been registered, the widow would be entitled to a dower right. If the election has been properly made, the widow would no longer retain her dower right. Please note that while as a current conveyancing consideration, dower and dower-related matters are ignored here, these will arise when reviewing title searches.

---

1. S.O. 1978, c. 2.
2. R.S.O. 1970, c. 135.
3. R.S.O. 1990, c. L.15, s. 25, as amended.
4. R.S.O. 1970, c. 129.
5. R.S.O. 1980, c. 143.

9.627—Family Law Reform Act: The Family Law Reform Act[1] applied to spouses who died on or after March 31, 1978, and up to but not including March 1, 1986. Under the Family Law Reform Act[2], the rights under Part III (matrimonial home) were for the benefit of a spouse, However, a spouse ceased to be a spouse on the death of the other spouse. This would make the provisions of Part III inapplicable because the widow or the widower would no longer be considered a "spouse" within the meaning of the Family Law Reform Act[3].

---

1. S.O. 1978, c. 2.
2. S.O. 1978, c. 2.
3. S.O. 1978, c. 2.

9.628—Family Law Act, R.S.O. 1990, c. F.3: Where the deceased died on or after March 1, 1986 and the lands that form part of the transaction constitute a matrimonial home, the provisions of the Family Law Act[1] must be considered. "Matrimonial Home" is defined in section 18[2] as follows:

> 18(1) Every property in which a person has an interest and that is or, if the spouses have separated, was at the time of separation ordinarily occupied by the person and his or her spouse as their family residence is their matrimonial home.

(2) The ownership of a share or shares, or of an interest in a share or shares, of a corporation entitling the owner to occupy a housing unit owned by the corporation shall be deemed to be an interest in the unit for the purposes of subsection (1).

(3) If property that includes the matrimonial home is normally used for a purpose other than residential, the matrimonial home is only the part of the property that may reasonably be regarded as necessary to the use and enjoyment of the residence.

In the context of estate conveyancing, the Family Law Act[3] is only of concern if, at the time of his or her death, the deceased was a spouse and the lands constituted a matrimonial home. If the Family Law Act[4] applies, the transaction may be affected in one or more of the following three circumstances.

9.628.1—Deemed Severance of a Joint Tenancy: Section 26(1) of the Family Law Act[5] provides as follows:

If a spouse dies owning an interest in a matrimonial home as a joint tenant with a third person and not with the other spouse, the joint tenancy shall be deemed to have been severed immediately before the time of death.

The effect of section 26(1)[6] is that immediately before the time of death, the joint tenancy is severed and therefore becomes a tenancy in common, which would devolve as either a testacy or intestacy unless one of the following statements can be made:

a)   the deceased and one of the surviving joint tenants were spouses of each other when the deceased died,

b)   the deceased was not a spouse at the time the deceased died; or

c)   the property was not a matrimonial home (within the meaning of Part II of the Family Law Act[7]) of the deceased at the time the deceased died.

9.628.2—Right to Occupy Matrimonial Home: Section 26(2) of the Family Law Act[8] provides as follows:

Despite clauses 19(2)(*a*) and (*b*) (termination of spouse's right of possession) a spouse who has no interest in a matrimonial home but is occupying it at the time of the other spouse's death, whether under an order for exclusive possession or otherwise, is entitled to retain possession against the spouse's estate, rent free, for sixty (60) days after the spouse's death.

If the closing of the transaction is within sixty (60) days following the date of the deceased's death, the property may be subject to the right referred to in section 26(2)[9] above.

9.628.3—Surviving Spousal Right of Election: Section 6 of the Family Law Act[10] provides for extensive rights on the part of the surviving spouse to make certain elections. Until the provisions dealing with the spousal right of election have been dealt with, no distribution of the deceased's estate may be made (see subsections 6(14), (15) and (19)). The prohibition against distribution in section 6 does not prohibit the sale of the property of the deceased. However, there are two instances where the sale of property may constitute a distribution. Pursuant to the provisions of section 17 of the Estates Administration Act[11], the personal representative may sell for the purpose of distributing the proceeds among persons beneficially entitled, or may sell for the purpose of distribution of the real property to or among persons beneficially entitled. In either of those situations, there would be a distribution, in which event the provisions of section 6 of the Family Law Act[12] would have to be observed. In most cases where there is a sale by a personal representative to a third party purchaser, section 6[13] does not usually present any additional requirements or complications. However, the requirements of section 26[14] referred to above must be considered. In the event the property is being conveyed for the purpose of distribution of the real property to or among persons beneficially entitled or for the purpose of distributing proceeds among persons beneficially entitled, the following considerations would apply:

a) if the conveyance takes place within six months after death:

   1) evidence that the deceased had no surviving spouse, or
   2) there is a court order authorizing such conveyance, or
   3) the consent of the surviving spouse has been obtained.

b) if the conveyance takes place six or more months after the time of death:

   1) evidence that the deceased had no surviving spouse, or
   2) a court order has been issued authorizing the transaction, or
   3) satisfactory evidence that no election has been made and no application under Part 1 of the Family Law Act[15] has been received, or
   4) where an application has been made under said Part 1[16], the consent of such applicant, presumably the surviving spouse, or
   5) satisfactory evidence that an election has been filed, the nature of the election, and that there is no application under Part 1 of the Family Law Reform Act[17] by the surviving spouse.

---

1. R.S.O. 1990, c. F.3.
2. *Ibid.*
3. *Ibid.*
4. *Ibid.*
5. *Ibid.*
6. *Ibid.*
7. *Ibid.*
8. *Ibid.*
9. *Ibid.*
10. *Ibid.*
11. R.S.O. 1990, c. E.22.
12. *Supra*, note 1.
13. *Supra*, note 1.
14. *Supra*, note 1.
15. *Supra*, note 1.
16. *Supra*, note 1.
17. S.O. 1978, c. 2.

Succession Duties

9.629—Provincial: Where the deceased died after December 31, 1969 and before April 11, 1979, succession duty may be payable. In this event, a certificate for registration is required, pursuant to section 53 of the Registry Act[1] or section 126 of the Land Titles Act[2]. Unless such certificate is registered, title will not pass (section 53(3) Registry Act[3] and section 126(1) Land Titles Act[4]). Under section 53(4) of the Registry Act[5] and section 126(2) of the Land Titles Act[6], provision is made whereby the Minster may, by regulation under The Succession Duty Act[7], prescribed any property that may be conveyed, transferred, or assigned without the consent of the Minister. No consent is required where land is held in joint tenancy, to the extent that an interest therein accrues by survivorship to the spouse of a deceased person and to any interest in property passing upon the registration of a discharge of a charge/mortgage. Both the Registry Act[8] and the Land Titles Act[9] provide that sections 48(3)-(7) and 126(1) and (2), respectively, do not apply where the deceased person died prior to the 1st day of January, 1970 or after the 10th day of April, 1979.

1. R.S.O. 1990, c. R.20.
2. R.S.O. 1990, c. L.5.
3. *Supra*, note 1.
4. *Supra*, note 2.
5. *Supra*, note 1.
6. *Supra*, note 2.
7. R.S.O. 1970, c. 449.
8. *Supra*, note 1.
9. *Supra*, note 2.

9.630—Federal: The lien and consent provision prescribed by sections 47 and 51 of The Estate Tax Act[1] as amended, and sections 25(3), 25(4) and 50 of The Dominion Succession Duty Act[2] were repealed by sections 26 and 23, respectively, of the Miscellaneous Statute Law Amendment Act, 1984[3]. Although the Miscellaneous Statute Law Amendment Act, 1984[4] was assented to June 29, 1984, the repeal of the noted sections of the Estate Tax Act[5] and The Dominion Succession Duty Act[6] were deemed effective as of May 28, 1980. Further provision is made that any lien that existed by virtue of these sections prior to May 28, 1980, no longer exists. Therefore, it is not necessary to apply for consent from the Minister of National Revenue with respect to federal succession duties.

1. R.S.C. 1970, c. E-9.
2. R.S.C. 1952, c. 89 (am. 1952, c. 317, ss. 1-8)
3. S.C. 1983-84, c. 40.
4. *Ibid.*

5. *Supra*, note 1.
6. *Supra*, note 2.

9.631—Land Transfer Tax: Generally speaking, there is no land transfer tax payable where the property is conveyed from the personal representative of a deceased person to a person beneficially entitled, provided there is no money or other consideration. This, of course, would not be the case in the event there is a sale to a third party who is not a person beneficially entitled. In those circumstances, land transfer tax would be payable on the full value of the consideration.

JOINT TENANCY

9.632—Where a joint tenant dies, the real property vests automatically in the surviving joint tenant(s) by operation of law, subject to the requirements of the Registry Act[1] or the Land Titles Act[2].

---

1. R.S.O. 1990, c. R.20.
2. R.S.O. 1990, c. L.5.

REGISTRY SYSTEM

9.633—Under the Registry Act[1], satisfactory evidence of death would be required, such as a death certificate of the deceased joint tenant. Depending on the date of death of the deceased and the relationship of the deceased to the surviving joint tenant, succession duties may be payable. In this event a certificate for registration would be required. Under the form of the Transfer/Deed of Land prescribed under the Land Registration Reform Act[2], affidavits may no longer be attached, other than the Affidavit of Residence and of Value of the Consideration. This precludes the usual practice of inserting a statement into the former Affidavit of Age and Spousal Status regarding the death of the deceased joint tenant. It would appear that any affidavits or declarations as to death or death certificates must be separately deposited by attaching them to a Form 4 Document General and by reciting the registration numbers thereof in a separate recital, included in a schedule attached to a Form 1 Transfer/Deed of Land.

Where there is actual notice that the joint tenancy has been severed (for example, only one joint tenant is mortgaging his or her undivided interest in the property), the foregoing would not apply. In such circumstances, the real property of the deceased tenant-in-common will devolve as a testacy or intestacy, as the case may be. In addition, please note the requirements of section 26(1) of the Family Law Act discussed above. This section applies equally to lands under the Registry or Land Titles Systems.

---

1. R.S.O. 1990, c. R.20.
2. R.S.O. 1990, c. L.4.

LAND TITLES SYSTEM

9.634—With respect to the requirements under the Land Titles Act[1], it is necessary to prepare a survivorship application under section 123 of the Act. Such application would include either a death certificate and an affidavit in support by the applicant, usually the surviving joint tenant, or a compliance with law statement incorporating the following statements:

    (i)   The applicant(s) held the property as (a) joint tenant(s) with the deceased, or

    (ii)   The applicant held the charge on joint account with right of survivorship with the deceased.

    (iii)   By right of survivorship, the applicant(s) is (are) entitled to be the owner(s), as a surviving joint tenant(s).

    (iv)   The date of death was (*insert date*).

In addition, a statement under subsection 26(1) of the Family Law Act must be included. All statements must be made by a solicitor. Upon the registration and acceptance of the survivorship application by the Land Registrar, the name of the deceased joint tenant will be crossed off the parcel register, leaving the surviving joint tenant free to deal with the property.

---

1. R.S.O. 1990, c. L.5.
2. R.S.O. 1990, c. L.5.

TESTACY

9.635—Where the deceased dies leaving a valid will, the provisions of the will are paramount. So long as the valid will contains an express or implied power of sale, the estate trustee is not bound by the provisions of section 17 of the Estates Administration Act. If the lands are under the Registry System, either a certified or notarial copy of the Certificate of Appointment of Estate Trustee With a Will of the deceased or the original will or a notarial copy thereof together with the prescribed statements and other documents required pursuant to section 53(1) of the Registry Act would be required. With respect to lands under the Land Titles System, a certified or notarial copy of the Certificate of Appointment of Estate Trustee With a Will would normally be required unless the value of the estate does not exceed $50,000.00. In that case, there are additional requirements which are set out in paragraph **9.639** below. From a conveyancing point of view, there are three general areas of interest in a will and they are:

a)　Whether there is a power of sale,

b)　Whether the property of the deceased has been devised to the executors upon trust or devised directly to the beneficiaries, and

c)　Whether there are any specific bequests involving the land being dealt with.

EXPRESS POWER OF SALE

9.636—Where there is an express power of sale in a will and there are no specific bequests involving the land being dealt with, the executor may sell the land without the consent of any beneficiary, and a purchaser in good faith and for value without notice will take the property free from debts. Where there is a specific bequest of the property being dealt with, then the release of the person to whom the specific bequest was made should be obtained and registered.

Implied Power of Sale

9.637—Where there is no express power of sale contained in the will, it will be necessary to determine whether or not such power of sale can be implied. Section 44 of the Trustee Act[1] provides as follows:

> 44(1) Where by any will coming into operation after the 18th day of September, 1865, a testator charges his land, or any specific part thereof, with the payment of his debts or with the payment of any legacy or other specific sum of money, and devises the land so charged to his executors or to a trustee without any express provision for the raising of such debt, legacy or sum of money out of such land, the devisee may raise such debt, legacy or money by a sale of such land or any part thereof, or by a mortgage of the same.
>
> (2) Purchasers or mortgagees are not bound to inquire whether the powers conferred by this section, or any of them, have been duly and correctly exercised by the person acting in virtue thereof.

The two requirements set out in the above section are that the land be devised to the executor and that the land be charged with payment. In these circumstances, a power of sale will normally be implied.[2]

1.　R.S.O. 1990, c. T.23.

2.　For a complete discussion on the implied power of sale, please refer to the lecture of W.G.C. Howland (as he then was) in the Special Lectures of the Law Society of Upper Canada, 1951 entitled "The Sale of Lands of a Deceased Owner".

No Power of Sale

9.638—Where there is no express or implied power of sale, then the executor must resort to the provisions of section 17(1) of the Estates Administration

Act[1] discussed below. Where there is no power of sale and no devise to the estate trustee, the real property will vest three years after the deceased's death, in the persons beneficially entitled unless a caution is registered against the real property, as per section 9(1) of the Estates Administration Act[2]. Where the real property has so vested, the conveyance must be from the persons beneficially entitled.

---

1. R.S.O. 1990, c. E.22.
2. *Ibid.*

Preparation of the Conveyance

9.639—Where there is a power of sale or a devise to an estate trustee upon trusts, then the conveyance must be from the estate trustee and not from the beneficiary. In such a case, there is no "automatic vesting" (discussed below) under section 9(1) of the Estates Administration Act[1]. However, it may be necessary to obtain the release of a beneficiary to whom a specific bequest of the land was made. After having determined the necessary parties to the conveyance, the following should be obtained:

- a) Certified or notarial copy of the Certificate of Appointment of Estate Trustee With a Will (or notarial copy of the will together with statements as required under section 53 of the Registry Act);
- b) Certificate for registration with respect to Succession Duty (where applicable);
- c) Transfer/Deed of Land (Form 1) including appropriate recitals which would be set out on a schedule and include the following:
  - the date of death of the deceased and the interest of the deceased in the real property being conveyed;
  - the registration particulars of the Certificate of Appointment of Estate Transfer With a Will;
  - the registration particulars of the certificate for registration (if applicable);
  - where the death occurred on or after March 1, 1986, the spousal status of the deceased at the time of death.

Under the Land Titles System, it will be necessary for the estate trustee to make a transmission application under section 120 of the Land Titles Act[3] to have the title registered in his or her name. An estate trustee has two options with respect to the supporting materials that must accompany the application. The estate trustee may provide an affidavit in support of the application or may provide a compliance with law statement in lieu of an affidavit. If the estate trustee chooses to submit an affidavit in support of the application the following would be required:

a)   Transmission application (incorporated into Form 4 Document General).

b)   Certified or notarial copy of the Certificate of Appointment of Estate Trustee With a Will of the deceased.

c)   Affidavit of applicant (required if deceased was a male and died prior to March 31, 1978 to deal with dower rights).

d)   Certificate for registration (Succession Duty), if necessary.

e)   Where the value of the estate does not exceed $50,000.00, a certified or notarial copy of the Certificate of Appointment of Estate Trustee With a Will is not required provided that the following are included in the Transmission Application:

   (i)   the original will, a notarial or certified copy therof,

   (ii) certificate of death or a notarial or certified copy or a statement of death,

   (iii) an affidavit or declaration that (A) the value of the estate does not exceed $50,000.00 and (B) the deceased was of the age of majority at the time of execution of the will and that the will is the last will of the deceased and has not been revoked by marriage or otherwise,

   (iv) a covenant to indemnify the Land Titles Assurance Fund from those beneficially entitled under the will.

As a matter of practice, it is suggested that the affidavit of the applicant include evidence to the effect that all debts of the deceased have been paid and that all creditors of the deceased have been notified. Although this is not necessary, it tends to expedite not only the initial registration of the transmission application but subsequent transactions as well. Please note that there is currently a one time waiver of the requirement of a certificate of appointment of estate trustee if the conveyance is the first dealing after the conversion by the Ministry from the Registry to the Land Titles system.

If the estate trustee chooses to submit a compliance with law statement in lieu of an affidavit in support of the transmission application, the statement, which must be made by a solicitor, must contain the following information:

   i.   The applicant is entitled to be the owner by law, as estate trustee, executor or administrator of the estate of the deceased owner.

   ii.   Name and date of death of registered owner.

   iii. Either that the property is subject to the debts of the deceased or the debts of the deceased are paid in full.

   iv.   One of the following:

      (a) The applicant is appointed as estate trustee with a will (*enter name of court*), under (*enter file number*), dated (*enter date*) which is still in force and effect, or

(b) The applicant is appointed as estate trustee without a will by *(enter name of court)*, under *(enter file number)*, dated *(enter date)* which is still in full force and effect, or

(c) No application was made for a certificate of appointment of an estate trustee as the total value of the estate of the deceased owner is not more than $50,000.00, and

(d) Documentation regarding the death of *(enter the deceased's name)* which is sufficient to deal with this transaction, is attached to registration number *(enter registration number)*.

---

1. R.S.O. 1990, c. E.22.
2. R.S.O. 1970, c. 129.
3. R.S.O. 1990, c. L.5.

Automatic Vesting

9.640—Where the death of the deceased occurred three or more years ago, the provisions of section 9(1) of the Estates Administration Act[1] may apply:

> 9(1) Real property not disposed of, conveyed to, divided or distributed among the persons beneficially entitled thereto under section 17 by the personal representative within three years after the death of the deceased is, subject to the Land Titles Act in the case of land registered under that Act and subject to subsections 53(3) and (5) of the Registry Act, and subject as hereinafter provided at the expiration of that period, whether probate or letters of administration (sic—now Certificates of Appointment of Estate Trustee With or Without a Will) have or have not been taken, thenceforth vested in the persons beneficially entitled thereto under the will or upon the intestacy or their assigns without any conveyance by the personal representative, unless such personal representative, if any, has registered, in the proper land registry office, a caution in Form 1 under his hand, and if a caution is so registered, the real property mentioned therein does not so vest for three years from the time of the registration of the caution or of the last caution if more than one was registered.

It is important to note that the automatic vesting provision applies in the case of testacies or intestacies. However, section 9 must be read in conjunction with section 10 of the Estates Administration Act[2] which provides as follows:

> 10 Nothing in section 9 derogates from any right possessed by an executor or administrator with the will annexed under a will or under the Trustee Act or from any right possessed by trustee under a will.

Generally speaking, the case law has held that where a will provides for an express or an implied power of sale, or where there has been a conveyance to the estate trustee upon trust, vesting will not occur pursuant to section 9 since it would interfere with the estate trustee's rights under the will.

---

1. R.S.O. 1990, c. E.22.
2. R.S.O. 1990, c. E.22.

Intestacy

9.641—Where the deceased dies not leaving a valid will or dies leaving a valid will not containing an express or implied power of sale, the powers of the personal representative of the deceased are found in the Estates Administration Act[1]. For the personal representative to exercise any of the powers under the Estates Administration Act a Certificate of Appointment of Estate Trustee Without a Will from an Ontario Court must be obtained. Section 17(1) of the Estates Administration Act[2] provides as follows:

> The powers of sale conferred by this Act on a personal representative may be exercised for the purpose of not only paying debts but also of distributing or dividing the estate among the persons beneficially entitled thereto, whether there are or are not debts, and in no case is it necessary that the persons beneficially entitled concur in any such sale except where it is made for the purpose of distribution only.

Because the powers of sale are limited, it is necessary in each case to ascertain the purpose of the sale.

---

1. R.S.O. 1990, c. E.22.
2. R.S.O. 1990, c. E.22.

Sales for the Purpose of Paying Debts

9.642—Where the personal representative is selling for the purpose of paying debts, he or she has the right to sell within 3 years of the death of the deceased (or longer if caution has been registered), without the concurrence of any beneficiaries regardless of whether the beneficiaries are minors or mentally incompetent. Under these circumstances, a purchaser for value without notice will get title free of the debts of the deceased.

Sales for the Purpose of Distributing the Proceeds Among Persons Beneficially Entitled

9.643—Where the purpose of the sale occurring within 3 years after death (or longer if a caution has been registered) is to distribute the proceeds of sale among persons beneficially entitled, the concurrence of a majority of those beneficially entitled representing together not less than one-half of all the interests therein is required, together with the approval of the Children's Lawyer on behalf of any minors. If the only persons interested in the real property being sold are minors, then the proper procedure is to make an application under the Children's Law Reform Act[1].

Where the estate has not yet been fully administered and some or all of the beneficiaries are minors, the Children's Lawyer may proceed under section 17(2) of the Estates Administration Act. According to section 17(2) of the Estates Administration Act[2], the Children's Lawyer may also concur on behalf of any mentally incompetent person, (unless the provisions of section 17(4) apply); any person whose consent cannot be obtained because his or her place of residence is unknown, and any person where in the opinion of the Children's Lawyer it would be inconvenient to require his consent. As a matter of practice, the Children's Lawyer must be convinced that all efforts to locate beneficiaries have been made, before approving on behalf of unfound beneficiaries. With respect to mentally incompetent persons, the Children's Lawyer will only approve if the consent of that mentally incompetent person is required to complete the majority of the beneficiaries. With respect to those beneficiaries whose consent it would be inconvenient to obtain, the Children's Lawyer will generally only consent when a court has determined that it would be inconvenient.

Unless the required approval is obtained, a purchaser will take title subject to the claims of the remaining beneficiaries as well as the debts of the deceased. It should be noted that where any of the beneficiaries are minors, mentally incompetent persons, or persons under any other mental disability, different limitation periods would apply, depending on the circumstances.[3] Where the required consents of the beneficiaries have been obtained, a purchaser for value without notice would get good title free of the debts of the deceased, save and except those of which the purchaser has actual notice.

It should be noted that although a beneficiaries' majority and the consent of the Children's Lawyer on behalf of minors will protect a purchaser for value without notice, the personal representative may still be liable to those beneficiaries who did not consent. For this reason, it would be advisable from the point of view of the personal representative to obtain the concurrence of all beneficiaries. In the event that this is not possible, a court order should be obtained dispensing with the consent of those beneficiaries who, for one reason or another, will not consent. While the foregoing may not be of particular concern to a purchaser, it is, of course, of concern when acting for the personal representative.

---

1. R.S.O. 1990, c. C.12.
2. R.S.O. 1990, c. E.22.
3. Refer to sections 36, 37, and 38 of Real Property Limitations Act, R.S.O. 1990, c. L. 15.

Sales or Conveyances for the Purpose of Distribution of the Real Property to or among Persons Beneficially Entitled

9.644—The personal representative may within 3 years of death (or longer if a caution has been registered) convey the property directly to those beneficially entitled either with or without a court order.

9.645—Without a Court Order: Where the conveyance is made without a court order, the concurrence of all persons beneficially entitled thereto, together with the approval of the Children's Lawyer on behalf of minors and mentally incompetent persons is required. However, such a conveyance does not free the property from the debts of the deceased owner. Section 17(8) of the Estates Administration Act[1] provides as follows:

> 17(8) The powers of a personal representative under subsection (2), (3) or (6) have heretofore been and shall hereafter be exercisable during the period of three years from the death of the deceased without an order of a judge, provided that,
>
> (a) real property conveyed, divided or distributed by virtue of such powers to or among the persons beneficially entitled thereto, shall be deemed to have been and to be liable for the payment of the debts of the deceased owner as if no conveyance, division or distribution had been made, even though it has subsequently during such three-year period been conveyed to a purchaser or purchasers in good faith and for value, but in the case of such purchaser or purchasers, such liability shall only continue after the expiry of such three-year period if some action or legal proceeding has been instituted by the creditor, his assignee or successor to enforce the claim and a "lis pendens" or a caution has, before such expiry, been registered against the property; and that
>
> (b) although such liability has applied and shall apply as aforesaid in respect of real property so conveyed, divided or distributed, any such purchaser, in good faith and for value, shall be deemed to have had and to have a right to relief over against the persons beneficially entitled, and where such conveyance, division or distribution was made by the personal representative with knowledge of the debt in respect of which claim is made, or without due advertisement for creditors, then against such personal representative; and that
>
> (c) upon the expiration of such three-year period where no "lis pendens" or caution has been registered, subsection 20(2) and section 22 apply as if such real property has become vested in the person beneficially entitled thereto under section 9.

As a matter of policy, the Children's Lawyer will not consent on behalf of anyone unless there is a court order.

---

1. R.S.O. 1990, c. E.22.

9.646—With a Court Order: Under section 17(5), before the expiration of three years from the death of the deceased the personal representative may apply for an order dividing or distributing the estate among the persons beneficially entitled. By operation of section 21(1) of the Estates Administration Act[1], "a person purchasing real property in good faith for value from a person beneficially entitled, to whom it has been conveyed by the personal representative, by leave of a judge, it is entitled to hold it freed and discharged from any debts and liabilities of the deceased owner, except such as are specifically charged thereon other than by his will . . .".

---

1. R.S.O. 1990, c. E.22.

Sales by Persons Beneficially Entitled

9.647—In addition to an administrator selling or conveying real property within 3 years of the death of the deceased (or longer if a caution has been registered) pursuant to the provisions of the Estates Administration Act[1], the person(s) beneficially entitled may, where the real property has been conveyed to them by the administrator, or where the real property has vested in them pursuant to section 9[2], and provided there are no minors involved, convey the property to third parties.

Where the real property has been conveyed to the person(s) beneficially entitled within the 3-year period following the death of the deceased without a court order, and the person(s) beneficially entitled in turn have conveyed the real property to a purchaser in good faith and for value, that purchaser takes the property subject to the debts of the deceased[3]. The liability of the purchaser, however, ends after the 3-year period has expired unless proceedings have been instituted and a certificate of pending litigation or a caution has been registered against the real property. Furthermore, if a purchaser is required to pay debts, that purchaser has the right to claim relief over against the person(s) beneficially entitled, and in certain circumstances can also claim against the personal representative. On the other hand, if the conveyance to the person(s) beneficially entitled was made pursuant to a court order, a purchaser obtaining a conveyance from such person(s) beneficially entitled takes the property free from the debts of the deceased[4].

It should be noted that where real property vests in the person(s) beneficially entitled pursuant to section 9(1) of the Estates Administration Act[5], the real property continues to be charged with the debts of the deceased owner, so long as it remains vested in such person or in any person claiming under him or her who is not a purchaser in good faith and for valuable consideration. However, a purchaser who has purchased from a person beneficially entitled, in whom real property has vested pursuant to section 9(1)[6], would be protected by section 23[7] which reads as follows:

23(1) A purchaser in good faith and for value of real property of a deceased owner that has become vested under section 9 in a person beneficially entitled thereto is entitled to hold it freed and discharged from the claims of creditors of the deceased owner except such of them of which he had notice at the time of his purchase.

(2) Nothing in subsection (1) affects the right of the creditor against the personal representative personally where he has permitted the real property to become vested in the person beneficially entitled to the prejudice of the creditor or against the person beneficially entitled.

---

1. R.S.O. 1990, c. E.22.
2. *Ibid.*, s. 9.
3. *Ibid.*, s. 17(8)(*a*).
4. *Ibid.*, s. 21(1).
5. *Supra*, note 1.
6. *Ibid.*, s. 9.
7. *Ibid.*, s. 23.

PREPARATION OF THE CONVEYANCE

9.648—Under the Registry System: Under the Land Registration Reform Act[1], section 5(1)3 sets out the implied covenants of a personal representative. These implied covenants would apply unless they are expressly amended. In this regard, it is suggested that the first implied covenant be amended by adding the words "except as the records of the land registry office disclose" so that the first implied covenant would read as follows:

> That the transferor has not done, omitted or permitted anything whereby the land is or may be encumbered or whereby the transferor is hindered from giving the transfer except as the records of the land registry office disclose.

Where the conveyance is by the persons beneficially entitled, the foregoing implied covenants would not apply. In their place, the usual covenants set out in section 5(1)1 of the Land Registration Reform Act[2] would apply. After having determined the necessary parties to the conveyance and prepared the Form 1 Transfer/Deed of Land in the usual manner, there should be included as a schedule all necessary recitals dealing *where applicable* with each of the following points:

(a) The date of death of the deceased and the interest of the deceased in the real property being conveyed.

(b) The registration particulars of the Certificate of Appointment of Estate Trustee Without a Will.

(c) The registration particulars of the certificate for registration.

(d)   The registration particulars of the caution (if any) pursuant to section 9 of the Estates Administration Act[3].

(e)   The spousal status of the deceased at death.

(f)   The purpose of the sale.

(g)   If the sale is for the purpose of paying debts, no further recital should normally be required.

(h)   If the purpose of the sale is to distribute the   proceeds of sale among persons beneficially entitled, the following additional recitals should be included:

- the listing of all surviving heirs-at-law and next-of-kin, their relationship to the deceased, and specification as to any minors or mentally incompetent persons;
- the consent and approval of the Children's Lawyer on behalf of specified minors and mentally incompetents; and
- a statement that all debts have been paid.
- where there is a surviving spouse, the appropriate recitals under "Surviving Spousal Right of Election", **Para. 9.628**, clause (a) or (b).

(i)   Where the purpose of the sale is to distribute the real property to those persons beneficially entitled, all of the foregoing recitals may be applicable and the following additional one:
- the registration particulars of the court order authorizing the distribution.

(j)   Where the sale is by the persons beneficially entitled, all of the foregoing recitals may be applicable.

As indicated previously, from a conveyancing point of view, it is advisable to have the recitals attested to by the personal representative or by one of the beneficiaries. However, the new forms do not appear to permit the insertion of an affidavit or declaration to that effect. Accordingly, it is suggested that a declaration or an affidavit by the person giving the conveyance be prepared and deposited in the usual manner and that the registration particulars of such deposit be recited in the schedule to the Transfer/Deed of Land.

---

1. R.S.O. 1990, c. L. 4.
2. Ibid.
3. R.S.O. 1990, c. E.22.

9.649—Under the Land Titles System: Section 68(1) of the Land Titles Act[1] provides that "no person, other than the registered owner, is entitled to transfer or charge registered freehold or leasehold land by registered disposition." Consequently, to that extent, the automatic vesting provision set out in section 9 of the Estates Administration Act[2] (which section 9 is expressed to be subject to the provisions of the Land Titles Act[3]) does not operate in favour of the person(s) beneficially entitled. It is necessary for a transmission application to be made, whereby the name of the personal representative or the person beneficially entitled would be entered as the registered owner on the parcel register. The relevant sections dealing with transmission applications on the death of a registered owner are sections 120 to 127, inclusive, of the Land Titles Act[4].

Transmission applicants may provide affidavit evidence or a compliance with law statement in support of their application.

Substantially the same information would be required under the Land Titles system as under the Registry system except that the form would be different. An application in the prescribed form is generally set out in Box 8 of the Form 4 Document General,[5] and is made to the appropriate Land Registrar. Attached to the Document General would be a notarial copy of the Certificate of Appointment of Estate Trustee Without a Will, any required ministerial consents, and an affidavit of the applicant or a compliance with law statement setting out the same sort of information as would be set out in the recitals under the Registry system. The forms are prescribed under the regulations made pursuant to the Land Titles Act[6].

Section 9.639 sets out the information that must be included in a compliance with law statement supporting a transmission application by an estate trustee (with or without a will). If no application for a certificate of appointment was made, a covenant to indemnify the Land Titles Assurance Fund is required to be filed with the office of the Director of Titles using the prescribed form 54 of Regulation 690.

If a devisee, or heir at law, is making the transmission application and chooses to submit a compliance with law statement in lieu of an affidavit in support of the application the following information must be included in the statement:

    i.   The name and date of the death of the owner.

    ii.   The applicant(s) is entitled to be the owner, as devisee or heir at law.

    iii.   The interest of the deceased is now vested in all of the beneficiaries of the estate of the deceased owner under the provisions of the Estate Administrations Act, the Succession Law Reform Act and the Family Law Act.

    iv.   The properties are subject to the debts of the deceased, or

    v.   The debts of the deceased are paid in full.

vi.   Title to the land is not subject to spousal rights under the Family Law Act, or

vii. Title to the land is subject to spousal rights of the spouse *(enter applicable name)*.

The statements required are consistent with those required for the electronic registration of a transmission application by a devisee, or heir at law, and can only be made by a solicitor. The solicitor must sign these statements.

The implementation of electronic registration has already begun in many of the land registry offices. The Land Registration Reform Act[7] was amended in 1994 to allow for electronic registration of documents and the passing of regulations in connection therewith. The specific requirements for estate conveyancing are set out below. By way of general observation, compliance with law statements made by solicitors will replace many of the affidavits, certificates and other supporting evidence that were previously registered. This does not mean that such affidavits, certificates and other supporting evidence are no longer required as part of a transaction. Solicitors must continue to ensure that all required affidavits, certificates and other supporting documentary evidence are completed prior to making any compliance with law statements. Therafter, it is important to retain all such documents in the event any compliance with law statements are questioned or challenged. Please note that electronic regulation only applies to lands registered under the Land Titles Act.[8]

Ontario Regulation 19/99[9] made under the Land Registration Reform Act sets out the general and specific requirements for electronic registration. The following is a brief summary:

(1)   Survivorship Application:

    (a)   the name of the deceased joint tenant;

    (b)   proof of death of the deceased satisfactory to the land registrar; and

    (c)   a statement by the applicant that the land affected by the application is not subject to any spousal right under the Family Law Act[10] with respect to the deceased.

2.   Transmission Application by an Estate Trustee, Executor or Administrator:

    (a)   the name and date of death of the owner;

    (b)   one of the following:

        (i)   The certificate of appointment or order confirming the appointment of the applicant as estate trustee, executor or administrator, as the case may be.

    (ii)   The date and court file number of the certificate or order.
    (iii)   Proof satisfactory to the Director of Titles that the value
             of the estate is less than $50,000.00; and

(c) the evidence described in subsection 36(2) of Regulation 690 of
     the Revised Regulations of Ontario, 1990 (which requires
     evidence of dower rights, spousal rights under the Family Act[11],
     the sex of the deceased, debts of the estate, the heirs of the
     deceased and whatever else the Director of Titles may specify)
     or all of the following statements;

    (i)   A statement that the land affected by the application is not
            subject to debts of the deceased, if that is the case.
    (ii)   A statement that the applicant as estate trustee, executor
            or administrator, as the case may be, is entitled by law to
            be registered as owner.

3. Transmission Application by Benificiary:

    (a) the name and proof of death of the owner satisfactory to the
         land registrar; and
    (b) the evidence described in subsection 36(2) of Regulation 690 of
         the Revised Regulations of Ontario, 1990[12] (as described above)
         or all of the following statements:

        (i)   A statement by the applicant that the land affected by the
                application is not subject to any spousal rights under the
                Family Law Act[13] with respect to the deceased.
        (ii)   A statement that the land affected by the application is not
                subject to debts of the deceased, if that is the case.
        (iii)   A statement that the land affected by the application has
                vested in the applicant.

4. Transfer Application by Estate Trustee, Executor or Administrator:

    (a) a statement that the transferor is entitled to transfer the land
         affected by the document under the terms of the will, if any, the
         Estates Administration Act[14] and the Succession Law Reform
         Act;[15]
    (b) a statement by the transferor that the land affected by the
         application is not subject to any spousal right under the Family
         Law Act[16] with respect to the deceased;
    (c) a statement that the transferor has obtained the consent of all
         required parties or that no consents are required; and
    (d) a statement that the land affected by the transfer is not subject
         to debts of the deceased, if that is the case.

5.   Transfer by Benificiary:

(a)   a statement that the transferee is not aware of any specific debts of the deceased, if that is the case.

Section 40(1) of Ontario Regulation 19/99[17] provides, in effect, that the compliance with law statements must be made by an Ontario solicitor.

---

1.   R.S.O. 1990, c. L.5.
2.   R.S.O. 1990, c. E.22.
3.   *Supra*, note 1.
4.   *Supra*, note 1.
5.   *Supra*, note 1, Reg. 688, Form 4.
6.   *Supra*, note 1.
7.   R.S.O. 1990, c. L.4, am. S.O. 1994, c. 27.
8.   R.S.O. 1990, c. L.5.
9.   O. Reg. 19/99.
10. R.S.O. 1990, c. F.3.
11. R.S.O. 1990, c. F.3.
12. R.R.O. 1990, Reg. 690 s. 36(2).
13. R.S.O. 1990, c. F.3.
14. R.S.O. 1990, c. E.22.
15. R.S.O. 1990, c. S.26.
16. R.S.O. 1990, c. F.3.
17. O. Reg. 19/99.

Secured Creditors, Receivers and Bankruptcy Trustees
General

9.650—Secured creditors and receivers (including receivers and managers), both those who are court appointed and those appointed pursuant to a specific security document, will be exercising remedies governed by one or a combination of the Ontario Personal Property Act[1], the Bank Act[2] the Bankruptcy and Insolvency Act ("BIA"),[3] or by court authority. Trustees in bankruptcy will be acting with the permission of the inspectors of the estate, pursuant to section 30 of the Bankruptcy and Insolvency Act.[3-1]

Consequently, it will be necessary to ensure that the requisite contractual and statutory authorities are observed, and that the vendor is properly conducting its sale in accordance with such legislation and the terms of the agreement with the debtor.

The secured party or its receiver exercising remedies pursuant to a security agreement governed by the Personal Property Security Act[4] will be required to observe Part V of that Act and effect its sale in a "commercially reasonable manner", having given the requisite notices of sale in the form and in the manner required by the Act. If no such notice of sale has been given in accordance with subsection 63(5)[5], then (i) the requisite subsection 63(7)[6] exception to the requirement for giving notice of sale should be proved or (ii) the consent of the debtor, its guarantors, and all other PPSA creditors with an interest in the collateral should be provided in writing, or (iii) the subsection 63(7)(e)[7] court order should be provided.

It is advisable to ensure that the security agreement is properly signed and perfected in accordance with the legislation by either registration or possession.

When purchasing goods from a bank, it may be exercising its remedies pursuant to the Bank Act[8]; specifically under subsection 427(3) of the Act which provides for power of sale remedies in the event of non-payment of any debt and allows the bank to apply the proceeds of sale against the borrower's indebtedness.

Subsection 428(7) and 428(8) of the Bank Act[9] provides that for sales of property other than livestock, there should be a sale by public auction after the requisite notice has been given to the debtor and public advertisement of such sale has been made. Subsection 428(10)[10] requires a standard of honesty and good faith in effecting sales or property pursuant to section 427 Bank Act[11] security, and requires the bank to deal with the property in a timely and appropriate manner, having regard to the nature of the property and the interest of the person by whom the security was given.

Failure of a secured creditor to observe the requirements of Part V of the PPSA[12], or the standard of care in section 428 of the Bank Act[13], may leave it vulnerable to damages claims from the debtor. Although bankruptcy trustees do not have such statutory standards the common law obliges them to conduct a sale to obtain a price that is fair in the circumstances.

The BIA[14] will also require additional notices be given. When a "receiver" as defined in section 243(2) of the BIA[15] has been appointed, such receiver must give notice of its appointment and make certain reports in accordance with sections 245 and 246[16]. In addition, the secured party must give notice of its intention to enforce its security over the inventory, accounts or substantially all other assets of the insolvent person, used or acquired for carrying on its business.

Given the BIA[17], the secured party will have to have completed the following:

a) given the debtor notice of any default for which the debtor has a grace or cure period, with a chance to cure such default;

b) given a demand letter giving reasonable demand in accordance with the common law. Such demand may be given alone, or in the appropriate circumstances, together with the section 244 BIA Form 89 [formerly

Form 115][18] notice of intention to enforce security. Some solicitors are giving the section 244[19] separately until after the reasonable demand has expired, being a point in time when the secured creditor can truly say it is entitled to enforce its security; and

c) notice of sale or other remedy under the PPSA[20] or land registration legislation.

You should have copies of all of these for your file. Section 247 of the BIA[21], like the PPSA[22], also requires that the secured party exercise its remedies, in a commercially reasonable manner, and in good faith.

In addition to ensuring compliance with all statutory requirements and common law standards imposed on a bankruptcy trustee or a secured creditor selling pursuant to security agreements, the solicitor needs to be very aware of the priorities of numerous statutory liens and trusts, which priorities may differ inside and outside of bankruptcy.

There have been recent amendments to legislation of note dealing with source deductions and Ontario retail sales and tobacco tax. These changes impose the burden of tax collection on secured creditors. An outline of these new priorities is as follows:

(a) Source Deduction Superpriority

The Supreme Court of Canada held in *Royal Bank of Canada v. Sparrow Electric Corp.*, [1997] 1 S.C.R. 411, that the statutory deemed trust under section 227(4) of the Income Tax Act on the property of the person required to remit source deductions (employee income tax, CPP and EI premiums; collectively "Source Deductions") only arises at the date a withholding or deduction is required to be made and is subordinate to a fixed charge created at a prior time.

The Court held that the Royal Bank of Canada's general security agreement and section 427 Bank Act security constituted fixed charges and had priority ahead of the federal Crown's claim for unremitted Source Deductions.

The Minister of Finance has amended the Income Tax Act section 227(4) to provide a "superpriority" for Source Deductions ranking ahead of all secured creditors, retroactively to June 15, 1994. Bill C-28 received Royal Assent on June 18, 1998.

Until these new provisions are interpreted by the Courts, it would be wise before purchasing assets or shares, to pay all Source Deduction arrears, at a full or negotiated rate, to ensure this superpriority is satisfied. Loan agreements should consider requiring monthly certificates from the borrower with evidence of payment of Source Deductions, to track this ongoing obligation.

(b)   Retail Sales and Tobacco Tax Priorities

On December 18, 1997 in a Red Tape bill,[23] Ontario amended both the Retail Sales Tax Act and the Tobacco Tax Act to provide for an increased penalty on secured creditors who seize assets of a debtor who is liable to remit taxes under either statute.

The revised section 22 of the Retail Sales Tax Act provides that if the seizing creditor does not obtain a tax clearance certificate from the Ontario Ministry of Finance prior to selling the goods seized, the seizing creditor becomes personally liable for all unpaid taxes, interest and penalties owing by the debtor effective from January 1, 1998. The seizing creditor would include a distraining landlord.

Note, that the personal liability imposed on the seizing creditor is not limited to the value of the property seized. Prior to the changes to section 22, the seizing creditor was only liable for the unpaid tax which had accrued over the prior year.

The changes to the Tobacco Tax Act are the same. The same changes have been made to the Fuel Tax Act and the Gasoline Tax Act.[24]

Such imposition applies to seizure of "property of the debtor"; it does not apply to goods subject to a conditional sale contract or lease. The position of the Ministry is that section 22 applies where the creditor has seized property owned by the subject debtor liable to remit the taxes. Consequently, if title has never transferred to the debtor, revised section 22 will not apply to the transaction.

Clients should be warned that outside of bankruptcy, there is a priority right for the Crown for which the secured creditor may be personally liable if the appropriate tax clearance certificate has not been obtained.

---

1.   R.S.O. 1990, c. P. 10.
2.   S.C. 1991, c. 46.
3.   R.S.C. 1985, c. B-3 as am.
3-1. R.S.C. 1985, c. B-3 as am.
4.   *Supra*, note 1.
5.   *Supra*, note 1, s. 63(5).
6.   *Supra*, note 1, s. 63(7).
7.   *Supra*, note 1, s. 63(7)(e).
8.   S.C. 1991, c. 46.
9.   *Supra*, note 2, s. 179(4)(a).
10. *Supra*, note 2, s. 179(5).
11. *Supra*, note 2, s. 178.

12. *Supra*, note 1.
13. *Supra*, note 2.
14. *Supra*, note 3.
15. *Supra*, note 3, s. 243(2).
16. *Supra*, note 3, ss. 245, 246.
17. *Supra*, note 3.
18. *Supra*, note 3, S.C. 1997, c. 12.
19. *Supra*, note 3, s. 244.
20. *Supra*, note 1.
21. *Supra*, note 1.
22. *Supra*, note 1.
23. Tax Credits to Create Jobs Act, S.O. 1997, c. 43.
24. An Act to Amend the Fuel Tax Act and the Gasoline Tax Act, S.O. 1998, c. 30.

Mortgagee of Land

General

9.651—When a mortgagor has defaulted under its obligations contained in a mortgage, the mortgagee has a number of remedies open to it. One of those remedies, and the remedy most commonly exercised, is the private power of sale. There are other situations in which a purchaser will find itself buying from a mortgagee. If the mortgagee has obtained a final order of foreclosure or a quit claim deed from the mortgagor, then title will have vested in the mortgagee and it will be able to convey title directly itself. These conveyances are not dissimilar to an ordinary purchase and sale transaction. Another situation in which a purchaser may find itself buying from a mortgagee is in a judicial sale action. Because the private power of sale is by far the most frequently exercised mortgage remedy, and because the rules governing power of sale are very precise and somewhat peculiar, this section deals only with the private power of sale mortgage remedy.

The Remedy Generally

9.652—A mortgagee may sell the mortgaged property under either the power of sale contained in the mortgage or pursuant to the power of sale provisions set out under the Mortgages Act[1]. The mortgage itself will usually contain a power of sale provision; that is, it permits the mortgagee to sell the mortgaged property privately upon default. The mortgagee has the right to convey the title to the property to a third-party purchaser and then to apply the sale proceeds to the outstanding mortgage debt (including all costs incurred in enforcing the mortgage). If the sale proceeds are less than the mortgage debt, the mortgagee has the additional right to sue the mortgagor for the deficiency. If, on the other hand, the sale produces a surplus, the mortgagee is obligated to turn over that surplus to the next party entitled to a share of the sale proceeds. The next entitled party would ordinarily be the encumbrancer, whose interest in the property is registered after the mortgagee's interest. It may also be a subsequent mortgagee, a lien claimant, an execution creditor, etc. If there are no other encumbrancers, the surplus from the sale is turned over to the mortgagor.

A mortgagee selling under power of sale thus assumes some responsibility in the nature of a trustee for the mortgagor and for subsequent encumbrancers, with respect to surplus funds resulting from the sale of the mortgaged property. The mortgagee has an obligation, upon completion of the sale, to render an accounting to any interested party so that that party is able to confirm proper disposal of the proceeds. The mortgagee also has a related obligation to obtain the best possible price for the property, given the particular circumstances of the sale. As a general proposition, and there is substantial case law on this issue, a mortgagee selling under private power of sale must take such steps and exercise such care in the selling process as would a reasonably prudent vendor of his or her own property. If the mortgagee fails to observe this obligation, it potentially may find itself involved with a subsequent encumbrancer and/or the mortgagor in an improvident sale action.

---

1. R.S.O. 1990, c. M. 40.

Results of a Power of Sale

9.653—When the mortgagee has completed the exercise of a power of sale, the mortgagee no longer retains an interest in the property. If the sale is conducted properly, it has the effect of extinguishing by operation of law the rights and interests in the property of all parties who held an interest subsequent in priority to the mortgagee's interest. The only remedy available to a mortgagor or to a subsequent encumbrancer whose interest has been extinguished by a power of sale proceeding, is to commence an action against the mortgagee for an improvident or improper sale. Those parties are also, as mentioned above, entitled to a strict accounting of the sale proceeds.

Any encumbrancer of the property whose interest was registered prior to the mortgage under which the power of sale is conducted is not affected by the sale.

The purchaser of a mortgaged property who buys under power of sale acquires good title to the property, subject only to encumbrances which existed prior to the mortgage, as long as the sale under the mortgage was completed in "professed compliance" with the Mortgages Act[1] and all proper parties were served with the notice of sale.

---

1. R.S.O. 1990, c. M.40.

Triggering of Power of Sale Proceedings

9.654—Before a mortgagee may commence power of sale proceedings there must be a default sufficient to trigger the proceedings. The power of sale provisions contained in the mortgage are usually determinative. Section 32 of the Mortgages Act[1] requires that a notice of sale may not be given until default has continued for a least 15 days. If default consists of failure to pay on a specified date (which is the usual default situation), determining the period of default is straightforward. Demand mortgages are more problematic in the sense that it may be difficult to establish the precise date on which default occurs. The case law suggests that a mortgagee will have to provide a "reasonable time" after demand has been made before power of sale proceedings can properly be commenced. In certain cases, the mortgage default is not a default of payment but, rather, a failure to observe some positive or negative mortgage covenant. In this type of situation, the mortgage provisions should be scrutinized to determine whether the particular default that has occurred is valid grounds for commencing a power of sale. As with demand mortgages, the case law supports a requirement that reasonable notice be provided by the mortgagee to the mortgagor to cure the non-payment default prior to commencement of power of sale proceedings.

---

1.   R.S.O. 1990, c. M.40.

Notice Requirement

9.655—Most mortgages contain a provision requiring a 35-day notice period once the period of default has expired. Section 32 of the Mortgages Act[1] reaffirms a minimum 35 day notice period. The terms of the mortgage will prevail if they specify longer default and notice periods. A notice of sale must be given either by personal service or by registered mail. Section 34 of the Mortgages Act[2] deems a notice of sale to be given on the day on which it is sent by registered mail. If a mortgage does not contain a power of sale provision, the mortgagee may utilize the statutory power of sale provisions set out in Part II of the Mortgages Act[3]. The time periods under Part II are longer than in the ordinary course. Section 24 of the Mortgages Act[4] provides that a sale cannot occur until at least 3 months after default in the payment of monies due under the mortgage, or failure to pay an insurance premium required to have been paid by the mortgagor under the terms of the mortgage. A sale under section 24 cannot be made until at least 45 days notice has been provided to all parties entitled to notice in accordance with Part III of the Mortgages Act[5]. If a mortgage contains its own power of sale provisions, the Part II provisions under the Mortgages Act[6] do not apply.

---

1. R.S.O. 1990, c. M.40.

2. *Ibid.*
3. *Ibid.*
4. *Ibid.*
5. *Ibid.*
6. *Ibid.*

Parties to be Served

9.656—Notice of sale must be served to the following parties:

(i) Because the effect of a sale under power of sale is to extinguish any interest subsequent to the mortgage being enforced, together with the interest of the mortgagor, it is essential that notice of the sale be sent to each of those parties. All of those appearing, from a review of the abstract index or parcel register, to have an interest in the mortgaged property subsequent to the mortgage itself, will have to be served, including:

(ii) The current registered owner of the property, together with the original mortgagor, must be served.

(iii) Execution creditors whose writs of execution were filed subsequent to the registration of the mortgage must be served with a notice of sale.

(iv) If the mortgagee has written notice of a statutory lien, the Crown or other public authority holding the lien should be provided with a notice of sale. Likewise, if the mortgagee has actual notice in writing of a construction lien claimant's unregistered potential lien claim, that claimant should also be served with a notice of sale.

(v) A tenant may or may not have to be served with a notice of sale. If a lease was entered into by the mortgagor, subsequent to the registration of the mortgage, and if the mortgagee did not acquiesce, the tenant should be provided notice, as it has a right to redeem. The mortgagee's right to possession of the property, however, supersedes the tenant's right to possession. If the lease was registered prior to the registration of the mortgage, or in certain situations if the tenant has possession of the property and the mortgagee has actual notice of the tenant's interest prior to taking its mortgage security, the tenant's leasehold interest will have priority over the mortgagee's interest.

In each case, the practical implications of a tenant in possession must be carefully considered. Very often a mortgagee will wish to sell a commercial property with tenants in place. If, for some reason, the mortgagee wishes to sell the property on a vacant basis, the mortgagee's rights vis-à-vis the tenant will have to be scrutinized to ensure that this can validly be effected. While it is beyond the scope of this paper, a mortgagee who deals with a tenant in possession (for example, by attorning rents), must be cognizant of the concept of "mortgagee in possession" and the implications that flow from it.

Manner of Serving Notice

9.657—Subsection 33(1) of the Mortgages Act[1] governs the service of a notice of sale. Subsection 33(1) reads as follows:

> A notice of exercising a power of sale shall be given by personal service or by registered mail addressed to the person to whom it is to be given at his usual or last known place of address, or, where the last known place of address is that shown on the registered instrument under which he acquired his interest, to such address, or by leaving it at one of such places of address, or where the mortgage provides for personal service only, by personal service, or, where the mortgage provides a specific address, to such address.

The most prudent approach in serving a notice of sale is to send it to every possible address for each party being served. The notice should be sent to any "address for service" noted on registered documents. The mortgagee should also be specifically asked to review a draft form of notice of sale in order to advise whether it is aware of any other, more current addresses for any of the parties being served. Notices should be sent not only to the parties, but also to their solicitors, where that information is available. A corporate search should be conducted against any corporate entities being served, in order to determine the registered/head office. It is also sometimes both possible, and prudent, to check for current addresses of parties in the telephone directory.

A notice of sale is deemed to be given on the day on which it is mailed, if sent by registered mail in Ontario. This rule applies notwithstanding that a notice is later returned. Under subsections 33(2) and 33(3) of the Mortgages Act[2] execution creditors and lien claimants may be served by sending the notice to their solicitors only. Again, however, in the interest of prudence, if an address for a lien claimant or execution creditor is available, the notice should be sent both directly to the party as well as to its solicitors.

---

1. R.S.O. 1990, c. M.40.
2. Ibid.

Form of Notice

9.658—The Mortgages Act[1] requires that a notice of sale must follow the Form referred to under subsections 26(1) and 31(1) of the Act. **[See 9F117].** The notice of sale must be completed with much care, since even relatively minor deficiencies will render it open to attack. If a court finds that notice of sale is in any way ambiguous or confusing, it will hold it to be invalid.

The notice should be completed in consultation with the mortgagee. The mortgagee's input will be especially critical in completing the amounts outstanding. Attention should also be paid to the interest rate specified in the notice. If the maturity date set out in the original mortgage has passed, it may be that the interest rate has been amended by registered or unregistered agreement. Another point to note is that if the notice is being issued pursuant to the statutory power of sale contained in the Mortgages Act[2], and not pursuant to a power of sale contained in the mortgage itself, the wording contained in the precedent will have to be appropriately amended. Care should be taken with respect to the legal description included in the notice of sale. This should be taken directly from the mortgage (with appropriate amendments should any part of the mortgaged property have been sold and a partial discharge provided). The date of the mortgage, the date of registration, and the instrument number should all be carefully checked. In addition to principal, interest, and legal costs incurred in connection with issuing the notice of sale, the mortgagee should be asked what, if any, costs it has incurred with respect to the property, so that these also can be included. For example, the mortgagee may have paid a realty tax instalment, an insurance premium, condominium common expenses, etc.. Pursuant to most standard mortgage provisions, payments such as these made by a mortgagee on behalf of a mortgagor may be included in the amounts secured by the mortgage and recovered in any enforcement proceeding.

---

1. R.S.O. 1990, c. M.40.
2. *Ibid.*

From Issuance of Notice to Sale

9.659—Once the notice of sale has been sent to the parties entitled to receipt of same, a period of statutorily imposed inactivity next follows. Section 42(1) of the Mortgages Act[1] prohibits any "further proceedings" being taken by a mortgagee during the notice period. This phrase has been judicially interpreted to include a multitude of mortgagee actions. A mortgagee is therefore best advised to do absolutely nothing during the notice period. If the mortgagor or another interested party has not redeemed the mortgage during the notice period, the mortgagee may then take steps to sell the property.

The first logical step in the selling process is the obtaining of appraisals. The standard practice is to obtain at least two independent appraisals. Again, while it is outside the scope of this title, it should be noted that the courts have set up a standard of care for a mortgagee enforcing its mortgage security by way of power of sale. The mortgagee must take all steps that a reasonable and prudent vendor would take in the ordinary course. After appraisals have been obtained, the next step that a mortgagee will usually take is to list the property with a reputable broker, preferably on a multiple listing service, and wait to see what offers are submitted. During this phase the role of the solicitor is ordinarily minimal. The mortgagee may require offers to be vetted by its solicitor. **[See 9F116 for a pro vendor/mortgagee**

form of agreement of purchase and sale]. The specific power of sale provisions included in the schedule to the agreement of purchase and sale are fairly typical. The provisions are, for the most part, self-explanatory. Typically, the mortgagee's position in selling a property under power of sale is that it does not have firsthand familiarity with the property, and therefore can provide very little in the way of warranties, representations, declarations of possession, etc. The mortgagee wants to sell on an "as is, where is" basis. It simply wants to recover its money from the property and to have no ongoing obligations. The purchaser will have to satisfy itself that the property that it is acquiring is a viable one. The agreement will provide time to have a search of title conducted and title requisitions submitted. However, a purchaser may wish to satisfy itself with respect to other matters (such as municipal work orders) before it submits its offer. It may also submit a conditional offer. As no ongoing representations or warranties are typically provided by mortgagees selling under power of sale (including the standard warranty with respect to urea formaldehyde), a purchaser would be well-advised to have a professional building inspector conduct a detailed inspection of the property before submitting an offer, or while the offer is in a conditional phase.

---

1. R.S.O. 1990, c. M.40.

Completion of the Sale

9.660—If the mortgaged property is located in the registry system, the solicitor acting for the purchaser will have to be particularly vigilant. If the property is in the land titles system, subsection 99(1) of the Land Titles Act[1] stipulates that "evidence specified by the Director of Titles" must be provided in order to give clear title. In the registry system, the standard practice is for 3 statutory declarations to be deposited on title prior to or at the time of closing. These declarations include the following:

(i)   a declaration regarding service of the notice of sale; [**See Forms 9F120 and 9F123**]

(ii)   a declaration of the mortgagee confirming default under the mortgage; [**See Forms 9F118 and 9F121**] and

(iii)   a declaration of the mortgagee or its solicitor (usually its solicitor) stating that the sale complies with Part III of the Mortgages Act[2]. [**See Forms 9F119 and 9F122**]

In the land titles system (either in paper-based jurisdictions or in jurisdictions governed by electronic registration), the transfer/deed shall include either similar statutory declarations, or, alternatively, prescribed solicitor statements attached to the transfer/deed.

Where statutory declarations are to be used, they generally must be scrutinized by the land registrar and are actually attached to the transfer/deed, rather than being separately deposited. It normally takes at least several days for these declarations to be reviewed. Care should therefore be taken to submit them well before closing so that sufficient time is available and any necessary amendments can be made. In jurisdictions governed by electronic registration, pre-approval of the transfer/deed and the declarations is not required.

In the alternative, prescribed solicitor statements[3] attached to the transfer/deed may be used. These statements are as follows:

1. A statement that the sale is authorized under the charge and the Mortgages Act.

2. A statement that the charge was in default at the time notice of sale was given and continues to be in default and that money has been advanced under the charge.

3. A statement that the sale proceedings comply with the charge, the Mortgages Act and if applicable the Bankruptcy and Insolvency Act (Canada), the Condominium Act, the Construction Lien Act, and the Farm Debt Review Act (Canada).

4. A statement identifying the instruments by instrument number and date of registration and writs of execution by name and writ number that rank subsequent to the charge and that are to be deleted from the parcel register as a result of the registration of the transfer.

5. A statement of spousal status under the Family Law Act with respect to every person whose spouse was not served with a notice under the Mortgages Act and whose interest is to be deleted on the registration of the transfer.

In jurisdictions governed by electronic registration, where these statements are used, the transfer/deed can only be registered by a lawyer since the statements made are law statements.

---

1. R.S.O. 1990, c. L.5.
2. R.S.O. 1990, c. M.40.
3. For jurisdictions governed by electronic registration, the authority for use of solicitor statements is found in section 20 of Regulation 19/99 (Electronic Registration) to the Land Registration Reform Act. For land titles properties in jurisdictions not governed by electronic registration, the authority for use of solicitor statements is found in Bulletin 98007 (December 18, 1998) issued by the Director of Land Titles pursuant to its authority under subsection 99(1) of the Land Titles Act.

9.661—Certain power of sale recitals will also be included in the transfer/deed where the property is registered in the registry system. These recitals should reference the following:

(i)   the particulars of the mortgage under which the sale is being conducted;

(ii)   the fact that a power of sale exists and the applicable default and notice periods;

(iii)   the fact that default has occurred and that notice has been given to all persons entitled thereto;

(iv)   that the notice period has expired and that default has not been remedied; and

(v)   that statutory declarations regarding the particulars of default, the service of notice of sale, and the sale proceedings have been deposited on title.

A vendor/mortgagee will ordinarily be reluctant to provide much in addition to the requisite statutory declarations. The vendor/mortgagee should provide a direction regarding payment of the balance due on closing, if not all funds are to be paid directly to it. An undertaking to readjust items set out in the statement of adjustments should also be provided. The undertaking of the vendor/mortgagee may also reference payment of utility accounts to closing and delivery of vacant possession and keys on closing. The purchaser may also request, and it would not be reasonable for the vendor/mortgagee to refuse to provide, a statement pursuant to section 116 of the Income Tax Act[1]. Aside from these basic documents, a vendor/mortgagee should not volunteer, and a purchaser should not expect to receive much, if anything, further. [**See Forms 9F124–9F128**]

---

1.   R.S.C. 1985, c. 1 (5th Supp.).

Power of Sale Under a Debenture

9.662—On occasion, especially for commercial properties, the mortgage pursuant to which a mortgagee is proceeding to exercise a power of sale is contained within   debenture. Section 41 of the *Mortgages Act* provides that the Part III requirements regarding a notice of sale under a mortgage do not apply to a "mortgage given by a corporation to secure bonds or debentures". The power of sale provision contained in a mortgage within a debenture typically does not reference an extended notice period. There has been some case law which casts shadow (albeit slight) over the validity of proceeding, in certain situations, under a debenture that has no notice requirement. The practical result is that most solicitors tend to treat a power of sale under a debenture the same as a power of sale under an ordinary mortgage. The Part III timing requirements are adhered to, a notice of sale is issued, the usually statutory declarations are prepared and registered, etc.

A purchaser acquiring a property subject to a debenture should ensure that a power of sale is being exercised by the debenture/holder rather than the property simply being sold by the debenture/holder (or by a receiver appointed by it) pursuant to a power of attorney. Most debentures contain a power of attorney from the corporation providing the debenture in favour of the debenture/holder. A sale of a property pursuant to a power of attorney will not have the same legal results as a sale pursuant to a power of sale. Depending on the circumstances, this may be acceptable but, in all cases, the purchaser and the purchaser's solicitor should be fully cognizant of the method of conveyance. [**See generally Forms 9F116–9F131**]

7. ORGANIZING THE PURCHASER

General

9.663—As part of the transaction, it may be necessary to organize a purchasing entity to effect the transaction. This may be the organization of partnership or limited partnership or the incorporation of a new company with all of the requisite requirements for its bylaws, resolutions and issuances of shares.

If the purchaser is an individual, he or she may need some tax and legal advice as to whether he or she should incorporate. He or she may also require some general advice concerning the benefits of a limited liability corporation, with regard to the provision of services or goods to the public.

If a partnership is intended, it may require the creation of a partnership agreement to document the relationship among the partners. If a limited partnership is intended, this also will need to be made subject to an agreement.

If there is to be an incorporation, instructions will be required with regard to the jurisdiction in which to incorporate and an understanding of the share capital that will best serve the individual shareholders.

[See Checklists 9C13–9C15 to assist the solicitor to take instructions to incorporate a purchaser, organize a shareholder agreement, or organize a partnership agreement.]

Banking

9.664—The purchaser will have to make an arrangement with its bank, credit union, trust company or other financial institution as to maintaining accounts for the business. If borrowings are needed from such financial institution, see "FINANCING THE DEAL" with regard to security for financing the purchase.

The client may be able to open its account on its own at its financial institution but may need to obtain from its solicitor true copies of the partnership agreement, limited partnership agreement or articles of incorporation to establish the nature of the busines operation, and, so that the financial institution may use the correct forms to document the account.

The client will then deliver to its bankers any of the following agreements:

(i)   agreements regarding operation of the account;

(ii)   certified copies of the borrowing by-law;

(iii)   certified copy of account operating resolution; and

(iv)   specimen signature cards.

Copies of the by-law and resolution should be delivered to the solicitor so that the original by-laws and resolutions are properly passed before certified copies are delivered to the institution. The client clearly needs to understand who will have signing authority and for what amounts.

Most agreements regarding operation of the account contain a provision that monthly statements must be revieed by the client within so many days (usually 30) of their issuance and any deficiencies or problems brought to the institution's attention within that time period. Failure to do so may cause the client to waive its rights for any such problems subsequently found as against the institution.

Business accounts need to have careful control of operation of signing authorities and preparation of cheques so as to ensure that fraud is not perpetrated against the client. Clients that are sloppy in the control of their finances may be found to have contributed to the forgery or fraud being perpetrated against them, relieving their bankers of liability for instruments honoured contrary to the banking agreement and specimen signatures.

The client may also require passage of further corporate resolutions to authorize corporate credit card accounts and other banking services such as payroll operation. It is important to check with the client so that all proceedings in the minute book are addressed.

EMPLOYEES

GENERAL

9.665—A purchaser who has acquired the business of a vendor by way of share purchase or asset purchase will have given consideration to many significant aspects of the transaction involving the employees of the business. A purchaser may want to refer to the items reviewed under the heading "DUE DILIGENCE AND INVESTIGATIONS—EMPLOYEES" and particularly **Para. 9.220 and Checklist 9C8.** There are numerous items contained within the checklist with which the purchaser may be concerned. Once the purchase has been completed, there are also a significant number of items that a purchaser will have to attend to in order to have the business functioning efficiently as soon as possible. Items requiring special attention are outlined in the points which follow.

Registrations

9.666—Workers' Compensation: New employers have a responsibility to register with the Workplace Safety and Insurance Board as soon as any workers are hired. Most employers are required to register on a compulsory basis while other employers, who are not compulsorily covered, may request coverage for their workers. Out-of-province employers may also be required to register. Employers must contact the board by telephone, letter, fax, or personal interview within 30 calendar days of hiring the first worker and return a completed employer's statement of payroll and their registration form within 45 days of these forms being issued to the employer by the board. An employer must advise the Board of the purchase or sale of a business or of assets within 10 days of the dispostion.

The Purchaser should also be aware that the Workplace Safety and Insurance Board can levy a penalty upon an employer for failing to register on time.

9.667—Canada Revenue Agency: The purchaser of an ongoing business with employees will need to ensure that the business employing the employees is properly registered with Canada Revenue Agency for the purposes of making source deductions for income tax, unemployment insurance premium contributions, and Canada Pension Plan contributions. The purchaser should register the business employing the employees with the nearest office of Canada Revenue Agency.

Failure to so register the business and to make appropriate source deductions will lead to significant financial liability and possible penalties for the purchaser.

9.668—Employer's Health Tax (Ontario): Employers who pay remuneration to employees in Ontario may be obligated to pay a tax for the purpose of providing health care in Ontario. Such health tax payments must be made to the Ontario Ministry of Revenue on either a quarterly or monthly instalment basis, depending on the size of an employer's payroll. An employer would need to register with the Ontario Ministry of Revenue and would be required to keep records and books of accounts at a permanent establishment of the employer in Ontario, or at such other place as is designated by the Minister of Revenue. An employer will also be required to deliver annual returns after the end of the year and remit any balance of tax payable for the year.

Pay Equity (Ontario)

9.669—If as a result of the purchase, the purchaser has acquired new employees formerly employed by the vendor, it would be prudent for the purchaser to re-evaluate the requirements of the Pay Equity Act[1]. The purchaser may be required to implement compensation adjustments provided for in the vendor's pay equity plan. The purchase may also require the purchaser to develop a new plan, or to negotiate a new plan with the union. New employers should implement new pay equity, immediately upon commencing operations. **[See Para. 9.280]**

---

1. R.S.O. 1990, c. P.7.

Union and Employee Notification

9.670—If a purchaser has acquired a business by way of share purchase, the purchaser should consider providing notice to any union that may hold bargaining rights or a collective agreement covering employees of the business, of the fact that the purchaser has bought the business formerly operated by the vendor. A general notice of the purchase might also be given to employees of the acquired business.

If a purchaser has acquired additional employees from the vendor through an asset purchase, the purchaser will, of necessity, have had to notify these employees of their new employment status with the purchaser. In the case of an asset purchase, a purchaser should not notify any union involved with the business operated by the vendor of the purchase, until the purchaser has had an opportunity to assess its position as to whether it would be considered a successor employer to the vendor. This should be done before the transaction is completed. At this juncture, the purchaser may wish to retain legal counsel to assess its position. If the purchaser acquires most of the significant assets of the vendor, takes over most or all of the employees and operates a similar type of business as an ongoing concern, it is likely that the purchaser would be found to be a successor to the vendor, and any union involved with the vendor's business could assert successor rights against the purchaser. While it may not be prudent for the purchaser to give notice to any union involved with the vendor's business that it has acquired significant assets of the vendor, the purchaser should be aware that the Labour Relations Act, 1985[1] essentially binds a successor employer to any collective agreements, bargaining agents or certification proceedings that were in place with the vendor, until the Ontario Labour Relations Board declares otherwise.

---

1. S.O. 1995, c. 1, Sched. A.

Occupational Health & Safety

9.671—A purchaser who has acquired a business by way of share purchase will stand fully in the shoes of the vendor with respect to any orders that immediately ensure compliance with all orders issued by an inspector or director under the Occupational Health & Safety Act[1]. If a purchaser acquires a business by way of an asset purchase, the purchaser will also want to ensure compliance with any orders of an inspector under the Occupational Health & Safety Act[2] that may pertain to the assets acquired. **[See Para. 9.290]**

---

1. R.S.O. 1990, c. O.1.
2. *Ibid.*

Employment Contracts

9.672—A purchaser who has acquired employees by way of an asset purchase from a vendor should give consideration to whether it wishes to enter into any written employment contracts with any of such employees. There are significant advantages to any employer in entering into an employment contract with an employee. In the event that the purchaser wishes to employ certain employees of the vendor on a speculative basis, employment contracts can be entered into with these employees at the commencement of their employment with the purchaser, limiting their rights to claim for damages on termination, in the event that they prove unsatisfactory in the future. **[See Para. 9.310]**

New Employers

9.673—A significant number of business purchasers may be new employers. Such a new employer may wish to give consideration to the following areas of concern:

(i) Workers' Compensation - A new employer will need to register with the Workplace Safety and Insurance Board and submit a Statement of Payroll in the prescribed form.

(ii) Canada Customs and Revenue Agency - A new employer will need to register with Canada Customs and Revenue Agency with respect to source deductions.

(iii) Employer's Health Tax - A new employer will need to register with the Ontario Ministry of Revenue and make appropriate instalment payments with respect to Employer's Health Tax.

(iv) Pay Equity - A new employer will need to establish immediate pay equity and maintain pay equity within its work force.

(v) Occupational Health & Safety - If more than five employees are regularly employed at a workplace, an employer will have to prepare, post, annually review, and maintain a program to implement a written Occupational Health & Safety Policy. In any workplace in which the number of workers regularly exceeds five, an employer will also need to have the workers select at least one Health & Safety Representative from among the workers at the workplace. In any workplace at which twenty (20) or more workers are regularly employed, an employer will need to establish a joint health and safety committee, instead of having the workers select health and safety representatives. Ontario's Occupational Health & Safety Act[1] places significant obligations upon all employers in Ontario and a new employer should acquaint itself with all the requirements of this statute as they may affect the employer's operations.

(vi) Employment Standards - A new employer should recognize that the Employment Standards Act[2] establishes minimum employment standards in a number of significant areas affecting the operations of most Ontario employers (for example, minimum wages, hours of work, and overtime requirements). The Employment Standards Act[3] also obligates an employer to prepare and keep in Ontario complete and accurate records for stipulated periods of time.

(vii) <u>Employment Contracts</u> - A new employer will want to give consideration to entering into written employment contracts with its employees. A particular advantage of a written employment contract is that it allows an employer to specify and limit the period of notice of termination that may be required. It is also desirable to have a system in which the employee affirms the contract from time to time during the course of employment. This affirmation could be confirmed by having the employee execute a new employment agreement when the employee changes his/her position or receives a salary increase. An employment agreement can also alter what would otherwise be the common law position as to the level of competence required of the employee, and the standard of "just cause" for dismissal. **[See Paras. 9.220-9.320]**

---

1. R.S.O. 1990, c. O. 1.
2. S.O. 20002, c. 41.
3. *Ibid.*

Licences, Permits, Tax Numbers

9.674—Prior to the purchase, the purchaser should obtain all requisite licences, permits, and tax numbers in order to immediately commence operation. Some licences may have been transferable from the vendor and completion of the recording of such transfers needs to be done. However, other licences such as liquor licences, nursing home licences, and agricultural quotas may not be transferable. In such cases the purchaser should effect its own filings with the requisite issuing bodies, in order to obtain its licences prior to closing, or should hire persons with the requisite licences such as pharmacists or engineers, to conduct that portion of the operations.

In order for the purchaser to carry on business it will need all requisite licences, permits, and tax numbers necessary to operate the business.

With respect to Canada Customs and Revenue Agency, the Ontario Ministry of Consumer and Commercial Relations will automatically forward to Canada Customs and Revenue Agency notice of creation of a new entity. Canada Customs and Revenue Agency then generates the necessary forms, which it sends directly to the registered office of the new corporation in order for it to properly complete the same to be registered with Canada Customs and Revenue Agency.

For Ontario provincial retails sales taxes, the purchaser fills out an Ontario Ministry of Revenue form number TR1, to be recorded with its records as an Ontario vendor.

8. FINANCING THE DEAL

Financing the Purchaser

Vendor Take Back Security

9.674.1—Part of the transaction may be the requirement that the vendor take back security to secure payment of all or a portion of the unpaid purchase price. Such may occur in either an asset or a share transaction. In an asset transaction, the vendor may take security such as a mortgage on freehold lands or a security agreement registered pursuant to the PPSA[1], either in first position or behind the bank and other financial institutions providing the operating line and other funding to the borrower. In a share deal, the vendor may take a pledge of the subject shares until the price therefor is paid in full.

---

1. R.S.O. 1990, c. P.10.

Other Lenders and Joint Representation

9.675—If the purchaser prefers to use its bank or other financial institution to obtain loans to finance the acquisition of the assets or shares, the solicitor will have the additional burden of negotiating two transactions at the same time, both the acquisition and the financing.

While acting as purchaser's counsel, the necessary due diligence will already have been performed, in order to assist the client to purchase the assets. Hence, there will be an inclination to having the same solicitor represent both the purchaser as borrower and the financial institution as lender, in order to save legal costs.

Many government departments and some banks, particularly for loans under $1,000,000, will be prepared to have one law firm represent both borrower and lender. In such situations, the lending institution usually issues a covering letter, stating they expect the firm to represent both parties and providing a list of instructions, standard form documentation, and possibly standard forms of reports expected from the firm on closing.[1]

It is preferable to have this consent signed by the borrower, the lender, and any third party guarantors or shareholders who will also be signing materials to be prepared. It is preferable to obtain the written consent from all appropriate parties prior to the commencement of work on the file. [**See**

Form 9F132 for a form of consent with respect to an acknowledgment of joint representation.]

---

1. In the event of representing both borrower and lender, please refer to Rule 5 of the Law Society of Upper Canada Rules of Professional Conduct. Rule 5 requires disclosure to all sides and the consent of all clients to the joint representation.

Commitment Letters and Loan Agreements

9.676—Frequently, the client will arrive at its solicitor's office with a commitment letter that has already been issued by the financial institution and accepted by the client. Occasionally, the client will bring the commitment letter in prior to execution by the borrower and seek legal advice with respect to its terms and conditions.

In providing advice with respect to commitment letters, it is helpful to bear in mind the following points:

(i) **The Cost of Money:** Is it possible for the client to obtain a lower rate of interest, longer amortization period, longer period between compounding of interest and/or reduction of commitment fees or standby fees?

(ii) **Overlapping of Security to be Provided:** Usually, banks will require security over inventory of the business taken under a combination of section 427 of the Bank Act[1], an inventory security agreement, a general security and/or a debenture, creating a charge on the inventories. It is sometimes possible to negotiate the removal of a duplication of mortgages, charges, and security interests.

(iii) **Covenants and Representations:** Are all the representations true and correct? Is it possible for the client to fulfill the covenants as stated, such as frequency of reporting requirements or financial ratios, without extreme difficulty, expense or inconvenience?

Frequently, the commitment letter as accepted by the borrower becomes the loan agreement. Demand loans generally use a commitment letter only, as the lender may demand to be repaid at any time. Term loans tend to use loan agreements to provide specific details on how the loan will be administered during the term, more extensive positive and negative covenants than the commitment letter, and numerous events of default and remedies.

---

1. S.C. 1991, c. 46.

Due Diligence

9.677—In timing the closing of the transaction, it must be remembered that the security documentation must be executed and delivered, and registration completed, with appropriate time left to enable subsearching to be done, all before funds will be available for the borrower. Remember that the PPSA[1] searching computer is usually operating two or three business days in arrears of real time and that it takes an additional business day to obtain a certified search printout. Consequently, if a document is registered by a financing statement filed on Monday, such registration may not appear on a search ordered on Thursday but available for pick-up on Friday.

To avoid some timing problems, preregister as permitted by subsection 45(3) of the PPSA[2], for deals not including consumer goods as collateral.

If acting for the borrower using the funds to acquire assets, the due diligence may need to cover two separate entities: (i) the vendor and title to the assets being acquired and subsequently charged in favour of the lender and (ii) the purchasing entity with respect to the priority of the charges being granted by it to the lender.

If any registrations or searches are to be made in other counties in Ontario, or in other provinces, ensure extra time for couriers, registrations, subsearches, and return couriers for opinions and registered materials. **[See also "DUE DILIGENCE AND INVESTIGATIONS" and Checklist 9C18.]**

---

1. R.S.O. 1990, c. P.10.
2. *Ibid.*

Security and Other Documents

9.678—**What assets are involved:** The nature of the assets involved will dictate which security documents will be required from the borrower. For example, the following:

(i) An interest in freehold land can be charged by a Charge/Mortgage form or under a debenture;

(ii) A leasehold interest in land may be charged by a mortgage of lease, an assignment of lease, and/or debenture;

(iii) Inventory can be charged under section 427 of the Bank Act[1], a security agreement, and/or debenture;

(iv) Equipment can be charged under a security agreement, debenture and fixtures notice registered against title where such equipment is located;

(v) Receivables can be charged under an assignment of book accounts document, security agreement, and/or debenture;

(vi) Intellectual property can be charged under a security agreement, a debenture or by assignments of specific patents, trade marks, trade names, or other intellectual property rights;

(vii) Stocks, bonds, and securities can be pledged by physical delivery;

(viii) Ships can be charged under ships mortgages; and

(ix) Rolling stock can be charged under the Canada Transportation Act.[2]

Consequently, the types of documents involved in these transactions depends on the nature of the assets involved.

---

1. S.C. 1991, c. 46.
2. S.C. 1996, c. 10.

9.679—Where assets are located: Each of the jurisdictions of Canada has its own statutes respecting the taking of and perfection of security in personal property and real property. Consequently, the location of the assets will also govern the documentation involved. For example, the following:

(i) Debentures, trust deeds and bonds are registrable in the appropriate government offices in each of the twelve jurisdictions of Canada. However, if any of the chattels and lands are located in the province of Quebec, a debenture form is inapplicable and a form of trust deed must be used, with the requisite affidavits and materials sworn before a notary public for the province of Quebec.

(ii) Assignments of book debts for registration in the province of Quebec need to be on legal length paper with specific margins and running on both sides of the page, and require execution before two witnesses for each of the borrower and the lender, with requisite affidavits of execution completed. They also require registration of notice of the granting of the assignment published in both an English language and a French language newspaper of general circulation in each registration district in which the assignment is registered.

(iii)   There is a PPSA Statute in all provinces and territories, except Quebec. Security agreements are registered by filing of financing statements in the PPSA[1] jurisdictions across Canada. Quebec has registration systems for leases, conditional sales and hypothecs under its civil code.[2]

The statutes for each jurisdiction should be consulted to confirm the details concerning place of registration, registration time limits, rules governing the naming of debtors, describing "motor vehicles" (as defined by that jurisdiction) and expiration dates. Local counsel will be required to assist in registration and searching if the lender requires opinions concerning due registration of the security in another jurisdiction and requires the results of local searches.

---

1. R.S.O. 1990, c. P.10.
2. A new Civil Code was proclaimed in January, 1994 which created a new personal property security registration system in Quebec.

9.680—Review of the documents: The documentation is usually prepared by lender's counsel or, in the case of joint representation of borrower or lender, usually the lender's standard preprinted forms are used. It is essential to review the documents to ascertain that they conform to the following points:

(i)   Do the security documents contain the same terms and conditions for the loan as outlined in the commitment letter? (For example, has the interest rate been stated at the specified rate and compounded at the appropriate time periods?)

(ii)   Are the representations and warranties true and correct as stated in the document, without amendment? Most borrowers will have prior registered encumbrances for such things as vehicle financing and equipment leases. If the borrower is to represent the assets being charged as free and clear, the document will need to be amended to have the prior existing charges accepted as prior permitted encumbrances, or else discharges will need to be obtained.

(iii)   Is the borrower able to fulfill all of the covenants? For example, will it be expensive or onerous to produce extensive financial records each month? Can the borrower meet specific financial ratios at all times of the year, including its seasonal slow period of business?

(iv)   Are the terms of the document more onerous than those contemplated in the commitment letter?

(v)   Are any particular terms unreasonable? For example, will the lender consider a grace period before an event of non-payment or breach of a covenant becomes an event of default?

It may be advisable to meet with the borrower or write to the borrower to point out portions of the documents which are considered onerous, and to obtain instructions to negotiate certain points with counsel for the lender.

9.681—Completion of the forms: It is worth the time and effort to ensure that each form is fully completed, and to complete all names, addresses, amounts, interest rates, and other details with precision. This will greatly facilitate the signing time required by the client to execute the documents, and will lessen the possibility of either a document being rejected by the lender as incomplete or being rejected by the government as incapable of registration, during the rush to close a transaction.

9.682—Names of the borrower, guarantors, and any shareholders or other third parties executing security documents should be verified by using the following documents:

A.   microfiche search or certified copy of the articles for a corporate borrower;

B.   copy of the partnership registration for partnership or limited partnership and copies of appropriate microfiches and/or birth certificates, Canadian citizenship papers or passports for individual partners; and

C.   birth certificate, Canadian citizenship papers or passport for any individual.

No part of the document is more essential than verifying the exact debtor name. Errors in the completion of the name on the document are likely to become errors in the completion of financing statements for registration pursuant to the Personal Property Security Act[1] (the "PPSA"). Refer to section 16 of the Regulation 912[2] under the PPSA respecting the required name of the debtor to be used when completing Ontario financing statements.

---

1. Personal Property Security Act, R.S.O. 1990, c. P.10.
2. R.R.O. 1990, Reg. 912.

9.683—Schedules: Contact the client promptly to obtain lists of equipment, copies of deeds containing legal descriptions of land, insurance particulars, copies of trademarks and patents, and other information needed to complete all schedules.

9.684—Number of copies: In preparing copies for execution, contemplate at least one copy for every party and each law firm involved in the transaction. Over and above these, additional copies may be required in order to deliver two copies to a government office enabling receipt of the duplicate registered instrument back for the file.

Normally, a borrower signs only one promissory note and one original delivery copy of a debenture. Further copies of each of these documents are marked with the word "copy", or in some other way indicated that it is "duplicate copy for registration purposes only". This is because each note and each debenture is a promise to pay an amount of monies to a named party and consequently, should not be duplicated by additional original forms.

9.685—Seals: It is generally prudent to affix the corporate seal to promissory notes and other documents issued by a corporate borrower. Although the Ontario Business Corporations Act[1] and the federal Business Corporations Act[2] do not require the use of a corporate seal, most financial institutions still maintain lending manuals which show the need for affixation of the corporate seal.

For documents given without consideration, such as guarantees, affix the corporate seal for a corporate guarantor and stationer's wafers for individual guarantors. If the corporation has no seal, add a stationer's wafer or draw a circle with "seal" written therein, to give evidence the party intended the document to be executed under seal.[3]

---

1. Business Corporations Act, R.S.O. 1990, c. B.16
2. Business Corporations Act, R.S.C. 1985, c. C-44
3. Do not let a lender add the seal afterward, as this is a material alteration voiding the guarantee. Bank of Montreal v. Scott (1987) 2 W.W.R. 404 (Alta. Q.B.).

9.686—Affidavits: Note that any affidavit being sworn in Ontario for a document for registration outside the province of Ontario must be sworn before a Notary Public for the province of Ontario. Swearing of the affidavit before a Commissioner for Oaths is insufficient for obtaining registration outside the province of Ontario.

Promissory Notes

9.687—Lenders generally provide their forms of pre-printed promissory notes. These can be demand notes, term notes, and/or grid notes. For operating lines, it is not uncommon for a financial institution to require the borrower to execute a large number of promissory notes in blank for the financial institution to complete as the loan balance fluctuates. **[See Forms 9F133 and 9F134 for samples of promissory notes for both fixed and floating interest rates]**

Security Agreements

GENERALLY

9.688—Financial institutions frequently have several forms of security agreements depending on the nature of the collateral involved. Some institutions have a security over inventory form of agreement governing only the inventory of the debtor and the proceeds thereof. Others have a general security agreement charging all present and future personalty of the borrower. Others have developed specific forms of security agreements respecting choses in action, intellectual property, and other forms for collateral that may also be pledged to be perfected by possession, such as stocks, bonds, and debentures.

It is important to ensure that the collateral is properly described[1] in the security agreement to comply with section 10 of the PPSA.[2] Before describing the collateral in the financing statement, ensure that the client's instructions are obtained, to avoid problems with subsection 46(3) of the PPSA regarding restriction of the collateral claimed by word descriptions.

Such security agreements are to be registered pursuant to the PPSA by the filing of a paper financing statement or electronic transmission, designating the appropriate classes of collateral charged by the agreement.[3] General information on registration is found in the Ontario Ministry of Consumer and Commercial Relations' "Registration and Enquiry Guide", but it is important to check the PPSA and its Regulations as well.

Although the agreement may not specify that there is an interest in proceeds, it is preferable to mark the box "other" on the financing statement to ensure that should some of the collateral be sold, transferred, or otherwise dealt with or damaged and give rise to insurance monies, the lender will retain a perfected security interest in any proceeds generated.

Instructions should also be obtained on the following:

(i) whether the lender will require a registration for each security agreement or will rely on a "blanket" filing as permitted by subsection 45(2), where no consumer goods are involved;

(ii)   the length of registration required (noting the subsection 51(5) five year limit on registrations including consumer goods);

(iii)   confirm whether solicitor or lender will provide the requisite copy of the registration to the debtor; and

(iv)   whether a section 54 fixtures notice is to be registered against title to the real property where any chattels have been or will be affixed.

Again, these instructions should be confirmed in writing to the financial institution. **[See Forms 9F135 to 9F137]**

---

1. See *Royal Bank of Canada v. Concorde Investments Corp.* (1991), 96 Sask. R. 43 (Q.B.), dealing with collateral descriptions.
2. R.S.O. 1990, c. P.10.
3. Since the decision of *Clinton's Flowers & Gifts Ltd., Re* (1992) 2 P.P.S.A.C. (2d) 139, prudent PPSA practice requires that the registrant check the Form 3C verification statement to ensure correct data entry before releasing opinions and closing the deal. While the Court of Appeal upheld the Bank's security in its decision released June 28, 1993, the high rate of government data entry errors in non-electronic registrations will place a strain on the limited insurance fund.

PMSIS

9.689—If the lender is providing funds or other extensions of credit, such as a banker's guarantee or letter of credit to allow the borrower to be able to acquire goods, it will be necessary to ensure that the security interest is properly perfected as a purchase-money security interest of "PMSI" in order to gain the benefit of the statutory priority afforded to PSMIs by section 33 of PPSA.

Carefully note that the procedure for effecting PMSI steps for "inventory" are different from those for any other kind of collateral, and that timing requirements as specified in subsection 33(1) for inventory are different from those for other types of collateral as specified in subsection 33(2).

Note that if you are obtaining a PMSI in inventory, the requisite form of PMSI notice must be sent by personal service or registered mail in accordance with the requirements of section 68. Subsection 68(4) provides that there is *no* deemed receipt for mailed PMSI notices. **[See Form 9F138]**

To ensure that the notices come to the attention of the appropriate person, observe the section 69 rules. For example, a PMSI notice addressed to the Royal Bank of Canada should not be sent to Royal Bank, Royal Bank Plaza, Toronto but should be more correctly sent to Royal Bank of Canada, Main Branch, Ground Floor, Royal Bank Plaza, Toronto, Attention: The Manager.

If effecting a PMSI on behalf of a lender and the vendor is also providing credit for the debtor to acquire the same goods, it must be brought to the attention of the lender that it will have a "second class PMSI" in accordance with subsection 33(3), that creates a PMSI priority for the vendor, ahead of the PMSI interest in the same goods of the lender.

Note for purposes of timing that subsection 33(1) and (2) refer to events that must occur before or within 10 days of the debtor or its agent obtaining possession. Consequently, if a shipping agent hired by the debtor is obtaining possession of the product, such possession will start the clock running for PMSI purposes.

It is always safest to complete all section 33 steps before permitting the debtor or its agent to obtain possession of the goods.

Assignment of Book Debts

9.690—Section 7(1) provides that a security interest in an "intangible", which includes accounts, is governed by the law of the jurisdiction when the debtor is located. Section 7(4) provides rules for location of the debtor. This is the mandatory PPSA registration to make for accounts.

Most institutions will also require additional registrations of an assignment of book debts in each jurisdiction where the borrower conducts business, although this may be reduced by negotiation, to registration only in each jurisdiction in which the borrower maintains an office where accounts receivable are collected by it or on its behalf.

[**See Forms 9F140 and 9F141** for a sample form for assignment of book debts, together with a sample financing statement for registration in the province of Ontario.]

Debentures and Trust Deeds

9.691—The original copy of the trust deed or debenture[1] is delivered to the financial institution. Duplicate copies of these documents may be required for registration purposes. The debenture is registered in PPSA jurisdictions by filing a financing statement. An original copy is registered in Quebec by the notary.

Where real property is also being charged, a copy of the debenture may be attached to a Form 2 Charge/Mortgage of Land. The debenture becomes a schedule to the form of Charge/Mortgage of Land, together with additional schedules indicating the description of the real property and any further schedules needed to conform the terms of the debenture to the standard terms of the form of Charge/Mortgage. Absent electronic registration capacity, two copies will be needed for each registration district in which the real properties are located.

In Quebec, trust deeds are registered instead of debentures. The documents are signed before a Notary for Quebec, who then takes the documents for appropriate recording and his or her issuance of certified copies.

If the assets are located outside the province of Ontario, it will be necessary to consult local counsel to obtain the appropriate affidavits and land registration documents to make the necessary registration under PPSA and land registration statutes.

---

1. Ensure the document is a "debenture". In *Acmetrack Ltd. v. Bank Canadian National* (1984), 12 D.L.R. (4th) 428 (Ont. C.A.); "debenture" was broadly interpreted to include an acknowledgment of a debt and promise to pay, whether or not a sum certain. Other cases had previously required an acknowledgment of a specific amount. See *Coopers & Lybrand Ltd. v. Ford Credit Canada Ltd.* (1983), 25 B.L.R. 14 (N.S.T.D.); and *Rollins Sports & Marine (1974) Ltd., Re* (1981), 37 C.B.R. (N.S.) 122.

Mortgages of Land

9.692—If freehold land is part of the security to be given to the lenders, the Form 2 Charge/Mortgage of Land forms are completed in duplicate so that the duplicate registered copy can be returned to the person filing from the registration offices. All other documents needed to satisfy requisitions of title will also be required.

Freehold land may also be charged in a debenture or trust deed, with such document attached as a Schedule to the Form 2 Charge/Mortgage of Land.

If the borrower's interest as tenant in occupation of real property is to be charged by way of mortgage of lease or assignment of lease, the lender may or may not have its own forms of mortgage of lease, assignment of lease, consent of land, and/or consent of mortgagee. A leasehold may also require notice of the lease be registered on title together with its charge on the lease. **[See Checklist 9C5** re: documents relating to giving notice of a lease, charging a lease, and consent of landlord.]

The lender shall also be asked for instructions on whether it will require a full search of title or will rely instead on a subsearch with respect to the mortgage of the lease.

It is necessary to review the head lease to determine if there is a prohibition against charging of the lease or assignment of all or a portion thereof.

Without the required consent of the landlord, the borrower may be in default of its obligations as tenant by breach of the covenant not to assign or mortgage, and the lender will be subject to the rights of distraint by a landlord under a commercial lease and the rights of prior registered mortgagees.

It is frequently difficult to obtain the consent of the landlord and/or the mortgagees to the creation of a charge on the leasehold interest in favour of the lender and to waiver of their respective rights. However, the request to obtain such consent and the effect on the loan should such consent not be provided, should be discussed with the financial institution and their instructions should be confirmed in writing.

Shareholder Postponements and Pledges of Shares

9.693—Frequently, a shareholder who has made a loan to the corporate borrower will be asked to postpone payment of his or her loan until the lender has been repaid in full. The lending institution may require a financing statement registered pursuant to the PPSA for such postponement document.

In addition, the lender may require the shareholder to pledge its shares in favour of the financial institution. **[See Forms 9F142 to 9F145 for sample forms that may be used for this purpose.]** In the event of a pledge of shares, it is important to have the share certificates delivered to the solicitor so they may be physically delivered to the lender to perfect the pledge to the lender. Such physical delivery for perfection may be done in addition to filing a financing statement.

For best protection, the shares should be issued in the lender's name and recorded in the share ledger of the subject company in the lender's name, with the appropriate authorizing resolution approving the transfer. This avoids subsequent realization problems with private company share restrictions.[1]

---

1. The issue of the secured's right to sell pledged shares has been discussed in both *Tureck v. Hanston Investments Ltd.* (1986), 56 O.R. (2d) 393 (Ont. H.C.J.); and *M.C. United Masonry Ltd., Re*; *Peat Marwick Ltd. v. Goldfarb (in trust)* (1982-83), 2 P.P.S.A.C. 237 (Ont. C.A.). The latter case also referred to two English cases dealing with sales of shares in private corporations where the share transfer provisions had not been fulfilled, being *Hunter v. Hunter* [1936] A.C. 222; and *Hawkes v. MacArthur* [1951] 1 All E.R. 22.

Section 427 Bank Act Security

9.694—Bank Act security documentation given to Canadian chartered banks pursuant to section 427 of the Bank Act[1] consists of four pre-printed forms.

As old section 178 states that a "person" may give section 178 security over specified assets, a partnership did not give such security in its own name. The individual partners, had to give the security.[2] This was changed in section 427 by the addition of definitions for "person" and "entities", solving this problem.

The Notice of Intention is completed in duplicate and tendered with the "appropriate agency" of the Bank of Canada for registration. Section 427 of the *Bank Act* specifies which agency of the Bank of Canada is the appropriate agency for registration purposes. Generally, where the borrower conducts business in more than one jurisdiction, the Notice of Intention is to be registered in the registration jurisdiction in which the borrower maintains its principal office. This one filing covers all of Canada.

Section 427 provides that this Notice of Intention must be registered with the appropriate agency before the remaining documents are completed. Consequently, borrower should complete the Notice of Intention and register the same as quickly as possible. The remaining documentation for delivery pursuant to section 427 may be completed and dated at a later date with the balance of the security documentation. As a minimum, there should be at least a one day difference in the date between when the Notice of Intention was registered and the date of execution of the remaining section 427 security documents. If this is not possible, an affidavit of execution should be done to verify the remaining documents were executed later in the day after the Notice of Intention was filed.

Again, it is prudent to affix the corporate seal, as banks' internal manuals still expect to see the seal on the standard form documentation.

Some banks also file a financing statement pursuant to the PPSA to record the section 427 documentation. Instructions should be obtained from the bank if registering on its behalf. These instructions should be confirmed in writing.

Some banks now have developed a policy providing that if the section 427 Notice of Intention is filed and the bank is also taking an inventory security agreement registered pursuant to the PPSA, the registration of a financing statement for the section 427 documentation is not required.[3]

---

1. Bank Act, S.C. 1991, c. 46.
2. See *Bank of Montreal v. Trapa Forest Products Ltd.*, unreported (B.C.S.C.).
3. Note that the Alberta and B.C. PPSA statutes exclude their statutes for applying to federal security under the Bank Act, S.C. 1991, c. 46.

Guarantees

9.695—Guarantees may be limited to a specific value or may be unlimited to cover all potential obligations of the borrower to the lender. It is important to use the guarantor's correct name by obtaining one of the documents specified earlier in this section. As a promise given without consideration to the guarantor, the document should be under seal.

Extreme care is needed when considering the giving or taking of "financial assistance" by means of guarantee, security or otherwise from a corporation. The solicitor needs to check the incorporating statute for the subject guarantor corporation and determine whether that statute contains any prohibitions or limitations on the corporation's capacity to issue guarantees or other like "financial assistance".

Prior to 1999 in Ontario, section 20 of the *Ontario Business Corporations Act*[1] made certain financial assistance void unless certain statutory exceptions existed or the corporation could meet a specific financial test. Generally speaking, a wholly owned subsidiary was able to guarantee its parent corporation and vice versa, but sister corporations could not guarantee each other unless the test was met.

The Canadian Institute of Chartered Accountants instructed its members not to issue opinions on whether the statutory financial test was met as the test was very vaguely worded. Hence, extreme care was required to qualify an opinion letter as might be necessary with respect to any statement as the enforceability of a corporate guarantee that did not fall squarely with one of the clear statutory permitted forms of financial assistance.

In December 1999, there was an amendment to section 20 of the *Ontario Business Corporations Act*[2] which followed a number of other jurisdictions and eliminated the financial test. Section 20 was again amended in December 2003.[3]

Following these two sets of amendments, generally speaking, a corporation may issue a guarantee or give financial assistance to its parent or to its wholly owned subsidiary or to its affiliated sister corporations.

Outside of those relationships, financial assistance is still permitted provided that disclosure has been made to the shareholders of the material financial assistance, giving the shareholders a description of the financial assistance, its terms and the amount of the assistance. A sample form to give this notice and resolution authorizing this notice is found at Form 147.

Section 44 of the *Canada Business Corporations Act*[4] which, like the old section 20 of the Ontario *Act*, had a financial test, was repealed in 2001, with nothing substituted therefor.

Many pre-printed forms of guarantee contain an assignment and postponement of debts clause in favour of the lender. The lender should be asked for its instructions as to whether it requires registration of a PPSA financing statement for such assignment of debts clause.

[See Forms 9F146 and 9F147 for a sample form of guarantee and an authorizing resolution and form to give shareholders the OBCA required notice.]

---

1. R.S.O. 1990, c. B.16.
2. Ontario Business Corporations Act, 1999, c.12, Sch. F, s. 3.
3. Ontario Business Corporations Act, 2000, c.26, Sch. B, s. 3.
4. Canada Business Corporations Act, 2001, c.14, s. 26.

Independent Legal Advice

9.696—Many institutions have their own forms of pre-printed certificates to be provided by a law firm that has represented a spouse or an elderly parent being asked for a guarantee and/or collateral mortgage and/or other security.[1] Such advice and the completion of the certificate of independent legal advice, must be done by an independent solicitor and not by another lawyer in the same firm that is representing the borrower and its principals. **[See Form 9F148]**

---

1. Lack of "ILA" may not invalidate the guarantee and security. Note *ASCU Community Credit Union Ltd. v. Dunstar* (1990), 75 O.R. (2d) 490 (Gen. Div.); where the guarantee of the wife was upheld despite lack of ILA, but only to the extent of the credit limit of which she was aware.

Insurance

On Assets

9.697—It will be necessary to obtain a certified copy of the policy or policies of insurance covering the assets being charged, naming the lender as loss payee. The lender will require the insurance policy to include a mortgagee clause giving the lender advance notice before the policy may be cancelled. It takes time for a certified copy of the policy to be delivered. Most lenders will advance funds if they have received a binder letter from the agent indicating that the lender has been added to the policy as loss payee and a statement that the certified policy will be provided in due course.

Assignment of Life Insurance

9.698—The lender may require "keyman insurance" be assigned in its favour. The lender and the insurer may each have their own forms for this purpose and the borrower may have to sign both forms before the insurer will record the assignment on its books. The original policy is delivered to the lender. The lender may also require proof from the agent that the premiums have been paid and confirmation should also be obtained from the insurer that the assignment has been recorded and that no other party holds an assignment of such policy.

Letters of Credit

9.699—There is a growing use of letters of credit issued to cover contingent obligations. For example, if some of the money is being advanced for real property development, a letter of credit may be posted as security for contingent liabilities under construction lien legislation. Again, if some of the purchase price in the acquisition is delayed or subject to adjustment for contingent events, a letter of credit may be used to ensure such payment is made. Letters of credit are issued or "opened" by financial institutions to the vendor as the "beneficiary" of the credit. They can be "accepted" or "confirmed" by a second lender (for a fee), if the opening institution is not one acceptable to the vendor.

The "L/C" is a contract between the vendor and the financial institution. The vendor obtains payment upon presenting the documents listed in the L/C to the institution. Hence, the name of "documentary letters of credit".

If the documents are not exactly as prescribed, the bank need not pay. Therefore, great care is needed to ensure that the vendor beneficiary will be able to produce the documents exactly as described in order to obtain payment.

The purchaser will have its own contracts with the opener to ensure the opener is paid if it honours the L/C. There are fees for the opening and the bank will want security for payment.

Corporate and Other Records

9.700—In addition to the security documentation, a number of corporate records will be required to enable the solicitor to give an opinion letter in favour of the lender. These items include the following:

(a)　Certificate of standing with respect to corporate borrower from each jurisdiction in which it carries on business.

(b)   Certified or notarial copies of the charter documentation and all by-laws.

(c)   Certificate of incumbency.

(d)   Certified copy of the resolution of directors (or shareholders in the event of a unanimous shareholders agreement) ratifying the commitment letter (which was probably signed before the meeting was held), and authorizing the creation of all promissory notes and security documentation being issued in favour of the lender.

In the event that a party is pledging shares in favour of the lender, there will also be required a resolution from the directors of the issuing corporation, respecting the approval of the pledge of shares by the shareholder in favour of the lender.

(e)   Certificate of an officer or director of the corporation certifying that there are no unanimous shareholder agreements or other restrictions on the ability of the corporation to borrow money and give security therefor. If it is a corporate guarantor, the same sorts of documentation will be required to prove the existence, good standing, and ability of the corporation to grant financial assistance. Regard should always be had to section 20 of the Ontario Business Corporations Act[1] with respect to the limitations on the ability of a corporation to give financial assistance.

(f)   If the borrower has not already done so, it will also need to create a bank account for the operation of the loan monies or operating line through the financial institution. Each institution has its own pre-printed forms for the operation of its accounts including the following documents:

  (i)   specimen signature cards;

  (ii)   list of officers and directors;

  (iii) the lender's form of borrowing by-law;

  (iv)   directors resolution specifying signing officers; and

  (v)   agreements regarding operation of the account.

  [See Para. 9.664 for further discussion on opening the bank account.]

(g)   Certificates of officer respecting facts upon which the solicitor is otherwise uninformed and upon which reliance is placed.

(h)   Directors for funds and undertakings by the borrower or others.

In that the loan proceeds are being used in whole or in part to acquire the assets from a vendor, a closing date must be coordinated to ensure that the assets acquisition is completed coincident with the borrowing from the lender. This will also necessitate the giving of directions for funds, to advance funds by the borrower's lender to the vendor and/or the vendor' financial institutions to repay the obligations of vendor to obtain clear title to the assets. Also required is a receipt of undertakings from the vendor's lenders, undertaking to discharge upon payment of specified sums of money on the closing date.

(i) Letter of acknowledgment from the lender accepting prior encumbrances. If any encumbrance is to remain, written consent should be obtained from the lender, agreeing to accept such encumbrance ranking in priority ahead of the leader.

---

1. R.S.O. 1990, c. B.16.

Opinion Letters and Reporting the Loan

9.701—Some financial institutions require delivery of their own pre-printed forms of reporting letters. Great care must be had that all appropriate qualifications are added to such pre-printed forms to ensure that nothing is said that cannot be legitimately given as an opinion.

It is advisable to recite in the opinion letter the documentation that has been obtained in order to complete the asset acquisition by the purchaser/borrower, to give comfort to the lender that the asset transaction has been completed and the lender's funds have been used to complete the acquisition as required in the commitment letter.

The opinion letter is also an excellent place to reiterate instructions received from a lender, such as the fact that the lender chose to take its own promissory notes directly from the borrower, it chose not to obtain a fixtures notice registered against title, it agreed to dispense with the consents of landlords and mortgagees, and it required PPSA registrations for X number of years.

It is important for the solicitor to recite in the opinion letter any certificates of offices upon which reliance was placed with respect to facts beyond his/her knowledge. Such certificates might incorporate such matters as lack of litigation against the borrower, lack of agreements being broken by the creation of the loan, and security documentation or in the case of a guarantor, the fact that the financial resources of a guarantor are sufficient to meet the test required by the statutes.

[See Forms 9F153 and 9F154 for sample forms of opinion letters given by borrower's counsel and lender's counsel. These opinions are given as examples only and care should be taken to ensure that each and every opinion letter is custom tailored to the particular facts of each transaction.]

If acting for a lending institution, which requires a loan "qualification" opinion letter, reference should be made to the federal and provincial loan, trust, and insurance companies and pension fund statutes respecting the lending capability for that type of institution. This opinion should be done first, to ensure the loan is capable of qualification, prior to spending time on the rest of the file.

When the transaction has closed, all post closing matters left to be completed should be listed, particularly undertakings given or received on closing, and these should be diarized for follow up.

Once the matters are fulfilled, such as registered discharges from the other lenders, the transaction should be reported to the borrower, or borrower and lender if both sides were represented.

If representing the lender, all original promissory notes, debentures, security documents, insurance papers, pledged share certificates, and duplicate registered documents should be delivered to it. The covering letter should note the expiry date for each registration which expires, with a strong warning to the lender to record such dates in its records with adequate advance notice, so that it may file renewals before that date. The lender should also be warned to record amendments as necessary, such as changes of debtor names and transfers of all or part of the collateral, to ensure maintenance of perfection of its security.

The letter to the borrower should remind it of when the first payment is due and of the convenants in the commitment letter or loan agreement respecting reporting required by the lender.

Closing books are time consuming to prepare, but worth the effort. The client has an easy source of reference for its auditors and use in completing its day-to-day affairs. The solicitor's copy will be of great assistance for subsequent transactions by this client and will greatly facilitate preparation of discharge documents without the expense of subsearching when the debt has been repaid or the client transfers financial institutions.

CHECKLISTS

9C1
CHECKLIST OF FREEHOLD INVESTIGATIONS

Note: For addresses, please consult the current edition of the Municipal Directory published by the Ministry of Municipal Affairs and available at the Ontario Government Bookstore (now called "Publications Ontario"). [**See 9F5–9F7 for sample search letters.**]

Searches	Ordered	Received	Comments
Title			
Planning Act[1]			
Executions			
Realty Taxes			
Water			
Gas			
Hydro			
Corporation Status			
Work Orders			
Zoning—			

Searches	Ordered	Received	Comments
Use			
Zoning— Survey Compliance			
Compliance with Municipal Agreements			
Compliance with Registered Restrictions			
Unregistered Hydro Easements			
Occupancy Permit			
Fire Department			
Elevator			
Health			
Ministry of Labour (Industrial Safety)			
Conservation Authority			
Environment (Provincial) Regional) Municipal)			
Ontario Heritage Act[2]			
Farm Tax Reduction			
Family Law Act,[3]			

Searches	Ordered	Received	Comments

Estoppel
Certificate

Rent Registry

Railway Act,[4]

---

1. R.S.O. 1990, c. P.13.
2. R.S.O. 1990, c. O.18.
3. R.S.O. 1990, c. F.3.
4. R.S.C. 1985, c. R-3.

9C2
PURCHASER'S CHECKLIST

(a) Obtain copies of all benefit plan texts, including all amendments, whether or not filed with applicable regulatory authorities, copies of any employee booklets describing benefits provided, and relevant board resolutions.1 Obtain copies of all funding agreements, any annual information returns and, where applicable, trust agreements relating to the plans and any trust fund financial statements.

(b) Consider cost of providing equivalent benefits for transferring employees, as well as the compatibility of benefits provided by the vendor with the purchaser's existing programs and benefits philosophy.

(c) Compare vendor's benefit programs to those maintained by purchaser. Can or should any plans be integrated? Determine potential cost of any change.

(d) If unionized employees are to be transferred, review provisions of collective agreement to determine benefits subject to agreement.

(e) Where pension or other benefit obligations are set out in employment contracts or collective agreements binding on the vendor, confirm whether the pension or other benefit plan text complies with the terms of the applicable contract or collective agreement.

(f) Determine whether there are any pending changes to the benefits provided.

(g) Ascertain jurisdiction in which any benefit plans are registered.

(h) Consider investment performance of any manager of plan funds, where plans to be assumed.

(i)   Determine whether plan documentation complies with applicable legislation or requires amendment.

(j)   Ascertain vendor's past practice as to the administration of benefits and the implementation of any ad hoc adjustments or other indexing arrangements.

(k)   Determine whether any undocumented arrangements exist and obtain copies of any employment contracts setting out supplementary benefits.

(l)   Determine funded status of plans and obtain copies of any actuarial valuations.

(m)   Determine means by which benefit coverage is to be continued to transferring employees pending establishment of purchaser's own benefit arrangements.

---

1. If the purchaser is considering adoption of the plan and is interested in the question of surplus entitlement, copies of all predecessor plan documentation should be obtained since this is critical to an assessment of surplus entitlement.

9C3
VENDOR'S CHECKLIST

(a)   Consider whether the purchaser will agree to assume vendor's benefit plans or to provide substantially similar benefits for employees to be offered employment by the purchaser.

(b)   Attempt to obtain covenant that any plans provided by purchaser will remain in place for a stated period after closing.

(c)   If assets are to be transferred to purchaser, consider any restrictions or penalties applicable to a transfer and any necessary notification periods where assets are to be withdrawn from investment manager.

(d)   If assets are to be transferred to the purchaser, consider the solvency of the purchaser and its ability to meet obligations undertaken and to cover indemnities given. Also, consider seeking compensation from purchaser if any part of such transferred amount represents pension plan surplus.

(e)   Preparation of necessary documentation to reflect nature of transaction:

　　　(i)   valuation of pension assets where necessary;

> (ii) preparation of amendments to plan and to funding documentation, where necessary:
>
> > (1) to reflect any change of name
> >
> > (2) to document any transfer of assets and liabilities to detail windup of any part of vendor's plan, where appropriate

(f) Consider adjustment for coverage of benefits to closing

(g) Consider coverage of employees from closing to commencement of coverage under plans provided by purchaser, where appropriate.

(h) Ensure all necessary documentation filed with Canada Customs and Revenue Agency, pension regulatory authorities and vendor's funding agent.

9C4
CONVEYANCING DOCUMENTS FOR ASSETS— LAND OWNED

[See Para 9.500]

(i) Form 1 Transfer/Deed of Land;

(ii) Statutory declaration of the vendor with respect to such items as:

> A. no urea-formaldehyde on the site;
>
> B. no additions or changes to the structures on the property since the survey was prepared;
>
> C. no repairs or renovations giving rise to construction liens;
>
> D. length of possession by this vendor;
>
> E. compliance with agreement and covenants registered against title;
>
> F. changes of the vendor's name by reason of corporate restructuring such as amalgamation or marriage;
>
> G. the vendor is not the same party as listed in particular executions against like names; and
>
> H. status of easements running in favour of the vendor;

(iii) Deposits to be prepared in the Form 4 Document General to be recorded against title, to request such matters as:

> A. amalgamations of corporate vendors;
>
> B. copies of death certificates for individuals;

(iv) Statement of adjustments allocating the purchase price among brokers' fees, deposits, assumptions of mortgages, repayment of mortgages, utilities, and municipal taxes, etc.;

(v) arrangements for practical matters such as delivery of keys, cancellation of vendor's insurance coverage, placement of purchaser's insurance coverage, delivery of access codes to security systems;
(vi) delivery of copy of survey; and
(vii) delivery of copies of reports of third parties such as environmental audits, elevator inspectors, fire department inspectors.

9C5
CONVEYANCING DOCUMENTS FOR ASSETS— LEASED REALTY

[See Forms 9F40-9F45]

(i)   Lease Assignment;
(ii)   Landlord's Certificate on Status of Lease;
(iii)   Landlord's Consent to Assignment;
(iv)   Landlord's Consent to Mortgage of Lease;
(v)   Non-Disturbance Agreement of Mortgagee;
(vi)   Non-Disturbance Agreement of Mortgagee to Tenant;
(vii)   Application for Leasehold Parcel (subsection 38(6) of *Land Titles Act*[1]);
(viii)   Notice of Lease (Subsection 22(7) of the *Registry Act*[2]);
(ix)   Notice of Mortgage of Lease (Subsection 22(7) of the *Registry Act*);
(x)   Notice of Lease (Subsection 111(1) of the *Land Titles Act*);
(xi)   Notice of an Interest in a Lease (Subsection 111(6) of the *Land Titles Act*);
(xii)   Charge/Mortgage of Leasehold.

---

1. R.S.O. 1990, c. L.5.
2. R.S.O. 1990, c. R.20.

9C6
CHECKLIST FOR LEASE COMMENTARY WHEN ACTING FOR TENANT

[See Paras. 9.160 and 9.500]

1. Report on title search including municipal and registered restrictions.
2. Advise whether notice of lease registered and if not, consider whether necessary to register notice.
3. Describe the premises demised and any appurtenant rights.
4. Term of lease.
5. Amount of rent and when and where payable.
6. Tenant's responsibility with respect to additional rent.
7. Report with respect to prior mortgages. Consider whether non-disturbance or postponement agreements should be obtained.
8. Advise with respect to renewal or purchase options and the provisions with respect to each.
9. Permited uses. Consider in light of applicable zoning.
10. Insurance Obligations.
11. Repair obligations.
12. Report and explanation with respect to fire and damage clauses.
13. Right to assign or sublet.
14. Security deposits.
15. Escalation clauses with respect to rent.
16. Ownersip and removal of fixtures and equipment.
17. Rights with respect to alterations and improvements.
18. Environmental Matters.

9C7
INTELLECTUAL PROPERTY ACQUISITION CHECKLIST

[See Paras. 9.190 and 9.520]

1. Purpose:	<ul><li>what is the purchaser's objective?</li><li>acquire new know-how? new marketing and sales mechanisms? name/brand recognition? eliminate a competitor</li><li>focus due diligence to meet the stated objective.</li></ul>

2. Confidentiality:	• ensure confidentiality agreements are in place between negotiating parties and people doing the investigations before anything is disclosed.
3. People:	• who are the key people at the target needed to achieve the objective? • is "know-how" in their heads as opposed to reduced to paper? • have they signed employment contracts? assigned inventions and/or copyright to employer? non-competition covenants? • what incentives exist to keep them (eg stock options)? • what if they won't join the purchaser?
4. Know-How/ Patents:	• did vendor develop the know-how? is it on paper or in people's heads? • have patents been applied for? where? get inventor's name; will inventor stay with purchaser? • get copies of applications and/or issued patents, patent numbers; are all government fees and maintenance fees required to preserve the registration paid? • did vendor purchase the know-how? are all assignments registered to show clear chain of title? • did vendor licence the know-how? get copy of licence; assignable? are all royalties paid? • has vendor vigorously defended its patent rights from infringers? • have technical advisors "kicked the tires" and advise on merits of the know-how as against competing methods? possible infringement on others' ideas?
5. Copyright:	• while listing all copyrighted works may be impossible, ensure you get a list of key publications, manuals, sales literature, advertisement copy, etc. and investigate these key items

	• are there any registered copyrights? get copies, registration numbers, date of first publication, authorship identified and all assignments of copyright to vendor and/or employment agreements assigning copyright to vendor • if vendor acquired third party's copyright, get copies of all assignments for good chain of title; are assignments registered? any copyright licenced for use?
6. Trademarks:	• identify key logos and business names purchaser wishes to acquire. • are they registered as trademarks? get copies of applications and/or issued trademarks, list classes of goods or services covered by the registration and compare with actual use; are all government fees and maintenance fees required to preserve the registration paid? • did vendor acquire these from third parties? are all assignments registered for good chain of title? licenced? are all licences in good standing? • is vendor defending its trademark from infringers? abandonment? are all users of the trademarks under licence from vendor?
7. Domain Names:[1]	• does vendor have a domain name? is it registered? where? • if it is a ".ca" domain name, was it re-registered before December 1, 2000 with the Canadian Internet Registration Authority ("CIRA") to preserve names previously registered with the defunct, volunteer run CDNnet.ca domain registry? • has a trademark been filed for the domain name? if not does the domain name infringe on someone else's trademark?

---

1. The California courts held in *Kremen v. Network Solutions Inc.* (2000), 99 F. Supp. 2d 1168, that a domain name was a service and not personal property. It is more akin to a telephone number in the control of the telephone company. The vendor cancels its registration and covenants not to re-register. The purchaser files afresh for that name.

8. Websites:	• if the vendor has a website, get copies of all hosting agreements, development agreements, content agreements; determine rights to all copyright for content on the site; linking agreements, rights to all trademarked materials • if the vendor sells on the website, how is a contract formed? terms and conditions for contracts on the site; what is the governing law? what provinces/states may assume jurisdiction over the transactions done through the site? steps taken to limit liability abroad? consumer protection issues? • security on the website for such issues as electronic signatures, PKIs and cryptography.
9. Licences to Third Parties:	• has Vendor licensed any of its IP to third parties? get copies of all licences; are licences in good standing? what right do licensees have? any options to purchase?
10. Security Interests:	• is any of the vendor's IP subject to a security interest? registered with the federal or provincial or USA registries? done as an assignment to the secured party with a licence back?
11. Privacy:	• is the vendor subject to any of the following, and if so has the vendor complied?: • federal *Personal Information Protection and Electronic Documents Act*, S.C. 2000, c. C-5 in effect January 1, 2001? • Quebec's *Act Respecting the Protection of Information in the Private Sector*, R.S.Q., c.P.39.1, as amended, in effect since 1994? • other provincial legislation as enacted; Ontario has a draft privacy proposal • released July 20, 2000.

	• does the vendor have the needed consents[2] to allow the "personal information" it maintains on employees, customers or others, in paper, electronically or on websites, to be transferred to purchaser? • vendor's security of its systems from unauthorized users, hackers. • vendor's website and email monitoring policies over its employees. • does the vendor's website use "cookies" to capture information about visitors to the site?
12. Claims and Litigation:	• has the vendor received or started any claims, disputes or litigation by or with third parties about the subject IP? nature of claims, dollar values, impact on vendor's cash flows; get copies of all litigation and settlements.
13. Representations and Warranties:	• the information obtained from your due diligence then gets drafted into the agreement of purchase and sale to ensure the purchaser gets what it bargained for, failing which specify the remedies available to purchaser, such as a reduced or eliminated earn out payment on the purchase price.

---

2. On July 21, 2000 the USA Federal Trade Commission ("FTC") reached a settlement with Toysmart.com Inc. After Toysmart ceased to carry on business, it endeavoured to sell its database of 190,000 customer names. Toysmart had posted on its website a statement that personal information given by visitors to the site would never be given to third parties. The FTC got Toysmart to agree that any purchaser of the data would keep it confidential and get the consent of each person to any change of use of that data.

9C8
EMPLOYMENT AND LABOUR LAW CHECKLIST

[See Paras. 9.150 and 9.220–9.330]

Federally and Provincially Regulated Employers

1. **Determine** whether the vendor is governed by federal or provincial statutes pertaining to labour relations and which precise statutes pertain to the vendor's operations.

2. For federally regulated employers who are obligated to comply with federal employment equity legislation, **obtain disclosure** of the vendor's most recent employment equity report, a copy of any agreement or undertaking relating to the implementation of employment equity, and disclosure of any plans, complaints, applications or orders concerning employment equity and disclosure of the status of same. If no employment equity plan is in place, obtain disclosure of the steps taken to implement employment equity.

3. **Obtain representation** that the vendor has complied with all applicable employment equity legislation, regulations, programs or policies.

4. **Obtain indemnification** for any costs or penalties attributable to non-compliance with employment equity legislation during the period prior to closing.

5. **Send** appropriate search letter to the federal Employment Equity authorities.

6. In the case of a vendor who is subject to provincial labour and employment legislation, **obtain disclosure** from the vendor concerning any outstanding federal contracts that have to be completed or whether there are any current bids for federal contracts that may contractually bind the vendor, and subsequently the purchaser, to federal fair wage, hours of work and employment equity requirements.

7. In the case of a vendor who is subject to provincial labour and employment legislation, **obtain representations** from the vendor that the vendor has been in compliance with federal fair wage, hours of work and employment equity requirements applicable to any work performed under contract with the federal government.

8. **Obtain indemnification** for liability for the vendor's failure to comply with federal fair wage, hours of work and employment equity requirements applicable to any work performed under contract with the federal government during the period prior to closing.

9. **Determine** whether the contemplated transaction falls within the ambit of the sale of business provisions of the Labour Relations Act, 1995 (Ontario) or the Canada Labour Code[1] (federal).

10. **Obtain disclosure** of any union certifications granted for employees of the vendor or any of its predecessors, any pending applications for

certification for any employees of the vendor, any voluntary recognition agreements signed with any union by the vendor or any of its predecessors, either directly or through a voluntary employer's organization, any union organizing campaigns currently in progress with respect to any employees of the vendor, and any collective agreements or accreditation orders to which the vendor may be bound.

11. **Obtain copies** of any collective agreements which may be binding upon the vendor.

12. **Obtain representations**

(a) that other than those disclosed, there have been no union certifications granted affecting the employees of the vendor, that no applications for certification are pending, that the vendor has not voluntarily recognized any trade unions, and that no unions are attempting to organize the vendor's employees;

(b) that the vendor is not bound to any collective agreement except for those disclosed to the purchaser; and

(c) that the vendor is not subject to any accreditation orders.

13. **Obtain disclosure** of copies of other documents, such as benefit plans, relevant to the terms of the collective agreement.

14. **Review** all collective agreements for unusual provisions. Watch for restrictions on the operation of the purchased business, such as a prohibition on subcontracting or limitations with respect to technological change. Ensure that benefit plans provided by the vendor comply with the terms of the collective agreement.

15. **Obtain disclosure** of all collective bargaining proposals and the status of ongoing bargaining (for example, is a strike or lockout likely in the near future). If the vendor is in negotiations (or if negotiations are imminent), obtain a commitment from the vendor and, if necessary, from the union to delay negotiations until the sale is completed or make other appropriate arrangements regarding the conduct of the negotiations pending the sale.

16. **Obtain disclosure** of any and all outstanding complaints, applications, proceedings, or orders involving the vendor or any pre-decessor of the vendor pursuant to any labour relations legislation.

17. **Obtain representations** that there are no outstanding labour relations proceedings or orders and that the vendor is not aware of any threatened proceedings.

18. **Obtain indemnification** for liability arising out of any outstanding or potential labour relations board proceedings or orders arising from the events that occurred prior to closing.

19. **Obtain disclosure** of any grievances outstanding at the time of the sale against the vendor or any predecessor of the vendor. Obtain copies of such grievances, quantify the financial liability related to such grievances, and ensure that informed personnel of the vendor are available, if necessary, to discuss the particulars of such grievances.

20. **Obtain disclosure** of any arbitration proceedings or awards pending at the time of the purchase.

21. **Obtain disclosure** of any arbitration awards outstanding at the time of the purchase that have not been complied with.

22. **Obtain disclosure** of all current seniority lists for unionized employees.

23. If the assets include a nursing home, retirement home or any other facility which is subject to the Hospital Labour Disputes Arbitration Act,[2] **obtain disclosure** of any outstanding or potential interest arbitration proceedings and of any unsatisfied interest arbitration awards.

24. **Obtain representations** that there are no outstanding grievances, arbitration proceedings, pending arbitration awards or unsatisfied awards except as have been disclosed to the purchaser.

25. **Obtain indemnification** for liability arising out of any outstanding or potential grievances, arbitration proceedings, arbitration awards or judicial proceedings arising from events that occurred prior to closing.

26. **Determine** whether the purchaser intends to intermingle the vendor's employees with its own and the implications thereof. Determine whether the transaction will result in conflicting bargaining rights and how such rights are to be resolved.

27. **Send** appropriate search letter to the Ontario Labour Relations Board and the Ministry of Labour Collective Agreements Library. For federally regulated employers, contact the Canada Industrial Relations Board.

28. **Determine** whether the contemplated transaction is subject to the sale of business provisions of the Employment Standards Act (Ontario) or the Canada Labour Code[3] (federal).

29. **Obtain disclosure** of any hours of work or overtime averaging agreements, any outstanding complaints, claims, applications, decisions or orders under any employment standards related legislation. Determine the status of any outstanding matters.

30. **Obtain representations** that the vendor has complied with all applicable employment standards obligations and that there are no outstanding complaints, claims, decisions, applications, orders or prosecutions under any employment standards related legislation except as disclosed to the purchaser.

31. **Obtain indemnification** for any outstanding or potential employment standards complaints, claims, decisions, applications, or orders arising from events that occurred prior to closing.

32. **Send** appropriate search letter to the Employment Standards Branch (Ontario) or to the Labour Program of Human Resources Development Canada (Federal).

33. Carefully **assess** the proposed transaction to determine whether the purchaser would be obligated to assume the Workplace Safety and Insurance Board liabilities of the vendor.

34. **Obtain disclosure** of all claims, all potential claims, current assess-ment rates, the existence of any actual or potential penalty assessments and the status of the vendor's workers' compensation accounts.

35. **Obtain representations** that there are no claims, potential claims or actual or potential penalty assessments except as disclosed, that all assessments have been paid to date and will be paid up to closing, and that there has been compliance with all applicable workers' compensation legislation.

36. **Obtain a purchase certificate** and written verification from the Workplace Safety and Insurance Board concerning the status of the vendor's workers' compensation board assessments and accounts, potential penalties, experience rating and accident claim history. Analyze the situation and the potential liability for penalties.

37. **Obtain indemnification** for any workers' compensation claims, assessments, surcharges or penalties attributable to the period prior to closing.

38. **Determine** whether the vendor may be obligated to re-employ any disabled employees under Workplace Safety and Insurance Act.[4] Consider whether the purchaser or the vendor will assume this responsibility.

39. **Send** appropriate search letters to the Workplace Safety and Insurance Board.

40. **Obtain disclosure** of any outstanding human rights complaints, investigations, proceedings, decisions or orders.

41. **Obtain representations** that there are no outstanding human rights complaints, investigations, proceedings, decisions or orders except as disclosed and that the vendor has complied with applicable human rights legislation.

42. **Obtain disclosure** of any accommodation that may be in place with respect to employees who may be otherwise incapable of performing or fulfilling the essential duties of their job because of handicap.

43. **Send** appropriate search letter to Ontario or Canadian Human Rights Commission.

44. **Obtain disclosure** of any pay equity plans and the status of their implementation. If no plan is in place, obtain disclosure of the steps taken to implement pay equity.

45. **Obtain disclosure** of any outstanding applications, complaints, investigations, orders of review officers, tribunal proceedings, tribunal orders or prosecutions concerning pay equity involving the vendor and the status of same.

46. **Obtain representations** that the vendor has complied with pay equity legislation and that there are no outstanding applications, complaints, investigations, orders of review officers, tribunal proceedings, tribunal orders or prosecutions concerning pay equity involving the vendor except as disclosed.

47. **Obtain indemnification** for any costs or penalties attributable to non-compliance with pay equity legislation during the period prior to closing.

48. **Send** appropriate search letter to Pay Equity Commission.

49. **Obtain disclosure** of

(a) any outstanding health and safety orders or instructions and outstanding or potential prosecutions under the Occupational Health and Safety Act (provincial) or Canada Labour Code[5] (federal). Discuss status of same with the vendor;

(b) inspection reports, testing results, records of health and safety audits, and minutes of meetings of any health and safety committee for the two years prior to the closing date; and

(c) all information pertaining to the use, control or storage of toxic, hazardous or designated substances by the vendor.

50. Have health and safety inspectors **inspect** all premises.

51. **Obtain representations**

(a) that there are no outstanding or potential inspection orders, violations or prosecutions under health and safety legislation or regulations;

(b) that, except as disclosed, there are no toxic materials used in the production processes or stored on the premises and that there are no materials which are hazardous or designated substances under health and safety legislation or regulations; and

(c) that the entire undertaking complies with all occupational health and safety legislation and regulations.

52. **Obtain indemnification** for any claims by employees, former employees or their families alleging adverse health consequences due to circumstances arising while the vendor was in control of the workplace.

53. **Obtain indemnification** for liability arising out of any outstanding or potential inspection orders under health and safety legislation or regulations arising from events that occurred or from circumstances that were present prior to closing.

54. **Send** appropriate search letter to Ministry of Labour (Occupational Health and Safety Branch) or to the Labour Program of Human Resources Development Canada for federally regulated operations.

55. **Obtain disclosure of**

(a) Employee Handbooks and statements concerning vendor's employment-related policies including, but not limited to, vacation and vacation pay policies;

(b) Group insurance policies, statements, agreements, and booklets;

(c) All pension-related documents including plans, trust agreements, summaries, and booklets;

(d) Any documentation concerning profit-sharing, commissions, bonus plans or policies, stock option plans, car allowances and travel allowances; and

(e) Claims history under any group insurance programs which are in place.

56. **Obtain representations** that the vendor has disclosed and fulfilled all of its obligations and commitments with respect to group insurance policies, pension plans, profit sharing plans, commissions, bonus plans or policies, stock option plans, and all other employee benefits and

allowances prior to the Closing Date. [**See Para. 9.349 describing other applicable representations to be obtained**]

57. **Obtain indemnification** for liability arising out of obligations and commitments with respect to group insurance policies, pension plans, profit sharing plans, commissions, bonus plans or policies, stock option plans, and all other employee benefits and allowances prior to the Closing Date.

58. **Obtain disclosure** of all employment, consulting, agency and management contracts. Require the vendor to provide a list of all employees, whether active, disabled or laid-off, giving
    (i) names,
    (ii) salaries or hourly rates,
    (iii) job descriptions,
    (iv) length of employment or hire date,
    (v) dates and amounts of most recent increases,
    (vi) amounts of bonus payments, commissions, accrued vacation pay, and other amounts owing to the individual employees.

59. **Obtain representation** that there are no employment, consulting, agency or management contracts other than those that have been disclosed.

60. **Determine** which current employees of the vendor, including inactive employees on long-term disability or workers compensation or those on lay-off subject to recall, are to be employed by the purchaser. If not all of the vendor's employees are to be employed, require the vendor to fulfil its statutory and common law duties with respect to the termination of the employment of those of the vendor's employees who will not be employed by the purchaser.

61. **Obtain indemnification** for any obligation arising in respect of employment prior to the closing date and with respect to claims by employees who are not to be retained.

62. **Obtain**
    (a) proof of payment of statutory amounts to redundant employees; and
    (b) releases or agreements with respect to settlements of any potential or actual wrongful dismissal or similar claims.

63. **Obtain representations** that the vendor has complied with its obligations to make appropriate source deductions for all employees and made the appropriate remittances to Canada Customs and Revenue Agency.

64. **Obtain indemnification** for liability arising out of the vendor's failure to make appropriate source deductions from all employees prior to closing or the employer's failure to make the appropriate remittances to Canada Customs and Revenue Agency.

65. **Send** appropriate search letter to Canada Customs and Revenue Agency.

66. **Obtain representations** that the vendor has complied fully with its obligations under the Employers Health Tax Act (Ontario)[6] and that there are no unpaid taxes, penalties, interest, garnishment orders, or other court orders pertaining to the vendor.

67. **Obtain** indemnification for liability arising from unpaid taxes, penalties, interest, garnishment orders, or other court orders pursuant to the Employer's Health Tax Act[7] arising during the period prior to closing.

68. **Send** appropriate search letter to provincial Ministry of Revenue.

[*General*]

69. **Obtain indemnification** for liabilities arising out of any employment-related matter not disclosed to the purchaser by the vendor.

70. **Obtain** sufficient information from the vendor concerning accrued vacation pay to allow for the calculation of an adjustment to the purchase price. Consider whether to request a similar adjustment based on the purchaser's assumption of the obligations to the employees, based on service with the vendor (e.g. termination or severance pay) or consider requiring indemnification for such liabilities.

71. Obtain an undertaking from the vendor not to change any significant term or condition of employment of an employee prior to closing without the purchaser's consent.

* *

---

1. R.S.C. 1985, c. L-2.
2. R.S.O. 1990, c. H.14.
3. R.S.C. 1985, c. L-2.
4. S.O. 1997, c. 16.
5. R.S.C. 1985, c. L-2.
6. R.S.O. 1990, c. E.11.
7. R.S.O. 1990, c. E.11.

9C9
CHECKLIST OF ENVIRONMENTAL ISSUES

[See Paras. 9.360-9.370]

[This checklist is fairly detailed, but obviously would not be appropriate in all cases. An experienced environmental practitioner should review this in the context of each unique transaction.]

The following information should be reviewed and questions should be answered to determine whether there are environmental concerns or issues that need further consideration.

1. Real Estate / Surrounding Lands

1. Physical description of the property, all buildings thereon and any areas that have been filled or graded by non-natural causes, or filled with material of unknown origin.

2. Detailed plans, maps and surveys available (i.e. historical maps, aerial photographs, fire insurance records, geological, topographic and use and soil maps, building plans, utility company records, land title and property assessment records).

3. A description of surrounding properties and past and present uses, if known, and any environmental risks associated with them.

4. Details of ground water and surface water uses and drainage issues in the area.

5. Check whether the property has ever been used for waste disposal or for the transfer, storage, recycling, or treatment of waste. If so, provide whatever particulars are available, including any licences or approvals and their supporting documentation.

6. Any evidence on the site of soil staining, vegetation damage, unusual odours, or surface water discolouration.

II. Specific Business Information

1. A description of the businesses and operations on site, including any industrial processes carried on.

2. Copies of all environmental certificates and permits.

3. Review of materials handling information (i.e. products received, inventoried, produced, generated, transported and stored). Check material safety data sheets ("MSDSs").

4. Copies of generator registration, details of any wastes generated on the site, where they are disposed of, and identity of the carrier(s).

5. Copies of licences for any pesticides or herbicides used on the property.

6. Details of waste water discharges, sewer by-law compliance issues, and copies of sewer permits.

7. Inventory of air emission and any odour release points.

8. Information on whether the operations on the property emit hazardous air pollution such as mercury, vinyl chloride, lead, asbestos, beryllium, benzene, CFCs or other refrigerants, or arsenic; and whether the property is in compliance with any applicable emission standards for such pollutants.

9. Describe air pollution control equipment installed (e.g. body shop, spray paint room).

10. For any substances used on the property that are specifically designated or regulated under occupational health and safety regulations, identify the substances and provide particulars of their use and any precautions taken and required programs in place with respect to worker exposure.

11. Employee, workers' compensation and occupational, health and safety records and concerns.

12. Verify that no vibration or noise problems exist.

III. Hazardous Substances

1. Records of any underground storage tanks, including inspections, upgrading, records of tanks removed and removal of any contaminated soil, any information filed and acknowledgements received.

2. Building inspection for signs of friable asbestos, including pipe wrapping, ceiling tiles, sprayed on fireproofing, or acoustical plaster.

3. Check building for Urea Formaldehyde Foam Insulation.

4. Details of any PCBs in active use, and details of any PCB storage sites on the property, including copies of licences.

5. Check whether any radioactive materials are stored on site or concern about the presence of radon in the area.

6. Check if there are any drums or containers storing chemicals on the site. If so, are they properly labelled and in compliance with Workplace Hazardous Materials Information Systems ("WHMIS").

7.   Description of solvents and degreasers used on the property, the volumes, storage prior to use, volume of spent solvents generated, and storage, recycling, and disposal practices for such spent solvents.

IV. Environmental Management Practices

1.   Review carefully all policies, practices, procedures and systems in place dealing with the management of environmental and related occupational health and safety, product liability and transportation of dangerous goods concerns (e.g. board of directors' resolutions, company policies, communication and reporting procedures, internal personnel involved, training and education programs in place, use of external experts, on-going compliance review and continuous improvement procedures, emergency response programs - spills/discharges, fires, accidents, investigations etc.).

2.   Obtain copies of any environmental audits, assessments, investigations or evaluations that have been done in the past.

3.   Review all waste reduction and recycling programs.

4.   Examine any energy efficiency programs.

5.   Discuss knowledge of environmental laws with plant personnel and systems in place to keep up-to-date and advised of upcoming changes in law or policies and practices of regulators.

V.   Regulatory or Civil Concerns

1.   Details of any spills or other incidents reported.

2.   Notices of any past or proposed orders or actions (including inspections and investigations) against the owners or occupants of the property.

3.   Details of any civil proceedings for environmental damage brought or threatened against the owners or occupants of the property or the surrounding area, if known.

4.   Review of environmental stakeholders involved in the business.

9C9:1
CHECKLIST OVERVIEW OF KEY ENVIRONMENTAL CONTRACTUAL PROVISIONS

[See Paras 9.360-9.365]

[As indicated in the discussion on environmental matters at paragraphs 9.360 to 9.365, environmental issues may be complex and if so, should be appropriately addressed by clear contractual arrangements. The following Checklist should be reviewed in connection with the Long Form of Asset Purchase Agreement (9F32) and Long Form of Share Purchase Agreement (9F78). For convenience references are made in this Checklist to the various specific precedent alternative clauses provided for environmental matters (9F35).]

I. Overview of Key Provisions Relating to Environmental Matters - Agreements of Purchase And Sale Representations and Warranties			
No./Ref*	Provision	Description	Importance & Special Concerns
1.	Parties	Proper legal name of parties involved.	Must always keep in mind the legal entities and what their net worth is now and what it might be in the future.
2.	Recitals	Introduction to document and transaction.	Not legally binding unless made so in the agreement.
3. See 9F35.6 (Representations and Warranties - Extensive Detailed)	Definitions	Defining certain key capitalized terms These need to be reviewed carefully in the context of each transaction	Makes the drafting of the agreement simpler and the agreement easier to read and understand. The following are possible key definitions: Governmental Authority Hazardous Substance Laws Notices Orders Permits Regulations Release Vendor's-Knowledge

No./Ref*	Provision	Description	Importance & Special Concerns
4. See 9F35:1 ("As is"), 9F35:5 (Broad-General) and 9F35:6 (Extensive - Detailed)	Representations and Warranties	Means of having parties give information that may be required and agreed upon as a basis to proceed. Also important for the allocation of risks and liability provisions contained in the indemnification section. These are statements regarding some past or existing facts or circumstances or state of affairs.	If not true, the following may result: (a) renegotiation of price or other terms of the transaction; (b) rescission or termination of contract; (c) damages for breach of warranty under indemnification clause. The following are examples of key topics that are often included as the subject matter of environmental representations and warranties: 1. Hazardous Substances 2. Release of Hazardous Substances 3. Offences 4. Orders 5. Reporting 6. Disposal Sites 7. Permits 8. Documents, Records and Audits 9. Adverse Environmental Conditions 10. Adverse Occupational Health and Safety Occurrences 11. Due Diligence/ Compliance Programs The following are key concerns that arise during the negotiation of appropriate representations and warranties: (i) the scope and breadth of the representations and warranties that the parties are willing and able to make;

No./Ref*	Provision	Description	Importance & Special Concerns
	Representations and Warranties (continued)		(ii) the details of specific exceptions to the general representations and warranties (usually by means of a disclosure schedule);
See 9F35:8 Limitations on Vendor's Environmental Obligations			(iii) the limitation on particular representations and warranties by: ` some sort of materiality basis;    ` "to the knowledge of the Vendor"; ` "to the best of the Vendor's knowledge after due inquiry";    ` limiting to actions taken by Vendor or arising during Vendor's ownership; ` exclusions for matters known by the Purchaser;
			(iv) any limitation on liability as to a specific dollar amount: ` as a floor (to eliminate claims for trifling amounts);    ` as a ceiling (usually something less than the purchase price);
			(v) the length of time that the representations and warranties survive following the closing;
			(vi) the mechanics as to the giving of notice of any breach to the Vendor by the Purchaser and allowing the Vendor either time to remedy the same or and opportunity to take action to minimize the damages.

No./Ref*	Provision	Description	Importance & Special Concerns
5.	Survival Clause	Sets out the period during which the representation and warranties can be relied on or a claim made thereunder.	The Vendor would like the representations and warranties to merge on closing so as not to have any possible continuing liabilities to the Purchaser. The Purchaser would like the representations and warranties to be open-ended. Liabilities at law to govern-ment or other third parties may not be "contracted out". Environmental liabilities or concerns may not be obvious or evident for many years unless a detailed environmental audit is conducted and discovers a problem or potential problem.
6. See 9F35.1 ("As Is") and 9F35.8 (Limitations on Vendor's environmental investigation that Environmental Obligations)	Exclusions	Means of having certain concerns excluded from the transaction.	The following are examples of matters that may be important in an environmental context: (i) exclusion of certain assets or part of the property to be purchased and sold; (ii) exclusion of certain liabilities to be assumed; (iii) limiting the scope of the may be conducted; (iv) limiting the extent of the representations and warranties.
7.	Covenants	Clauses setting out agreements made to do or not to do something in the present or in the future.	Examples of covenants that are important in an environmental context include:

No./Ref*	Provision	Description	Importance & Special Concerns
See 9F35:2 (Environmental Access and Testing) See 9F34 (Confidentiality Solicitor-Client Privilege Clause)	Covenants (continued)		(i) representations and warranties true and correct at closing; (ii) conditions performed or complied with; (iii) actions until closing; (iv) ongoing disclosure; (v) access for inspection or environmental audit and provisions regarding scope, costs, reports, involvement with regulations; (vi) special confidentiality provisions - solicitor-client privilege; (vii) further assurances
8.	Financial Security Arrangements	Provisions for some sort of security or other arrangements to ensure that the parties will be able to fulfil their obligations.	(i) Extended Payment Terms (ii) Escrow (iii) Guarantees (iv) Letters of Credit (v) Performance Bonds (vi) Insurance
9. See 9F35:7 Vendor's Continuing Responsibilities and Indemnification	Indemnities	Provisions that expressly provide for the protection against loss or damage and the reimbursement for loss, damage and injury	Express contractual arrangement between the parties: (a) confirming their direct obligations, and (b) providing for resolution of third party claims.

No./Ref*	Provision	Description	Importance & Special Concerns
			An indemnity may be quite complex, including any one or more of the following features: (i) conditions precedent to recovery by the claimant; (ii) threshold or deductible claim amounts ` to provide for the "de minimus factor" and avoid costly administrative time and effort;  (iii)  maximum claim amounts:     ` the total price (or percentage thereof) received; (iv) mechanics for settling and paying claims: ` notification of claims     ` participation in settlement of claims ` cooperation by parties     ` lead counsel ` settlement rights
10.	Conditions of Closing	Provisions that expressly provide for closing requirements and arrangements for a waiver thereof or rescission rights under the contract.	The following conditions may be important in an agreement with respect to environmental matters: (i) the condition that the representations and warranties contained in the agreement shall be true and correct at the time of closing with the same force and effect as if made at and as of such time as well as on the date of the agreement;

No./Ref*	Provision	Description	Importance & Special Concerns
			(ii) that the other party shall have performed or complied with all of the terms, covenants and conditions of the agreement to be performed or complied with by it at or prior to the time of closing;
			(iii) that a certificate or other instrument of the party or its officers be delivered to confirm that its representations and warranties are true and correct at the time of closing;
			(iv) that the exercising of rights of access and inspection shall not affect or mitigate the covenants, representations and warranties otherwise also made under the contract;
			(v) that no material change shall have occurred to the business being acquired prior to the closing or to the laws relating to the business or the property;
			(vi) that the purchaser is able to obtain financing for the transaction;
			(vii) that a satisfactory environmental audit has been performed;

No./Ref*	Provision	Description	Importance & Special Concerns
See 9F35:3 (General) and 9F35:4 (Extensive - Detailed) Environmental Audit and Clean-up			(viii) that an appropriate clean-up agreement or environmental agreement be entered into by the parties providing for an allocation of the responsibilities of the parties to address any environmental problems that have been discovered prior to closing; (ix) that any consents required under contracts or from regulatory authorities have been obtained.
11.	Boiler Plate Clauses	Standard General or Miscellaneous provisions dealing with routine matters that are important for environmental matters	(i) Further Assurances (ii) Time of the Essence (iii) Public Announcements (iv) Benefit of the Agreement (v) Entire Agreement (vi) Amendments and Waiver (vii) Assignment (viii) Notices (ix) Governing Law

II. Overview of Key Provisions Relating to Environmental Matters - Leases		
No.	**Clauses**	**Comments**
1.	Use	Open / Closed
2.	No nuisance	No ___ yes___
3.	Cleanliness and no wastes	No ___ Yes ___
4.	Compliance	Laws, regulations, orders, policies?
5.	Payments - additional rent	Utilities and services; repairs, landlord's work
6.	Landlord entry	Inspection rights
7.	Landlord work	Repairs, clean up
8.	Landlord remedies	Termination; do repairs work
9.	Assignment/subletting	Landlord consent - No___ Yes ___
10.	Environmental audit rights	Base line; during; on termination
11.	Notice of environmental matters	Investigations, orders, inspections
12.	Hazardous substances provisions	Notice, general and / or specific compliance, clean up
13.	Indemnity Provisions	General and/or specific
14.	Financial security provisions etc	Performance bond letter of credit
15.	Specific environmental covenants / representations warranties	Taylor made to deal
16.	Survival clause	General and /or specific

III. Overview of Key Environmental Lenders' Procedures and Documentation			
No.	**Lenders' Due Diligence Procedures**	**No.**	**Lenders' Special Environmental Covenants**
1.	Internal awareness and training programs.	1.	Compliance with applic-able environmental laws.
2.	Knowing the customer and the business.	2.	Obligation to ensure representations and warranties remain true and correct.
3.	Environmental risk rating.	3.	Obligation to advise of any non-compliance or breaches of representations and warranties.
4.	Borrower questionnaires and signed compliance certificates.	4.	Obligation to provide compliance certificates.
5.	Environmental site assessments and "audits." Environmental management review.	5.	Obligation to provide information or to conduct environmental audits as may be required.
6.	More extensive borrower contractual provisions.	6.	Access for inspection and testing by Bank representatives.
7.	Careful consideration of range and type of security.	7.	Authorization for government information.
8.	Agreements with the environmental regulators.	8.	Indemnification provisions.
9.	Careful enforcement and realization procedures.	9.	Insurance requirements.

9C10
ASSET PURCHASE AGREEMENT CHECKLIST

1.   Name of Vendor:

2.   Name of Purchaser:

3.   Closing Date:

4.   Included Assets

    (a)   real property; include municipal address and legal description

    (b)   inventory

    (c)   equipment

    (d)   vehicles, rolling stock and mobile equipment

    (e)   receivables, cash and securities

    (f)   intellectual property (patents, trade marks, trade names, industrial design and copyright)

    (g)   books and records, including software

    (h)   goodwill and customer lists

    (i)   supply contracts

    (j)   purchase contracts

    (k)   leases of real property

    (l)   leases of personal property

    (m)   material contracts and licenses.

5.   Excluded Assets

6.   Shared Assets

7.   Purchase Price

    (a)   amount of purchase price

    (b)   amount of deposit, if any

    (c)   method of payment on closing

    (d)   security for balance

(e)   allocation of purchase price:

    (i)   lands

    (ii)   buildings

    (iii)   depreciable property (recapture)

    (iv)   capital property

    (v)   goodwill and intangibles

    (vi)   receivables

    (vii)   inventory

    (viii)   prepaids

(f)   adjustments to the purchase price

(g)   deferred consideration; earn-outs

(h)   taxes exigible on sale/tax elections

(i)   responsibility for legal accounting and other fees

8.   Assumption of Liabilities

9.   Valuation of Inventory

10.   Representations and Warranties:
      from Vendor

(a)   Organization and good standing

(b)   Bankruptcy

(c)   Capacity to carry on business

(d)   Due authorization

(e)   Absence of conflicting agreements

(f)   Enforceability of obligations

(g)   Accurate description of assets

(h)   Net Worth

(i)   Title to assets

(j)   Machinery and equipment

(k)   Conditions of assets

(l)   Location of assets

(m)   Real property and use in compliance with law

(n)   Accounts Receivable – good and valid

(o)   Inventory in good standing and merchantable condition

(p)   Intellectual property

(q)   Buildings

(r)   Guarantees and indebtedness

(s)   Material contracts in good standing

(t)   No options

(u)   Expropriation

(v)   Insurance

(w)   Bank Accounts

(x)   Books and records

(y)   Financial statements

(z)   Contracts

(aa)   Product Liability

(bb)   Liabilities

(cc)   Absence of changes

(dd)   Absence of unusual transactions

(ee)   Ordinary and usual course

(ff)   Capital expenditures

(gg)   Dividends and Repurchase of shares

(hh)   Management Bonuses

(ii)   Leases

(jj)   No default or litigation

(kk)   Employees and details of terms

(ll)   Government withholdings

(mm)   Employment payments

(nn)   Workers' Compensation

(oo)   Labour matters

(pp)   Pension Plan

(qq)   Benefit Plan

(rr)   Health and safety

(ss)   Environmental matters

(tt)   Third Party Consents

(uu)   Licenses and permits

(vv)   Governmental consents

(ww)   Residence

(xx)   Total assets and gross revenues

(yy)   GST registration

(zz)   Tax matters

from Purchaser:

(a)   Organization and good standing

(b)   Due authorization

(c)   Absence of conflicting agreements

(d)   Enforceability of obligations

(e)   Investment Canada Act

(f)   Governmental consents

(g)   Total assets and gross revenues

(h)   Financing

(i)   GST registration

11.   Employees

(a)   liability for employee payments

(b)   list of employees to be hired

(c)   employees on short and long term disability

(d)   grievance and arbitration

(e)   terminations – responsibility

12.   Environmental Matters

(a)   access to property

(b)   environmental audit

13.   Access to book, records and real property during Interim Period

14.   Conditions Precedent to Closing

    (a)   truth and accuracy of reps and warranties

    (b)   delivery of closing documents

    (c)   consents obtained

    (d)   certificate of status of assets

    (e)   delivery of purchase price

15.   Non-Competition Agreement

    (a)   Description of Business

    (b)   Territory

    (c)   Time Period

16.   Other agreements:

    (a)   allocation of purchase price and tax filings

    (b)   tax treatment of receivables

    (c)   transfer taxes, including GST (i.e. s.167 filing)

    (d)   WSIB Compliance

    (e)   Bulk Sales Act Compliance

    (f)   Indemnification Provisions

    (g)   Thirty Party Claims

    (h)   Product Liability Claims

17.   Confidentiality

18.   Survival of Representations and Warranties

19.   Press Releases

20.   Insurance

21.   Operation of Business until Closing

22.   Disaster

23.   Documentation to be Delivered on Closing

24.   Assignment

25. Governing Laws

26. Arbitration

27. Schedule Agreements (e.g. Non-Comp, Supply Agreements, Transitional Services Agreement)

9C10:1
PURCHASE AGREEMENT CHECKLIST
For both Asset Purchase and Share Purchase Agreements

1. Proper Corporate Name of Vendor(s)/Purchaser(s)

    1.1 Obtain copies of all articles of vendor(s)/purchaser(s).

2. Closing Date

    2.1 Anticipated closing date, outside date for closing.

3. Assets [only in asset sale agreement. In share sale assets owned by the corporation are described in schedules or in representations. Obtain same information as below for insertion in schedules, where applicable.]

4. Description of included Assets

    4.1 real property; include municipal address and legal description

    4.2 inventory

    4.3 equipment

    4.4 vehicles, rolling stock and mobile equipment

    4.5 receivables, cash and securities

    4.6 intellectual property (patents, trade marks, trade names, industrial design and copyright)

    4.7 books and records, including software

    4.8 goodwill and customer lists

    4.9 supply contracts

    4.10 purchase contracts

    4.11 leases of real property

4.12   leases of personal property

4.13   material contracts and licenses

5.   <u>Excluded Assets</u>

5.1   description <u>of</u> excluded assets (if applicable, add provision re removal)

6.   <u>Shared Assets</u>

6.1   description of assets shared by different divisions (if applicable, add provision for treatment)

7.   <u>Purchase Price</u>

7.1   amount of purchase price

7.2   amount of deposit, if any

7.3   method of payment on closing

7.4   security for balance

7.5   allocation of purchase price [only asset sale]:

     (i)   lands

     (ii)   buildings

     (iii)   depreciable property (recapture)

     (iv)   capital property

     (v)   goodwill and intangibles

     (vi)   receivables

     (vii)   inventory

     (viii) prepaids

7.6   adjustments to the purchase price

7.7   taxes exigible on sale/tax elections

7.8   responsibility for legal accounting and other fees

8.   <u>Assumption of Liabilities</u>

8.1   list number of liabilities to be assumed. [only asset sale]

9.   <u>Valuation of Inventory</u>

9.1   method of valuation

10. Representations and Warranties

(a)   From Vendor:

All of the following representations are to be true and correct as of the date of execution of the agreement and at closing:

(i)   Organization and Good Standing – due incorporation, organization and compliance with incorporating statute by vendor and or corporation to be acquired.

[Asset and share purchase – if vendor is a corporation and it is not properly incorporated or organized, it may not have the ability to sell. If vendor is not in compliance, it may be dissolved and will have no ability to sell. If purchaser is acquiring shares, it may be acquiring shares of a dissolved corporation. The assets of a dissolved corporate escheat to the Crown. All matters may ascertained by corporate searches; however, government records are generally six weeks out of date.]

(ii)   Bankruptcy – not insolvent, or filed or petitioned into bankruptcy.

[Asset and share sale – if vendor is bankrupt, it does not have ability to sell. May be checked by searches, but records are usually four to six weeks out of date.]

(iii)   Capacity to carry on business – there are no restrictions on the ability of vendor and/or corporation to be acquired; to carry on the business to be acquired (either by articles, by-laws, agreement (i.e. non-compete) or order (court or tribunal).

[Asset and share sale – may affect ability to sell, if acquiring shares may not be able to carry on business.]

(iv)   Due Authorization – the vendor has the requisite authority to sell (directors approval and/or shareholders).

[Asset and share sale – sales outside the ordinary course of business must be approved by directors and where substantially all of the assets of a corporation are being sold, it must also be approved by the shareholders. This may also be a condition of closing.]

(v)   Absence of Conflicting Agreements – no agreements which prohibit sale (either which the vendor is a party and/or corporation to be acquired).

[Share and asset sale – representation that there are no restrictions on the vendor's ability to sell or transfer title.]

(vi)   Enforceability of obligations – the obligations of the vendor under the agreement are enforceable in accordance with its terms.

[Asset and share sale – representation that agreement and terms (i.e. non-competition agreement) are enforceable. Lawyer may instead give opinion, except with respect to non-competition agreement.]

(vii)   Accurate description of assets – the assets are accurately described.

[Share and asset sale – if asset transaction affects what purchaser has acquired, if shares acquired affects valuation, and control of assets.]

(viii) Net Worth – financial tests with respect to working capital, debt to equity ratio and net worth of corporation.

[Share only – to ensure value, limit new debt, stripping of cash and ensure adequate working capital on closing.]

(ix)   Title to Assets – vendor or corporation to be acquired has good title to the assets, there are no encumbrances against assets.

[Asset and shares – there is no personal property registry in Ontario, therefore, must rely on representation and searches to determine title.]

(x)   Machinery and Equipment – forming part of the assets are in good operating condition and have been maintained in accordance with manufacturers recommendations.

(xi)   Conditions of Assets – [Share and asset sale – to ensure condition of assets.]

        Title to Shares – the vendor is the beneficial owner of all the shares, free and clear of all liens, charges or encumbrances. Number of shares authorized, issued and outstanding.

[Shares only – confirms that vendor owns shares, is not holding any shares in trust for beneficial owner.]

(xii)   Location of Assets – all locations where assets stored or used.

[Asset and share – to order searches in proper jurisdictions and for asset control.]

(xiii) Real property and use in compliance with law – the vendor has good and marketable title free and clear of any liens, charges and encumbrances, and the use of the real property is in compliance with all laws. The real property is unrestricted lands as defined under the Land Transfer Act (Ontario).

[Assets and shares – representation of title and that purchaser or corporation may use property for intended use. Non-residents such as Lafarge and Standard Aggregates pay 20% land transfer tax *if* real property is restricted lands.]

(xiv)　　Accounts Receivable – good and valid – all accounts receivable are *bona fide* and good and collectible within 60 days of the closing date. Only relevant to asset sale if purchaser is acquiring receivables. If the receivables are not good and valid, the purchaser is entitled to seek damages.

(xv)　　Inventory in good and merchantable condition – [Assets and shares–relevant only in asset sale if inventory is acquired. If inventory is not in merchantable condition, purchaser entitled to claim damages, may also affect working capital requirements on start up.]

(xvi)　　Intellectual property – good title, not infringing on anyone else's intellectual property.

[Asset and share – assurance of title and to confirm that there are no potential lawsuits affecting intellectual property, especially necessary if intellectual property is an important asset.]

(xvii) Buildings – in good repair, no asbestos or copper wiring.

[Asset and shares – substantial removal costs.]

(xviii) Guarantees and indebtedness – vendor or corporation is not a party to any guarantees or other indebtedness with respect to business.

[Asset and shares – representation as to liabilities which may become purchaser's responsibility. Also discloses obligations, i.e., bonds, etc. which purchaser may require to operate the business.]

(b)　　Material contracts in good standing – [Shares and assets – only necessary in asset sale if acquiring business as a going concern.]

(c)　　No options – no person has any right, privilege or option to acquire any of assets; or if share sale; any shares in the capital of the corporation.

[Share and asset – affects title to assets or shares and may affect ownership percentage acquired.]

(d)　　Expropriation – none of assets have been expropriated nor has the vendor notice received of intention to expropriate.

[Asset and shares – Affects what assets are acquired and discloses potential future expropriation.]

(e)   Insurance – the assets and business to be acquired are adequately insured and the insurance will be continued to closing date (or assumed by purchaser).

[Assets or shares – if assets damaged or destroyed before or after closing, ensures insurance sufficient to compensate purchaser.]

(f)   Bank Accounts – list of and signing authority, funds on deposit.

[Shares and assets – only relevant in an asset sale if purchaser is acquiring bank accounts and funds.]

(g)   Books and records – fairly and accurately disclose financial condition of the business and material transactions.

[Share and asset. Share sale – valuation of corporation, results of operations. Asset Sale – valuation, if acquiring as a going concern.]

(h)   Financial statements – prepared in accordance with generally accepted accounting principles applied on a consistent basis and levels of sales and earnings accurate.

[Assets and shares. Share sale – valuation of corporation, results of operations. Asset Sale – valuation, if acquiring as a going concern.]

(i)   Contracts – no material purchase commitments in excess of ordinary business requirements, no sales contracts for X% below list price.

[Asset and share – only relevant in asset sale if assuming contracts.]

(j)   Product Liability – no contingent or actual liabilities relating to inventory or product sold, adequate insurance coverage.

[Assets and shares – to determine possible lawsuits.]

(k)   Liabilities – no liabilities to which the Purchaser may become liable (or the corporation to be acquired is liable), no liabilities not shown in last financial statements.

[Asset and share sale – disclosure of liability.]

(l)   Absence of changes – no material changes from date of last financial statement (i.e. damage to assets, material adverse change in business) to date of closing.

[Assets and share – only relevant in asset sales if purchaser is acquiring the business as a going concern, affects valuation and operation of business.]

(m) Absence of unusual transactions – no unusual transactions from date of last financial statements (transfer of assets, incurring of debts or security interests).

[Share sale – to determine changes in business.]

(n) Ordinary and usual course – business carried on in the ordinary and usual course since date of last financial statements.

[Assets and shares – only relevant in asset sale if the business is acquired as a going concern. Assurance that vendor has done nothing that may adversely affect the business.]

(o) Capital expenditures – the corporation has not made or committed to any capital expenditures since date of last financial statement and will not do so after the date of the agreement.

[Shares only – may affect liabilities and working capital.]

(p) Dividends and Repurchase of Shares – the corporation has not declared any dividends or redeemed or repurchased any of its shares since the date of the last financial statements.

[Shares only – affects issued cash and capital, prevents stripping of cash through dividends, etc.]

(q) Management Bonuses – the corporation has not declared or paid any management bonuses since the date of the last financial statements and has no agreement to do so.

[Shares only – affects cash requirements after closing, prevents stripping of cash.]

(r) Leases – no leases except as disclosed.

[Shares only – affects liabilities, title to assets.]

(s) No default or litigation – no default under any agreements, no litigation.

[Assets and shares – only relevant in asset sale if agreements are acquired or litigation affects title to assets or the ability of the vendor to transfer title. If share sale, litigation stays with the acquired corporation. Defaults may result in penalties, litigation or loss of material contracts.]

(t) Employees and details of terms of employment – list of employees and terms of employment. Any employees receiving workers compensation, long or short term disability.

[Assets and shares – only relevant in asset sale if purchaser is retaining employees. Provides disclosure of number of employees and remuneration, liability if terminated.]

(u) Government Withholdings – all government withholdings with respect to employees have been made and remitted.

[Assets and Shares – these liabilities remain an obligation of corporation but failure to remit can create superpriority lien on assets.]

(v) Employment payments to date of closing – all wages, vacation pay made to the date of closing.

[Assets and shares – only relevant in asset if retaining employees, may become an obligation of purchaser, remains an obligation of the corporation.]

(w) Workers' Compensation – all levies paid, claims experience or agreement that purchaser may order history of claims experience.

[Assets and shares – if employees are retained, assists in determining existing and future liability (penalties, etc.).]

(x) Labour matters – status or existence of complaints/strikes, outstanding certifications, grievances, arbitrations, negotiations, claim for benefits for short or long term disability.

[Assets and shares – if employees retained, to determine state of labour relations, costs, details of collective or other employment agreements.]

(y) Pension Plan – there is no pension plan or the only pension plan is disclosed in the schedules, no default under obligations under plan or law.

[Assets and shares – if retaining employees. Disclosure of obligations and costs.]

(z) Benefit Plan – there are no benefit plans or only benefit plan(s) disclosed in schedules.

[Asset and shares – if retaining employees. Disclosure of obligations and costs.]

(aa) Health and safety – business premises are in compliance with health and safety legislation. There are no orders or directions from any sanitation or occupational health and safety authority or board.

[Assets and shares – if real property (sale or lease) acquired. Determines compliance requirements, costs, possible charges for non-compliance.]

(bb) Environmental matters – the vendor or the corporation to be acquired:

   (i)   is in compliance with laws and holding of all necessary permits;

   (ii)   has not violated any laws relating to the environment;

   (iii)   has handled environmental contaminants in accordance with law;

   (iv)   there are no orders respecting the real property;

   (v)   there has been no release of environmental contaminants and the real property has not used as a landfill or waste disposal site nor are there any underground surface storage tanks on the real property;

   (vi)   there are no claims, proceedings and investigations with respect to the property;

   (vii)   is in compliance with reporting and inspection requirements;

   (viii) all operating records and reports of the business are in accordance with law.

[Asset and share – if real property acquired. Confirms that real property has not been contaminated by the owner which may result in clean-up requirements. The Ministry of the Environment may require present owner to clean up property and that the present owner seek compensation from the former owner or owners. If shares are acquired, the corporation remains liable for non-compliance with environmental laws. We recommend an environmental audit and testing be undertaken and professional's report addressed to lawyer to protect confidentiality.]

(cc) Consents to complete the transaction – there are no consents of any third parties required to carry out transactions.

      [Assets and shares – if licences or agreements assumed discloses consents required to assign material arguments.]

(dd) Licenses and permits – the business holds all licences required and are listed in schedule.

[Assets and share – disclosure of licencing requirements to carry on business.]

(ee) Governmental consents – no regulatory consents required to carry out transaction.

[Assets and share – disclosure of government consents to be acquired prior to closing.]

(ff) Residence – vendor is not a non-resident of Canada as that term is defined in the Income Tar Act (Canada).

[Assets and Share – if vendor is a non-resident, vendor must deliver a s.116 certificate under the Income Tax Act (Canada) or purchaser must withhold and remit 33 1/3% of purchase price to Revenue Canada.]

(gg) Total assets and gross revenues – disclosure of total assets and gross revenues in last fiscal period as disclosed in audited (if available) financial statements.

[Assets and shares – to determine if pre-merger notification under Competition Act (Canada) is required.]

(hh) GST registration – the vendor is registered for 1st purposes.

[Asset – the purchaser and vendor are only entitled to an exemption from (1ST on the sale if vendor is registered.]

(ii) Tax Matters – the corporation has paid all federal, provincial or municipal tax, and is compliance in filing of returns and payments of taxes, the date of last assessment for taxes received by the corporation was for the fiscal period ended 20__.

[Shares – to determine compliance and outstanding taxes which will remain with corporation.]

(i) From Purchaser:

(jj) Organization and good standing – the purchaser has been duly incorporated, organized and is in compliance with incorporating statute.

[Assets and shares – affects ability of purchaser to complete transaction and fulfil continuing obligations, if any.]

(kk) Due authorization – the purchaser is duly authorized to purchase (directors approval).

[Asset and share – affects ability to complete transaction. Must be approved by board of directors, may also be a condition of closing.]

(ll) <u>Absence of conflicting agreements</u> – no agreements which prohibit purchase.

[Asset and share – representation of no restriction on ability to complete transaction.]

(mm) <u>Enforceability of obligations</u> – the obligations of the purchaser under the agreement are enforceable in accordance with its terms.

[Assets and shares – representation that agreement and terms are enforceable, lawyer may give this opinion instead.]

(nn) *Investment Canada Act* – the purchaser is not a non-Canadian as that term is defined under the *Investment Canada Act* (Canada)

[Asset and share – if review under Act required, approval must be obtained prior to closing.]

(oo) <u>Governmental consents</u> – no regulatory consents required to carry out transaction.

[Asset and share – disclosure of government consents to be acquired prior to closing, unusual except Investment Canada and pre-merger notification.]

(pp) <u>Total assets and gross revenues</u> – level of assets and gross revenues in last fiscal period as disclosed in audited (if available) financial statements.

[Assets and shares – to determine if pre-merger notification under Competition Act (Canada) is required.]

(qq) <u>Financing</u> – the purchaser has obtained a binding commitment of financing from XYX Bank.

[Assets and shares – only when financing necessary for purchaser to complete sale, if not obtained, vendor may incur costs needlessly.]

(rr) <u>Status of tax accounts</u> – vendor reps as to existence, amounts and age of loss carryforwards or availability of tax credits (e.g., SRD credits).

[Share – to allow purchaser to determine possible future tax advantageous accounts.]

(ss) <u>GST Registration</u> – the purchaser is registered for GST purposes.

[Asset – vendor and purchaser are only entitled to exemption from GST if both vendor and purchaser are registered for GST purposes.]

11. Employees

Clauses to be inserted relating to:

11.1 The purchaser hiring all or some of the employees, and on what terms and conditions or vendor's responsibility to terminate.

11.2 Assignment of written employment contracts to be acknowledged by employees.

11.3 Allocation of liability between vendor and purchaser for wages, commissions, remittances, benefits, claims, etc. for employees pre and post closing.

11.4 Employment or consulting contracts with key personnel to acquire know-how.

11.5 Grievances and arbitrations – how dealt with.

11.6 Employees on long and short term disability – who assumes responsibility.

12. Environment Matters

12.1 Access to real property to inspect, carrying out tests and take soil samples (professional audits and testing). If environmental problem, what is purchaser's right (i.e. clean up by vendor, reduction in purchase price, no transaction).

13. Access

13.1 Determine right of access to inspect books, record facilities, soil, inspections by purchaser and/or government officials, requests for information from governmental bodies.

14. Conditions Precedent to Closing

14.1 Specify the conditions that must be completed on or before closing before the vendor is obliged to sell or the purchaser is obliged to purchase, such as:

(a) Title to real property and assets or shares.

(b) No material adverse change in the business.

(c) Compliance with applicable laws in the operation of the business.

(d) Compliance with the *Bulk Sales Act*

(e) Compliance with the *Employment Standards Act* or Ontario or Canada labour legislation.

(f) Discharges or Consents of secured creditors.

(g)   Directors' approval of sale.

(h)   Shareholder's approval of sale.

(i)   Employment of the vendor or other key employees.

(j)   Releases of claim by employees of the vendor, if being dismissed.

(k)   Consents of regulatory bodies to acquisition of assets.

(l)   Consents to assignments of key contracts.

(m)   Investment Canada approval.

(n)   Filing with Competition Bureau and expiry of wait periods, or advance ruling certificate or no action letter.

(o)   Evidence vendor is not a non-resident or delivery of s. 116 certificate.

(p)   Conduct of parties prior to closing.

(q)   The ability of purchaser to obtain a licence necessary to carry on the business, or obtain funding.

(r)   Provide for waiver of conditions or event to occur if conditions unfulfilled.

15. Non-Competition

15.1 Agreement regarding non-competition between the vendor and purchaser in the same or similar business, territory and time period.

16. Confidentiality

16.1 Agreement regarding non-disclosure of confidential information prior to or post closing, or in the event of no closing.

17. Survival of Representations and Warranties

17.1 Length of time may claim against vendor for breach (untruth) of a representation or warranty. [Purchaser should require a period of not less than two years and if tax matters involved should survive for period may be reassessed.)

18. Press Releases

18.1 Any press releases, consent of both parties to press releases.

19. Insurance

19.1 Who is to carry insurance until closing (usually vendor).

19.2   Will vendor's policies assigned or new policies for purchaser.

20. Operation of Business until Closing

20.1   Agreement as to vendor or purchaser operating the business until closing.

20.2   At whose expense, allocation of costs.

20.3   No sales or contracts outside of normal course of business.

21. Disaster

21.1   Agreement as to whether purchaser must close the deal if disaster befalls all or part of the assets prior to closing.

22. Documents to be Delivered on Closing

Specify essential documents to be delivered, which may include (*Assets only, **Shares only):

22.1   s.6 certificate under the Retail Sales Tax Act.*

22.2   Deeds of real property.*

22.3   Assignments of contracts, with the necessary consents of the other parties to the contracts.*

22.4   Assignments of leases with the landlord's consents.*

22.5   Assignments of vehicles, boats and aircraft in the prescribed forms.*

22.6   Certificate of mechanical fitness of vehicles (unless purchaser agreed to obtain).*

22.7   Assignments of trade marks, copyrights and patents in the forms required by the applicable statutes.*

22.8   General conveyance of assets.*

22.9   Bulk sales affidavits, consents or orders.*

22.10 Assignment of accounts receivables.*

22.11 Assignment of securities with requisite consents and guarantees of signatures.*

22.12 Minister's certificate under s.1 16 of the Income Tax Act by non-resident vendor.

22.13 Investment Canada approval.

22.14 Bureau of Competition Policy approval.

22.15 Certified copies of requisite shareholders' resolution.

22.16   Undertaking of corporate vendor to change its name and consent of vendor to permit corporate purchaser to take the name.*

22.17   Certificate of officer of vendor regarding representations and warranties as at closing.

22.18   Environmental condition of property.

22.19   Other evidence required by the agreement to be delivered on closing.

22.20   Share certificates.**

22.21   Transfers and assignments.**

22.22   Directors resolution approval of transfers.~

22.23   Opinions.

22.24   Miscellaneous.

22.25   Assignment.

22.26   Governing law.

22.27   Arbitration.

9C11
SHARE PURCHASE AGREEMENT CHECKLIST

[See Para. 9.620]

1.   SHARES

—   description of issued and authorized capital of target corporation

—   list of all shares issued and registered owners thereof

2.   PRICE

—   currency to be used

—   deposit (escrow arrangements; refundable or not)

—   funds on closing (cash; securities; assumption of liabilities)

—   security for balance owing

—   adjustment of price on closing

—   commissions, fees and expenses of the transaction

3.   REPRESENTATIONS AND WARRANTIES

From Vendor

—   all of the following representations to be true and correct as of the date of execution of the agreement at closing:

(i)   vendor is a duly incorporated, organized and subsisting corporation, has corporate authority to carry on the business as now conducted and sale is authorized by all necessary corporate actions

(ii)   no other agreements, options or rights of third parties to acquire the shares

(iii)   that the attached financial statements have been prepared in accordance with generally accepted accounting principles applied on a basis consistent with prior periods and fairly represent the financial position of the business as of the date of the balance sheet and the operations of the business being acquired for the periods covered by the profit and loss statements, and that there has been no lease, acquisition, or disposition of any fixed or principal assets, no increase in employee remuneration, and no material adverse change (financial or otherwise) to the business, its management, or assets since that date, and that the vendor is aware of nothing that would make books and records of the business not true and correct in all material respects;

(iv)   all shares being purchased are owned by vendor;

(v)   no other person has a right or option to require issuance of further shares;

(vi)   no prohibition in any shareholders agreement prohibiting the sale;

(vii)   the corporation has filed all necessary tax returns and no tax claims outstanding;

(viii)   target corporation is duly incorporated and organized and in good standing and has made all necessary filings and registrations in all jurisdictions in which it has assets or carries on business, which require the same;

(ix)   there are no subsidiaries of the target corporation;

(x)   records of the corporation provide full disclosure and minute books and share ledgers are accurate and up to date;

(xi)   no outstanding guarantees or indemnities for any person;

(xii)   no payments to non-arm's length persons and no dividends or bonuses paid since last financial statements;

(xiii) no debt obligations except as revealed on financial statements and attached schedules;

(xiv) no capital expenditures since last financial statements;

(xv) no changes in business and no revocations of all necessary licences;

(xvi) that the accounts receivable of the target company (full particulars of which will be delivered on closing) are fully collectable, subject to the reserve for bad debts as shown on the balance sheet, are not subject to any right of set off, are only for trade accounts;

(xvii) the marketability of the inventory;

(xviii) that the assets are in good operating condition;

(xix) target company has title to its assets and undertaking free and clear of any mortgage, lien, charge, claim or other encumbrance;

(xx) that each lease, conditional sales agreement, chattel mortgage, insurance policy, employment agreement, collective bargaining agreement, licence, and other material contract of the target company is described in the agreement, is in good standing, no party thereto is in default and there are no grievances or arbitration proceedings pending with respect thereto;

(xxi) compliance with all applicable legislation in the operation of the business and specifying any legislation applicable to the target business (including no liability for funding of past service portions of pension plans, registration of pension and profit sharing plans and qualification of the investment thereof);

(xxii) between the date of the agreement and closing, the business shall have been operated in the ordinary course and no new material contracts created or variations in practice;

(xxiii) requisite director and shareholder approvals of the sale of the shares;

(xxiv) Canadian residency of the vendor Income Tax Act, section 116);[1]

(xxv) that the agreement does not constitute a default of any agreement to which the vendor is a party;

(xxvi) that there is no litigation affecting the target company, nor any pending to the knowledge of the vendor or its officers (if a corporation);

(xxvii) that there are no claims against the target company with respect to warranties furnished with its products;

(xxviii) appropriate environmental provisions; and

(xxix) that all material facts that would influence a purchaser in making the decision to purchase the shares, have been disclosed to the purchaser.

From the Purchaser

- (i)   purchaser is a corporation duly incorporated, organized and validly subsisting and has taken all corporate action necessary to authorize the purchase; and
- (ii)   that it is not a non-eligible person within the meaning of the Investment Canada Act.

4.   CONDITIONS PRECEDENT TO CLOSING

—   specify the conditions that must be completed on or before closing before the vendor is obliged to sell or the purchaser obliged to purchase, such as:
- (i)   titles;
- (ii)   no material adverse change;
- (iii)   compliance with laws applicable to the operation of the business including all employment legislation;
- (iv)   consents of secured creditors;
- (v)   shareholder approvals of sale;
- (vi)   Investment Canada and/or Corporations Act[2] consents;
- (vii)   vendor not a non-resident for Income Tax Act;[3]
- (viii) conduct of parties prior to closing;
- (ix)   consents of regulatory bodies to the purchaser acquiring the shares;
- (x)   ability of purchaser to obtain funding;
- (xi)   environmental audit or clean-up requirements.

—   provide for evidence of compliance such as certificates of auditors or government bodies;

—   provide for waiver of conditions or event to occur if conditions unfulfilled.

5.   NON-COMPETITION

—   agreements regarding non-competition between the vendor and purchaser in the same business and/or territory post closing and for how long.

6.   CONFIDENTIALITY

—   agreement regarding non-disclosure of confidential information prior to or post closing, or in the event of no closing

—   press releases

7.   DOCUMENTS TO BE DELIVERED ON CLOSING

—   specify essential documents to be delivered, which may include:
- (i)   section 6 certificate under the Retail Sales Tax Act[4]
- (ii)   Minister's certificate under section 116 of the Income Tax Act[5] for non-resident vendor;
- (iii)   Investment Canada approval;
- (iv)   certified copies of requisite shareholders' resolution;

(v)   certificate of officer of vendor regarding representations and warranties as at closing; and

(vi)   other evidence required by the agreement to be delivered on closing.

8.   OPERATION OF BUSINESS UNTIL CLOSING

—   agreement as to vendor or purchaser operating the business until closing

—   at whose expense; allocation of costs and profits

—   no sales or contracts outside of normal course of business

—   purchaser's ability to inspect books, records, operations, learn the trade secrets.

9.   DISASTER

—   agreement as to whether or not purchaser must close the deal if disaster befalls all or part of the business prior to closing

10.   MISCELLANEOUS

—   notices

—   tender

—   assignment

—   governing law

—   further assurances

—   binding on successors

—   arbitration

—   access to records post closing for vendor

—   special provisions to terminate target company's participation in any of vendor's pension or other employee benefit plans

---

1. S.C. 1970-71-72, c. 63, as amended.
2. R.S.O. 1990, c. C.38.
3. *Supra,* note 1.
4. R.S.O. 1990, c. R.31.
5. Supra, note 1.

9C12
PURCHASER'S CHECKLIST FOR EFFECTIVE CONVEYANCE

[See Para. 9.650]

Given the foregoing, purchaser's counsel should observe the following in order to obtain an effective conveyance for the purchasing client:

(a)   Review of the authority pursuant to which the vender is effecting its sale -

(i)   if purchasing from a secured creditor under a PPSA security agreement, obtain true copies of the security agreement, the financing statement, the section 63 notice of sale, and proof that such notice has been properly sent by registered mail or personal service to all requisite parties. If purchasing pursuant to a document to which the old *Corporation Securities Registration Act* applied, under the new Part VII of the PPSA, such "prior law" may still be deemed to apply. It may therefore also be necessary to ensure that the old instrument had been properly registered pursuant to the *Corporation Securities Registration Act* by means of filing the requisite affidavit within 30 days of execution of the debenture or other corporate instrument, and that such registration has been properly recorded, with any requisite financing change statements, under the PPSA since October 10, 1989, as required by that statute. Copies of the BIA section 244 Notice of Intention to Enforce, and the Notice of Appointment of the Receiver will also be needed, if applicable;

(ii)   if purchasing from a privately appointed receiver, in addition to the foregoing, be sure to review the security documentation giving the secured party the right to appoint the receiver, the letter of appointment, as amended, the BIA Notice of Appointment of the Receiver, and the powers for the receiver to sell and the manner in which the sale may be made;

(iii)   if purchasing from a court apppointed receiver, review the court order appointing the receiver to ensure that it is exercising its powers as required by the court and that the assets are those that the receiver is able to sell in the manner in which the sale is being conducted. It may be necessary to obtain a further court approval for the specific transaction to be conducted; and

(iv)   if purchasing from a bankruptcy trustee, ensure a bankruptcy has occurred by obtaining a true copy of the assignment or receiving order and a copy of the resolution of the inspectors approving this sale.

(b)   Obtain a general conveyance or bill of sale from the receiver or secured party with as many representations and warranties as the secured party or the receiver are prepared to make, including the representations and warranties that such receiver has been properly appointed, that the party had the right to convey the assets described in the conveyance, and that they have not encumbered such assets. Such sales are, however, usually made "as is, where is".

(c)   Make sure to conduct corporate and other encumbrance searches against the debtor and any of its predecessor names to ensure that there are no other third parties with a prior charge to the interest of the secured party or the receiver. If possible, try to determine if any third parties are holding a purchase money security interest or a repair and storage lien claim that would rank ahead of the interest of the receiver or secured party.

(d)   Obtain from the secured party, the receiver, or the authorized agent from a bank pursuant to the *Bank Act*, a statutory declaration that the debtor's indebtedness remains outstanding to the creditor; that demand was made and dishonoured; that the security remains in force; that the appointment of the receiver remains in force; that the receiver consented to the appointment; and that the requisite notices were given pursuant to the PPSA, the *Bank Act* and the BIA. Also obtain proof of delivvry of any requisite notices or publication of any required notice to the public. [**See Forms 9F111–9F115**]

9C13
INCORPORATION CHECKLIST
[See Paras. 9.663-9.674]

INCORPORATION/ORGANIZATION DATA FORM
NON-OFFERING CORPORATION

INSTRUCTIONS

1.   Part A of this form may be used for incorporation.

2.   Part B may be used for organization.

DEFINITIONS

1.   "OBCA" – Business Corporations Act (Ontario)

2.   "CBCA" – Canada Business Corporations Act

3.   "BNA" – Business Names Act

A.   INFORMATION REQUIRED TO COMPLETE APPLICATION FOR INCORPORATION

---

1.   INCORPORATION JURISDICTION

1.1

Ontario

Canada

Other

1.2   Date Required (if any):_____

1.3 If Canada, please indicate consent to receiving electronic communication.

Yes _____

No _____

Address

2. NAME OF CORPORATION

2.1 First Choice:_____

Alternative Choice:_____

French Name, if any:[1] ___

Should we obtain a translation:

Yes

No

Foreign Language name, if any:_____

2.2 Will consents be available:

Yes

No

3. ADDRESSES[2]

3.1 Registered Office Municipality:

City of Toronto _____

Other: _____

3.2 Registered Office Street Address:

_____

_____

Telephone No.:_____ Fax No.:_____ E-mail add.:_____

Name of Contact:_____

3.3 Mailing Address (where correspondence is addressed)

_____

_____

Name of Contact:_____

Telephone No.:_____ Fax No.:_____ E-mail add.:_____

3.4 Place(s) of Business (if different from mailing address)

_____

_____

Name of Contact:_____

Telephone No.:_____ Fax No.:_____ E-mail add.:_____

4. DIRECTORS

4.1 Floating Board

   (a) Minimum/Maximum Number   1-10; or

       Other:_____

   (b) Fixed Number_____

4.2 Fixed Board

       Number _____

4.3 First Directors - Note - Resident Canadian[3]
    [OBCA = Majority; CBCA = 25%]

Full Name (First, Middle & Last)	Residence Address, Telephone, Fax and E-mail	Address for Service, Telephone, Fax and E-mail (Ontario Corporations Only)	Citizenship

5.   NATURE OF BUSINESS

5.1   Description of Business of Corporation:

_____

_____

5.2   Activity Code:

_____(A)	Agricultural and Related Service Industries		_____(J)	Retail Trade Industries
_____(B)	Fishing/Trapping Industries		_____(K)	Finance/Insurance Industries, including Holding & Investment Companies
_____(C)	Logging/Forestry Industries		_____(L)	Real Estate Operator/Insurance Agent Industries
_____(D)	Mining (including Milling), Quarrying and Oil Well Industries		_____(M)	Business Service Industries
_____(E)	Manufacturing Industries		_____(O)	Education Service Industries
_____(F)	Construction Industries		_____(P)	Health/Social Service Industries
_____(G)	Transportation/Storage Industries		_____(Q)	Accommodation/Food/ Beverage Service Industries
_____(H)	Communication/Other Utility Industries		_____(R)	Other Service Industries
_____(I)	Wholesale Trade Industries		_____(X)	None of the above

5.3   Is there any restriction on the Corporation's business?

Yes (Please specify)

_____

No (standard)

5.4   Are any approvals required for the incorporation:

No

Yes   List: _____

6.   **AUTHORIZED CAPITAL**

6.1   Are only Common Shares required?

Yes

Unlimited Number (standard)
Limited Number _____

6.2   If more than one class of shares list classes.

Common

    No share attributes (standard)

Preferred
Other (Please specify) _____

6.3   List share attributes on Schedule A.

6.4   Are holders of fractional shares to have voting rights and dividend entitlement (O.B.C.A. s. 57(3); C.B.C.A. s.49(17))

    Yes
    No (standard)

6.5   Restrictions on Transfer

Standard[4] (see below)
See attached

6.6   Restrictions on Class or Series Vote

If there is more than one class of shares, is clause restricting separate class or series voting rights upon a proposal to amend articles to be included? (O.B.C.A. s.170(1) C.B.C.A. s.176(1)).

(Note: This may remove right to dissent on such amendments for non-voting shares.)

    Yes
    No (standard)

7.   **SPECIAL PROVISIONS**

7.1   Include Usual Closely-Held Other Provisions in addition to the standard transfer restriction in 6.5 as follows:

Yes (Standard)
No

1.   The outstanding securities of the Corporation may be beneficially owned, directly or indirectly, by not more than 35 persons or companies, exclusive of:

    i)   persons or companies that are, or at the time they last acquired securities of the Corporation were, accredited investors as such term is defined in the Ontario Securities Commission ("OSC") Rule 45-501 Exempt Distributions as amended from time to time; and

ii) current or former directors, officers or employees of the Corporation or an affiliated entity of the Corporation, or current or former consultants as defined in OSC Rule 45-503 Trades to Employees, Executives and Consultants as amended from time to time, who in each case beneficially own only securities of the Corporation that were issued as compensation by, or under an incentive plan of, the Corporation or an affiliated entity of the Corporation;

provided that:

A. two or more persons who are the joint registered holders of one or more securities of the Corporation are counted as one beneficial owner of those securities; and

B. a corporation, partnership, trust or other entity is counted as one beneficial owner of securities of the Corporation unless the entity has been created or is being used primarily for the purpose of acquiring or holding securities of the Corporation, in which event each beneficial owner of an equity interest in the entity or each beneficiary of the entity, as the case may be, is counted as a separate beneficial owner of those securities of the Corporation.

Note: If there is a beneficial security holder that is not resident in Ontario, these standard provisions must be reviewed by a securities lawyer to ensure compliance with applicable securities laws. It may be advisable to use old "private company" restrictions in some circumstances.

7.2 Other Provisions

Lien for indebtedness (standard)

Voting for fractional shares

Paramountcy of Unanimous Shareholder Agreement

B.   INFORMATION REQUIRED TO COMPLETE ORGANIZATION

8.   DATE OF ORGANIZATION

8.1

Day of Incorporation
other _____

9.   PRE-INCORPORATION CONTRACTS

Are there any pre-incorporation contracts to be adopted by the Corporation? If so, please attach copy.

Yes
No

9.1 Does the Corporation require a corporate seal?

Yes
No (standard)

10. **PERMANENT DIRECTORS**[5] (Written consent to act must be obtained before elections or within 10 days after election).

10.1 If a floating board, is precise number to be fixed by

directors   OR
shareholders (standard)

10.2 Quorum for directors' meetings:

majority (standard) OR
(state number)

10.3 Notice for directors' meetings

48 hours (standard)   OR
(state notice required)

10.4 Does chairman have casting vote?

Yes
No (standard)

10.5 **PERMANENT DIRECTORS**[6]

Full Name (include first name, all middle name(s) in full)	Residence Address Telephone, Fax and E-mail	Address for Service Telephone, Fax and E-mail (Ontario Corporations)	Citizenship

11.   **PERMANENT OFFICERS**[7] (Ontario Corporations - only the five most senior officers will be recorded on the public record- please indicate priority).

Office (in order of seniority)_	Full Name, Middle Initial and Surname	Residence Address Telephone, Fax and E-Mail	Address for Service Telephone, Fax and E-mail (Ontario Corporations)
Chairman			
President			
Vice-President			
Secretary			
Treasurer			
Other			

11.1   Managing Director[8]

Yes
No

11.2   Do you wish a Unanimous Shareholder Agreement restricting the powers of the directors?

Yes
No

11.3   Do you wish indemnities prepared for the directors who are not office directors?

No
Yes

If so, please name:_____

_____

12.   REGISTERED AND BENEFICIAL SECURITY HOLDERS[9]

12.1(a)   Registered Shareholders:

Full Name, Address and Email Address	Accredited Investor (Y/N)	Accredited Investor (Category under OSC Rule 45-501)	Class	Number	Aggregate Price Paid

12.1(b)   Canada Corporation Only:

Will the above shareholders consent to electronic communications.

Yes
No

If yes, please indicate email address above.

12.2   Beneficial Shareholders:

Full Name, Address and Email Address	Accredited Investor (Y/N)	Accredited Investor (Category under OSC Rule 45-501)	Class	Number	Aggregate Price Paid

12.3 Registered Holders of Other Securities (e.g. Promissory Note, Debenture):

Full Name, Address and Email Address	Accredited Investor (Y/N)	Accredited Investor (Category under OSC Rule 45-501)	Class	Number	Aggregate Price Paid

12.4 Beneficial Holders of Other Securities (e.g. Promissory Note, Debenture):

Full Name, Address and Email Address	Accredited Investor (Y/N)	Accredited Investor (Category under OSC Rule 45-501)	Class	Number	Aggregate Price Paid

12.5 If any of the securities are to be beneficially owned, directly or indirectly, by a person or company that is an accredited investor (see attached Schedule B), these persons or companies need not be included in the "35" beneficial security holder limitation if they have acquired their securities as principal.[10]

All accredited investors have purchased as principal.

Yes

No   If no, please provide details:_____

_____

_____

12.6 If any of the securities are to be beneficially owned, directly or indirectly, by a person who is a current or former director, officer or employee of the Corporation or an affiliated entity of the Corporation or current or former consultants as defined in OSC Rule 45-503 AND in each case who beneficially owns only securities of the Corporation that were issued as compensation by or under an incentive plan of the

Corporation or an affiliated entity, those persons need not be included in the "35" beneficial security holder limitation.[11]

All such persons have acquired all securities beneficially owned by them as compensation.

Yes

No   If no, please provide details:_____

_____

_____

12.7 Has the Corporation provided an offering memorandum in connection with the issuance of any of the above securities (provide copies):

Yes

No

12.8 If a share is to be issued for consideration other than money - (Note: OBCA S23(4), CBCA s.25(3)), please provide:

(a)   the amount of money the corporation would have received if the share had been issued for money;

_____

(b)   EITHER:

(i)   the fair value of the property or past service in consideration of which the share is issued:

_____

_____

OR:

(ii)   confirm that such property or past service has a fair value that is not less than the amount of money referred to in (a) above.

AND:

(c)   confirm amount to be added to stated capital: $ _____

12.9 Quorum at Shareholders' meetings:

The holders of a majority of the shares entitled to vote at a meeting, whether present in person or represented by proxy (standard)

Other _____

12.10 Notice of Shareholders' meetings:

Not less than 10 days, not more than 50/60 days (OBCA s.96(1); (CBCA s.135(1) (standard))

Other _____

12.11 Does Chairman have a casting vote?

Yes
No (standard)

13. <u>AUDIT INFORMATION</u>

13.1 Name and address of:[12]

Auditors
Accountants

_____

_____

Contact:_____ Telephone No.___

Facsimile No._____ E-mail add._____

13.2 Financial year end: _____

14. <u>BANKING</u>

14.1 Bank and branch (include address and name of contact):

_____

Contact:_____ Telephone No.___

Facsimile No._____ E-mail add._____

14.2 Signing officers for Corporation's account. (Please note any monetary restrictions.)

_____

15. <u>EXECUTION OF DOCUMENTS</u>

15.1 Any one of the directors or officers

Other (specify)

_____

_____

16. BUSINESS NAME REGISTRATION

16.1 List of business names to be registered (BNA s.2(1))

Name:_____

   Business address if different from registered office:

   _____

   Activity carried on under business name (not more than 40 characters): _____

   Date of first use of name:_____

   Province of registration:[13] _____

Name:_____

   Business address if different from registered office:

   _____

   Activity carried on under business name (not more than 40 characters): _____

   Date of first use of name:_____

   Province of registration: _____

16.2 Business Name Banking:

   Bank (include address): _____

   Signing officers: _____

17. EXTRA-PROVINCIAL REGISTRATIONS[14]

17.1 Indicate where corporation is to be registered to carry on business:

Alberta

Northwest Territories

British Columbia

Ontario

Manitoba

Quebec

New Brunswick

Saskatchewan

Newfoundland

Yukon

Nova Scotia

Prince Edward Island

Nunavut

17.2 Name and address of registered attorney:

Miller Thomson LLP Agent

See attached

18. **OTHER MATTERS**

advice on creditor-proofing assets

lease or other occupancy arrangements

trade-mark or domain name registrations

securing accounts receivable

insurance

employment contracts or manuals

notification under the Investment Canada Act

securing shareholder loans

shareholder agreement / unanimous shareholder agreement

contribution or indemnity for guarantees of corporate obligations

sales contracts and commercial credit guarantees

form of purchase order

health, safety and environmental matters

incentive plans

exempt financings

19. BUSINESS REGISTRATIONS

19.1 Indicate if any of the following are required:

Ontario: Vendor's Permit

WSIB Registration

Employer Health Tax

Federal: Business Number Application

GST Account

Payroll Account

Corporate Tax Account

Import/Export Account

Other:

20. **GENERAL**

20.1 Where are the corporate records to be kept?

Miller Thomson LLP[15]

Client

20.2 Do you wish a corporate seal?

- Yes • No

20.3 List all related corporations and show the appropriate relationship and percentage of ownership from the following:

Ultimate Holding Corporation (UHC)

Holding Corporation (HC)

Wholly Owned (WO)

Partly Owned (0-50%) (PO)

Associate (51-100%) (A)

Independent (I)

Sister

Name of Corporation	Relationship	Percent Ownership	GIP %

20.4 Group Name:

20.5 Does the Corporation have its own General Counsel?

Yes
No

SCHEDULE A

CHECKLIST - SHARE PROVISIONS (if applicable)

	Maximum Number to be issued - if applicable	Cumulative Dividends - rate - priority - frequency	Non-cumulative Dividend - rate - priority - frequency	Redemption Price	Retraction Price	Participation on wind-up - priority - amount	Voting/ Non-voting	Convertible into _____ Shares
Common								
Preferred								

SCHEDULE B

Accredited Investor means:

(a)   a bank listed in Schedule I or II of the Bank Act (Canada), or an authorized foreign bank listed in Schedule III of that Act;

(b)   the Business Development Bank incorporated under the Business Development Bank Act (Canada);

(c)   a loan corporation or trust corporation registered under the Loan and Trust Corporations Act or under the Trust and Loan Companies Act (Canada), or under comparable legislation in any other jurisdiction;

(d)   a co-operative credit society, credit union central, federation of caisses populaires, credit union or league, or regional caisse populaire, or an association under the Cooperative Credit Associations Act (Canada), in each case, located in Canada;

(e)   a company licensed to do business as an insurance company in any jurisdiction;

(f)   a subsidiary of any company referred to in paragraph (a), (b), (c), (d) or (e), where the company owns all of the voting shares of the subsidiary;

(g)   a person or company registered under the Actor securities legislation in another jurisdiction as an adviser or dealer, other than a limited market dealer;

(h)   the government of Canada or of any jurisdiction, or any crown corporation, instrumentality or agency of a Canadian federal, provincial or territorial government;

(i)   any Canadian municipality or any Canadian provincial or territorial capital city;

(j)   any national, federal, state, provincial, territorial or municipal government of or in any foreign jurisdiction, or any instrumentality or agency thereof;

(k)   a pension fund that is regulated by either the Office of the Superintendent of Financial Institutions (Canada) or a provincial pension commission or similar regulatory authority;

(l)   a registered charity under the Income Tax Act (Canada);

(m)   an individual who beneficially owns, or who together with a spouse beneficially own, financial assets having an aggregate realizable value that, before taxes but net of any related liabilities, exceeds $1,000,000;

(n)   an individual whose net income before taxes exceeded $200,000 in each of the two most recent years or whose net income before taxes combined with that of a spouse exceeded $300,000 in each of those years and who, in either case, has a reasonable expectation of exceeding the same net income level in the current year;

(o)   an individual who has been granted registration under the Act or securities legislation in another jurisdiction as a representative of a person or company referred to in paragraph (g), whether or not the individual's registration is still in effect;

(p)   a promoter of the issuer or an affiliated entity of a promoter of the issuer;

(q)   a spouse, parent, grandparent or child of an officer, director or promoter of the issuer;

(r)   a person or company that, in relation to the issuer, is an affiliated entity or a person or company referred to in clause (c) of the definition of distribution in subsection 1(1) of the Act;

(s)   an issuer that is acquiring securities of its own issue;

(t)   a company, limited partnership, limited liability partnership, trust or estate, other than a mutual fund or non-redeemable investment fund, that had net assets of at least $5,000,000 as reflected in its most recently prepared financial statements;

(u)   a person or company that is recognized by the Commission as an accredited investor;

(v)   a mutual fund or non-redeemable investment fund that, in Ontario, distributes its securities only to persons or companies that are accredited investors;

(w)   a mutual fund or non-redeemable investment fund that, in Ontario, distributes its securities under a prospectus for which a receipt has been granted by the Director;

(x)   a managed account if it is acquiring a security that is not a security of a mutual fund or non-redeemable investment fund;

(y)   an account that is fully managed by a trust corporation registered under the Loan and Trust Corporations Act;

(z)   an entity organized outside of Canada that is analogous to any of the entities referred to in paragraphs (a) through (g) and paragraph (k) in form and function; and

(aa)   a person or company in respect of which all of the owners of interests, direct or indirect, legal or beneficial, are persons or companies that are accredited investors.

Exemption for a Trade to an Accredited Investor

Sections 25 and 53 of the Act do not apply to a trade in a security if the purchaser is an accredited investor and purchases as principal.

---

1. French name required if the Corporation will be operating in Quebec.
2. Please give street & number or R.R. #, municipality and postal code. OBCA - must be in Ontario. CBCA -province in Canada
3. Resident Canadian is defined as:
   CBCA
   i. a Canadian citizen ordinarily resident in Canada;
   ii. a Canadian citizen not ordinarily resident in Canada who is a member of a prescribed class of person; or

   iii. a permanent resident within the meaning of the Immigration Act (Canada), and ordinarily resident in Canada, except a permanent resident who has been ordinarily resident in Canada for more than one year after the time at which they first became eligible to apply for Canadian citizenship.

OBCA

   i. a Canadian citizen ordinarily resident in Canada;

   ii. a Canadian citizen not ordinarily resident in Canada who is a member of a prescribed class of persons; or

   iii. a permanent resident within the meaning of the Immigration Act (Canada) and ordinarily resident in Canada.

4. (a)   the approval of the directors of the Corporation expressed by a resolution passed by the board of directors of the Corporation at a meeting of the directors or by an instrument or instruments in writing signed by a majority of the directors; or

   (b)   the approval of the holders of a majority of the voting shares of the Corporation for the time being outstanding expressed by a resolution passed at a meeting of shareholders or by an instrument or instruments in writing signed by the holders of a majority of such shares.

5. OBCA 118(3) - **Directors to be resident Canadians** - A majority of the directors of every corporation other than a non-resident corporation shall be resident Canadians but where a corporation has only one or two directors, that director or one of the two directors, as the case may be, shall be a resident Canadian.

CBCA 105(3) - **Residency** - At least 25% must be resident Canadian except if less than 4 at least 1 must be resident Canadian.

CBCA 105(4) - **Exception for holding corporation** - Notwithstanding subsection (3), not more than one-third of the directors of a holding corporation need be resident Canadians if the holding corporation earns in Canada directly or through its subsidiaries less than 5% of the gross revenues of the holding corporation and all of its subsidiary bodies corporate together as shown in:

   (a) the most recent consolidated financial statements of the holding corporation referred to in section 157; or

   (b) the most recent financial statements of the holding corporation and its subsidiary bodies corporate as at the end of the last completed year of the holding corporation.

6. 1.   Management approval must be obtained for a Miller Thomson LLP lawyer to act as a director.

   2.   Indemnities are automatically prepared for all office directors.

7. None of the officers need be a director (OBCA s. 133, CBCA s. 121).

8. Must be director and resident Canadian, OBCA s.127(1), CBCA s.115(1)

9. In order to issue securities in reliance on the "closely-held issuer exemption":

   a) The restrictions on transfer (see above item 6.5, note 4) and the definition under 7.1 must be complied with.

   b) The Corporation may not receive consideration in excess of $3,000,000 Cdn. for securities issued in reliance on that exemption on or after November 30, 2001.

   c) If the Corporation is to receive consideration in excess of $3,000,000 Cdn. another exemption must be identified.

   d) If there is a beneficial security holder that is not resident in Ontario, the standard provisions in 7.1 hereof must be reviewed to ensure compliance with applicable securities laws.

   e) No selling or promotional expenses can be paid in connection with the issuance (except for services performed by a registered dealer).

   f) A promoter of the Corporation cannot act as a promoter of any other issuer that has relied on this exemption in the last 12 months.

g) The Corporation must provide a purchaser with a prescribed "don't buy" statement (Form 45-501F3) at least four days prior to the trade unless the issuer will not have more than five beneficial holders following the trade.

h) The Corporation must "share" the $3 million dollar cap with all other issuers engaged in a "common enterprise". The term is not defined. The Ontario Securities Commission notes that the term "common Enterprise" is intended to operate as an anti-avoidance mechanism to the extent that multiple business entities are organized for the purposes of financing what is essentially a single business enterprise in order to benefit from continued or excessive use of the closely-held issuer exemption. The Commission takes the view that commonality of ownership combined with commonality of business plans will be particularly indicative of a "common enterprise".

10. To satisfy the Corporation's due diligence obligations, the Corporation will require any "accredited investor" to certify as to its status.

11. To satisfy the Corporation's due diligence obligations, the Corporation will require any such person to certify as to beneficial ownership of securities.

12. OBCA s. 148(1) "Exemption from Audit requirements - In respect of a financial year of a corporation, the corporation is exempt from the requirements of this Part regarding the appointment and duties of an auditor.
   (a)   where:
      (i) the corporation is not an offering corporation; and
      (ii) all of the shareholders of the corporation consent thereto in writing in respect of that year."
   CBCA also allows all shareholders of a non-distributing corporation to waive the audit requirement on an annual basis.

13. Extra-provincial registrations are generally required in the provinces and territories prior to registering a business name.

14. Federal corporations are not necessarily exempt from the requirement to obtain an extra-provincial registration or licence.

15. Our standard report letter advises client that annual resolutions are automatically prepared annually.

9C14
SHAREHOLDER AGREEMENT CHECKLIST

[See Para 9.663]

1.	Identity of Shareholders	— describe authorized capital and all issued shares
		— describe each shareholder
2.	Identity of Subject Corporation	— describe business being operated

3.   Restrictions on Transfer   — who may transfer or issue new and
      Shares and Issuance of   Issuance of shares? when?
      Shares

                                     — restrictions on corporate shareholder
                                         transferring to related corporations?

                                     — permit transfers by individual share-
                                         holder to his or her holding company?

                                     — restrictions on ability to pledge or
                                         encumber shares

4.   Rights of Transmission   — a)   on death:

                                     —   sale to whom? terms of sale?

                                     —   keyman insurance to fund
                                              purchase?

                                     —   calculation of price? when
                                              payable?

                                  —   b)   on retirement or permanent
                                              disability or ceasing to be an
                                              employee:

                                     —   definition of terms?

                                     —   sale to whom? terms of sale?

                                     —   calculation of price? when
                                              payable?

                                  —   c)   sale to third parties:

                                     —   rights of first refusal to others
                                     —   rights of others to piggyback on
                                              outsider's offer

                                      d)   sale to each other:

                                     —   shotgun provisions

5.   Directors and Officers   —   identity of board of directors

                                     —   nominees of each shareholder?

                                     —   identity of officers

                                     —   job descriptions of officers

		—	remuneration of officers and directors
6.	Day-to-Day Operations	—	persons to run daily operations
		—	salary levels, bonuses and benefits
		—	signing authority for contracts, banking and borrowing
		—	only shareholders to approve certain matters? e.g. dividends, issuances of shares, borrowing, hiring of family members, salaries above $X, change of business, sales of assets, etc.
7.	Profits	—	how to approve dividends?
		—	shareholder loans policies
8.	Non-Competition	—	in what geographic areas and for how long?
9.	Indemnities	—	for shareholder's security to lenders
		—	fees for guarantees of shareholders? (tax deductibility)
10.	Shareholders' Rights to Information	—	access to securities book and financial records at reasonable times
11.	Remedies on Default	—	arbitration? litigation?
12.	Process to Value Shares	—	average from two accountants?
		—	auditors?
		—	book value at last year end?

9C15
PARTNERSHIP AGREEMENT CHECKLIST

[See Para. 9.663]

1.	Effective Date	— start of business
2.	Describe Partners	— percentage of partnership each to have
		— each partner represents own interests
		— designate nominee to represent corporate partners
3.	Firm Name	— specify name
4.	Terms of Partnership	— at will of partners or specific length
5.	Description of Business	— type of business to be operated
6.	Daily Management	— describe scope of authority of each partner
		— will there be an administrative partner
		— banking and cheque signing
		borrowing
		— signing of contracts
7.	Place of Business	—
8.	Death or Disability of a Partner	— return of capital
		— buyout
		— long term disability insurance coverage
		— keyman insurance to fund
9.	Retirement	— return of capital
		— buyout
10.	Capital Contributions	— how much
		— interest earned
		— how and when repayable

9C16
PENSION CONSIDERATIONS CHECKLIST

SHARE TRANSACTION

General Rule — corporation continues under the control of the new shareholder and, as a consequence, any pension plan sponsored by the corporation will continue without any action required by either Seller or Buyer.

Seller's Concerns — what representations and warranties is it prepared to give
— surplus value taken into account in purchase price

Buyer's Concerns — seeking protection through representations and warranties given by Seller, particularly with respect to:
— pre-purchase administration of pension fund
— funded status of the plan
— registration status of the plan
— no illegal use or withdrawal of surplus, including contribution holidays
— entitlement to surplus, particularly if surplus taken into account in purchase price

Special Situations — corporation's pension fund assets held in master trust arrangement with pension fund assets of other plans sponsored by Seller and/or corporations related to Seller
— Buyer or Seller generally obligated to cause corporation to establish new funding arrangement
— purchased corporation a participating employer in Seller's (or other related corporation's) pension plan
    e.g.   — A owns 100% of shares of B
        — A sponsors pension plan in which B is participating employer
        — A sells shares of B to C, who is unrelated to A
        — A will act to remove B from participation in its pension plan
        — onus on C to establish successor plan or risk constructive dismissal claims

9C17
PENSION CONSIDERATIONS CHECKLIST

(ASSET TRANSACTIONS)

Summary of Relevant Pension Benefits Act (Ontario) Provisions

A.   Buyers Provides No Successor Plan

s. 69(1)   Superintendent of Financial Services may, by order, require the windup of a pension plan in whole or in part where, . . .

(f)   all or part of the employer's business or all or part of the assets of the employer's business are sold, assigned or otherwise disposed of and the person who acquires the business or assets does not provide a pension plan for the members of the employer's pension plan who become employees of the person;

B.   Buyer Provides a Successor Plan

s. 80(1)   Where an employer who sponsors a pension plan disposes of all or part of its business or assets, a plan member who, as a result of the disposition, becomes an employee of the successor employer and a participant in the successor employer's pension plan,

(a)   remains entitled to benefits provided under the former employer's plan to the effective date of the transaction, without further accrual [unless successor assumes liability for these benefits; s. 80(2)];

(b)   is entitled to credit in the successor's plan for the period of membership in the former employer's plan for the purposes of eligibility for participation in or entitlement to benefits under the successor plan;
[i.e. period of <u>membership</u> in Seller's plan counts toward eligibility for participation in, and vesting/locking-in of benefits under, Buyer's plan]; and

(c)   is entitled to credit in the former employer's plan for the period of employment with the successor employer for the purpose of determining entitlement to benefits under the former plan.
[i.e. period of <u>employment</u> with Buyer counts toward vesting/locking-in of benefits earned under Seller's plan]
. .

(3)   Where a transaction described in (1) above occurs, the employee's employment is deemed not to have terminated.

(4)   Where successor assumes liability for benefits under the former employer's plan, no transfer of assets may be made from former to successor plan without consent of the Superintendent.

(5)   Superintendent shall refuse to consent to asset transfer that does not protect the benefits of members and former members of the transferring plan or otherwise meet prescribed requirements.
       — PCO Policy Statement 2 - Transfer of Assets Resulting from Sale of a Business

Seller's Concerns

— compel Buyer to offer employment to   employees of purchased business on "substantially the same terms and conditions" to avoid constructive dismissal claims
— compel Buyer to maintain/establish a successor plan so as to avoid implications of order under s. 69(1) of PBA, being:
  - partial wind-up (different provincial rules)
  - accelerated vesting and funding implications
  - potential surplus distribution
  - compliance costs - filing and notice requirements
— protect interests in surplus or obtain value for same

Buyer's Concerns

— understand the nature of, and costs associated with, obligation it assumes re: transferred employees
— acknowledge obligations of "successor employer" under provisions of any collective bargaining agreement
— make informed decision on pension arrangements provided for transferred employees with regard not only to Seller's practice, but other design considerations, such as:
  -Buyer's current compensation/benefit policies
  -cost sharing policies
  -competition
  -costs
  -union negotiations
  -employee characteristics
  -legislation
  -government benefits - CPP/OAS

Alternative Arrangements

1. **Buyer Establishes Plan for Future (Post-Closing) Service Only**

   Advantages
   - simple to document and administer
   - Buyer assumes no liability for pre-closing benefits
   - less reliance for Buyer on Seller's representations and warranties
   - no costs borne by Seller or Buyer re: valuing liabilities
   - Seller retains any surplus and rights relating thereto
   - rights and obligations of Seller and Buyer prescribed under PBA

   Disadvantages
   - Seller retains administrative obligations re: former employees - benefit statements, record-keeping, etc.
   - Buyer's failure to establish or maintain plan may trigger partial termination of Seller's plan
   - Buyer loses some control over pension arrangements for its new employees
   - employees may be significantly prejudiced
     - must look to 2 sources for pension
     - no further accrual of benefit earned in Seller's plan in respect of future salary increases (i.e. in career or final average earnings plan)

   Considerations
   - all above issues
   - defined benefit vs. defined contribution plan

2. **Buyer's Plan "Wraps Around" Seller's Plan**

Average Earnings — B

C

Average Earnings at Closing — A

Closing Date · Total Service

A = Seller's Liability

B + C = Buyer's Liability

Advantages
- same as Alternative 1 from Seller's perspective
- employee is "made whole" with respect to amount of pension ultimately payable
- allows Buyer to maintain separate but comparable plan without prejudice to new employees

Disadvantages
- employees must still look to separate sources for pension
- Buyer assumes some liability for benefits earned in respect of pre-closing service, without a corresponding asset transfer from Seller's plan
- same as Alternative 1 from Seller's perspective

Considerations
- only relevant to defined benefit plan
- is Buyer prepared to incur expense?
- why not have Buyer assume all liabilities?

3.   **Seller Assigns and Buyer Assumes Entire Plan and Fund**
(applicable only where transferred employees constitute all of the participants in Seller's plan)

Advantages
- Seller relieved of all ongoing liabilities/obligations
- Seller avoids expense of winding up plan
- employees need only look to one source for pension payment employees bear no risk of part of pension being calculated at closing date
- Buyer has full control over all pension benefits for new employees
- Seller may receive value for surplus

Disadvantages
- Seller may give up right to surplus without adequate compensation
- Buyer assumes all risk of Seller's past administration and must obtain representations and warranties from Seller, particularly with respect to:
  - funded status of the plan
  - registration status of the plan
  - no illegal use or withdrawal of surplus

Considerations
- representations and warranties Seller prepared to give
- ad hoc increases

- defined benefit vs. defined contribution
- ownership of surplus
- interim administrative arrangements

4. Buyer Assumes Pension Liabilities in Respect of Transferred Employees with Corresponding Asset Transfer from Seller's Plan

Advantages
- same as Alternative 3 from perspective of Seller, Buyer and employees

Disadvantages
- same as Alternative 3
- compliance with Policy Statement 2 of the Pension Commission of Ontario (now the Financial Services Commission of Ontario) time and cost considerations
- actuarial valuation of assumed liabilities required

Considerations
- defined benefits vs. defined contribution plan
- representations and warranties Seller prepared to give
- does Buyer have existing defined benefit plan?
- will Buyer assume liabilities for non-active employees?
- settlement of actuarial assumptions to be used in valuation of defined benefits
- surplus entitlement issue
- does finding arrangement for Seller's plan permit prohibit complicate asset transfer?
- interim administrative arrangements

9C18
BABE'S PPSA COMMANDMENTS

[See Paras. 9.178 and 9.677]

1. I will read sections 3 and 4 of the PPSA and ensure that the PPSA is the correct statute governing the collateral and the collateral is in fact personal property:

    e.g. ships, rolling stock, intellectual property, insurance policies, quotas and licences, real property leases and rents.

2. I will read sections 5, 6, 7 and 8 of the PPSA (the conflict of law rules) and check to ensure that it is the Ontario PPSA that applies.

3. I will read section 11 of the PPSA and ensure that my client's security interest has "attached" to the collateral because:

    (a) the debtor has signed a security agreement that contains a description of the collateral sufficient to allow it to be identified;

    (b) "value" as defined in the Act has been given by my client; and

    (c) the debtor has rights in the collateral.

4. I will read section 33 of the PPSA and ensure I have done the necessary PMSI steps and timing based on the debtor's use of the collateral (watching out for ineligible sales and lease backs).

5. I will ensure that I have properly registered the financing statement to "perfect" my client's security interest by checking the regulations *every* time I register to ensure:

    (a) I have named the debtor(s) as specified in the regulations with a copy of the necessary document in my file to confirm I have the required name;

    (b) I have described "motor vehicles" used by the debtor as "consumer goods" or "equipment" as required in the Act and regulations.

6. I have not limited the scope of my client's security interest by placing words in the optional collateral description area without first warning my client about section 46(3).

7. I will always remember that the PPSA computer runs in arrears of real time and plan my closings accordingly. I will register as soon as I can (noting no registration before signing the agreement for "consumer goods" by section 45(2)), so that I may obtain a post registration certified search before advancing funds.

8. I will ensure a copy of each registration I do is sent to the debtor as required by the Act (section 46(6)).

9. I will report the registration to my client noting *the client* must file a financing change statements to:

    (a) renew before the registration expiry date;

    (b) record changes of debtor names within 15 days;

    (c) record transfers of collateral to third parties within 30 days; and

    (d) re-register elsewhere if the collateral leaves Ontario or the debtor moves out of Ontario.

10. I will double check myself by reading the commentary to the CBA-O Personal Property Security Opinion Report or calling the LSUC practice advisory hotline.

FORMS AND PRECEDENTS

9F1
LETTER OF INTENT

[See Para. 9.100]

(*date*)

Ms. Jane Doe, in trust
123 White Street
Toronto, Ontario

Dear Ms. Doe:

Re: Purchase of Target Ltd.

1. We confirm the intention of Vendor Inc. (the "Vendor") to sell its ABC Chemical division to you in trust, for a corporation to be incorporated, including the following assets:

    (a) the land and buildings comprising Part of Lots 1 and 2, Plan 55R-12345, City of Toronto, known as 3 Dundas St. East, Toronto (the "Realty"); and

    (b) the business, undertaking, assets and equipment as a going concern of the ABC Chemical division operated on the Realty by the Vendor (hereinafter referred to as the "Business"), including:

        (i) the saleable inventory of chemicals and the consumables used in the operation of the Business;

        (ii) all accounts receivable outstanding as at the date of closing in respect of the operation of the Business, excluding any accounts outstanding over ninety (90) days;

        (iii) all prepaid expenses in respect of the operation of the Business; and

        (iv) the goodwill of the Business including the right to carry on business in succession to the Business under the name and style "ABC Chemicals".

    For greater certainty, all monies in the bank, certificates of deposit and cash on hand shall be excluded from the Agreement of Purchase and Sale.

2.   The purchase price for the Realty referred to in paragraph 1(a) shall be the sum of $_____, subject to the usual adjustments, payable:

    (a)   as to $ _____in cash or by certified cheque payable to the Vendor on the date of execution of a formal agreement of purchase and sale, to be held as a deposit pending closing and to be credited to the purchase price on the date of closing;

    (b)   as to $_____, subject to the adjustments provided for in paragraph 2, above, in cash or by certified cheque payable to the Vendor on the date of closing;

    (c)   the balance of the purchase price in the amount of $_____ by way of a mortgage back of the Realty to the Vendor, such mortgage to be for a term of five (5) years and to contain the following terms:

        (i)   interest to accrue from the date of closing at a rate of ____% per annum, calculated half-yearly not in advance;

        (ii)   accrued interest to be payable quarterly, in arrears;

        (iii)   principal to be payable in equal consecutive quarterly instalments in the amount of $_____, the first such instalment becoming due and payable on the last day of the third month immediately following the date of closing and the balance of the principal becoming due and payable on maturity; and

        (iv)   the Purchaser to be entitled to prepay the whole or any part of the principal sum outstanding on any principal payment date, at any time or times without notice, bonus or penalty.

3.   (a)   The purchase price for the remaining assets of the Business referred to in paragraph 1(b) shall be an amount equal to the sum of:

        (i)   the amount of the accounts receivable relating to the operation of the Business recorded in the books of the Vendor as at the closing date;

        (ii)   the value of all inventory on hand as of the closing date calculated at cost on a first in, first out basis;

        (iii)   the value of prepaid expenses recorded in the books of the Vendor as of the closing date; and

        (iv)   the full amount of the trade accounts payable outstand-ing on the books of the Vendor incurred in the ordinary course of the Business.

    (b)   The purchase price for the Business shall be allocated among the various assets in accordance with the amounts as recorded in the books of the Vendor.

    (c)   The purchase price for the Business shall be payable as to an amount equal to the sum of the outstanding trade accounts payable by the Purchaser assuming the liability of the Vendor for payment of such accounts and the balance of such purchase price shall be paid in cash or by certified cheque on the closing date.

4.   (a)   The Purchaser shall covenant and agree that the principal sum and interest outstanding under the mortgage back shall, at the option of the Vendor, accelerate and immediately become due and payable on the occurrence of any sale, transfer or assignment of the Realty, or the controlling interest in the legal or beneficial interests comprising the legal entity of the Purchaser.

  (b)   The events of default referred to in paragraph 4(a) above, shall be incorporated into the mortgage back of the Realty.

5.   The person(s), firm(s) or corporation(s) for whom Ms. Doe is acting as trustee shall be identified in and named as the Purchaser in the formal agreement of purchase and sale.

6.   The Purchaser shall waive compliance with the Bulk Sales Act (Ontario).

7.   The Purchaser shall assume and continue the employment of all employees of the Business as of the date of closing as agreed between the parties.

8.   The Realty shall be transferred free and clear of all liens, charges or encumbrances and the Vendor shall covenant and agree that it is, and as of the date of closing, will be the owner of the equipment and assets comprising the Business free and clear of any liens, charges or encumbrances of any nature or kind.

9.   Upon acceptance of this letter, the Trustee shall deliver a certified cheque payable to the Vendor in the amount of $_____ as a negotiating deposit to offset the legal and accounting fees to be incurred by the Vendor. If the transaction fails to proceed for any reason, including a failure of the parties to agree upon the terms to be incorporated into the formal agreement of purchase and sale, this negotiation deposit shall be non-refundable and may be retained by the Vendor. Upon execution of a formal agreement of purchase and sale, the amount of the negotiation deposit shall be credited to the deposit referred to in paragraph 2(a), above.

10.   The closing of the transaction of purchase and sale shall take place on or before the _____ day of _____, 19____.

A binding agreement, otherwise than as provided above regarding the negotiation deposit, is subject to the preparation and execution of a formal Agreement of Purchase and Sale incorporating the above and such other terms and conditions as are necessary or advisable. If you are in agreement with the above terms, please sign the copy of this letter where indicated below, return same to the undersigned together with your certified cheque in the amount of $_____, whereupon we will instruct our solicitors to prepare a formal Agreement of Purchase and Sale.

Yours truly,

VENDOR INC.

Per: _____

President

The above terms are agreed to and accepted this _____ day of _____, 19_____.

_____
Jane Doe, in trust

9F2
OPTION AGREEMENT - PERSONALTY

[See Para. 9.110]

THIS AGREEMENT made the _____ day of _____, 19_____

B E T W E E N :

VENDOR INC., a corporation incorporated under the laws of the Province of Ontario,

(hereinafter called "Vendor"),

OF THE FIRST PART,

-and-

PURCHASER INC., a corporation incorporated under the laws of the Province of Ontario,

(hereinafter called "Purchaser"),

OF THE SECOND PART.

WHEREAS Vendor is the owner of certain assets more particularly described herein;

AND WHEREAS Purchaser wishes to purchase the said assets upon the terms and conditions herein set out;

AND WHEREAS Vendor deems it advisable to grant to Purchaser an option to purchase the said assets on the same terms and conditions contained herein;

NOW THEREFORE THIS AGREEMENT WITNESSETH that in consideration of the mutual covenants and agreements hereinafter contained, and of the sum of Two ($2.00) Dollars paid by each party hereto to the other, the receipt of which is hereby acknowledged, the parties hereto mutually covenant and agree as follows:

1. **Option.** Vendor hereby grants to Purchaser the right and option, which option shall be exercised in accordance with the provisions of Section 2 herein, to purchase the following assets belonging to Vendor at the prices set out as follows opposite the said assets, which option shall remain open up to and including the _____ day of _____, 19_____.

The fixed assets set out in schedule A hereto	_____ Dollars ($_____), provided however that if any such assets are deleted from the final agreement of purchase and sale, by agreement of the parties hereto, the said amount of _____ Dollars ($_____) shall be reduced by the fair market value of any such assets deleted.
Inventory	Lower of original cost of replacement value as at _____, 19_____ (to be determined).
Intangibles (Goodwill, Trade Name, Customer Lists, etc.)	One ($1.00) Dollar

2. **Exercise of Option.** The option granted in Section 1 herein shall be validly exercised by Purchaser upon the delivery by Purchaser of written notice of its exercise of the option in the form annexed hereto as Schedule B.

3. **Termination of Option.** The option granted in Section 1 shall automatically and irrevocably terminate on the ____ day of _____, 19____ if at that time Purchaser has not exercised the said option in accordance with the provisions of Section 2.

4. **Acknowledgement and Covenant of Vendor.** Vendor expressly agrees and acknowledges that subsequent to the date of execution herein, and prior to the exercise by Purchaser of the option granted in Section 1 herein, Purchaser shall seek the following:

(a) an opinion of (*name of Vendor's valuators*) as to the value of all of Vendor's fixed assets;

(b) an opinion of (*name of Vendor's accountant*), that the financial statements of Vendor dated the ____ day of _____, 19_____ fairly represent the financial position of Vendor as at the said date;

(c) an opinion of (*name of Vendor's Solicitors*) that Vendor possesses good and marketable title to the assets set out in Schedule A herein;

(d) financing with respect to the purchase of the assets of Vendor upon terms satisfactory to Purchaser;

(e) approval of the board of directors of Purchaser with respect to the exercise of the said option; and

(f) a lease with respect to the premises currently occupied by Vendor for the purpose of carrying on its business in a form satisfactory to Purchaser.

Vendor covenants that between the date of execution herein and the _____ day of _____, 19_____, it will use its best efforts to comply with any reasonable requests by Purchaser, whichrequests are designed to assist Purchaser with respect to any of the matters enumerated in sub-clauses (a) to (f) of this Section 4.

5. **Deposit Payment.** On the date of execution herein, Purchaser hereby covenants and agrees to pay the sum of Five Thousand ($5,000) Dollars to Vendor, which amount shall be held in escrow by Vendor until either:

(a) the option granted in Section 1 is exercised by Purchaser, at which time Vendor shall apply the said Five Thousand ($5,000) Dollars against the total purchase price to be paid for the assets set out in Section 1; or

(b) the option granted in Section 1 is terminated in accordance with Section 3, at which time Vendor shall refund the said Five Thousand ($5,000) Dollars to Purchaser.

6. **Option Non-Assignable.** The parties hereto covenant and agree that the option granted in Section 1 shall not be transferred, assigned, pledged or hypothecated in any way, whether by operation of law or otherwise, and shall not be subject to execution, attachment or similar process.

7. **Canadian Dollars.** All dollar amounts referred to in this agreement are in Canadian funds.

8. **Headings.** Section headings are not to be considered part of this Agreement and are included solely for reference purposes and are not intended to be full or accurate descriptions of the contents thereof.

9. **Schedules.** The following schedules are annexed hereto and form an integral part of this agreement:

   Schedule A — Fixed Assets
   Schedule B — Exercise of Option

10. **Entire Agreement.** This agreement constitutes the entire agreement between the parties hereto pertaining to the subject matter hereof and supersedes all prior and contemporaneous agreements, understandings, negotiations and discussions, whether oral or written, of the parties, and there are no warranties, representations and other agreements between the parties in connection with the subject matter hereof. No supplement, modification, waiver or termination of this agreement shall be binding unless executed in writing by the party to be bound thereby.

IN WITNESS WHEREOF this agreement has been executed by the parties hereto as of the date first above written.

VENDOR INC.

Per: _____ c/s

PURCHASER INC.

Per: _____ c/s

SCHEDULE A
(insert schedule)

SCHEDULE B

EXERCISE OF OPTION

TO: Vendor Inc.

We hereby exercise the Option provided for in an agreement dated the _____ day of _____, 20____ (the "Option Agreement") to purchase certain assets upon the terms and conditions contained therein.

DATED the _____ day of _____, 20_____.

PURCHASER INC.

Per: _____ c/s

9F3
OPTION AGREEMENT — REAL ESTATE

[See Para. 9.120]

This Agreement made the _____ day of _____, 20____.

BETWEEN

A

(hereinafter called the "Vendor"),

OF THE FIRST PARTAND

B

(hereinafter called the "Purchaser"),

OF THE SECOND PART

WHEREAS

A. The Purchaser wishes to obtain an option to purchase certain lands and premises in the _____ of _____ in the _____ of _____ more particularly described in Schedule "A" attached hereto, known municipally as _____ and herein referred to as the Subject Property;

B. The Vendor has agreed to grant an option to the Purchaser to purchase the Subject Property on the terms and conditions hereinafter set forth.

WITNESSETH that in consideration of the premises, other good and valuable consideration and the sum of $_____ paid by the Purchaser to the Vendor (the receipt and sufficiency of which is hereby acknowledged by the Vendor), the Vendor and Purchaser agree as follows:

1. OPTION

The Purchaser shall have the exclusive right and option to purchase the Subject Property for the purchase price of _____ (herein referred to as the Purchase Price").

2. TERM AND EXERCISE

This option may be exercised by the Purchaser on or before the ____ day of _____, _____, by notice in writing from the Purchaser to the Vendor advising the Vendor that the Purchaser intends to purchase the Subject Property and such notice shall be accompanied by a deposit payable to the Vendor in the amount of $_____ which deposit shall be held by the Vendor in trust pending completion or other termination of this Agreement and to be credited towards the Purchase Price on completion as hereinafter set out. In the event this option is not exercised in accordance with the provisions of this paragraph, this option shall terminate, any rights under this Agreement shall become null and void and all liabilities of the Purchaser and the Vendor pursuant to this Agreement shall be released and forever discharged.

3. NOTICES

Any notices given under this Agreement or pursuant to any law or governmental regulation shall be in writing. Such notice shall be deemed given if personally delivered, or sent by prepaid registered mail, posted in the ____ of ____;

(a) To the Vendor at the following address:

or such other address as the Vendor may designate by notice to the Purchaser

(b)　To the Purchaser at the following address:

or such other address as the Purchaser may designate by notice to the Vendor.

Any notice referred to above, if delivered, shall be deemed to have been given or made on the date on which it was personally delivered, or if sent by prepaid registered mail shall be deemed to have been given or made on the third business day on which mail is distributed to the recipient by the post office in the Province of Ontario following the date on which it was so mailed. During the period of any postal strike or other interference with the mails, personal delivery shall be substituted for prepaid registered mail.

4.　MISCELLANEOUS

(a) Right to Inspect: The Purchaser and all persons authorized by it shall have the right at all reasonable times to enter on the Subject Property for the purposes of inspection, conducting soil tests and preparing surveys and plans. In the event this option is not exercised or if exercised and the agreement of purchase and sale is not completed (other than as a result of the Vendor's breach) the Purchaser shall at its sole cost and expense restore the Subject Property as nearly as practicable to its condition existing prior to such inspection or soil tests being carried out.

(b) Authorizations: The Vendor covenants to provide the Purchaser and execute without charge to the Purchaser such authorizations, directions and other documents as may be required by the Purchaser to bring an application for (*choose appropriate option: rezoning/minor variance/severance/ building and demolition permit*) provided that all costs thereof and liabilities in relation thereto shall be the sole responsibility of the Purchaser.

(c) Assignment: The Purchaser shall have the right to assign this option and all its rights hereunder by giving notice of such assignment to the Vendor whereupon all references herein to the Purchaser shall then be references to its assignee provided that the Purchaser shall continue to be liable hereunder. [*The Purchaser may assign its rights under this option and upon such assignment and upon the assignee or assignees executing an agreement to assume the Purchaser's obligations hereunder, the assignee or assignees shall stand in the place and stead of the Purchaser as if the assignee or assignees were originally the Purchaser and the Purchaser shall be relieved of any further liability and obligation hereunder.*]

(d) Planning Act Provided that this option shall be effective to create an interest in the Subject Property only if the provisions of the Act are complied with on or before the Closing Date (as hereinafter defined). The Vendor covenants with the Purchaser not to acquire any lands abutting the Subject Property that would result in the conveyance of the Subject Property pursuant to this Agreement being contrary to the provisions of section 50 of the Planning Act.

5.   AGREEMENT OF PURCHASE AND SALE

In the event of and upon the exercise of the option by the Purchaser pursuant to the provisions of paragraph 2 herein, this Agreement shall then become a binding agreement of purchase and sale between the parties hereto, upon the following terms:

(a) Purchase Price

The Purchase Price of $ _____ shall be payable as follows:

(i)   By the Purchaser paying the sum of $ _____ which sum shall have been submitted as a deposit upon the exercise of this option by the Purchaser, to be held in trust pending completion or other termination of this Agreement which deposit (herein referred to as the "Deposit") shall be credited on account of the Purchase Price on the Closing Date (as hereinafter defined).

(ii) By the Purchaser paying the sum of _____ DOLLARS by certified cheque or bank draft (subject to the adjustments as set out in paragraph 5(g) on the Closing Date and delivery of a valid and registrable transfer/deed to the Subject Property as herein set forth.

(iii) By the Purchaser giving back to the Vendor, and the Vendor taking back from the Purchaser a first mortgage for the balance of the Purchase Price having a term of _____ years repayable in _____ calculated _____ at the rate of _____% per annum, which mortgage shall be open for repayment in whole or in part at any time or times without notice or bonus, and which mortgage shall, at the option of the Vendor, become due and payable upon any sale of the Subject Property after the Closing Date.

(b) Closing Date

This Agreement shall be completed on the sixtieth (60th) day next following the giving of the notice of exercise of the option pursuant to paragraph 2 above. In the event the sixtieth day shall fall on a day that is a Saturday, Sunday or other day on which the applicable Land Registry Office shall not be open, then this Agreement shall be completed on the day next following when the applicable Land Registry Office shall be open. Such day of completion shall be referred to herein as the Closing Date. The closing shall be held at the Land Registry Office for the _____ Division of _____ on the Closing Date between the hours of 9:30 a.m. and 4:30 p.m. local time.

(c) Warranties and Representations

The Vendor hereby represents and warrants to the Purchaser subject to the limitations, if any, expressed hereby as follows:

(i)   The Vendor is now and at the Closing Date will be a body corporate existing in good standing under the laws of the Province of Ontario with full corporate power, authority and capacity to accept this Agreement and to carry out the transaction contemplated hereby;

(ii)   The Vendor will at the Closing Date have full and absolute right and power to convey and transfer to the Purchaser or cause to be conveyed or transferred to the Purchaser the Subject Property;

(iii)   [*That no part of the Subject Property nor any part of the common elements of (   ) Condominium Plan No. (   ) (hereinafter called the "Condominium") has been or is now insulated in whole or in part with asbestos, urea formaldehyde foam or any similar type substance or insulation;*]

(iv)   [*That there are no special assessments contemplated by (   ) Condominium Corporation No. ( ) (the "Condominium Corporation") and that there are no legal actions pending or contemplated by or against the said Condominium Corporation; and*]

(v)   [*That the Vendor has not received any notice convening a special or general meeting of the Condominium Corporation respecting the termination of the Condominium, any alteration in or addition to the common elements or the renovation thereof or any substantial change in the assets or liabilities of the Condominium Corporation. The Vendor covenants that if he receives any such notice prior to the Closing Date, it shall forthwith notify the Purchaser in writing and the Purchaser may thereupon at its option declare this Agreement to be null and void and the Deposit shall be returned to the Purchaser forthwith.*]

(d) Covenants

The Vendor covenants and agrees with the Purchaser as follows:

(i)   In addition to the documentation referred to in this Agreement, to provide the following documents on the Closing Date:

A.   Transfer/Deed of Land.

B. Declaration of the Vendor (or an officer of the Vendor in the case of a corporation) declaring unequivocally that the Vendor's ownership of the Subject Property has not been challenged by anyone and that there are no adverse or possessory claims against the Vendor or the Subject Property.

C. Bill of Sale with respect to all chattels (if any).

(ii) That the Purchaser shall not be liable or responsible in any way for any agent's or broker's fees in connection with the Agreement;

(iii) To provide the Purchaser with vacant possession of the Subject Property on the Closing Date;

(iv) To provide the Purchaser on the Closing Date evidence in a form satisfactory to the Purchaser that on the Closing Date the Vendor is the beneficial owner of the Subject Property and is a resident of Canada for purposes of determining its liability for tax pursuant to the Income Tax Act. The Vendor shall also provide satisfactory evidence on the Closing Date of compliance with the provisions of the Family Law Act.

(v) To discharge at its sole cost and expense, all mortgages, liens and encumbrances registered on title to the Subject Property on or before the Closing Date, save and except the mortgage back referred to in paragraph 5(a)(iii) above, the encumbrances and other interests described in paragraph 5(h); and

(vi) To convey to the Purchaser all fixtures and chattels affixed to, located on and used in conjunction with the Subject Property on the Closing Date, all such fixtures and chattels to be free and clear of all encumbrances.

(e) Purchase Price Allocation

The Purchase Price is hereby allocated among the various properties comprising the Subject Property as follows:

Land:	$ _____
Buildings:	$ _____
Chattels:	$ _____

The parties hereto acknowledge and agree that the foregoing allocation is reasonable in the circumstances. Each of the parties hereto covenants with the other that in reporting the purchase and sale herein to the Minister of National Revenue in any return of income for any relevant taxation year for federal or provincial income tax purposes, it will report the proceeds of disposition or cost of acquisition, as the case may be, using the amounts allocated herein.

(f) Income Tax Act

Purchaser shall be credited towards the Purchase Price with the amount, if any, which it shall be necessary for the Purchaser to pay to the Receiver General of Canada in order to satisfy Purchaser's liability in respect of tax payable by the Vendor under the non-residency provisions of the Income Tax Act by reason of the sale. Purchaser shall not claim such credit if the Vendor delivers on the Closing Date, the prescribed certificate or a statutory declaration from an office of the Vendor that it is not, as of the Closing Date, a non-resident of Canada.

(g) Adjustments

Real property taxes on the basis of the calendar year for which assessed, water and utilities (unless metered) shall be apportioned and allowed to the Closing Date, it being agreed that the expenses and revenues of the Closing Date shall be allocated to the Purchaser. [*There shall be no adjustment for the Vendor' share of any of the assets or liabilities of the Condominium Corporation including any reserve or contingency fund to which the Vendor may have contributed prior to the Closing Date.*]

(h) Title

The Purchaser shall be allowed up to and including the tenth day prior to the Closing Date to examine the title to the Subject Property at its own expense. Title to the Subject Property shall be good and marketable and free and clear of all restrictions, liens, encumbrances, charges, tenancies, occupancies and other possessory rights except the following:

If within the time allowed for examining the title any valid objection to title is made in writing to the Vendor and which the Vendor is unable or unwilling to remove, remedy or satisfy and which the Purchaser will not waive, this Agreement, notwithstanding any intermediate action, negotiations in respect of such objections, shall be at an end and the Deposit shall be returned to the Purchaser forthwith without deduction and neither party shall have any further rights or obligations hereunder. Save as to any objection made within such time, and any objection going to the root of title the Purchaser shall be conclusively deemed to have accepted the Vendor's title to the Subject Property.

(i) Planning Act

Provided that this Agreement shall be effective to create an interest in the Subject Property only if the provisions of the Planning Act are complied with by the Vendor on or before the Closing Date and the Vendor covenants to proceed diligently at its expense to obtain any necessary consents and approvals on or before the Closing Date. The Vendor covenants that the prescribed statements pursuant to subsection 50(22) of the Planning Act shall be properly completed by it and its solicitors on the Closing Date.

(j) Damage

The Subject Property and all other things being purchased shall be and remain until the Closing Date at the risk of the Vendor. Vendor shall hold all insurance policies, if any, and the proceeds thereof in trust for the parties as their interests may appear and in the event of damage, Purchaser may either terminate this Agreement whereupon the Deposit shall be returned forthwith to the Purchaser or else take the proceeds of any insurance and complete the transaction.

(k) GST

The Purchaser agrees that it will be as at the Closing Date a registrant for Goods and Services Tax (G.S.T.) under the Excise Tax Act, R.S.C. 1985, as amended, and will provide evidence of same in form and substance reasonably satisfactory to the Vendor or its solicitors at the Closing Date, including without limitation, a statutory declaration sworn by a senior officer of the Purchaser confirming the Purchaser's G.S.T. registration number and that such registration continues to be in full force and effect and an indemnity to the Vendor for any GST claimed from the Vendor in the event the Purchaser does not pay the GST payable by it in respect of this transaction. In the event that the Purchaser shall fail to deliver such evidence and such indemnity to the Vendor, then the Purchaser shall pay to the Vendor, in addition to the Purchase Price herein, in pursuance of the Purchaser's obligation to pay and the Vendor's obligation to collect G.S.T. under the said Act, an amount equal to seven (7%) per cent of the Purchase Price or such other amount as is required pursuant to the said Act on the Closing Date.

(l) Electronic Registration

The Vendor and Purchaser acknowledge that the Teraview Electronic Registration System ("TERS") is operative and mandatory in the Land Registry Office for the Land Titles Division of Halton. The Purchaser and Vendor shall each retain legal counsel who are authorized TERS users and who are in good standing with the Law Society of Upper Canada. The Vendor and Purchaser shall each authorize their respective legal counsel to enter into a document registration agreement in the form as adopted by the joint LSUC-CBAO Committee on Electronic Registration of Title Documents on March 28, 2001. The delivery and exchange of documents and closing funds and the release thereof to the Vendor and Purchaser, as the case may be:

(a)   shall not occur contemporaneously with the registration of the transfer/deed of land (and other registrable documentation, if any); and

(b)   shall be governed by the document registration agreement pursuant to which legal counsel receiving any documents or funds will be required to hold same in escrow and will not be entitled to release except in strict accordance with provisions of the document registration agreement.

(m) Miscellaneous

(i)   This is the entire agreement between the parties and there are no other terms, obligations, covenants, representations, warranties, statements or conditions oral or otherwise of any kind whatsoever.

(ii)   Notwithstanding any presumption to the contrary, all covenants, conditions, warranties and representations contained in this Agreement which by their nature either impliedly or expressly involve performance in any particular after the Closing Date or which cannot be ascertained to have been fully performed until after the Closing Date shall survive the Closing Date.

(iii)   Time shall in all respects be of the essence of this Agreement. This Agreement shall be binding upon and enure to the benefit of the Vendor and Purchaser and their respective successors and assigns. Any tender of documents or money hereunder may be made upon the Vendor or Purchaser or their respective solicitors on the Closing Date.

(iv)   All captions and headings herein are intended only as a matter of convenience and for reference and in no way define, limit or describe the scope of this Agreement or the intent of any provisions hereof.

IN WITNESS WHEREOF the Vendor and the Purchaser have executed this Agreement on the day and date first above written.

SIGNED, SEALED AND DELIVERED in the presence of:

}_____
}   Purchaser
}_____
}   Vendor

9F3:1
PRIVACY AND NON-SOLICITATION AGREEMENT

[See Para. 9.079.1.2]

(*Date*)

Purchaser Inc.

Attention: (*Title*)

In connection with your consideration of a possible acquisition by you of part of, or investment in, by way of merger, a sale of assets or stock, or otherwise (a "Transaction"), you requested personal information concerning the [*employees, pensioners, customers, officers, directors, shareholders and guarantors*] of Target Inc., including, without limitation, the personal information held by Target Inc. listed in Schedule A hereto.

(__) are acting as adviser to Target Inc., as more particularly named in Schedule B hereto.

In this agreement, "personal information" is defined as information about an individual, as defined in the federal Personal Information Protection and Electronic Documents Act ("PIPEDA").

As a condition to you being furnished with the personal information, you agree that both:

(i)   any personal information furnished to you by or on behalf of Target Inc., whether furnished to you before or after the date of this agreement; and

(ii)   all analyses, compilations, and other documents prepared by you or any of your directors, officers, employees, agents or advisers (including, without limitation, lawyers, accountants, actuaries, consultants, bankers, financial advisers and any representatives of your advisers) (collectively referred to as the "Evaluation Material");

will be subject to and held by you and your advisors in accordance with the provisions of this agreement.

You hereby agree that all personal information and the Evaluation Material will be used solely for the purpose of evaluating a possible Transaction between Target Inc. and you and that all such information will be kept confidential by you, except to the extent that disclosure of such information:

1.   is required by law, regulation, supervisory authority or other applicable judicial or governmental order; or

2.   your advisors need to know such information for the purpose of evaluating any such possible Transaction between Target Inc and you; and

3.   your advisors have been advised of this agreement and shall have agreed in writing to be bound by the provisions hereof.

In any event, you shall be responsible for any breach of this agreement by any of your advisors and you agree, at your sole expense, to take all reasonable measures (including but not limited to court proceedings) to restrain your advisors from any prohibited or unauthorized disclosure or use of the personal information and Evaluation Material.

In the event that you are requested or required by law, regulation, supervisory authority or other applicable judicial or governmental order to disclose any personal information or Evaluation Material, you will provide Target Inc. with prior written notice of such request or requirement so that Target Inc. may seek the appropriate protective order. If, failing the entry of a protective order, you are, in the opinion of your counsel, compelled to disclose the personal information or Evaluation Material, you may disclose that portion of the personal information or Evaluation Material that is being disclosed. In any event you will not oppose action by Target Inc. to obtain an appropriate protective or other reliable assurance that confidential treatment will be accorded to the personal information and Evaluation Material.

If a Transaction is completed between us, you agree that the personal information provided to you by Target Inc. may only be used by you pursuant to the consent granted by each person to Target Inc. as to the disclosure and use of his or her personal information.

If no Transaction is completed between us, you agree that all copies of the personal information and all Evaluation Material, whether in paper or other mediums, must either be returned to Target Inc. or certified by one of your senior officers, as having been destroyed by you and by all of your advisors.

Having been given access to the personal information of Target Inc.'s employees and customers, you agree not to solicit:

(i)   for employment any of the current employees of Target Inc. to whom you had been directly or indirectly introduced or had other contact with as a result of your consideration of a Transaction so long the employees are employed by Target Inc.;

(ii)   customers, clients, or accounts of Target Inc., during the period in which there are discussions conducted between us and for a period of one year thereafter, without the prior written consent of Target Inc.

You hereby agree to indemnify Target Inc. and save it harmless for any and all losses, expenses, costs, including legal costs, and damages resulting directly or indirectly from the actions of:

(i)   your officers, employees and agents; or

(ii)   any other party who obtains access to the personal information and Evaluation Materials as a result of the failure to comply with the terms of this agreement by you or your advisors.

This indemnification shall survive the termination of this agreement and shall not detract in any way from any other rights or remedy which the Client may have under this agreement or otherwise in law or in equity.

You hereby acknowledge and expressly agree that any breach of this agreement which does or may result on loss of confidentiality of the personal information and the Evaluations Materials would cause Target Inc. irreparable harm for which damages would not be an adequate remedy and, therefore, you hereby agree that, in the even of any breach by you of this agreement, Target Inc. shall have the right to seek injunctive relief against the continuing or further breach by you or your advisors, without the necessity of proof of damages. This right to seek injunctive relief without necessity of proof of damage shall be in addition to any other right which Target Inc. may have under this agreement or otherwise in law or in equity.

IN WITNESS WHEREOF the parties have executed this agreement.

Target Inc.

Per: _____

Purchaser Inc.

Per: _____

The foregoing is agreed and accepted:

Advisor #1

Per: _____
Date: _____

Advisor #2

Per: _____
Date: _____

9F4

SEARCH LETTER—EMPLOYMENT STANDARDS

[See Paras. 9.150–9.160 and 9.250–9.253]

Director
Employment Standards Branch
Ministry of Labour
400 University Avenue
9th Floor
Toronto, Ontario
M7A 1T7

Dear Sir:

Re: (*Corporate Name*)

We are the solicitors for a client who is considering purchasing the above-named corporation (the "Corporation"). Among other things, the purchase is conditional upon there being no outstanding applications or complaints filed with you with respect to the Corporation. Would you please advise the writer as to whether any such complaints or applications have been filed under the Employment Standards Act against the Corporation.

The Corporation is the successor corporation to _____ (or carries on business under the name _____). Could you, therefore, conduct your search as against _____ as well as against the Corporation and inform us of your findings.

As the closing date for this transaction is rapidly approaching, we would appreciate receiving your written reply not later than _____.

Thank you for your consideration in this matter.

Yours very truly,

9F5

SEARCH LETTER—LABOUR RELATIONS/ OCCUPATIONAL HEALTH AND SAFETY ACT

[See Paras. 9.150 and 9.290–9.291]

Registrar
Ontario Labour Relations Board
Ministry of Labour
505 University Avenue
2nd Floor
Toronto, Ontario
M5G 2P1

Dear Sir:

Re: (*Corporate Name*)

We are the solicitors for a client who is considering purchasing _____ (the "Corporation"). Among other things, the purchase is conditional upon there being no outstanding applications or complaints filed with you with respect to the Corporation. Would you please inform the writer as to whether any such complaints or applications have been filed within the last year under the Labour Relations Act, the Occupational Health and Safety Act or any other relevant legislation.

The Corporation is the successor corporation to _____ (or carries on business under the name _____). Could you, therefore, conduct your search as against _____ as well as against the Corporation and inform us of your findings.

As the closing date for this transaction is rapidly approaching, we would appreciate receiving your written reply not later than _____.

Thank you for your consideration in this matter.

Yours very truly,

9F6

SEARCH LETTER—INDUSTRIAL HEALTH AND SAFETY BRANCH—INSPECTIONS

[See Paras. 9.150 and 9.290–9.291]

Regional Manager
Industrial Health & Safety Branch
Ministry of Labour

Dear Sir:

Re: Purchase of (*Corporate Name and Address*)

We are the solicitors for a client who is considering purchasing the assets of _____ (the "Corporation") which presently carries on business at the above-noted address. As such, we would ask that your branch carry out the appropriate inspection of the Company's premises at the above address and notify the writer of any contraventions of the Occupational Health and Safety Act or the Regulations made under the Act which your inspection may uncover.

We would also ask you to review your files and advise us if there are any outstanding orders on file as against the Company or against the above noted property. In particular, please advise us whether or not any orders have been issued under section 29 of the Occupational Health and Safety Act.

To that end, please find enclosed herewith our firm cheque in the amount of _____ as well as a consent and authorization executed on behalf of the Company.

As the closing date for this transaction is rapidly approaching, we would appreciate receiving your written reply not later than _____.

I trust that this meets your present requirements. Please contact the writer if you have any further questions.

Yours very truly,

9F7

SEARCH LETTER—MINISTRY OF AGRICULTURE AND FOOD

[See Para. 9.150]

Ministry of Agriculture and Food
Policy Analysis Branch
1 Stone Road West
2nd Floor
Guelph, ON N1G 4Y2

Dear Sirs:

Re:

We act for _____ who is purchasing the above described land from _____ closing on the _____.

Please advise us of the status of the account of Farm Tax Reduction and Managed Forest Tax Reduction on the above mentioned lands. In particular, we would appreciate information as to the amount of tax reduction for the current year and amounts paid for the previous nine years.

Yours very truly,

9F7:1
SEARCH LETTER—REALTY TAXES

[See Para. 9.150]

Dear Sirs:

Re:

We act for the _____ in the above noted transaction, closing the _____. We would appreciate receiving a tax certificate for the above mentioned property setting out:

1.   All charges for realty taxes now outstanding against the subject property, including taxes for the current year;

2.   Any local improvement charges;

3.   Any charges for work orders, snow shovelling, demolition, hydro, water, or other public utility, or charges under the Telephone Act, the Fire Marshall's Act, the Public Health Act, or the Weed Control Act;

4.   Any charges or special rates under the Tile Draining Act;

5.   Any charges under the Shoreline Property Assistance Act;

6.   Any other charges forming a lien by the Municipality against the property.

Enclosed is our cheque for _____ payable to _____ , which we understand to be your fee in this matter.

Yours very truly,

9F7:2
SEARCH LETTER—ZONING & WORK ORDERS
(WITH SURVEY)

[See Para. 9.150]

Dear Sirs:

Re:

We enclose a copy of a survey of the above noted property together with our cheque in the amount of $_____ and would appreciate your assistance by providing us with the following information at your earliest convenience:

1.   Whether the building erected on the above lands conforms to all set back, lot area, lot frontage and lot depth requirements as set out in the current building and zoning by-laws of the _____ affecting the above property.

2.   Whether there are any work orders outstanding against the above noted property.

3.   Whether the property is subject to any development or redevelopment control under section 40 of the Planning Act.

4.   What the permitted uses are with respect to the subject property.

5.   Whether the terms and provisions of all site plan, development and subdivision agreements have been complied with to date and whether you hold sufficient security to ensure completion of all outstanding obligations thereunder.

Yours very truly,

9F7:3
SEARCH LETTER—ZONING AND WORK ORDERS
(NO SURVEY)

[See Para. 9.150]

Dear Sirs:

Re:

We enclose our cheque in the amount of $_____ and would appreciate your assistance by providing us with the following information at your earliest convenience:

1.   Whether there are any work orders outstanding against the above noted property.

2.   Whether the property is subject to any development or redevelopment control under section 40 of the *Planning Act*.

3.   What the permitted uses are with respect to the subject property.

We would also appreciate receiving a copy of the relevant section   of the zoning by-laws. We thank you for your kind help in this matter.

Yours very truly,

9F7:4
SEARCH LETTER—LOCAL HYDRO

[See Para. 9.150]

Dear Sirs:

Re:

We act on behalf of the _____ in the above noted transaction and as such wish to provide you with the following information:

1.   Final meter reading to be taken on the closing date which is the _____.

2.   Final bill to be prepared and sent to: _____

3.   New account to be opened in the name(s) of: _____

Please provide us with your written advice prior to the closing date with respect to the following:

1.   Whether there are any arrears with respect to the account(s) for the supply of hydro to the above property.

2.   Whether there is any equipment on the above property belonging to you or on which you have a charge or other interest.

We enclose our firm cheque payable to _____ in the amount of $_____, representing your fee herein.

Thank you in advance for your assistance.

Yours very truly,

9F7:5
SEARCH LETTER—WATER

[See Para. 9.150]

Dear Sirs:

Re:

We act on behalf of the _____ in the above noted transaction and as such wish to provide you with the following information:

1.   Final meter reading to be taken on the closing date which is the _____.

2.   Final bill to be prepared and sent to: _____

3.   New account to be opened in the name(s) of: _____

Please provide us with your written advice prior to the closing date with respect to the following:

1.   Whether there are any arrears with respect to the account(s) for the supply of water to the above property.

2.   Whether there is any equipment on the above property belonging to you or on which you have a charge or other interest.

Enclosed is our cheque payable to _____ in the amount of $_____, representing your fee herein.

Thank you in advance for your assistance.

Yours very truly,

9F7:6
SEARCH LETTER—GAS (CONDOMINIUM)

[See Para. 9.150]

Dear Sirs:

Re:

We act on behalf of the _____ in the above noted transaction.

May we request your advice whether there are any outstanding gas charges owing against the property referred to above. In the event there is any equipment on the premises that is rented by the present owner, we would appreciate your advice in this regard.

We realize that in most condominium developments gas charges are billed on a bulk basis. If the billing is in fact done on a bulk basis, we would nevertheless appreciate your advice as to the status of the account.

Thank you in advance for your assistance.

Yours very truly,

9F7:7
SEARCH LETTER—WATER (CONDOMINIUM)

[See Para. 9.150]

Dear Sirs:

Re:

We act on behalf of the _____ in the above noted transaction.

May we request your advice whether there are any outstanding water charges owing against the property referred to above. In the event there is any equipment on the premises that is rented by the present owner, we would appreciate your advice in this regard.

We realize that in most condominium developments water charges are billed on a bulk basis. If the billing is in fact done on a bulk basis, we would nevertheless appreciate your advice as to the status of the account.

Enclosed is our cheque payable to _____ in the amount of $_____, representing your fee herein.

Thank you in advance for your assistance.

Yours very truly,

9F7:8
SEARCH LETTER—HYDRO (CONDOMINIUM)

[See Para. 9.150]

Dear Sirs:

Re:

We act on behalf of the _____ in the above noted transaction.

May we request your advice whether there are any outstanding hydro charges owing against the property referred to above. In the event there is an electric hot water heater on the premises that is rented by the present owner, we would appreciate your advice in this regard.

We realize that in most condominium developments hydro charges are billed on a bulk basis. If the billing is in fact done on a bulk basis, we would nevertheless appreciate your advice as to the status of the account.

We enclose our firm cheque payable to _____ in the amount of $_____, representing your fee herein.

Thank you in advance for your assistance.

Yours very truly,

9F7:9
SEARCH LETTER—STATUS CERTIFICATE
(CONDOMINIUM)
[See Para. 9.150]

Dear Sirs:

Re:

We are the solicitors for the purchaser(s) in the above noted transaction which is scheduled to be completed on the _____. Enclosed is our firm cheque in the amount of _____ and we would appreciate receiving from you at your earliest convenience a status certificate as well as a copy of all condominium documents and financial statements as prescribed by the Condominium Act, 1998.

Yours very truly,

9F7:10

SEARCH LETTER—ELEVATORS

[See Para. 9.150]

Ministry of Consumer and Business Services
Technical Standards and Safety Authority
4th Floor, West Tower
3300 Bloor Street West
Toronto, Ontario
M8X 2X4

Dear Sirs:

Re:

We are solicitors for the purchaser in the above noted matter.

Would you please confirm whether or not the building and its installations and equipment with which you are concerned fully comply with your requirements and as to whether or not there are any fees outstanding.

You will find enclosed the authorization of the solicitors for the owner permitting you to release the necessary information to us.

In addition, we enclose our cheque to the Treasurer of Ontario, in the amount of _____ for each elevator to cover your charge.

Yours very truly,

9F7:11
SEARCH LETTER—FIRE DEPARTMENT

[See Para. 9.150]

Dear Sirs:

Re:

We act for the _____ in connection with the above captioned matter, which is scheduled to be completed the _____.

Please advise if there are any work orders or deficiency notices with respect to the premises. If an inspection has not been carried out recently, would you kindly inspect the premises.

Enclosed is the consent of the owner. Thank you for your anticipated co-operation herein.

Yours very truly,

9F7:12
SEARCH LETTER—DEPARTMENT OF PUBLIC HEALTH

[See Para. 9.150]

Department of Public Health
(*address*)

Dear Sirs:

Re:

We act for the _____ in connection with the above captioned matter, which is scheduled to be completed the _____ .

Please advise if there are any work orders or deficiency notices with respect to the premises. If an inspection has not been carried out recently, would you kindly inspect the premises.

Enclosed is the consent of the owner. Thank you for your anticipated co-operation herein.

Yours very truly,

9F7:13
SEARCH LETTER—AGREEMENT COMPLIANCE LETTER

[See Para. 9.150]

Clerks' Department

Dear Sir:

Re:

We act on behalf of _____ in the above noted transaction. Our search of title has revealed the following agreements:

_____

_____

We would appreciate your early written advice whether these agreements have been complied with to date, whether any of them have been breached and whether there remain any financial or other obligations outstanding under any of these agreements. Please advise whether you are holding sufficient security to ensure completion of any outstanding obligations.

In the event any of these matters are not under your administration, we would appreciate it if you would forward this letter or a copy to the appropriate departments.

Thank you for your kind assistance. We enclose our cheque in the amount of _____.

Yours very truly,

9F7:14
SEARCH LETTER—ENVIRONMENTAL

[See Para. 9.364]

Ministry of Environment and Energy

(*Local/Regional Office*)

Dear Sirs:

Re: (*Corporate Name and Address and Legal Description of Property*)

We are the solicitors for a client who is considering purchasing [*the assets of*] the above-noted corporation which carries on business at the property indicated above (the "Property").

Would you please advise the writer of the following concerning the legislation that your Ministry administers and the records and public information that you may have with respect to the Property and the persons whose names appear on the attached schedule who have been involved with the Property:

1. Were these lands ever used for the disposal of waste?

2. Have any approvals, licenses, permits, etc. been issued with respect to any equipment, processes or operations located at the Property?

3. Is the Property registered as a PCB waste storage or disposal site?

4. Have any orders, decisions or prohibitions been issued concerning the Property or any business conducted thereon by the persons noted in the schedule hereto?

5. Have any prosecutions been commenced, or convictions entered, with respect to any business conducted by the persons noted in the schedule hereto?

6. Have you been advised of any spills and/or discharges having occurred on, or of any other environmental problems or concerns with respect to, the Property?

7.   Have you been advised of any spills and or discharges having occurred on, or of any other environmental problems or concerns with respect to, any property or business being conducted near to the Property?

As the closing date for this transaction is rapidly approaching we would appreciate receiving your written reply not later than _____.

Thank you for your consideration in this matter.

Yours very truly,

cc: The Clerk [Local Municipality]

9F7:15
SEARCH LETTER—CONSERVATION AUTHORITY

[See Para. 9.150]

Dear Sirs:

Re:

We act for the _____ in the above-noted transaction which is scheduled to close the _____.

Please advise whether any part of the property is an area subject to the provisions of any regulations passed pursuant to the provisions of the Conservation Authorities Act.

Please advise us if there is any directive, order, or other breach of regulations with respect to the building or current use of the property. Enclosed is our cheque for $_____ payable to _____, which we understand to be your fee in this matter, together with a copy of the survey for the above property.

Yours very truly,

9F7:16
SEARCH LETTER—UNREGISTERED HYDRO EASEMENTS

[See Para. 9.150]

Dear Sirs:

Re:

We act for the _____ in connection with the above-noted transaction.

Please advise if there are any unregistered easements over the above property claimed by the Hydro-Electric Power Commission of Ontario pursuant to section 42 of the *Power Corporation Act*.

Would you please make an on-site inspection.

Please advise us if any rights to unregistered easements have been transferred to the local Hydro.

Yours very truly,

9F7:17
SEARCH LETTER—HISTORICAL PROPERTIES

[See Para. 9.150]

Dear Sirs:

Re:

We act for the _____ in the above-noted transaction, closing the _____.

Please search your register maintained pursuant to the provisions of the Ontario Heritage Act and advise use whether or not the above mentioned property is a "designated property" within the meaning of the said Act, or if any by-law designating the property is in any way proposed or pending.

If the property is designated, we would appreciate receiving the relevant extract from the register.

Yours very truly,

9F7:18
SEARCH LETTER—UTILITIES

[See Para. 9.150]

Dear Sirs:

Re:

MUNICIPAL ADDRESS:

VENDOR'S FULL NAME:

PURCHASER'S FULL NAME:
(If this is a business, we require Owner's name, address and phone #).

CLOSING DATE:

FOR TENANTS WHO WILL REMAIN:
(Landlord's Name address, phone number is required).

TENANTS WHO WILL VACATE: Yes/No

FOR FINAL BILL:
(Vendor's name, address or vendor's solicitor).

MORTGAGE ONLY: Yes/No

Thank you in advance for your assistance.

Yours very truly,

9F8

CHANGE OF NAME ENQUIRY

[See Paras. 9.172–9.175]

_____, 19__

COURIER

Office of the Registrar General
Ontario Ministry of Consumer and
   Business Services
189 Red River Road
P.O. Box 4600
Thunder Bay, Ontario
P7B 6L8

Attention: Change of Name Section

Dear Sirs:

Re: Change of Name of _____

We are the solicitors acting on behalf of a client with respect to [a judgment debtor examination of _____/ a secured financing involving _____/ a purchase of land from _____]. In order to accurately complete the searches and documentation in connection with that matter, we require information concerning the exact present and past names of the person named above.

We therefore request a search of the Registrar General's Change of Name Index respecting the person named above. Please find enclosed our cheque in the amount of $____, being the Registrar's fee for such service.

The information we have concerning the person named above is as follows:

Present Name:

Past Name:

Date of Birth:

Address:

Additional Information:

To enable us to complete our investigations against the above named person, we need the results of this search as promptly as possible. When the search results are available, please telephone the writer's direct dial number and we will arrange for a courier to collect the same.

Thank you for your prompt assistance in this matter.

Yours very truly,

9F9

SEARCH REQUEST FORM

[See Para. 9.170]

CORPORATE SEARCH REQUEST FORM

TO: DATE: _____

FROM: DATE DUE: _____

CLIENT/MATTER NAME & NUMBER: _____

NAME(S) TO BE SEARCHED:

(1) _____

(2) _____

(3) _____

	Date Ordered	Date Picked Up
1. ONTARIO CORPORATIONS — HEAD OFFICE, DIRECTORS, ETC. (minimum 48 hours)	_____	
— MICROFICHE ONLY (minimum 24 hours)	_____	
— CERTIFICATE OF STATUS If specific date required, please specify _____ (minimum 6 business days)	_____	

— CERTIFIED COPIES   _____
     (specify which articles & dates)
(minimum 6 business days)

2. FEDERAL CORPORATIONS

— CERTIFICATE OF COMPLIANCE   _____
     (minimum 5 business days)
— CERTUNCERT COPIES   _____
     Specify which articles & dates
(minimum 5 business days)
   — CORPORATE HISTORY   _____
                                    (minimum 3 to 4 weeks)

3. PARTNERSHIPBUSINESS STYLE:

—   PHOTOCOPIES OF ALL

REGISTRATIONS   _____
                          (minimum 24 hours)
—   INACTIVE SEARCH

                             _____
                          (minimum 1 week)

4. PPSA:

— CERTIFICATE PRINTOUT   — VERBAL PRINTOUT   _____
                  (24 hours)   (same day)

— OBTAIN PARTICULARS OF CSRA REGISTRATIONS

5. SECTION 178:

— CERTIFICATE   — MANUAL   _____
                          (minimum 24 hours)

6. BANKRUPTCY: OFFICIAL RECEIVER
— CERTIFICATE — MANUAL VERBAL ONLY_____
                         AVAILABLE
                  (minimum 24 hours)

7. EXECUTIONS

— YORK — OTHER   _____
                     (minimum 48 hours)

Specify jurisdiction   1. _____
                       2. _____

8. BILL OF SALE:
— YORK — OTHER   _____
                     (minimum 48 hours)

Specify jurisdiction   1. _____
                       2. _____

9. BULK SALES:

— YORK — OTHER   _____
                     (minimum 48 hours)

Specify jurisdiction   1. _____

                               2. _____

10. ACTION SEARCH — (instruct litigation clerk)   _____

                                                    (minimum 48 hours)

Times shown are minimum turnaround;
complex searches may take longer.

<h2 style="text-align:center">9F10
SEARCH REPORT FROM CLERK</h2>

<h3 style="text-align:center">[See Para. 9.170]</h3>

1.   C.S.R.A.   SEARCH DATE: ____   UPDATED: ____
   Inst. No.   _____   _____
   Debtor   _____   _____
   Sec. Party   _____   _____
   Exec. Date   _____   _____
   Filing Date: _____   _____
   Sec. Amt. & Int.   _____   _____
   Due Date   _____   _____
   Collateral   _____   _____

2.   S. 427   SEARCH DATE: ____   UPDATED: ____
   Number   _____   _____
   Debtor   _____   _____
   Sec. Party   _____   _____
   Date   _____   _____

3.   BANKRUPTCY SEARCH DATE: _____   UPDATED: _____

     Registrar (circle one and attach particulars):
(a) Petition   (b) Receiving Order   (c) Proposal   (d) Assignment   (e) clear

     Official Receiver (circle one and attach particulars):
(a) Petition   (b) Receiving Order   (c) Proposal   (d) Assignment   (e) Clear

4. EXECUTION SEARCH DATE: _____ UPDATED: _____
    Exec. No. _____ _____
    Plaintiff _____ _____
    Defendant _____ _____
    Action No. _____ _____
    Amount _____ _____
    Jud. District _____ _____

5. BILLS OF SALE SEARCH DATE: _____ UPDATED: _____
    Number _____ _____
    Bargainor _____ _____
    Bargainee _____ _____
    Date _____ _____
    Assets Trnsfrd _____ _____

6. BULK SALES SEARCH DATE: _____ UPDATED: _____
    Number Vendor _____ _____
    Purchaser _____ _____
    Date _____ _____
      _____ _____

7. P.P.S.A FILE CURRENCY DATE: _____
                     Registrations: Yes_____ No _____
                     Particulars attached.

9F11
SEARCH SUMMARY FOR CLIENT

[See Para. 9.170]

SUMMARY OF SEARCHES IN ONTARIO ON:

ACME GROUP INC.

As of: April 22, 1992 (April 20, 1992 for PPSA)
From: May 1, 1970

Addresses: 1. 1 First Avenue West, Suite 900, Downsview (York)
2.   2 Second Street, Mississauga (Peel)

1. CORPORATE

Jurisdiction: Ontario (#567890)

Created: Articles of Amalgamation; December 31, 1989

Regd. Office: 1 First Ave. West, Ste. 900, Downsview M1A 2B3
Directors: 2

1.   John Doe—Secretary   2.   Jane Doe—President

Last Form 1:   March 20, 1991

Bus. Styles: Acme Group

Amalgamated: 2 corporations

1.   <u>123456 Ontario Limited</u>

Jurisdiction:Ontario (#123456)
Created: Articles of Incorporation; December 10, 1982
Regd. Office: Downsview
Bus. Styles: 1.   Acme Designs
                              2.   Acme Resources

2.   <u>Acme Group Limited</u>

Jurisdiction: Ontario (#234567)
Created: Articles of Amalgamation; April 18, 1985
Regd. Office: Toronto
Amalgamated: 2 corporations

A)   <u>Better Acme Limited</u>

Jurisdiction: Ontario (#345678)
Created: Letters patent; May 1, 1970
Original Name: <u>345678 Ontario Limited</u>
Changed: October 5, 1979
To: Better Acme Limited
Regd. Office: Toronto
Bus. Styles: Acme Toronto

B)   <u>Acme Designs Limited</u>

Jurisdiction:Ontario (#456789)
Created: Articles of Incorporation; Dec. 31/84
Regd. Office: Toronto

Searches therefore conducted on:

1.   Acme Designs Limited

2.   345678 Ontario Limited

3.   Better Acme Limited

4.   Acme Group Limited

5.   123456 Ontario Limited

6.   Acme Group Inc.

7.   all business styles

2.   BANKRUPTCY

clear for Toronto offices of the Supreme Court of Ontario and Ottawa Office of the Official Receiver

3.   SECTION 427, BANK ACT

for Toronto agency of the Bank of Canada:

i)   #13579
     Debtor: 123456 Ontario Limited
     Dated: March 26, 1985
     Secured: _____ Bank

ii) #24680
     Debtor: Acme Group Limited
     Dated: March 29, 1988
     Secured: _____ Bank

4.   EXECUTIONS

clear in Judicial Districts of York and Peel

5.   BULK SALES

clear in Judicial Districts of York and Peel

6.   BILL OF SALE

clear in Judicial Districts of York and Peel

7.   PERSONAL PROPERTY SECURITY ACT

Note: 1.   Registrations filed before October 10, 1989 expire in 3 years; registrations filed on or after that date expire when indicated.

     2.   CSRA filings (if any) have been entered in chronological order, but this does not determine priority.

i)   CSRA #75697; Demand Debenture
PPSA File #900756972

Dated:	April 18, 1985
Filed:	April 18, 1985
Debtor:	Better Acme Limited
Secured:	_____ Bank
Amount:	$3,000,000
Interest:	25%
Collateral:	fixed charge on lots 29 and 30, Plan M–121, Toronto

on Merton Street, and floating charge on all other present and future assets

ii)   860731 0913 88 4408

Debtor:	234567 Ontario Limited
Secured:	_____ Bank
	Yonge & Eglinton, Toronto
Collateral:	Book Debts, Other
Renewed:	890626 0921 88 0047
Amended:	900330 1121 0088 2371
Reason:	Change of Debtor's name to Acme Group Inc.
Amended:	910918 0930 0088 9940
Reason:	Change of Secured's address to
	Yonge & Sheppard, North York

iii)   860731 0912 88 4369

Debtors:	1. 234567 Ontario Limited
2. Acme Designs	
Secured:	_____ Bank
Collateral:	Book Debts, Other
Renewed:	890626 0921 88 0048
Amended:	900330 1121 0088 2372
Reason:	Change of Debtor's name to Acme Group Inc.

iv)　890419 0811 88 0726

　　　Debtor:　　　　Acme Group Inc.
　　　Secured:　　　_____ Bank
　　　Yonge & Sheppard, North York
　　　Collateral:　　Book Debts, Other
　　　Renewed:　　920304 0925 0088 7681
　　　For:　　　　　5 years

v)　890419 0813 88 0802

　　　Debtor:　　　　Acme Group Limited
　　　Secured:　　　_____ Bank
　　　Collateral:　　Inventory, Equipment, Book Debts, Other, Motor
　　　Vehicle
　　　Amended:　　900312 0918 0088 6330
　　　Reason:　　　Record Debtor's change of name to:
　　　Acme Group Inc.
　　　Renewed:　　920304 0927 0088 7730
　　　For:　　　　　5 years

vi)　890929 0834 88 9505

　　　Debtors:　　　1. 234567 Ontario Limited
　　　　　　　　　　2. Acme Designs
　　　Secured:　　　_____ Bank
　　　Collateral:　　Inventory, Equipment, Book Debts, Other, Motor
　　　Vehicle
　　　Description:　Late renewal of 860731 0913 88 4407
　　　Amended:　　900313 0955 0088 1908
　　　Reason:　　　Debtor's name changed to:
　　　　　　　　　　Acme Group Inc.

9F12
SEARCH LETTER - LABOUR CANADA

[See Para. 9.230]

(Date)

Regional Director
HRDC
Labour Program
4900 Yonge Street
2nd Floor
North York, Ontario
M2N 6A8

Dear

Re: (*Corporate Name*)

We are the solicitors for a client who is considering purchasing the above-named corporation (the "Corporation") which carries on business in (location of business). Among other things, the purchase is conditional upon there being no outstanding claims, applications or complaints filed with you with respect to the Corporation. Would you please advise the writer as to whether any such claims, complaints or applications have been filed under the Canada Labour Code against the Corporation. We also request that you advise the writer whether the Corporation is in compliance with its occupational health and safety obligations under the Canada Labour Code.

The Corporation is the successor corporation to _____ (or carries on business under the name _____). Could you, therefore, conduct your search as against _____ as well as against the Corporation and inform us of your findings.

As the closing date for this transaction is rapidly approaching we would appreciate receiving your written reply not later than _____.
Thank you for your consideration in this matter.

Yours very truly,

9F13
SEARCH LETTER—
CANADA INDUSTRIAL RELATIONS BOARD

[See Para. 9.230]

(Date)

Canada Industrial Relations Board
C.D. Howe Building
4th Floor West
240 Sparks Street
Ottawa, Ontario
K1A 0X8

Attention: P. Sioui-Thivierge, Registrar

Dear Sir:

Re: (*Corporate Name*)

We are the solicitors for a client who is considering purchasing _____ (the "Corporation"). Among other things, the purchase is conditional upon there being no outstanding applications, complaints or other proceedings under Part I of the Canada Labour Code filed with you with respect to the Corporation. Would you please inform the writer concerning any such matters under the Canada Labour Code or any other relevant legislation, involving the Corporation.

The Corporation is the successor corporation to _____ (or carries on business under the name _____). Could you, therefore, conduct your search as against _____ as well as against the Corporation and inform us of your findings.

As the closing date for this transaction is rapidly approaching, we would appreciate receiving your written reply not later than (_____).

Thank you for your consideration in this matter.

Yours very truly,

9F14
SEARCH LETTER—
CANADIAN HUMAN RIGHTS COMMISSION

[See Para. 9.230]

(Date)

Canadian Human Rights Commission
175 Bloor St. East
South Tower
10th Floor, Suite 1002
Toronto, Ontario
M4W 3R8

Attention: Mr. Mervin Witter, Toronto Regional Director

Dear Sir:

Re: (*Corporate Name*)

We are the solicitors for a client who is considering purchasing the above-named corporation (the "Corporation") which carries on business in (location of business). Among other things, the purchase is conditional upon there being no outstanding orders or complaints under the provisions of the Canadian Human Rights Act with respect to the Corporation. Would you please advise the writer as to whether there are any such orders or complaints under the Canadian Human Rights Act existing with respect to the Corporation.

We have enclosed a consent and authorization to release this information to us.

As the closing date for this transaction is rapidly approaching, we would appreciate receiving your written reply not later than _____.

Thank you for your consideration in this matter.

Yours very truly,

9F15
CONSENT AND AUTHORIZATION
CANADIAN HUMAN RIGHTS COMMISSION

[See Para 9.230]

TO: THE CANADIAN HUMAN RIGHTS COMMISSION

The undersigned, on behalf of _____ (the "Corporation"), hereby consents to the release to (*insert firm name*), Barristers and Solicitors of any and all information with respect to any outstanding orders or complaints under the provisions of the Canadian Human Rights Act involving the Corporation.

This document shall be your good and sufficient authority to release to (*insert firm name*) the information referred to above.

DATED this _____ day of _____ , 20___.

(*Proper corporate name*)

per:_____

9F16
SEARCH LETER — EMPLOYMENT EQUITY

[See Para. 9.230]

(*Date*)

Public Inquiries Centre
Public Affairs Branch
Human Resources Development Canada
140 Promenade du Portage, Phase IV
Hull, QC K1A 0J9

Dear Sirs:

Re: (*Corporate Name*)

We are the solicitors for a client who is considering purchasing the above-named corporation (the "Corporation") which carries on business in (*location of business*). Among other things, the purchase is conditional upon whether the Corporation is in full compliance with its obligations under the Employment Equity Act. Would you please advise the writer whether the Corporation is in compliance with its obligations under the Employment Equity Act.

As the closing date for this transaction is rapidly approaching, we would appreciate receiving your written reply not later than _____.

Thank you for your consideration in this matter.

Yours very truly,

9F17

SEARCH LETTER—ONTARIO LABOUR RELATIONS BOARD

[See Paras. 9.240 and 9.241]

Mr. T. Parker
Director & Registrar
Ontario Labour Relations Board
Ministry of Labour
505 University Avenue
2nd Floor
Toronto, Ontario
M5G 2P1

Dear Mr. Parker:

Re: (*Corporate Name*)

We are the solicitors for a client who is considering purchasing _____(the "Corporation"). Among other things, the purchase is conditional upon there being no outstanding applications or complaints filed with you with respect to the Corporation. Would you please inform the writer as to whether any complaints or applications have been filed within the last year under the Labour Relations Act, the Occupational Health and Safety Act or any other relevant legislation.

The Corporation is the successor corporation to ( ) and ( ). Could you, therefore, conduct your search as against ( ) as well as against the Corporation and inform us of your findings.

As the closing date for this transaction is rapidly approaching, we would appreciate receiving your written reply not later than _____.

Thank you for your consideration in this matter.

Yours very truly,

9F18

SEARCH LETTER — ONTARIO MINISTRY OF LABOUR

[See Paras. 9.241 and 9.242]

(Date)

Office of Collective Bargaining Information
Ontario Ministry of Labour
400 University Avenue, 9th Floor
Toronto, Ontario
M7A 1T7

Attention: Mr. Nirmal Karan

Dear Ms. Matthews:

Re: (*Corporate Name*)

We are the solicitors for a client who is considering purchasing the above-named corporation (*the "Corporation"*) which carries on business in (*location of business*). Would you please advise the writer as to whether there are any collective agreements pertaining to the Corporation on file in your library and provide us with the date of the most recent collective agreements on file.

The Corporation is the successor corporation to _____ (or carries on business under the name _____). Could you, therefore, conduct your search as against (_____) as well as against the Corporation and inform us of your findings.

As the closing date for this transaction is rapidly approaching, we would appreciate receiving your written reply not later than _____.

Thank you for your consideration in this matter.

Yours very truly,

9F19
SEARCH LETTER—EMPLOYMENT STANDARDS

[See Paras. 9.250–9.253]

(Date)

Director's Area
Employment Practices Branch
400 University Avenue
Tower B
9th Floor
Toronto, Ontario
M7A 1T7
Dear Mr. Evans:

Re: (*Corporate Name*)

We are the solicitors for a client who is considering purchasing the above-named corporation (*the "Corporation"*) which carries on business in (*location of business*). Among other things, the purchase is conditional upon their being no outstanding claims, prosecutions, orders, applications or complaints filed with you with respect to the Corporation pursuant to the Employment Standards Act. Please advise the writer whether there are any such matters outstanding against the Corporation. In addition, please advise the writer if any approvals or permits have been granted under the Employment Standards Act.

The Corporation is the successor corporation to _____ (or carries on business under the name _____). Could you, therefore, conduct your search as against as well as against the Corporation and inform us of your findings.

As the closing date for this transaction is rapidly approaching, we would appreciate receiving your written reply not later than _____.

Thank you for your consideration in this matter.

Yours very truly,

9F20
SEARCH LETTER—WORKPLACE SAFETY AND INSURANCE BOARD

[See Paras. 9.260–9.263]

(*Date*)

Revenue Branch
Workplace Safety and Insurance Board
200 Front Street West,
11th Floor,
Toronto ON M5V 3J1

Dear Sir or Madam:

Re: (*Insert Proper Company Name and W.S.I.B. Account and Firm No.*)

We are the solicitors for a client who is considering purchasing _____ (the "Company"). We are enclosing herewith a written authorization properly executed on behalf of the Company authorizing you to release to us the following information:

1. Written verification as to the present status of the Company's account with the Workplace Safety and Insurance Board;

2. Whether any certificates with respect to unpaid assessments have been filed with any court or the clerk of any municipality pursuant to the Workplace Safety and Insurance Act;

3. If the Company is participating in experience rating, a history of accident claims and a forecast of its experience rating;

4. A statement of the Company's accident costs and frequency for the last three years and the current year for the purpose of determining whether a section 103(8) Assessment is likely.

As the closing date for this transaction is rapidly approaching, we would appreciate receiving your written response to this letter no later than _____, 20__.

Thank you for your attention to this matter.

Yours very truly,

9F21
CONSENT AND AUTHORIZATION—
WORKPLACE SAFETY AND INSURANCE BOARD

[See Paras. 9.260–9.263]

TO: WORKPLACE SAFETY AND INSURANCE BOARD

The undersigned, on behalf of _____ (the "Company"), hereby authorizes the Workplace Safety and Insurance Board (the "Board") to release to (*insert firm name*), Barristers & Solicitors, any and all information requested by (*insert firm name*) pertaining to the status of the Company's account with the Board. The Company's firm and account numbers are _____. In particular, we authorize the Board to release to (*insert firm name*), information pertaining to the status of the Company's account with the Board and we authorize the Board to provide (*insert firm name*) with a history of accident claims, a forecast of the Company's experience rating and a statement of the Company's accident costs and frequency for the last three years and the current year for the purpose of determining the likelihood of an assessment. This document shall be your good and sufficient authority to release to (*insert firm name*) the information referred to above.

DATED this _____ day of _____ , 20___.

(*Proper Corporate Name*)

Per: _____

9F22
SEARCH LETTER—
ONTARIO HUMAN RIGHTS COMMISSION

[See Para. 9.270]

(*Date*)

Ontario Human Rights Commission
180 Dundas Street West
8th Floor
Toronto, ON M7A 2R9

Attention: Regional Manager

Dear Sir or Madam:

Re: (*Corporate Name*)

We are the solicitors for a client who is considering purchasing the above-named corporation (the "Corporation") which carries on business in (*location of business*). Among other things, the purchase is conditional upon there being no outstanding orders or complaints under the provisions of the Ontario Human Rights Code with respect to the corporation. Would you please advise the writer as to whether there are any such orders or complaints under the Ontario Human Rights Code existing with respect to the corporation.

We have enclosed a Consent and Authorization to release this information to us.

As the closing date for this transaction is rapidly approaching, we would appreciate receiving your written reply not later than _____.

Thank you for your consideration in this matter.

Yours very truly,

Encl.

9F23
CONSENT AND AUTHORIZATION—
ONTARIO HUMAN RIGHTS COMMISSION

TO: ONTARIO HUMAN RIGHTS COMMISSION

The undersigned, on behalf of _____ (the "Corporation"), hereby consents to the release to (*insert firm name*), Barristers and Solicitors of any and all information with respect to any outstanding orders or complaints under the provisions of the Ontario Human Rights Code involving the Corporation.

This document shall be your good and sufficient authority to release to (*insert firm name*) the information referred to above.

DATED: This _____ day of _____ , 20 ___ .

(*Proper Corporate Name*)

per: _____

9F24
SEARCH LETTER—PAY EQUITY COMMISSION

[See Para. 9.280]

(*Date*)

Pay Equity Commission
400 University Avenue
11th Floor
Toronto ON M7A 1T7

Dear

Re: (*Corporate Name*)

We are the solicitors for a client who is considering purchasing the above-named corporation (the "Corporation") which carries on business in (*location of business*). Among other things, the purchase is conditional upon there being no complaints, investigations, orders by review officers, tribunal proceedings or orders or prosecutions outstanding with respect to the Corporation. Would you please advise the writer concerning any such matters which may be outstanding.

As the closing date for this transaction is rapidly approaching, we would appreciate receiving your written reply not later than

_____.

Thank you for your consideration in this matter.

Yours very truly,

[*Note: The Pay Equity Hearings Tribunal is now administered separately from the Pay Equity Commission. Therefore, a separate letter in the above form should be sent to the following address:*

Registrar
Pay Equity Human Rights Tribunal
400 University Avenue
11th Floor
Toronto ON M7A 1T7]

9F25
SEARCH LETTER—INDUSTRIAL
HEALTH AND SAFETY

[See Paras. 9.290–9.291]

(*Date*)

Regional Manager
Industrial Health and Safety Branch
Ministry of Labour

Dear Sir or Madam:

Re: Purchase of (*Corporate Name and Address*)

We are the solicitors for a client who is considering purchasing the assets of (*the Corporation*) which presently carries on business at the above-noted address. As such, we would ask that your branch carry out the appropriate inspection, as indicated in the accompanying request form, and notify the writer of any contraventions of the Occupational Health and Safety Act or the Regulations which your inspection may uncover. We would also ask you to inform the writer whether the Corporation is in compliance with its obligations under the Occupational Health and Safety Act or its Regulations and if there are any outstanding prosecutions, orders or directives involving the Corporation under the Occupational Health and Safety Act or its Regulations. In addition, we would ask that your branch forward to us copies of any and all previous inspection reports, testing results and health and safety audits which you may have on file pertaining to the Corporation.

Pursuant to our request, please find enclosed our firm cheque in the amount of $500 as well as a Consent and Authorization executed on behalf of the Corporation. As the closing date for this transaction is rapidly approaching, we would appreciate receiving your written response to this letter no later than _____.

I trust this meets your present requirements. Please contact the writer if you have any further questions.

Yours very truly,

Encl.

9F26
REQUEST FORM—INDUSTRIAL HEALTH AND SAFETY

[See Paras. 9.290–9.291]

Name/Company of
Requester _____

Details Concerning Information Requested:

Name of Establishment _____

Address of Premises   _____
                        _____

Specific Information
required   _____

- OPTION ONE   Inspection of the premises and access to copy of
                resulting report.

        Please return this slip with written permission of the owner, plus
        the fee made payable to "TREASURER OF ONTARIO" to:

        Field office of the Industrial Health and Safety Branch, Ministry of
        Labour in closest proximity to the requested company.

- OPTION TWO   Copies of inspection reports and testing results
                pertaining to the premises. (Please stipulate time-span of
                information requested e.g. last 2 years).

        Please return this slip to:

        Christopher Berzins
        Manager
        Freedom of Information and Privacy
        Protection Office
        Ontario Ministry of Labour
        400 University Avenue
        7th floor
        Toronto, ON M7A 1T7
        Tel. (416) 326-7786
        Signature of Requester

9F27
CONSENT AND AUTHORIZATION—
INDUSTRIAL HEALTH AND SAFETY

[See Paras. 9.290–9.291]

TO: INDUSTRIAL HEALTH AND SAFETY BRANCH
     MINISTRY OF LABOUR

The undersigned, on behalf of (the "Company"), hereby consents to an inspection being conducted by the Industrial Health and Safety Branch, Ministry of Labour (the "Branch") and authorizes the Branch to inspect the Company's premises _____ at for the purposes of determining whether the Occupational Health and Safety Act or the Regulations made pursuant to that Act have been or are being contravened. The Company hereby further authorizes the Branch to release to (*insert firm name*), Barristers & Solicitors, the results of that inspection and any information relevant to any contraventions of the Act or the Regulations that are disclosed by that inspection.

The Company hereby further authorizes the Branch to release to (*insert firm name*) any information requested by (*insert firm name*) concerning outstanding orders made by the Branch relating to the above-mentioned premises.

This document shall be your good and sufficient authority to conduct the search referred to above and to release the aforementioned information to (*insert firm name*).

DATED this _____ day of _____, 20__.

(*Proper Corporate Name*)

Per: _____

9F28
SEARCH LETTER—CANADA REVENUE AGENCY

[See Para. 9.320]

(*Date*)

[**Note:** The search letter should be sent to the proper address as determined by the BIN number. Inquiries regarding the proper mailing address should be directed to the CRA's information line at 1-800-959-5525.]

Dear Sir or Madam:

Re: (*Corporate Name and Address*)

We are the solicitors for a client who is considering purchasing the above-mentioned Corporation (the "Corporation"). Among other things, the purchase is conditional upon the Corporation having complied with the source deduction requirements of the Canada Pension Plan, the Employment Insurance Act, and the Income Tax Act. Would you please inform the writer as to whether there has been such compliance. Attached please find a form of consent and authorization, duly executed by the Corporation, authorizing you to release this information to us.

As the closing date for this transaction is rapidly approaching, we would appreciate receiving your written reply not later than _____.

Yours very truly,

9F29
CONSENT AND AUTHORIZATION — CANADA REVENUE AGENCY

[See Para. 9.320]

CONSENT AND AUTHORIZATION

To: Canada Revenue Agency

Re: (*Corporate Name*)

This shall be your good and sufficient authority to release to (*insert firm name*), Barristers & Solicitors, information regarding the compliance by with the source deduction requirements of the Canada Pension Plan, the Employment Insurance Act and the Income Tax Act.

DATED this _____ day of _____, 20 ____.

(Corporate Name)

Per:_____

9F30
SEARCH LETTER—EMPLOYERS' HEALTH TAX

[See Paras. 9.330 and 9.430]

(Date)

The Director
Employer Health Tax Branch
Ministry of Finance
33 King Street West
1st Floor
Oshawa, ON L1H 8H5

Dear Sir or Madam:

Re: *(Purchaser)* of _____ shares of *(Employer corporation)* from *(vendor)*

We are the solicitors for *(Purchaser)* in the above transaction. *(Purchaser)* is located at *(address)* and is the holder of Employer Health Tax account number *(account number)* (or where account number is unavailable, is the holder of federal source deduction number *(number)*). *(Purchaser)* will, pursuant to the terms of the transaction, acquire *(set out briefly the transaction)*.

We hereby request written verification that *(employer corporation)* does not have any outstanding obligations or liabilities for unpaid taxes, penalties, interest or any garnishment notice or other court order issued against it pursuant to the provisions of the Employer Health Tax Act and regulations. If any such obligation, liability or orders exist, we request that the nature and amount of such liabilities or orders be disclosed to us.

Enclosed for your information is a consent for the release of the above information duly signed by [employer corporation] pursuant to subsection 27(c) of the Employer Health Tax Act.

As this transaction is scheduled to close on (date) your early attention to this matter would be appreciated.

Yours very truly,

9F31
CONSENT—EMPLOYER'S HEALTH TAX

[See Paras. 9.460 and 9.430]

TO: The Director
Employer Health Tax Branch
The undersigned hereby consents to the release of any and all information in respect of any outstanding liabilities or obligations of the undersigned for unpaid taxes, penalties, interest or in respect of any garnishment notice or other court order against the undersigned imposed pursuant to the provisions of the Employer Health Tax Act and regulations. The undersigned authorizes you to release any and all such information to (*insert firm name*), Barristers & Solicitors and, without limiting the generality of the foregoing, [*lawyer*] of that firm.

The foregoing consent is made pursuant to subsection 27(c) of the Employer Health Tax Act.

(*Employer*)

Per: _____

9F32
LONG FORM OF ASSET PURCHASE AGREEMENT

[See Paras. 9.470, 9.470–9.610 generally and Forms 9F80–9F81 and 9F88]

THIS AGREEMENT made the _____ day of _____, 19___.

B E T W E E N:

> VENDOR LTD., a corporation incorporated under the laws of the Province of Ontario,
>
> (the "Vendor")

OF THE FIRST PART

-and-

> PURCHASER INC., a corporation incorporated under the laws of the Province of Ontario,
>
> (the "Purchaser")

OF THE SECOND PART

WITNESSETH THAT:

WHEREAS the Vendor carries on the business of manufacturing soaps and cleaning products under the name "ABC Chemicals" (the "Business");

AND WHEREAS the Vendor has agreed to sell to the Purchaser and the Purchaser has agreed to purchase from the Vendor substantially all the assets, property and undertakings of and pertaining to the Business, upon and subject to the terms and conditions of this Agreement;

NOW THEREFORE, in consideration of the premises and mutual agreements contained in this Agreement and of other good and valuable consideration (the receipt and sufficiency of which are acknowledged by each Party hereto), the Parties agree with one another as follows:

1. INTERPRETATION

(1) Definitions

Whenever used in this Agreement, unless there is something in the subject matter or context inconsistent therewith, the following words and terms shall have the respective meanings ascribed to them in this section 1(1):

(a)   **"Affiliate", "Associate", "Body Corporate", "Subsidiary" and "Voting Securities"** shall have the respective meanings ascribed to those terms by the *Business Corporations Act* (Ontario);

(b)   **"Agreement"** means this asset purchase agreement and all instruments supplemental to or in amendment or confirmation of this asset purchase agreement, and all references to this Agreement shall include the attached Schedules and "Article", "Section", "Sub-section", or "Paragraph" means and refers to the specified article, section, subsection, or paragraph of this asset purchase agreement;

(c)   **"Assumed Liabilities"** means all the debts, liabilities (whether accrued, absolute or contingent or whether liquidated or unliquidated) and obligations of the Business or the Purchased Assets existing or incurred on or after the Effective Date, other than Excluded Liabilities, including, without limiting the generality of the foregoing, the liabilities and obligations of the Vendor:

[*List specific relevant Assumed Liabilities — liabilities which are often assumed by purchasers include accounts payable, bank indebtedness, obligations under contracts and leases, purchase and supply orders and warranty claims.*]

(d)   **"Assumption Agreement"** means the assumption and indemnity agreement to be issued by the Purchaser to the Vendor in the form attached as Schedule "A";

(e)   **"Audited Financial Statements"** means the consolidated financial statements of the Vendor for its fiscal period ended on 199_____;

(f)   **"Auditors"** means collectively, the Vendor's Auditors and the Purchaser's Auditors;

(g)   **"Bank Prime"** means the rate per annum charged by the Vendor's Bank at its principal office in Toronto, Ontario for loans of Canadian dollars to its customers in Canada, and said to be its "prime rate", as the same is adjusted from time to time;

(h)   **"Benefit Plans"** has the meaning ascribed in Subsection 4(1)(ag);

(i)   **"Book Value of Assets"** means the total book value of the Purchased Assets as shown in the Effective Date Financial Statements; and **"Book Value of Assumed Purchased Liabilities"** means the total book value of the Assumed Liabilities as shown in the Effective Date Financial Statements;

(j)   **"Business"** has the meaning ascribed in the recitals to this Agreement;

(k)   **"Business Day"** means any day, other than a Saturday, Sunday or any other day on which the principal chartered banks located in the City of Toronto are not open for business during normal banking hours;

(l)   **"Closing"** means the completion of the sale to, and the purchase by the Purchaser of, the Purchased Assets under this Agreement by the transfer and delivery of documents of title to the Purchased Assets and the payment of the Purchase Price;

(m)   **"Closing Date"** means _____, 19_____, or such other date as the Parties may agree in writing as the date upon which the Closing shall take place; [*Alternate: The *day next following the day on which this transaction of purchase and sale may be completed under the _____ Act*].

(n)   **"Closing Documents"** means collectively the documents referred to in Article 7;

(o)   **"Closing Time"** means 10:00 o'clock in the forenoon on the Closing Date or such other time on such date as the Parties may agree as the time at which the Closing shall take place;

(p)   **"Collective Agreements"** means the collective agreements and related documents including all benefit agreements, letters of understanding, letters of intent and other written communications with bargaining agents which impose any obligations upon the Vendor or set out the understanding of the parties with respect to the meaning of any provisions of the collective agreements entered into by the Vendor with respect to the Business as are listed in Schedule "F";

(q) **"Contracts"** means those contracts, agreements, commitments, entitlements and engagements of the Vendor relating to the Business and the Purchased Assets other than relating to the Excluded Assets (and, for greater certainty, not including Collective Agreements, Leases and Equipment Leases) whether with suppliers, customers or otherwise and including all unfilled orders from customers; all forward commitments for supplies or materials; all orders for new machinery and equipment as yet undelivered; all equipment and construction guarantees and warranties; negative covenants with employees; and all other contracts described in Schedule "E";

(r) **"Deposit"** has the meaning ascribed in Section 3(11);

(s) **"Effective Date"** means _____, 199_____, or such other date as the parties may agree in writing as the date at which the Auditors prepare the Effective Date Financial Statement;

(t) **"Effective Date Financial Statements"** means the consolidated financial statements of the Business for the fiscal period ended on the Effective Date, prepared in accordance with generally accepted accounting principles consistently applied, consisting of balance sheet as at such date, and statements of earnings and retained earnings and of changes in financial position for such period, together with the Vendor's Auditors notes at such date on those statements, addressed to the Vendor;

(u) **"Employees"** has the meaning ascribed in Subsection 5(6)(a);

(v) **"Employment Agreement"** has the meaning ascribed in Section 5(18);

(w) **"Equipment Leases"** means those equipment leases, conditional sales contracts, title retention agreements and other agreements between the Vendor and third Persons relating to equipment used by the Vendor in connection with the Business including those that are listed in Schedule "G";

(x)   **"Excluded Assets"** means:

    (i)   all cash, bank balances, monies in possession of banks and other depositaries, term or time deposits and similar cash items of, owned or held by or for the account of the Vendor;

    (ii)   the corporate, financial, taxation and other records of the Vendor not pertaining exclusively or primarily to the Business or Purchased Assets;

    (iii) all extra-provincial, sales, excise or other licences or registrations issued to or held by the Vendor, whether in respect of the Business or otherwise;

    (iv) all deferred income taxes and income taxes recoverable; and

    (v)   all proceeds receivable from life insurance policies on the life of any director, officer, employee or shareholder of the Vendor;

[*List any other Excluded Assets*]

(y)   **"Excluded Liabilities"** means the following debts, liabilities (whether assumed, absolute or contingent or whether liquidated or unliquidated) and obligations of the Business or the Purchased Assets existing or incurred on or after the Effective Date:

    (i)   deferred income tax of the Vendor;

    (ii)   except as specifically contemplated in the Agreement all other taxes, duties or similar charges (including penalties, fines and interest) payable by the Vendor;

    (iii) those liabilities and obligations, whether accrued, absolute or contingent, liquidated or unliquidated or disclosed or undisclosed, which relate to the Excluded Assets;

    (iv) all costs and expenses of the Vendor incurred in the preparation, execution and delivery of this Agreement and the transaction contemplated by this Agreement;

    (v)   any liability under the Benefit Plans;

    (vi) any liability under the Pension Plan(s);

    (vii) any liability of the Vendor to the Purchaser arising after the date of this Agreement out of any misrepresentation or breach of any warranty of the Vendor contained in this Agreement;

    (viii) any obligation or liability of the Vendor to the extent that the Vendor shall be indemnified by an insurer under a policy of insurance;

    (ix) any liability for any personal injuries or product liability claims arising by reason of the occurrence on or before to the Closing Date of an injury, accident or other alleged damage-causing event with respect to the operations of the Vendor on or prior to the Closing Date or relating to products manufactured or sold by the Vendor on or before the Closing Date that provide the basis for a personal injury or product liability claim after the Closing Date;

(x) any liability of the Vendor to any bank or other financial institution by way of loan or other credit facility; and

(xi) any liability of the Vendor to its shareholders, affiliates or associates or any other Person not dealing at arm's length with any of them;

[*List any other Excluded Liabilities.*]

(z) **"GAAP"** has the meaning ascribed in Section 1(8);

(aa) **"General Assignment"** has the meaning ascribed in Subsection 2(5)(b);

(ab) **"GST"** means the Goods and Services Tax payable under the Excise Tax Act;

(ac) **"Intellectual Property Rights"** means all patents and inventions, trade marks, including those described in Schedule "H", all trade names and styles, including the trade names or styles "ABC Soaps", "ABC Chemicals", and "ABC Cleansers", logos and designs, trade secrets, technical information, engineering procedures, designs, knowhow and processes (whether confidential or otherwise), software, and other industrial property (including applications for any of these) in each case used or reasonably necessary to permit satisfactory operation of the Business as presently constituted;

(ad) **"Interim Period"** means the period beginning on the Effective Date to and including the Closing Date;

(ae) **"Inventories"** means all inventories of every kind and nature and wheresoever situate owned by the Vendor and pertaining to the Business including, without limitation, all inventories of raw materials, work-in-progress, finished goods, operating supplies and packaging materials of or pertaining to the Business;

(af) **"Leases"** means all leases of Leasehold Properties;

(ag) **"Licences"** means all transferable licences, registrations, qualifications, permits and approvals, issued by any government or governmental unit, agency, board, body or instrumentality, whether federal, provincial or municipal, relating to the Business, including those listed in Schedule "I", together with all applications for such licences or permits

(*) ["**Net Book Value of Assets**" *means the Book Value of Assets, excluding the book value of the good will of the Business, minus the Book Value of Assumed Liabilities, as determined from the Effective Date Balance Sheet in accordance with generally accepted accounting principles; —Note: This definition is used if the Purchase Price is determined based on Net Book Value. In this precedent agreement, the Purchase Price is the Book Value of Assets and the Assumed Liabilities are assumed in part payment of the Purchase Price*]

(ah) **"Non-Competition Agreement"** means the non-competition agreement in the form of Schedule "C";

(ai) **"Parties"** means the Vendor and the Purchaser, collectively, and "Party" means either one of them;

(aj) **"Pension Plan(s)"** has the meaning ascribed in Subsection 4(1)(af);

(*) [*"**Permitted Encumbrances**" means those liens, charges and encumbrances listed in Schedule "_____"; [Note: In this precedent agreement, it is provided that all Purchased Assets are being sold free and clear of all encumbrances. This definition is applicable if the Purchased Assets are sold subject to encumbrances, such as in the case where the Purchaser may be assuming the Vendor's bank indebtedness or equipment financing obligations*]

(ak) **"Person"** includes an individual, corporation, partnership, joint venture, trust, unincorporated organization, the Crown or any agency or instrumentality thereof or any other juridical entity;

(al) **"Purchase Price"** means the purchase price to be paid by the Purchaser to the Vendor for the Purchased Assets, all as provided in Section 3(1);

(am) **"Purchased Assets"** means the following properties, assets and rights:
    (i)   **Real Property** — all of the Real Properties;

(ii)   **Inventories** — all the Inventories;

(iii) **Contracts and Equipment Leases** — all right, title and interest of the Vendor in, to and under and the full benefit and advantage of the Contracts and the Equipment Leases and the full benefit of all service contracts relating to any Equipment Leases or any equipment or other assets covered by the Equipment Leases and all options, including, without limitation, options to purchase, under the Contracts or Equipment Leases;

(iv)   **Fixed Assets, Equipment, etc.** — all fixed assets, machines, machinery, equipment, fixtures, furniture, furnishings, vehicles, dies, tools, and other tangible property and facilities owned or held by the Vendor and used in the Business whether located in or on the premises of the Vendor or elsewhere, including, without limitation, those described in Schedule "D"

(v)   **Goodwill of Business** — the right, title and interest of the Vendor in the goodwill of the Business, and all right, title and interest of the Vendor in, to and in respect of the names "ABC Soaps", "ABC Chemicals", and "ABC Cleansers";

(vi)   **Prepaid Expenses** — all prepaid expenses including, without limitation, taxes, business taxes, rents, telephone and insurance incurred by the Vendor but excluding income, capital and other taxes which are personal to the Vendor or not incurred in connection with the Business;

(vii) **Accounts Receivable** — all accounts receivable, bills receivable, trade accounts, book debts, and other amounts due, owing or accruing due to the Vendor in connection with the Business, including for greater certainty, the amounts due, owing or accruing due to the Vendor by Subco Inc. and the benefit of all security (including cash deposits), guarantees and other collateral held by the Vendor in respect of any accounts receivable;

(viii) **Intellectual Property Rights** — all right, title and interest of the Vendor in the Intellectual Property Rights;

(ix)   **Leases** — all right, title and interest of the Vendor in the Leases;

(x)   **Proceeds of Litigation** — the right, title and interest of the Vendor in all rights and causes of action and proceeds therefrom in respect of litigation that is related exclusively to the Business;

(xi)   **Investments** — all the investments of the Business in other corporations or businesses (other than investments forming part of the Excluded Assets), specifically including the 1,000 issued and outstanding common shares of Subco Inc.:

(xii) **Licences** — all the Licences;

(xiii) **Books and Records** — all business books and records used in the conduct of the Business, including without limitation, all financial, operating, inventory, legal, personnel, payroll, and customer records and all sales and promotional literature, correspondence and files; and,

(xiv) **General** — all other rights, properties and assets (other than Excluded Assets) of the Vendor used primarily in the Business, including telephone numbers, of whatsoever nature or kind and wherever situated;

[*List any other Purchased Assets*]

(an) **"Purchaser's Auditors"** means [*Purchaser's auditors*], Chartered Accountants;

(ao) **"Purchaser's Note"** means the promissory note of the Purchaser in favour of the Vendor in the amount of $_____ dated the Closing Date, in the form attached as Schedule "B";

(ap) **"Real Properties"** means all freehold, leasehold, and other interests in real and immoveable properties owned or used by the Vendor in connection with the Business, including, without limitation,

(i)   the freehold lands and premises described in Schedule "J", and all plant, buildings, sidings, parking lots, roadways, structures, erections, improvements, fixed machinery, fixed equipment, appurtenances, and fixtures situate on or forming part of such lands and premises (collectively the "Owned Properties"),

(ii) the leasehold and other interest described in Schedule "K" including all fixtures and improvements owned by the Business relating to those leasehold and other interest (collectively the "Leasehold Properties");

(aq) **"Settlement Date"** means the day 10 days after the delivery of the final Settlement Statement under Section 3(7), or such other day to which the Parties may agree;

(ar) **"Settlement Statement"** means a statement prepared under Section 3(2) showing the particulars of the calculations of the Purchase Price and its allocation, including the Book Value of Assets and the

Book Value of Assumed Liabilities and other adjustments, if any, to which the Purchaser is entitled under the provisions of Sections 3(8), 3(9) and 3(10);

(as) **"Statement of Adjustments"** has the meaning ascribed in Section 3(10);

(at) **"Statements"** has the meaning ascribed in Section 3(2);

(au) **"to the best of the knowledge"** when used in reference to:
  (i)   the Vendor means the knowledge of the senior officers [*name specific officers*] of the Vendor; and,
  (ii) the Purchaser means the knowledge of the senior officers [*name specific officers*] of the Purchaser;

(av) **Undertaking to Readjust"** has the meaning ascribed in Section 3(10);

(aw) **"Vendor's Auditors"** means Chartered Accountants.

(ax) **"Vendor's Bank"** shall mean the _____ Bank;

(2) Gender and Number

In this Agreement, words importing the singular include the plural and vice versa and words importing gender include all genders.

(3) Entire Agreement

This Agreement, including Schedules "A" to "V", together with the agreements and other documents to be delivered under this Agreement constitute the entire agreement between the Parties pertaining to the subject matter of this Agreement and supersede all prior agreements, understandings, negotiations and discussions, whether oral or written, of the Parties and there are no warranties, representations or other agreements between the Parties in connection with the subject matter of this Agreement except as specifically set forth in this Agreement. No supplement, modification or amendment to this Agreement and no waiver of any provision of this Agreement shall be binding on any Party unless executed by such Party in writing. No waiver of any of the provisions of this Agreement shall be deemed or shall constitute

(4) Article and Section Headings

Article and Section headings contained in this Agreement are included solely for convenience, are not intended to be full or accurate descriptions of the content of any Article or Section and shall not be considered to be part of this Agreement.

(5) Schedules

The following Schedules are an integral part of this Agreement:

Schedule A—Assumption Agreement
Schedule B—Purchaser's Note
Schedule C—Non-competition Agreement
Schedule D—Fixed Assets and Equipment
Schedule E—Contracts
Schedule F—Collective Agreements
Schedule G —Equipment Leases
Schedule H—Intellectual Property Rights
Schedule I—Licences
Schedule J—Owned Properties
Schedule K—Leases
Schedule L—General Assignment
Schedule M—Vendor's previous names
Schedule N—Locations of Purchased Assets
Schedule O—Employees
Schedule P—Pension Plan(s)
Schedule Q—Benefit Plans
Schedule R—Employees on compensation or disability
Schedule S—Undertaking of Vendor's bank
Schedule T—Licences and permits
Schedule U—Purchaser's financing commitment
Schedule V—Employment Agreement

(6) Applicable Law

This Agreement shall be governed by and construed in accordance with the laws of the Province of Ontario and the federal laws of Canada applicable in the Province of Ontario and shall be treated, in all respects, as an Ontario contract. Each Party to this Agreement irrevocably attorns to and submits to the jurisdiction of the Courts of Ontario with respect to any matter arising under or relating to this Agreement.

(7) Currency

Unless otherwise indicated, all dollar amounts referred to in this Agreement are in Canadian funds.

(8) Accounting Terms

All accounting terms not otherwise defined have the meanings assigned to them, and all calculations are to be made and all financial data to be submitted are to be prepared, in accordance with the generally accepted accounting principles "GAAP" approved from time to time by the Canadian Institute of Chartered Accountants, or any successor institute applied on a consistent basis.

(9) Arm's Length

For purposes of this Agreement, Persons are not dealing "at arm's length" with one another if they would not be dealing at arm's length with one another for purposes of the Income Tax Act.

(10) Business Days

Whenever any action or payment to be taken or made under this Agreement shall be stated to be required to be taken or made on a day other than a Business Day, and payment shall be made or such action shall be taken on the next succeeding Business Day.

(11) Statutory Instruments

Unless otherwise specifically provided in this Agreement, any reference in this Agreement to any law, by-law, rule, regulation, order, act or statute of any government, governmental body or other regulatory body shall be construed as a reference to those as amended or re-enacted from time to time or as a reference to any successor to those.

(12) Materiality

In this Agreement "Material" means, when used as an adjective, that any breach, default or deficiency in the satisfaction of any covenant, representation or warranty so described might reasonably:

    (a)   give rise to an aggregate remedial cost (including consequential loss and loss of profit) of more than \$_____, in any individual instance, or more than \$_____ collectively in any greater number of instances, where all such instances arise pursuant to multiple breaches of the same covenant, representation or warranty; or

(b)   where no adequate remedy is reasonably available, result in disturbance in the ordinary conduct of the Business of an aggregate cost properly attributable to such disturbance (including consequential loss and loss of profit) of more than $_____, and "Materially" shall have the corresponding meaning.

2. PURCHASE AND SALE OF PURCHASED ASSETS

(1) Purchase and Sale of Purchased Assets

Upon and subject to the terms and conditions of this Agreement, the Vendor shall sell, transfer, assign and set over to the Purchaser and the Purchaser shall purchase and acquire from the Vendor at the Closing Time, the Purchased Assets for the Purchase Price payable as provided in Section 3(4) [*Note: An alternative method of structuring the purchase and sale is to provide for the purchase and sale of all the assets and undertaking of a defined "Purchased Business". See alternative clauses*]

(2) Excluded Assets

For greater certainty, the Excluded Assets shall be specifically excluded from the Purchased Assets whether or not they form part of the property and assets of the Business. Within 30 days following the Closing Date, the Vendor shall at its own expense remove all tangible Excluded Assets, if any, from the premises of the Business. [*Note: This provision regarding re-moval of assets by the Vendor is appropriate where the premises of the Business are acquired by the Purchaser, as is the case assumed under this precedent agreement.*]

(3) Assumed Liabilities

The Purchaser agrees to assume and become liable only for the Assumed Liabilities at the Closing Time by executing and delivering the Assumption Agreement to the Vendor.

(4) Excluded Liabilities

For greater certainty, it is understood that the Purchaser will assume no liabilities of the Business other than those described in or forming part of the Assumed Liabilities that, without limitation, do not include the Excluded Liabilities.

(5) Non-Assignable Contracts

This Agreement and any document delivered under this Agreement shall not constitute an assignment or an attempted assignment of any Contract, Equipment Lease, Lease or Licence contemplated to be assigned to the Purchaser under this Agreement;

(a)   which is not assignable without the consent of a third party if such consent has not been obtained and such assignment or attempted assignment would constitute a breach of such contract or agreement; or

(b)   in respect of which the remedies for the enforcement of such contract or agreement available to the Vendor would not pass to the Purchaser.

The Vendor shall use its best efforts to obtain the consents of third parties as may be necessary for the assignment of the Contracts, the Equipment Leases, the Leases and the Licences except that the Vendor shall not be obliged to make any payments to those third parties in addition to those required to be made under those contracts or agreements in order to obtain such consents, unless the Purchaser reimburses the Vendor for such payments at the time that they are made. To the extent that any of the foregoing items are not assignable by their terms or where consents to their assignment cannot be obtained as provided in this Section 2(5), such items shall be held by the Vendor in trust for the Purchaser and the covenants and obligations under those contracts or agreements shall be performed by the Purchaser in the name of the Vendor and all benefits and obligations existing therein shall be for the account of the Purchaser. The Vendor shall take or cause to be taken such action in its name or otherwise as the Purchaser may reasonably require so as to provide the Purchaser with the benefits of those contracts or agreements and to effect collection of money to become due and payable under such items and the Vendor shall promptly pay over to the Purchaser all money received by the Vendor in respect of all of the foregoing items. Upon the Closing, the Vendor and the Purchaser shall execute and deliver a general assignment of contracts, leases and licences agreement (the "General Assignment") in the form attached as Schedule "L", under which the Vendor shall authorize the Purchaser, at the Purchaser's expense, to perform all of the Vendor's obligations under the foregoing items and constitute the Purchaser its attorney to act in the name of the Vendor with respect to those items, and the Purchaser shall agree to assume those obligations.

Nothing in this Section 2(5) shall limit the effect of Subsection 7(1)(f) regarding consents to assignments.

3. PURCHASE PRICE AND PAYMENT

(1) Purchase Price

The Purchase Price payable by the Purchaser under this Agreement for the Purchased Assets shall be, subject to the adjustments provided in this Article 3, an aggregate sum equal to the Book Value of Assets, other than Goodwill, as shown on the Effective Date Financial Statements and $1.00 for Goodwill.

(2) Preparation of Effective Date Financial Statement

At the same time as the execution and delivery of this Agreement, the Vendor and the Purchaser shall instruct their respective Auditors to jointly prepare the Effective Date Financial Statement and the Settlement Statement (collectively, the "Statements"). The following generally accepted accounting principles will be applied in preparing the Effective Date Financial Statement:

    (a)   all fixed assets will be valued at actual cost less accumulated depreciation taken;

    (b)   the accounts receivable will be net of an allowance for doubtful accounts established on a basis consistent with the prior practice of the Business; and

    (c)   inventories will be valued at the lower of cost and net realizable value and will be net of an allowance for obsolete and slow-moving items.

The fees and expenses charged by the Auditors for and in connection with the preparation of the Statements shall be paid equally by the Purchaser and the Vendor.

(3) Effective Date

The sale and purchase contemplated under this Agreement shall, when completed on the Closing Date, take effect as of the close of business on the Effective Date and from such time to the Closing Date the Business shall be carried on by the Vendor in the ordinary course for the account of the Purchaser.

(4) Payment of Purchase Price

The Parties expect that the Purchase Price will be approximately $_____.
At the Closing Time, the Purchaser shall pay on account of the Purchase
Price the amount of $_____, to be satisfied by:

    (a)   assumption by the Purchaser of the Assumed Liabilities, which the
Parties estimate will be $_____ at the Closing Time;

    (b)   application of the Deposit;

    (c)   a certified cheque or bank draft of the Purchaser payable to or to
the order of the Vendor in the amount of $_____; and,

    (d)   execution and delivery to the Vendor by the Purchaser of the
Purchaser's Note.

The Purchaser acknowledges that the Purchase Price does not include GST
payable, if any, as a result of the purchase and sale of the Purchased Assets.

(5) Draft Statements

Before issuing the Statements in final form, the Auditors shall submit final
drafts to the Parties for consideration and comment. The Parties agree to
comment promptly on the final draft Statements and, in any event, within 15
days of receiving them.

(6) Preparation of Final Statements

The Auditors shall amend the final draft Statements to the extent they
consider appropriate in the light of the comments of the Parties. If the
Auditors fail to reach agreement as to their reports on the Statements, a third
chartered accountant (who shall be selected by the Vendor's Auditors and
the Purchaser's Auditors) shall, with all reasonable dispatch, finally
determine the Statements. If the Auditors are unable to agree as to the third
chartered accountant, he shall be selected by lot from the two nominees
proposed by the Auditors. In making his determination, the third chartered
accountant shall act as an expert and not as an arbitrator. The resulting
Statements, including as finally determined by the third chartered
accountant, are binding on the parties to this Agreement and all other
interested Persons.

(7) Delivery of Final Statements

The final Statements shall not be completed and delivered to the Parties by
the Auditors until adjustments provided under Section 3(9) and 3(10) have
been reported to the Auditors and incorporated into the final Statements, but

in no case shall the final Statements be delivered to the Parties more than 100 days after Closing Date, unless otherwise agreed by the Parties.

(8) Adjustment of Purchase Price

On the Settlement Date the Parties agree to make the necessary adjustments to the Purchase Price based on any discrepancy between the amount paid by the Purchaser on the Closing Date and the Book Value of Assets and Book Value of Assumed Liabilities disclosed on the Effective Date Financial Statements and on the results of the count of Inventories and Receivables under Section 3(9) and other adjustments under Section 3(10). [*Note: Consider a hold-back by the Purchaser in case of downward adjustments to the Purchase Price where all the Purchase Price is otherwise payable at Closing. In this precedent agreement, part of the Purchase Price is payable by promissory note, for which a downward adjustment in the principal amount could be provided.*]

(9) Determination of Inventory Value and Uncollectable Accounts Receivable

Within 90 days of the Closing Date, the Vendor and the Purchaser shall jointly make a physical count of the Inventories and an audit of accounts receivable and identify obsolete Inventories and the uncollectable accounts receivable. The Vendor and the Purchaser shall, either directly or through their respective Auditors or representatives, promptly take such action as is necessary to determine the actual value of the Inventories and accounts receivable in accordance with the principles contained in Section 3(2). Before the Settlement Statement is finalized, the Parties shall report the amount of any necessary adjustments under this Section 3(9) to the Auditors so that the Settlement Statement incorporates that adjustment. Any accounts receivable or Inventories determined by the Vendor and the Purchaser to be uncollectable, or obsolete, as the case may be, shall be returned by the Purchaser to the Vendor. [*Note: With respect to accounts receivable, the key issue is determining which party is responsible for collection and collection costs and which party takes the risk of non-collection—See alternative clauses.*]

(10) General Adjustments

In addition to the adjustments under Section 3(8) and 3(9), the usual adjustments as of the Effective Time (including adjustments for rents, realty taxes, local improvement charges, water and unmetered utility charges and cost of fuel) shall be made and allowed either to the Vendor or the Purchaser, as the case may be, on the Closing Date and a statement of adjustments (the "Statement of Adjustments") shall be prepared and delivered by the Parties on the Closing Date. The amounts adjusted in the

Statement of Adjustments shall be subject to readjustment on the Settlement Date and to further readjustment from time to time thereafter under mutual undertakings to readjust (the "Undertakings to Readjust") to be executed and delivered by the Parties on the Closing Date.

(11) Deposit

(a)   A deposit of $_____ on account of the Purchase Price (the "Deposit") has been made by the Purchaser, by depositing that amount in a trust account with the *[Purchaser's solicitors]*, who shall not permit such moneys to be released from trust without the approval of the *[Vendor's solicitors]*. The interest payable on the deposit is payable to the Purchaser.

(b)   If the Purchaser fails to complete this transaction by reason of the non-fulfilment by the Vendor of any of the conditions set forth in Section 7(1), the Vendor is not entitled to the Deposit and it shall be released to the Purchaser no later than one day after the scheduled Closing Date. If the Purchaser fails to complete this transaction for any other reason, the Deposit may be retained by the Vendor as liquidated damages and shall be obtained by the Vendor by making the requisite demand upon the *[Vendor's solicitors]* and the *[Purchaser' solicitors]*.

(12) Cash Reconciliation

The parties acknowledge that in the Interim Period the cash receipts and disbursements received or made by the Vendor in respect of the Business shall be deposited into or made from a bank account maintained by the Vendor. At the Closing Time the Vendor shall deliver to the Purchaser a cash reconciliation statement showing all cash receipts and disbursements relating to the Business for the Interim Period. The Vendor shall pay to the Purchaser any net positive balance shown on such reconciliation statement and the Purchaser shall pay to the Vendor any net negative balance shown on such reconciliation statement. Any such payments required to be made under this Section 3(12) shall be made at the Closing Time.

(13) Allocation of Purchase Price and Tax Returns

The Vendor and the Purchaser covenant and agree with each other that the Purchase Price shall be allocated among the Purchased Assets as provided in the Settlement Statement. The Vendor and the Purchaser agree to cooperate in the filing of such elections under the *Income Tax Act*, the *Corporations Tax Act* (Ontario) and such other taxation statutes as may be necessary or desirable to give effect to said allocation for tax purposes. In addition the Vendor and the Purchaser agree to prepare and file their respective tax returns in a manner consistent with those allocations and elections. If either party fails to file its tax returns in the agreed manner, it shall indemnify and save harmless the other of them, in accordance with Article 6, in respect of any additional tax, interest, penalty, legal or accounting costs paid or incurred by the other of them as a result of the failure to file.

(14) Transfer Taxes

Subject to Sections 5(7), 5(11) and 5(16), the Purchaser shall be liable for and shall pay at the Closing Date, in addition to the Purchase Price, all sales and value added taxes and all registration charges and other transfer fees or taxes properly payable upon and in connection with the sale and transfer of the Purchased Assets, including, without limitation, GST and Ontario retail sales tax, but specifically excluding any taxes based on the net income of the Vendor.

(15) Employees

Despite anything to the contrary in this Article 3, all payments, assumptions of liabilities and adjustments concerning any amount with respect to the Transferred Employees shall be calculated and dealt with between the Parties in accordance with Section 5(6). [Note: See alternative clauses for sample provisions concerning security for the unpaid balance of the Purchase Price.]

4. REPRESENTATIONS AND WARRANTIES

(1) Representations and Warranties of the Vendor

The Vendor hereby represents and warrants to the Purchaser as follows and acknowledges that the Purchaser is relying on these representations and warranties in entering into this Agreement and the transactions contemplated under this Agreement: [Note: The precedent representations and warranties in this agreement are generally unqualified, but all representations and warranties are subject to appropriate qualifications to which the Parties may agree. Commonly used qualifications include Materiality thresholds, knowledge qualifications, specific exceptions listed in attached schedules.]

(a) Organization and Good Standing—The Vendor is a corporation duly incorporated, organized and validly existing in good standing under the laws of [jurisdiction of incorporation].

(b)   Bankruptcy, etc.—No bankruptcy, insolvency or receivership proceedings have been instituted or are pending against the Vendor and the Vendor is able to satisfy its liabilities as they become due.

(c)   Previous Names—Set out in Schedule "M" is a list of all corporate predecessors of the Vendor and all previous corporate [*and business*] names of the Vendor and its predecessors.

(d)   Capacity to Carry on Business—The Vendor has all necessary corporate power, authority and capacity to own its property and assets to carry on the Business as presently owned and carried on by it, and the Vendor is duly licensed, registered and qualified as a corporation to do business and is in good standing in each jurisdiction in which the nature of the Business and the Purchased Assets make such qualification necessary and all such licences, registrations and qualifications are valid and subsisting and in good standing and none of them contains any burdensome term, provision, condition or limitation which has or may have an adverse effect on the Purchased Assets.

(e)   Due Authorization, etc.—The Vendor has all necessary corporate power, authority and capacity to enter into this Agreement and to perform its obligations hereunder; the execution and delivery of this Agreement and the consummation of the transactions contemplated by this Agreement have been duly authorized by all necessary corporate action on the part of the Vendor.

(f)   Absence of Conflicting Agreements—Except for the Contracts, the Equipment Leases, and the Leases, the consent to the assignment or transfer of which may be required from lessors or other third parties thereunder in connection with the completion of the transactions contemplated by this Agreement and except for various financing and security agreements with the Vendor's Bank all of which will be terminated before Closing or all of which will be waived by the Vendor's Bank in respect of the transactions contemplated in this Agreement, the Vendor is not a party to, bound or affected by or subject to any indenture, mortgage, lease, agreement, instrument, statute, regulation, arbitration award, charter or by-law provisions, order or judgment which would be violated, contravened, breached by, or under which any default would occur as a result of the execution and delivery of this Agreement or the consummation of any of the transactions contemplated under this Agreement.

(g)   Enforceability of Obligations—This Agreement constitutes a valid and binding obligation of the Vendor enforceable against it in accordance with its terms, provided that enforcement may be limited by bankruptcy, insolvency, liquidation, reorganization, reconstruction and other similar laws generally affecting enforceability of creditors's rights and that equitable remedies such as specific performance and injunction are in the discretion of the court from which they are sought.

(h)   Purchased Assets—The Purchased Assets referred to in any Schedule to this Agreement are accurately described. The Purchased Assets comprise all the assets, property and undertakings necessary to carry on the Business. All machines, machinery, equipment or other moveable or mechanical property forming a part of the Purchased Assets are in good operating condition and are in a state of good repair and maintenance, reasonable wear and tear excepted. [*Except for the representations and warranties contained in this Subsection 4(1)(h), the Vendor makes no further representations or warranties to the Purchaser of any kind, character or nature, whether express or implied, statutory or otherwise with respect to the Purchased Assets, including without limitation, any representations or warranties regarding merchantability or fitness for a particular purpose.*] [*Note: See alternative clauses for a representation and warranty clause where assets are sold on an "as is, where is" basis.*]

(i)   Title to Purchased Assets—Except for [*Permitted Encumbrances*] encumbrances in favour of the Vendor''s Bank shall be discharged or waived in writing by the Vendor's Bank on or before Closing), the Vendor is, or will be on the Closing Date, subject to Section 2(5), and the Purchaser shall become, on Closing, subject to Section 2(5), the absolute beneficial owner of the Purchased Assets, with good and marketable title to the Purchased Assets, free and clear of any title defects, mortgages, pledges, hypothecs, security interests, deemed trusts, liens, charges, encumbrances or rights or claims of others of any kind whatsoever and the Vendor is exclusively entitled to possess and dispose of the same (subject only to obtaining any necessary consents to transfer in the case of the Contracts, the Equipment Leases and the Leases), and in particular, without limiting the generality of the foregoing, there has been no assignment, subletting or granting of any licence (of occupation or otherwise) of or in respect of any of the Contracts, the Equipment Leases or the Leases.

(j)   Location of Assets—All material tangible assets of the Vendor used in or in connection with the Business are all normally situate only in the Provinces of _____ and _____ and the State of _____ the municipalities in which such assets are normally situate are set forth in Schedule "N".

(k)   Real Property—The Real Properties and their existing and prior uses comply with, and at all material times have complied with, and the Vendor is not in violation of or has violated in connection with the ownership, use, maintenance or operation of the Real Properties, any applicable federal, provincial or municipal laws, regulations or by-laws or orders of any governmental authorities. There are no currently outstanding work orders or directions requiring any work, repairs, construction or capital expenditures with respect to the Real Properties and no such orders or directions are pending or threat-ened. [*Note: See alternative clause for more environmental representations and warranties and* **see Paras. 9.120-9121 and 9.580** *of this Text for a more detailed review of considerations and precedents concerning the purchase and sale of real property.*]

(l)   Insulation—The buildings and structures located on the Real Properties have not been insulated with a urea formaldehyde foam type of insulation.

(m)   Accounts Receivable—All accounts receivable, trade accounts, bills receivable and book debts and other debts due or accruing to the Vendor in connection with the Business are bona fide and good and subject to an allowance for doubtful accounts taken in accordance with GAAP are collectible without setoff or counterclaim.

(n)   Inventories—The Inventories are in good and merchantable condition and are usable or saleable in the ordinary course of business for the purposes for which they are intended and are carried on the books of the Vendor at the lower of cost and net realizable value.

(o)   Intellectual Property—All patents, trade-marks, trade names, brand names, trade designs, service marks and copyrights and all licences and similar rights and property which are necessary or incidental to the conduct of the Business as the same is presently being carried on are listed in Schedule "H", and are valid and subsisting and held by the Vendor with good and marketable title and are in good standing free and clear of all security interests, claims, liens, objections and infringements of every nature and kind (other than in favour of the Vendor's Bank) and all registrations therefor have been kept renewed and are in full force and effect. The operations of the Business, the manufacture, storage, use and sale by it of its products and the provision by it of its services do not involve infringements or claimed infringement of any patent, trade-mark, trade name or copyright. No employee of the Vendor owns, directly or indirectly in whole or in part, any patent, trade-mark, trade name, brand name, copyright, invention, process, know-how, formula or trade secret which the Vendor is presently using or the use of which is necessary for the Business.

(p) Guarantees and Indebtedness—The Vendor is not a party to or bound by any guarantee, indemnification, surety or similar obligation (except such as are granted in the ordinary course of business) in respect of the Business.

(q) Material Contracts—Except for the Contracts, the Equipment Leases, the Leases and various loan and security agreements with the Vendor's Bank, the Vendor is not a party to or bound by any material contract or commitment relating to the Business whether oral or written. The Contracts, the Leases, and the Equipment Leases are all in good standing and in full force and effect unamended and no Material default or breach exists in respect of them on the part of any of the parties to them and no event has occurred which, after the giving of notice or the lapse of time or both, would constitute such a default or breach; the foregoing includes all the presently outstanding material contracts entered into by the Vendor in the course of carrying on the Business.

(r) No Options—No Person other than the Purchaser has any agreement or option or any right capable of becoming an agreement or option for the purchase from the Vendor of any of the Purchased Assets, other than purchase orders accepted by the Vendor in the ordinary course of business.

(s) Expropriation—No part of the Purchased Assets has been taken or expropriated by any federal, provincial, state, municipal or other authority nor has any notice or proceeding in respect thereof been given or commenced nor is the Vendor aware of any intent or proposal to give such notice or commence any such proceedings.

(t)   Insurance—The Vendor maintains such policies of insurance, issued by responsible insurers, as are appropriate to the Business and its property and assets, in such amounts and against such risks as are customarily carried and insured against by owners of comparable businesses, properties and assets; all such policies of insurance are in full force and effect, and will continue to be so until the Closing Date, and the Vendor is not in default, whether as to the payment of premium or otherwise, under the terms of any such policy, nor has the Vendor failed to give any notice or present any claim under any such insurance policy in due and timely fashion. [*Note: If desired, provide a list of insurance policies in a schedule with particulars or copies of insurance policies.*]

(u)   Bank Accounts—All of the bank accounts operated in connection with the Business are maintained and operated solely in the name of the Vendor. There are no bank accounts operated in the name of any division or business or trade name or style of the Vendor.

(v)   Books and Records—The books and records of the Vendor fairly and correctly set out and disclose in all material respects, in accordance with GAAP, the financial position of the Vendor as at the date of this Agreement and all material financial transactions of the Vendor relating to the Purchased Business have been accurately recorded in Vendor's books and records.

(w)   Audited Financial Statements—The items reported in the Audited Financial Statements are reported in accordance with GAAP applied on a basis consistent with that of the preceding period and present fairly:
   (i)   all of the assets of the Business as at _____, 199_____ that are of a nature customarily reflected or reserved against in a balance sheet,
   (ii)   all of the liabilities of the Business as at _____, 199_____ that are of a nature customarily reflected or reserved against in a balance sheet, and
   (iii) the sales and earnings from operations of the Business for the _____ month period ended _____, 199_____.

[The financial position of the Vendor is now at least as good as shown or reflected in the Audited Financial Statements]

For greater certainty, the Audited Financial Statements do not include any additions or deductions for income taxes and interest.

(x)   Liabilities—There are no liabilities of the Vendor of any kind whatsoever, whether or not accrued and whether or not determined or determinable, in respect of which the Purchaser may become liable on or after the Effective Date other than the Assumed Liabilities.

(y)   Absence of Changes—Since _____, 199_____ there has not been:
   (i)   any Material change in the condition or operations of the Business other than changes in the ordinary and normal course of business and other than changes resulting from a general deterioration of markets in the industries in which the Business is engaged; or
   (ii) any damage, destruction or loss, labour trouble or other event, development or condition of any character (whether or not covered by insurance) Materially and adversely affecting the Business.

(z)   **Absence of Unusual Transactions**—Since _____, 19_____, the Vendor has carried on the Business in its usual and ordinary course, and in particular the Vendor has not:
   (i)   transferred, assigned, sold or otherwise disposed of any of the assets used in the Business except in the ordinary and usual course of business;
   (ii)   discharged or satisfied any lien or encumbrance, or paid any obligation or liability (fixed or contingent) other than liabilities included in the balance sheet to the Audited Financial Statements and liabilities incurred since the date of the Audited Financial Statements in the ordinary and normal course of business;
   (iii) suffered an extraordinary loss, or waived any rights of Material value, or entered into any Material commitment or transaction not in the ordinary and usual course of business;
   (iv)   made any general wage or salary increases or other payments in respect of personnel which it employs except in the ordinary course of business;
   (v)   declared or paid any dividends or declared or made any other distribution on any of its securities or shares of any class, and

451

has not directly or indirectly, redeemed, purchased or otherwise acquired any of its securities or shares of any class or has agreed to do so;

(vi) made any capital expenditure, except in the usual and ordinary course of business, and no capital expenditure will be made or authorized after the date of this Agreement by the Vendor with respect to the Business without the prior written consent of the Purchaser;

(vii) mortgaged, pledged, subjected to lien, granted a security interest in or otherwise encumbered any of the Purchased Assets other than in favour of the Vendor's Bank; or

(viii) authorized or agreed or otherwise become committed to do any of the foregoing;

(aa) Employees, etc.—Set forth in Schedule "O" is a list showing the names of all the Employees, and their current annual salaries or hourly rates, job descriptions, length of employment or date of hire, dates and amounts of the most recent increases in salary, the amounts of any bonus payments, commissions, accrued vacation pay and other amounts owing to all Employees. This list includes all full-time, part-time, temporary, seasonal and casual employees of the Vendor, including, without limitation, all persons who may be considered, pursuant to applicable workers' compensation, employment standards or similar legislation or otherwise at law or in equity to be employees of the Vendor and all employees of the Vendor who have been laid off but retain recall or reinstatement rights pursuant to any Collective Agreements or statute.

[*Note: See alternative clauses for more sample representations and warranties concerning employees*]

(ab) Employment Contracts and Government Withholdings—Subject to applicable statutory rights, the Vendor is not a party to any written contracts of employment with any of its employees (other than union employees governed by the Collective Agreements) or any oral contracts of employment which are not terminable on the giving of reasonable notice and/or severance pay in accordance with applicable law and no inducements to accept employment with the Vendor were offered to any such employees which have the effect of increasing the period of notice of termination to which any such employee is entitled. The Vendor has deducted and remitted to the relevant governmental authority or entity all income taxes, unemployment insurance contributions, Canada Pension Plan contributions, Ontario employer health tax remittances and any taxes or deduction or other amounts which it is required by statute or contract to collect and remit to any governmental authority or other entities entitled to receive payment of such deduction.

(ac) Employment Payments by the Vendor to Date of Closing—The Vendor has paid to the date of this Agreement all amounts payable on account of salary, bonus payments and commission (other than accrued vacation pay which shall be adjusted in accordance with Subsection 5(6)(g)) to or on behalf of any and all Employees;

(ad) Workers' Compensation—All levies under Workplace Safety and Insurance Act, 1997 (Ontario), or under the workers' compensation legislation of any other jurisdiction where the Business is carried on by the Vendor, have been paid by the Vendor.

(ae) Labour matters:

(i) there is no unfair labour practice complaint under [*The Canada Labour Code or Ontario Labour Relations Act*] against the Vendor pending before the [*federal or*] provincial labour tribunals or any similar agency or body having jurisdiction therefor;

(ii) there is no labour strike threatened against or involving the Vendor;

(iii) there is no certification application outstanding respecting the Employees;

(iv) there is no grievance or arbitration proceeding or governmental proceeding relating to the Employees pending, nor is there any such proceeding threatened against the Vendor which might have a material adverse effect on the Vendor or on the conduct of the Business;

(v) no collective bargaining agreement is currently being negotiated by the Vendor;

(vi) there are no Employees in receipt of or who have claimed benefits under any weekly indemnity, long term disability or workers' compensation plan or arrangement or any other form of disability benefit programme, other than those Employees or former employees identified on Schedule "R".

(af) Pension Plan—The pension plan(s) described in Schedule "P" (the "Pension Plan(s)") is the only pension plan maintained by the Vendor for the Employees, and the Vendor is not in default of any of its obligations under the Pension Plan or prescribed by law;
[*Note: See Form* **9F36** *for more representations and warranties concerning pension plans. Many of these representations and warranties may also apply to benefit plans.*]

(ag) Benefit Plans—The Vendor is not a party to any management agreement, pay equity plan, vacation or vacation pay policy, employee insurance, hospital or medical expense programme or pension, retirement, profit sharing, stock bonus or other employee benefit plan, programme or arrangement or to any executive or key personnel incentive or other special compensation arrangement or to other contracts or agreements with or with respect to officers, employees or agents other than the Pension Plan and those listed and described in Schedule "Q" (the "Benefit Plans").
[*Note: Other specific benefit plans include deferred profit sharing plans, supplemental retirement or unemployment benefits, group RRSPs, disability insurance, dental service plans. These benefit plans may be funded or unfunded. See Form 9F36*-Alternative Clauses]

(ah) Health and Safety—The business premises located on the Real Properties are in compliance with applicable sanitation, health and safety legislation and regulations and are not subject to any orders or directions of a sanitation or occupational health and safety authority or similar body.

(ai) Litigation—There is no suit, action, litigation, arbitration, proceeding, governmental proceeding, including appeals and applications for review in progress, pending or threatened against or involving the Vendor, and there is not presently outstanding against the Vendor any judgment, decree, injunction, rule or order of any court, governmental department, commission, agency, instrumentality or arbitrator.

(aj) Environmental Matters—[*Note: See alternative clauses for some environmental representations, warranties and covenants.*] [**See Form 9F35**]

(ak) Consents—Except for Contracts, Equipment Leases and Leases requiring the consent to assignment of third parties and with respect to the licences or permits referred to in Subsection 4(1) (am), there are no consents, authorizations, licences, franchise agreements, permits, approvals or orders of any person or government required to permit the Vendor to complete this transaction with the Purchaser.

(al) Licences and Permits—All of the licences, registrations, qualifications, permits, bonds and approvals (other than environmental licences or permits) issued by any government or governmental unit, agency, board, body or instrumentality, whether federal, provincial or municipal, related to the Business or necessary for the conduct of the Business are listed on Schedule "T".

(am) Governmental Consents —[*Except for approvals under* _____ *list regulatory approvals, Investment Canada Act, Competition Act*] No governmental or regulatory authorizations, consents, approvals, filings or notices pertaining to Purchaser are required to be obtained or given or waiting period is required to expire in order that the purchase and sale of the Assets may be consummated by the Purchaser or for the Purchaser to carry out its obligations set out in this Agreement.

(an) Residence—The Vendor is not a non-resident of Canada within the meaning of the Income Tax Act.
[*Note: See alternate clauses for provisions concerning the delivery of a section 116 clearance certificate or remittance to Revenue Canada when the Vendor is a non-resident of Canada*]

(ao) Total assets and gross revenues—The Vendor and all of its affiliates have combined assets in Canada, or combined gross revenues from sales in or from Canada, of $_____, in aggregate value. [*Note: The purpose of this representation and warranty is to assist in ascertaining whether the* Competition Act *thresholds have been exceeded.*]

(ap) GST Registration—The Vendor is a registrant for purposes of GST and its GST registration number is R _____;

(aq) Tax Matters—The Business is not in arrears or in default in respect of the filing of any required federal, provincial, or municipal tax or other return; and,
    (i)   all taxes, filing fees, and other assessments due and payable or collectable from the Business have been paid or collected;
    (ii)   no claim for additional taxes, filing fees, or other amounts and assessments has been made that has not been paid; and,

(iii) to the best of the Vendor's knowledge, no such return contains any misstatement or conceals any statement that should have been included therein.

[*Note: For an extensive treatment of tax representations, warranties and covenants, see E. G. Kroft, "Tax Clauses in Acquisition Agreements", Corporate Management Tax Conference, 1990, 9:1, Toronto: Canadian Tax Foundation, 1991*]

(ar) Subsidiaries:

(i) The only Subsidiary of the Vendor is Subco Inc.;

(ii) The authorized capital of Subco Inc. is an unlimited number of common shares, of which 1,000 are validly issued to the Vendor and are outstanding as fully paid and non-assessable and are the only outstanding shares of Subco Inc.;

(iii) There is not any agreement or option existing pursuant to which Subco Inc. is or might be required to issue any further shares of its capital;

(iv) Each of the representations and warranties contained in this Section 4(1) is applicable, *mutatis mutandis*, to Subco Inc.

[*Note: Subco Inc. may be made a party to this Agreement and will then give all representations, warranties and covenants itself.*]

(as) Vendor's Security—The Vendor has obtained from the Vendor's Bankers or other financial institutions an undertaking to discharge all security held by Vendor's Bankers or other financial institutions over the assets of the Business other than Excluded Assets, a copy of which undertaking is attached as Schedule "S".

(at) Rights, Privileges etc.—There are no rights, privileges or advantages presently enjoyed by the Business which might be lost as a result of the consummation of the transactions contemplated under this Agreement.

(au) Disclosure—None of the foregoing representations, warranties and statements of fact contains any untrue statement of material fact or omits to state any material fact necessary to make any such representation, warranty or statement not misleading to a prospective purchaser of the Purchased Assets seeking full information concerning the matters which are the subject of such representations, warranties and statements.

(2) Representations and Warranties of the Buyer

The Purchaser hereby represents and warrants to the Vendor as follows:

(a) Organization and Good Standing—The Purchaser is a corporation duly incorporated, organized, and validly existing and in good standing under the laws of [*jurisdiction of incorporation*].

(b) Authority Relative to this Agreement, etc.—The Purchaser has all necessary corporate power, authority and capacity to enter into this Agreement and to perform its obligations under this Agreement; the execution and delivery of this Agreement and the consummation of the transactions contemplated by this Agreement have been duly authorized by all necessary corporate action on the part of the Purchaser.

(c) Absence of Conflicting Agreements—The Purchaser is not a party to, bound or affected by or subject to any indenture, mortgage, lease, agreement, instrument, charter or by-law provision, statute, regulation, order, judgment, decree or law which would be violated, contravened or breached by, or under which any default would occur as a result of the execution and delivery by it of this Agreement or the consummation of the transactions contemplated under this Agreement, except as disclosed in this Agreement.

(d) Enforceability of Obligations—This Agreement constitutes a valid and binding obligation of the Purchaser enforceable against it in accordance with its terms provided that enforcement may be limited by bankruptcy, insolvency, liquidation, reorganization, reconstruction and other similar laws generally affecting enforceability of creditors' rights and that equitable remedies such as specific performance and injunction are in the discretion of the court from which they are sought.

(e) *Investment Canada Act*—The Purchaser is not a non-Canadian within the meaning of the Investment Canada Act.

(f) *Land Transfer Tax Act*—The Purchaser is not a non-resident person as defined in the Land Transfer Tax Act (Ontario).

(g) Governmental Consents —[*Except for approvals under—list regulatory approvals, Investment Canada Act, Competition Act.*] No governmental or regulatory authorizations, consents, approvals, filings or notices pertaining to Purchaser are required to be obtained or given or waiting period is required to expire in order that the purchase and sale of the Assets may be consummated by the Purchaser or for the Purchaser to carry out its obligations set out in this Agreement. [*Note: Purchaser may have to make necessary applications to acquire necessary licenses because certain licenses or permits may not be transferable.*]

(h)   Total assets and gross revenues—The Purchaser and its affiliates have combined assets in Canada, or combined gross revenues from sales in or from Canada, of $_____, in aggregate value. [*Note: The purpose of this representation and warranty is to assist in ascertaining whether the Competition Act thresholds have been exceeded.*]

(i)   Financing—The Purchaser has obtained a commitment from [*XYZ*] to provide it with the necessary financing or equity to enable it to complete the transactions contemplated hereunder. A copy of the commitment letter of [*XYZ*] is attached hereto as Schedule "U".

(j)   GST Registration—The Purchaser is a registrant for purposes of GST and its GST registration number is R _____.

(3) Commission

Each Party represents and warrants to the other Party that no Person is entitled to a brokerage commission, finder's fee or other like payment in connection with the purchase and sale contemplated by this Agreement.

(4) Non-Waiver

No investigations made by or on behalf of the Purchaser at any time shall have the effect of waiving, diminishing the scope of or otherwise affecting any representation or warranty made by the Vendor in this Agreement or pursuant hereto. No waiver by the Purchaser of any condition, in whole or in part, shall operate as a waiver of any other condition.

(5) Nature and Survival of Representations and Warranties

All statements contained in any certificate or other instrument delivered by or on behalf of a Party pursuant to or in connection with the transactions contemplated by this Agreement shall be deemed to be made by that Party under this Agreement. All representations, warranties, covenants and agreements contained in this Agreement on the part of each of the Parties shall survive the Closing, the execution and delivery hereunder of any bills of sale, instruments of conveyance, assignments or other instruments of transfer of title to any of the Purchased Assets and the payment of the consideration contemplated under this Agreement, except that the representations and warranties contained in this Agreement shall only survive for [*two*] years following Closing (except for the Vendor' representations and warranties relating to tax matters which shall survive for the period of time during which the taxes to which such representations and warranties relate may be reassessed by the relevant taxation authority, unless the Vendor has been fraudulent in filing a return or supplying information to any taxation authority under any taxation legislation [*or unless the Vendor has agreed to extend by waiver the period in which tax reassessments may be made*], in which case the survival of those representations and warranties relating to tax matters shall be unlimited [*in the case of fraud, or shall continue to the expiry of the extended reassessment period, as the case may be,*]) after which period of time, if no claim shall, prior to the expiry of such period, have been made under this Agreement against a Party with respect to any incorrectness in or breach of any representation or warranty made in this Agreement by such Party, such Party shall have no further liability under this Agreement with respect to such representation or warranty.

5. OTHER COVENANTS OF THE PARTIES

(1) Conduct of Business Prior to Closing

During the Interim Period, the Vendor shall do the following:

(a) Conduct Business in Ordinary Course—Except as otherwise contemplated or permitted by this Agreement, the Vendor shall conduct the Business in the ordinary and normal course and shall not, without the prior written consent of Purchaser, enter into any transaction which, if entered into before the date of this Agreement, would cause any representations or warranties of the Vendor contained in this Agreement to be incorrect or constitute a breach of any covenant or agreement of the Vendor contained in this Agreement. The Vendor shall use its best efforts to preserve intact the Business and the relationship existing between the customers of the Business and those of the Vendor that carry on the Business.

(b) Continue Insurance—The Vendor shall continue in force all insurance maintained by it in respect of the Business.

(c)   Perform Obligations—The Vendor shall comply with all applicable laws, regulations, by-laws and other governmental requirements of each jurisdiction in which the Business is carried on.

(d)   Material Changes—The Vendor shall not take any action which would result in any Material adverse change, which shall be deemed to include the circumstances specified in Subsection 4(1)(y), in or to the Purchased Assets or sell, transfer or dispose of any of the Purchased Assets, other than in the ordinary course of business.

(e)   Liens—The Vendor shall not suffer or permit any mortgages, pledges, hypothecs, security interests, deemed trusts, liens, charges, rights or claims of other Persons, or any other encumbrances whatsoever, to attach to or affect the Purchased Assets other than security interests in favour of the Vendor's Bank, all of which shall be discharged or waived in writing by the Vendor's Bank on or prior to the Closing.

(f)   Wage Increases, Hiring and Firing—The Vendor shall not make or commit to make any wage increases or grant any bonuses to any of the non-union Employees of the Business, nor employ any new Employees in the Business without the Purchaser's consent nor terminate the employment of any key Employees of the Business, including *and*, without the Purchaser's consent.

(2) Access for Investigation

The Vendor shall permit the Purchaser and its employees, agents, counsel and accountants or other representatives, between the date of this Agreement and the Closing Time, without interference to the ordinary conduct of the Business, to have access during normal business hours to the premises and to all the books, accounts, records and other data of the Business (including, without limitation, all corporate and accounting records of the Vendor relating exclusively to the Business) and to furnish to the Purchaser such financial and operating data and other information with respect to the Business, as the Purchaser shall from time to time reasonably request to enable confirmation of the matters warranted in Section 4(1). Specifically, within _____ Business Days of the execution of this Agreement by the Parties, the Vendor agrees to deliver to or make available for inspection by the Purchaser of the following: [*List specific documents and other due diligence materials to be disclosed, which may include copies of Contracts, Equipment Leases, Leases, Collective Agreements, Pension Plans, Benefit Plans, Licences, Insurance Policies, other Material plans and contracts.*]

(3) Delivery of Books and Records

At the Time of Closing, the Vendor shall deliver to the Purchaser the following documents: (i) lists of suppliers and customers of the Vendor which relate to the Business; (ii) employee records with respect to employees of Vendor hired by Purchaser; (iii) advertising, promotional and marketing materials which relate to the Business; and (iv) files relating to the Purchased Assets including, without limitation, the maintenance records for each item of equipment or machinery included in the Pur-chased Assets. The Purchaser agrees that it will preserve the documents, books and records so delivered to it for a period of six years from the Closing Date, or for such other period as is required by any applicable law, and will permit the Vendor or its authorized representatives reasonable access to those books and records in connection with the affairs of the Vendor relating to any tax matters, workers' compensation or litigation matters. The Vendor agrees that it will preserve the documents, books and records which are not delivered to the Purchaser for a period of six years from the Closing Date, or for such longer period as is required by applicable law, and will permit the Purchaser or its authorized representatives reasonable access to those books and records in connection with the affairs of the Purchaser relating to any tax, workers' compensation or litigation matters.

(4) Actions to Satisfy Closing Conditions

Each Party hereby agrees to take all such actions as are within its power to control, and to use its best efforts to cause other actions to be taken which are not within its power to control, so as to ensure compliance with any conditions set forth in Article 7 which are for the benefit of the other Party.

(5) Business Names

Immediately after the Closing Date, the Vendor shall change its corporate name and shall discontinue further use of the names "ABC Chemicals", "ABC Soaps", and "ABC Cleansers" and agrees not to use names similar to those names after the Closing Date. If requested by the Purchaser, the Vendor shall also take such action as may be necessary in order to assist the Purchaser or any of its affiliates to change their corporate names to names including any of the Vendor's former names.

(6) Employees [*Note: See alternative clauses for more extensive covenants concerning employees.*]

(a)   Offer to Employment—The Purchaser will offer employment, effective from the Closing Date, to all of the Vendor's employees who are active employees of the Business and all of the Vendor's employees who are employees of the Business on temporary leave of absence or layoff or disability (collectively the "Employees") on terms and conditions of employment including salary, incentive compensation, benefits, positions and responsibilities which are substantially similar and in any event no less favourable than those presently paid to the employees now engaged in the Business. The Purchaser shall recognize the service of the employees with the Vendor or its predecessors up to the Closing Date for all purposes as if such service had occurred with the Purchaser. The Purchaser acknowledges that it will be bound by the provisions of the Collective Agreements. The Vendor will co-operate with the Purchaser in giving notice to the Employees of the matters referred to in this Section 5(6) as is considered reasonable in the circumstances by the Purchaser.

(b)   Wages and Benefits—The Vendor shall be responsible for all wages, bonuses, earned vacations, sick leave, pensions, source deductions and other remuneration benefits for all the Employees accruing up to the Effective Date. Purchaser shall be responsible, conditional on Closing, for all such benefits of the Employees accruing on or after the Closing Date. All such benefits payable in the Interim Period shall be accounted for in the cash reconciliation under Section 3, and shall be for the account of the Vendor for Employees who do not accept the Purchaser's offer of employment and for the account of the Purchaser for Employees who accept the Purchaser's offer of employment.

(c)   Employees Refusing Offer—The Vendor shall be liable for the payment of all legal obligations relating to the termination of employment of any Employee who does not accept the Purchaser's offer of employment ("Refusing Employee"). The Vendor's liability shall extend to all amounts required either by statute or at common law to be paid to all Refusing Employees including pay in lieu of notice, termination pay, severance pay, vacation pay and all other outstanding amounts. The termination of any Refusing Employment shall be effective on the later of the day that he leaves his employment in the Interim Period or the Closing Date.

(d)   Employees Accepting Offer—The Purchaser shall be liable for the payment of all legal obligations relating to the termination of employment after the Closing Date of any Employee who accepts the Purchaser's offer of employment ("Accepting Employee"). The extent of the liability of the Purchaser with respect to the Accepting Employees shall be the same as that of the Vendor with respect to the Refusing Employees described in Subsection 5(6)(c).

(e) Employee Lists—Before and on the Closing Date the Vendor shall provide the Purchaser with an updated list containing the information set forth in Schedule "O".

(f) Deductions and Withholding—In the Interim Period, the Vendor will make all deductions required by law or by contract to be made from employee wages or salaries and will remit the amounts deducted and all related employer contributions required to the authorities or entities entitled to receive payment of such amounts.

(g) Accrued Vacation Pay Credits—The Vendor shall quantify the amount of accrued vacation pay due and owing to the Employees as of the Effective Date, and such amount shall be an adjustment to the Purchase Price to the Purchaser's credit.

(7) Pension and Benefit Plans

Immediately after the Closing, the Vendor shall take all steps necessary to wind up the Vendor's Pension Plan [in respect of the Employees] and to terminate the Employees' participation in the Benefit Plans.

[*Note: See alternative clauses for sample clauses concerning the transfer of pension plans and the transition of pension and benefit plans for employees of the Vendor to be employed by the Purchaser.*]

(8) Bulk Sales

If required by the Purchaser's bankers and/or other creditworthy financial resources prior to Closing, the Vendor shall comply with all bulk sales legislation in each jurisdiction in which the Purchased Assets are located in connection with the transactions contemplated under this Agreement; otherwise the Purchaser shall waive compliance with the provisions of the Bulk Sales Act (Ontario) or any other applicable bulk sales legislation in respect of the purchase and sale of the Purchased Assets, on the condition that the Vendor shall indemnify and save harmless the Purchaser as provided in Article 6.

(9) Removal of Purchased Assets

The Vendor shall permit access by the Purchaser following Closing to those locations not leased or assigned to the Purchaser to enable the Purchaser to remove Purchased Assets from such locations.

(10) Workers' Compensation

On or before Closing, the Vendor shall provide a clearance or purchase certificate or other similar documentary evidence from the worker's compensation authority in each jurisdiction where the Vendor carries on business certifying that there are no outstanding assessments, penalties, fines, levies, charges, surcharges or other amounts due or owing to those authorities. The Vendor shall be and remain responsible for any and all worker's compensation assessments, penalties, fines, levies, charges, surcharges or other amounts due or owing to those authorities. The Vendor shall be and remain responsible for any and all worker's compensation assessments, penalties, fines, levies, charges, surcharges or ' compensation or similar legislation in respect of any period prior to Closing.

(11) GST Election

The Vendor and the Purchaser shall elect jointly pursuant to the provisions of subsection 167(1) of the Excise Tax Act by completing at or prior to Closing all prescribed forms and related documents in such manner as is prescribed, so that for purposes of the Excise Tax Act, no GST is payable in respect of the purchase and sale of the Purchased Assets. The Purchaser covenants that, at the time of Closing, it will file with Revenue Canada, Customs and Excise, the joint election made under section 167 of the Excise Tax Act by registered mail, and will provide the Vendor with written confirmation of such filing.

(12) *Competition Act*/Investment Canada Act

[*Note: See alternative clauses for sample provisions concerning Investment Canada Act and the Competition Act. Consider, as well, all other necessary regulatory consents and approvals and provide details as to the responsibility for, the timing of and the costs involved in obtaining these consents or approvals.*]

(13) Confidentiality

The Purchaser shall keep confidential all confidential technology and any other confidential information (unless readily available from public or published information or sources or required to be disclosed by law) obtained from the Vendor. If this Agreement is terminated without completion of the transactions contemplated in this Agreement then, promptly after such termination, all documents, work papers and other written material obtained from the Vendor in connection with this Agreement shall be returned by the Purchaser to the Vendor.

[*Note: See alternative clauses for another example of a confidentiality provision.*]

(14) Consents Required in Contracts

The Purchaser shall be responsible for obtaining any consent to assignment which may be required for the assignment of any Contract, Lease or Equipment Lease which are included in the Assets as a result of the consummation of transactions contemplated by this Agreement. If the Purchaser is unable to obtain such consent, such Contract, Lease or Equipment Lease shall not be assigned and the Vendor shall, to the extent legally possible, hold its right, title and interest in, to and under such Contract, Lease or Equipment Lease in trust for the benefit of the Purchaser until such consent is obtained.

(15) Section 22 Election

The Purchaser and the Vendor agree to elect, in the prescribed manner and form and within the prescribed time to have section 22 of the Income Tax Act apply to the transfer of the accounts receivable comprised in the Assets and transferred under this Agreement. The parties shall file all necessary elections or filings under all corresponding provincial tax legislation to make the transfer of the accounts receivable transferred hereunder effective on the same basis as contemplated by section 22 of the Income Tax Act.

(16) Retail Sales Tax

The Vendor agrees to deliver to the Purchaser on the Closing Date a clearance certificate under section 6 of the Retail Sales Tax Act (Ontario) and similar clearance certificates, if available, from the retail sales tax authorities in all jurisdictions where the Business is carried on by the Vendor or the Purchased Assets are located. [*If applicable, the Purchaser may deliver to the Vendor the appropriate purchase exemption certificate or certificates, to exempt this transaction, in whole or in part, from the application of retail sales tax in any jurisdiction.*]

(17) Non-Competition

The Vendor covenants and agrees that it will not, from and after the Closing Date until the fifth anniversary of the Closing Date, carry on in Canada any business of a nature of or in competition with the Business. At Closing, the Vendor shall execute and deliver to the Purchaser the Non-Competition Agreement.

(18) Employment Agreement

The Vendor agrees to cause (*name of key employee*) to enter into an employment agreement with the Purchaser, to be entered into at Closing in the form attached as Schedule "U" (the "Employment Agreement").

[*Note: See alternative clauses for covenants concerning key customer visits before the Closing Date.*]

6. INDEMNIFICATION

(1) Indemnification by Vendor

(a)   If the transactions contemplated by this Agreement are consummated, the Vendor agrees to indemnify and hold the Purchaser harmless against and in respect of any loss, damage, claim, cost or expense whatsoever, including any and all incremental out-of-pocket costs, including, without limitation, all reasonable legal and accounting fees, which the Purchaser may incur, suffer or be required to pay, pursuant to any claim, demand, action, suit, litigation, charge, complaint, prosecution or other proceeding (collectively, a "Claim") that may be made or asserted against or affect the Purchaser, provided, however, that the subject matter of any such Claim relates to or arises out of or in connection with the following matters:

   (i)   any misrepresentation or breach of any warranty, agreement, covenant or obligation of the Vendor contained in this Agreement or in any agreement, schedule, certificate or other document required to be entered into or delivered by the Purchaser;

   (ii)   any bulk sales or similar legislation concerning creditors' rights;

   (iii) failure by the Vendor to comply with its agreements under Section 3(13);

   (iv)   any amount payable to or in respect of any Employee for which the Vendor is responsible under Section 5(6);

   [(v)   *any and all liability of any nature whatsoever under any Worker's Compensation or similar legislation or regulation in any jurisdiction for the period prior to the Effective Date, including any experience rating assessments, surcharges or levies based on or related to the Vendor's record or history of workplace injuries*];

   (vi)   the Excluded Assets or the Excluded Liabilities;

   [(vii) Environmental matters]

[*Note: List other specific matters for which Vendor will indemnify Purchaser.*]

(b) The obligation of the Vendor to indemnify the Purchaser as set forth in Paragraph 6(1)(a)(i) for any loss, damage, claim, cost or expense shall be subject to the limitation period referred to in Section 4(5) with respect to survival of representations and warranties. [*Note: List any other applicable limitation periods for other indemnities.*]

(2) Indemnification by Purchaser

(a) If the transactions contemplated by this Agreement are consummated, the Purchaser agrees to indemnify and hold the Vendor harmless against and in respect of any loss, damage, claim, cost or expense whatsoever, including any and all incremental out-of-pocket costs, including, without limitation, all reasonable legal and accounting fees, which the Vendor may incur, suffer or be required to pay, pursuant to any claim, demand, action, suit, litigation, charge, complaint, prosecution or other proceeding of any nature or kind whatsoever (collectively a "Claim") that may be made or asserted against or affect the Vendor, provided, however, that the subject matter of any such claim relates to or arises out of or in connection with the following matters:

    (i)   any misrepresentation or breach of any warranty, agreement, covenant or obligation of the Purchaser contained in this Agreement or in any agreement, schedule, certificate or other document required to be entered into or delivered by the Purchaser;

    (ii) the Purchaser's failure to fulfil the terms of any of the Customer Contracts, Equipment Leases or Leases which are assigned to the Purchaser and which the Purchaser has assumed pursuant to the Purchase Agreement;

    (iii) failure by the Purchaser to comply with its agreements under Section 3(13);

    (iv) any amount payable to or in respect of any Employee for which the Purchaser is responsible under Section 5(6);

    (v) the Purchased Assets or the Assumed Liabilities.

    (vi) failure by the Purchaser to file the election pursuant to section 167 of the *Excise Tax Act* in the manner and within the time limits prescribed under the *Excise Tax Act*.

[*Note: List other specific matters for which Purchaser will indemnify Vendor.*]

(b)   The obligation of the Purchaser to indemnify the Vendor as set forth in Paragraph 6(2)(a)(i) for any loss, damage, claim, cost or expense shall be subject to the limitation period referred to in Section 4(5) with respect to survival of representations and warranties. [*Note: List any other applicable limitation periods for other indemnities.*]

(3) Claims by Third Parties

(a)   For the purposes of this Section 6.3 "Third Party Claim" means any demand which has been made on, or communicated to, the Vendor or the Purchaser by or on behalf of any Person other than the persons mentioned above in this definition and which, if maintained or enforced, might reesult in a loss, liability or expense of the nature described in either Subsection 6(1)(a) or Subsection 6(2)(a).

(b)   Promptly upon receipt by either the Purchaser or the Vendor (the "Indemnitee") of notice of any Third Party Claim in respect of which the Indemnitee proposes to demand indemnification from the other party to this Agreement (the "Indemnitor", the Indemnitee shall forthwith give notice to that effect to the Indemnitor.

(c)   The Indemnitor shall have the right, exercisable by giving notice to the Indemnitee not later than 30 days after receipt of the notice described in Subsection 6(3)(b), to assume the control of the defence, compromise or settlement of the Third Party Claim, provided that:
   (i)   the Indemnitor shall first deliver to the Indemnitee its written consent to be joined as a party to any action or proceeding relating thereto; and,
   (ii)   Indemnitor shall at the Indemnitee's request furnish it with reasonable security against any costs or other liabilities to which it may be or become exposed by reason of such defence, compromise or settlement.

(d)   Upon the assumption of control by the Indemnitor as aforesaid, the Indemnitor shall, at its expense, diligently proceed with the defence, compromise or settlement of the Third Party Claim at the Indemni-tor's sole expense, including employment of counsel reasonably satisfactory to the Indemnitee, and in connection with such proceedings, the Indemnitee shall co-operate fully, but at the expense of the Indemnitor, to make available to the Indemnitor all pertinent information and witnesses under the Indemnitee's control and to make such assignments and take such other steps as in the opinion of counsel for the Indemnitor are necessary to enable the Indemnitor to conduct such defence, provided always that the Indemnitee shall be entitled to reasonable security from the Indemnitor for any expense, costs or other liabilities to which it may be or may become exposed by reason of such co-operation.

(e)   The final determination of any such Third Party Claim, including all related costs and expenses, will be binding and conclusive upon the Parties as to the validity or invalidity, as the case may be, of such Third Party Claim against the Indemnitor.

(f)   Should the Indemnitor fail to give notice to the Indemnitee as provided in Subsection 6(3)(b), the Indemnitee shall be entitled to make such settlement of the Third Party Claim as in its sole discretion may appear advisable, and such settlement or any other final determination of the Third Party Claim shall be binding upon the Indemnitor.

(4) Details of Claims

With respect to any claim provided for under Subsections 6(1)(a) and 6(2)(a), no ndemnity under this Agreement shall be sought unless written notice providing reasonable details o the reasons for which the indemnity is sought is provided to the Vendor or the Purchaser, as the case may be, before the expiration of the limitation dates provided for in Subsections 6(1)(b) and 6(2)(b), respectively, as applicable.

[Note: See alternative clauses for additional indemnification clauses concerning subroga-tion, limitation on recovery, indemnification sole remedy, tax adjustment and de minimis.]
[Note also that in some cases, the delivery of separate indemnity agreements at Closing may be provided for.]

(5) Goods and Services Tax Gross-up on Indemnification

Where an amount is payable by the Purchaser or Vendor as indemnification pursuant to the terms of this Agreement and the Excise Tax Act provides that GST is deemed to have been collected by the payee thereof, the amount so payable as determined without reference to this paragraph (the "Indemnification Amount") shall be increased by an amount equal to the rate of GST applied to the Indemnification Amount in accordance with the Excise Tax Act.

7. CONDITIONS PRECEDENT TO THE PERFORMANCE BY THE PURCHASER AND THE VENDOR OF THEIR OBLIGATIONS UNDER THIS AGREEMENT

(1) Purchaser's Conditions

The obligation of the Purchaser to complete the transactions contemplated by this Agreement shall be subject to the satisfaction of, or compliance with, at or before the Closing Time, each of the following conditions precedent (each of which is hereby acknowledged to be inserted for the exclusive benefit of the Purchaser and may be waived by it in whole or in part):

(a)　Truth and Accuracy of Representations of the Vendor at the Closing Time—All of the representations and warranties of the Vendor made in or under this Agreement, including, without limitation, the representations and warranties made by the Vendor and set forth in Section 4(1), shall be true and correct in all material respects as at the Closing Time and with the same effect as if made at and as of the Closing Time (except as such representations and warranties may be affected by the occurrence of events or transactions expressly contemplated and permitted by this Agreement) and the Purchaser shall have received a statutory declaration [*certificate*] from a senior officer of the Vendor confirming the truth and correctness in all material respects of the representations and warranties of the Vendor.

(b)　Performance of Obligations—The Vendor shall have performed or complied with, in all material respects, all their obligations, covenants and agreements under this Agreement.

(c)　Receipt of Closing Documentation—All instruments of conveyance and other documentation and assurances relating to the sale and purchase of the Purchased Assets including, without limitation, share certificates, assignments of the Contracts, the Leases, the Equipment Leases and the Licences (and consents to such assignments, where required), bills of sale, motor vehicle transfers and documentation, and all actions and proceedings taken on or prior to the Closing in connection with performance by the Vendor of their obligations under this Agreement shall be satisfactory to the Purchaser and their counsel, acting reasonably, and the Purchaser shall have received copies of all such documentation or other evidence as it may reasonably request in order to establish the consummation of the transactions contemplated under this Agreement and the taking of all corporate proceedings in connection under those transactions in compliance with this Subsection 7(1)(c), in form (as to certification and otherwise) and substance satisfactory to the Purchaser and its counsel.

(d) Closing Documentation—Without limiting the generality of Subsection 7(1)(c), the Purchaser shall have received at or before the Closing Time sufficient duly executed original copies of the following:

    (i) certified copy of a resolution of the shareholders of the Vendor approving this Agreement and the transactions contemplated under this Agreement;

    (ii) statutory declaration of a senior officer of the Vendor concerning residence of the Vendor, the matters referred to in Subsection 7(1)(a) and confirming that all conditions under this Agreement in favour of the Vendor have been either fulfilled or waived;

    (iii) certificate of incumbency of the Vendor;

    (iv) certificate of status of the Vendor;

    (v) bill of sale [*general conveyance*];

    (vi) General Assignment;

    (vii) Transfer/Deed of Land;

    (viii) Assignment of trade-marks [*assignments of patents and copyrights*];

    (ix) Non-Competition Agreement;

    (x) Employment Agreement;

    (xi) Statement of Adjustments;

    (xii) Undertaking to Readjust;

    (xiii) election under section 22 of the *Income Tax Act*;

    (xiv) election under subsection 167(1) of the *Excise Tax Act*;

    (xv) clearance certificate under section 6 of Retail Sales Tax Act (Ontario);

(e) Opinion of Counsel for Vendor—The Purchaser shall have received an opinion dated the Closing Date, in form and substance satisfactory to the Purchaser, from counsel for the Vendor, confirming the matters warranted in Subsections 4(1)(a), 4(1)(d), 4(1)(e) and 4(1)(g), which opinion may rely on opinions of counsel in other jurisdictions with respect to matters of law in those jurisdictions. In giving such opinion, counsel to the Vendor may rely on certificates of senior officers of the Vendor as to factual matters.

(f) Consents to Assignment—All consents or approvals from or notifications to any lessor or other third Person required under the terms of any of the Contracts, Equipment Leases, the Leases or the Licences with respect to their assignment to the Purchaser, or otherwise in connection with the consummation of the transactions contemplated under this Agreement, shall have been duly obtained or given, as the case may be, on or before the Closing Time.

(g)   Consents, Authorizations and Registrations—All consents, approvals, orders and authorizations of or from governmental or regulatory authorities required in connection with the completion of the transactions contemplated in this Agreement shall have been obtained on or prior to the Closing Time including:

[*Note: Describe particular consents or approvals required.*]

(h)   Planning Act—If the provisions of section 29 of the Planning Act (Ontario) apply to the Agreement, the provisions of that section shall have been complied with so that the conveyance of the Owned Property under this Agreement is effective to create in the Purchaser a freehold interest in the Owned Property;

(i)   Vendor's Security—The Vendor shall have delivered to the Purchaser the undertaking provided for in Subsection 4(1)(as).

(j)   Financing—The Purchaser shall have completed all necessary financing, to permit the Purchaser to complete the transactions contemplated under this Agreement, in accordance with the commitment from *XYZ* described in Subsection 4(2)(i).

(k)   Bulk Sales—If required by the Purchaser's bankers and/or other financial resources, the Vendor shall have complied with all bulk sales legislation in each jurisdiction in which the Purchased Assets are located in respect of the sale by the Vendor to the Purchaser of the Purchased Assets under this Agreement.

(l)   Certificate as to Status of Assets—A senior officer of the Vendor shall have executed and delivered to the Purchaser, in a form satisfactory to the Purchaser, a certificate stating that, as of the Closing Date, there has been no Material damage to or adverse change in the condition of the Purchased Assets.

(m)   No Actions Taken Restricting Sale—No action or proceeding in Canada by law or in equity shall be pending or threatened by any person, firm, corporation, government, governmental authority, regulatory body or agency to enjoin, restrict or prohibit the purchase and sale of the Purchased Assets contemplated under this Agreement.

(n)   Directors of Subco Inc.—There shall have been delivered to the Purchaser on or before the Closing Time, the resignations, effective as and from Closing, of all of the directors of Subco Inc., together with comprehensive releases from each such person of all their claims respectively, except for any claims for unpaid remuneration.

(o)   Employment Offers Accepted—The Purchaser shall be satisfied that senior employees of the Purchased Business _____ and _____, will accept the offer of employment by the Purchaser under Section 5(6).

(2) Vendor's Conditions

The obligations of the Vendor to complete the transactions contemplated by this Agreement shall be subject to the satisfaction of, or compliance with, at or before the Closing Time, each of the following conditions precedent (each of which is hereby acknowledged to be inserted for the exclusive benefit of the Vendor and may be waived by the Vendor in whole or in part):

(a)   Truth and Accuracy of Representations of the Purchaser at Closing Time—All of the representations and warranties of the Purchaser made in or under this Agreement, including, without limitation, the representations and warranties made by the Purchaser and set forth in Section 4(2) of this Agreement, shall be true and correct in all material respects as at the Closing Time and with the same effect as if made at and as of the Closing Time (except as such representations and warranties may be affected by the occurrence of events or transactions contemplated and permitted by this Agreement) and the Vendor shall have received a statutory declaration [*certificate*] from a senior officer of the Purchaser confirming the truth and correctness in all material respects of such representations and warranties of the Purchaser.

(b)   Performance of Agreements—The Purchaser shall have performed or complied with, in all respects, all their other obligations, covenants and agreements under this Agreement.

(c)   Closing Documents—The Vendor shall have received at or before the Closing Time sufficient duly executed original copies of the following:

   (i)   certified copy of a resolution of the board of directors of the Purchaser approving this Agreement and the transactions contemplated under this Agreement;

   (ii)   statutory declaration of a senior officer of the Vendor concerning residence of the Vendor, the matters referred to in Subsection 7(2)(a), its status for purposes of the Investment Canada Act and confirming that all conditions under this Agreement in favour of the Purchaser have been either fulfilled or waived;

   (iii) certificate of incumbency of the Purchaser;

   (iv)   certificate of status of the Purchaser;

   (v)   Assumption Agreement

   (vi)   Statement of Adjustments;

   (vii) Undertaking to Readjust;

   (viii) election under section 22 of the Income Tax Act;

   (ix)   election under subsection 167(1) of the Excise Tax Act.

(d)   Opinion of Counsel for Purchaser—The Vendor shall have received an opinion dated the Closing Date, in form and substance satisfactory to the Vendor, from counsel to the Purchaser confirming the matters warranted in Subsections 4(2)(a), 4(2)(b) and 4(2)(d). In giving such opinion, counsel to the Purchaser may rely on certificates of senior officers of the Purchaser as to factual matters and may rely on opinions of counsel in other jurisdictions with respect to matters of law in those jurisdictions.

(e)   No Actions Taken Restricting Sale—No action or proceeding in Canada by law or in equity shall be pending or threatened by any person, firm, corporation, government, governmental authority, regulatory body or agency to enjoin, restrict or prohibit the purchase and sale of the Purchased Assets contemplated under this Agreement.

(f)   Payment of Purchase Price—The Purchaser shall have tendered to the Vendor the Purchaser's Note and a certified cheque or bank draft for the balance of the Purchase Price.

(g)   Consents, Authorizations and Registrations—All consents, approvals, orders and authorizations of or from governmental or regulatory authorities required in connection with the completion of the transactions contemplated in this Agreement shall have been obtained on or prior to the Closing Time including:

[*Note: Describe particular consents or approvals required.*]

(h)   Release of Directors of Subco Inc.—Subco Inc. shall have executed and delivered to each of the directors of Subco Inc., comprehensive releases with respect to any claims by Subco Inc. against such directors.

[*Note: There may be a class of condition applicable to a transaction which is solely for the benefit of neither party and is therefore not waivable independently by any party. These conditions are "true conditions precedent", upon the fulfilment of which the transaction is dependent. Certain government approvals may fall into this category. In such cases, a separate section for true conditions precedent may be appropriate.*]

(3) Failure to Satisfy Conditions

If any condition set forth in Sections 7(1) or 7(2) is not satisfied on or before the Closing time, the Party entitled to the benefit of such condition (the "First Party") may terminate this Agreement by notice in writing to the other Party and in such event the First Party shall be released from all obligations under this Agreement, and unless the First Party can show that the condition or conditions which have not been satisfied and for which the First Party has terminated this Agreement are reasonably capable of being performed or caused to be performed by the other Party then the other Party shall also be released from all obligations under this Agreement, except that the First Party shall be entitled to waive compliance with any such conditions, obligations or covenants in whole or in part if it sees fit to do so without prejudice to any of its rights of termination in the event of non-performance of any other condition, obligation or covenant, or whole or in part.

(4) Destruction or Expropriation

Up to the Closing Time, all risk of loss or damage by fire or other cause or hazard to the Purchased Assets shall remain with the Vendor and the Vendor shall hold all insurance policies and any proceeds thereof in trust for the Vendor and the Purchaser. If, prior to the Closing Time, there occurs any Material destruction or damage by fire or other cause or hazard to any of the Purchased Assets, or if the Purchased Assets or any Material part of them are expropriated or forcefully taken by any governmental authority or if notice of intention to expropriate a Material part of the Purchased Assets has been filed in accordance with applicable legislation, then the Purchaser may, at its option;

(a)   terminate this Agreement by notice to the Vendor; or

(b)   elect to complete the purchase and sale of the Purchased Assets, in which event all insurance proceeds or expropriation proceeds, as the case may be, shall be assigned and/or paid by the Vendor to the Purchaser; or

(c)   elect to complete the purchase and sale subject to the Purchase Price being reduced to reflect such change or expropriation, such reduction to be based on the Book Value of the Assets.

8. CLOSING ARRANGEMENTS

(1) Time and Place of Closing

The completion of the transactions contemplated by this Agreement shall take place at the Closing Time on the Closing Date at the offices of _____ Ontario, or at such other place as may be agreed upon between the Parties.

(2) Closing Arrangements

At the Closing Time, upon fulfilment of all the conditions under this Agreement which have not been waived in writing by the Purchaser or the Vendor respectively:

(a)   Purchase and Sale of Purchased Assets—The Vendor shall sell and the Purchaser shall purchase the Purchased Assets and for the Purchase Price payable under this Agreement.

(b)   Delivery of Closing Documents—The Parties shall respectively deliver the Closing Documents.

(c)   Actual Possession—The Vendor shall deliver actual possession of the Purchased Assets to the Purchaser.

(d)   Payment of Purchase Price—On the fulfilment of the foregoing terms of this Article 8, the Purchaser shall pay and satisfy the Purchase Price as provided in Section 3.4.

(3) Tender

Any tender of documents or money hereunder may be made upon the Parties or their respective counsel and money may be tendered by official bank draft drawn upon a Canadian chartered bank or by negotiable cheque payable in Canadian funds and certified by a Canadian chartered bank or trust company.

9. NOTICES

Any notice, direction or other instrument required or permitted to be given by either party under this Agreement shall be in writing and shall be sufficiently given if delivered personally, sent by prepaid first class mail or transmitted by telecopier or other form of electronic communication during the transmission of which no indication of failure of receipt is communicated to the sender:

(a)   in the case of a notice to the Vendor at:

_____

_____

_____

_____

Attention: Chairman of the Board

Fax No. (   )

(b)   in the case of a notice to the Purchaser at:

_____

_____

_____

_____

Attention: President

Fax No. (   )

Any such notice, direction or other instrument, if delivered personally, shall be deemed to have been given and received on the date on which it was received at such address, or, if sent by mail, shall be deemed to have been given and received on the date which is five days after which it was mailed, provided that if either such day is not a Business Day, then the notice shall be deemed to have been given and received on the Business Day next following such day. Any notice transmitted by telecopier or other form of electronic communication shall be deemed to have been given and received on the date of its transmission provided that if such day is not a Business Day or if it is received after the end of normal business hours on the date of its transmission at the place of receipt, then it shall be deemed to have been given and received at the opening of business in the office of the recipient on the first Business Day next following the transmission thereof. If normal mail service, telex, telecopier or other form of electronic communication is interrupted by strike, slowdown, *force majeure* or other cause, a notice, direction or other instrument sent by the impaired means of communication will not be deemed to be received until actually received, and the party sending the notice shall utilize any other such service which has not been so interrupted to deliver such notice.

10. GENERAL

(1) Expenses

All costs and expenses (including, without limitation, the fees and disbursements of legal counsel) incurred in connection with this Agreement and the transaction contemplated under this Agreement shall be paid by the Party incurring such expenses.

(2) Time

Time shall be of the essence of this Agreement.

(3) Assignment/Successors and Assigns

Neither this Agreement nor any rights or obligations under this Agreement shall be assignable by either Party without the prior written consent of the other Party. Subject to that condition, this Agreement shall enure to the benefit of and be binding upon the Parties and their respective heirs, executors, administrators, successors (including any successor by reason of amalgamation of any Party) and permitted assigns.

(4) Further Assurances

Each Party agrees that upon the written request of any other Party, it will do all such acts and execute all such further documents, conveyances, deeds, assignments, transfers and the like, and will cause the doing of all such acts and will cause the execution of all such further documents as are within its power to cause the doing or execution of, as the other Party may from time to time reasonably request be done and/or executed as may be required to consummate the transactions contemplated under this Agreement or as may be necessary or desirable to effect the purpose of this Agreement or any document, agreement or instrument delivered under this Agreement and to carry out their provisions or to better or more properly or fully evidence or give effect to the transactions contemplated under this Agreement, whether before or after the Closing.

(5) Public Notices

All notices to third parties and all other publicity concerning the transactions contemplated by this Agreement shall be jointly planned and coordinated by the Vendor and the Purchaser and no Party shall act unilater-ally in this regard without the prior approval of the other Party (such approval not to be unreasonably withheld), except where required to do so by law or by the applicable regulations or policies of any provincial or Canadian or other regulatory agency of competent jurisdiction or any stock exchange.

(6) Counterparts

This Agreement may be executed by the Parties in separate counterparts each of which when so executed and delivered shall be an original, and all such counterparts shall together constitute one and the same instrument.

IN WITNESS WHEREOF the Parties have duly executed this Agreement under authority of their respective Boards of Directors.

VENDOR INC.

Per: _____ c/s

PURCHASER LTD.

Per: _____ c/s

9F33
Short Form of Asset Purchase Agreement

[See Paras. 9.470 and 9.470–9.610 generally]

B E T W E E N:

PURCHASER INC., a corporation incorporated under the laws of the Province of Ontario

(hereinafter called "Purchaser")

OF THE FIRST PART

- and -

VENDOR INC., a corporation incorporated pursuant to the laws of Canada

(hereinafter called "Vendor")

OF THE SECOND PART

The Purchaser agrees to purchase from the Vendor the assets as hereinafter described on the following terms and conditions:

1. Purchased Assets

The assets to be sold or assigned to the Purchaser include:

(a)   all assets used by the Vendor in its ABC Chemical division (the "Division");

(b)   all equipment owned or leased by the Vendor for the Division including vehicles and the office equipment located at 1 White Street, Toronto and at the Hamilton business office at 2 Hughson Street South, Hamilton;

(c)   all inventories used in connection with the Division, including office supplies and training supplies;

(d)   the lease of 2 Hughson Street South, Hamilton, being the business office occupied by the Vendor as tenant;

(e)   the Vendor's rights in all contracts dealing with the Division, including contracts of employment for persons engaged in work for the Division. The Vendor undertakes to provide to the Purchaser a list of all such contracts and to make available to the Purchaser copies of such contracts; and

(f)   all intellectual property owned or used by the Vendor in connection with the Division, including but not limited to logos, trade-marks, trade-names and the goodwill associated with the name "ABC Chemicals".

2. Excluded Assets

Excluded from this sale are the following assets of the Vendor:

(a)   the equipment owned or leased by the Vendor to operate its soap business at 4 Brown Street, Toronto, and other rights granted to the Vendor by its landlord with respect to use and occupation of the said premises; and

(b)   any and all receivables owed to the Vendor, including without limiting the generality of the foregoing, accounts receivable owing to the Vendor from 123456 Ontario Limited.

3. Purchase Price

The price for the assets shall be _____ dollars ($_____). $_____ shall be paid upon execution of this agreement and the balance on closing on _____, 19_____.

4. Liabilities

The Vendor shall be responsible for all expenses and liabilities associated with the running of the Division up to the closing date. Without limiting the generality of the foregoing, the Vendor shall remain liable for all wages of employees of the Division, including statutory vacation pay and all monies due to players under contract up to the closing date. Thereafter the Purchaser shall be responsible for all costs involved in the operation of the Division, with the exception of any deferred salary payments owed by the

Vendor to employees prior to the closing date, and any loans made by the Vendor to employees prior to the closing date, both of which shall remain the sole liability of the Vendor.

5. Employees

On or before closing, the Purchaser will:

(a)   offer to employ the employees of the Vendor engaged in services for the Division, whether or not such persons are under contract, on substantially the same terms and conditions as they presently enjoy (excepting employee loans); and

(b)   indemnify the Vendor with respect to any liability associated with the employment of such persons as a result of this transaction.

The Vendor will remain liable for such employees until the closing date. Thereafter, the Vendor shall be solely liable only with respect to any loans made by the Vendor to these employees, as such loans shall not be assumed by the Purchaser. The Vendor shall supply to the Purchaser a list of names of all employees engaged in services for the Division, setting out therein their terms of employment and the length of time each employee has been employed by the Vendor.

6. Conditions Precedent to Closing

The closing of this transaction is subject to the following conditions precedent:

(a)   the Board of Directors of the Vendor approving the transfer of the Division to the Purchaser from the Vendor;

(b)   the Vendor providing a Court order exempting this transaction for the Bulk Sales Act;

(c)   Jane Doe accepting employment to operate the Division; and

(d)   the Purchaser obtaining a loan of $_____ from _____ Bank.

7. Closing

Closing shall occur on _____, 19_____ or another date mutually satisfactory to both Purchaser and Vendor after the fulfilment of all of the aforesaid conditions precedent, which date shall be no more than 10 days after the fulfilment of the last of the aforesaid conditions precedent. On closing, the Vendor will provide all bills of sale and other documents, to transfer to you free and clear title to the assets owned by the Vendor.

The Vendor will also provide assignments to the Purchaser of all leases of equipment and realty, to the extent the same are assignable, and use its best efforts to obtain consents to such assignments from the third parties thereto.

8. Access to Records and Confidentiality

After the signing of this agreement, the Vendor shall afford the Purchaser and the Purchaser's professional advisers, access to the books and records of the Vendor related to the Division. Each of the Vendor and the Purchaser, and our respective servants and professional advisers, are to keep confidential the terms of this agreement, and the books and records of the Vendor. This agreement of confidentiality shall remain binding on the aforesaid parties, whether or not this transaction is consummated. Each party shall be responsible for its own professional fees and other expenses arising in connection with this letter of intent, any approvals, consents or investigations in connection herewith, and the negotiation and completion of this transaction.

9. Termination of this Agreement

In addition, this agreement will be at an end:

(a)   if the Purchaser has not obtained the funding from _____ Bank on or before _____, 19_____; or

(b)   if all of the other conditions precedent listed in paragraph 6 are not completed on or before _____, 19_____.

In either event:

(i)   the deposit of _____ dollars ($_____) shall be returned to the Purchaser;

(ii)   the Vendor shall be at liberty to seek another purchaser for the Division; and

(iii) the confidentiality obligations set out in paragraph 8 hereof shall continue to be binding on all parties listed therein.

IN WITNESS WHEREOF the parties hereto have signed this agreement this _____ day of _____, 19_____.

PURCHASER INC.

per:_____

VENDOR INC.

per: _____

9F34
CONFIDENTIALITY — SOLICITOR-CLIENT PRIVILEGE CLAUSE

[See Para. 9.364]

It is understood and agreed that, we as environmental consultants, are being retained to perform the above-noted work to provide your general legal counsel, and your special environmental legal counsel, (collectively "Counsel") with the necessary professional/technical assistance so that Counsel can provide you with legal advice respecting compliance with all applicable laws and regulations and possible litigation or regulatory proceedings respecting the present and past use and development of the site. We will treat as confidential and will not disclose or communicate to anyone other than you or Counsel, either orally or in writing, any information developed or obtained during the performance of the work hereunder without the prior written consent of you or Counsel. All such information will remain your exclusive property and be held in trust and confidence and used only as may be required for the purposes of our work. All information, including copies thereof, will be delivered up to Counsel or you on request. We will mark all our written materials *"Privileged and Confidential — Prepared for Legal Counsel"* and keep the same in separate files also marked *"Privileged and Confidential — Prepared for Legal Counsel"*. All written communications will be sent to Counsel and as Counsel may direct. All draft or final documents and reports will be prepared only after discussing the same with Counsel in advance.

9F35
ALTERNATIVE CLAUSES — ENVIRONMENTAL MATTERS

9F35:1
SALE OF PROPERTY
ON AN "AS IS" BASIS

Broad General Provisions

(1) It is understood and agreed that the property is being sold to the Purchaser "as is". The Purchaser acknowledges that it has inspected the property and conducted an independent investigation of current and past uses of the property; and that the Purchaser has not relied on any representations by the Vendor concerning any condition of the property, environmental or otherwise.

(2) The Purchaser shall from and after the closing date assume any and all environmental liabilities relating to the property, including but not limited to any liability for clean-up of any hazardous substances on or under the property. The Purchaser shall indemnify and save harmless the Vendor from and against any claims, demands, liabilities, losses, damages and expenses suffered by the Vendor arising out of or in connection with any and all environmental liabilities relating to the property.

Broad Specific Provisions

The Purchaser acknowledges that the property has been used as a plant for the manufacture and storage of X and that such use may have resulted in the existence or leakage of toxic, hazardous, dangerous or potentially dangerous substances or conditions into the soil or the structures located on the property. The Vendor makes no representations or warranties whatsoever regarding the fitness of the property for any particular use or regarding the presence or absence on the property or any surrounding or neighbouring lands of or the leakage or emission from or onto the property of any toxic, hazardous, dangerous, or potentially dangerous substance or condition, including, without limitation any urea formaldehyde foam type insulation, asbestos, PCB's, lead, radioactive materials, or gasoline. The Purchaser will satisfy itself as to the condition of the property and the fitness for its intended use. If the Purchaser does not elect to terminate the agreement during the inspection period provided for herein, the Purchaser shall be deemed to have accepted the condition of the property and the existence of any toxic, hazardous, dangerous, or potentially dangerous substances or conditions thereon or the leakage or emission thereof from or onto the property, and will be solely responsible for any work desirable or necessary or ordered by reason thereof, and all liabilities, claims, demands, and obligations arising therefrom of any such substances from the property. The Purchaser shall indemnify and hold harmless the Vendor from and against any claims, demands, liabilities, losses, damages and expenses suffered by the Vendor arising out of or in connection with any and all such environmental liabilities relating to the property. If the Purchaser elected to terminate the agreement during the approval period described in section X above, the Vendor's obligations under the agreement shall be at an end and the Purchaser shall not be entitled to make any claim for damages arising out of any breach of any warranty contained herein or for any costs or expenses incurred by it in connection with the identification of the property, the entering into of the agreement or in connection with any inspections or investigations carried out by the Purchaser in connection with the property.

9F35:2
ENVIRONMENTAL ACCESS AND TESTING

GENERAL

The Vendor shall permit the Purchaser and its authorized representatives reasonable access to the property for the purpose of making soils, ground-water, environmental or other tests, measurements or surveys in, on or below the property provided that the Purchaser shall do so at its own expense and at its own risk and shall not interfere with the operations of the Vendor at the property and shall return the property to the state in which it was before the commencement of such action. No action taken by the Purchaser hereunder shall constitute a trespass or a taking of possession.

DETAILED

(a) Access—The Vendor shall forthwith make available to the Purchaser and its authorized representatives all title documents, abstracts of title, deeds, surveys, leases, . . . and the Vendor shall, if reasonably requested, provide copies, at the cost of the Purchaser, of the following records maintained in connection with the purchased business: . . . information relating to any environmental matters affecting the property or assets   or their use including permits, licences or approvals, and results of any tests or surveys. The Vendor shall give the Purchaser and its authorized representatives every reasonable opportunity to have access to and to inspect the property and assets. The exercise of any rights of access or inspection by or on behalf of the Purchaser under this section shall not affect or mitigate the covenants, representations and warranties of the Vendor hereunder which shall continue in full force and effect.

(b) Authorization—The Vendor hereby authorizes and directs all municipal, provincial and federal governments, boards, agencies, or departments having jurisdiction to release any and all information in their possession respecting the property to the Purchaser, and further hereby authorizes each of them to carry out inspections of the property upon the request of the Purchaser. The Vendor agrees to execute any specific authorization pursuant to this paragraph within two (2) days of being requested to do so by the Purchaser.

(c) Objections—The Purchaser shall have X days from the date hereof to investigate the title of the lands at its own expense and to satisfy itself that there are no outstanding municipal work orders, deficiency notices or adverse environmental conditions affecting the property or assets and that the present use of the lands may be lawfully continued, and the Purchaser must within the time deliver to the Vendor or its counsel any objection that the Purchaser may have to such title or condition.

(d) Confidentiality—Both prior to the closing date and, if the sale and purchase of the assets hereunder fails to occur for whatever reason, thereafter the Purchaser shall not disclose to anyone or use for its own or for any purpose other than the purpose contemplated by this agreement any information concerning the Vendor, the property or the assets obtained by the Purchaser pursuant hereto, and the Purchaser shall keep all such information in the strictest confidence and, if the sale and purchase of the assets hereunder fails to occur for whatever reason, shall return all documents, records and all other information or data relating to the purchased business which the Purchaser obtained pursuant hereto, including the results of any soils, groundwater or environmental tests, surveys or measurements of the property or assets.

9F35:3
ENVIRONMENTAL AUDIT AND
CLEAN-UP—GENERAL

Prior to the closing, the Vendor shall provide the Purchaser with access, during reasonable business hours and on reasonable prior notice, to the purchased real estate for the purpose of conducting an environmental assessment of the purchased real estate and all permits related thereto, provided that such assessment is conducted after prior arrangement with the Vendor and in a manner which will not interfere with the Vendor's operations. Such environmental assessment shall be at the Purchaser's sole expense.

In the event that the environmental assessment conducted by the Purchaser pursuant to this section indicates that all the requirements of Environmental law (as hereinafter defined) are not being met or the previous and/or on-going release of hazardous substances at or under the site (hereinafter "Adverse Environmental Conditions"), then the Vendor and the Purchaser shall proceed under the terms of (a) or (b) below:

(a)   if the parties agree upon the nature and extent of the remediation of the Adverse Environmental Conditions, the Vendor may elect to commence, and subsequently continue, the remediation measures, in which event the closing shall take place when all conditions precedent are satisfied, with such remediation to be completed as soon as practicable after the closing; or

(b)   if the parties hereto are unable to agree upon the nature and extent of such remedial measures or if the Vendor shall elect not to commence agreed-upon remediation actions, the Purchaser may terminate this agreement without liability to the Vendor, or complete the transaction contemplated by this agreement and accept the property and assets with knowledge of such conditions.

"Environmental Laws" means the common law and all applicable federal, provincial, local, municipal or other applicable laws, statutes, ordinances, by-laws, regulations, orders, decisions, directives, permits, licences, certificates, approvals, authorizations, or the like relating to the environment or occupational health and safety or transportation matters.

9F35:4
ENVIRONMENTAL AUDIT AND
CLEAN-UP—EXTENSIVE DETAILED

1. Environmental Audit

(a) Vendor's Consultant—The Vendor will undertake at its cost an environmental audit (the "Audit") of the property by an independent consultant (the "Vendor's Consultant") to develop an estimate of material adverse environment conditions, if any, affecting the soil and ground water on the property; the work required to remedy any such adverse conditions (the "Remedial Work); and the Vendor's estimate of the costs of the remedial work (the "Estimated Costs"). The Vendor shall furnish to the Purchaser a draft copy of the audit; the Remedial Work, and the Estimated Costs forthwith after each becomes available. Prior to receipt, the Purchaser shall execute and deliver to the Vendor a confidentiality agreement with regard thereto in the form attached.

(b) Agreement on Audit, Remedial Work and Estimated Costs—The Vendor and Purchaser shall each review the Audit, the Remedial Work and the Estimated Costs, forthwith after these become available and confer with each other concerning proposed changes in any of the foregoing. The Vendor and Purchaser shall use their best efforts to reach an agreement on any changes in the Audit, the Remedial Work and Estimated Costs not later than X days after receipt by the Purchaser of drafts of such items.

(c) Arbitration—If the Vendor and Purchaser cannot agree within the time specified in section 1.1(b) on the Audit, the Remedial Work or the Estimated Costs, the matter shall be immediately submitted to an independent environmental consultant mutually acceptable to the Vendor and Purchaser (the "Independent Consultant"), with instructions to resolve such dispute within thirty (30) days. The cost of the Independent Consultant shall be shared equally by the Vendor and Purchaser.

(d) Extension of Closing Date—If the Audit, the Remedial Work and the Estimated Costs are not determined within X days from the date of this agreement, then either the Vendor or the Purchaser may postpone the closing date in order that they may be determined.

2. Vendor's Performance of the Remedial Work.

Provided the agreement has not been terminated in accordance with section 1.4(b) or 1.4(c), the Vendor shall proceed, at its cost, subject to reimbursement by the Purchaser as provided in section 1.3, to perform, or cause to be performed, the Remedial Work. To the extent the Remedial Work must be performed after the closing, the Purchaser shall grant the Vendor and its contractors and consultants access to the property without cost in order to perform such work. The Vendor shall use reasonable efforts to perform the Remedial Work so as not to interfere with the Purchaser's activities on the property.

3. Sharing of Costs

(a)   Vendor's and Purchaser's Share of Costs—Provided that the Vendor has provided the Purchaser with the Audit, the Remedial Work and the Estimated Costs as provided in section 1.1(a), and provided that the agreement has not been terminated in accordance with section 1.4(b) or 1.4(c), then the Vendor shall invoice the Purchaser for X% of the costs of the Remedial Work that it actually incurs from time to time (the "Actual Costs") in excess of $X and the Vendor shall be responsible for the remaining percentage of the actual costs. Unless either party has elected to assume the other party's percentage of the Actual Costs in excess of the maximum as provided in section 1.4(b), then the Vendor and Purchaser shall share the Actual Costs above the maximum in accordance with their respecting percentages. The Purchaser shall reimburse the Vendor for such amounts owed under this section 1.3(a) within X days after receipt of the Vendor's invoice.

(b)   Purchaser's Letter of Credit—As a condition of closing, the Purchaser shall deposit with the Vendor a letter of credit ("Letter of Credit") in the form attached for an amount equal to the percentage of the Estimated Costs in excess of $X for which the Purchaser is responsible as security for the Purchaser's obligations under section 1.3(a). If at any time the letter of credit shall prove insufficient to meet the Purchaser's share of the Actual Costs, the Purchaser shall within X days after written notice increase the letter of credit accordingly.

4. Right to Terminate

(a) Mutual Right to Terminate—If the Estimated Costs exceed $X (the "Maximum"), then either party may terminate this agreement by sending written notice to the other party (a "Notice of Termination"), within X days after final determination of the Estimated Costs.

(b) Right to Void Termination—Within X days after receipt of a Notice of Termination, the receiving party may void the Notice of Termination by advising the sending party in writing that it will assume that party's percentage (as defined in section 1.3(a)) of the Actual Costs in excess of the maximum in which case the agreement shall remain in effect. If the receiving party does not void the Notice of Termination within such period, this agreement shall be terminated.

(c) Purchaser's Right to Terminate—Notwithstanding anything to the contrary in section 1.3(a) or 1.4(b), the Purchaser shall have the unilateral right to terminate the agreement upon written notice to the Vendor within X days after the Purchaser's Receipt of the Estimated Costs, if the Estimated Costs exceed $X.

(d) Effect of Termination—If this agreement is terminated under section 1.4(b) or 1.4(c), the deposit shall be returned to the Purchaser without further obligation of any party hereto, except as expressly reserved in this agreement.

5. Completion of Remedial Work

The Remedial Work shall be deemed to be completed only upon receipt by both the Vendor and the Purchaser of a report from the Vendor's Consultant outlining the Remedial Work that was to be done; confirming the completion of such work; and stating that the property is appropriate for the Purchaser's intended use; and a letter from the Ministry of Environment and Energy addressed to the Vendor stating that based upon the Vendor's Consultant's report, the property is appropriate for the Purchaser's intended use.

9F35:5
REPRESENTATIONS AND WARRANTIES—BROAD GENERAL

Except as disclosed in Schedule _____ there are no facts, circumstances, or conditions that directly or indirectly relate to the Purchased Assets or the past or present conduct of the Business with respect to environmental, health or safety matters that have existed or now exist and already have had or may have a material adverse effect on the operation of the Business or use of the Purchased Assets or that may give rise to any significant liability on the Purchaser concerning the protection, preservation or remediation of the natural environment, whether air, land, surface water or groundwater.

9F35:6
REPRESENTATIONS AND WARRANTIES—EXTENSIVE DETAILED

Environmental Schedule

Definitions

For the purpose of this Schedule:

"Governmental Authority" means any federal, provincial, regional, municipal, local or other political subdivision or agency thereof and any entity or person exercising executive, legislative, judicial, regulatory or administrative functions of, or pertaining to, government;

"Hazardous Substance" means any substance or material that is on the date hereof prohibited, controlled or regulated by any Governmental Authority including, without limitation, any contaminant, pollutant, dangerous substance, toxic substance, designated substance, controlled product, hazardous waste, subject waste, hazardous material, dangerous good or petroleum, its derivatives, by-products or other hydrocarbons, all as defined in or pursuant to any Laws, Regulations, or Orders;

"Laws" means all applicable laws, statutes, or ordinances of any Governmental Authority in effect on the date hereof, relating to environmental, occupational health and safety or transportation matters;

"Notice" means any citation, Order, claim, litigation, investigation, proceeding, judgment, letter or other communication, written or oral, actual or threatened, from any person, including any Governmental Authority;

"Orders" means all applicable orders, decisions, directives, directions or the like rendered by any Governmental Authority as in effect on the date hereof;

"Permits" means all permits, licences, certificates, approvals, authorizations, registrations or the like issued pursuant to any Laws or Regulations by any Governmental Authority;

"Regulations" means all rules, regulations, policies, guidelines or the like as in effect on the date hereof promulgated under or pursuant to any Laws;

"Release" includes release, discharge, add, deposit, emit, spill, leak, pump, pour, empty, inject, escape, leach, migrate, disperse, dispose or dump;

"Vendor's knowledge" means any information, fact or matter known to any of _____ relating to the business of the Vendor, or which with reasonable diligence would reasonably be expected to be within the knowledge of such persons given their role or function.

Representations and Warranties

With respect to environmental and occupational health and safety matters, the Vendor hereby represents and warrants to the Purchaser that, except as disclosed in the Appendix hereto and, without limiting the generality of the representations and warranties of Section _____ of the asset purchase agreement to be entered into and completed between _____ (the "Vendor") and _____ (the "Purchaser"):

Hazardous Substances

(1)   The Vendor has not used the business facility, or property, or permitted them to be used, to generate, manufacture, refine, treat, transport, store, handle, dispose, transfer, produce or process Hazardous Substances, except in substantial compliance with all Laws, Regulations, Orders and Permits. There are no Hazardous Substances stored or disposed of in or on or below any of the Vendor's business facility or property except as listed in the Appendix hereto which also describes any designated substance control programs in effect in relation thereto.

Release of Hazardous Substances

(2)   The Vendor has not caused or permitted, nor has the Vendor any knowledge of, the Release of any Hazardous Substances on or offsite of the Vendor's business facility or property, or, of any Release from a facility or property owned or operated by third parties, including previous owners, but with respect to which the Vendor is alleged to or may have liability.

Offences

(3)   The Appendix hereto lists and describes any prosecutions of the Vendor for an offence for non-compliance with any Laws, Regulations, or Orders and any convictions, settlements or other disposition of such prosecutions short of conviction.

Orders

(4)   The Appendix hereto lists and describes any Orders issued with respect to the environmental and occupational health and safety matters relating to the business of the Vendor within the last five years and all Orders that are still in full force and effect on the date hereof. The Vendor has received no written Notice, nor is it aware of any facts which could give rise to any Notice that any such Orders will be issued against the Vendor in the near future.

Reporting

(5)   To the best of the Vendor's knowledge, the Vendor has not defaulted in reporting to the proper Governmental Authority on the happening of an occurrence which it is or was required by Law, Regulation, or Order to do so relating to environmental or occupational health and safety matters or environmental conditions affecting the business of the Vendor. The Vendor has disclosed all such reporting to the Purchaser occurring during the last three years and provided details thereof to the Purchaser.

Disposal Sites

(6)   The Vendor has received no written Notice, nor is it aware of any facts which could give rise to any Notice, that the Vendor is a party potentially responsible for a cleanup site or corrective action under any Law, Regulation, or Order. The Vendor has not received any written request for information in connection with any inquiry by any Governmental Authority concerning disposal sites or other environmental matters. The Ap-pendix hereto identifies all locations where Hazardous Substances used in whole or in part previously or at present by the business of the Vendor are being stored or disposed of other than the business facility or property of the Vendor.

Permits

(7)   The Appendix hereto lists all the Permits issued with respect to the environmental and occupational health and safety matters relating to the business of the Vendor, which Permits are valid and subsisting and in good standing and are all the Permits necessary or required to enable the Vendor's business to be carried as now conducted and none of the same contains or is subject to any term, provision, condition or limitation which has or may have an adverse effect on the operation of the business.

Documents, Records and Audits

(8)
(i)   The Vendor has maintained all documents and records relating to environmental and occupational health and safety matters substantially in the manner and for the time periods required by any Laws, Regulations or Orders.

(ii)   The Vendor has never had conducted an audit relating to environmental or occupational health and safety matters. For the purposes of this section, such audit shall mean any inspection, investigation, assessment, study or test performed at the request of or on behalf of a Governmental Authority, including, without limitation, a member of a joint health and safety committee, but does not include normal or routine inspections, assessments, studies or tests which do not relate to a threatened or pending charge, Order, revocation of any permit or any work stoppage issues.

Adverse Environmental Conditions

(9)   To the best of the Vendor's knowledge, there are no conditions that, directly or indirectly, relate to environmental matters and may adversely affect the business of the Vendor or the use thereof (whether on, above or below the lands or any structures, building or facilities, now or formerly owned, operated or used by the Vendor, or by adjoining properties or businesses) including, without limitation, being located within an environmentally sensitive area as determined by any Governmental Authority, the condition of the soil or groundwater in the area, the use of urea formaldehyde foam insulation, asbestos fireproofing or insulation, PCBs, radio-active substances or underground storage tanks.

Adverse Occupational Health and Safety Occurrences

(10)   There have been no occupational health or safety occurrences affecting the business of the Vendor of a nature or type, including without limitation the presence of any industrial disease or any long term occupational illness in the workplace or among any of the employees or former employees which could or did result in an action or claim against the vendor by any of the employees, former employees or their respective dependents, heirs or legal personal representatives or under any applicable insurance programs, workers' compensation Laws or other Laws, Regulations or Orders except as listed and described in the Appendix hereto and, without limiting the generality of the foregoing, any issues discussed at or arising out of meetings of the Joint Health and Safety Committee have been reviewed and completed to the satisfaction of the committee as properly recorded in its minutes.

Due Diligence/Compliance Programs

(11)   The Vendor has provided to the Purchaser description of and all appropriate information available concerning the system(s), program(s), policies and procedures established and maintained concering the assurance of, and monitoring compliance with, all legal requirements regarding environmental and occupational health and safety matters.

9F35:7
VENDOR'S CONTINUING RESPONSIBILITIES AND INDEMNIFICATION

Vendor's Continuing Responsibility for Environmental Matters

(a)   After the closing, the Vendor covenants at its sole cost and expense, to remove or take remedial action with regard to any materials released to the environment at, on or near the property prior to the closing for which any removal or remedial action is required pursuant to law, regulation, order or governmental action, provided that no such removal or remedial action shall be taken except after reasonable   advance written notice to the Purchaser; any such removal or remedial action shall be   undertaken in a manner so as to minimize any impact on the business conducted at the property.

(b)   The Vendor shall at all times retain any and all liabilities arising from the handling, treatment, storage, transportation or disposal of environmental contaminants by the Vendor or by any of the Vendor's contractors.

Vendor's Indemnification

The Vendor shall indemnify and save harmless the Purchaser from and against any and all liabilities, losses, claims, damages (including, within limitation, lost profits, consequential damages, interest, penalties, fines and monetary sanctions), and costs (hereinafter "Loss"), and lawyers', on a solicitor and his own client basis, and environmental consultants' fees and expenses, court costs and all other out-of-pocket expenses (the "Expense") incurred or suffered by the Purchaser by reason of, resulting from, in connection with, or arising in any manner from the breach of any warranty or covenant or the inaccuracy of any representation of the Vendor contained or referred to in this agreement.

9F35:8
LIMITATIONS ON VENDOR'S ENVIRONMENTAL OBLIGATIONS

The representations and warranties of the Vendor are subject to the following limitations:

(a) Exclusive Benefit of Purchaser—The Vendor's representations and warranties are for the exclusive benefit of the Purchaser and shall not be for the benefit of any other person or entity. Any substantial change in use as proposed by the Purchaser or redevelopment of the property shall terminate the Vendor's liability to the Purchaser.

(b) Knowledge of Purchaser—The Vendor shall have no liability to the Purchaser for the falsity of any representation or the breach of any warranty to the extent that the Purchaser, or any employee, contractor or agent of the Purchaser (the "Purchaser's Agent"), had knowledge of the falsity of such representation or of the breach of such warranty when made; or fails to give written notice to the Vendor of the breach as soon as the Purchaser or the Purchaser's Agent acquires such knowledge.

(c) Expiration Period of Representations and Warranties—The Vendor's representations and warranties under section _____ shall survive for X year(s) after closing.

(d) Limitation on Damages—In no event shall the Vendor be liable under section _____ for incidental, special, exemplary or consequential damages including, but not limited to, loss of profits or revenue, interference with business operations; loss of tenants; lenders; investors or buyers; diminution in value of the property; or inability to use the property.

[(e) *Knowledge of Vendor—Any representations or warranties made as to "the knowledge of the Vendor" or to the "best of the Vendor's knowledge" or words of like import shall be deemed to be breached only if the most senior management official assigned full time to the Vendor's facility at the property at the date of this agreement had actual knowledge of the falsity of such representation or of the breach of such warranty.*]

9F36

ALTERNATIVE CLAUSES: REPRESENTATIONS AND WARRANTIES FOR PENSION AND BENEFIT PLANS

Pension Plan -

(a) The pension plan described in Schedule "_____" (the "Pension Plan") is the only pension plan maintained by the Vendor for the benefit of the Employees.

(b) The Vendor has delivered to the Purchaser true and complete copies of each of the following documents:

(i) a copy of the most current text of the Pension Plan, including all amendments made thereto;

(ii) a copy of all employee communications relating to the Pension Plan, whether or not such communications have been filed with any applicable regulatory authority;

(iii) a copy of the trust or other funding agreement maintained in connection with the Pension Plan, including all amendments made thereto and the latest financial statements thereof;

(iv) a copy of the annual information return filed in respect of the Pension Plan with any applicable regulatory authority for each of the two most recently completed plan years;

(v) a copy of the two most recently completed actuarial reports filed in respect of the Pension Plan with any applicable regulatory authority;

(vi) a copy of any statement of investment policies and procedures prepared in respect of the Pension Plan, including all amendments made thereto, whether or not such statement has been filed with any applicable regulatory authority; and

(vii) the most recent letters of confirmation of registration of the Pension Plan pursuant to the applicable provincial pension legislation and the Income Tax Act (Canada).

(c) The Vendor has delivered to the Purchaser evidence acceptable to the Purchaser that the Pension Plan and each of the amendments made thereto have been accepted for registration under the Income Tax Act (Canada) and the applicable provincial pension legislation, and the Pension Plan has been established, administered, maintained and invested in compliance in all material respects with all applicable federal and provincial statutory and regulatory requirements.

(d)   All contributions required to be made to the Pension Plan to the date hereof in order for the Pension Plan to comply with the minimum funding standards imposed by applicable provincial pension legislation and the regulatory requirements prescribed thereunder have been made. [The Pension Plan is fully funded on a "going-concern" basis, as determined in accordance with the actuarial methods and assumptions used in the most recent actuarial report accepted for filing by the applicable regulatory authority—depending on the funding status of the plan.] All employee contributions to the Pension Plan to the date hereof have been properly withheld from the remuneration of the Employees, or otherwise received from the Employees, by the Vendor and have been remitted to the funding arrangement for the Pension Plan in a timely fashion.

(e)   There has been no improper withdrawal by the Vendor of assets held under the Pension Plan or transfer of assets from the pension or fund, and there has been no partial wind-ups or any application by the Vendor of surplus assets held under the Pension Plan to offset contributions otherwise required to be made thereto by the Vendor has been permitted under the terms of the Pension Plan and the funding agreement maintained in connection therewith, and under all applicable legislation.

(f)   There are no outstanding actions, suits or claims pending or threatened concerning the assets held in the fund for the Pension Plan (other than routine claims for the payment of benefits submitted by members or beneficiaries in the normal course, and there is no litigation, legal action, suit, investigation, claim, counterclaim or proceeding pending or threatened against or affecting any Pension Plan which could have a material adverse effect on the vendor or on any Pension Plan.

(g)   Neither the vendor nor its agents have been in breach of any fiduciary obligation with respect to the administration of the Pension Plan or fund.

Benefit Plans -

(a) The Vendor is not a party to any management agreement, pay equity plan, vacation or vacation pay policy, or any bonus, deferred compensation, incentive compensation, stock purchase or option, severance or termination pay, hospitalization or medical expense benefits, employee life or other insurance, supplemental unemployment benefits, profit sharing or retirement plan, program, agreement or arrangement, or to any executive or key personnel incentive or other special compensation arrangement, or to other contracts or agreements with or with respect to officers, employees or agents other than the Pension Plan and those plans, programs, agreements and arrangements listed and described in Schedule "Q" (the "Benefit Plans"). The Vendor does not have any formal plan or commitment to create any additional Benefit Plan or to modify or amend any existing Benefit Plan that would affect any Employee, other than such modification or amendment as may be required to secure the continued registration of an existing Benefit Plan with any applicable regulatory authority.

(b) With respect to each of the Benefit Plans, the Vendor has delivered to the Purchaser true and complete copies of each of the following documents:

   (i)   a copy of the most current text of the Benefit Plan, including all amendments made thereto;

   (ii)   a copy of all employee communications relating to the Benefit Plan;

   (iii) a copy of the trust or other funding agreement, including all amendments made thereto in respect of any of the Benefit Plans which are funded, and the latest financial statements prepared in respect of such funds; and

   (iv)   each contract relating to the Benefit Plan pursuant to which the Vendor may have any liability, including insurance contracts, investment management agreements, administration or record-keeping agreements and the like.

(c) Except as disclosed in Schedule "_____", none of the Benefit Plans provide benefits, including, without limitation, life insurance or medical benefits, to Employees following their retirement or other termination of service.

(d) There are no pending, threatened or anticipated claims against, or otherwise involving, any of the Benefit Plans by an Employee or a beneficiary, or otherwise, other than routine claims for benefits payable under the Benefit Plan.

9F37
ALTERNATIVE CLAUSES: PENSION PLANS

Alternative 1 — Buyer Covenants to Establish Pension Plan for Transferring Employees with No Assumption of Pre-Closing Benefit Accruals

Pension Plan

(a) The Vendor agrees to maintain responsibility for all benefits accrued by Accepting Employees [*as that term is defined in subsection 5(6)(d) of the Asset Purchase Agreement*] under the Pension Plan in respect of service with the Vendor prior to the Closing Date. The Vendor further agrees to take all steps necessary to secure such pension benefits as may be required pursuant to the terms of the Pension Plan and in accordance with the provisions of applicable pension standards legislation.

(b) As soon as practicable after the Closing Date [*but in any case within 90 days thereof*], and effective as of the Closing Date, the Purchaser shall, at its own expense, establish and submit for registration with the applicable regulatory authorities a pension plan for the Accepting Employees (the "Purchaser's Plan"). The Purchaser's Plan shall provide benefits for the Accepting Employees which are substantially similar to, and in any event no less favourable than, the benefits currently provided to Employees under the Pension Plan. The Purchaser's Plan shall recognize the period of service with the Vendor of each Accepting Employee who participated in the Pension Plan as service with the Purchaser for the purposes of eligibility for participation in, and the vesting of benefits, under, the Purchaser's Plan, but not for the purposes of benefit accrual thereunder.

(c) As soon as practicable following the Closing Date [*but in any case within 90 days thereof*] the Vendor shall furnish to the Purchaser a schedule of the credited service under the Pension Plan of all Accepting Employees for the purposes of the Purchaser's Plan.

(d) The Purchaser agrees to provide to the Vendor evidence satisfactory to the Vendor that the Purchaser has established and filed for registration with the applicable regulatory authorities the

Purchaser's Plan. The Purchaser further agrees to provide such information as may be reasonably requested by the Vendor concerning service by the Accepting Employees with the Purchaser for the purposes of calculating benefits payable to such Accepting Employees under the Pension Plan, but the Purchaser shall otherwise have no obligation to the Vendor or any of the Accepting Employees in respect of the Pension Plan.

Alternative 2 — Purchaser Accepts Assignment of Entire Pension Plan of Vendor (*appropriate only where all participants in Vendor's pension plan transfer to the Purchaser*)

Pension Plan

(a)   As soon as practicable after the Closing Date, but effective as of the Closing Date, the Vendor agrees to assign to the Purchaser, and the Purchaser agrees to assume the Pension Plan, including all rights, obligations, assets and liabilities thereunder. In order to effect such assignment, the Vendor and the Purchaser agree to take such steps, to prepare and execute such documents and to seek such approvals of the applicable regulatory authorities as may be necessary or desirable.

(b)   Subject to the approval of the applicable regulatory authorities and the funding agent for the Pension Plan, the Vendor agrees to assign to the Purchaser, and the Purchaser agrees to accept all of the rights and obligations of the Vendor under the funding agreement maintained in respect of the Pension Plan (the "Funding Agreement"), including all of the Vendor's rights in respect of the assets held under the Funding Agreement.

(c)   Notwithstanding the provisions of paragraphs (a) and (b) hereof, the Purchaser's administrative responsibility for the Pension Plan shall become effective only upon the assignment to the Purchaser by the Vendor of the rights and obligations of the Vendor under the Funding Agreement.

(d)   The Vendor agrees to administer the Pension Plan until the date upon which the assignment contemplated by paragraph (b) hereof is completed (the "Assignment Date") in the same manner as it is being administered at the Closing Date, but for the account of, and at the expense of, the fund maintained under the Funding Agreement, or, where any such charge to the pension fund is not permitted by applicable legislation or the terms of the Funding Agreement, the Purchaser. For greater certainty, the Vendor shall not be obligated to pay any amounts to or in respect of the Pension Plan and the fund established thereunder after the Closing Date, except for the account of, and at the expense of, the Purchaser.

(e)   Until the Assignment Date, the Vendor agrees to receive and deposit contributions, if any, by the Purchaser and the participants in the Pension Plan to the fund held under the Funding Agreement. Until the Assignment Date, the assets held in the pension fund shall be invested under the supervision of the Vendor and the funding agent appointed under the Funding Agreement. The Vendor and such funding agent shall act with reasonable diligence and prudence in the investment of such funds, and provided that they so act, neither the Vendor nor the funding agent shall be liable for the performance of the investments held in such pension fund.

(f)   As soon as practicable after the Closing Date, and in any event forthwith upon the completion of the assignments contemplated hereunder, the Vendor shall provide to the Purchaser such information and records, and access to such personnel, as may reasonably be required by the Purchaser in order to administer the Pension Plan.

(g)   All statutory and regulatory reporting, filing and disclosure requirements applicable to the Pension Plan in respect of the plan years ending prior to the Closing Date shall remain the responsibility of the Vendor, and all such requirements applicable in respect of plan years ending on or after the Closing Date shall be the responsibility of the Purchaser.

Alternative 3—   Purchaser Covenants to Establish Pension Plan and to Assume Liabilities for Accepting Employees from Vendor's Pension Plan.

Pension Plan

(a)   As soon as practicable after the Closing Date, but effective as of the Closing Date, the Vendor shall assign to the Purchaser, and the Purchaser shall assume all of the Vendor's liability and responsibility under the Pension Plan in respect of accrued pension benefits for the Accepting Employees [*as that term is defined under Subsection 5(6)(d)*]. As soon as practicable after the Closing Date, but effective as of the

Closing Date, the Purchaser shall establish and register with the applicable regulatory authorities a pension plan for the Accepting Employees (the "Purchaser's Plan") which shall contain benefit provisions which are equivalent in all material respects to those provided under the Pension Plan. The Purchaser's Plan shall recognize, for the purposes of eligibility for participation therein and the vesting and accrual of benefits thereunder, all periods of service of an Accepting Employee recognized for such periods under the Pension Plan.

(b)   The Purchaser agrees to provide the Vendor with such documentation and information as the Vendor may reasonably require to satisfy itself that the Purchaser's Plan and the fund therefor have been properly established in accordance with paragraph (a) hereof.

(c)   As soon as practicable after the Closing Date [*but in any case within 90 days thereof*], the Vendor shall cause the actuary for the Pension Plan to calculate the actuarial present value of the accrued benefits of the Accepting Employees as at the Closing Date (the "Assumed Liabilities") which shall be determined on a going-concern basis using the actuarial methods and assumptions specified in Schedule _____ and applying the provisions of the Pension Plan in effect at the Closing Date. Immediately upon receipt thereof, the Vendor shall provide to the Purchaser a copy of the report of the actuary for the Pension Plan showing the amount of the Assumed Liabilities, together with such other information and data as may be reasonably required by the Purchaser to permit a review of such calculations. The Purchaser shall be entitled to employ at its expense a qualified actuary to review the calculation of the Assumed Liabilities. If the actuary for the Pension Plan and the actuary retained by the Purchaser cannot agree on the calculation of the Assumed Liabilities, such calculation shall be referred to and settled by [*insert name of independent actuarial consulting firm*], and the cost and expenses of such independent actuary shall be borne equally by the Purchaser and the Vendor.

(d)   The Vendor agrees to administer the Pension Plan in respect of the Accepting Employees until the date on which the transfer of the value of the Assumed Liabilities to the fund for the Purchaser's Plan has been completed in accordance with paragraph (e) hereof (the "Transfer Date") in the same manner as it is being administered at the Closing Date, but for the account of, and at the expense of, the Purchaser. Until the Transfer Date, the Vendor agrees to cause the funding agent for the Pension Plan to receive and deposit contributions, if any, by the Purchaser and the Accepting Employees to the trust fund for the Pension Plan. Such contributions shall be credited with interest at [____%] and shall be reflected in an adjustment to the value of the Assumed Liabilities. Until the Transfer Date, the Vendor shall cause the funding agent for the Pension Plan to pay benefits becoming due under the terms of the Pension Plan or the Purchaser's Plan to any Accepting Employee prior to the Transfer Date, and the amount of such payments shall be deducted from the value of the Assumed Liabilities. Until the Transfer Date, the trust fund for the Pension Plan shall continue to be invested under the supervision of the Vendor and the funding agent for the Pension Plan, and the value of the Assumed Liabilities shall be credited with interest at a rate equal to [____%] from the Closing Date to the Transfer Date.

(e) Immediately upon the approval of the calculation of the Assumed Liabilities, the Vendor shall apply to the applicable regulatory authorities for approval to transfer such amount from the pension fund held under the Pension Plan to the fund established for the Purchaser's Plan. Immediately following receipt of the approval of such applicable regulatory authorities, the Vendor shall cause the funding agent for the Pension Plan to transfer to the fund for the Purchaser's Plan a lump sum cash payment [*or assets*] equal to the Assumed Liabilities, adjusted to take into account the contributions thereto and payments therefrom as contemplated under paragraph (d) hereof. In the event that such regulatory authority approves the transfer of an amount from the Pension Plan which is less than the value of the Assumed Liabilities as determined hereunder, such difference shall be paid by the Vendor to the Purchaser in the form of a lump sum cash payment.

9F38
ASSIGNMENT OF AGREEMENT
OF PURCHASE AND SALE

[See Para. 9.470]

THIS AGREEMENT made in duplicate this   day of   , 19 .

BETWEEN:

VENDOR INC., a corporation incorporated under the laws of the Province of Ontario,

(hereinafter called the "Assignors"),

OF THE FIRST PART,

- and -

PURCHASER INC., a corporation incorporated under the laws of the Province of Ontario,

(hereinafter called the "Assignee"),

OF THE SECOND PART.

WHEREAS the Assignors are the owners of property in the (*insert city*) in the (*insert municipality*) of _____, comprising a hotel and an apartment building known _____ Hotel ("_____ Hotel");

AND WHEREAS the Assignors have entered into an Agreement of Purchase and Sale with _____ dated _____ (the "Agreement of Purchase and Sale") providing for the sale of _____ Hotel and the business carried out thereon, and providing further for the assignment of all contracts set out in Schedule "A" attached hereto;

AND WHEREAS _____ has assigned all of its right, title and interest in the Agreement of Purchase and Sale to the Assignee.

NOW THEREFORE THIS AGREEMENT WITNESSETH that in consideration of the sum of TWO DOLLARS ($2.00) and other good and valuable consideration and in consideration of the Assignee accepting the within assignment and assuming the Assignors' obligations under the contracts, the Assignors do hereby set over, assign, transfer, release and quit claim unto the Assignee all of their right, title and interest whatsoever in and to all contracts set forth in Schedule "A" attached hereto.

TO HAVE AND TO HOLD unto the Assignee, its successors and assigns, all benefits and advantages accruing thereon under the contracts set out in Schedule "A" attached hereto.

THE ASSIGNORS covenant, represent and warrant that they have full power and authority to set over the aforesaid contracts.

THIS AGREEMENT shall enure to and be binding upon the parties hereto, their respective successors and assigns.

DATED at (*city*), (*province*), this _____.

IN WITNESS WHEREOF the parties hereto have hereunto caused to be affixed their corporate seals duly attested to by the hands of their respective proper signing officers authorized in that behalf.

VENDOR INC.

Per: _____

PURCHASER INC.

Per: _____

9F39
ASSIGNMENT OF WARRANTIES

[See Para. 9.470]

THIS AGREEMENT made in duplicate this _____.

BETWEEN:

> Hereinafter called the "Assignors",

OF THE FIRST PART,

- and -

> Hereinafter called the "Assignee",

OF THE SECOND PART,

- and -

> Hereinafter called the "Parties",

OF THE THIRD PART.

WHEREAS the Assignors are the owners of property in the City of (*insert city*), in the Municipality of (*insert municipality*), comprising a hotel and an apartment building known as _____ Hotel ("_____ Hotel");

AND WHEREAS the Assignors have entered into an Agreement of Purchase and Sale with _____ dated _____ (the "Agreement of Purchase and Sale") providing for the sale of _____ Hotel and the business carried out thereon, and providing further for the assignment of any guarantees, warranties and indemnities pertaining to _____ Hotel, to the extent permitted;

AND WHEREAS _____ has assigned all of its right, title and interest in the Agreement of Purchase and Sale to the Assignee.

NOW THEREFORE THIS AGREEMENT WITNESSETH that in consideration of the sum of TWO DOLLARS ($2.00) and other good and valuable consideration the Assignors and Parties of the Third Part do hereby set over, assign, transfer, release and quit claim unto the Assignee all of their right, title and interest whatsoever in or to all guarantees, warranties and indemnities, if any, to the extent assignable, whatsoever pertaining to _____ Hotel and being sold by the Assignors to the Assignee under the Agreement of Purchase and Sale.

TO HAVE AND TO HOLD unto the Assignee, its successors and assigns, all benefits and advantages accruing therefrom from the date hereof.

THE ASSIGNORS and the Parties of the Third Part covenant, represent and warrant that they have full power and authority to set over the guarantees, warranties and indemnities to the extent assignable.

THIS AGREEMENT shall enure to and be binding upon the parties hereto, their respective successors and assigns.

DATED at (*city*), (*province*), this _____.

IN WITNESS WHEREOF the parties hereto have hereunto caused to be affixed their corporate seals duly attested to by the hands of their respective proper signing officers authorized in that behalf.

ASSIGNOR(S)

Per: _____

ASSIGNEE(S)

Per: _____

[*THIRD PARTIES*

_____]

9F39:1
APPLICATION FOR LEASEHOLD PARCEL

[See Para. 9.583]

Document General

Form 4 — Land Registration Reform Act, 1984

D

(1) Registry ☐   Land Titles ☒   (2) Page 1 of ____ pages

(3) Property Identifier(s) ____ Block ____ Property ____

(4) Nature of Document

APPLICATION FOR LEASEHOLD PARCEL
(SUBSECTION 38 (6) OF THE ACT)

(5) Consideration ____ Dollars $

(6) Description

Parcel ° , Section °

being Block ° , Plan °

Town of Anywhere

Regional Municipality of Anywhere

Land Titles Division of ____ (No.)

(7) This Document Contains   (a) Redescription New Easement Plan/Sketch ☐   (b) Schedule for Description ☐ Parties ☐ Other ☐

(8) This Document provides as follows :

(B) is entitled for his own benefit to a leasehold estate for a term of ° years from ° and two (2) consecutive renewal periods of five (5) years each thereafter in Parcel ° , Section ° (and other lands under the Registry System) registered in the Land Registry Office for the Land Titles Division of ° being the freehold land registered as Parcel ° , Section °. It hereby applies to be the registered owner of the leasehold lands.

The evidence in support of this application consists of the lease, notice of which is registered as Instrument No. ° in the said Land Registry Office.

Continued on Schedule ☐

(9) This Document relates to instrument number(s)

NOTICE OF LEASE, °

(10) Party(ies) (Set out Status or Interest)

Name(s)	Signature(s)	Date of Signature Y M D
(B)	Per: I.N. President	
(TENANT)	I have authority to bind the Corporation	

(11) Address for Service   100 Bay Street, Somewhere, Ontario

(12) Party(ies) (Set out Status or Interest)

Name(s)	Signature(s)	Date of Signature Y M D

(13) Address for Service

(14) Municipal Address of Property

20 Lease Lane
Somewhere, Ontario

(15) Document Prepared by

I.N. Solicitor
Law Firm
20 Queen Street
Everywhere, Ontario

Fees and Tax

Registration Fee ____

Total ____

510

9F39:2
NOTICE OF LEASE (REGISTRY ACT)
[See Para. 9.583]

Document General
Form 4 — Land Registration Reform Act, 1984

D

(1) Registry ☒ Land Titles ☐	(2) Page 1 of pages

(3) Property Identifier(s)   Block   Property   Additional See Schedule ☐

(4) Nature of Document
NOTICE OF LEASE SECTION 2X(7) OF THE REGISTRY ACT

(5) Consideration   Dollars $

(6) Description

Part Lot 6
Concession 1
City of Anywhere
Regional Municipality of Anywhere
Being Part 1, Reference Plan ***

New Property Identifiers   Additional See Schedule ☐

Executions   Additional See Schedule ☐

(7) This Document Contains: (a) Redescription New Easement Plan/Sketch ☐ (b) Schedule for Description ☐ Additional Parties ☐ Other ☒

(8) This Document provides as follows:

EXECUTED NOTICE OF LEASE ATTACHED

Continued on Schedule ☐

(9) This Document relates to instrument number(s)

(10) Party(ies) (Set out Status or Interest)
Name(s)   Signature(s)   Date of Signature Y M D

(A)
(LANDLORD)

(11) Address for Service   25 Main Street West, Anywhere, Ontario

(12) Party(ies) (Set out Status or Interest)
Name(s)   Signature(s)   Date of Signature Y M D

(B)   Per:
(TENANT)   I.M. Solicitor

By its solicitors, Law Firm

(13) Address for Service   100 Bay Street, Somewhere, Ontario   Attention: **

Municipal Address of Property
20 Lease Lane
Somebere, Ontario

(15) Document Prepared by
I.M. Solicitor
Law Firm
20 Queen Street West
Everywhere, Ontario

Fees and Tax
Registration Fee

REGISTRY ACT, R.S.O. 1990, c. R.20

NOTICE OF LEASE (SUBSECTION 22(7) OF THE ACT)

NOTICE IS HEREBY GIVEN of an unregistered lease dated as of the * day of *, 19* and made

B E T W E E N:

(A)
as Landlord

- AND -

(B)
as Tenant

affecting part of the land described on page 1 which part is cross-hatched with solid lines on Schedule A attached hereto (herein referred to as the "Demised Land") under which the Landlord leased the Demised Land to the Tenant and which lease contains inter alia the following terms and provisions:

1. Landlord: (A)

2. Tenant: (B)

3. Date of Lease   *

4. Term   * years expiring the * date of *, 19*
                        (subject to the Tenant's option to renew set out below).

5. Right or Option
   to Purchase: None.

6. Option to Renew: * years at the Tenant's option exercised at least * prior to the
                        expiry of the term.

7. Landlord's Address: 25 Main Street West, Anywhere, Ontario

8. Tenant's Address: At the Demised Land with a copy to:
                        100 Bay Street, Somewhere, Ontario
                        Attention: *

The Tenant is prepared to produce the lease to which this Notice relates for inspection by any person who can establish that he has an interest in the Demised Land.

DATED at Everywhere, the * day of *, 19*.

(B)
By its solicitors, Law Firm

Per:_____
            I.M. Solicitor

9F39:3
NOTICE OF MORTGAGE OF LEASE
[See Para. 9.583]

Document General
Form 4 — Land Registration Reform Act, 1984

D

(1) Registry ☐   Land Titles ☐   (2) Page 1 of   pages

(3) Property Identifier(s)

(4) Nature of Document

NOTICE OF MORTGAGE OF LEASE (SUBSECTION 22 (7) OF THE REGISTRY ACT

(5) Consideration

Dollars $

(6) Description

Part Lot *
Plan *
City of Anywhere
Regional Municipality of Anywhere

SEE SCHEDULE ATTACHED

(7) This Document Contains   (a) Redescription New Easement Plan/Sketch ☐   (b) Schedule for: Description ☐ Additional Parties ☐ Other ☐

(8) This Document provides as follows:

Notice is hereby given of an unregistered mortgage of lease dated as of *, made between (B), as Charger and (D), as Chargee, affecting the land described in Box 6 and page 2 hereof (herein referred to as the mortgaged land) under which the Charger mortgaged and assigned to the Chargee the Charger's right, title and interest in the mortgaged land and in a lease dated *, notice of which was registered on *, as Instrument No. *, as continuing collateral security for the payment of unlimited indebtedness by the Charger to the Chargee.

The Chargee is prepared to produce the mortgage of lease to which this notice relates for inspection by any person who can establish that he has an interest in the mortgaged land.

Continued on Schedule ☐

(9) This Document relates to Instrument number(s)

Notice of Lease No. *

(10) Party(ies) (Set out Status or Interest)
Name(s)   Signature(s)   Date of Signature

(B)   Per:
I. M. President
I have authority to bind the Corporation

(11) Address for Service   25 Main Street West, Anywhere, Ontario

(12) Party(ies) (Set out Status or Interest)
Name(s)   Signature(s)   Date of Signature

(D)
By its solicitors,   Per:
I. M. Solicitor
Law Firm

(13) Address for Service   100 Bay Street, Somewhere, Ontario   Attention: **

(14) Municipal Address of Property   (15) Document Prepared by:

20 Lease Lane
Somewhere, Ontario

I.M. Solicitor
Law Firm
20 Queen Street West
Everywhere, Ontario

Fees and Tax
Registration Fee

Total

9F39:4
NOTICE OF LEASE (LAND TITLES ACT)
[See Para. 9.583]

Document General
Form 4 — Land Registration Reform Act, 1984

D

(1) Registry ☐   Land Titles ☒   (2) Page 1 of   pages

(3) Property
Identifier(s)   Block   Property

(4) Nature of Document
**NOTICE OF LEASE (SUBSECTION 111(1)
OF THE LAND TITLES ACT**

(5) Consideration
Dollars $

(6) Description

Parcel *
Section *
Being part Lot *
Concession *
City of Anywhere
Regional Municipality of Anywhere
designated as Part * on *

(7) This
Document
Contains   (a) Redescription
New Easement
Plan/Sketch ☐   (b) Schedule for
Description ☐   Parties ☐   Other ☒

(8) This Document provides as follows:

(B) hereby applies for the entry of a notice of
the lease produced herewith in respect of the land
described above as Parcel *, in the Register for
Section * of which (A) is the registered owner
being the whole of the parcel.

The evidence in support of this application
consists of an executed copy of the lease.

Continued on Schedule ☐

(9) This Document relates to instrument number(s)

(10) Party(ies) (Set out Status or Interest)
Name(s)   Signature(s)   Date of Signature

(A)

(LANDLORD)

(11) Address
for Service   25 Main Street West, Anywhere, Ontario

(12) Party(ies) (Set out Status or Interest)
Name(s)   Signature(s)   Date of Signature

(B)

(TENANT)

Per:
I.M. President

I have authority to bind
the Corporation

(13) Address
for Service   100 Bay Street, Somewhere, Ontario   Attention: **

(14) Municipal Address of Property   (15) Document Prepared by: Fees and Tax

20 Lease Lane
Somewhere, Ontario

I.M. Solicitor
Law Firm
20 Queen Street West
Everywhere, Ontario

Registration Fee

Total

9F39:5
NOTICE OF AN INTEREST IN A LEASE (LAND TITLES ACT)

[See Para. 9.583]

9F39:6

CHARGE/MORTGAGE OF LAND

Charge/Mortgage of Land

Form 2 — Land Registration Reform Act, 1984

B

(1) Registry **X** Land Titles	(2) Page 1 of 10 pages

(3) Property Identifier(s)   Block   Property

(4) Principal Amount   Dollars $

(5) Description

Part Lot 6
Concession 1
City of Anywhere
Regional Municipality of Anywhere
Being Part 1, Reference Plan ***

(7) Interest/Estate Charged
Leasehold

(8) Standard Charge Terms — The parties agree to be bound by the provisions in Standard Charge Terms filed as number **N/A** and the Chargor(s) hereby acknowledge(s) receipt of a copy of these terms.

(9) Payment Provisions

Principal Amount $	Interest Rate SEE SCHEDULE % per annum	Calculation Period SEE SCHEDULE
Interest Adjustment Date	Payment Date and Period SEE SCHEDULE	First Payment Date
Payment Date	Amount of Each Payment SEE SCHEDULE	Dollars $
Balance Due Date	Insurance SEE SCHEDULE	Dollars $

(10) Additional Provisions

SEE SCHEDULE ATTACHED

Continued on Schedule

(11) Chargor(s) The chargor hereby charges the land to the chargee and certifies that the chargor is at least eighteen years old and that

The chargor acknowledges receipt of a true copy of this charge

Name(s)
(B)

Signature(s)
Per:
    I.M. President

I have authority to bind
the Corporation

Date of Signature

(12) Spouse(s) of Chargor(s) I hereby consent to this transaction
Name(s)   Signature(s)   Date of Signature

(13) Chargor(s) Address for Service
25 Main Street West, Anywhere, Ontario

(14) Chargee(s)
(D)

(15) Chargee(s) Address for Service
100 Bay Street, Somewhere, Ontario Attention: **

(16) Assessment Roll Number of Property Cty Mun Map Sub Par		
Municipal Address of Property	(18) Document Prepared by	Fees
20 Lease Lane Somewhere, Ontario	I.M. Solicitor Law Firm 20 Queen Street West Everywhere, Ontario	Registration Fee
		Total

---

* Reprinted with permission of Dye & Durham Co. Ltd.

THIS INDENTURE made the   day of   ,

B E T W E E N:

>   (hereinafter called the Chargor)

OF THE FIRST PART;

>   -and-

(hereinafter called the Chargee)

OF THE SECOND PART

1.   WHEREAS by Indenture of lease dated the _____ day of _____, 19_____ and registered in the Land Registry Office for the _____ Division of as No. _____ (the "lease") _____ as lessor therein, (the "lessor"), did demise and lease unto the Chargor, as lessee, all and singular that certain parcel or tract of land and premises described on page 1 (and, if applicable, Schedule A hereto), for a term of (_____) years, computed from the _____ day of _____, 19_____ subject to the yearly rental as therein provided and to the further covenants, terms and conditions as therein set out and including the right to renew.

2.   AND WHEREAS the Chargor has at the request of the Chargee agreed to give this Charge as a continuing collateral security for payment and satisfaction to the Chargee of all obligations, debts and liabilities, present or future, direct or indirect, absolute or contingent, matured or not, extended or renewed at any time owing by the Chargor to the Chargee or remaining unpaid by the Chargor to the Chargee heretofore or hereafter incurred or arising, and whether incurred by or arising from agreement or dealings between the Chargee and the Chargor or from any agreement or dealings with any third party by which the Chargee may be or become in any manner whatsoever a creditor of the Chargor, or however otherwise incurred or arising anywhere within or outside Canada and whether the Chargor be bound alone or with another or others and whether as principal or surety and any ultimate unpaid balance thereof and whether the same is from time to time reduced and thereafter increased or entirely extinguished and thereafter incurred again (such obligations, debts and liabilities being hereinafter called the "liabilities") but it being agreed that this Charge at any one time will secure only that portion of the aggregate principal component of the liabilities outstanding at such time does not exceed the sum of _____ dollars together with any interest or com-pound interest accrued on the principal at such time at the rate hereinafter set forth.

3.   NOW THEREFORE as general and continuing collateral security for the payment and performance of the liabilities, the Chargor does hereby grant, mortgage, charge and assign to the Chargee and create a security interest in all of the right, title and interest of the Chargor in and to the lease and the leasehold interest of the Chargor thereunder (collectively, the "mortgaged premises"), to have and to hold unto the Chargee for and during the unexpired term of years granted by the lease and any renewals thereof, subject to the exception as to the last day thereof, and the proviso for redemption hereinafter contained.

4.   PROVIDED THIS CHARGE to be void upon the Chargor paying on demand to the Chargee the ultimate balance of the liabilities in full, as and when due, including the principal component of such liabilities together with interest thereon at a rate equal to _____% per annum, calculated and payable monthly as well after as before maturity, default and judgment, with interest on overdue interest at the same rate as on the principal sum, and all other amounts payable by the Chargor hereunder and paying any taxes, rates, levies, charges or assessments upon the mortgaged premises no matter by whom or what authority imposed, and observing and performing all covenants, provisos and conditions herein contained.

5. *Trust Provisions*

As further security and for the consideration aforesaid, the Chargor hereby covenants and declares, as a condition hereof, to henceforth stand possessed of the mortgaged premises for the residue vested in the Chargor of the term of lease, upon trust for the Chargee or for the nominee of Chargee for the purpose of these presents, and will assign and dispose thereof as Chargee or its nominee shall for such purposes direct; and upon any sale or sales of the mortgaged premises or any part thereof in the due exercise of the powers hereby granted or otherwise available to the Chargee, the Chargee, for the purpose of vesting the residue of such term in any purchaser or purchasers thereof, shall be entitled by deed or writing to nominate such purchaser or purchasers or any other person or persons as a new trustee or trustees of the aforesaid residue of the term in place of the Chargor and upon any such nomination the same shall vest forthwith in the new trustee or trustees as nominated, and the Chargor further authorizes and empowers the Chargee to appoint any other person or body corporate as substitute attorney for the Chargee for all or any of the said purposes.

6. *Taxes*

The Chargor will pay as they fall due all taxes, rates and assessments, municipal, local, parliamentary and otherwise which now are or may hereafter be imposed, charged or levied upon the mortgaged premises and which are required to be paid by the Chargor under the lease and will, forthwith on payment, produce to the Chargee at its office, at Toronto, Ontario, or as it might otherwise direct, receipted bills for the said taxes, rates and assessments, or at the Chargor's expense, will obtain and furnish to the Chargee proof to the Chargee's satisfaction that all such taxes, rates and assessments due and owing up to the time of each request have been paid in full. Untill all the liabilities have been fully paid and satisfied, the Chargee is hereby empowered and shall from time to time have the right (but shall not be obligated so to do) to pay the taxes either before or after due, including interest and penalties imposed, if any, required to be paid by the Chargor under the lease on the mortgaged premises in full or in part for each year, and the whole amount so paid shall be added to the liabilities hereby secured and shall bear interest calculated at the rate stipulated above and payable monthly and shall be payable forthwith. The Chargee shall also have the right from time to time to estimate the amount of taxes on the mortgaged premises for each year required to be paid by the Chargor under the lease, and to require the Chargor to pay in each month one-twelfth of such estimated amount in addition to the monthly instalments herein mentioned; and the Chargor covenants and agrees when so required to pay to the Chargee in addition to the monthly instalments herein mentioned one-twelfth of the said estimated amount of taxes with each of the twelve succeeding monthly installments herein mentioned next falling due and the Chargor shall also pay to the Chargee on demand the amount, if any, by which the actual taxes payable by the Chargor under the lease exceed such estimated amount. Provided, however, that if, before any sum or sums so paid to the Chargee shall have been so applied, there shall be default by the Chargor in respect of any payment of the liabilities, the Chargee may apply such sum or sums in or towards payment of such liabilities. The Chargor further covenants and agrees to transmit to the Chargee immediately after receipt of the same, all tax bills, receipts, assess-ment notices and other notices affecting the imposition of taxes. Provided, however, that the Chargee may deduct from the principal money advanced hereunder an amount sufficient to pay all taxes which have or may become due during the calendar year in which the final advance of moneys secured by this mortgage is made. When taxes are in arrears, the Chargee may similarly require the Chargor to pay monthly, one-twelfth of the arrears, plus interest and penalties in addition to the aforesaid monthly instalments for principal, interest and taxes.

7. *Covenant to Pay and to keep Lease in good Standing*

The Chargor covenants and agrees to pay or cause to be paid to the Chargee the liabilities when due, and to keep, observe and perform the covenants, terms and conditions herein contained and also (unless and until upon default the Chargee does not enter upon, lease or sell the mortgaged premises) that the Chargor will pay the said rents, taxes, premiums of insurance, payments and charges and keep, perform and observe all the covenants, terms and conditions expressed or implied in the lease and indemnify and save the Chargee harmless against payment of any rents, rates, taxes, premiums of insurance, payments and charges and against all loss, costs, damages and forfeiture whatsoever occasioned by or by reason of or consequent upon any non-payment, non-performance or non-observance thereof. If the Chargor does make default in payment of any such rent, rates, taxes, charges, premiums of insurance or payments and the Chargee does pay the same or any part thereof, the Chargor will pay to it the amount so paid with interest at the said rate and the mortgaged premises shall stand charged therewith upon this security; and further, will not do, cause or permit any matter or thing to be done or be left undone which would cause or give ground for the termination of the lease or render the same void or voidable, and will not surrender the lease or render the same void or voidable, and will not surrender the lease nor make any change, amendment, modification or alteration with respect thereto without the prior written consent of the Chargee; and further, will forthwith after receipt thereof furnish to the Chargee a true copy of any notice or demand received in respect of the Lease, provided that nothing herein shall prevent the Chargor from subletting the mortgaged premises or any part thereof, subject to the rights of the Chargee hereunder.

8. Lease Valid and Power to Mortgage

The Chargor covenants and warrants to the Chargee that:

(a)   The lease is as of the date hereof a good, valid and subsisting lease in the law and not surrendered, forfeited or become void or voidable; and that the rents and covenants therein reserved and contained have been duly paid and performed by the Chargor up to the day of the date hereof; and that, subject to the terms of the lease, the Chargor now has in itself good right, full power and lawful and absolute authority to grant, mortgage, bargain, sell, assign or sublet the mortgaged premises in manner aforesaid and according to the true intent and meaning of this mortgage.

(b)   The Chargor has full power and authority to execute and deliver this mortgage and any other agreements or documents related thereto which are being executed by it.

9. Default in Payment and other Covenants

Provided that in the case of default in payment of any of the liabilities or in the keeping, observance or performance of the covenants, terms and conditions herein contained, the Chargee may enter into and upon and hold and enjoy the mortgaged premises for the residue of the term of years of the lease and any renewal or renewals thereof for its own use and benefit without any other person whomsoever subject to the terms of this mortgage and the lease; and that free and clear and freely and clearly acquitted, exonerated and discharged or otherwise by and at the expense of the Chargor well and effectually saved, defended and kept harmless, of, from and against all former and other gifts, grants, bargains, sales, leases and other encumbrances whatsoever. Except as disclosed to the Chargee, the Chargor has not made, done, committed or suffered any act, deed, matter or thing whereby or by reason whereof the mortgaged premises or any part thereof have or has been or may be in anywise charged, affected or encumbered.

10. *Further Assurances*

The Chargor and all other persons claiming any interest in the mortgaged premises by or under the lease shall and will from time to time, and at all times hereafter, at the request of the Chargee, make, do and execute, or cause and procure to be made, done and executed, all such further acts, deeds, assignments and assurances in the law for more effectually assigning and assuring the lease and the mortgaged premises to the Chargee, according to the true intent and meaning of this mortgage as the Chargee shall reasonably request.

11. *Insurance*

(a) The Chargor covenants that it will forthwith insure   or cause to be insured during the continuance of this mortgage and will keep insured with loss payable to the Chargee against loss or damage by fire and, as the Chargee may reasonably require, against loss or damage by explosion, tempest, tornado, cyclone, lightning and other risks or hazards as the Chargee may require, with provision for permission to occupy and with automatic vacancy permit, each and every building on the mortgaged premises and which may hereinafter be erected thereon, both during erection and thereafter, for the full replacement value thereof in a company or companies approved by the Chargee. The Chargor shall forthwith place and continue to maintain in amounts equal to the full replacement value of the mortgaged premises including all improvements thereon, boiler and pressure vessels insurance. The Chargor will, at the request of the Chargee, forthwith assign, transfer and deliver over unto the Chargee the policy or policies of insurance or certificates in respect thereof. If a Chargee's original copy of the policy is not available from the insurance company, the Chargee shall be permitted reasonable access to the relevant policies from time to time for review purposes and receipts thereto appertaining. If the Chargor shall neglect to keep the said buildings or any of them insured as aforesaid, or to deliver such policies, certificates and receipts or to produce to the Chargee at least thirty days before the termination of any insurance, evidence of renewal thereof, the Chargee shall be entitled but shall not be obliged to insure the said buildings or any of them. The Chargor shall forthwith on the happening of any loss or damage, furnish at its own expense all necessary proofs and do all necessary acts to enable the Chargee to obtain payment of the insurance monies;

(b) The Chargor further covenants that it will forthwith insure or cause to be insured and during the continuance of this mortgage keep insured with loss payable to the Chargee and the Chargor (and, if required, the Lessor) as their interests may appear against loss of rental income resulting from loss or damage caused by any of the perils against which the Chargor is required to insure under clause (a) of this paragraph 11 to the value of not less than two years' rent;

(c) The Chargor further covenants that each insurer providing insurance hereunder will waive any right it may have to be subrogated to the rights of the Chargee. No such policy shall contain a co-insurance clause except a stated amount clause.

(d) The Chargor further covenants that it will maintain   during the continuance of this mortgage liability insurance in amounts satisfactory to the Chargee.

12. Release

The Chargor does release unto the Chargee all its claims upon the mortgaged premises and the term of years hereof, except as aforesaid, subject to the said proviso for repayment.

13. Powers to Lease or Sell

It is hereby further agreed and provided that the Chargee, on default of payment of the liabilities for at least fifteen days, may on at least ten days' notice enter on and lease the mortgaged premises, or on default of payment for at least fifteen days may on at least thirty-five days' notice sell the mortgaged premises and term of years thereof. Such notice shall be given to such persons and in such manner and form and within such time as provided under Part III of the Mortgages Act, R.S.O. 1990, c. M.40, as amended. In the event that the giving of such notice shall not be required by law or to the extent that such requirements shall not be applicable, it is agreed that notice may be effectually given by mailing it in a registered letter addressed to the Chargor at its last known address.

Provided further, without prejudice to the statutory powers of the Chargee under the foregoing proviso, that in case default be made in the payment of the liabilities or any part thereof, and such default continues for one month after any payment of either falls due, then the Chargee may without consent or concurrence of the Chargor and without notice to the Chargor, enter into possession of the mortgaged premises and receive and take the rents, issues, and profits thereof and whether in or out of possession may make any such lease thereof or any part thereof as it shall think fit. The Chargee may also sell and absolutely dispose of the mortgaged premises and the then unexpired term of years and rights of renewal and reversion, or any part or parts of any term thereof, by public auction or private contract of sale without being responsible for any loss, costs or deficiency thereby occasioned and may make such terms as to credit and otherwise and such conditions of sale or agreements as to title, price and all other matters whatsoever as it may deem expedient and may transfer, assign or secure the same when so sold to the purchaser or purchasers and his, her or their executors, administrators and assigns; it being understood and agreed, however, that if the giving of notice by the Chargee shall be required by law, then notice shall be given to such persons and in such manner and form and within such time as is required by law. Provided that the Chargee shall stand possessed of the mortgaged premises and the rents and profits thereof until sale, and then of the proceeds of sale in trust, firstly, to pay all costs, charges, expenses and disbursements of getting and keeping possession of the mortgaged premises and of repairs and of and about the leasing or selling thereof; secondly, to pay all moneys and interest hereby secured; and lastly, on entitlement, to pay the surplus, if any, to the Chargor or others entitled thereto claiming under the Chargor and to re-assign or transfer to the Chargor, the remaining mortgaged property or term of years if any.

The cost of any sale proceedings hereunder whether such sale proves abortive or not, and all costs, charges and expenses incurred in taking, recovering or keeping possession of the mortgaged premises or in enforcing the remedies under this mortgage, shall be payable by the Chargor forthwith on demand, shall be a charge on the mortgaged premises and shall bear interest at the rate hereinbefore provided.

The Chargee shall not, nor shall its agents or attorneys, be liable by reason of any entry into possession of the mortgaged premises or any part hereof to account as Chargee in possession or for anything except actual receipts or be liable for any loss on realization or for any act for commission which a Chargee in possession might be liable; the Chargee shall not be virtue of this mortgage be deemed a Chargee in possession of the mortgaged premises; and the Chargee shall be liable to account for only such receipts as actually come into its hands, less reasonable collection charges in respect thereof.

14. Foreclosure

Provided always and it is hereby agreed by and between the parties that notwithstanding the power of sale and the other powers and provisions contained herein, the Chargee shall have and be entitled to its right of foreclosure of the equity of redemption of the Chargor in the mortgaged premises as fully and effectually as it may have exercised and enjoyed the same, in case the power of sale and other provisions and trust incidental hereto had not been herein contained.

15. Repair

The Chargor further covenants with the Chargee that it will keep the mortgaged premises in good and substantial condition and repair according to the nature and description thereof respectively, to the satisfaction of the Chargee, and that the Chargee may whenever it deems necessary by its surveyor or agent, and always during reasonable business hours, enter upon and inspect the mortgaged premises, and, that if the Chargor or those claiming under it neglect to keep the mortgaged premises in good and substantial condition and repair or commit any act of waste of the mortgaged premises or make default as to any of the covenants, terms or conditions herein contained and such act, neglect or default continue for thirty days after written notice thereof from the Chargee to the Chargor, then the liabilities hereby secured shall at the option of the Chargee forthwith become due and payable; and in default of payment of the same the powers of entering and leasing or selling hereinbefore given may be exercised accordingly and the Chargee may make any such repairs as it reasonably may deem necessary and the cost thereof shall be payable forthwith by the Chargor to the Chargee and until so paid shall be a charge upon the mortgaged premises prior to all claims thereon subsequent to these present.

16. Distress

It is further agreed and provided that the Chargee may distrain for arrears in payment of the liabilities in the event the Chargor shall make default in payment of any part of the liabilities herein secured, and it shall be lawful for the Chargee to distrain therefor and by distress warrant to recover by way of rent reserved, so much of such interest as shall from time to time be in arrears and unpaid, together with all costs, charges and expenses, as in like cases of distress for rent.

17. *Quiet Enjoyment*

Provided further that until default in payment of any part of the liabilities hereby secured or in the doing, observing or keeping any of the covenants, terms or conditions herein, it shall, subject to the terms of this mortgage, be lawful for the Chargor to hold, occupy, possess and enjoy the mortgaged premises and all appurtenances thereto, without any molestation, interruption or disturbance of, from or by the Chargee or any person claiming under it.

18. *Costs and Prior Encumbrances*

It is further stipulated, provided and agreed that the Chargor shall pay all legal fees and disbursements incurred by any party in connection with the preparation, execution, registration (where required) and carrying out this mortgage and all other documents related thereto and all accounts for utilities and operating and maintenance costs relating to the mortgaged premises and will perform all legally enforceable obligations imposed by any governmental body or agency and will forthwith on demand by the Chargee furnish evidence thereof to the Chargee, and further that the Chargee may pay the amount of any encumbrance, lien or charge now or hereafter existing, or to arise or be claimed upon the mortgaged premises having priority over this mortgage, including any taxes or other rates on the lands or any of them and all accounts for utilities and operating and maintenance costs relating to the mortgaged premises which the Chargor fails to pay, and may pay all costs, charges and expenses and all solicitors' charges or commissions, as between a solicitor and its client, which may be incurred in taking, recovering and keeping possession of the mortgaged premises and generally in any proceedings or steps of any nature whatever properly taken in connection or to realize this security, or in respect of the collection of any overdue interest, principal, insurance premiums or any other money whatsoever payable by the Chargor hereunder, whether any action or any judicial proceedings to enforce such payments has been taken or not, and the amount so paid and insurance premiums for fire or other risks or hazards and any other monies paid hereunder by the Chargee, together with any unpaid legal fees and disbursements hereinbefore in this paragraph required to be paid by the Chargor, shall be added to the liabilities hereby secured and be a charge on the mortgaged premises and shall bear interest at the rate aforesaid, and shall be payable forthwith by the Chargor to the Chargee, and the non-payment of such amount shall be a default of payment within the meaning of those words in the proviso contained in paragraph 9 hereof, and shall entitle the Chargee to exercise the powers under such proviso. In the event of the Chargee paying the amount of any such encumbrance, lien or charge, taxes or rates, either out of the monies advanced on the security of this mortgage or otherwise, it shall be entitled to all the rights, equities and securities of the person or persons, company or corporation or government so paid off, and is hereby authorized to retain any discharge thereof, without registration, for a longer period than six months if it thinks proper to do so.

19. Buildings and Fixtures

It is hereby mutually covenanted and agreed by and between the parties hereto, that all erections and improvements fixed or otherwise now on or hereafter put upon the mortgaged premises, including but without limiting the generality of the foregoing, all buildings, fences, heating, piping, plumbing, aerials, air-conditioning, ventilation, lighting and water heating equipment, cooking and refrigeration equipment, window blinds, radiators and covers, fixed mirrors, fitted blinds, storm windows and storm doors, window screens and screen doors, shutters and awnings, floor coverings and all apparatus and equipment appurtenant thereto are and shall, in addition to other fixtures thereon, be and become fixtures and an accession to the freehold and a part of the realty as between the parties hereto and all persons claiming by, through or under them, and shall be a portion of the security for the liabilities, subject to the provisions of the lease.

20. Non-Apportionment

And it is also agreed and declared that every part or lot into which the mortgaged premises are or may hereafter be divided does and shall stand charged with the whole of the liabilities hereby secured and no person shall have any right to require the mortgage monies to be apportioned upon or in respect of any such part or lots and the Chargee may discharge any part or parts from time to time of the mortgaged premises for such consideration as it shall think proper or without consideration as it sees fit and no discharge shall diminish or prejudice this security as against the part or parts remaining undischarged or as against any person whomsoever.

21. Short Forms of Mortgages Act

If any of the forms of words contained herein are substantially in the form of words contained in column one of Schedule B of the Short Form of *Mortgages Act*, R.S.O. 1990, c. M.40 and distinguished by a number therein, this mortgage shall be deemed to include and shall have the same effect as if it contained the form of words in column two of Schedule B of the said Act distinguished by the same number, and this Charge shall be interpreted as if the Short Forms of Mortgages Act were still in full force and effect. If any such form of words or any other terms of this mortgage are inconsistent with any of the covenants provided for in Section 7 of the Land Registration Act, 1984, any such covenant so provided for in the Land Registration Reform

Act, 1984 to the extent that it is so inconsistent is expressly excluded from the terms of this Charge.

The Chargor and the Chargee covenant and agree each with the other that the covenants, terms or conditions of this mortgage added to the short form clauses shall not derogate from the Chargee's right under the long form clauses in the Short Forms of Mortgages Act, but shall be in addition thereto or in substitution for part or parts thereof as the Chargee may elect and all shall have the force of covenants or conditions in accordance with the context.

22. Right of Entry to Cure Default

The chargor covenants and agrees with the Chargee that in the event of default in the payment of any money payable hereunder by the Chargor or on breach of any covenant, proviso or agreement herein contained, the Chargee may, at such time or times as the Chargee may deem necessary and without the concurrence of any person, enter upon the mortgaged premises and may make such arrangements for completing the construction, repairing or putting in order any buildings or other improvement to the mortgaged premises, or for inspecting, taking care of, leasing, collecting the rents of and managing generally the mortgaged premises, or for remedying any breach or default of the Chargor hereunder, as the Chargee may deem expedient, without thereby becoming a Chargee in possession hereunder, and all reasonable costs, charges and expenses, including allowance for the time and service of any employee of the Chargee or other person appointed for the above purposes, shall be forthwith payable to the Chargee and shall be a charge upon the mortgaged premises and shall bear interest at the rate stipulated above until paid.

23. Discharge

The Chargee shall have a reasonable time after payment of the liabilities and other monies owing hereunder in full within which to prepare and execute a discharge of this mortgage, and interest as aforesaid shall continue to run and accrue until actual payment in full has been received by the Chargee and all legal and other expenses for the preparation and execution of such discharge shall be borne by the Chargor.

24. Not to Prejudice Other Securities

This mortgage is in addition to and not in substitution for any other security held by the Chargee for all or any part of the liabilities secured hereunder, and it is understood and agreed that the Chargee may pursue its remedies thereunder or hereunder concurrently or successively at its option. Any judgment or recovery hereunder or under any other security held by the Chargee for the monies secured hereunder shall not affect the right of the Chargee to realize upon this or any other such security.

25. Receiver and Manager

If the Chargor should make default under any of the terms and provisions of this mortgage, the Chargee may be instrument in writing appoint any person or persons, whether an officer or officers or an employee or employees of the Chargee or not, to be a receiver or receivers of all or any part of the mortgaged premises and may remove any receiver or receivers so appointed, and may appoint another or others in his or their stead. Any such receiver shall, so far as concerns responsibility for his acts, be deemed the agent of the Chargor and in no event the agent of the Chargee, and the Chargee shall not be in any way responsible for any misconduct, negligence or nonfeasance on the part of any such receiver. Subject to the provisions of the instrument appointing such receiver, any such receiver or receivers so appointed shall have power to take possession of the mortgaged premises or any part thereof and to carry on or concur in carrying on the business of the Chargor and to sell, assign or sublet or concur in selling, assigning or subletting all or any part of the mortgaged premises and in such event the Chargee shall not be deemed a Chargee in possession of the mortgaged premises. Except as may be otherwise directed by the Chargee, all monies from time to time received by such receiver shall be in trust for and paid over to the Chargee. Such receiver may make arrangements for completing the construction, repairing or putting in order of any building or other improvement on the mortgaged premises, or for inspecting, taking care of, managing, leasing and collecting the rents therefor; and all reasonable costs, expenses, charges, solicitors' fees and expenses (as between solicitor and his own client) including proper allowance for the time of service of an employee of the Chargee, charged at the same rate as if such service had been rendered to the Chargor in respect of property not subject to a mortgage held by the Chargee, or for the time and service of any other person or receiver appointed for the above purposes, shall be forthwith payable by the Chargor and shall be a charge on the mortgaged premises and shall bear interest at the rate aforesaid until paid. The rights and powers conferred by this paragraph are in supplement of and not in substitution for any rights or power the Chargee may from time to time have as the Chargee of this mortgage, and every such receiver may in the discretion of the Chargee be vested with all or any of the rights and powers of the Chargee. The term "receiver" as used in this paragraph includes a receiver and manager.

26. Expropriation

The process of any expropriation, condemnation, eminent domain or like proceeding or the sale in lieu of or in reasonable anticipation thereof of the whole or any part of the mortgaged premises to which the tenant under the lease might otherwise be entitled shall, at the option of the Chrgee, be paid to the Chargee in priority to any claims of any other party and shall be applied in reduction of the liabilities and other monies hereby secured.

27. General

(a) Provided that no sale or other dealing by the Chargor with the lease or mortgaged premises or any part thereof shall in any way change the liability of the Chargor or in any way alter the rights of the Chargee as against the Chargor or any other person liable for payment of the monies hereby secured.

(b) Provided and it is hereby agreed, that all rights, advantages, privileges, immunities, powers and things hereby secured to the Chargee shall be equally secured to and exercisable by its or their successors and assigns, and that all covenants, liabilities, rights and obligations entered into or imposed hereunder upon the Chargor shall be equally binding upon their successors and assigns, and that all such covenants, liabilities, rights and obligations shall be joint and several.

(c) The Chargor agrees that neither the preparation execution nor registration of this mortgage shall bind the Chargee to advance the money hereby intended to be secured, nor shall the advance of part of such money bind the Chargee to advance the balance thereof, but nevertheless the estate hereby conveyed shall take effect forthwith on the execution hereof.

IN WITNESS WHEREOF the Chargor has executed these presents.

SIGNED, SEALED AND
DELIVERED
in the presence of

9F40
LEASE ASSIGNMENT

[See Paras. 9.501 and 9.160]

THIS AGREEMENT made as of and effective from the _____ day of _____, 19_____

A M O N G

(A)

(hereinafter referred to as the "Assignor")

OF THE FIRST PART

- A N D -

(B)

(hereinafter referred to as the "Assignee")

OF THE SECOND PART

- A N D -

(C)

(hereinafter referred to as the "Landlord")

OF THE THIRD PART

RECITALS

A.   By lease dated _____ (the "Lease") the Landlord leased to the Assignor as tenant for and during a term (the "Term") of _____ years commencing on the _____ day of _____, 19_____ and expiring on the   day of , 19_____ certain premises (the "Leased Premises") comprising an area of _____ square feet and shown outlined in red on a plan attached to the Lease;

B.   Notice of the Lease was registered in the Land Registry Office for the _____ Division of _____ on _____ as Instrument No. _____ ;

C.   The Assignor has agreed to assign the Lease to the Assignee subject to obtaining the Landlord's consent to such assignment;

D.   The Assignor has applied to the Landlord for the Landlord's consent to assign the Lease to the Assignee, subject to and upon the terms and conditions herein set out; and

E.   The Landlord has agreed to grant its consent to this assignment as and from the _____ day of _____, 19_____ (the "Effective Date") subject to the terms and conditions herein set out.

1. CONSIDERATION

The mutual covenants and agreements among the parties herein set out and the sum of TEN ($10.00) CANADIAN DOLLARS that has been paid by each of the parties to each of the others (the receipt and sufficiency of which is hereby acknowledged) are the consideration for this Agreement.

2. RECITALS

The parties hereto acknowledge, confirm and agree that the foregoing recitals are true in substance and fact.

3. ASSIGNMENT

The Assignor hereby transfers, sets over and assigns to the Assignee as of and from the Effective Date, the Leased Premises and all privileges and appurtenances thereto belonging together with the unexpired residue of the Term thereof and the Lease and all benefits and advantages to be derived therefrom. To have and to hold the same unto the Assignee, subject to the payment of rent and other payments thereunder as may hereafter become due and payable under the terms of the Lease, and the observance and performance of the covenants and conditions of the tenant contained in the Lease.

4. ASSIGNOR'S COVENANTS

The Assignor covenants and agrees with the Assignee that:

(a)   Despite any act of the Assignor, the Lease is a good, valid, and subsisting lease and subject only to a final determination by the Landlord of additional rent attributable to the Leased Premises for the 19___ lease year, all rents and other payments thereunder and thereby reserved have been duly paid up to but not including the

Effective Date and the covenants and conditions therein contained have been duly observed and performed by the Assignor.

(b)   The Assignor has good right, full power and absolute authority to assign the Lease in the manner aforesaid according to the true intent and meaning of this Agreement, free and clear of all liens, mortgages, charges and encumbrances of any kind whatsoever.

(c)   Subject to the payment of rent and all other payments thereunder and to the observance and performance of the terms, covenants and conditions contained in the Lease on the part of the tenant therein to be observed and performed, the Assignee may enter into and upon and hold and enjoy the Leased Premises for the residue of the Term granted by the Lease for its own use and benefit without interruption by the Assignor or by any person whomsoever claiming through or under the Assignor.

(d)   The Assignor will indemnify and save harmless the Assignee from all actions, suits, costs, losses, charges, demands and expenses for and in respect of any non payment, non observance or non performance arising, accruing or occurring up to but not including the Effective Date.

(e)   The Assignor will from time to time hereafter at the request and cost of the Assignee promptly execute such further assurances as the Assignee may reasonably require.

5. ASSIGNEE'S COVENANTS

(1)   The Assignee covenants with the Assignor that:

(a)   It will at all times during the balance of the Term of the Lease pay the rent and other payments under the Lease and observe and perform the terms, covenants and agreements contained in the Lease respectively reserved and contained on the part of the Assignor therein to be observed and performed; and

(b)   It will indemnify and save harmless the Assignor from all actions, suits, costs, losses, charges, demands and expenses for and in respect of any such non payment, non–observance or non–performance arising or occurring from and including the Effective Date.

(2) The Assignee covenants with the Landlord that:

(a) It will at all times during the balance of the Term of the Lease pay all rent and all other payments to be paid by the tenant therein, at the times and in the manner provided for in the Lease. The Assignee will observe and perform all of the terms, covenants and conditions contained in the Lease on the part of the tenant therein to be observed and performed, as and when the same are required to be observed and performed including without limitation, the provisions of the Lease relating to the permitted use of the Leased Premises;

(b) It will indemnify and save harmless the Landlord from all actions, suits, costs, losses, charges, demands and expenses for and in respect of any such non payment, non observance or non performance.

(3) The Assignee acknowledges that it has received a copy of the executed Lease and is familiar with its terms, covenants and conditions.

6. LANDLORD'S CONSENT

The Landlord hereby consents to the assignment of the Lease from the Assignor to the Assignee upon and subject to the following terms and conditions, that:

(a) This consent does not in any way derogate from the rights of the Landlord under the Lease nor operate to release the Assignor from making all payments becoming due under the Lease or from the non-observance or non-performance of all of the terms, covenants and conditions in the Lease on the part of the Assignor to be observed and performed. Regardless of the assignment, the Landlord shall have all of its rights and remedies arising as a result of any such non-observance or non-performance by the Assignor and the Assignor shall remain liable during the balance of the Term of the Lease for the observance and performance of all of the terms, covenants and conditions contained in the Lease. The Assignor shall not be liable for such observances and performances during any extension or renewal subsequently negotiated between the Landlord and the Assignee;

(b) This consent does not constitute a waiver of the necessity for consent to any further assignment or transfer of the Lease (which for the purpose of this consent includes any assignment, subletting, mortgaging or encumbering of the Lease or parting with or sharing possession of all or any part of the Leased Premises) which must be completed in accordance with the terms of the Lease. If the Assignee proposes to effect a further transfer or assignment of the Lease, the terms of the Lease with respect to such transfer or assignment shall apply to any such further transfer or assignment;

(c) The Assignor releases and waives any and all rights and remedies to which it may be entitled at law, in equity or as tenant under the Lease including, without limitation, the right to apply for relief from forfeiture or to obtain any reassignment of the Lease;

(d) This consent is given upon the expressed understanding that the Assignor shall hereafter be responsible for and shall save the Landlord harmless and indemnify it from and against all costs, including all costs incurred by the Landlord in connection with the preparation of this Agreement and any additional documentation related thereto and the Landlord's consent to this Agreement;

(e) By giving its consent pursuant to this Agreement, the Landlord does not hereby acknowledge or approve of any of the terms of this Agreement as between the Assignor and the Assignee except for the assignment of the Lease itself;

(f) This assignment of the Lease is deemed not to have been delivered to the Assignee by the Assignor until the consent of the Landlord has been evidenced by the execution and delivery of this Agreement by the Landlord to both the Assignor and the Assignee;

(g) The Assignor and the Assignee shall, at their expense, promptly execute such further documentation with respect to the Leased Premises as the Landlord reasonably requires from time to time; and

(h) The Assignee acknowledges and agrees that:
    (i) It is accepting possession of the Leased Premises in an "as is" condition as of the Effective Date;
    (ii) The Landlord has no responsibility or liability for making any renovations, alterations or improvements in or to the Leased Premises; and

(iii) All further renovations, alterations, or improvements in or to the Leased Premises are the sole responsibility of the Assignee and shall be undertaken and completed at the Assignee's expense and strictly in accordance with the provisions of the Lease.

7. CONFIRMATION

(a) The Assignor hereby confirms that the Lease is in full force and effect, unchanged and unmodified except in accordance with this Agreement including the recitals aforesaid it being understood and agreed that all terms and expressions when used in this Agreement have the same meaning as they have in the Lease.

(b) The Assignor confirms that the Landlord is not in default of any of the Landlord's covenants, obligations or agreements under the Lease.

(c) The Assignor and the Landlord confirm that the Landlord holds the sum of $_____ in accordance with Section _____ of the Lease and the Landlord further confirms that the Assignee will not be responsible for any defaults arising or incurred prior to the Effective Date of any of the tenant' covenants, obligations or agreements under the Lease and the Assignee only can treat the Lease as not being in default up to but not including the Effective Date.

8. BINDING EFFECT

This Agreement shall enure to the benefit of the Landlord, Assignor and Assignee, their respective successors and assigns and shall be binding upon each of them and their successors and assigns respectively.

IN WITNESS WHEREOF the parties hereto have duly executed this Agreement as of the Effective Date by affixing their respective corporate seals under the hands of their proper signing officers duly authorized in that regard.

(A)

Per: _____

(Assignor)

(B)

Per: _____

(Assignee)

C)

Per: _____

(Landlord)

9F41
LANDLORD'S CERTIFICATE ON STATUS OF LEASE

[See Para. 9.150]

TO: (B)
AND TO: _____, its solicitors
RE: Assignment of Lease dated _____
       (the "Lease") between (C) (the "Landlord") and
       (A) (the "Assignor")

CERTIFICATE

The Landlord hereby confirms and acknowledges as follows:

1.   The Lease has been validly executed and delivered by the Landlord.

2.   The Lease constitutes a valid and subsisting obligation of the Landlord enforceable in accordance with its terms.

3.   There have been no oral or written variations, modifications or alterations of the Lease and the Lease is now in full force and effect.

4.   The Lease contains all of the terms agreed to between the Landlord and the Assignor and none of the Landlord's obligations under the Lease has been waived or released.

5.   The Landlord does not hold any security deposit for damages and there has been no prepayment of rent or other payments other than rent for the current period. All rent and other amounts payable are as stated in the Lease.

6.   The term of the Lease commenced on _____. All rent and other payments required to be made by the Assignor to the Landlord pursuant to the Lease up to and including the date of this certificate have been made, all audits in connection therewith have been completed to the satisfaction of the Landlord and there are no outstanding rent, payments or other liabilities due, owing or accruing under the Lease that are the responsibility of the Assignor except as set out below:

7.   The term of the Lease expires on _____ subject to the rights of the Landlord and the Assignor's right to renew under the Lease. There are no defaults by either the Landlord or the Assignor under the Lease.

8.   There has been no prior assignment of the Lease by the Assignor.

The Landlord acknowledges that you are relying on the truth and accuracy of this certificate in completing the assignment of the Lease from the Assignor to the Assignee.

DATED at _____ this _____ day of _____, 19__

(C)

per: _____c/s

per: _____

9F42
LANDLORD'S CONSENT TO ASSIGNMENT

[See Paras. 9.501 and 9.160]

TO: (B)
AND TO: , its solicitors

RE: Assignment of Lease dated

(the "Lease") between (C) (the "Landlord") and (A) (the "Assignor")

CONSENT

The Landlord hereby consents to the assignment of the Lease from the Assignor to the Assignee upon and subject to the following terms and conditions, that:

1.   This consent does not in any way derogate from the rights of the Landlord under the Lease nor operate to release the Assignor to make all payments from time to time becoming due under the Lease and from the non-observance or non-performance of all of the terms, covenants and conditions in the Lease on the part of the Assignor therein to be observed and performed (and the Landlord's rights and remedies arising as a result of any such non-observance or non-performance), and notwithstanding such assignment (or any disaffirmance or disclaimer of the said assignment) the Assignor shall remain liable during the balance of the term of the Lease for the observance and performance of all of the terms, covenants and conditions contained in the Lease but the Assignor shall not be liable therefor during any extension or renewal thereof, if any, subsequently negotiated between the Landlord and the Assignee.

2.   This consent does not constitute a waiver of the necessity for consent to any further assignment or transfer of the Lease (which for the purpose of this consent includes any assignment, subletting, mortgaging or encumbering of the Lease or parting with or sharing possession of all or any part of the premises referred to in the Lease) which must be completed in accordance with the terms of the Lease. If the Assignee proposes to effect a further transfer or assignment of the Lease, the terms of the Lease with respect to such transfer or assignment shall apply to any such further transfer or assignment.

DATED at _____ this _____ day of (*month*), (*year*)

         (C)

         per: _____c/s

         per: _____

9F43
LANDLORD'S CONSENT
TO MORTGAGE OF LEASEHOLD

[See Paras. 9.501 and 9.160]

CONSENT

TO: (D)
AND TO: , its solicitors

RE: (D) (insert name of the "Lender")—Mortgage of Leasehold from (A)
     (insert name of the "Borrower")—address

(C) (*insert name of the "Landlord"*) HEREBY CONSENTS to the mortgage granted by the Borrower to the Lender of a lease (the "Lease") dated _____ made between the Landlord as landlord and the Borrower as tenant and notice of which was registered in the Land Registry Office for the _____ Division of _____ as Instrument No. _____ on _____ as security for the Borrower's past and future obligations to the Lender pursuant to the terms of the said mortgage of lease.

The Landlord HEREBY DECLARES that:

(a) The Lease is presently in good standing and that all payments have been made to date;

(b) No modifications have been made in the Lease to date except as disclosed by the registered title; and

(c) There are no existing defaults of which the Landlord has knowledge.

This consent shall not be deemed to waive or modify in any respect any of the rights of the Landlord under the terms and conditions of the Lease or to relieve the tenant from the observance and performance of any and all of the covenants and conditions of the Lease, except that the Landlord agrees that if there shall be any default made by the tenant, the Landlord will not exercise such rights or remedies to which it may be entitled thereunder by reason of such default, without first giving the Lender ten (10) days' notice in writing at:

(D)

address

Attention:

within which to remedy such default, and if such default is remedied or reasonable steps are taken to remedy such default, the Landlord shall not be entitled to terminate the Lease. If the default of the Borrower is by its nature not capable of rectification or remedy, so long as the Lender shall pay the rent reserved by the Lease and shall perform the other covenants of the tenant under the Lease, the Landlord shall not be entitled to terminate the Lease and the Lender may at its option require that the Landlord execute and deliver a new lease of the leased premises to the Lender on the same terms and conditions as the Lease, for the balance of the stated term of the Lease and any renewal period. If the Lender enforces any of the Lender's security or enters into a new lease pursuant hereto, the Lender shall have the right to sell, assign, sublet or otherwise dispose of the Lease with the consent of the Landlord, such consent not to be unreasonably withheld, and shall upon such sale, assignment, sublease or other disposition be relieved from all obligations under the Lease or any such new lease.

DATED at the City of _____, this _____ day of _____ 19 ____.

(C)

Per: _____

9F44
NON-DISTURBANCE AGREEMENT

[See Paras. 9.501 and 9.160]

THIS AGREEMENT made the _____ day of _____, 19____ .

A M O N G:

(hereinafter referred to as "Mortgagee")

OF THE
FIRST PART

-and-

(C)

(hereinafter referred to as "Landlord")

OF THE SECOND PART

-and-

(A)

(hereinafter referred to as "Tenant")

OF THE THIRD PART

WHEREAS:

By a lease dated _____, (the "Lease") the Landlord leased to the Tenant certain premises located at _____ (the "Premises") more particularly described in Schedule A attached hereto.

Notice of the Lease was registered in the Land Registry Office for the _____ Division of _____ on _____ as Instrument No. _____ ; and

The Mortgagee registered a charge in the said Land Registry Office against the Premises on _____ as Instrument No. _____ .

NOW THIS AGREEMENT WITNESSETH that in consideration of the premises and of TWO DOLLARS ($2.00) now paid by the Landlord and the Tenant to the Mortgagee, the receipt and sufficiency whereof is hereby acknowledged by the Mortgagee, the Mortgagee covenants and agrees with the Landlord and the Tenant as follows:

1. So long as the Tenant is not in default in the payment of rent or in the performance of any of the covenants under the Lease and the period for curing such default has not expired, the Tenant's possession of the Premises and the Tenant's rights and privileges under the Lease or any renewal thereof shall not be diminished or interfered with by the Mortgagee.

2. In the event that the Mortgagee succeeds to the interest of the Landlord under the Lease, the Tenant shall be bound to the Mortgagee under all of the terms of the Lease for the balance of the term thereof remaining with the same force and effect as if the Mortgagee were the landlord under the Lease, and the Tenant hereby attorns to the Mortgagee as its landlord, such attornment to be

effective without the execution of any further instrument on the part of either of the parties hereto, immediately upon the Mortgagee succeeding to the interest of the landlord under the Lease. Notwithstanding anything herein to the contrary, the Tenant shall be under no obligation to pay rent to the Mortgagee until the Tenant receives written notice from the Mortgagee that it has succeeded to the interest of the landlord under the Lease. The respective rights and obligations of the Tenant and the Mortgagee upon such attornment shall, to the extent of the then remaining balance of the term of the Lease, be the same as now set forth therein, it being the intention of the parties hereto for this purpose to incorporate the Lease in this Agreement by reference with the same force and effect as if set forth at length herein.

3. In the event that the Mortgagee succeeds to the interest of the landlord under the Lease, the Mortgagee shall be bound to the Tenant under all of the terms of the Lease, and the Tenant shall, from and after such event, have the same remedies against the Mortgagee for the breach of any agreement contained in the Lease that the Tenant might have had under the Lease against the prior landlord thereunder. In no event shall the Mortgagee be liable for any act or omission of any prior landlord, or be subject to any offsets or defences which the Tenant might have against any prior landlord.

IN WITNESS WHEREOF the Mortgagee has duly executed this Agreement _____ this _____ day of _____, 19__.

Per: _____

Per: _____

We have the authority to bind the Corporation

9F45
NON-DISTURBANCE AGREEMENT
WITH LEASEHOLD MORTGAGEE

[See Paras. 9.501 and 9.160]

THIS AGREEMENT made the _____ day of , 19__.

A M O N G:

(hereinafter referred to as "Mortgagee")

OF THE FIRST PART

-and-

(C)

(hereinafter referred to as "Landlord")

OF THE SECOND PART

-and-

(A)

(hereinafter referred to as "Tenant")

OF THE THIRD PART

-and-

(D)

(hereinafter referred to as the "Leasehold Mortgagee")

OF THE FOURTH PART

WHEREAS:

1. By a lease dated the _____ day of _____, 19__, (the "Lease") the Landlord leased to the Tenant certain premises located at _____ (the "Premises") more particularly described in Schedule A attached hereto.

2. Notice of the Lease was registered in the Land Registry Office for the _____ Division of _____ on _____ as Instrument No_____.

3. The Mortgagee registered a charge in the said Land Registry Office against the Premises on _____ as Instrument No_____.

4. The Tenant mortgaged the Lease and its interest thereunder to the Leasehold Mortgagee pursuant to a mortgage of lease dated _____ notice of which was registered in the said Land Registry Office on _____ as Instrument No_____.

NOW THIS AGREEMENT WITNESSETH that in consideration of the premises and of TWO DOLLARS ($2.00) now paid by the Landlord, the Leasehold Mortgagee and the Tenant to the Mortgagee, the receipt and sufficiency whereof is hereby acknowledged, the Mortgagee covenants and agrees with the Landlord, the Leasehold Mortgagee and the Tenant:

1. So long as the Tenant is not in default in the payment of rent or in the performance of any of the covenants under the Lease and the period for curing such default has not expired, the Tenant's possession of the Premises and the Tenant's rights and privileges under the Lease or any renewal thereof shall not be diminished or interfered with by the Mortgagee.

2. In the event that the Mortgagee succeeds to the interest of the Landlord under the Lease, the Tenant shall be bound to the Mortgagee under all of the terms of the Lease for the balance of the term thereof remaining with the same force and effect as if the Mortgagee were the landlord under the Lease, and the Tenant hereby attorns to the Mortgagee as its landlord, such attornment to be effective without the execution of any further instrument on the part of either of the parties hereto, immediately upon the Mortgagee succeeding to the interest of the Landlord under the Lease. Notwithstanding anything herein to the contrary, the Tenant shall be under no obligation to pay rent to the Mortgagee until the Tenant receives written notice from the Mortgagee that it has succeeded to the interest of the Landlord under the Lease. The respective rights and obligations of the Tenant and the Mortgagee upon such attornment shall to the extent of the then remaining balance of the term of the Lease be the same as now set forth therein, it being the intention of the parties hereto for this purpose to incorporate the Lease in this Agreement by reference with the same force and effect as if set forth at length herein.

3. In the event that the Mortgagee succeeds to the interest of the Landlord under the Lease, the Mortgagee shall be bound to the Tenant under all of the terms of the Lease, and the Tenant shall, from and after such event, have the same remedies against the Mortgagee for the breach of any agreement contained in the Lease that the Tenant might have had under the Lease against the prior Landlord thereunder. In no event shall the Mortgagee be liable for any act or omission of any prior landlord, or be subject to any offsets or defences which the Tenant might have against any prior landlord.

4. The Mortgagee acknowledges receipt of the consent of the Landlord (a true copy of which is attached hereto as Schedule B) with respect to the said mortgage of lease and other matters. In the event that the Mortgagee succeeds to the interest of the Landlord under the Lease, the Mortgagee shall be bound to the Leasehold Mortgagee under all of the terms of the said consent.

IN WITNESS WHEREOF the Mortgagee has duly executed the within Agreement as of the day and date above written.

Per: _____

Per: _____

We have the authority to bind the Corporation

9F46
BILL OF SALE

[See Para. 9.510]

THIS INDENTURE made the _____ day of _____, 19__.

B E T W E E N :

Vendor Inc., a corporation incorporated under the laws of the Province of Ontario, with an office at:

_____

(hereinafter referred to as the "Vendor")

OF THE FIRST PART

A N D :

Purchaser Inc., a corporation incorporated under the laws of the Province of Ontario, with an office at:

_____

(hereinafter referred to as the "Purchaser")

OF THE SECOND PART

WHEREAS the Vendor and the Purchaser have entered into an agreement of purchase and sale dated as of the _____ day of _____, 19____ (the "Asset Purchase Agreement"), wherein the Vendor has agreed, inter alia, to sell, assign and transfer to the Purchaser and the Purchaser has agreed to purchase from the Vendor certain of the property and assets of the Vendor.

NOW THEREFORE THIS INDENTURE WITNESSETH that for good and valuable consideration and the sum of _____ Dollars ($_____) now paid by the Purchaser to the Vendor pursuant to the Asset Purchase Agreement, the receipt and sufficiency of which is hereby acknowledged by the Vendor, which consideration includes the consideration for the transfer of the goods and chattels hereinafter referred to, the Vendor hereby grants, bargains, sells, assigns, transfers, conveys and sets over unto the Purchaser, its successors and assigns, all those items listed in Schedule "A" attached hereto.

The Vendor covenants, promises and agrees with the Purchaser that the hereby sold, assigned and transferred goods and chattels are owned by the Vendor as beneficial owner thereof with a good and marketable title thereto, free and clear of all mortgages, liens, charges, pledges, security interests, encumbrances or other claims whatsoever.

The Vendor covenants and agrees with the Purchaser, its successors and assigns, that it will, from time to time and at all times hereafter, upon every reasonable request of the Purchaser, its successors and assigns, make, do and execute or cause and procure to be made, done and executed all such further acts, deeds or assurances as may be reasonably required by the Purchaser, its successors and assigns, for more effectively and completely vesting in the Purchaser, its successors and assigns, the goods and chattels hereby sold, assigned and transferred in accordance with the terms hereof.

All terms with initial capitals used herein and not otherwise defined herein shall have the respective meanings ascribed thereto in the Asset Purchase Agreement.

This Indenture is subject to the provisions contained in the Asset Purchase Agreement.

This Indenture shall be governed by and construed in accordance with the laws of the (*Province*) and the laws of Canada applicable therein.

IN WITNESS WHEREOF this Indenture has been executed by the Vendor as of the day and year first above-mentioned.

Vendor Inc.

SIGNED, SEALED AND DELIVERED
  in the presence of:

Per:_____
Per:_____

NB: Add affidavits of execution by Vendor and bona fides of Purchaser in form for local laws, sworn before a notary, for registration outside of Ontario.

SCHEDULE "A"

Equipment

_____

_____

_____

_____

_____

9F46:1
ELECTION CONCERNING THE ACQUISITION OF A BUSINESS OR PART OF A BUSINESS

[See Para. 9.042]

TITLE 9: SALE OF A BUSINESS [9F46:1]

APPLICATION OF ELECTION

This section applies only to the acquisition of a business or part of a business where, under the agreement, the recipient acquired all or substantially all of the property required to carry on the business.

APPLICATION DU CHOIX

Ce choix s'applique uniquement à l'acquisition d'une entreprise ou d'une partie d'une entreprise, lorsque, en vertu de la convention l'acquéreur a acquis la totalité, ou presque, des biens requis pour exploiter l'entreprise ou une partie de l'entreprise.

GENERAL DEFINITIONS

"all or substantially all"	generally means 90 per cent or more;
"business"	includes a profession, calling, trade, manufacture or undertaking of any kind whatever, whether the activity or undertaking is engaged in for profit, and any activity engaged in on a regular or continuous basis that involves the supply of property by way of lease, licence or similar arrangement, but does not include an office or employment;
"property"	means any property, whether real or personal, movable or immovable, tangible or intangible, corporeal or incorporeal, and includes a right or interest of any kind, a share and a chose in action, but does not include money;
"recipient"	of a supply of property or a service means

(a) where consideration for the supply is payable under an agreement for the supply, the person who is liable under the agreement to pay that consideration,

(b) where paragraph (a) does not apply and consideration is payable for the supply, the person who is liable to pay that consideration, and

(c) where no consideration is payable for the supply,

    (i) in the case of a supply of property by way of sale, the person to whom the property is delivered or made available,

    (ii) in the case of a supply of property otherwise than by way of sale, the person to whom possession or use of the property is given or made available, and

    (iii) in the case of a supply of a service, the person to whom the service is rendered,

and any reference to a person to whom a supply is made shall be read as a reference to the recipient of the supply;

"registrant"	means a person who is registered, or who is required to be registered, under Subdivision d of Division V;
"supplier"	in respect of a supply, means the person making the supply;
"supply"	means, subject to sections 133 and 134, the provision of property or a service in any manner, including sale, transfer, barter, exchange, licence, rental, lease, gift or disposition;

DÉFINITIONS GÉNÉRALES

«totalité ou presque totalité»	En général, s'entend d'une proportion de 90 p. 100 ou plus
«enterprise»	Sont compris parmi les entreprises les commerces, les industries, les professions et toutes affaires quelconques avec ou sans but lucratif, ainsi que les activités exercées de façon régulière ou continue qui comportent la fourniture de biens par bail, licence ou accord semblable. En sont exclus les charges et les emplois
«bien»	À l'exclusion d'argent, tous biens – meubles et immeubles – tant corporels qu'incorporels, y compris un droit quelconque, une action ou une part
«acquéreur»	

a) Personne qui est tenue, aux termes d'une convention portant sur une fourniture, de payer la contrepartie de la fourniture;

b) personne qui est tenue, autrement qu'aux termes d'une convention portant sur une fourniture, de payer la contrepartie de la fourniture;

c) si nulle contrepartie n'est payable pour une fourniture:

    (i) personne à qui un bien, fourni par vente, est livré ou à la disposition de qui le bien est mis,

    (ii) personne à qui la possession ou l'utilisation d'un bien, fourni autrement que par vente, est transférée ou à la disposition de qui le bien est mis,

    (iii) personne à qui un service est rendu.

Par ailleurs, la mention d'une personne au profit de laquelle une fourniture est effectuée vaut mention de l'acquéreur de la fourniture.

«inscrit»	Personne inscrite, ou tenue de l'être, aux termes de la sous-section d de la section V.
«fournisseur»	Relativement à une fourniture, la personne qui effectue la fourniture.
«fourniture»	Sous réserve des articles 133 et 134, livraison de biens ou prestation de services, notamment par vente, transfert, troc, échange, louage, licence, donation ou aliénation.

9F47
GENERAL CONVEYANCE

[See Para. 9.510]

THIS INDENTURE made as of the _____ day of _____, 19__.

BETWEEN:

VENDOR INC., a corporation incorporated under the laws of the Province of Ontario

(hereinafter called the "Vendor")

OF THE FIRST PART

-and-

PURCHASER INC., a corporation incorporated under the laws of the Province of Ontario

(hereinafter called the "Purchaser")

OF THE SECOND PART

WHEREAS the Vendor agreed to sell and the Purchaser agreed to purchase as at and from the close of business on _____, 19__, as a going concern the undertaking and assets (the "Assets") of the Vendor relating to the Chemical Division of the Vendor (the "Business");

NOW THIS INDENTURE WITNESSETH that for good and valuable consideration now paid by the Purchaser to the Vendor (the receipt and sufficiency of which is hereby acknowledged) the Vendor hereby grants, bargains, sells, assigns, transfers, conveys and sets over onto the Purchaser, its successors and assigns as a going concern as at and from the close of business on _____, 19__ the undertaking and the Assets of the Business have and except the excluded assets of the foregoing the following Assets of the Business:

1.   inventory;

2.   fixed assets (including machinery and equipment);

3. goodwill;

4. vehicles;

5. prepaid expenses;

6. leasehold interests;

7. registered and unregistered trade marks and the name "ABC Chemicals";

8. contracts and customer lists;

9. trade accounts receivable; and

10. books and records.

TO HOLD the said hereby sold, assigned, transferred or conveyed undertaking and Assets and all right, title and interest of the Vendor thereto and therein unto and to the use of the Purchaser, its successors and assigns.

AND the Vendor doth hereby covenant, promise and agree with the Purchaser in the manner following, that is to say:

THAT the Vendor is now rightfully and absolutely possessed of and entitled to the said hereby sold, assigned, transferred or conveyed undertaking and Assets of the Business and that the Vendor now has in it good right, title and authority to assign the same unto the Purchaser, its successors and assigns, according to the true intent and meaning of these presents and that the Purchaser shall immediately upon the execution and delivery of these presents have possession of and may from time to time and at all times hereafter peaceably and quietly have, hold, possess and enjoy the said hereby sold, assigned, transferred or conveyed undertaking and Assets of the Business and every part thereof to and for its own use and benefit without any manner of hindrance, interruption, molestation, claim or demand whatsoever, of, from or by the Vendor or any person whomsoever and with good and marketable title thereto, free and clear and absolutely released and discharged from and against all former and other bargains, sales, gifts, grants, mortgages, pledges, security interests, adverse claims, liens, charges and encumbrances of any nature or kind whatsoever.

The Vendor covenants and agrees with the Purchaser, its successors and assigns, that it will from time to time and at all times thereafter, upon every reasonable request of the Purchaser, its successors or assigns, make, do and execute or cause and procure to be made, done and executed all such further acts, deeds or assurances as may be reasonably required by the Purchaser, its successors or assigns, whether for more effectually and completely vesting in the Purchaser, its successors or assigns, the undertaking, and Assets of the Business hereby sold, assigned, transferred or conveyed in accordance with the terms hereof or for the purpose of registration or otherwise.

The Vendor hereby declares that, as to any property and assets or interest in any property or assets of the Vendor intended to be transferred, assigned, conveyed, bargained, sold and set over to the Purchaser, its suc-cessors and assigns, hereby and the title to which may not have passed to the Purchaser, its successors and assigns, by virtue of this indenture or any transfers or conveyances which may from time to time be executed and delivered in purchase of the covenants aforesaid, the Vendor holdsthe same in trust for the Purchaser, its successors or assigns, to convey, assign and transfer the same as the Purchaser may from time to time direct.

IN WITNESS WHEREOF this indenture has been executed by the Vendor and the Purchaser.

VENDOR INC.

Per: _____c/s

PURCHASER INC.

Per: _____c/s

9F48
ASSIGNMENT OF LEASED EQUIPMENT

[See Para. 9.510]

To: Purchaser Inc.

In consideration of the closing of the transactions specified in the agreement of purchase and sale made between us dated _____, 19___, the undersigned hereby assigns and transfers to you all of the undersigned's right, title and interest in and to the following leased equipment held by the undersigned as lessee:

Lessor: Lessor Inc.
Address: _____
Contact Party: _____
Phone No.:   _____
Lease No.:   _____
Equip. Description: _____
Lease Term Expires: _____
Rental Per Month: _____
Option to Purchase: Yes/No
Option Price: $_____

DATED at _____ this _____ day of _____, 19___.

VENDOR INC.

per:_____

per: _____

The foregoing assignment is hereby acknowledged and agreed to this _____ day of _____, 19__.

LESSOR INC.

per: _____

per: _____

9F49
STATUTORY DECLARATION OF VENDOR RE ENCUMBRANCES

[See Para. 9.510]

TO: Purchaser Inc. ("Purchaser")

AND TO: Messrs. _____
         solicitors for the Purchaser

RE: Sale of assets of Vendor Ltd. to Purchaser pursuant to an agreement of purchase and sale dated the _____ day of _____ , 19__ (the "Agreement")

I,_____ , of the _____ of _____, Province of Ontario, make oath and say:

1.   I am the _____ of Vendor Ltd. (the "Corporation") and as such have personal knowledge of the matters herein declared.

2.   None of the assets transferred by the Corporation to Purchaser pursuant to the closing of the above-noted transaction are encumbered by any of the security interests represented by the following registrations pursuant to the Personal Property Security Act (Ontario) and the Bank Act (Canada):

REGISTRATION NUMBER   **SECURED PARTY**

_____

_____

_____

_____

_____

And I make this solemn declaration conscientiously believing it to be true and knowing that it is of the same force and effect as if made under the Canada Evidence Act.

SWORN BEFORE ME at the _____
of _____, in the ____
of _____ this____
day of _____, 19___

_____

A Commissioner etc.

_____

9F50
LIABILITIES ASSUMPTION AGREEMENT

[See Para. 9.510]

THIS AGREEMENT made as of the _____ day of _____, 19__.

B E T W E E N :

VENDOR LTD., a corporation incorporated under the laws of the Province of Ontario

(hereinafter called the "Vendor")

OF THE FIRST PART

A N D :

JANE DOE

(hereinafter called the "Purchaser")

OF THE SECOND PART

WHEREAS the Vendor has agreed to sell to the Purchaser and the Purchaser has agreed to purchase from the Vendor pursuant to an agreement dated as of the _____ day of _____, 19__ (the "Purchase Agreement"), the undertaking, property and assets of the Vendor on the Closing Date (the "Business").

NOW THEREFORE, in consideration of the premises and the sum of Two Dollars ($2.00) of lawful money of Canada and of other good and valuable consideration (the receipt and sufficiency whereof is hereby acknowledged by the parties hereto), the parties covenant and agree as follows:

1. Defined Terms—Unless the context otherwise requires, all words and phrases defined in the Purchase Agreement and used herein shall have the same meaning herein as in the Purchase Agreement.

2.   (a)   Assumption of Liabilities—The Purchaser hereby assumes and becomes liable for, and shall pay, satisfy, assume, discharge, observe, perform, fulfil, and indemnify the Vendor against, the liabilities described in Schedule "A" hereto.

     (b)   In connection therewith, the Purchaser shall:
         (i)   indemnify and save the Vendor harmless from all and any costs, damages or expenses that may be paid or incurred by the Vendor following any suit or action taken by any other party because of the failure of the Purchaser to discharge and perform all or any of the obligations, covenants, agreements and obligations forming part of the liabilities assumed hereunder; and

         (ii)   if any suit or action is commenced against the Vendor in connection with any of the assumed liabilities or in respect of any covenant, condition, agreement or obligation assumed hereby, assume the conduct of the Vendor's case and will provide to the Vendor such further indemnification from all costs, damages or expenses the Vendor may reasonably require.

3. Further Assurances—The Purchaser will, from time to time, and at all times hereafter upon the reasonable request of the Vendor, its successors and assigns, or its solicitors and at the cost of the Purchaser, do and execute or cause to procure to be made, done and executed all such further acts, deeds and assurances for more effectually and completely assuming and becoming liable for the liabilities assumed in accordance with this Agreement.

4. Governing Law—The provisions shall be governed and construed in accordance with the laws of the Province of Ontario.

5. Succession—This Agreement shall enure to the benefit of and be binding upon the parties hereto and their respective successors and assigns.

IN WITNESS WHEREOF this Agreement has been executed by the parties hereto.

SIGNED, SEALED AND
DELIEVERED in the presence of

_____

_____

Jane Doe

VENDOR LTD.

Per: _____

Per: _____

9F51
ASSIGNMENT OF TRADE-MARKS

[See Paras. 9.520 and 9.190]

THIS ASSIGNMENT AGREEMENT entered into this _____ day of _____ , 19__.

B E T W E E N :

VENDOR INC., (*address*), a corporation incorporated under the laws of the Province of Ontario

(hereinafter referred to as the "Assignor")

OF THE FIRST PART

-and-

PURCHASER INC., (*address*), a corporation incorporated under the laws of the Province of Ontario

(hereinafter referred to as the "Assignee")

OF THE SECOND PART

WHEREAS under and by virtue of an agreement of purchase and sale, dated as of the _____ day of _____, 19___ between the Assignor and the Assignee, the Assignor sold to the Assignee certain assets as more particularly described in the said agreement, including without limitation the trade marks described in Schedule "A" attached hereto (the "Trade-marks");

AND WHEREAS the Assignee is desirous of acquiring the right to use the Trade Marks;

NOW THEREFORE THIS AGREEMENT WITNESSETH that in consideration of the sum of Ten Dollars ($10.00) and other good and valuable consideration now paid by the Assignee to the Assignor, the receipt and sufficiency of which is hereby acknowledged, the parties hereto agree as follows:

1. The Assignor hereby sells, assigns, and transfers to the Assignee the whole right, title, and interest of the Assignor in and to the Trade-marks and the registrations thereof, together with the goodwill of the business relating to the goods andor services in respect of which the Trade-marks are registered to the Assignor, the same to be held as fully by the Assignee as the same would have been held by the Assignor had this Assignment not been made.

2. The Assignor hereby represents and warrants that the Assignor is now rightfully possessed of and entitled to, and now has good right, title and authority to sell, assign and transfer unto the Assignee the Trade-marks and goodwill hereinbefore described and that the Assignor is registered as owner of the Trade-marks.

3. The Assignor covenants and agrees with the Assignee, its successors, and assigns, that it will from time to time and at all times hereafter, upon every reasonable request of the Assignee, its successors and assigns, make, do and execute or cause and procure to be made, done and executed all such further acts, deeds or assurances as may be reasonably required by the Assignee, its successors and assigns, for more effectually and completely vesting in the Assignee, its successors and assigns, the Trade-marks and goodwill hereby sold, assigned and transferred in accordance with the terms hereof.

4. The Assignee hereby appoints (*solicitors*) whose full post office address in Canada is (*address*), as the firm to which any notice in respect of any application or registration may be sent, and upon which service of any proceedings in respect of any application or registration may be given or served with the same effect as if they had been given to or served upon the Assignor.

5. This Agreement shall enure to the benefit of and be binding upon the parties hereto and their respective successors and assigns.

IN WITNESS WHEREOF this Agreement has been executed by the Assignor and the Assignee on the day and the year first above written.

VENDOR INC.

per: _____ c/s
           per: _____

PURCHASER INC.

per: _____ c/s

per: _____

SCHEDULE "A"

	Trade Mark	Canadian Registration Number
1.	ACME	123,456
2	WIDGET	234,567
3	BLACK	345,678

		United States Registration Number
1.	ACME	567,890

9F52
UNDERTAKING OF CORPORATE VENDOR TO MINISTRY TO CHANGE ITS NAME

[See Para. 9.520]

CONSENT TO CORPORATE NAME
AND UNDERTAKING BY CORPORATION

TO: The Minister of Consumer and Commercial Relations.

RE: The Ontario *Business Corporations Act* and the proposed incorporation of Vendor's Corporate Property Inc.

Vendor Inc., incorporated under the laws of Ontario by articles of incorporation dated the (day) of (month, year) hereby consents to the incorporation of a corporation under the name Vendor's Corporate Property Inc. or any variation thereof, articles of incorporation of which are filed herewith, and hereby undertakes to cease to carry on business or activities under the name of Vendor Inc. or to change such name to some dissimilar name within 6 months of the incorporation of the proposed corporation.

DATED the (*day*) of (*month, year*).

VENDOR INC.

Per: _____

June Brown
President

9F53
UNDERTAKING OF VENDOR
TO CHANGE ITS NAME

[See Para. 9.520]

UNDERTAKING

TO: Purchaser Inc.

AND TO: Messrs. _____
         solicitors for Purchaser Inc.

RE: Sale of assets of Vendor Ltd. to Purchaser Inc. pursuant to an
       agreement of purchase and sale dated the _____ day of _____,
       19__ (the "Agreement")

IN CONSIDERATION OF AND NOTWITHSTANDING the closing of
the above-captioned transaction, the undersigned hereby undertakes to file
Articles of Amendment and do all other acts and things necessary to
change its name to a name that does not resemble in sound, form or
substance as that of within thirty (30) days of the date hereof and to
provide a notarial copy of the said Articles of Amendment, as filed, to
_____.

DATED at _____ this _____ day of _____, 19__.

VENDOR LTD

Per: _____

Per: _____

9F54
EMPLOYMENT AGREEMENT

[See Paras. 9.530 and 9.310]

MEMORANDUM OF AGREEMENT made as of the _____ day of _____, 19__

BETWEEN:

JANE DOE, of the city _____ of , in the (province) of _____, Executive

(hereinafter called the "Executive")

OF THE FIRST PART

- and -

PURCHASER INC., a corporation incorporated under the laws of the Province of _____

(hereinafter called "Purchaser")

OF THE SECOND PART

- and -

TARGET INC., a corporation incorporated under the laws of the Province of _____

(hereinafter called the "Company")

OF THE THIRD PART

WHEREAS the Executive has entered into an agreement dated _____, 19____ with the Purchaser (the "Share Purchase Agreement") providing for the sale by the Executive to the Purchaser of Common and Class B Preference Shares in the capital of the Company;

AND WHEREAS, pursuant to the Share Purchase Agreement, the Executive and the Purchaser have entered into an agreement dated as of _____ 19__, (the "Shareholders' Agreement") providing, *inter alia,* for options to purchase and sell the remaining Common Shares and Class B Preference Shares of the Company owned by the Executive;

AND WHEREAS the Executive owns and will continue to own a majority of the Common Shares and Class B Preference Shares in the capital of the Company until the aforesaid options provided for in the Shareholders' Agreement have been exercised;

AND WHEREAS under the terms of the Share Purchase Agreement the Executive agreed to enter into this agreement;

NOW THEREFORE THIS AGREEMENT WITNESSETH THAT in consideration of the premises and the respective covenants and agreements herein set out, it is agreed by and between the parties as follows:

1. The Executive shall serve as the President, Chief Executive and Chief Operating Officer of the Company and shall perform such duties and exercise such powers as are normally performed by persons holding such office and as may from time to time be determined by resolution of the board of directors of the Company or vested in her by the by-laws of the Company.

2. The employment of the Executive hereunder shall commence on the date hereof and shall continue until _____, 19__ and thereafter for such period as the parties may agree provided that the Executive may, at her option, relinquish the position of Chief Executive Officer of the Company at any time after _____, 19__.

3. The employment of the Executive hereunder may be terminated by the Company only (i) for cause by notice in writing from the Company; or (ii) if the Executive shall by reason of illness or mental or physical disability or incapacity fail, for any six consecutive calendar months in any calendar year or for nine months in the aggregate in any two successive calendar years, to perform her duties hereunder, then by not less than six months' notice in writing from the Company to the Executive. In either case, the employment of the Executive may not be terminated by the Company without the express prior written approval of the board of directors of the Company, expressed by a resolution passed by the directors at a meeting of the directors of each Company which is called for the purpose of considering such a resolution.

4. For the purposes of this agreement "cause" shall mean (i) wilful misfeasance, bad faith, gross negligence or an act of dishonesty of the Executive in the performance of her obligations, responsibilities, powers, discretions or authorities hereunder or (ii) the Executive's reckless disregard of her obligations or responsibilities hereunder.

5. The employment of the Executive hereunder may be terminated at any time by the Executive by not less than six months' notice in writing from the Executive to the Company. The employment of the Executive hereunder shall automatically cease upon her death.

6. The Executive shall devote the whole of her working time, attention and ability to the business and affairs of the Company and the Executive shall well and faithfully serve the Company during the continuance of her employment hereunder and shall use her best efforts to promote the interests of the Company.

7. During the Executive's employment hereunder, the remuneration of Executive for her services hereunder shall be payable in equal monthly instalments in arrears on the last business day of each calendar month. The annual rate of remuneration of the Executive for the first twelve (12) months of her employment hereunder shall be $_____, plus a bonus equal to an amount determined by reference to the aggregate of the net income of the Company for the fiscal year ended _____, 19__ as shown on the audited financial statements of the Company as follows:

(a)   a bonus of 5% of the amount of net income if net income is $200,000 or more and is less than $300,000; or

(b)   a bonus of 6.5% of the amount of net income if net income exceeds $299,999 and is less than $400,000; or

(c)   a bonus of $30,000 if net income is $400,000 or more.

The remuneration of the Executive for the second twelve (12) months of her employment hereunder shall be equal to the aggregate of the remu-neration paid to the Executive in respect of the first twelve (12) months. Thereafter, the annual rate of remuneration of the Executive shall be subject to annual review and increase by the board of directors of the Company. For the purposes of this paragraph, the term "net income" means the income of the Company calculated before income taxes and before deduction of bonus. The Company shall, from time to time, review the sharing of the remuneration and the cost of employee benefits and expenses and agree upon the proportion to be borne by each of them.

8. During the Executive's employment hereunder the Executive shall from time to time be entitled to vacations of five (5) weeks in each consecutive twelve month period commencing on the date hereof. Such vacations shall be taken at such times as are appropriate having regard to the operations of the Company.

9. In addition to the remuneration provided for in clause 7, the Company shall provide the Executive with a suitable current model automobile for her use and shall pay the cost of operation, maintenance, parking and insurance in connection therewith and shall provide the Executive with all of the benefits generally available to the senior executive employees of the Company, which benefits shall include Company-paid group life insurance, group medical and dental insurance and long-term disability insurance.

10. The Executive covenants and agrees that she will not, except as an officer and/or executive of the Company at any time during the period that the Executive is receiving and accepting remuneration from the Company hereunder and for a period of two (2) years thereafter, either individually or in partnership or jointly or in conjunction with any person or persons, firm, association, syndicate, company or corporation, as principal, agent, shareholder or in any other manner whatsoever, carry on or be engaged in or concerned with or interested in, or advise, lend money to, guarantee the debts or obligations of, or permit her name or any part thereof to be used or employed by or associated with, any person or persons, firm, association, syndicate, company or corporation engaged in or concerned with or interested in the business of an advertising agency in the Province of _____ or the Province of _____.

11. Any notice in writing required or permitted to be given to the Execu-tive hereunder shall be sufficiently given if delivered to the Executive or mailed by registered mail, postage prepaid, addressed to the Executive at her last residential address known to the Secretary of the Company. Any such notice mailed as aforesaid shall be deemed to have been received by the Executive on the third business day following the date of mailing. Any notice in writing required or permitted to be given to the Company hereunder shall be sufficiently given if delivered to the Company or mailed by registered mail, postage prepaid, addressed to the Company at (*address*). Any such notice mailed as aforesaid shall be deemed to have been received by the Company on the third business day following the date of mailing. Any such address for the giving of notices hereunder may be changed by notice in writing given hereunder.

12. The provisions of this agreement shall be governed by and interpreted in accordance with the laws of the Province of _____ and the laws of Canada in force in such province and each of the parties hereto hereby irrevocably attorns to the jurisdiction of the courts of such province.

13. The provisions of this agreement shall enure to the benefit of and be binding upon the heirs, executors, administrators and legal personal

representatives of the Executive and the successors and assigns of the Company, respectively.

IN WITNESS WHEREOF this agreement has been executed by the parties hereto.

_____

JANE DOE

PURCHASER INC.

per: _____
　　　President

TARGET INC.

per: _____
　　　President

9F55
PENSION ASSUMPTION AGREEMENT

[See Para. 9.530]

THIS AGREEMENT made this _____ day of _____ , 19__.

A M O N G:

"X"

(hereinafter referred to as the "Vendor")

OF THE FIRST PART

-and-

"Y"

(hereinafter referred to as the "Purchaser")

OF THE SECOND PART

-and-

"Z"

(hereinafter referred to as the "Trustee")

OF THE THIRD PART

WHEREAS the Vendor sponsored the [*name of the plan*] Pension Plan (the "Plan") for its employees;

AND WHEREAS the assets of the Plan are held by the Trustee pursuant to the terms of a trust agreement between the Vendor and the Trustee dated the _____ day of _____, 19__ (the "Trust Agreement);

AND WHEREAS pursuant to an agreement between the Vendor and the Purchaser dated , the Vendor has agreed to sell to the Purchaser and the Purchaser agreed to purchase from the Vendor substantially all of the assets, property and undertakings of the Vendor;

AND WHEREAS the Vendor and Purchaser have agreed that, as soon as practicable after the completion of such transaction, the Vendor shall assign and transfer to the Purchaser its rights, obligations, and liabilities under, and in relation to, the Plan and the aforesaid trust pursuant to which the Plan assets are administered (the "Trust") and the Purchaser shall accept such assignment and transfer and shall assume all duties and responsibilities required of it under the Plan and Trust as the successor Plan sponsor;

AND WHEREAS the parties have agreed that from the Closing Date to the date hereof the Vendor and the Trustee shall administer the Plan and Trust on the Purchaser's behalf.

NOW THEREFORE in consideration of the premises and of the mutual covenants and agreements contained herein, the parties hereto covenant and agree as follows:

1. Effective [insert Closing Date], the Vendor hereby assigns and transfers to the Purchaser its respective rights, obligations and liabilities under, and in

relation to, the Plan and the Trust including, without limitation, its rights, obligations and liabilities as Plan sponsor in relation to the "Members" (as defined in the Agreement of Purchase and Sale). The Purchaser hereby accepts such assignment and transfer and assumes all duties and responsibilities required of it under the Plan and Trust as the successor Plan sponsor.

2. In accordance with the foregoing, the Trustee hereby confirms its acceptance of the Purchaser as the successor Plan sponsor and as party to the Trust in the place and stead of the Vendor, effective [insert effective date] and the Purchaser hereby confirms the Trustee's appointment as Trustee of the Trust, subject to the terms and conditions of the Trust Agreement.

3. The parties hereto confirm that the Plan and Trust are to continue in accordance with the terms thereof and acknowledge that nothing contained in this Agreement nor in its implementation shall operate in any way as a discontinuance or wind-up of such Plan or Trust.

4. The Plan and the Trust Agreement shall be considered to be amended, where required, to give full effect to this Agreement and the parties hereto shall co-operate fully with each other in connection with the implementation of such amendments. Furthermore, the parties hereto agree that all requisite filings shall be made with the appropriate provincial and federal regulatory authorities.

5. Attached hereto as Schedule "A" is a list of the names and specimen signatures of those officers or employees of the Purchaser, who are authorized to give instructions and directions to the Trustee in relation to all matters pertaining to the Plan and the Trust.

6. This Agreement may be amended by written agreement of the parties hereto and shall enure to the benefit of and be binding upon the parties hereto and their respective successors and assigns.

7. The provisions of the Agreement shall be governed by and construed in accordance with the laws of the Province of _____ and the laws of Canada applicable therein.

IN WITNESS WHEREOF the parties hereto have executed the Agreement as of the date first above written.

VENDOR

Per:_____

PURCHASER

Per:_____

TRUSTEE

Per:_____

9F56
NOTICE OF PENSION ASSIGNMENT

[See Para. 9.520]

To: The Insurer

NOTIFICATION OF ASSIGNMENT

For the sum of one dollar, and for other valuable consideration, the receipt of which is hereby acknowledged, we, (*Vendor*), do hereby assign and convey to (*Purchaser*) all (*Vendor's*) right, title, and interest in Group Policy No. _____, issued by (*the Insurer*) to (*Vendor*) with effect from   to provide for the purchase of retirement incomes under the (*name of pension plan*), established by (*Vendor*) for its employees.

IN WITNESS WHEREOF, (*Vendor*), has hereto affixed its corporate seal, attested by the hands of its duly authorized officers this _____ day of _____, 19__.

(*Vendor*)

Per: _____

[*Purchaser*] hereby accepts the assignment of the above-described Group Policy in accordance with the terms set forth in the Agreement of Purchase and Sale made as of the _____ day of _____, 19__ between (*Vendor*) and (*Purchaser*).

(*Purchaser*)

Per: _____

9F57
AGREEMENT RE ESTABLISHMENT OF NEW PLAN

[See Para. 9.530]

THIS AGREEMENT made as of the _____ day of ____, 19__

B E T W E E N:

"X"

(hereinafter referred to as the "Vendor")

OF THE FIRST PART

- and -

"Y"

(hereinafter referred to as the "Purchaser")

OF THE SECOND PART

WHEREAS the Vendor has agreed to sell, and the Purchaser has agreed to purchase certain assets of the Vendor's business [*insert the "Acquired Business"*];

AND WHEREAS the Vendor provides pension and other benefits to its employees pursuant to the [*name of Pension Plan*] (the "Vendor's Pension Plan");

AND WHEREAS pursuant to the agreement between the Vendor and the Purchaser dated _____ (the "Purchase Agreement"), the Vendor agreed to retain responsibility for the provision of pension and other benefits under the Vendor's Pension Plan accrued up to and including the Date of Closing, for employees of the Acquired Business (the "Transferred Employees") who are continued in employment by the Purchaser;

AND WHEREAS pursuant to the Purchase Agreement the Purchaser has agreed to implement one or more Plans which would provide pension and other benefits to the Transferred Employees that are substantially similar to or superior to the pension and other benefits currently provided to the Transferred Employees under the Vendor's Pension Plan;

AND WHEREAS the parties hereto desire to give effect to the provisions of the Purchase Agreement;

NOW THEREFORE in consideration of the mutual premises set out herein and for good and valuable consideration, the receipt and sufficiency of which is hereby acknowledged, the parties hereto agree as follows:

1. The Vendor shall be responsible for the satisfaction of its obligations with respect to the pension and other benefits for the Transferred Employees accrued under the Vendor's Pension Plan, up to and including the Date of Closing, in accordance with the terms of the Vendor's Pension Plan, the applicable collective agreement, and applicable regulatory requirements.

2. No further pension or other benefits under the Vendor's Pension Plan shall, from and after the Date of Closing, accrue to the credit of the Transferred Employees.

3. The Purchaser shall be responsible for the provision and satisfaction of pension and other benefits for the Transferred Employees, accruing from and after the Date of Closing, and the Purchaser shall establish, effective as of and from the Date of Closing, a pension plan that shall provide to the Transferred Employees, pension and other benefits which are substantially similar or superior to the pension and other benefits provided under the Vendor's Pension Plan for such employees as at the Date of Closing.

4. The Vendor agrees to indemnify and save harmless the Purchaser from and against any claims, demands, actions, damages, liabilities, losses, expenses or costs that the Purchaser may suffer or incur in connection with, or in respect of, the pension and other benefits of Transferred Employees accrued under the Vendor's Pension Plan, up to and including the Date of Closing.

5. The Purchaser agrees to indemnify and save harmless the Vendor from and against any claims, demands, actions, damages, liabilities, losses, expenses or costs that the Vendor may suffer or incur in connection with or in respect of the pension and other benefits of the Transferred Employees accrued from and after the Date of Closing.

IN WITNESS WHEREOF the parties hereto have duly executed this agreement as of the day and year first above written.

[*VENDOR*]

By:_____

[PURCHASER]

By: _____

9F58
DIRECTIONS TO ACCOUNT DEBTORS

[See Para. 9.550]

(*Date*)To the Customers of Vendor Inc. (*"Vendor"*)

Dear Customer:

Please be advised that (*the Vendor*) has sold all of the assets and undertakings of its ABC Division to Purchaser Inc. (*the "Purchaser"*) on (*today's date*), including the contract made between the (*Vendor*) and (*you*).

You are hereby directed to make all payments due under this contract commencing _____, 19__ to the (*Purchaser*) at its address at (*address*). The (*Purchaser*) has moved into the premises formerly occupied by the ABC Division and is undertaking the business of the (*Vendor*) in supplying chemicals and serving their chemical handling equipment.

You are hereby directed to make all payments due under this contract on or before _____, 19__ to (*the Vendor's*) at (*address*) (Attention: Mr. B. Smith).

Should you require further information or assistance, please contact (*name*) of Purchaser at (*telephone number*).

Yours very truly,

VENDOR INC.

per:_____

9F59
PPSA REGISTRATION
FOR ABSOLUTE ASSIGNMENT OF ACCOUNTS

[See Para. 9.550]

Financing Statement/Claim for Lien
État de financement/Demande de privilège
Form
Formule **1C**OCR

053808975

P 3

VENDOR INC.

2 QUEEN ST. WEST   TORONTO   ONT   M1A 2B3

PURCHASER INC.

2 ASH ROAD   DOWNSVIEW   ONT   N2B 3C4

X   X $ .00

ABSOLUTE ASSIGNMENT OF CERTAIN ACCOUNTS AND CHATTEL

PAPER AND THE PROCEEDS THEREOF

PURCHASER INC.
BY ITS SOLICITORS:

PER:

9F60
SELLER'S AFFIDAVIT

[See Paras. 9.560 and 9.074]

Statement and Affidavit, B.S.A. — Page 1   DYE & DURHAM CO. INC. — FORM NO. 246

Bulk Sales Act

STATEMENT AS TO SELLER'S CREDITORS

Statement showing names and addresses of all unsecured trade creditors and secured trade creditors of

JUNE BROWN and JAMES BROWN   of the   City

of   Mississauga in the   Regional Municipality of Peel

c.o.b. as The Best Pizza   and the amount of the indebtedness or liability due, owing,

payable or accruing due, or to become due by   them to each of them.

UNSECURED TRADE CREDITORS

NAME OF CREDITOR	ADDRESS	AMOUNT	
NIL	NIL	NIL	

Statement and Affidavit, B.S.A. — Page 2   DYE & DURHAM CO. INC. — FORM NO. 246

SECURED TRADE CREDITORS

Name of Creditor	Address	Amount		Nature of Security	Due or becoming due on the date fixed for the completion of the sale
NIL	NIL	NIL		NIL	NIL

X'X   We,   JUNE BROWN and JAMES BROWN, both   of the City of Mississauga   in the Regional Municipality of Peel in the Province of Ontario make oath and say:

1.   That the foregoing statement is a true and correct statement
   (a)   of the names and addresses of all the unsecured trade creditors of the said *The Best Pizza* and of the amount of the indebtedness or liability due, owing, payable or accruing due or to become due and payable by the said *The Best Pizza*   to each of the said unsecured trade creditors; and
   (b)   of the names and addresses of all the secured trade creditors of the said *The Best Pizza* and of the amount of the indebtedness or liability due, owing, payable or accruing due or to become due and payable by the said *The Best Pizza*   to each of the said secured creditors, the nature of their security and whether they are or in the event of sale will become due and payable on the date fixed for the completion of the sale.

and, if the
seller is a
corporation

Sworn before me at the City

of Toronto
in the Municipality of
Metropolitan Toronto

this   day of   19____

A Commissioner, etc.

June Brown

James Brown

9F61
BUYER'S AFFIDAVIT

[See Paras 9.560 and 9.074]

AFFIDAVIT UNDER THE BULK SALES ACT

PROVINCE OF ONTARIO

) IN THE MATTER OF
the sale in bulk of the
assets of _____ LIMITED
(the "Vendor") to
_____INC.
(the "Purchaser") AND IN THE
MATTER OF the Bulk Sales Act,
R.S.O. 1990, c. B.14.

AFFIDAVIT

1. (*name*), of the City of (   ), in the Municipality of (
)

DO SOLEMNLY DECLARE THAT:

1. I am a solicitor with the firm (   ), which firm rep-resented the Purchaser in the above-named transaction and as such have knowledge of the matters hereinafter set forth;

2. The buyer is _____ Inc. of (*insert address*).

3. The seller is _____ Limited, (*insert address*), which formerly operated a car dealership at (*insert address*).

4. The buyer has purchased from the seller certain chattels and equipment situated in the seller's former place of business at (*insert address*) and (*insert address*).

5. The sale was completed on the _____ day of _____, 19__.

6. Annexed hereto and marked as Exhibit "A" to my affidavit is a true copy of the statement as to the Vendor's creditors prescribed by section 4 of the Bulk Sales Act, executed by the Vendor.

7. This affidavit is made pursuant to the Bulk Sales Act, and is made for no improper purpose.

AND I make this solemn Declaration conscientiously believing it to be true and knowing that it is of the same force and effect as if made under oath.

SWORN BEFORE ME AT THE
CITY OF _____, IN THE
MUNICIPALITY OF _____ THIS   _____
_____day of _____, 19__.   (*name*)

_____
A COMMISSIONER, ETC.

9F62
MATERIALS FOR EXEMPTION ORDER

[See Paras. 9.560 and 9.074]

Court File No. _____

SUPERIOR COURT OF JUSTICE

IN THE MATTER OF ABC Inc.

AND IN THE MATTER OF the Bulk Sales Act, R.S.O. 1990, c. B.14

B E T W E E N:

ABC INC.

Applicant

-and-

123456 ONTARIO LIMITED

Respondent

NOTICE OF APPLICATION

TO THE RESPONDENT:

A LEGAL PROCEEDING HAS BEEN COMMENCED by the Applicant. The claim made by the Applicant appears on the following page.

THIS APPLICATION will come on for a hearing before a judge on _____, 19__ at 10:00 o'clock at Osgoode Hall, Toronto.

IF YOU WISH TO OPPOSE THIS APPLICATION, you or an Ontario lawyer acting for you must forthwith prepare a notice of appearance in Form 38C prescribed by the Rules of Civil Procedure, serve it on the Applicant's lawyer or, where the Applicant does not have a lawyer, serve it on the Applicant, and file it, with proof of service, in this court office, and you or your lawyer must appear at the hearing.

IF YOU WISH TO PRESENT AFFIDAVIT OR OTHER DOCUMEN-TARY EVIDENCE TO THE COURT OR TO EXAMINE OR CROSS-EXAMINE WITNESSES ON THE APPLICATION, you or your lawyer must, in addition to serving your notice of appearance, serve a copy of the evidence on the Applicant's lawyer or, where the Applicant does not have a lawyer, serve it on the Applicant, and file it, with proof of service, in the court office where the application is to be heard as soon as possible, but not later than 2 p.m. on the day before the hearing.

IF YOU FAIL TO APPEAR AT THE HEARING, JUDGMENT MAY BE GIVEN IN YOUR ABSENCE AND WITHOUT FURTHER NOTICE TO YOU.

IF YOU WISH TO OPPOSE THIS APPLICATION but are unable to pay legal fees, legal aid may be available to you by contacting a local Legal Aid office.

Date: _____, 19__   Issued by _____
                                              Local Registrar

                                              Address of court office:

                                              145 Queen Street West
                                              Toronto, Ontario
                                              M5H 2N9

TO: *(Name and Address of Each Respondent or Party Receiving Notice if any)*

* * * * *

APPLICATION

1.   The Applicant makes application for:

(a)   an order exempting a sale in bulk from ABC Inc. to 123456 Ontario
        Limited from the provisions of the Bulk Sales Act, R.S.O. 1990 c. B.14
        (the "Act"), save section 7 thereof.

2.   The grounds for the application are:

(a)   The sale is advantageous to the seller, ABC Inc. and will not impair the
        seller's ability to pay creditors in full.
(b)   Section 3 of the Act.

3.   The following documentary evidence will be used at the hearing of the
        application:

(a)   the Affidavit of Jane Doe, filed, and the exhibits thereto.
(b)   such further and other material as counsel may advise and this
        Honourable Court permit.

Date: _____ , 19__

                              (*firm*)
                              (*address*)]
                              Solicitors for the Applicant

                              Court File No. _____

SUPERIOR COURT OF JUSTICE

     IN THE MATTER OF ABC Inc.

     AND IN THE MATTER OF the Bulk Sales Act, R.S.O. 1990, c. B.14

B E T W E E N:

                              ABC Inc.

                                                              Applicant

                              -and-

                         123456 ONTARIO LTD.

                                                              Respondent

                         A F F I D A V I T

I, Jane Doe, of the City of Toronto, in the Municipality of Metropolitan Toronto, MAKE OATH AND SAY AS FOLLOWS:

1.   For a period of over _____ years, I have been President of the Applicant, ABC Inc.and as such, have knowledge of the matters hereinafter deposed to.

2.   ABC Inc. carries on a number of businesses. Through its chemical division, it carries on business under the name "ABC Chemicals" at premises in Toronto, Ontario. On _____, 19__, ABC Inc. entered into an Agreement of Purchase and Sale with 123456 Ontario Limited (the "Purchaser" whereby ABC Inc. agreed to sell all of the assets of its chemical division to the Purchaser. The closing is scheduled for _____, 19__.

3.   A copy of the Agreement of Purchase and Sale is attached hereto as Exhibit "A" to this my Affidavit. As set out in Exhibit "A", the asset purchase is at book value.

4.   The chemical division, in the normal course of its business, orders materials and products from trade suppliers on a daily or weekly basis. The accounts of trade creditors are similarly paid. As of _____, 19__, the chemical division had 111 trade creditors who were owed an aggregate of $_____. Given the number of such trade creditors and the changing identity of such creditors from day to day, it is not practical to receive consents from trade creditors as a means of complying with the Bulk Sales Act.

5.   The trade creditors of the chemical division will be fully protected after the sale to the purchaser. First, the Purchaser, under Exhibit "A", has agreed to assume liability for the payment to trade creditors and it is expected that the trade creditors will be paid in the usual course. Second, should the Purchaser for some reason fail to pay the trade creditors, the trade creditors will have recourse against ABC Inc. Attached hereto as Exhibit "B" to this my Affidavit is a copy of the latest audited financial statements for ABC Inc. dated _____, 19__. As set out in Exhibit "B", ABC Inc. had a net worth by way of shareholder's equity of $_____ million as at _____, 19__. As the sale of the chemical division is at book value, the shareholder's equity of ABC Inc. will be unaffected by the sale. ABC Inc. both before and after the sale, will have more than sufficient assets to pay the trade creditors of the chemical division.

6.   There has been no material change in the financial condition of the chemical division since _____, 19__. There has been no material change in the financial condition of ABC Inc. since _____, 19__. The ability of _____ to pay the trade creditors of the chemical division

will thus not be significantly altered from its ability as demonstrated by the figures cited above in this Affidavit.

7. This Affidavit is sworn in support of an exemption order pursuant to section 3 of the Bulk Sales Act and for no improper purpose.

Sworn before me at the City of
Toronto, in the Municipality of
Metropolitan Toronto, this _____
day of_____, 19 ___.

_____
A Commissioner for
Taking Affidavits, etc.

_____
JANE DOE

*****

Court File No. _____

SUPERIOR COURT OF JUSTICE

THE HONOURABLE   _____DAY, THE _____DAY
JUSTICE   OF_____, 19___

IN THE MATTER OF ABC Inc.

AND IN THE MATTER OF the Bulk Sales Act, R.S.O. 1990, c. B.14

B E T W E E N:

ABC INC.

Applicant

-and-

123456 ONTARIO LIMITED

Respondent

J U D G M E N T

THIS APPLICATION was heard this day without notice in the presence of counsel for the Applicant, ABC Inc.

ON READING THE NOTICE OF APPLICATION AND THE EVIDENCE FILED BY THE PARTIES, including the Affidavit of Jane Doe, filed, and on hearing the submissions of counsel for the Applicant,

1. **THIS COURT ORDERS** that the sale in bulk by ABC Inc. to 123456 Ontario Limited be, and the same is hereby, exempted for the application of the Bulk Sales Act, save Section 7 thereof.

9F63
CREDITOR'S WAIVER

[See Paras. 9.560 and 9.072]

BULK SALES ACT

(Section 8(1)(c))

IN THE MATTER OF the sale in bulk between

_____ (the "Seller") and

_____ (the "Buyer")

WAIVER

_____, an unsecured trade creditor of the above-named Seller hereby waives the provisions of the Bulk Sales Act that requires that adequate provisions be made for the immediate payment in full of my claim forthwith after the completion of the sale, and I hereby acknowledge and agree that the Buyer may pay or deliver the proceeds of the sale to the Seller and thereupon acquire the property of the Seller in the stock, without making provision for the immediate payment of my claim, and that any right to recover payment of my claim may, unless otherwise agreed, be asserted against the Seller only.

DATED at _____ this _____ day of _____, 19___.

_____
Name

9F64
CREDITOR'S CONSENT

[See Paras. 9.560 and 9.074]

BULK SALES ACT

(Section 8(2)(a) and 9(1)(a))

CONSENT

IN THE MATTER OF THE SALE IN BULK

B E T W E E N

_____
(hereinafter called the "Purchaser")

-and-

_____
(hereinafter called the "Vendor"

I, _____ , of the _____ of , _____ in the _____ of _____, an unsecured trade creditor of the above-named Vendor, hereby   acknowledge and agree:

1.   That I have received

(a)   a copy of the statement showing the names and addresses of the unsecured trade creditors and the amount of the indebtedness or liability due, owing, payable or accruing due or to become due and payable by the Vendor, and showing the names and addresses of the secured trade creditors, the nature of their security and whether their claims are or, in the event of sale, become due on the date fixed for the completion of the sale, and the amount of the indebtedness or liability due, or owing, payable or accruing due or to become due and payable by the Vendor;

(b)   a statement of the affairs of the Vendor; and

(c)   a copy of the agreement of the sale in bulk.

2.   That I consent to the sale; and

3.   That I consent to the appointment of _____ as trustee.

DATED at this _____ day of _____, 19___.

WITNESS

_____

9F65
CLOSING AGENDA—ASSET PURCHASE

[See Paras. 9.570 and 9.470–9.610 generally]

CLOSING AGENDA

TRANSACTION: Sale of assets by Vendor Ltd. to Purchaser Inc.

DATE: _____

TIME: _____

PLACE: Offices of (*firm*) Messrs. Miller Thomson (*address*)

PARTIES:

Vendor Ltd. (the "VENDOR")
represented by:

_____

Messrs. _____ ("*Vendor's Counsel* ")
represented by:

_____

(Purchaser Inc.) (*the "Purchaser "*)
represented by:

_____

Messrs. _____ ("*Purchaser's Counsel* ")
represented by:

_____

TERMS OF ESCROW:

All deliveries, payments and corporate proceedings, called for in the Closing Agenda shall be in escrow until all items therein have been completed and those persons involved have acknowledged satisfaction with same, at which time the escrow will be released and all documents and monies may be taken up by the respective parties herein and the corporate proceedings will thereupon be effective, save for such partial releases from escrow as agreed upon from time to time during the closing.

DEFINITIONS:

All defined terms (denoted with initial capital letters) have the meaning assigned to them in an Agreement of Purchase and Sale dated the _____ day of _____, 19___ between the Vendor and the Purchaser providing for the sale of substantially all of the assets of the Vendor to the Purchaser (*the "Agreement "*).

Document		Executed by:
1	Asset Purchase Agreement	Vendor, Purchaser
2.	Certified copy of resolution of the directors Vendor, of the Purchaser authorizing the Agreement and all ancillary matters.	Vendor
3.	Certified copy of resolution of the directors of the Purchaser, authorizing the Agreement and all ancillary matters.	Purchaser
4.	Consent of Landlord to transfer of all rights, title and interest of the Vendor in its leasehold interest in property known municipally as _____ to the Purchaser, pursuant to section _____ of the Agreement.	Vendor
5.	Assignment Agreement with respect to leasehold interest in property known municipally as _____ pursuant to section _____ of the Agreement.	Vendor, Purchaser
6.	Proof of insurance required under _____ (to be delivered to_____)	Purchaser
7.	Consent of _____ to transfer of all rights, title and interest of the Vendor in _____	Vendor
8.	Closing declaration of the Vendor pursuant to section _____ of the Agreement confirming (i) that representations and warranties are true; (ii) that all closing conditions for the Vendor's benefit have been fulfilled; and (iii) incumbency.	Vendor
9.	Closing declaration of the Purchaser pursuant to section _____ of the Agreement confirming (i) that representations and warranties are true; (ii) that all closing conditions for the Purchaser's benefit have been fulfilled; and (iii) incumbency.	Purchaser
10.	Documentation pursuant to the Bulk Sales Act (Ontario) pursuant to section _____ of the Agreement.	Vendor

11.	Bill of Sale pursuant to section _____ of the Agreement.	Vendor
12.	Specific Conveyances where required (i.e., receivables, motor vehicles plus mechanical fitness certificates).	Vendor
13.	Deeds or Transfers by the Vendor of the real estate in registrable form, including Planning Act Affidavit and Declaration of Residency, pursuant to section _____ of the Agreement.	Vendor
14.	Certificate: section 6 of the Retail Sales Tax Act (Ontario) pursuant to section _____ of the Agreement.	Vendor
15.	Indemnification Agreement in favour of the Purchaser pursuant to section _____ of the Agreement.	Vendor
16.	Indemnification Agreement in favour of the Vendor.	Purchaser
17.	Non-competition agreement in favour of the Purchaser pursuant to section _____ of the Agreement.	Vendor
18.	Undertaking to change corporate name pursuant to section _____ of the Agreement.	Vendor
19.	Releases, discharges and/or Consents of any secured parties having liens or encumbrances against the Purchased Assets not being assumed by the Purchaser.	Vendor
20.	Election under section 22 of the Income Tax Act in respect of the Receivables	Vendor/Purchaser
21.	Statement of Adjustments	Vendor, Purchaser
22.	Direction re: Funds	Vendor
23.	Certified cheque payable to Vendor for balance of the Purchase Price.	Purchaser

24.	Receipt of the Vendor for the purchase price		Vendor
25.	Payment of Sales Tax applicable to transaction		Purchaser
26.	Payment of GST applicable to transaction		
27.	Security Agreement with respect to unpaid portion of purchase price		Purchaser/Vendor
28.	(a)	Financing Statement with respect to Vendor Security Agreement	Vendor
	(b)	Receipt of Purchaser for copy of PPSA registration	
29.	Undertaking to adjust		Vendor
30.	Undertaking to adjust		Purchaser

9F66
AUTHORIZING RESOLUTION

[See Paras. 9.570–9.571]

RESOLUTION OF THE SHAREHOLDERS
OF

_____

Sale of Assets of _____

    BE IT RESOLVED THAT the Corporation do enter into an agreement to sell certain assets of the Corporation in the form annexed hereto as Schedule "A", and the execution and delivery of the said agreement by the President of the Corporation be, and is hereby ratified and affirmed, in such form and with such additions, amendments, deletions or variations thereto as the President may approve, execution by such officer to be conclusive evidence for such approval. The President of the Corporation alone be, and is hereby authorized and directed to take such actions and execute and deliver such documents under the corporate seal of the Corporation or otherwise, as the President in his sole discretion may consider it necessary or desirable to implement the foregoing.

It is hereby certified by the undersigned President of _____ that the foregoing is a true and correct copy of a resolution consented to be the Shareholders of the Corporation on the _____ day of _____, 19___ and that the said resolutions are in full force and effect, unamended.

DATED this _____ day of , 19___.

_____

, President

9F67
POST-CLOSING TRUST AGREEMENT
TO SETTLE FUNDS

[See Paras. 9.570–9.571 and 9.470–9.610 generally]

THIS AGREEMENT made this _____ day of _____, 19___

AMONG:

> PURCHASER LTD. (*the "Purchaser"*)
>
> and
>
> VENDOR LIMITED (*the "Vendor"*)
>
> and
>
> (*the "Trustee"*)

WHEREAS by an Agreement of Purchase and Sale dated as of _____, 19___ the Purchaser has acquired all of the issued and outstanding shares owned by the Vendor in the capital of Target Ltd. (the "Company");

AND WHEREAS it was agreed between the Vendor and Purchaser that the sum of $_____ (the "Holdback") be withheld from payment of the purchaser price;

AND WHEREAS the parties are entering into this agreement to evidence the terms and conditions with respect to the Holdback;

NOW THEREFORE the parties hereto agree as follows:

1.   The parties acknowledge that the foregoing recitals are true and correct.

2.   The Vendor and the Purchaser hereby agree that the Purchaser shall pay the amount of the Holdback to the Trustee in trust to hold the same in trust for both of them under the terms of this agreement.

3.   The Purchaser has been in control of the operations of the day-to-day business of the Company since _____, 19____. The Purchaser agrees to monitor the collection of the $_____ of doubtful accounts listed on the books and records of the Company as of _____, 19____ for the 90-day-period from _____ to , 19____ inclusive. At the end of such period, the Vendor shall prepare an accounting of such doubtful accounts for which the Purchaser received payment during the aforesaid 90-day period.

4.   On or before _____, 19___ the Vendor shall deliver to the Purchaser a statement reflecting the aforesaid doubtful accounts for which it received payment during the 90-day period. On or before _____, 19____, the Vendor shall indicate to the Purchaser whether or not it is in agreement with such statement.

5.   If the Purchaser and the Vendor are in agreement with the statement provided by the Purchaser, they shall both sign a copy of such statement and deliver the same to the Trustee with their direction of the Trustee make payment of the principal of the Holdback as follows:

      (a)   an amount equal to the doubtful receivables received by the Purchaser shall be paid to the Vendor; and

      (b)   an amount equal to the doubtful receivables not collected by the Purchaser shall be paid to the Purchaser.

6.   The Trustee shall deposit the Holdback in an interest-bearing account. Any interest earned on the Holdback shall be paid pro rata to the Vendor and the Purchaser in the same proportions as the principal of the Holdback.

7.   The signed copy of the statement from the Vendor and the Purchaser shall be delivered to the Trustee on or before _____, 19___ and upon receipt the Trustee shall forthwith make payment of the principal and interest of the Holdback in accordance with this agreement.

8.   In the event that the Vendor and the Purchaser do not agree with respect to the Purchaser's statement of collection of the doubtful accounts, one or

both of them shall so notify the Trustee on or before _____, 19___ and the Purchaser's statement shall be delivered to the auditors of the Company for their determination as to the proper accounting, which determination shall be final and binding upon the parties. A copy of the auditor's report shall be forwarded to the Trustee as soon as it is available and the payments shall be made by the Trustee to the Vendor and the Purchaser of the principal and interest on the Holdback in accordance with the auditor's report.

9.   The Vendor and the Purchaser agree that the Trustee shall have no liability with respect to the Holdback other than to make payment in accordance with the signed statement from the Vendor and the Purchaser or in accordance with the report of the auditors, as the case may be.

IN WITNESS WHEREOF the parties hereto have executed this agreement this ___ day of _____, 19___ .

VENDOR INC.

Per:_____ c/s

PURCHASER LTD.

Per: _____

Per: _____

(*firm*)

Per: _____

(*Solicitor*)

9F68
INDEMNIFICATION AGREEMENT

[See Paras. 9.570–9.571 and 9.470–9.610 generally]

THIS INDEMNIFICATION AGREEMENT made as of the _____ day of _____, 19___ .

B E T W E E N:

Vendor Inc. and Seller Ltd.

(hereinafter collectively called the "Vendors")

OF THE FIRST PART

AND

Purchaser Inc.

(hereinafter called the "Purchaser")

OF THE SECOND PART

WHEREAS by an agreement of purchase and sale dated the _____ day of _____, 19___ (the "Agreement of Purchase and Sale"), the Vendors agreed to sell, and the Purchaser agreed to purchase, certain assets of the Vendors upon the terms and conditions therein contained;

AND WHEREAS the Agreement of Purchase and Sale provides for indemnification to the extent and in the manner hereinafter provided for.

NOW THEREFORE THIS INDENTURE WITNESSETH THAT in consideration of the premises, the sum of Ten Dollars ($10.00) and other good and valuable consideration, the receipt and sufficiency whereof is hereby mutually acknowledged, the parties hereto hereby covenant and agree the one with the other as follows:

1. For the purposes of this agreement, unless otherwise specifically herein set forth, defined terms shall have the same meanings as those ascribed thereto by the Agreement of Purchase and Sale.

2. The Vendors hereby jointly and severally covenant and agree to indemnify and save harmless the Purchaser at all times against and in respect of any

and all claims, demands, actions, or proceedings and legal and other expenses by reason of any liability arising out:

(a) a material event which occurred prior to Closing but which became known subsequent to Closing with respect to the Business; and

(b) any and all assessments, re-assessments, penalties or other claims or prosecutions by Revenue Canada, Customs, Excise and Taxation or any other person or entity against them, or any of them, for or in respect of any matter not properly reflected in the Financial Statements, tax filings made by the Companies or the Vendors pertaining to the Business or otherwise pertaining to the ownership by the assets of the Business.

3. The Vendors shall jointly and severally reimburse the Purchaser for any payment made by the purchaser, at any time in respect of any liability or claim against it, arising out of the said transaction to which the foregoing indemnity relates provided that:

(a) it shall be a condition of any obligation of the Vendors under this paragraph that the Purchaser shall have given written notice to the Vendors of any such liability, loss or claim for damages as soon as is reasonably possible after the same shall have come to the attention of the Purchaser and shall have advised the Vendors by such notice whether the Purchaser intends to dispute the liability or cause such liability to be disputed;

(b) upon receipt of such notice from the Purchaser, the Vendors shall have the right individually or collectively to undertake the entire defence of any such claims by giving to the Purchaser notice of such intention within fifteen (15) days thereafter;

(c) failing notice from all of the Vendors of their intention to defend, the Purchaser shall be at liberty to defend the said claim at the cost and expense of the Vendors; and

(d) should the Vendors elect to dispute the said claim, they shall jointly and severally indemnify and save harmless the Purchaser of and from all costs and expenses of the defence.

(e) Where an amount is payable by the Purchaser or Vendor as indemnification pursuant to the terms of this Agreement and the Excise Tax Act provides that GST is deemed to have been collected by the payee thereof, the amount so payable, as determined without reference to this paragraph (the "Indemnification Amount"), shall be increased by an amount equal to the rate of GST applied to the Indemnification Amount in accordance with the Excise Tax Act.

4. Time shall be of the essence of this agreement and every part thereof.

5. Any notice, direction or other instrument required or permitted to be given to the Vendors or to the Purchaser shall be in writing and shall be given in accordance with the provisions of paragraph ____ of the Agreement of Purchase and Sale.

6. This agreement shall not be amended, altered or qualified, except by memorandum in writing signed by all of the parties hereto and any amendment, alteration, or qualification hereof shall be null and void and shall not be binding upon any party who has not given his written consent as aforesaid.

7. This agreement may be executed in counterpart and the counterparts together shall constitute the entire agreement.

IN WITNESS WHEREOF the parties hereto have hereunto caused to be affixed their corporate seals duly attested to by the hands of their respective proper signing officers, authorized in that behalf as of the date and year first above written.

PURCHASER INC.

Per: _____

Per: _____

VENDOR INC.

Per: _____

Per: _____

SELLER LTD.

Per: _____

Per: _____

9F69
STATUTORY DECLARATIONS RE REPRESENTATIONS AND CORPORATE AUTHORITY

[See Paras. 9.570–9.571 and 9.470–9.610 generally]

STATUTORY DECLARATIONS
OF
_____

TO: Purchaser Inc. ("Purchaser")

AND TO: Messrs. _____
             solicitors for the Purchaser

RE: Sale of assets of Vendor Ltd. to Purchaser Inc. pursuant to an agreement of purchase and sale dated the _____ day of _____, 19___ (the "Agreement")

I, _____ , of the _____ of _____, Province of Ontario, make oath and say:

1.   I am the _____ of Vendor Ltd. (the "Corporation") and as such have personal knowledge of the matters herein declared.
2.   All of the covenants, representations and warranties of the Corporation contained in the Agreement are true and correct as of the date of execution herein without qualification.
3.   All of the conditions of closing, for the benefit of the Corporation, as provided for in the Agreement, have been fulfilled.
4.   The officers and directors of the Corporation are as follows:

DIRECTORS	**OFFICERS**	**OFFICE**
_____	_____	_____
_____	_____	_____
_____	_____	_____
_____	_____	_____
_____	_____	_____

And I make this solemn declaration conscientiously believing it to be true and knowing that it is of the same force and effect as if made under the Canada Evidence Act.

SWORN BEFORE ME AT THE

_____of _____, in the

_____of _____ this

_____ day of _____, 19___.

_____

A Commissioner etc.

_____

9F70
VENDOR'S STATUTORY DECLARATION

[See Paras. 9.570–9.571 and 9.470–9.610 generally]

STATUTORY DECLARATION

TO: Purchaser Inc.
AND TO:

Messrs. _____

solicitors for Purchaser Inc.

RE: Sale of assets of Vendor Ltd. to Purchaser Inc. pursuant to an agreement of purchase and sale dated the _____ day of _____, 19____ (the "Agreement").

I, _____ , of the _____ of Vendor Ltd., Province of _____, make oath and say:1.   I   am   the   _____   of   _____   (the "Corporation") and as such have personal knowledge of the matters herein declared.

2.   The Corporation was incorporated under the laws of the Province of _____ on the _____ day of , 19____.

3.   The Corporation has carried on business in Canada since its incorporation and is resident in Canada within the meaning of the Income Tax Act.

4.   The assets to be sold pursuant to the Agreement do not con-
     stitute all or substantially all of the property of the Corporation.

And I make this solemn declaration conscientiously believing it to be true
and knowing that it is of the same force and effect as if made under the
Canada Evidence Act[2]

SWORN BEFORE ME at the _____
_____ of , in the _____ of ____
this _____ day of _____, 19___

_____

A Commissioner, etc.

_____

9F71
UNDERTAKING TO ADJUST

[See Paras. 9.570–9.571 and 9.470–9.610 generally]

TO: Vendor Ltd.

AND TO:
     Messrs. _____
     solicitors for Vendor Ltd.

RE: Sale of assets of Vendor Ltd. to Purchaser Inc. pursuant to an
     agreement of purchase and sale dated the ____ day of _____, 19___
     (the "Agreement")

   IN CONSIDERATION of and notwithstanding the closing of the above
transaction, Purchaser Inc. hereby undertakes to readjust, if neces-sary,
forthwith upon request by _____ all adjustments to the Purchase Price in
this transaction. Where an adjustment has not been finally determined by the
Closing Date, Purchaser Inc. agrees to further adjust such adjustment
forthwith upon request by Vendor Ltd. In this Undertaking, the terms
"Closing Date" and "Purchase Price" have the meanings attributed to them
in the above-noted Agreement.

   DATED at _____, this _____ day of _____, 19____.

PURCHASER INC.

per:_____

9F72
DIRECTION RE: TITLE

[See Paras. 9.570–9.571 and 9.470–9.610 generally]

TO: _____

AND TO:
    Messrs. _____
    solicitors for _____

RE: Sale of assets of _____ to _____ pursuant to an agreement of
      purchase and sale dated the _____ day of _____, 19___ (the
      "Agreement")

Please accept this as your good, sufficient, and irrevocable authority to accept *(insert name of corporation designated to be owner of the asset)* as the corporation designated by the undersigned for purposes of the Agreement.

DATED at _____, *(province)* this _____ day of _____, 19___.

_____

(Signature)

_____

(Name— Please Print)

9F73
DIRECTION RE: FUNDS

[See Paras 9.570–9.571 and 9.470–9.610 generally]

TO: _____
AND TO: Messrs. _____
solicitors for _____

RE: Sale of assets of Vendor Ltd. to Purchaser Inc. pursuant to an agreement of purchase and sale dated the _____ day of _____, 19___

Please accept this as your good, sufficient and irrevocable authority to make payment of the proceeds due on closing of the above noted transaction payable to:

1. _____,   as to $_____
2. _____,   as to $_____
3. _____,   as to $_____

DATED at _____, (*province*) this ____ day of _____, 19___.

_____

Per: _____

Per: _____

9F74
NON-COMPETITION AGREEMENT

[See Paras. 9.570–9.571 and 9.470–9.610 generally]

TO: _____
(herein called the "Purchasers")

WHEREAS the Purchasers have completed the purchase of substan-tially all of the assets of the business of Seller Inc. and Vendor Ltd. (col-lectively the "Vendors") (the "Purchased Business") pursuant to an agreement of purchase and sale between the Purchasers and Vendor dated the _____ day of _____, 19____ (the "Asset Purchase Agreement");

AND WHEREAS pursuant to the Asset Purchase Agreement it is a condition of closing that the undersigned enter into this instrument in favour of the Purchasers;

NOW THEREFORE THIS INSTRUMENT WITNESSES that in consideration of the premises and other good and valuable consideration and the sum of One Dollar ($1.00) of lawful money of Canada now paid to each of the undersigned by the Purchasers (the receipt and adequacy whereof is hereby acknowledged by the undersigned), each of the undersigned hereby covenant and agree with the Purchasers as follows:

1.   Each of the undersigned shall not at any time within the period of _____ (   ) years from the date of execution herein, either individually or in partnership or in conjunction with any person or persons, firm, association, syndicate, company or corporation, as principal, agent, director, officer, employee, investor or in any other manner whatsoever, directly or indirectly, carry on, be engaged in, be interested in, or be concerned with, or permit any of their names or any part thereof to be used or employed by any such person or persons, firm, association, syndicate, company or corporation, carrying on, engaged in, interested in or concerned with, a business which is similar to the Purchased Business within _____ (   ) miles of _____ .

For the purpose of this instrument "Purchased Business" also means the solicitation of and sale to the present customers of the Purchased Business of any services performed by the Purchased Business at the date hereof.

2.   Each of the undersigned shall not at any time within the period of _____ ( ) years from the date of execution herein, directly or indirectly, induce or attempt to induce any employee of the Purchased Business to leave the employ of the Purchasers or _____ or to become employed by any person other than the Purchasers or _____.

3.   The undersigned acknowledges that they have reviewed the provisions of sections 1 and 2 herein and that they have turned their minds to the reasonableness of the scope thereof, both as to geographical area and time period, that they have consulted the law firm of Messrs. _____, who have explained the implications of the said sections to them, and that they fully understand the implications of such restrictive covenants, and that they are entirely satisfied that the provisions of such sections are both necessary and reasonable for the protection of the legitimate interests of the Purchasers and that they reflect the mutual desire and intent of the Purchasers and the

undersigned that such provisions be upheld in their entirety and be given full force and effect.

4.   The undersigned acknowledge and agree that the breach by them of any of the restrictions set out in sections 1 and 2 of this instrument would cause irreparable harm to the Purchasers which could not be adequately compensated for by damages, and in the event of a breach or a threatened breach of any of the said provisions, the undersigned hereby acknowledge that the Purchasers shall be entitled to specific performance of this Agreement and to an injunction being issued against any of the undersigned restraining the said party or parties from any breach or further breach of such restrictions, but this sentence shall not be construed so as to be in derogation of any other remedy which the Purchasers may have in the event of such a breach or threatened breach. In order to obtain such relief, it shall not be necessary for the Purchasers to establish irreparable harm which cannot be satisfied by an award of damages.

5.   This instrument shall be construed in accordance with the laws of the Province of Ontario. This instrument shall extend to and enure to the benefit of the successors and assigns of the Purchasers and shall be binding upon each of the undersigned and their heirs, representatives, successors and assigns.

DATED this _____ day of _____, 19___.

SIGNED, SEALED AND
DELIVERED in the presence of:

_____   _____

_____   _____

VENDOR LTD.

Per: _____

Per: _____

SELLER INC.

Per: _____

Per: _____

9F75
RECEIPT

[See Paras. 9.570–9.571 and 9.470–9.610 generally]

TO: _____

AND TO: Messrs. _____
solicitors for _____

RE: Sale of assets of Vendor Ltd. to Purchaser Inc. pursuant to an agreement of purchase and sale dated the ____ day of _____, 19___ (the
"Agreement")

Receipt is hereby acknowledged of payment of the amount of _____
Dollars ($_____), in satisfaction of the purchase price payable pursuant
to the Agreement.

DATED at _____, (*province*) this _____ day of _____, 19___.

_____

Per: _____

Per: _____

9F76
CONFIDENTIALITY AGREEMENT

[See Paras. 9.570–9.571 and 9.470–9.610 generally]

_____, 19___

To: Vendor Ltd. ("Vendor")

Re: Confidentiality Agreement

In connection with our consideration of a possible purchase of all or
substantially all of the assets of the Vendor's chemical division pursuant to
our agreement (the "Agreement") made the ____ day of _____, 19___, the

undersigned confirms that it has requested Vendor to disclose certain confidential information pertaining to the chemical division pursuant to the Agreement, which confidential information includes and extends to, without limitation, the confidential documents listed in Schedule "A" attached hereto, the confidential information contained therein and all documents, materials and information (whether oral, written or otherwise) relating to the chemical division which are given or disclosed to us in the course of the transactions contemplated hereunder and/or which are obtained by us as a result of or in the course of any visit to any facility or location owned or occupied by the Vendor (hereinafter collectively referred to as the "Confidential Information").

In consideration of your furnishing the Confidential Information to us and as a condition to such disclosure, the undersigned party (the "Purchaser") agrees as follows:

1. Unless the context otherwise requires, the word "Purchaser" includes the undersigned, its affiliated corporations and their respective directors, officers, employees, agents, representatives and advisers.

2. The Purchaser will not disclose or release any of the Confidential Information to any third party, without the prior written consent of the Vendor.

3. Without the prior written consent of the Vendor, the Purchaser will not disclose to any third party either the fact that discussions or negotiations are taking place with respect to the sale of the chemical division, or any facts with respect to any such possible transaction, including the status thereof.

4. All records and other documents and all copies thereof relating to such Confidential Information, whether delivered to the Purchaser by the Vendor, or copies, summaries, analyses or notes thereof made by the Purchaser, shall be given to the Vendor, upon request, if a transaction of purchase and sale with respect to the chemical division is not completed. Return of such documents shall in no event relieve the Purchaser of any obligation of confidentiality contained herein respecting the Confidential Information.

5. Without the prior written consent of the Vendor, the Purchaser shall not use, directly or indirectly, any of the Confidential Information received or obtained from the Vendor in furtherance of its business (except in negotiation of the subject transaction) or the business of anyone else,

unless such information has become public other than as a result of acts by the Purchaser.

6. The Purchaser accepts all Confidential Information furnished and to be furnished concerning the chemical division, subject to these provisions of this letter. The Purchaser understands that neither the Vendor nor any of its agents, representatives or employees makes any representation or warranty as to the accuracy or completeness of the Confidential Information. This letter agreement shall be governed by the laws of the Province of _____ and constitutes our entire agreement with respect to the subject matter of this letter. The Purchaser acknowledges that it has consulted its counsel prior to and with respect to the implications of the execution of this letter.

Yours truly,

PURCHASER INC.

Per: _____

_____
Name (please print)

_____

Title

9F77
SHARE PURCHASE CLOSING AGENDA

[See Para. 9.620]

**PURCHASER LTD.
PURCHASE OF SHARES IN
TARGET LTD.
FROM
VENDOR LTD.**

_____, 19_____

CLOSING AGENDA

Time: 1:00 p.m. EST

Place: Offices of (*firm*), (*address*)

Parties Present: 1.   On behalf of Purchaser Ltd. ("Purchaser")

    —

    —

    —

2.   On behalf of Vendor Ltd. ("Vendor") and Target Ltd. ("Company")

    —

    —

3.   On behalf of (*firm*) ("MT"), counsel to Purchaser and Lender

    — (*name*)

4.   On behalf of Black and White ("BW"), counsel to Vendor and Company

Escrow: All deliveries, payments and the proceedings called for at closing shall be in escrow until all items on the closing agenda have been completed and all persons tendering or receiving documents at the closing acknowledge satisfaction with the same, at which time the escrow may be taken up by the respective parties described below and the proceedings will thereupon be effective.

No.		Document Description	Party Tabling	No. of Copies
1.	a)	Agreement of Purchase and Sale, complete with Schedules	Purchaser	4
	b)	Certified copy of resolution of directors of Vendor authorizing sale	Vendor	4
2.	a)	Federal Certificate of Standing for Company	Company	1+3P

No.	Document Description	Party Tabling	No. of Copies
	b) Ontario Certificate of Status for Company	Company	1+3P
3.	Certified copy of resolution of directors of Company authorizing transfer of shares	Company	4
4.	Share certificate no. 4 issued to Vendor endorsed for transfer and marked cancelled	Vendor	1+3P
5.	New share certificate no. 5 issued to Purchaser	Vendor	4
6.	Copy of updated share ledger	Vendor	4
7.	a) Resignation of Vendor's nominee directors and officers of Company	Vendor	4
	b) Resignation of remaining officers	Vendor	4
	c) Mutual Release of Company by Vendor's nominee directors and officers and Vendor as shareholder	Vendor	4
8.	Election of directors by Purchaser	Purchaser	4
9.	Election of new officers by new directors	Purchaser	4
10.	Federal and Provincial Corporations Information filings re: change of directors and officers	Purchaser	4

No.	Document Description	Party Tabling	No. of Copies
11.	Section 116 Income Tax Act declaration of Vendor re: residency	Vendor	4
12.	a) Indemnity of Vendor re: activities and litigation of Company	Vendor	4
	b) Delivery of $25,000 term deposit receipt by Vendor re: indemnity, including ABC litigation	Vendor	4
	c) Pledge of term deposit receipt by Vendor	MT	4
	d) Copy of latest audited annual and unaudited quarterly financial statements of Vendor	Vendor	4P of each
13.	Delivery of Minute Book, Share Ledgers and seal of the Company	Vendor	as necessary
14.	a) Opinion letter of counsel to Vendor	Vendor	4
	b) Certificate of officer of Vendor as to certain facts	Vendor	4
15.	Financial statements of Company as at _____. 19__ .	Vendor	4
16.	a) Undertaking re: delivery of Section 6 Retail Sales Tax Act certificate	Vendor	4
	b) Copy of _____, 19_____ payment for RST	Purchaser	4P

No.	Document Description	Party Tabling	No. of Copies
17.	Direction re: purchase price to BW, in trust	Vendor	4
18.	Statement of calculation of purchase price	Vendor/Purchaser	4
19.	a) MT's trust cheque to BW, in trust for $_____ for purchase price for common shares less $_____ holdback, less $_____ deposit	Purchaser	1+3P
	b) Copy of Purchaser's cheque for $_____ deposited to Company's account on _____ , 19___		
20.	Agreement of Vendor, Purchaser and MT regarding holdback of $_____ to be paid to Vendor and Purchaser on _____, 19 __ upon resolution of 90 day receivables	MT	4

Post Closing

No.	Document Description	Party Tabling	No. of Copies
1.	Delivery of statements on 90 day receivables, signed as accepted by Vendor and Purchaser	Purchaser	4
2.	MT's cheques for portion of $____ plus interest thereon as may be due to Vendor and/or Purchaser	MT/Purchaser/ Vendor	4
3.	Delivery of Section 4 Retail Sales Tax Act certificate	BW	

9F78
LONG FORM SHARE PURCHASE AGREEMENT

[See Para. 9.620]

THIS AGREEMENT made the _____ day of _____, 19___.

BETWEEN

> PURCHASER INC., a corporation incorporated under the laws of Canada
>
> (hereinafter referred to as the "Purchaser")
>
> OF THE FIRST PART

- and -

> JANE DOE, of the City of _____, in the Province of _____
>
> (hereinafter referred to as the "Vendor")
>
> OF THE SECOND PART

- and -

> TARGET LIMITED, a corporation incorporated under the laws of _____
>
> (hereinafter referred to as the "Company")
>
> OF THE THIRD PART

WITNESSETH THAT:

WHEREAS the Vendor is the legal and beneficial owner of all the issued and outstanding shares in the capital of the Company; and

AND WHEREAS the Vendor has agreed to sell to the Purchaser and the Purchaser has agreed to purchase from the Vendor all of the issued and outstanding shares in the capital of the Company upon and subject to the terms and conditions of this Agreement;

NOW THEREFORE, in consideration of the premises and mutual agreements herein contained and of other good and valuable consideration (the receipt and sufficiency of which are acknowledged by each Party hereto), the Parties agree with one another as follows:

INTERPRETATION

(1) Definitions

Whenever used in this Agreement, unless there is something in the subject matter or context inconsistent therewith, the following words and terms shall have the respective meanings ascribed to them in this Section 1(1):

(a) **"Affiliate", "Associate", "Body Corporate", "Subsidiary" and "Voting Securities"** shall have the respective meanings ascribed to those terms by the Business Corporations Act (Ontario) on the date hereof;

(b) **"Agreement"** means this share purchase agreement and all instruments supplemental to or in amendment or confirmation of this share purchase agreement, and all references to this Agreement shall include the attached Schedules and "Article", "Section", "Subsection", or "Paragraph" means and refers to the specified article, section, subsection, or paragraph of this share purchase agreement;

(c) **"Assets"** means the undertaking, property and assets of the Company relating to the Business as going concern, of every kind and description and wheresoever situated;

(d) **"Audited Financial Statements"** means the consolidated financial statements of the Company for its fiscal period ended on _____, 19___;

(e) **"Auditors"** means collectively, the Company's Auditors, the Vendor's Auditors and the Purchaser's Auditors;

(f) **"Bank Prime"** means the rate per annum charged on loans by the Vendor's Bank at its principal office in _____, Ontario for loans of Canadian dollars to its customers in Canada, and said to be its "prime rate", as the same is adjusted from time to time;

(g) **"Benefit Plan"** has the meaning ascribed in Section 4(1)(ab);

(h) **"Book Value of Assets"** means the total book value of the Assets as shown in the Effective Date Balance Sheet; and **"Book Value of Assumed Purchased Liabilities"** means the total book value of the liabilities as shown in the Effective Date Balance Sheet;

(i) **"Business"** means the operations of the Company in [*description of type of business*] and all operations related thereto;

(j) **"Business Day"** means any day, other than a Saturday, Sunday or any other day on which the principal chartered banks located in the City of _____ are not open for business during normal banking hours;

(k) **"Claim"** means any claim, demand, action, suit, litigation, charge, complaint, prosecution or other proceeding for which one Party can seek indemnification from the other Party pursuant to Sections 6(1) or 6(2);

(l) **"Closing"** means the completion of the sale to, and the purchase by the Purchaser of, the Shares and the completion of the transactions contemplated by this Agreement including the transfer and delivery of all documents of title to the Shares and the payment of the Purchase Price;

(m) **"Closing Date"** means _____, 19____, or such other date as the Parties may agree in writing as the date upon which the Closing shall take place; [*Alternative: The* _____ *day following the day on which this transaction of purchase and sale may be completed under the Act.*]

(n) **"Closing Documents"** has the meaning ascribed in Article Seven;

(o) **"Closing Time"** means 10:00 o'clock in the forenoon on the Closing Date or such other time on such date as the Parties may agree as the time at which the Closing shall take place;

(p) **"Collective Agreements"** means the collective agreements and related documents including all benefit agreements, letters of understanding, letters of intent and other written communications with bargaining agents which impose any obligations upon the Company or set out the understanding of the parties with respect to the meaning of any provisions of such Collective Agreements entered into by the Company as are listed in Schedule "A";

(q) **"Company's Auditors"** means [*company's auditors*], Chartered Accountants;

(r) **"Company's Bank"** means the _____ Bank;

(s) **"Contracts"** means those contracts, agreements, commitments, entitlements and engagements of the Company relating to the Business and the Assets (and, for greater certainty, not including Collective Agreements, Leases and Equipment Leases) whether with suppliers, customers or otherwise and including all unfilled orders from customers; all forward commitments for supplies or materials; all orders for new machinery and equipment as yet undelivered; all equip-ment and construction guarantees and warranties; negative covenants with employees; and all other contracts described in Schedule "B";

(t) **"Deposit"** has the meaning ascribed in Section 3(2);

(u) **"Effective Date"** means _____, 19___, or such other date as the parties may agree in writing as the date the Auditors prepare the Effective Date Financial Statement;

(v) **"Effective Date Financial Statements"** means the consolidated financial statements of the Company for the fiscal period ended on the Effective Date, prepared in accordance with generally accepted accounting principles consistently applied, consisting of balance sheet as at such date, and statements of earnings and retained earnings and of changes in financial position for such period, together with notes thereto as at such date of the Company's Auditors thereon addressed to the Company;

(w) **"Employees"** has the meaning ascribed in Section 4(1)(r);

(x) **"Employment Agreement"** has the meaning ascribed in Section 5(12);

(y)   **"Equipment Leases"** means those equipment leases, conditional sales contracts, title retention agreements and other agreements between the Company and third Persons relating to equipment used by the Company including those that are listed in Schedule "C";

(z)   **"GAAP"** has the meaning ascribed in Section 1(8);

(aa)   **"GST"** means the Goods and Services Tax payable under the Excise Tax Act;

(ab)   **"Intellectual Property Rights"** means all patents and inventions, trade-marks, including those described in Schedule "D", all trade names and styles, including the trade names or styles _____, _____, and _____, logos and designs, trade secrets, technical information, engineering procedures, designs, know-how and processes (whether confidential or otherwise), software, and other industrial property (including applications for any of these) in each case used or reasonably necessary to permit satisfactory operation of the Business as presently constituted;

(ac)   **"Interim Period"** means the period beginning on the Effective Date to and including the Closing Date;

(ad)   **"Inventories"** means all inventories of every kind and nature and wheresoever situate owned by the Company and pertaining to the Business including, without limitation, all inventories of raw materials, work-in-progress, finished goods, operating supplies and packaging materials of or pertaining to the Business;

(ae)   **"Leases"** means all leases of Leasehold Properties including those listed in Schedule "E"

(af)   **"Licences"** means all transferable licences, registrations, qualifications, permits and approvals, issued by any government or governmental unit, agency, board, body or instrumentality, whether federal, provincial or municipal, relating to the Business, including those listed in Schedule "F", together with all applications for such licences or permits;

(ag) **"Non-Competition Agreement"** means the non-competition agreement in the form of Schedule "G"

(ah) **"Parties"** means the Vendor, the Purchaser and the Company, collectively, and "Party" means any one of them;

(ai) **"Person"** includes an individual, corporation, partnership, joint venture, trust, unincorporated organization, the Crown or any agency or instrumentality thereof or any other juridical entity;

(aj) **"Pension Plan"** has the meaning ascribed in Section 4(1)(aa);

(ak) **"Purchase Price"** means the purchase price to be paid by the Purchaser to the Vendor for the Shares, all as provided in Section 3(1);

(al) **"Purchaser's Auditors"** means [*purchaser's auditors*], Chartered Accountants;

(am) **"Purchaser's Note"** means the promissory note of the Purchaser in favour of the Vendor in the amount of $_____ date the Closing Date, in the form attached as Schedule "H";

(an) **"Real Properties"** means all freehold, leasehold, and other interests in real and immoveable properties owned or used by the Company in connection with the Business, including, without limitation,
  (i)   the freehold lands and premises described in Schedule "I", and all plants, buildings, sidings, parking lots, roadways, structures, erections, improvements, fixed machinery, fixed equipment, appurtenances, and fixtures situate on or forming part of such lands and premises (collectively the **"Owned Properties"**);
  (ii) the leasehold and other interest described in Schedule "J" including all fixtures and improvements owned by the Company relating to those leaseholds and other interests (collectively the **"Leasehold Properties"**);

(ao) **"Settlement Date"** means the day ten days after the delivery of the final Settlement Statement under Section 3(10), or such other day to which the Parties may agree;

(ap) **"Settlement Statement"** means a statement prepared under Section 3(6) showing the particulars of the calculations of the Purchase Price and its allocation, including the Net Book Value of Assets and the Net Book Value of Liabilities and other adjustments, if any, to which the Purchaser is entitled under the provisions of Sections 3(11) and 3(12) of this Agreement;

(aq) **"Shares"** means all of the issued and outstanding common shares [*and preference shares*] in the capital of the Company, to be sold by the Vendor to the Purchaser pursuant to the terms of this Agreement;

(ar) **"Statements"** has the meaning ascribed in Section 3(6);

(as) **"Third Party Claim"** means for the purposes of Section 6(3) any demand which has been made on, or communicated to either of the Vendor or the Purchaser by or on behalf of any Person other than the persons mentioned above in this definition and which, if maintained or enforced, might result in a loss, liability or expense of the nature described in either Section 6(1) or Section 6(2);

(at) **"to the best of the knowledge"** when used in reference to:
    (i) the Vendor means the knowledge of the Vendor; and
    (ii) the Purchaser means the knowledge of the senior officers [*name officers*] of the Purchaser;

(au) **"Vendor's Auditors"** means [*vendor's auditors*], Chartered Accountants.

(av) **"Vendor's Bank"** means the _____ Bank.

(2) Gender and Number

In this Agreement, words importing the singular include the plural and vice versa and words importing gender include all genders.

(3) Entire Agreement

This Agreement, including Schedules "A" to "AA", together with the agreements and other documents to be delivered under this Agreement constitute the entire agreement between the Parties pertaining to the subject matter of this Agreement and supersede all prior agreements, understandings, negotiations and discussions, whether oral or written, of the Parties and there are no warranties, representations or other agreements between the Parties in connection with the subject matter of this Agreement except as specifically set forth in this Agreement. No supplement, modification or amendment to this Agreement and no waiver of any provision of this Agreement shall be binding on any Party unless executed by such Party in writing. No waiver of any of the provisions of this Agreement shall be deemed or shall constitute a waiver of any other provision (whether or not similar) nor shall such waiver constitute a continuing waiver unless otherwise expressly provided.

(4) Article and Section Headings

Article and Section headings contained in this Agreement are included solely for convenience, are not intended to be full or accurate descriptions of the content of any Article or Section and shall not be considered to be part of this Agreement.

(5) Schedules

The following Schedules are an integral part of this Agreement:

Schedule "A"	—	Collective Agreements [S.1(1)(p)]
Schedule "B"	—	Contracts [S.1(1)(s)]
Schedule "C"	—	Equipment Leases [S.1(1)(y)]
Schedule "D"	—	Intellectual Property Rights [S.1(1)(ab), 4(1)(aq)]
Schedule "E"	—	Leases [S.1(1)(ae)]
Schedule "F"	—	Licenses[S.1(1)(af), 4(1)(ao)]
Schedule "G"	—	Non-Competition Agreement [S.1(1)(ag), S.5(11)]
Schedule "H"	—	Purchaser's Note [S.1(1)(am)]
Schedule "I"	—	Owned Properties [S.1(1)(an)(i)]
Schedule "J"	—	Leasehold Properties [S.1(1)(an)(ii)]
Schedule "K"	—	Predecessor Corporations and Previous Corporate Names [S.4(1)(c)]
Schedule "L"	—	Jurisdictions of Business and Extra-provincial Licenses [S.4(1)(d)]
Schedule "M"	—	Unusual Transactions [S.4(1)(p)]
Schedule "N"	—	Location of Assets [S.4(1)(q)]
Schedule "O"	—	Employees [S.4(1)(r)]
Schedule "P"	—	Pension Plans [S.4(1)(aa)]
Schedule "Q"	—	Benefit Plans [S.4(1)(ab)]
Schedule "R"	—	Labour Matters [S.4(1)(v)]
Schedule "S"	—	Litigation [S.4(1)(af)]
Schedule "T"	—	Undertaking to Release Vendor's Security S.4(1)(ai)]

Schedule "U"	—	Guarantees and Indebtedness of Company [S.4(1)(ak)]
Schedule "V"	—	Banks [S.4(1)(ap)]
Schedule "W"	—	Material Fixed Assets, Machinery and Equipment [S.4(1)(bf)]
Schedule "X"	—	Purchaser's Commitment Letter Regarding Financing [S.4(2)(h)]
Schedule "Y"	—	Employment Agreement [S.5(12)]
Schedule "Z"	—	Opinion of Vendor's Counsel [S.7(1)(e)]
Schedule "AA"	—	Opinion of Purchaser's Counsel [S.7(2)(e)]

(6) Applicable Law

This Agreement shall be governed by and construed in accordance with the laws of the Province of _____ and the federal laws of Canada applicable in the Province of Ontario and shall be treated, in all respects, as an _____ contract. Each Party to this Agreement irrevocably attorns to and submits to the jurisdiction of the Courts of _____ with respect to any matter arising under or relating to this Agreement.

(7) Currency

Unless otherwise indicated, all dollar amounts referred to in this Agreement are in Canadian funds.

(8) Accounting Terms

All accounting terms not otherwise defined have the meanings assigned to them, and all calculations are to be made and all financial data to be submitted are to be prepared, in accordance with the generally accepted accounting principles ("GAAP") approved from time to time by the Canadian Institute of Chartered Accountants, or any successor institute applied on a consistent basis.

(9) Arm's Length

For purposes of this Agreement, Persons are not dealing "at arm's length" with one another if they would not be dealing at arm's length with one another for purposes of the Income Tax Act.

(10) Business Days

Whenever any action or payment to be taken or made under this Agreement shall be stated to be required to be taken or made on a day other than a

Business Day, any payment shall be made or such action shall be taken on the next succeeding Business Day.

(11) Statutory Instruments

Unless otherwise specifically provided in this Agreement any reference in this Agreement to any law, by-law, rule, regulation, order, act or statute of any government, governmental body or other regulatory body shall be construed as a reference to those as amended or re-enacted from time to time or as a reference to any successor to those.

(12) Materiality

In this Agreement "Material" means, when used as an adjective, that any breach, default or deficiency in the satisfaction of any covenant, representation or warranty so described might reasonably:

(a)   give rise to an aggregate remedial cost (including consequential loss and loss of profit) of more than $_____, in any individual instance, or more than $_____ collectively in any greater number of instances, where all such instances arise pursuant to multiple breaches of the same covenant, representation or warranty; or

(b)   where no adequate remedy is reasonably available, result in disturbance in the ordinary conduct of the Business of an aggregate cost properly attributable to such disturbance (including consequential loss and loss of profit) of more than $_____, and "Materially" shall have the corresponding meaning.

2. PURCHASE AND SALE OF SHARES

(1) Purchase and Sale of Shares

Upon and subject to the terms and conditions of this Agreement, the Vendor shall sell, transfer, assign and set over to the Purchaser and the Purchaser shall purchase and acquire from the Vendor at the Closing Time, the Shares for the Purchase Price payable as provided in Section 3(1).

(2) Non-Assignable Contracts

(Note: In a share purchase agreement, it is not generally necessary to address the issue of the assignment of contracts, except in the case where agreements provide that they may be terminated upon a change of control. The following provisions address this situation.)

This Agreement and any document delivered under this Agreement shall not constitute an assignment or an attempted assignment of any Contract, Equipment Lease, Lease or Licence contemplated to be assigned to the Purchaser under this Agreement;

(a) *which is not assignable through the change of control of the Company without the consent of a third party if such consent has not been obtained and such assignment or attempted assignment would constitute a breach of such contract or agreement; or*

(b) *in respect of which the remedies for the enforcement of such contract or agreement available to the Vendor would not pass to the Purchaser.*

The Vendor shall use its best efforts to obtain the consents of third parties as may be necessary for the change of control of the Company for the assignment of the Contracts, the Equipment Leases, the Leases and the Licences where necessary except that the Vendor shall not be obliged to make any payments to those third parties in addition to those required to be made under those contracts or agreements in order to obtain such consents, unless the Purchaser reimburses the Vendor for such payments at the time that they are made. To the extent that any of the foregoing items are determined not to be assignable by their terms or where consents to their assignment cannot be obtained as provided in this Section 2(2), the Parties agree that the Purchase Price shall be adjusted to account to the Purchaser for the value of the benefits of those items lost to the Company.

Nothing in this Section 2(2) shall limit the effect of Section 7(1)(f) regarding consents to assignments.]

3. PURCHASE PRICE AND PAYMENT

(1) Payment of Purchase Price

The Parties agree that the Purchase Price, subject to the adjustments provided in this Agreement, will be \$_____. At the Closing Time, the Purchaser shall pay on account of the Purchase Price the amount of \$_____, to be satisfied by:

(a) application of the Deposit;

(b) a certified cheque or bank draft of the Purchaser payable to or to the order of the Vendor in the amount of \$_____; and,

(c) execution and delivery to the Vendor by the Purchaser of the Purchaser's Note.

The Purchaser acknowledges that the Purchase Price does not include GST payable, if any, as a result of the purchase and sale of the Shares.

(2) Deposit

(a) A deposit of $_____ on account of the Purchase Price (the "Deposit") has been made by the Purchaser, by depositing that amount in a trust account with the Purchaser's solicitors, who shall not permit such moneys to be released from trust without the approval of the Vendor's solicitors. The interest payable on the deposit is payable to the Purchaser.

(b) If the Purchaser fails to complete this transaction by reason of the non-fulfilment by the Vendor of any of the conditions set forth in Section 7(1), the Vendor is not entitled to the Deposit and it shall be released to the Purchaser no later than one day after the scheduled Closing Date. If the Purchaser fails to complete this transaction for any other reason, the Deposit may be retained by the Vendor as liquidated damages and shall be obtained by the Vendor by making the requisite demand upon the Vendor's solicitors and the Purchaser's solicitors.

(3) Delivery of Certificates, etc.

The Vendor shall transfer and deliver to the Purchaser at the Closing Time, share certificates representing the Shares duly endorsed in blank for transfer, or accompanied by irrevocable security transfer powers of attorney duly executed in blank, with the signatures thereon guaranteed by a Canadian chartered bank or trust company and shall cause the Company to enter the Purchaser or its nominee(s) on the books of the Company as the holder of the Shares and to issue one or more share certificates to the Purchaser or its nominee(s) representing the Shares.

(4) Place of Closing

The Closing shall take place at the Closing Time at the office of _____, (*city*) (*province*), or at such other place as may be agreed upon by the Vendor and the Purchaser.

(5) Tender

Any tender of documents or money hereunder may be made upon the Parties or their respective counsel and money may be tendered by official draft drawn upon a Canadian chartered bank or trust company or by negotiable cheque payable in Canadian funds and certified by a Canadian chartered bank.

(6) Preparation of Effective Date Financial Statement

At the same time as the execution and delivery of this Agreement, the Vendor and the Purchaser shall instruct their respective Auditors to jointly prepare and deliver the Effective Date Financial Statement and the Settlement Statement (collectively, the **"Statements"**). The following generally accepted accounting principles will be applied in preparing the Effective Date Financial Statement:

(a)   all fixed assets of the Company will be valued at actual cost less accumulated depreciation taken;

(b)   the accounts receivable of the Company will be net of an allowance for doubtful accounts established on a basis consistent with the prior practice of the Company; and,

(c)   inventories will be valued at the lower of cost and net realizable value and will be net of an allowance for obsolete and slow-moving items.

The fees and expenses charged by the Auditors for and in connection with the preparation of the Statements shall be paid equally by the Purchaser and the Vendor.

(7) Draft Statements

Before issuing the Statements in final form, the Auditors shall submit final drafts to the parties to this Agreement for consideration and comment. The parties to this Agreement agree to comment promptly on the final draft Statements and, in any event, within 15 days of receiving them.

(8) Preparation of Final Statements

The Auditors shall amend the final draft Statements to the extent they consider appropriate in the light of the comments of the parties hereto. If the Auditors fail to reach agreement as to their reports on the Statements, a third chartered accountant (who shall be selected by the Vendor's Auditors and the Purchaser's Auditors) shall, with all reasonable dispatch, finally determine the Statements. If the Auditors are unable to agree as to the third chartered accountant, he or she shall be selected by lot from the two nominees proposed by the Auditors. In making his or her determination, the third chartered accountant shall act as an expert and not as an arbitrator. The resulting Statements, including as finally determined by the third chartered accountant, are binding on the Vendor and Purchaser and all other interested Persons.

In connection with the audit, it is acknowledged that the Vendor's Auditors may require the assistance of the accounting and clerical staff of the Company, who shall continue in the employment with the Company pursuant to this Agreement. It is agreed that the Purchaser shall, during the period of three months following the Closing Date, allow representatives of the Vendor and its auditors the use of an office on the premises of the Company and, to the extent the Company has staff available, shall, at the expense of the Vendor, allow such staff to perform any functions reasonably required by the Vendor in connection with the audit.

(9) Effective Date

The sale and purchase contemplated under this Agreement shall, when completed on the Closing Date, take effect as of the close of business on the Effective Date and from such time to the Closing Date the Business of the Company shall be carried on by the Vendor in the ordinary course for the account of the Purchaser.

(10) Delivery of Final Statements

The final Statements shall not be completed and delivered to the Parties by the Auditors until adjustments provided under Section 3(12) have been reported to the Auditors and incorporated into the final Statements, but in no case shall the final Statements be delivered to the Parties more than 100 days after Closing Date (the "Settlement Date").

(11) Adjustment of Purchase Price

On the Settlement Date the Parties agree to make the necessary adjustments to the Purchase Price based on any discrepancy between the amount paid by the Purchaser on the Closing Date and the Book Value of Assets and Book Value of liabilities disclosed on the Effective Date Financial Statements and on the results of the count of Inventories and accounts receivable under Section 3(12) and other adjustments under this Section 3(11). [*Note: Consideration should be given to a hold-back by the Purchaser in the event of a downward adjustment to the Purchase Price where the entire Purchase Price is payable at Closing. In this precedent agreement part of the Purchase Price is payable by promissory note, for which a downward adjustment in the principal amount could be provided.*]

(12) Determination of Inventory Value and Uncollectible Accounts Receivable

Within 90 days of the Closing Date, the Vendor and the Purchaser shall jointly make a physical count of the Inventories and an audit of accounts receivable and identify obsolete Inventories and the uncollectable ac-counts receivable. The Vendor and the Purchaser shall, either directly or through their respective Auditors or representatives, promptly take such action as is necessary to determine the actual value of the Inventories and accounts receivable in accordance with the principles contained in Section 3(6). Before the Settlement Statement is finalized, the Parties shall report the amount of any necessary adjustments under this Section 3(12) to the Auditors so that the Settlement Statement incorporates that adjustment.

[(13) *Allocation of Purchase Price and Tax Returns*

[Note: Generally in a share purchase the issue of allocation of the Purchase Price will not arise, unless different classes of the shares are being acquired, in which case an allocation may be necessary so that the Parties' tax values with respect to those shares can be determined]

The Vendor and the Purchaser covenant and agree with each other that the Purchase Price shall be allocated among the Shares as provided in the Settlement Statement. The Vendor and the Purchaser agree to cooperate in the filing of such elections under the Income Tax Act, the Corporations Tax Act (Ontario) and such other taxation statutes as may be necessary or desirable to give effect to said allocation for tax purposes. In addition the Vendor and the Purchaser agree to prepare and file their respective tax returns in a manner consistent with the aforesaid allocations and elections. If either party fails to file its tax returns as aforesaid, it shall indemnify and save harmless the other of them in respect of any additional tax, interest, penalty, legal or accounting costs paid or incurred by the other of them as a result of the failure to file as aforesaid.]

[Note: See alternative clauses for sample provisions concerning security for the unpaid balance of the Purchase Price.]

4. REPRESENTATIONS AND WARRANTIES

(1) Representations and Warranties of the Vendor

The Vendor hereby represents and warrants to the Purchaser as follows and acknowledges that the Purchaser is relying on these representations and warranties in entering into this Agreement and the transactions contemplated under this Agreement:

[Note: The precedent representations and warranties in this agreement are generally unqualified, but all representations and warranties are subject to appropriate qualifications to which the Parties may agree. Commonly used qualifications include

Materiality thresholds, knowledge qualifications, specific exceptions listed in attached schedules.]

(a) Organization and Good Standing—The Company is a corporation duly incorporated, organized and validly existing in good standing under the laws of [*jurisdiction of incorporation*].

(b) Bankruptcy, etc.—No bankruptcy, insolvency or receivership proceedings have been instituted or are pending against the Company and the Company is able to satisfy its liabilities as they become due.

(c) Previous Names—Set out in Schedule "K" is a list of all corporate predecessors of the Company and all previous corporate names of the Company and its predecessors and present business name registrations.

(d) Capacity to Carry on Business—The Company has all necessary corporate power, authority and capacity to own its property and assets and to carry on the Business as presently owned and carried on by it, and the Company is duly licensed, registered and qualified as a corporation to do business and is in good standing in each jurisdiction in which the nature of the Business make such qualification necessary, and all such licences, registrations and qualifications are valid and subsisting and in good standing and none of them contains any burdensome term, provision, condition or limitation which has or may have an adverse effect on the Company. All of the jurisdictions in which the Company conducts business and for which the necessary licences have been obtained are listed in Schedule "L".

(e) Due Authorization, Company etc.—The Company has all necessary corporate power, authority and capacity to enter into this Agreement and to perform its obligations under this Agreement; the execution and delivery of this Agreement and the consummation of the transactions contemplated hereby have been duly authorized by all necessary corporate action on the part of the Company.

(f) Authorized and Issued Capital of the Company—The authorized capital of the Company consists of an unlimited number of common shares of which [#] common shares have been validly issued and are outstanding as fully paid and non-assessable shares. The authorized capital of the Subsidiary consists of an unlimited number of common shares of which [#] common shares have been validly issued and are outstanding as fully paid and non-assessable shares.

(g)   Title to Shares—Except for encumbrances in favour of the Vendor's Bank (all of which encumbrances shall be discharged or waived in writing by the Vendor's Bank on or before Closing) the Vendor is the legal and beneficial owner of the number of common shares of the Company set forth opposite her name below:

Registered Shareholder	No. of Common Shares Owned
Jane Doe	[#]

and on Closing the Purchaser shall acquire good and marketable title to the Shares, free and clear of all agreements, mortgages, pledges, charges, hypothecs, claims, liens, security interests, encumbrances and rights of other Persons. The Shares constitute all of the issued and outstanding shares in the capital of the Company. No options, warrants or other rights for the purchaser, subscription or issuance of shares or other securities of the Company or securities convertible into or exchangeable for shares of the Company have been authorized or agreed to be issued or are outstanding. There are no restrictions on the transfer of the Shares except those set forth in the Articles.

(h)   Title to Shares—The Company is the legal and beneficial owner of the number of common shares of the Subsidiary set forth opposite its name below:

Registered Shareholder	No. of Common Shares Owned
Company	[#]

and on Closing the Purchaser, indirectly through the Company, shall acquire good and marketable title to the shares of the Subsidiary, free and clear of all agreements, mortgages, pledges, charges, hypothecs, claims, liens, security interests, encumbrances and rights of other Persons. The Shares together constitute all of the issued and outstanding shares in the capital of the Subsidiary. No options, warrants or other rights for the purchase, subscription or issuance of shares or other securities of the Subsidiary or securities convertible into or exchangeable for shares of the Subsidiary have been authorized or agreed to be issued or are outstanding. There are no restrictions on the transfer of the Shares except those set forth in the Articles.

(i) *Family Law Act*—No order has been given under the Family Law Act (Ontario) (the "FLA") nor is there any application pending under the FLA by the spouse of the Vendor which would or does affect the Shares in any manner whatsoever.

(j) Absence of Conflicting Agreements—Except for the Contracts, the Equipment Leases, and the Leases, the consent to the consent to the change of control of the Company which may be required from lessors or other third parties thereunder in connection with the completion of the transactions contemplated by this Agreement and except for various financing and security agreements with the Vendor's Bank all of which will be terminated before Closing or all of which will be waived by the Vendor's Bank in respect of the transactions contemplated by this Agreement, neither the Vendor nor the Company is not a party to, bound or affected by or subject to any indenture, mortgage, lease, agreement, instrument, statute, regulation, arbitration award, charter or by-law provisions, order or judgment which would be violated, contravened, breached by, or under which any default would occur as a result of the execution and delivery of this Agreement or the consummation of any of the transactions contemplated under this Agreement.

(k) Absence of Guarantees—The Company has not given or agreed to give, nor is it a party to or bound by, any guarantee of indebtedness or other obligations of third parties nor any other commitment by which the company is, or is contingently, responsible for such indebtedness or other obligations.

(l) Enforceability of Obligations—This Agreement constitutes a valid and binding obligation of the Vendor and the Company enforceable against both in accordance with its terms, provided that enforcement may be limited by bankruptcy, insolvency, liquidation, reorganization, reconstruction and other similar laws generally affecting enforceability of creditors' rights and that equitable remedies such as specific performance and injunction are in the discretion of the court from which they are sought.

(m) Books and Records—The books and records of the Company fairly and correctly set out and disclose in all material respects, in accordance with GAAP, the financial position of the Company as at the date of this Agreement and all material financial transactions of the Company relating to the Business have been accurately recorded in such books and records.

[Alternative Representation

(m) *Books and Records—The Company's books and records are fully and accurately maintained and its books of account provide for all excise, sales, business and property taxes and other rates, charges, assessments, levies, duties, taxes, contributions, fees, licenses and other governmental charges of whatsoever kind and nature that have become or may become due and payable on or before the Closing Time. The provisions and reserves in the books of account of the Company in respect of same, together with the provisions and reserves in the books of account of the Company in respect of taxes charged upon its income for which returns have been filed but for which no assessments have yet been received or determined, are adequate and the Vendor does not know of any basis for any additional assessment for any of such years for which adequate provision has not been made. The minute books of the Company are complete and accurate and reflect all material actions taken and resolutions passed by the directors and shareholders of the Company since the date of its incorporation and all such meetings were duly called and held and the share certificate books, register of shareholders, register of transfer and registers of directors are complete and accurate.]*

(n) Audited Financial Statements—The items reported in the Audited Financial Statements are reported in accordance with GAAP applied on a basis consistent with that of the preceding period and present fairly:

    (i) all of the assets of the Company as at _____, 199___ that are of a nature customarily reflected or reserved against in a balance sheet,

    (ii) all of the liabilities of the Company as at _____, 199___ that are of a nature customarily reflected or reserved against in a balance sheet, and

    (iii) the sales and earnings from operations of the Company for the _____ month period ended _____, 199___.

The financial position of the Company is now at least as good as shown or reflected in the Audited Financial Statements. For greater certainty, the Audited Financial Statements do not include any additions or deductions for income taxes and interest.

(o) Absence of Changes—Since _____, 19___, there has not been:

    (i) any Material change in the condition or operations of the Company other than changes in the ordinary and normal course of business and other than changes resulting from a general deterioration of markets in the industries in which the Company is engaged; or

(ii)   any damage, destruction or loss, labour trouble or other event, development or condition of any character (whether or not covered by insurance) materially and adversely affecting the Company.

(p)   Absence of Unusual Transactions—Except as listed in schedule "M" since _____, 19___, the Company has carried on the Business in its usual and ordinary course, and in particular the Company has not:

(i)   transferred, assigned, sold or otherwise disposed of any of the assets shown in the Effective Date Balance Sheet except in the ordinary and usual course of business;

(ii)   discharged or satisfied any lien or encumbrance, or paid any obligation or liability (fixed or contingent) other than liabilities included in the balance sheet to the Audited Financial Statements and liabilities incurred since the date of the Audited Financial Statements in the ordinary and normal course of business;

(iii)   suffered an extraordinary loss, or waived any rights of Material value, or entered into any Material commitment or transaction not in the ordinary and usual course of business;

(iv)   made any general wage or salary increases or other payments in respect of personnel which it employs except in the ordinary course of business;

(v)   declared or paid any dividends or declared or made any other distribution on any of its securities or shares of any class, and has not directly or indirectly, redeemed, purchased or otherwise acquired any of its securities or shares of any class or has agreed to do so;

(vi)   made any capital expenditure, except in the usual and ordinary course of business, and no capital expenditure will be made or authorized after the date of this Agreement by the Company with respect to the Business without the prior written consent of the Purchaser;

(vii) mortgaged, pledged, subjected to lien, granted a security interest in or otherwise encumbered any of the assets of the Company other than in favour of the Company's Bank;

(viii) incurred or assumed any obligation or liability (fixed or contingent), except secured and unsecured current obligations and liabilities incurred in the ordinary and normal course of business, particulars of which have been disclosed in writing to the Purchaser or its representatives;

(ix)   except as provided in this Agreement, issued or sold any shares in its capital or any warrants, bonds, debentures or other securities of the Company or issued, granted or delivered any right, option or other commitment for the issuance of any such securities;

(x) amended or changed or taken any action to amend or change its Articles or by-laws; or

(xi) authorized or agreed or otherwise become committed to do any of the foregoing.

(q) Location of Assets—All material tangible assets of the Company used in or in connection with the Business are all normally situate only in the Provinces of _____ and _____ and the State of _____; the municipalities in which such assets are normally situate are set forth in Schedule "N".

(r) Employees, etc.—There are set forth in Schedule "O":

(i) the names and titles of all salaried personnel and unionized office workers paid on an hourly basis, employed or engaged by the Company on a full- or part-time basis and including, without limitation, all individuals who may be considered to be employees of the Company pursuant to applicable law or equity, notwithstanding that they may have been laid off or terminated, (the "Employees") together with the location of their employment;

(ii) the date each such employee was hired by the Company or its predecessor corporations;

(iii) the hourly rate and rate of annual remuneration of each such employee as at the date hereof and the dates and amounts of the most recent salary increases; and

(iv) particulars of all other material terms and conditions of employment or engagement of such employees, including benefits and positions held.

[*Note: See alternative clauses for sample representations and warranties concerning employees.*]

(s) Employment Contracts and Government Withholdings—Subject to applicable statutory rights, the Company is not a party to any written contracts of employment with any of its employees (other than union employees governed by the Collective Agreement) or any oral contracts of employment which are not terminable on the giving of reasonable notice and/or severance pay in accordance with applicable law and no inducements to accept employment with the Company were offered to any such employees which have the effect of increasing the period of notice of termination to which any such employee is entitled. The Company has deducted and remitted to the relevant governmental authority or entity all income taxes, unemployment insurance contributions, Canada Pension Plan contributions, provincial employer health tax remittances and any taxes or deductions or other amounts which it is required by statute or contract to collect and remit to any governmental authority or other entities entitled to receive payment of such deduction.

(t) Employment Payments by the Company to Date of Closing—The Company has paid to the date of this Agreement all amounts payable on account of salary, bonus payments and commission to or on behalf of any and all Employees;

(u) Workers' Compensation—All levies under the Workplace Safety and Insurance Act, 1997 (Ontario), or under the workers' compensation legislation of any other jurisdiction where the Company carries on the Business, have been paid by the Company.

(v) Labour Matters—Except as listed in Schedule "R" there is no:

   (i) unfair labour practice complaint under [*The Canada Labour Code or Ontario Labour Relations Act*] *against the Company pending before the* [*federal or*] provincial labour tribunals or any similar agency or body having jurisdiction therefor;

   (ii) labour strike threatened against or involving the Company;

   (iii) certification application outstanding respecting the Employees;

   (iv) grievance or arbitration proceeding or governmental proceeding relating to the Employees pending, nor is there any such proceeding threatened against the Company which might have a material adverse effect on the Company or on the conduct of the Business;

   (v) collective bargaining agreement currently being negotiated by the Company; and

   (vi) Employee in receipt of or who has claimed benefits under any weekly indemnity, long term disability or workers' compensation plan or arrangement or any other form of disability benefit programme.

(w) Material Contracts—Except for the Contracts, the Equipment Leases, the Leases and various loan and security agreements with the Company's Bank, the Company is not a party to or bound by any material contract or commitment relating to the Business whether oral or written. The Contracts, the Leases, and the Equipment Leases are all in good standing and in full force and effect unamended and no Material default or breach exists in respect of them on the part of any of the parties to them and no event has occurred which, after the giving of notice or the lapse of time or both, would constitute such a default or breach; the foregoing includes all the presently outstanding material contracts entered into by the Company in the course of carrying on the Business.

[*Note: Expand covenant as necessary re: investigation to provide obligation to deliver copies of due diligence documents to Purchaser.*]

(x) Residence—The Vendor is not a non-resident of Canada within the meaning of the Income Tax Act.

[*Note: See alternative clauses for provisions concerning the delivery of a section 116 clearance certificate or remittance to Revenue Canada when the Vendor is a non-resident of Canada*]

(y) Insurance—The Company maintains such policies of insurance, issued by responsible insurers, as are appropriate to the Business and its property and assets, in such amounts and against such risks as are customarily carried and insured against by owners of comparable businesses, properties and assets; all such policies of insurance are in full force and effect, and will continue to be so until the Closing Date, and the Company is not in default, whether as to the payment of premium or otherwise, under the terms of any such policy, nor has the Company failed to give any notice or present any claim under any claim under any such insurance policy in due and timely fashion. (Note: May provide schedule with particulars or copies of insurance policies.)

(z) Compliance with Applicable Laws—The Company has conducted and is conducting the Business in compliance in all material respects with all applicable laws, rules and regulations of each jurisdiction in which the Business is carried on and are not in breach of any such laws, rules or regulations, except for breaches which are not Material.

(aa) Pension Plan—The pension plan described in Schedule "P" (the "Pension Plan") is the only pension plan maintained by the Company for the Employees, and the Company is not in default of any of its obligations under the Pension Plan or prescribed by law;

[*Note: See* **Form 9F36** *re: alternative clauses for extensive sample representations and warranties concerning Pension Plans. Many of these representations and warranties may also apply to benefit plans.*]

(ab) Benefit Plans—The Company is not a party to any management agreement, pay equity plan, vacation or vacation pay policy, employee insurance, hospital or medical expense programme or pension, retirement, profit sharing, stock bonus or other employee benefit plan, programme or arrangement or to any executive or key personnel incentive or other special compensation arrangement or to other contracts or agreements with or with respect to officers, employees or agents other than the Pension Plan and those listed and described in Schedule "Q" (the "Benefit plans").

[*Note: Other specific benefit plans include deferred profit sharing plans, supplemental retirement or unemployment benefits, group RRSP's, disability insurance, and dental service plans. These benefit plans may be funded or unfunded.*] **[See Form 9F36.]**

(ac) Total Assets and Gross Revenues—The Company and all of its affiliates have combined assets in Canada, or combined gross revenues from sales in or from Canada, of $ _____ in aggregate value.

(ad) Health and Safety—The business premises located on the Real Properties are in compliance with applicable health and safety legislation and regulations and are not subject to any orders or directions of an occupational health and safety authority or similar body.

(ae) Litigation—Except as provided in Schedule "S" there is no suit, action, litigation, arbitration, proceeding, governmental proceeding, including appeals and applications for review in progress, pending or threatened against or involving the Company, and there is not presently outstanding against the Company any judgment, decree, injunction, rule or order of any court, governmental department, commission, agency, instrumentality or arbitrator.

[*Alternative Representations*]

(ae) (i) *Litigation—Company—Except as disclosed in Schedule "S", there is no suit, action, litigation, arbitration proceeding or governmental proceeding, including appeals and applications for review, in progress, pending or, to the best of the knowledge, information and belief, after due enquiry, of the Vendor, threatened against or relating to the Company, affecting its properties or Business which if determined adversely to the Company might materially and adversely affect the properties, business, future prospects or financial condition of the Company and, except as shown in Schedule "S", there is not presently outstanding against the Company any judgment, decree, injunction, rule or order of any court, governmental department, commission, agency, instrumentality or arbitrator. Except as disclosed in Schedule "S", the Company has not received any notices to the effect that the operations or the assets of the Company on the Real Property are (i) not in full compliance with all of the requirements of applicable federal, provincial or local environmental, health and safety statutes and regulations, or (ii) the subject of any federal or provincial remedial or control action or order, or any investigation or evaluation as to whether any remedial action is needed to respond to a release or threatened release of any contaminant into the environment or any facility or structure.*

(ae)   *(ii) Litigation—Shares—Except as disclosed in Schedule "S", there is no suit, action, litigation, arbitration proceeding or governmental proceeding, including appeals and applications for review, in progress, pending or, to the best of the knowledge, information and belief, after due enquiry, of the Vendor, threatened against or relating to the Shares and, except as shown in Schedule "S", there is not presently outstanding against the Vendor any judgment, decree, injunction, rule or order of any court, governmental department, commission, agency, instrumentality or arbitrator which would affect the Vendor's ability to sell the Shares as provided for in this Agreement.]*

(af)   Real Property—The Real Properties and their existing and prior uses comply with, and at all material times have complied with, and the Company is not in violation of or has violated in connection with the ownership, use, maintenance or operation of the Real Properties, any applicable federal, provincial or municipal laws, regulations or by-laws or orders of any governmental authorities which exist as of the date of this Agreement. There are no currently outstanding work orders or directions requiring any work, repairs, construction or capital expenditures with respect to the Real Properties and no such orders or directions are pending or threatened.

[*Note: See alternative clauses for more environmental representations and warranties.*]

(ag)   Insulation—The buildings and structures located on the Real Properties have not been insulated with a urea formaldehyde foam type of insulation.

(ah) Vendor's Security—The Vendor has obtained from the Vendor's Bankers or other financial institutions an undertaking to discharge all security held by Vendor's Bankers or other financial institutions over the Shares, a copy of which undertaking is attached as Schedule "T".

(ai) Accounts Receivable—All accounts receivable, bills receivable and book debts and other debts due or accruing to the Company are bona fide and good and subject to an allowance for doubtful accounts taken in accordance with GAAP are collectible without set-off or counterclaim.

(aj) Guarantees and Indebtedness—Except as disclosed in Schedule "U" the Company is not a party to or bound by any guarantee, indemnification, surety or similar obligation (except such as are granted in the ordinary course of business).

(ak) Environmental Matters—[*Note: See alternative clauses for environmen-tal representations, warranties and covenants.* **See Form 9F35**]

(al) Rights, Privileges etc.—There are no rights, privileges or advantages presently enjoyed by the Company which might be lost as a result of the consummation of the transactions contemplated under this Agreement.

(am) Consents—Except for Contracts, Equipment Leases and Leases requiring the consents to the change of control of the Company and with respect to the licenses or permits referred to in Section 4(1)(ac), there are no consents, authorizations, licenses, franchise agreements, permits, approvals or orders of any person or government required to permit the Vendor to complete this transaction with the Purchaser.

[*Note: regulatory approvals, Investment Canada, Competition Act*]

(an) Licenses and Permits—All of the licences, registrations, qualifica-tions, permits, bonds and approvals (other than environmental licences or permits) issued by any government or governmental unit, agency, board, body or instrumentality, whether federal, provincial or municipal, related to the Company or necessary for the conduct of the Business are listed on Schedule "F".

(ao) Banks—Schedule "V" contains a true and complete list (including address and account number) of each bank, trust company or similar institution in which the Company has an account or a safety deposit box and the names of all persons, including any person or firm holding a power of attorney, authorized to draw thereon or to have access thereto and a description of all credit facilities, lines of credit, loan agreements and the like which the Company has with any financial institution. All of the bank accounts operated in connection with the Business are maintained and operated solely in the name of the Company. There are no bank accounts operated in the name of any division or business or trade name or style of the Company. [*Note: list security registrations against Company*]

(ap) Intellectual Property—All patents, trade-marks, trade names, brand names, trade designs, service marks and copyrights and all licenses and similar rights and property which are necessary or incidental to the conduct of the Business as the same is presently being carried on are listed in Schedule "D", and are valid and subsisting and held by the Company with good and marketable title and are in good standing free and clear of all security interests, claims, liens, objections and infringements of every nature and kind (other than in favour of the Company's Bank) and all registrations therefor have been kept renewed and are in full force and effect. The operations of the Business, the manufacture, storage, use and sale by it of its products and the provision by it of its services do not involve infringements or claimed infringement of any patent, trademark, trade name or copyright. No employee of the Company owns, directly or indirectly in while or in part, any patent, trade-mark, trade name, brand name, copyright, invention, process, know-how, formula or trade secret which the Company is presently using or the use of which is necessary for the Business.

(aq) Inventories—The Inventories are in good and merchantable condition and are usable or saleable in the ordinary course of business for the purposes for which they are intended and are carried on the books of the Company at the lower of cost and net realizable value.

(ar) Expropriation—No part of the assets of the Company as disclosed in the Audited Financial Statements have been taken or expropriated by any federal, provincial, state, municipal or other authority nor has any notice or proceeding in respect thereof been given or commenced nor is the Company aware of any intent or proposal to give such notice or commence any such proceedings.

(as) Tax Matters—Except to the extent reflected in or reserved against in the Audited Financial Statements or the Effective Date Financial Statements, the Company is not liable for any taxes, levies, duties, assessments, charges, penalties, interest, fines or other imposts of any nature or kind due and unpaid at the date hereof in respect of its income, business or property or for the payment of any tax instalment due in respect of its current taxation year and, except as aforesaid, no such taxes, assessments, imposts, levies, charges, fines or penalties are required to be reserved against. If any such reservation has been made or taken, it is adequate to provide for taxes payable by the Vendor for its current period for which tax returns are not yet required to be filed. The Company is not in default in filing any returns or reports covering any Canadian federal, provincial, punicipal or local taxes, levies, duties, assessments or other reports in respect of its income, business or property. The Company has filed all reports or returns with respect to income, capital, sales (including goods and services and Ontario employer health tax reports), excise, business and property taxes and all other taxes and customs duties which are required to be filed by it up to the date of this Agreement (and all such returns and reports are correct and complete in all material respects) and has paid, or where permitted by law, provided security for, all taxes and duties as shown on such reports or returns to the extent such taxes or duties are payable or have or may become due and has paid, or where permitted by law, provided security for, all assessments received by it. The Company has withheld from any amounts payable, including without limiting the generality of the foregoing, from any salaries, bonuses or dividends paid by it all deductions required by law to be made therefrom and has remitted the same to the proper tax or other authorities. Federal Canadian income tax assessments have been issued to the Company covering all past periods through the fiscal year ended _____, 19_____ (and such assessments, if any amounts were owing in respect thereof, have been paid or, where permitted by law, security therefor has been provided [*or the Vendors are challenging such assess-ments with Revenue Canada (Taxation) in good faith*]). There are no currently outstanding reassessments, suits, actions, proceedings, in-vestigations, claims or questions which have been issued or raised by an governmental authority relating to any such reports or tax returns except for those provided in the Audited Financial Statements or the Effective Date Financial Statements and the Company does not have any negotiations or discussions in progress with respect to any eventual assessment or reassessment with any such authority. The Company has not executed or filed with any taxing authority any waiver or agreement extending the period for assessment or collection of any income or other taxes.

[*Note: For an extensive treatment of tax representations, warranties and covenants, see E.G. Kroft, "Tax Clauses in Acquisition Agreements", Corporate Management Tax Conference, 1990 9:1, (Toronto: Canadian Tax Foundation) 1991.*]

[Tax Data — Information as to the cost for Canadian income tax purposes of the assets of the Company is set forth in Schedule "____"].

(at)   Subsidiaries:

(i)   The only Subsidiary of the Company is Subco Inc.:

(ii)   The authorized capital of Subco Inc. is an unlimited number of common shares, of which [#] are validly issued to the Company and are outstanding as fully paid and non-assessable and are the only outstanding shares of Subco Inc.;

(iii) There is not any agreement or option existing pursuant to which Subco Inc. is or might be required to issue any further shares of its capital;

(iv)   Each of the representations and warranties contained in this Section 4(1) is applicable, *mutatis mutandis*, to Subco Inc.

[Note: Subco Inc. may be made a party to this Agreement and will then give all representations, warranties and covenants itself.]

(au)   Disclosure—None of the foregoing representations, warranties and statements of fact contains any untrue statement of material fact or omits to state any material fact necessary to make any such representation, warranty or statement not misleading to a prospective purchaser of the Shares seeking full information concerning the matters which are the subject of such representations, warranties and statements.

(av)   Undisclosed Liabilities—The Company has no liabilities (whether accrued, absolute, contingent or otherwise) of any kind except liabilities incurred in the ordinary course of business since _____ which are not inconsistent with past practice, are not, in the aggregate, Material and adverse to the business, assets, financial condition or results of operations of the Company, and do not Materially violate any covenant contained in this Agreement or constitute a Material misrepresentation or breach of warranty made in or pursuant to this Agreement. Without limiting the foregoing, there were reflected or reserved against in the Effective Date Balance Sheet, and the Audited Financial Statements all Material liabilities of a type required to be so reflected or reserved against under Generally Accepted Accounting Principles applied consistently with prior years by the Company which the Vendor knows or had reasonable grounds to know there was a basis for asserting against the Company.

(aw) Non-Arm's Length Transactions—The Company has not entered into any contracts, agreements, options, or arrangements or incurred or assumed any obligation or liability (whether fixed or contingent) with, on behalf of, or with respect to the Vendor or other "non-arm's length person" (as that term is defined in the *Income Tax Act* or a Related Person, whether jointly or severally.

(ax) Accountants—Since incorporation of the Company the accountants of the Company have been the firm of "Messrs _____, Chartered Accountants, of the City of _____.

(ay) No Change in Remuneration—Since _____, 19_____, the salaries whether in the form of salary, dividends, bonus or commission paid by the Company or paid on behalf of the Company to the Vendor has not exceeded $_____ per fiscal year of the Company; provided, however, that to the extent that the Operating Profits of the Company, between _____, 19_____ and _____, 19_____ exceed $_____, such Operating Profits in excess of $_____ have been or will after Closing be distributed by way of salary, bonus or dividend to the Vendor and any dividends declared have been declared and paid in accordance with the Business Corporations Act[13] (Ontario).

(az) Retained Earnings—Notwithstanding anything herein to the contrary the retained earnings of the Company on the Closing Date, as reflected in the Statement of Retained Earnings on the Effective Date Financial Statements shall be not less than $_____which amount includes a reserve of not less than $_____ with respect to lost products.

(ba) Restrictions on Business—The Company is not a party to any agreement, indenture, mortgage, debenture, security agreement, lease, agreement or instrument, or subject to any restriction in the Articles or by-laws or subject to any restriction imposed by regulatory authorities having jurisdiction over it or subject to any statute, order, regulation or rule or to any writ, judgment, injunction or decree of any court or federal, provincial, municipal or other governmental department, commission, board of instrumentality which might prevent or interfere with the use of its Assets or which may limit or restrict or otherwise adversely affect the Business, properties, assets or financial condition, other than statutory provisions and restrictions of general application to its particular business. The Business is the only business carried on by the Company on the date hereof.

(bb) Titles to Properties—Except for any liens, charges or encumbrances or other minor imperfections of title which are not in the aggregate material and which do not materially impair the use of the property or assets subject thereto and except for the Leases listed on Schedule "E" and except as disclosed in the Effective Date Balance Sheet and the Audited Financial Statements or in Schedules "C" and "J", the Company has good and marketable title to all its properties, interests in properties and assets, real and personal, including without limitation those reflected in the Effective Date Balance Sheet and the Audited Financial Statements or acquired since the date of the Effective Date Balance Sheet (except as otherwise permitted in the Agreement or as since transferred, sold or otherwise disposed of in the ordinary and usual course of business), free and clear of all mortgages, pledges, charges, hypothecs, liens, title retention agreements, security interests, encumbrances or rights of other Persons, of any kind or character.

(bc) Real Property—The Company is not a party to or bound by any leases of real property other than the Leases. Where applicable, all rental and other payments required to be paid by the Company pursuant to the Leases have been duly paid and the Company is not in default or in breach of any material term or provision of the Leases.

(bd) Leased Equipment—Schedule "C" sets forth a true and complete list of all equipment, other personal property and fixtures in the possession or custody of the Company which, as of the date hereof, is leased or held under licence or similar arrangement and of the leases, licences, agreements or other documentation relating thereto.

(be) Condition of Assets—All material tangible Assets of the Company used in or in connection with the Business are in good condition, repair and, where applicable, working order, having regard to the use and age thereof. A complete description of all material fixed assets, machinery and equipment and all vehicles is shown in Schedule "W".

(bf) Purchase Commitments—No purchase commitment of the Company is in excess of its normal business requirements or at any excessive price. The Company is not obligated in any manner whatsoever to purchase widgets from any supplier.

(bg) Securities Legislation—The Company is a private company within the meaning of the *Securities Act* (Ontario) and the sale of the Shares by the Vendor to the Purchaser will be made in compliance with all applicable securities legislation.

(bh) Copies of Agreements, etc.—True, correct and complete copies of all mortgages, debentures, security agreements, leases, agreements, instruments and other documents listed in Schedule "B", "C", "E", "F" and "V" and of the policies of insurance referred to herein have been delivered to the Purchaser.

(bi)   Powers of Attorney—No person has any tax or other power of attorney from the Company with respect to any matter.

(bj)   Product Liability Claims—There is no pending or threatened product liability or similar claim which relates to the products manufactured, distributed or sold by the Company which is not covered fully by insurance.

(2)   Representations and Warranties of the Purchaser

The Purchaser hereby represents and warrants to the Vendor as follows:

(a)   Organization and Good Standing—The Purchaser is a corporation duly incorporated, organized, and validly existing and in good standing under the laws of [*jurisdiction of incorporation*].

(b)   Authority Relative to this Agreement, etc.—The Purchaser has all necessary corporate power, authority and capacity to enter into this Agreement and to perform its obligations hereunder; the execution and delivery of this Agreement and the consummation of the transactions contemplated hereby have been duly authorized by all necessary corporate action on the part of the Purchaser.

(c)   Absence of Conflicting Agreements—The Purchaser is not a party to, bound or affected by or subject to any indenture, mortgage, lease, agreement, instrument, charter or by-law provision, statute, regulation, order, judgment, decree or law which would be violated, contravened or breached by, or under which any default would occur as a result of the execution and delivery by it of this Agreement or the consummation of the transactions contemplated herein, except as disclosed in this Agreement.

(d)   Enforceability of Obligations—This Agreement constitutes a valid and binding obligation of the Purchaser enforceable against it in accordance with its terms provided that enforcement may be limited by bankruptcy, insolvency, liquidation, reorganization, reconstruc-tion and other similar laws generally affecting enforceability of creditors' rights and that equitable remedies such as specific performance and injunction are in the discretion of the court from which they are sought.

(e) Investment Canada Act—The Purchaser is not a non-Canadian within the meaning of the Investment Canada Act.

(f) Governmental Consents—No governmental or regulatory authorizations, consents, approvals, filings or notices pertaining to the Purchaser are required to be obtained or given or waiting period is required to expire in order that the purchase and sale of the Shares may be consummated by the Purchaser or for the Purchaser to carry out its obligations set out in this Agreement.

[*Note: Purchaser may have to acquire necessary licences even if no consent or approval is needed, or if licences or permits are not transferable.*]

(g) Total Assets and Gross Revenues—The Purchaser and its affiliates have combined assets in Canada, or combined gross revenues from sales in or from Canada, of $_____ in aggregate value.

(h) Financing—The Purchaser has obtained a commitment from *XYZ* to provide it with the necessary financing or equity to enable it to complete the transactions contemplated hereunder. A copy of the commitment letter of XYZ is attached hereto as Schedule "X".

(3) Commission

Each Party represents and warrants to the other Parties that no Person is entitled to a brokerage commission, finder's fee or other like payment in connection with the purchase and sale contemplated hereby.

(4) Non-Waiver

No investigations made by or on behalf of the Purchaser at any time shall have the effect of waiving, diminishing the scope of or otherwise affecting any representation or warranty made by the Vendor herein or pursuant hereto. No waiver by the Purchaser of any condition, in whole or in part, shall operate as a waiver of any other condition.

(5) Nature and Survival of Representations and Warranties

All statements contained in any certificate or other instrument delivered by or on behalf of a Party pursuant to or in connection with the transactions contemplated by this Agreement shall be deemed to be made by that Party under this Agreement. All representations, warranties, covenants and agreements contained in this Agreement on the part of each of the Parties shall survive the Closing, the execution and delivery hereunder of any bills of sale, instruments of conveyance, assignments or other instruments of transfer of title to any of the Shares and the payment of the consideration contemplated under this Agreement, except that the representations and warranties contained in this Article shall only survive for [*two*] years following Closing (except for the Vendor's representation and warranties relating to tax matters which shall survive for the period of time during which the taxes to which such representations and warranties relate may be reassessed by the relevant taxation authority, unless the Vendor has been fraudulent in filing a return or supplying information to any taxation authority under an taxation legislation [*or unless the Vendor has agreed to extend by waiver the period in which tax reassessments may be made*], in which case the survival of those representations and warranties relating to tax matters shall be unlimited [*in the case of fraud, or shall continue to the expiry of the extended reassessment period, as the case may be,*]) after which period of time, if no claim shall, prior to the expiry of such period, have been made under this Agreement against a Party with respect to any incorrectness in or breach of any representation or warranty made herein by such Party, such Party shall have no further liability under this Agreement with respect to such representation or warranty.

5. COVENANTS OF THE PARTIES

(1) Conduct of Business Prior to Closing

During the period from the date of this Agreement to the Closing Time, the Vendor shall do or cause the Company to do the following:

(a) Conduct Business in Ordinary Course—Except as otherwise contemplated or permitted by this Agreement, the Company shall conduct the Business in the ordinary and normal course and shall not, without the prior written consent of Purchaser, enter into any transaction which, if entered into before the date of this Agreement, would cause any representations or warranties of the Vendor contained in this Agreement to be incorrect or constitute a breach of any covenant or agreement of the Vendor contained in this Agreement. The Vendor shall use its best efforts to preserve intact the Company and the Business and the relationship existing with the customers of the Company.

(b) Continue Insurance—The Company shall continue in force and in good standing all existing insurance maintained by it.

(c)   Perform Obligations—The Company shall comply with all applicable laws, regulations, by-laws and other governmental requirements of each jurisdiction in which the Business is carried on.

(d)   Material Changes—The Company shall not take any action which would result in any Material adverse change, which shall be deemed to include the circumstances specified in Section 4(1)(p), in or to the Business or sell, transfer or dispose of any of the assets of the Company, other than in the ordinary course of business.

(e)   Liens, Vendor—The Vendor shall not suffer or permit any mortgages, pledges, hypothecs, security interests, deemed trusts, liens, charges, rights or claims of other Persons, or any other encumbrances whatsoever, to attach to or affect the Shares other than security interests in favour of the Vendor's Bank, all of which shall be discharged or waived in writing by the Vendor's Bank on or prior to the Closing.

(f)   Liens, Company—The Company shall not suffer or permit any mortgages, pledges, hypothecs, security interests, deemed trusts, liens, charges, rights or claims of other Persons, or any other encumbrances whatsoever, to attach to or affect the assets of the Company other than security interests which are not Material in amount and which are granted in the ordinary course of business.

(g)   Wage Increases, Hiring and Firing—The Company shall not make or commit to make any wage increases or grant any bonuses to any of the non-union employees of the Company, nor employ any new employees in the Company without the Purchaser's consent nor terminate the employment of any key employees of the Company, including [*name key employees*], nor amend or discontinue the Pension Plan or any of the Benefit Plans, without the Purchaser's consent.

(h)   Accounts Receivable—Provide to the Purchaser on the third Business Day prior to the Closing Date, an up-to-date list (accurate to within 45 days of the Closing Date) of all outstanding accounts receivable and not write off any existing account receivable without the prior written consent of the Purchaser except for usual adjustments made in the ordinary course of business for prompt payment.

(i)   Financial Statements—To use their best efforts to cause the Auditors to commence with the preparation of the Effective Date Financial Statements.

(2)   Access for Investigation

The Vendor and the Company shall permit the Purchaser and its employ-ees, agents, counsel and accountants or other representatives, between the date of execution of this Agreement and the Closing Time, without interference to the ordinary conduct of the Business, to have access during normal business hours to the premises and to all the books, accounts, records and other data of the Company (including, without limitation, all corporate and accounting records of the Vendor relating exclusively to the Company) and to furnish to the Purchaser such financial and operating data and other information with respect to the Company, as the Purchaser shall from time to time reasonably request to enable confirmation of the matters warranted in Section 4(1). Specifically, within [_____] Business Days of the execution of this Agreement by the Parties, the Vendor and the Company agree to deliver to or make available for inspection by the Purchaser of the following:
[*List specific documents and other due diligence materials to be disclosed which may include copies of Contracts, Equipment Leases, Leases, Collective Agreements, Pension Plans, Benefit Plans, Licenses, insurance policies and other Material plans and contracts.*]

(3)   Delivery of Books and Records

At the Time of Closing, the Vendor and the Company shall deliver to the Purchaser the following documents: (i) lists of suppliers and customers of the Company; (ii) employee records with respect to the Employees; (iii) advertising, promotional and marketing materials which relate to the Company; and (iv) files relating to the assets of the Company including, without limitation, the maintenance records for each item of equipment or machinery owned or leased by the Company. The Purchaser agrees that it will preserve the documents, books and records so delivered to it for a period of six years from the Closing Date, or for such other period as is required by any applicable law, and will permit the Vendor or her authorized representatives reasonable access to those books and records in connection with the affairs of the Vendor relating to any tax matters, workers' compensation or litigation matters. The Vendor agrees that she will preserve the documents, books and records which are not delivered to the Purchaser for a period of six years from the Closing Date, or for such longer period as is required by applicable law, and will permit the Purchaser or its authorized representatives reasonable access to those books and records in connection with the affairs of the Company relating to any tax, workers' compensation or litigation matters.

(4) Actions to Satisfy Closing Conditions

Each Party agrees to take all such actions as are within its power to control, and to use its best efforts to cause other actions to be taken which are not within its power to control, so as to ensure compliance with any conditions set forth in Article Seven which are for the benefit of the other Party.

(5) Workers' Compensation

On or before Closing, the Company shall provide a clearance certificate or other similar documentary evidence from the Worker's Compensation authority in each jurisdiction where the Company carries on business certifying that there are no outstanding assessments, penalties, fines, levies, charges, surcharges or other amounts due or owing to those authorities.

(6) Competition Act

[Note: See alternative clauses for sample provisions concerning Investment Canada Act and the Competition Act. Consider, as well, all other necessary regulatory consents and approvals and provide details as to the responsibility for, the timing of and the costs involved in obtaining these consents and approvals.]

(7) Confidentiality

The Purchaser shall keep confidential all confidential technology and any other confidential information (unless readily available from public or published information or sources or required to be disclosed by law) obtained from either the Vendor or the Company. If this Agreement is terminated without completion of the transactions contemplated herein then, promptly after such termination, all documents, work papers and other written material obtained by the Purchaser from the Vendor or the Company in connection with this Agreement shall be returned by the Purchaser to the party from whom such materials were obtained. [Note: See alternative clauses for another example of a confidentiality provision.]

(8) Consents Required in Contracts

The Purchaser shall be responsible for obtaining any consent for any Contract, Lease or Equipment Lease where such consent is required upon a change of control of the Company as a result of the consummation of transactions contemplated by this Agreement. If the Purchaser is unable to obtain such consent, such Contract, Lease or Equipment Lease shall not be assigned and the Vendor or the Company shall, to the extent legally possible, hold its right, title and interest in, to and under such Contract, Lease or Equipment Lease in trust for the benefit of the Purchaser until such consent is obtained.

(9)   Retail Sales Tax

[*Note: Ontario retail sales tax applies only to transfers of tangible personal property and therefore does not apply to the sale of shares, but as part of the purchaser's due diligence, it may still wish to obtain a clearance certificate so that the Vendor's liabiltiy, if any, concerning retail sales tax can be determined*]

The Vendor agrees to deliver to the Purchaser on the Closing Date a clearance certificate respecting the Company under section 6 of the Retail Sales Tax Act (Ontario) and similar clearance certificates, if available, from the retail sales tax authorities in all jurisdictions where the Business is carried on by the Vendor or the Purchased Assets are located.

(10) Non-Competition

The Vendor covenants and agrees that she will not, from and after the Closing Date until the fifth anniversary of the Closing Date, carry on in Canada any business in the nature of or in competition with the Business. At Closing, the Vendor shall enter into a non-competition agreement in support of the covenant under this Section 5(11), in the form attached as Schedule "G" (the "Non-Competition Agreement").

(11) Employment Agreement

The Vendor agrees to cause [*key employee*] to enter into an employment agreement with the Purchaser, to be entered into at Closing in the form attached as Schedule "Y" (the "Employment Agreement").

(12) Co-operation to Obtain Governmental Approvals

Between the Agreement Date and the Closing Date both the Purchaser and the Vendor shall take such steps as are reasonably necessary and within their respective control to obtain all governmental actions and approvals necessary to the execution, delivery and performance of this Agreement by the Purchaser, including without limitation, the satisfaction of the conditions set forth in Section 7(1)(g) respecting the Competition Act and the Investment Canada Act. The Purchaser acknowledges that it has made application to the appropriate governmental authorities for requisite approvals pursuant to the Competition Act and the Investment Canada Act.

6. INDEMNIFICATION

(1) Indemnification by Vendor

(a)   Subject to this Article Six, if the transactions contemplated by this Agreement are consummated, the Vendor agrees to indemnify and hold the Purchaser harmless against and in respect of any loss, damage, claim, cost or expense whatsoever, including any and all incremental out-of-pocket costs, including, without limitation, all reasonable legal and accounting fees, which the Purchaser may incur, suffer or be required to pay, pursuant to any Claim that may be made or asserted against or affect the Purchaser, provided, however, that the subject matter of any such Claim relates to or arises out of or in connection with the following matters:

   (i)   any misrepresentation or breach of any warranty, agreement, covenant or obligation of the Vendor contained in this Agreement or in any agreement, schedule, certificate or other document required to be entered into or delivered by the Purchaser;

   (ii)   any reassessment for income, corporate sales, excise or other tax (and all interest and/or penalties relating thereto) in respect of which tax returns have been filed before the Closing Time which result in the payment of tax in excess of the amount accrued or reserved for in the Audited Financial Statements or the Effective Date Financial Statements;

[*Note: List other specific matters for which Vendor will indemnify Purchaser including Environmental Matters (see alternate clauses for indemnification concerning environmental matters.)*]

(b)   The obligation of the Vendor to indemnify the Purchaser as set forth in Section 6(1)(a)(i) for any loss, damage, claim, cost or expense shall be subject to the limitation period referred to in Section 4(5) with respect to survival of representations and warranties. [*Note: List any other applicable limitation periods for other indemnities.*]

(2) Indemnification by Purchaser

(a)   Subject to this Article Six, if the transactions contemplated by this Agreement are consummated, the Purchaser agrees to indemnify and hold the Vendor harmless against and in respect of any loss, damage, claim, cost or expense whatsoever, including any and all incremental out-of-pocket costs, including, without limitation, all reasonable legal and accounting fees, which the Vendor may incur, suffer or be required to pay, pursuant to any Claim, that may be made or asserted against or affect the Vendor, provided, however, that the subject matter of any such claim relates to or arises out of or in connection with the following matters:

(i)   any misrepresentation or breach of any warranty, agreement, covenant or obligation of the Purchaser contained in this Agreement or in any agreement, schedule certificate or other document required to be entered into or delivered by the Purchaser; or

[*Note: List other specific matters for which Purchaser will indemnify Vendor*].

(b)   The obligation of the Purchaser to indemnify the Vendor as set forth in Section 6(2)(a)(i) for any loss, damage, claim, cost or expense shall be subject to the limitation period referred to in Section 4(5) with respect to survival of representations and warranties. [*Note: List any other applicable limitation periods for other indemnities.*]

(3) Claims by Third Parties

(a)   Promptly upon receipt by either the Purchaser or the Vendor (herein referred to as the "Indemnitee") of notice of any Third Party Claim in respect of which the Indemnitee proposes to demand indemnification from the other party to this Agreement (the "Indemnitor"), the Indemnitee shall forthwith give notice to that effect to the Indemnitor.

(b)   The Indemnitor shall have the right, exercisable by giving notice to the Indemnitee not later than 30 days after receipt of the notice described in Sections 6(3)(a), to assume the control of the defence, compromise or settlement of the Third Party Claim, provided that:

(i)   the Indemnitor shall first deliver to the Indemnitee its written consent to be joined as a party to any action or proceeding relating thereto; and,

(ii)   the Indemnitor shall at the Indemnitee's request furnish it with reasonable security against any costs or other liabilities to which it may be or become exposed by reason of such defence, compromise or settlement.

(c)   Upon the assumption of control by the Indemnitor as aforesaid, the Indemnitor shall, at its expense, diligently proceed with the defence, compromise or settlement of the Third Party Claim at the Indemnitor's sole expense, including employment of counsel reasonably satisfactory to the Indemnitee, and in connection with such proceedings, the Indemnitee shall co-operate fully, but at the expense of the Indemnitor, to make available to the Indemnitor all pertinent information and witnesses under the Indemnitee's control and to make such assignments and take such other steps as in the opinion of counsel for the Indemnitor are necessary to enable the Indemnitor to conduct such defence, provided always that the Indemnitee shall be entitled to reasonable security from the Indemnitor for any expense, costs or other liabilities to which it may be or may become exposed by reason of such co-operation.

(d) The final determination of any such Third Party Claim, including all related costs and expense, will be binding and conclusive upon the Parties as to the validity or invalidity, as the case may be, of such Third Party Claim against the Indemnitor.

(e) Should the Indemnitor fail to give notice to the Indemnitee as provided in Section 6(3)(b), the Indemnitee shall be entitled to make such settlement of the Third Party Claim as in its sole discretion may appear advisable, and such settlement or any other final determination of the Third Party Claim shall be binding upon the Indemnitor.

(f) Where an amount is payable by the Purchaser or Vendor as indemnification pursuant to the terms of this Agreement and the Excise Tax Act provides that GST is deemed to have been collected by the payee thereof, the amount so payable, as determined without reference to this paragraph (the "Indemnification Amount"), shall be increased by an amount equal to the rate of GST applied to the Indemnification Amount in accordance with the Excise Tax Act.

(4) Indemnification Sole Remedy

The provisions of this Article Six shall constitute the sole remedy to the Vendor and the Purchaser against the other party to this Agreement with respect to any and all breaches of any agreement, covenant, representation or warranty made by such party in this Agreement.

(5) Details of Claims

With respect to any claim provided for under Sections 6(1) and 6(2), no indemnity under this Agreement shall be sought unless written notice providing reasonable details of the reasons for which the indemnity is sought is provided to either of the Vendor or the Purchaser, as the case may be, before the expiration of the limitation dates provided for in Section 6(1) and 6(2) respectively, as applicable.

(6)   Limit on Indemnity

Notwithstanding any other provision of this Agreement, the Vendor and the Purchaser agree that they shall not assert against the other any claim or claims with respect to the breach of any representation, warranty, covenant or agreement under this Agreement unless the aggregate amount of the claim or claims asserted to that date, including the claim or claims then being asserted, is at least $_____ .

No Indemnifying Party shall be liable to an Indemnified Party under either Sections 6(1) or 6(2) unless the aggregate amount of all Indemnified Losses incurred by the Indemnified Party exceed (*insert amount*) whereupon the Indemnifying Party will be liable for all Indemnified Losses incurred in excess of such (*insert amount*) amount.

[*Note: See alternative clauses for additional indemnification clauses concerning subrogation, limitation on recovery, indemnification sole remedy, tax adjustment and de minimis.*]

[*Note also that in some cases, the delivery of separate indemnity agreements at Closing may be provided for.*]

7.   CONDITIONS PRECEDENT TO THE PERFORMANCE BY THE PURCHASER AND THE VENDOR OF THEIR OBLIGATIONS UNDER THIS AGREEMENT

(1)   Purchaser's Conditions

The obligation of the Purchaser to complete the transactions contemplated by this Agreement shall be subject to the satisfaction of, or compliance with, at or before the Closing Time, each of the following conditions precedent (each of which is hereby acknowledged to be inserted for the exclusive benefit of the Purchaser and may be waived by it in whole or in part):

(a)   Truth and Accuracy of Representations of the Vendor at the Closing Time — All of the representations and warranties of the Vendor made in or under this Agreement, including, without limitation, the representations and warranties made by the Vendor and set forth in Section 4(1), shall be true and correct in all material respects as at the Closing Time and with the same effect as if made at and as of the Closing Time (except as such representations and warranties may be affected by the occurrence of events or transactions expressly contemplated and permitted by this Agreement) and the Purchaser shall have received a statutory declaration [*certificate*] from the Vendor confirming the truth and correctness in all material respects of the representations and warranties of the Vendor.

(b)　Performance of Obligations — The Vendor shall have performed or complied with, in all material respects, all their obligations, covenants and agreements under this Agreement.

(c)　Receipt of Closing Documentation — All instruments of conveyance and other documentation and assurances relating to the sale and purchase of the Shares including, without limitation, share certificates (the "Closing Documents") and all actions and proceedings taken on or prior to the Closing in connection with performance by the Vendor of her obligations under this Agreement shall be satisfactory to the Purchaser and its counsel, acting reasonably, and the Purchaser shall have received copies of all such documentation or other evidence as it may reasonably request in order to establish the consummation of the transactions contemplated under this Agreement and the taking of all corporate proceedings in connection with those transactions in compliance with this Section 7(1), in form [as to certification and otherwise] and substance satisfactory to the Purchaser and its counsel.

(d)　Closing Documentation — Without limiting the generality of Section 7(1)(c), the Purchaser shall have received at or before the Closing Time sufficient duly executed original copies of the following:

(i)　certified copy of a resolution of the board of directors of the Company approving this Agreement and the transactions contemplated under this Agreement;

(ii)　statutory declaration of the Vendor concerning residence of the Vendor, the matters referred to in subsection 7(1)(a) and confirming that all conditions under this Agreement in favour of the Vendor have been either fulfilled or waived;

(iii)　certificate of incumbency of the Company;

(iv)　certificate of status of the Company;

(v)　share certificates representing the Shares;

(vi)　books and records of the Company;

(vii)　Non-Competition Agreement; and

(viii)　Employment Agreement.

(e)　Opinion of Counsel for the Vendor — The Purchaser shall have received an opinion dated the Closing Date, in the form attached as Schedule "Z" from counsel for the Vendor, confirming the matters warranted in subsections (a), (d), (e), (g) and (p) of Section 4(1) which opinion may rely on opinions of counsel in other jurisdictions with respect to matters of law in those jurisdictions. In giving such opinion, counsel to the Vendor may rely on certificates of the Vendor as to factual matters.

(f) Consents to Assignment — All consents or approvals from or notifications to any lessor or other third Person required under the terms of any of the Equipment Leases, the Leases or the Assignable Licences with respect to the acquisition of control of the Company by the Purchaser, or otherwise in connection with the consummation of the transactions contemplated under this Agreement, shall have been duly obtained or given, as the case may be, on or before the Closing Time.

(g) Consents, Authorizations and Registrations — All consents, approvals, orders and authorizations of or from governmental or regulatory authorities required in connection with the completion of the transactions contemplated in this Agreement shall have been obtained on or prior to the Closing Time including: [*Note: Describe particular consents or approvals required.*]

[*Alternative Language*]

(g) Governmental Actions and Approvals — There shall have been obtained, from all appropriate federal, provincial, municipal or other governmental or administrative bodies, such approvals or consents as are required to permit the change of ownership and due registration of the Shares contemplated by this Agreement, including, without limitation, the following:
   (i)   Investment Canada — The Purchaser shall have either received a receipt issued under subsection 13(1) of the Investment Canada Act certifying that a complete notice in prescribed form in respect of the acquisition has been received and advising that such acquisition is not reviewable; or a notice from the Minister of Industry, Science and Technology issued under Sections 21, 22 or 23 of the Investment Canada Act indicating that such Minister is, or is deemed to be, satisfied that the acquisition is likely to be of net benefit to Canada.
   (ii) Competition Act— (i) The Purchaser and the Vendor shall each have filed all notices and information required under Part IX of the Competition Act (Canada), satisfied any requests for additional information from the Director of Investigation and Research appointed under the Competition Act (the "Director") and the Director shall have issued confirmation that he does not intend to refer the transaction contemplated herein to the Competition Tribunal pursuant to Section 92 of the said Act; or (ii) the Director shall have issued an Advance Ruling Certificate

under the Act with respect to the acquisition contemplated herein.

(h)   Vendor's Security — The Vendor shall have delivered to the Purchaser the undertaking of the Vendor's Bank to release its security interest in the Shares in the form of Schedule "T".

(i)   Financing — The Purchaser shall have complete all necessary financing, to permit the Purchaser to complete the transactions contemplated under this Agreement, in accordance with the commitment from XYZ described in Section 4(2)(h).

(j)   Non-objection of Major Customers — Within five Business Days of the date of execution of this Agreement, Purchaser shall have satisfied itself that none of the major customers of the Company, have any objections to the transaction of purchase and sale contemplated by this Agreement and Purchaser shall forthwith thereafter confirm in writing to the Vendor its satisfaction or failure to achieve such satisfaction, as the case may be.

(k)   Certificate as to Status of Assets — A senior officer of the Company shall have executed and delivered to the Purchaser, in a form satisfactory to the Purchaser, a certificate stating that, as of the Closing Date, there has been no Material damage to or adverse change in the condition of the Assets or to the nature of the Business.

(l)   No Actions Taken Restricting Sale — No action or proceeding in Canada by law or in equity shall be pending or threatened by any person, firm, corporation, government, governmental authority, regulatory body or agency to enjoin, restrict or prohibit the purchase and sale of the Shares contemplated under this Agreement.

(m)   Directors of Company — There shall have been delivered to the Purchaser on or before the Closing Time, the resignations, effective as and from Closing, of all of the directors of the Company, together with comprehensive releases from each such person of all their claims respectively, except for any claims for unpaid remuneration.

(n)   Directors of Subco Inc. — There shall have been delivered to the Purchaser on or before the Closing Time, the resignations, effective as and from Closing, of all of the directors of Subco Inc., together with comprehensive releases from each such person of all their claims respectively, except for any claims for unpaid remuneration.

(o) Employment Offers Accepted — The Purchaser shall be satisfied that senior employees of the Company, _____, _____ and _____, will continue in the employ of the Company as provided for in Section 5(12).

(p) Status of Vendor — The Vendor has delivered to the Purchaser reasonable and satisfactory evidence that the Vendor is at the Closing Date a resident of Canada within the meaning of the Income Tax Act, [*or failing such evidence, has delivered the requisite certificate with a certificate limit in proper amount as provided for by the Income Tax Act* (Canada)—*See alternative clauses*].

(q) Change of Control Filing — The Vendor shall prepare at its expense and provide to the Company and the Purchaser to be filed within the time period prescribed by the Income Tax Act and any other applicable legislation all tax returns and tax filings required to be made by the Company consequent upon the acquisition of control of the Company by the Purchaser. The Vendor shall indemnify and hold harmless the Company and the Purchaser in respect of liability of the Company for Taxes relating to all fiscal periods of the Company commencing prior to the Effective Completion Time. In its return for the fiscal period ending on the acquisition of control of the Company by the Purchaser, the Company shall elect not to have subsection 256(9) of the Income Tax Act (and other similar provisions under provincial law) apply.

(2) Vendor's Conditions

The obligations of the Vendor to complete the transactions contemplated by this Agreement shall be subject to the satisfaction of, or compliance with, at or before the Closing Time, each of the following conditions precedent (each of which is hereby acknowledged to be inserted for the exclusive benefit of the Vendor and may be waived by the Vendor in whole or in part);

(a) Truth and Accuracy of Representations of the Purchaser at Closing Time — All of the representations and warranties of the Purchaser made in or under this Agreement, including, without limitation, the representations and warranties made by the Purchaser and set forth in Section 4(2), shall be true and correct in all material respects as at the Closing Time and with the same effect as if made at and as of the Closing Time (except as such representations and warranties may be affected by the occurrence of events or transactions contemplated and permitted hereby) and the Vendor shall have received a statutory declaration [*certificate*] from a senior officer of the Purchaser confirming the truth and correctness in all material respects of such representations and warranties of the Purchaser.

(b)   Performance of Agreements — The Purchaser shall have performed or complied with, in all respects, all of its other obligations, covenants and agreements under this Agreement.

(c)   Receipt of Closing Documentation — All instruments of conveyance and other documentation and assurances relating to the sale and purchase of the Shares including, without limitation, share certificates and all actions and proceedings taken on or prior to the Closing in connection with performance by the Purchaser of its obligations under this Agreement shall be satisfactory to the Vendor and her counsel, acting reasonably, and the Vendor shall have received copies of all such documentation or other evidence as she may reasonably request in order to establish the consummation of the transactions contemplated under this Agreement and the taking of all corporate proceedings in connection with those transactions in compliance with this Section 7(2), in form (as to certification and otherwise) and substance satisfactory to the Vendor and her counsel.

(d)   Closing Documentation — Without limiting the generality of Section 7(2)(c), the Vendor shall have received at or before the Closing Time sufficient duly executed original copies of the following:

   (i)   certified copy of a resolution of the board of directors of the Purchaser approving this Agreement and the transactions contemplated under this Agreement;

   (ii)   statutory declaration of a senior officer of the Vendor concerning residence of the Vendor, the matters referred to in subsection 7(2)(a), its status for purposes of the Investment Canada Act and confirming that all conditions under this Agreement in favour of the Purchaser have been either fulfilled or waived;

   (iii)   certificate of incumbency of the Purchaser; and

   (iv)   certificate of status of the Purchaser.

(e)   Opinion of Counsel for Purchaser — The Vendor shall have received an opinion dated the Closing Date, in the form attached as Schedule "AA" from counsel for the Purchaser, confirming the matters warranted in subsections (a), (b) and (d) of Section 4(2), which opinion may rely on opinions of counsel in other jurisdictions with respect to matters of law in those jurisdictions. In giving such opinion, counsel to the Purchaser may rely on certificates of the Purchaser as to factual matters.

(f)   No Actions Taken Restricting Sale — No action or proceeding in Canada by law or in equity shall be pending or threatened by any person, firm, corporation, government, governmental authority, regulatory body or agency to enjoin, restrict or prohibit the purchase and sale of the Shares contemplated under this Agreement.

(g)   Payment of Purchase Price — The Purchaser shall have tendered to the Vendor the Purchaser's Notes and certified cheques or bank drafts for the balance of the Purchase Price payable to the Vendor.

(h)   Consents, Authorizations and Registrations — All consents, approvals, orders and authorizations of or from governmental or regulatory authorities required in connection with the completion of the transactions contemplated in this Agreement shall have been obtained on or prior to the Closing Time including: [*Note: Describe particular consents or approvals required.*]

(i)   Governmental actions and Approvals — There shall have been obtained, from all appropriate federal, provincial, municipal or other governmental or administrative bodies, such approvals or consents as are required to permit the change of ownership and due registration of the Shares contemplated by this Agreement, including, without limitation, the following:

    (i)   Investment Canada — The Purchaser shall have either received a receipt issued under subsection 13(1) of the Investment Canada Act certifying that a complete notice in prescribed form in respect of the acquisition has been received and advising that such acquisition is not reviewable; or a notice from the Minister of Industry, Science and Technology issued under Sections 21, 22 or 23 of the Investment Canada Act indicating that such Minister is, or is deemed to be, satisfied that the acquisition is likely to be of net benefit to Canada.

    (ii)   Competition Act — (i) The Purchaser and the Vendor shall each have filed all notices and information required under Part IX of the Competition Act, satisfied any requests for additional information from the Director of Investigation and Research appointed under the Act (the "Director") and the Director shall have issued confirmation that he does not intend to refer the transaction contemplated herein to the Competition Tribunal pursuant to Section 92 of the said Act; or (ii) the Director shall have issued an Advance Ruling Certificate under the Competition Act with respect to the acquisition contemplated herein.

(j) Release of Directors of the Company — The Company shall have executed and delivered to each of the directors of the Company, comprehensive releases with respect to any claims by the Company against such directors.

(k) Release of Directors of Subco Inc. — Subco Inc. shall have executed and delivered to each of the directors of Subco Inc., comprehensive releases with respect to any claims by Subco Inc. against such directors.

(l) Release of Guarantee — The guarantee granted by the Vendor to the Company's Bank, as more particularly described in item @ of Schedule "T", has been released, and the Company's Bank has released the Vendor from any and all obligations under such guarantee or in respect thereto.

(m) Release of Existing Mortgage — The Vendor has been released from any and all obligations under the mortgage more particularly described in item @ of Schedule "T".

[*Note: There may be a class of condition applicable to a transaction which is for the benefit of neither party and is therefore not waivable independently by any party. These conditions are "true conditions precedent", upon the fulfilment of which the transaction is dependent. Certain government approvals may fall into this category. In such cases, a separate section for true conditions precedent may be appropriate.*]

(3) Failure to Satisfy Conditions

If any condition set forth in Sections 7(1) or 7(2) is not satisfied on or before the Closing Time, the Party entitled to the benefit of such condition (the "First Party") may terminate this Agreement by notice in writing to the other Party and in such event the First Party shall be released from all obligations under this Agreement, and unless the First Party can show that the condition or conditions which have not been satisfied and for which the First Party has terminated this Agreement are reasonably capable of being performed or caused to be performed by the other Party then the other Party shall also be released from all obligations under this Agreement, except that the First Party shall be entitled to waive compliance with any such conditions, obligations or covenants in whole or in part if it sees fit to do so without prejudice to any of its rights of termination in the event of non-performance of any other condition, obligation or covenant, or whole or in part.

(4) Destruction or Expropriation

If, prior to the Closing Time, there occurs any material destruction or damage by fire or other cause or hazard to any of the properties or assets of the Company, or if such properties or assets or any material part of them are expropriated or forcefully taken by any governmental authority or if notice of intention to expropriate a material part of such properties or assets has been filed in accordance with applicable legislation, then the Purchaser may, at its option, terminate this Agreement by notice to the other Parties.

8. CLOSING ARRANGEMENTS

(1) Time and Place of Closing

The completion of the transactions contemplated by this Agreement shall take place at the Closing Time on the Closing Date at the offices of _____, Ontario, or at such other place as may be agreed upon between the Parties.

(2) Closing Arrangements

At the Closing Time, upon fulfilment of all the conditions under this Agreement which have not been waived in writing by the Purchaser or the Vendor respectively:

(a) Purchase and Sale of Purchased Assets — The Vendor shall sell and the Purchaser shall purchase the Shares for the Purchase Price payable under this Agreement.

(b) Delivery of Closing Documents — The Parties shall respectively deliver the Closing Documents.

(c) Actual Possession — The Vendor shall deliver actual possession of the Shares to the Purchaser.

(d) Payment of Purchase Price — On the fulfilment of the foregoing terms of this Article Eight, the Purchaser shall pay and satisfy the Purchase Price as provided in Section 3(1).

(3) Tender

Any tender of documents or money hereunder may be made upon the Parties or their respective counsel and money may be tendered by official bank draft drawn upon a Canadian chartered bank or by negotiable cheque payable in Canadian funds and certified by a Canadian chartered bank or trust company.

9. NOTICES

(1) Delivery of Notice

Any notice, direction or other instrument required or permitted to be given by either party under this Agreement shall be in writing and shall be sufficiently given if delivered personally, sent by prepaid first class mail or transmitted by telecopier or other form of electronic communication during the transmission of which no indication of failure of receipt is communicated to the sender:

(a)   in the case of a notice to the Vendor at:

_____

_____

_____

_____

Attention: President

Fax No. (   )

(b)   in the case of a notice to the Purchaser at:

_____

_____

_____

_____

Attention: President

Fax No. (   )

Any such notice, direction or other instrument, if delivered personally, shall be deemed to have been given and received on the date on which it was received at such address, or, if sent by mail, shall be deemed to have been given and received on the date which is five days after which it was mailed, provided that if either such day is not a Business Day, then the notice shall be deemed to have been given and received on the Business Day next following such day. Any notice transmitted by telecopier or other form of electronic communication shall be deemed to have been given and received on the date of its transmission provided that if such day is not a Business Day or if it is received after the end of normal business hours on the date of its transmission at the place of receipt, then it shall be deemed to have been given and received at the opening of business in the office of the recipient on the first Business Day next following the transmission thereof. If normal mail service, telex, telecopier or other form of electronic communication is interrupted by strike, slowdown, *force majeure* or other cause, a notice, direction or other instrument sent by the impaired means of communication will not be deemed to be received until actually received, and the party sending the notice shall utilize any other such service which has not been so interrupted to deliver such notice.

10. GENERAL

(1) Expenses

All costs and expenses (including, without limitation, the fees and disbursements of legal counsel) incurred in connection with this Agreement and the transaction contemplated under this Agreement shall be paid by the Party incurring such expenses.

(2) Time

Time shall be of the essence hereof.

(3) Assignment/Successors and Assigns

Neither this Agreement nor any rights or obligations under this Agreement shall be assignable by either Party without the prior written consent of the other Party. Subject to that condition, this Agreement shall enure to the benefit of and be binding upon the Parties and their respective heirs, executors, administrators, successors (including any successor by reason of amalgamation of any Party) and permitted assigns.

(4) Further Assurances

Each Party agrees that upon the written request of any other Party, it will do all such acts and execute all such further documents, conveyances, deeds, assignments, transfers and the like, and will cause the doing of all such acts and will cause the execution of all such further documents as are within its power to cause the doing or execution of, as the other Party may from time to time reasonably request be done and/or executed as may be required to consummate the transactions contemplated under this Agreement or as may be necessary or desirable to effect the purpose of this Agreement or any document, agreement or instrument delivered under this Agreement and to carry out their provisions or to better or more properly or fully evidence or give effect to the transactions contemplated under this Agreement, whether before or after the Closing.

(5) Public Notices

All notices to third parties and all other publicity concerning the transactions contemplated by this Agreement shall be jointly planned and coordinated by the Vendor and the Purchaser and no Party shall act unilaterally in this regard without the prior approval of the other Party (such approval not to be unreasonably withheld), except where required to do so by law or by the applicable regulations or policies of any provincial, federal or other regulatory agency of competent jurisdiction or any stock exchange.

(6) Counterparts

This Agreement may be executed by the Parties in separate counterparts each of which when so executed and delivered shall be an original, and all such counterparts shall together constitute one and the same instrument.

IN WITNESS WHEREOF the Parties have duly executed this Agreement as of the date and year first above written.

SIGNED, SEALED AND DELIVERED
in the presence of:

_____   _____ I/s
Witness: JANE DOE

PURCHASER LTD.

Per: _____ c/s

TARGET LIMITED

Per: _____ c/s

9F79
SHORT FORM PURCHASE AGREEMENT

[See Para. 9.620]

MEMORANDUM OF AGREEMENT made as of the _____ day of
_____, 19____

A M O N G

> VENDOR INC., a corporation incorporated pursuant to the laws of
> the State of Delaware
>
> (hereinafter referred to as the "Vendor")

OF THE FIRST PART

> - and -
>
> PURCHASER LTD., a corporation incorporated under the laws of
> Ontario
>
> (hereinafter referred to as the "Purchaser")

OF THE SECOND PART

> - and -
>
> TARGET LTD., a corporation incorporated under the laws of the
> Province of _____
>
> (hereinafter called the "Corporation")

OF THE THIRD PART

WHEREAS the authorized capital of the Corporation consists of 100
common voting shares without par value of which 10 have been issued and
are outstanding as fully paid and non-assessable;

AND WHEREAS Vendor controls the 10 aforesaid issued and
outstanding common shares;

AND WHEREAS the Purchaser has agreed with the Vendor to purchase the 10 issued and outstanding shares controlled by the Vendor in the capital stock of the Corporation;

THIS AGREEMENT WITNESSETH that in consideration of the covenants, agreements, warranties and payments herein set out and provided for, the parties hereto hereby respectively covenant and agree as follows:

1. Purchased Shares

Subject to the terms and conditions hereof, the Vendor covenants and agrees to sell, assign, and transfer to the Purchaser and the Purchaser covenants and agrees to purchase from the Vendor all (and not less than all) of the issued and outstanding shares in the capital stock of the Corporation controlled by the Vendor (the "Purchased Shares") for the purchase price (the "Purchase Price") payable as set out in Article 2 hereof.

2. Purchase Price

(1) The Purchase Price shall be the sum of _____ dollars ($_____) of lawful money of Canada.

(2) The Purchase Price shall be payable to or to the order of the Vendor by certified cheque payable at the Closing.

(3) The Purchaser shall be entitled to reduce its payment of the foregoing amounts, for amounts payable to Revenue Canada for withholding taxes, by reason of the Vendor being a non-resident within the meaning of the Income Tax Act, unless Vendor delivers to Purchaser on the Closing Date a Section 116 Income Tax Act certificate issued by Revenue Canada for this transaction. If such certificate is not available on the Closing Date, such amount so withheld, shall be paid to Messrs. _____ in trust, to hold until such Section 116 Certificate is received, or to forward such monies to Revenue Canada if such Section 116 Certificate is refused.

3. Closing Arrangements

(1) The closing of this transaction shall take place at the offices of Messrs. _____ Barristers and Solicitors, located at (*address*), on _____, 19____ or at such other date(s) as the parties hereto may agree (the "Closing Date").

(2) On the Closing Date, upon fulfilment of all the conditions set out herein, the Vendor shall deliver to the Purchaser the certificates representing all the Purchased Shares duly endorsed in favour of the Purchaser.

4. Representations and Warranties of the Vendor

(1) The Vendor covenants, represents and warrants as follows as of the date hereof and as of the Closing Date and it acknowledges that the Purchaser is relying upon such covenants, representations and warranties in connection with the purchase by the Purchaser of the Purchased Shares:

(2) The authorized capital of the Corporation consists of 100 common voting shares without par value of which 10 have been duly issued for an aggregate purchase price of $_____ and are outstanding as fully paid and non-assessable.

(3) The shareholders of record are as follows:

Vendor Inc. — 10 common shares

and such shares are owned by the Vendor, are held with good and marketable title, free and clear of all mortgages, liens, charges, security inter-ests, adverse claims, pledges, encumbrances and demands whatsoever.

(4) No person, firm or corporation has any agreement or option or any right (whether by law, pre-emptive or contractual and including convertible securities, warrants or convertible obligations of any nature) for the purchase or the issue of either the Purchased Shares or any unissued shares in the capital stock of the Corporation.

(5) The entering into of this agreement and the transactions contemplated hereby will not result in the violation of any of the terms and provisions of the constating documents or by-laws of the Vendor or of any indenture or other agreement, written or oral, to which the Vendor may be a party.

(6) This agreement has been duly executed and delivered by the Vendor and is a valid and binding obligation of the Vendor enforceable in accordance with its terms.

(7) The Vendor is a non-resident within the meaning of the Income Tax Act.

(8) To the Vendor's knowledge, there are no existing or threatened legal actions or claims against the Corporation.

(9) The Corporation, on _____, 19____, entered into an agreement (the "Services Agreement") with Services Ltd. ("Services"), under which agreement Services provides replacement parts on behalf of the Corporation to fulfill its warranty claims for purchasers of the Corporation's heating and air conditioning products. To the Vendor's knowledge, there are no existing or pending warranty claims with respect to such products. Vendor shall assume liability to Services for payment for all warranty parts supplied by Services under the Services Agreement on valid warranty claims received from arms-length third parties, in respect of such products of the Corporation sold prior to the Closing Date that are still under warranty as provided in the Services Agreement.

(10) As at _____, 19____, there is approximately Cdn $_____ in the Corporation's bank accounts.

(11) There are no liens, charges or encumbrances of any kind whatsoever on the assets of the Corporation.

(12) The audited financial statements of the Corporation dated _____, 19____, a copy of which is attached hereto as Schedule "A", prepared by ABC, Chartered Accountants, fairly represent the financial position of the Corporation as at _____, 19____. The Vendor represents that the tax loss carry forwards set forth in Schedule "A" are correct as to their amount and expiry. The Vendor makes no representations or warranties and assumes no responsibility as to the usability by the Purchaser of such tax losses nor as to any fees, interest charges or penalties that may arise from the actual or attempted use of such tax losses by the Purchaser.

5. Covenants of the Vendor

(1) The Vendor covenants and agrees with the Purchaser that on or before the Closing Date, it will do or will cause to be done the following:

(2) Take all necessary steps and proceedings to permit all of the Purchased Shares to be duly and regularly transferred to the Purchaser.

(3) The three nominee directors of the Vendor shall resign as directors and officers of the Corporation in favour of nominees of the Purchaser, such resignations to be effective as at the Closing Date.

(4) The Vendor shall have made application to Revenue Canada for a Section 116 Income Tax Act Certificate for this transaction.

(5) At closing, Vendor will notify the Purchaser in writing of the name of Vendor's employee who will be Purchaser's contact for any warranty claims or other matters regarding the Corporation.

6. Covenants of the Purchaser

(1) The Purchaser covenants and agrees with Vendor that on, before or following the Closing Date, it will do or will cause to be done the following:

(2) The Purchaser shall cause the Corporation to cease using the Vendor's trade-name and trade-mark, "Heating". Existing sales literature may be imprinted or labelled with the Corporation's new name, "Heating Ltd.", address and telephone number only. The Purchaser agrees that subsequent sales literature developed by the Corporation shall be redesigned so as not to imitate, resemble or otherwise infringe on the Vendor's trade name, trade-marks or other intellectual property.

(3) The Purchaser shall enter into its own agreement with Services or on its own behalf perform all services and supply all materials with respect to warranty claims arising from arms-length third party purchasers of the Corporation's products, which claims relate to products sold subsequent to the Closing Date. The Purchaser acknowledges that Services is an affiliated corporation of the Purchaser within the meaning of the Business Corporations Act (Ontario).

7. Survival of Representations and Warranties

The representations and warranties of the Vendor and Purchaser contained in this agreement and contained in any document or certificate given pursuant hereto shall survive the closing of the purchase and sale of the Purchased Shares herein provided for, for a period of two years from the Closing Date.

8. Indemnification

The Vendor hereby indemnifies and saves the Corporation, Services, and the Purchaser harmless of and from any cause or claim arising with respect to the Corporation or its activities prior to the Closing Date. Vendor shall remain liable to defend at its expense any such actions or claims that may arise with respect to the Corporation or its activities, concerning the time period prior to the Closing Date. Such indemnity is conditional upon Purchaser and/or Services not entering into any claim or action in an adverse position to Vendor.

9. Notices

Any notice, direction or other instrument required or permitted to be given to the Vendor hereunder shall be in writing and may be given by mailing the same postage prepaid or delivering the same addressed to the Vendor at:

(*address*)

Any notice, direction or other instrument required or permitted to be given to the Purchaser or the Corporation hereunder shall be in writing and may be given by mailing the same postage prepaid or delivering the same addressed to the Purchaser or the Corporation at:

(*address*)Any notice, direction or other instrument aforesaid if delivered, shall be deemed to have been given or made on the date on which it was delivered or if mailed, shall be deemed to have been given or made on the fifth business day following the day on which it was mailed.

10. Costs

(1) The parties hereto agree that there are no broker's or finder's fees due or payable with respect to this transaction.

(2) Each of the parties hereto shall pay its own legal, accounting and other costs and expenses associated with this transaction and this agreement.

(3) The Purchaser shall be responsible for all expenses and costs in connection with the Corporation from and after the Closing Date, except those specific costs relating to the Services Agreement as set forth in section 4(9) hereof, and to legal actions and claims as set forth in section 8 hereof, for which the Vendor has assumed liability hereunder.

11. Entire Agreement

This agreement constitutes the entire agreement between the parties hereto. There are not and shall not be any verbal statements, representations, warranties, undertakings or agreements between the parties hereto and this agreement may not be amended or modified in any respect except by written instrument signed by the parties hereto.

12. Proper Law of Contract

This agreement shall be construed and enforced in accordance with, and the rights of the parties shall be governed by, the laws of the Province of

_____. Each of the parties hereto hereby irrevocably submits and attorns to the jurisdiction of the courts of the Province of _____.

13. Benefit and Binding Nature of the Agreement

This agreement shall enure to the benefit of and be binding upon the parties hereto and their respective successors and assigns.

IN WITNESS WHEREOF this agreement has been executed by the parties hereto.

VENDOR INC.

By: _____ c/s

President

PURCHASER LTD.

By: _____ c/s

President

TARGET LTD.

By: _____ c/s

By: _____

9F80
ALTERNATIVE CLAUSE: NON-RESIDENT VENDOR—DISPOSITION OF TAXABLE PROPERTY

The Vendor covenants and agrees with the Purchaser as follows:

(a)   the Vendor shall deliver to the Purchaser on or before the Closing Time a certificate issued by the Minister of National Revenue under subsection 116(2) of the Income Tax Act;

(b)   if a certificate is so delivered to the Purchaser, the Purchaser shall be entitled to withhold from the purchase price payable at the time of closing 33 1/3 percent of the amount, if any, by which the cost to the Purchaser of the property so acquired exceeds the certificate limit as defined in subsection 116(2) of the Income Tax Act and fixed by the Minister of National Revenue in such certificate;

(c) if a certificate is not so delivered, the Purchaser shall be entitled to withhold from the purchase price payable at the time of closing an amount equal to 33 1/3 percent of the purchase price;

(d) where the Purchaser has withheld any amount under the provisions of paragraph (c) above and the Vendor delivers to the Purchaser, after the closing date and within 30 days after the end of the month in which the Purchaser acquired the property, certificate issued by the minister of national revenue under subsection 116(2) of the Income Tax Act, the Purchaser,

    (i) shall pay forthwith to the Receiver General of Canada 33 1/3 percent of the amount, if any, by which the purchase price exceeds the certificate limit fixed in such certificate; and

    (ii) shall pay forthwith to the Vendor any amount that the Purchaser has withheld and is not required to pay to the Receiver General of Canada in accordance with subparagraph (i) above; and

(e) where the Purchaser has withheld any amount under Paragraph (b) or under Paragraph (c) and no certificate has been delivered to the Purchaser by the Vendor in accordance with the provisions of Paragraph (d), such amount shall be paid by the Purchaser to the Receiver General of Canada under subsection 116 of the Income Tax Act.

(f) The Purchaser shall not remit the amounts referred to in Paragraph (e) before the [*third*] Business Day before the 30th day of the month following the month in which the Purchaser acquired the property.

– or –

(f) The Purchaser and the Vendor acknowledge and agree that the amount required to be withheld under Paragraph (e) must be remit-ted by the Purchaser to the Receiver General of Canada on or before the 30th day of the month following the month in which the Purchaser acquired the property (the "Remittance Date"). The Purchaser agrees to hold the amount required to be withheld under sec-tion 116 of the *Income Tax Act in trust for the account of the Vendor in an interest bearing account at a financial institution as directed by the Vendor until the* [*fifth*] Business Day before the Remittance Date. The amount held in trust will be paid by the Purchaser to the Vendor if the Vendor delivers a section 116 clearance certificate to the Purchaser before the Remittance Date [*and provided that the certificate limit of the section 116 certificate is not less than the Purchase Price in which case the Purchaser shall only pay to the Vendor that proportion of the amount withheld that the certificate limit if to the Purchase Price*] If the Vendor has failed to deliver to the Purchaser a section 116 certificate before the Remittance Date, the amount withheld shall be remitted to the Receiver General of Canada in accordance with section 116 of the Income Tax Act.

(g)   Any amount paid by the Purchaser to the Receiver General of Canada under Paragraphs (d) or (e) shall be credited to the Purchaser as a payment to the Vendor on account of the Purchase Price.

[**Note:** *If the property being sold by the non-resident involves a life insurance policy in Canada, a Canadian resource property, real property that is inventory, a timber resource or depreciable property the rate of withholding by the purchaser is 50% and the clearance certificate would be obtained under subsection 116(5.2) of the Income Tax Act. In this case, corresponding amendments must be made to the above precedent clauses.*][**Note:** *The Vendor should prepare the application for the section 116 certificate as soon as possible before Closing as Revenue Canada normally takes 6 to 8 weeks to process a section 116 certificate application.*]

9F81
ALTERNATIVE CLAUSE:
REPRESENTATIONS AND WARRANTIES

Condition of Purchased Assets — The parties intend that the Purchased Assets sold, transferred and assigned pursuant to this Agreement are being sold, transferred and assigned on an "as is, where is" basis and that no representation or warranty is given by the Seller with respect to the condition or state of repair of the Purchased Assets.

Automated Systems — Schedule _____ lists and describes all computer software owned, licensed or used by the Vendor in the Purchased Business. The core software used in the Purchased Business is the _____ System which provides the basis for inventory management. The Vendor has maintained the _____ System to a standard of Material functionality. Other software used by the Purchased Business requires enhancements.

9F81:1
ALTERNATIVE CLAUSE:
LABOUR RELATIONS AND EMPLOYMENT
PRECEDENTS
Representations and Warranties by Vendor

(a) Except as disclosed in Schedule X, none of the vendor's employees are represented by a trade union or other organization representing employees. There is no current campaign or attempt by any trade union or other employee organization to organize the employees of the vendor. There are no applications for certification pending and no outstanding proceedings or orders of any labour relations board, tribunal or similar body concerning any of the vendor's employees nor is the vendor aware of any potential complaints or applications pursuant to any labour relations legislation. The vendor is not subject to any accreditation orders.

(b) Except as disclosed on Schedule X, the vendor is not a party to or bound to any collective agreement or to any oral or written agreement concerning its employees, either individually or collectively. The vendor has not agreed to voluntarily recognize any trade union or any other organization which represents employees.

(c) Except as disclosed on Schedule X, there are no outstanding grievances, outstanding arbitration proceedings or unsatisfied arbitration awards to which the vendor is a party. The vendor is not a party to any outstanding proceedings, charges, claims, complaints, decisions, orders, applications, investigations, or prosecutions concerning the vendor under any employment-related legislation, by-laws or statutory regulations nor are there any unsatisfied judgments, directions, awards, orders, or decisions of any court, tribunal or agency involving the vendor and any of its current or former employees.

(d) The vendor has disclosed to the purchaser all ongoing negotiations or pending negotiations with any trade union or organization representing employees of the vendor. The vendor has not made any commitment, either orally or in writing, to any trade union, employee association, employee or group of employees with respect to any future agreements.

(e) The vendor has conducted its operations and its relations with its employees in compliance with all applicable employment and labour standards legislation. Except as disclosed on Schedule[___], there are no outstanding complaints, applications, claims, decisions, orders or prosecutions pursuant to any employment or labour standards legislation.

(f) Except as disclosed on Schedule [___], no employee or former employee of the vendor is in receipt of, or may have a potential claim for, benefits under any weekly indemnity, sickness and accident, long term disability or workers' compensation plan or arrangement or any other form of disability benefit program. All actual or potential assessments, penalties, fines, levies, charges, surcharges, premiums or other amounts relating to such disability or workers' compensation benefits arising during or related to the period prior to closing have been disclosed to the purchaser and paid by the vendor. The vendor has conducted its operations in compliance with applicable workers' compensation legislation.

(g) The vendor has conducted its operations and relations with its employees in compliance with all human rights legislation and requirements. Except as disclosed in Schedule [___], there are no outstanding or potential human rights complaints, investigations or proceedings, nor are there any unsatisfied judgments, orders, decisions or awards of any tribunal or court relating to any human rights matters.

(h) The vendor has complied with any applicable pay equity legislation. Except as disclosed on Schedule [___], there are no pay equity plans nor are there any complaints, applications, investigations, orders, prosecutions, or proceedings, actual, potential or pending, pursuant to any pay equity legislation.

(i) The premises to be assumed by the purchaser are safe for employment and are in compliance with applicable health and safety legislation and regulations and there are no outstanding or potential orders, directions, violations or prosecutions   under any occupational health and safety legislation or regulations. Except as has been disclosed by the purchaser, there are no toxic, hazardous or designated substances as defined by the applicable health and safety legislation or regulations used in the production processes or stored on the premises.

(j) Except as has been disclosed to the purchaser, the vendor is not a party to any written or oral labour agreement, management agreement, consulting agreement, employment agreement or agency agreement. Except as disclosed, the vendor has not announced or implemented any employment-related policy; employee insurance; hospital or medical expense program; pension or retirement plan; profit-sharing, commission, bonus, or stock option plan; or other employee benefit plan, policy, program, allowance or arrangement. There are no executive or key personnel incentives or other special compensation arrangements, contracts or agreements with or with respect to any officers, employees or agents of the vendor.

(k) During the period prior to closing, the vendor has made all deductions required by law or by contract to be made from employee wages or salaries and has remitted the amounts deducted and all related employer contributions required to the authorities or entities entitled to receive payment of such amounts.

(l) The vendor has complied with all applicable employment equity legislation, regulations, programs or policies.

(m) All obligations, commitments and amounts payable on account of wages, salary, bonus payments, commissions, group insurances, pensions, profit-sharing, stock option plans, payment in lieu of notice of termination, severance pay, retirement allowances, vacation pay and any other payments, benefits or allowances, to any employee or former employee accruing or arising prior to closing, have been paid or met or shall be paid or met prior to closing.

(n) The vendor has complied with all federal fair wages, hours of work and employment equity requirements applicable to any contracts for work which it obtained from the federal government.

(o) The vendor is in compliance with its obligations under the Employer's Health Tax Act and there are no unpaid taxes, penalties, interest, garnishment orders or other court proceedings outstanding or pending pursuant to the Employer's Health Tax Act.
[See Paras. 9.530 and 9.480]

Covenants

(a) Prior to closing, the purchaser shall advise the vendor of the names of any employees of the vendor that the purchaser does not intend to employ. With respect to such employees, the vendor shall meet all legal obligations relating to the termination of employment. Without limiting the generality of the foregoing, the vendor shall pay all amounts required either by statute or at common law to be paid to such employees including pay in lieu of notice, termination pay, severance pay, vacation pay and all other outstanding amounts. The termination of such employees will be effective on or before the closing date.

(b)   The vendor shall co-operate with the purchaser in giving such notice to the employees of the vendor who will be retained by the purchaser as is considered reasonable in the circumstances by the purchaser.

(c)   Between the date hereof and the closing date, the vendor shall not increase the compensation payable to any employee or pay any discretionary bonuses to any employee except with the specific written consent of the purchaser. The vendor will bear the cost of any such bonus payments.

(d)   On or before the closing date, the vendor shall provide documentary evidence from the appropriate Workers' Compensation authority certifying there are no outstanding claims, assessments, penalties, fines, levies, charges, surcharges or other amounts due or owing to the said Workers' Compensation authority.

(e)   With respect to ongoing negotiations or pending negotiations with any trade union or organization representing employees of the vendor, the vendor will co-operate with the purchaser in ensuring the achievement of terms and conditions of unemployment satisfactory to the purchaser. The vendor will not enter into any memorandum of agreement, collective agreement or other agreement, arrangement or understanding with any trade union or employee organization orf with any employee or group of employees without the specific written consent of the purchaser. Prior to closing, the vendor will make senior employees of the vendor who are knowledgeable with respect to labour relations and employment matters available for the purposes of discussing such matters.

(f)   The vendor shall not implement or agree to any pay equity plan or resolve any pay equity complaint or application without the written consent of the vendor.

(g)   Prior to closing, the vendor will provide the purchaser with a complete list of any toxic, hazardous or designated substances stored or in use in the work   place. The vendor will further provide the purchaser with copies of the vendor's inventory of controlled products, the vendor's health and safety policy and with copies of the minutes of the meetings of the Joint Health and Safety Committee for the two years prior to the closing date. The vendor will make available appropriate, informed officials to discuss health and safety matters, if required by the purchaser. The vendor will co-operate with the purchaser and provide any required consent with respect to any inspection required by the purchaser by a government health and safety inspector.

(h) Prior to closing, the vendor will provide the purchaser with a copy of all employee handbooks and written policies relating to terms and conditions of employment. The vendor will further provide copies of all group insurance policies, statements, agreements and booklets and of any and all documentation relating to any pension plans including the plans, trust agreements, summaries and booklets. The vendor will provide the purchaser with any documentation relating to any profit-sharing, bonus or commission plans or other compensation arrangements, agreements or policies.

(i) Prior to closing, the vendor will provide the purchaser with a list showing the names of all of the vendor's employees, current annual salaries or hourly rates, job descriptions, length of employment or date of hire, dates and amounts of the most recent increases in salary, the amounts of any bonus payments, commissions, accrued vacation pay and other amounts owing to all employees of the vendor. The list shall include all full-time, part-time, temporary, seasonal and causal employees including, without limitation, all persons who may be considered, pursuant to applicable Workers' Compensation, employment standards or similar legislation or otherwise at law or in equity to be employees of the vendor and all employees who have been laid off but retain recall or reinstatement rights pursuant to any collective agreement or statute. Prior to closing, the vendor will provide the purchaser with a copy of all current seniority lists.

(j) Prior to closing, the vendor will provide the purchaser with a copy of the vendor's most recent employment equity report, if any, and a copy of any agreement or undertaking relating to the implementation of employment equity.

(k) During the period prior to closing, the vendor will make all deductions required by law or by contract to be made from employee wages or salaries and will remit the amounts deducted and all related employer contributions required to the authorities or entities entitled to receive payment of such amounts.

(l)　The vendor shall quantify the amount of accrued vacation pay due and owing to its employees as of the closing date. Such amount shall be an adjustment to the purchase price of the purchaser's credit.

9F83
ALTERNATIVE CLAUSES: ACCOUNTS RECEIVABLE

[See Forms 9F32–9F33]

Alternative I

There shall be specifically excluded from the Purchased Assets the accounts receivable as at the Closing Date and the Purchaser agrees to use its best efforts to collect on behalf of the Vendor such outstanding accounts receivable and to remit such in accordance with the Vendor's reasonable instructions.

Alternative II

(1) The Purchaser agrees that the accounts receivable owing as at the Closing Date ("Receivables") do not form part of the Purchased Assets and the Purchaser shall collect the same on behalf of the Vendor and shall remit such in accordance with the Vendor's reasonable instructions, it being agreed that all moneys collected on account of Receivables shall be applied firstly to past debts for payment to the Vendor, and only thereafter to the account of the Purchaser and the Purchaser shall in any event hold such Receivables in trust for the Vendor and shall retain them in a separate bank account designated for such purpose. The obligations of the Purchaser under this paragraph shall be to exercise all reasonable efforts to effect collection in a timely and orderly fashion in accordance with the usual business practices of the industry.

(2) At the reasonable direction and cost of the Vendor, and in the event of failure to collect and remit the Receivables as hereinbefore set out, the Purchaser shall recover all possible amounts owing on account of the Receivables on behalf of the Vendor by taking appropriate legal action for recovery in the name of both the Vendor and the Purchaser, all recoveries and collections to be paid to the Vendor until such time as the Vendor has

been fully paid for the receivables due and owing as at the Date of Closing for the particular debtor against which recovery is being made.

Alternative III

(1) The Purchaser shall re-assign to the Vendor any of the Accounts Receivable which have not been collected at the end of six months from the Closing Date.

(2) The Purchaser shall take diligent steps during such six-month period to collect all of the Accounts Receivable, shall provide the Vendor with a monthly listing of such of the Accounts Receivable that remain outstanding and shall extend to the Vendor an opportunity to assist in the collection thereof and shall provide the Vendor reasonable access on an ongoing basis to the records of the Purchased Business pertaining to the Accounts Receivable so that the Vendor may effectively assist in the collection thereof.

(3) If the amount collected by the Purchaser on account of the Accounts Receivable exceeds the value thereof determined from the balance sheet of the Vendor on the Closing Date, the Purchaser shall pay to the Vendor the amount of such excess on receipt thereof.

(4) For the purposes of the preceding section _____, all payments received from any customer by whom any amount is owing on account of the Accounts Receivable shall be applied in respect of the amount owing by such customer which is included in the Accounts Receivable unless such customer had disputed in writing all or any part of the amount owing by him on account of the Accounts Receivable. If any such customer so disputes only a part of such of the Accounts Receivable as is owing by him, payments by such customer after Closing shall be applied first as against such of the Accounts Receivable owing by him as are not disputed, and therefore as against any other trade accounts receivable owing by such customer to the Purchaser.

(5) If any customer of the Purchased Business who owes any amount on account of the Accounts Receivable disputes the amount owing by him:

(a)   the Purchaser shall give to the Vendor written notice thereof within 10 business days from the date upon which the Purchaser becomes aware of such dispute;

(b)   the Vendor shall be given access to all of the records of the Purchased Business necessary to deal with any of the Accounts Receivable in respect of which there is a dispute;

(c)   the Purchaser shall not settle any of such disputed Accounts Receivable for less than its face value; and

(d)   the Vendor shall be given a reasonable opportunity to settle the dispute with such customer.

If the Purchaser fails to comply with the terms of this section _____, payments by such customer shall be applied in respect of the Accounts Receivable as if no dispute existed.

9F84
ALTERNATIVE CLAUSE: SECURITY FOR INSTALMENT PAYMENTS OF THE PURCHASE PRICE

As security for the payment of the balance of the Purchase Price evidenced by the Promissory Note and in order to secure the due perform-ance by the Purchaser of the obligations hereunder, the Purchaser agrees to provide the following security on or before the Closing Date (the "Security Documents"):

(a)   a debenture containing both a fixed and floating charge in substantially the form of the draft debenture attached hereto as Schedule _____;

(b)   a letter of credit drawn on a Canadian chartered bank in the amount of _____ Dollars ($_____) expiring on _____ substantially in the form of the draft attached hereto as Schedule _____;

(d)   a security agreement in a form acceptable to the solicitors for the Vendor, and providing security on all of the Purchased Assets;

(e)   a share pledge agreement substantially in the form of the draft attached hereto as Schedule _____, pledging and assigning the shares in the capital of the Purchaser in favour of the Vendor.

[The Security Documents shall all be expressed to be subordinated and postponed to any security granted by the Purchaser to its bank, and if requested by such bank, the Vendor shall enter into a priority agreement with such bank for the purposes of confirming such subordination and postponement

- or -

Any security for the payment of the balance of the Purchase Price is, or will be, subject to and in subordination to all security and any claims thereunder made by any lending institution which is financing the purchase of the Purchased Business or the Purchased Assets or providing financing assistance in the ordinary course of the business of the Purchaser.

- or -

The security in favour of any bank with respect to the present and future indebtedness and liability of the Purchaser to the bank shall take priority over any security arrangements pursuant to this Agreement and the Vendor agrees to execute any necessary documents that may be required from time to time to evidence the priority arrangements.

For valuable consideration, the receipt and sufficiency of which is hereby acknowledged, the Guarantor hereby agrees that in order to further secure the obligation of the Purchaser hereunder he shall enter into and deliver to the Vendor a guarantee (the "Guarantee") in a form acceptable to the solicitors for the Vendor guaranteeing performance in full of all obligations of the Purchaser hereunder.

- or -

For valuable consideration, the receipt and sufficiency of which is hereby acknowledged, the Guarantor hereby agrees that in order to further secure the obligations of the Purchaser hereunder he shall enter into and deliver to the Vendor a guarantee substantially in the form of the draft attached hereto as Schedule _____.]

9F85
ALTERNATIVE CLAUSE: CONFIDENTIALITY

If the purchase and sale transaction contemplated under this Agreement is not completed, the Purchaser agrees that it will not, directly or indirectly, use for its own purposes any information, trade secrets or confidential data relating to the Vendor or any of its businesses, including the customers, the operations and the methods of conducting its businesses discovered or acquired by the Purchaser, its representatives or any of them, as a result of the Vendor making available to the Purchaser, and its representatives, any information, books, accounts, records or other data and information relating to the Vendor or its businesses and the Purchaser agrees that it will not disclose, divulge or communicate orally, in writing or otherwise, any such information, trade secrets or confidential data so discovered or acquired to any other person, firm or corporation.

9F86
ALTERNATIVE CLAUSE:
CONDITIONS IN FAVOUR OF PURCHASER

The guarantee granted by the Vendor to the Bank, as more particularly described in Schedule _____, has been released and the Vendor has been released by the Bank from any and all obligations thereunder or in respect thereto and the security agreements described in Schedule _____ have been discharged.

9F87
ALTERNATIVE CLAUSE:
CONDITIONS IN FAVOUR OF VENDOR

The Vendor has been released from any and all obligations under the mortgage more particularly described in Schedule _____.

9F88
ALTERNATIVE CLAUSE: PROPERTY AND ASSETS
TO BE PURCHASED AND SOLD

[See Forms 9F32–9F33]

[Note: This clause may be used in conjunction with the Long or Short Asset Purchase Agreements.]

Subject to the terms and conditions of this Agreement, the Vendor agrees to sell, assign and transfer to the Purchaser and the Purchaser agrees to purchase from the Vendor as a going concern, as, at and from the close of business on the Closing Date, the undertaking and all the property and assets of the Purchased Business of every kind and description and wheresoever situate (except as provided in section _____.2), including without limiting the generality of the foregoing:

[list particular assets being purchased and sold]

The following assets of the Vendor are specifically excluded from the assets purchased and sold under this Agreement:

[list excluded assets]

To the extent any undertaking, property and assets, wherever located, used or held for use in connection with the Purchased Business, are currently owned, or are hereafter acquired prior to the Closing Date, by any associate or affiliate of the Vendor including, without limitation, Associate Inc., they shall be included within the term "Purchased Assets" if those assets would have been included had they been owned or been hereafter acquired by the Vendor prior to the closing date, and in such case such associate or affiliate shall be deemed to be included within the term "Vendor" and the Vendor shall cause each such associate and affiliate, on or prior to the Closing Date, to convey such assets to the Purchaser, or to the Vendor for conveyance to the Purchaser, in accordance with the provisions of this Agreement.

9F89
ALTERNATIVE CLAUSE: COVENANTS RE GOVERNMENTAL ACTIONS AND APPROVALS

Alternative I

There shall have been obtained, from all appropriate federal, provincial, municipal or other governmental or administrative bodies, such approvals or consents as are required to permit the change of ownership and due registration of the Purchased Assets contemplated under this Agreement, including, without limitation, the following:

(a) Investment Canada—The Purchaser shall have either received a receipt issued under subsection 13(1) of the Investment Canada Act certifying that a complete notice in prescribed form in respect of the acquisition has been received and advising that such acquisition is not reviewable; or a notice from the Minister of Industry, Science and Technology issued under Sections 21, 22 or 23 of the Investment Canada Act indicating that such Minister is, or is deemed to be, satisfied that the acquisition is likely to be of net benefit to Canada.

(b) Competition Act—(i) The Vendor and the Purchaser shall each have filed all notices and information required under Part IX of the Competition Act (Canada), satisfied any requests for additional information from the Director of Investigation and Research appointed under the Competition Act (the "Director") and the Director shall have issued confirmation that he does not intend to refer the transaction contemplated under this Agreement to the Competition Tribunal pursuant to Section 92 of the said Act; or (ii) the

Director shall have issued an Advance Ruling Certificate under the Competition Act with respect to the acquisition contemplated under this Agreement.

Alternative II

Investment Canada Act—The Purchaser shall complete and file a notice of the transaction of purchase and sale under this Agreement in the form and within the applicable time periods prescribed by Section 12 of the Investment Canada Act. [*This clause is applicable for transaction only if notifiable, and notice may be sent after closing.*]

Competition Act

(a)   Prenotification Requirements—Each of the Vendor and the Purchaser shall file or cause to be filed with the Director of Investigation and Research appointed under the Competition Act immediately after the execution of this Agreement any notifications or applications required to be filed under Section 114 of the said Act and the rules and regulations thereunder with respect to the transactions contemplated under this Agreement.

(b)   Waiting Periods—The Vendor and the Purchaser will use their best efforts to make such filings promptly, to respond to any request for additional information made by the said Director (or any person on his behalf), and generally to seek to cause the waiting periods under the said Act to terminate to expire at the earliest possible date; provided, however, that if the Purchaser has diligently prosecuted all notifications and applications as aforesaid and the said waiting periods have not terminated or expired on or before _____, 199__, either party to this Agreement may, by written notice to the other party, terminate this Agreement.

If the Vendor terminates this Agreement under this Section, the Vendor shall be released from all obligations under this Agreement [*(other than any obligations provided for under the confidentiality agreement between the Vendor and the Purchaser, entered into contemporaneously with this Agreement)*] and unless the Vendor can show that the condition giving rise to the right of the Vendor to terminate this Agreement was reasonably capable of being performed or caused to be performed by the Purchaser, then the Purchaser shall also be released from its obligations under this Agreement [*(other than under the confidentiality agreement).*]

In the event that the Purchaser terminates this Agreement under this Section, the Purchaser shall be released from all obligations under this Agreement [(*other than any obligations provided for under the confidentiality agreement between the Vendor and the Purchaser, entered into contemporaneously with this Agreement)*] and unless the Purchaser can show that the condition giving rise to the right of the Purchaser to terminate this Agreement was reasonably capable of being performed or caused to be performed by the Vendor, then the Vendor shall also be released from its obligations under this Agreement [(*other than under the confidentiality agreement)*].

(c)   Co-operation—Each Party shall supply the other with a copy of all notices and information (other than such notices or information as are confidential to the former party) supplied or filed by it after the date of this Agreement under the Competition Act immediately after the notices or information are supplied or filed and shall indicate thereon the date of supply or filing. Each Party shall also supply the other with a copy of all notices or other correspondence (other than such as are confidential to the former party) received from or the details of any communications with the Director of Investigation and Research or on his behalf forthwith after receipt of the notices or other correspondence or the occurrence of the communications.

9F90
ALTERNATIVE CLAUSE:
COVENANT RE CUSTOMER MEETINGS

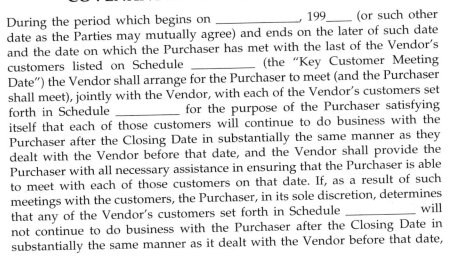

During the period which begins on _____, 199____ (or such other date as the Parties may mutually agree) and ends on the later of such date and the date on which the Purchaser has met with the last of the Vendor's customers listed on Schedule _____ (the "Key Customer Meeting Date") the Vendor shall arrange for the Purchaser to meet (and the Purchaser shall meet), jointly with the Vendor, with each of the Vendor's customers set forth in Schedule _____ for the purpose of the Purchaser satisfying itself that each of those customers will continue to do business with the Purchaser after the Closing Date in substantially the same manner as they dealt with the Vendor before that date, and the Vendor shall provide the Purchaser with all necessary assistance in ensuring that the Purchaser is able to meet with each of those customers on that date. If, as a result of such meetings with the customers, the Purchaser, in its sole discretion, determines that any of the Vendor's customers set forth in Schedule _____ will not continue to do business with the Purchaser after the Closing Date in substantially the same manner as it dealt with the Vendor before that date, the Purchaser shall have the op-tion, exercisable at or before 12:00 o'clock Noon (local Toronto time) on the day after the Key Customer Meeting Date, to terminate this Agreement by delivery of written notice of termination to the Vendor. If the Purchaser does not deliver to the Vendor a notice of termination under this Section _____.1 at or before that time, this Agreement shall remain binding upon both the Vendor and the Purchaser subject to the terms and conditions contained in this Agreement.

9F91
ALTERNATIVE CLAUSES: INDEMNIFICATION

Indemnification Sole Remedy

The provisions of this Article _____ shall constitute the sole remedy to the Vendor and the Purchaser against the other party to this Agreement with respect to any and all breaches of any agreement, covenant, representation or warranty made by such party in this Agreement or in any agreement, schedule, certificate or other document required to be entered into or delivered by such party under this Agreement.

Tax Adjustment

It is the intent of the Parties that no Indemnitee receiving a payment from the Indemnitor under Sections _____ or _____ should receive a tax benefit or incur a tax cost in computing its income for Canadian income tax purposes, as a result of:

(a) the Indemnitee being permitted to deduct any outlay or expenditure made by it with respect to any Claim, but not having to include in its income an amount with respect to such Claim received from the Indemnitor; or

(b) the Indemnitee not being permitted to deduct any outlay or expenditure made by it with respect to any Claim, but having to include in its income an amount with respect to such Claim received from the Indemnitor.

In such case, the amount payable to the Indemnitee by the Indemnitor shall be adjusted so as to neutralize any such tax benefit or tax cost to the Indemnitee.

Subrogation

The Indemnitor shall be subrogated to the claims and rights of the Indemnitee as against other Persons, and shall be entitled to contribution from any such Person, with respect to any Claim paid by the Indemnitor, but only after the Indemnitee shall have received payment in full of its claim with interest.

Limitation

Notwithstanding any other provision of this Agreement, the liability of either Party shall be limited to the amount of the Purchase Price.

De Minimis

Notwithstanding any other provision of this Agreement, the Vendor and the Purchaser agree that they shall not assert against the other any claim or claims with respect to the breach of the representations, warranties, covenants and agreements under this Agreement unless the aggregate amount of the claim or claims asserted to that date, including the claim or claims then being asserted, is at least $_____. [*Note: This clause may be amended to provide either that the $25,000 is a deductible, or that after aggregate claims reach $25,000, all claims are payable.*]

9F92
FORM OF SHARE TRANSFER

[See Para. 9.620]

TO: SUBJECT CORPORATION
            (the "Corporation")

AND TO: The directors thereof.

FOR VALUE RECEIVED, the undersigned hereby sells, assigns and transfers unto Purchaser Limited ownership of 1 Common Share in the capital of the Corporation registered in the name of the undersigned and does hereby irrevocably constitute and appoint the Secretary of the Corporation attorney to transfer such shares on the books of the Corporation, with full power of substitution in the premises.

DATED the day of (*month, year*).

VENDOR INC.

Per: _____

June Brown
President

9F93
SHARE CERTIFICATE OF VENDOR

[See Para. 9.620]

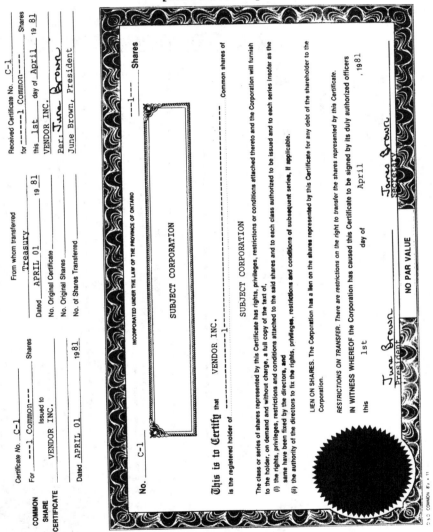

687

9F94
NEW SHARE CERTIFICATE FOR PURCHASER

[See Para. 9.620]

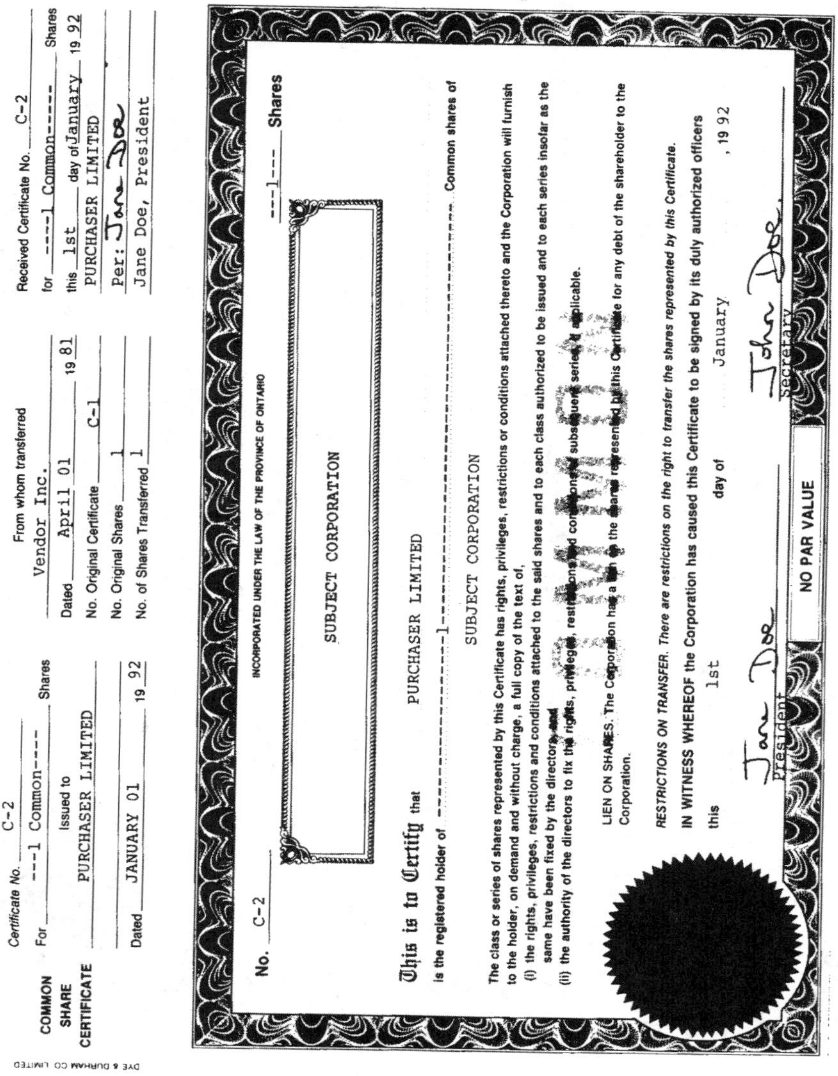
COMMON SHARE CERTIFICATE

Certificate No. C-2
For ---1 Common---- Shares
Issued to PURCHASER LIMITED
Dated JANUARY 01 19 92

From whom transferred Vendor Inc.
Dated April 01 19 81
No. Original Certificate C-1
No. Original Shares 1
No. of Shares Transferred 1

Received Certificate No. C-2
for ----1 Common------ Shares
this 1st day of January 19 92
PURCHASER LIMITED
Per: Jane Doe
Jane Doe, President

DYE & DURHAM CO LIMITED

No. C-2

INCORPORATED UNDER THE LAW OF THE PROVINCE OF ONTARIO

SUBJECT CORPORATION

---1--- Shares

COMMON

This is to Certify that PURCHASER LIMITED
is the registered holder of ----------1---------- Common shares of
SUBJECT CORPORATION

The class or series of shares represented by this Certificate has rights, privileges, restrictions or conditions attached thereto and the Corporation will furnish to the holder, on demand and without charge, a full copy of the text of,
(i) the rights, privileges, restrictions and conditions attached to the said shares and to each class authorized to be issued and to each series insofar as the same have been fixed by the directors, and
(ii) the authority of the directors to fix the rights, privileges, restrictions and conditions of subsequent series, if applicable.

LIEN ON SHARES: The Corporation has a lien on the shares represented by this Certificate for any debt of the shareholder to the Corporation.

RESTRICTIONS ON TRANSFER. *There are restrictions on the right to transfer the shares represented by this Certificate.*

IN WITNESS WHEREOF the Corporation has caused this Certificate to be signed by its duly authorized officers
this 1st day of January, 19 92

Jane Doe
President

John Doe
Secretary

NO PAR VALUE

9F95
RESOLUTION OF DIRECTORS
APPROVING SHARE TRANSFER

[See Para. 9.620]

RESOLUTION OF THE BOARD OF DIRECTORS

OF

SUBJECT CORPORATION
(the "Corporation")

TRANSFER OF SHARES

RESOLVED that the following transfer of shares is approved effective the 1st day of January, 1992:

Transferor	Transferee	Number and Class of Shares
Vendor Inc.	Purchaser Limited	1 Common Share

The foregoing resolution is passed by all of the directors of the Corporation pursuant to the Ontario Business Corporations Act, the _____ day of (*month, year*).

_____   _____

June Brown   James Brown

9F96
RESIGNATION OF PRIOR DIRECTORS

[See Para. 9.620]

R E S I G N A T I O N

TO: SUBJECT CORPORATION
   (the "Corporation")

AND TO: The shareholders thereof.

I hereby tender my resignation as a director of the Corporation, such resignation to be effective immediately.

DATED the _____ day of (*month, year*).

_____
June Brown

9F97
RESIGNATION OF PRIOR OFFICERS

[See Para. 9.620]

R E S I G N A T I O N

TO: SUBJECT CORPORATION
   (the "Corporation")

AND TO: The shareholders thereof.

I hereby tender my resignation as a director of the Corporation, such resignation to be effective immediately.

DATED the _____ day of (*month, year*).

_____
June Brown

9F98
ELECTION OF NEW DIRECTORS

[See Para. 9.620]

RESOLUTION OF THE SOLE SHAREHOLDER

OF

SUBJECT CORPORATION
(the "Corporation")

ELECTION OF DIRECTORS

RESOLVED that the following persons are elected the directors of the Corporation for the ensuing year or until their respective successors are elected or appointed:

> Jane Doe
> John Doe.

The foregoing resolution is hereby passed by the sole shareholder of the Corporation pursuant to the Ontario Business Corporations Act, the _____ day of (*month, year*).

PURCHASER LIMITED

Per: _____

June Brown
President

9F99
ELECTION OF NEW OFFICERS

[See Para. 9.620]

RESOLUTION OF THE BOARD OF DIRECTORS

OF

SUBJECT CORPORATION
(the "Corporation")

APPOINTMENT OF OFFICERS

RESOLVED that the following persons are appointed to the following respective offices in the Corporation, to hold such offices at the pleasure of the directors:

President:	Jane Doe
Secretary:	John Doe.

The foregoing resolution is passed by all of the directors of the Corporation pursuant to the Ontario Business Corporations Act, the _____ day of (*month, year*).

_____   _____

Jane Doe   John Doe

9F100
ONTARIO CORPORATIONS INFORMATION ACT
FORM 1 —
NOTICE OF CHANGE

[See Para. 9.620]

Ministry of / Ministère de la / Companies Branch / Direction des compagnies
Consumer and / Consommation / 375 University Avenue, 8 Floor / 375, avenue University, 8° étage
Commercial / et du / Toronto ON M7A 2H6 / Toronto ON M7A 2H6
Relations / Commerce

Form 1 - Ontario Corporation/
Formule 1 - Personnes morales en Ontario

Initial Notice/Notice of Change/
Avis initial/Avis de modification
Corporations Information Act/Loi sur les
renseignements exigés des personnes morales

All information must be typewritten in block capital letters using black ink in 10 or 12 pitch.
Tous les renseignements doivent être dactylographiés en caractères d'imprimerie à l'encre noire, en 10 ou 12 points.

For Ministry Use Only
À l'usage du ministère seulement
Page/Page 1 of/de _____

	Notice of Change
1.	Initial Notice / Notice of Change
Business Corporations/Société par actions	Avis initial / modification
Not-For-Profit Corporation/Personne morale sans but lucratif	X

For Ministry Use Only / À l'usage du ministère seulement	2. Ontario Corporation Number / Numéro matricule de la personne morale en Ontario	3. Offering / Appel à l'épargne Yes/Oui No/Non	4. Date of Incorporation/Amalgamation or Continuation/ Date de constitution/fusion ou prorogation Year/Année Month/Mois Day/Jour	For Ministry Use Only / À l'usage du ministère seulement
	000000	X	1981 04 01	

5. Corporation Name Including Punctuation/Raison sociale de la personne morale, y compris la ponctuation

SUBJECT CORPORATION

6. Address of Registered or Head Office/Adresse du siège social

c/o / attn
JANE DOE

Street Number/Numéro civique | Street Name/Nom de la rue | Suite/Bureau
123 | 45TH STREET

Street Name (cont'd)/Nom de la rue (suite)

City/Town/Ville
TORONTO ONTARIO, CANADA

Postal Code/Code postal
M1A 2X3

7. Principal Place of Business in Ontario/Adresse du bureau d'affaire principal en Ontario

| X | Same as Registered or Head Office/ Même que celle du siège social |
| | Not Applicable/ Ne s'applique pas |

Street Number/Numéro civique

Street Name/Nom de la rue

Street Name (cont'd)/Nom de la rue (suite) | Suite/Bureau

City/Town/Ville ONTARIO, CANADA

Postal Code/Code postal

8. Activity Classification Code/Code de classification des activités

A B C D E F G H I J K L M O P Q R

9. Language of Preference/Langue préférée

English - Anglais [X]   French - Français   None of the Above / Aucun de ces choix [X]

10. Information on Directors/Officers must be completed on Schedule A. If additional space is required, photocopy Schedule A./Renseignements relatifs aux administrateurs/dirigeants doivent être inscrits à l'annexe A. Si vous avez besoin de plus d'espace, photocopiez l'annexe A.

Number of Schedule A(s) submitted/Nombre d'annexes A présentées [2] (At least one Schedule A must be submitted/Au moins une annexe A doit être présentée)

11.
I, Je soussigné (Type name in full/inscrire les noms et prénoms en caractères d'imprimerie)
JANE DOE
certify that the information set out herein, is true and correct.
Atteste que les renseignements précités sont véridiques et exacts.

Signature
Jane Doe

Check appropriate box
Cocher la case pertinente

D) [X] Director/Administrateur
O) [ ] Officer /Dirigeant
P) [ ] Other individual having knowledge of the affairs of the Corporation/Autre personne ayant connaissance des activités de la personne morale

NOTE/REMARQUE: Sections 13 à 14 of the Corporations Information Act provide penalties for making false or misleading statements or omissions. Les articles 13 à 14 de la Loi sur les renseignements exigés des personnes morales prévoient des peines en cas de déclaration fausse ou trompeuse, ou d'omission.

FOR MINISTRY USE ONLY / À L'USAGE DU MINISTÈRE SEULEMENT

See Deficiency Letter enclosed
Voir l'avis d'irrégularité ci-joint

07200(05/92)

Form 1 - Ontario Corporation/Formule 1 - Personnes morales en Ontario

Schedule A/Annexe A

For Ministry Use Only
À l'usage du ministère seulement
Page/Page ____ of/de ____

All information must be typewritten in block capital letters using black ink in 10 or 12 pitch.
Tous les renseignements doivent être dactylographiés en caractères d'imprimerie à l'encre noire, en 10 ou 12 points.

For Ministry Use Only À l'usage du ministère seulement	Ontario Corporation Number Numéro matricule de la personne morale en Ontario	Date of Incorporation/Amalgamation or Continuation Date de constitution, fusion ou prorogation Year/Année - Month/Mois Day/Jour	For Ministry Use Only À l'usage du ministère seulement
⎵	000000	1981 | 04 | 01	

DIRECTOR / OFFICER INFORMATION - RENSEIGNEMENTS RELATIFS AUX ADMINISTRATEURS/DIRIGEANTS

Full Name and Residential Address/Nom et adresse personnelle au complet

Last Name/Nom de famille	First Name/Prénom	Middle Names/Autres prénoms
DOE	JANE	

Street Number/Numéro civique
999

Street Name/Nom de la rue
86TH STREET

Street Name (cont'd)/Nom de la rue (suite)   Suite/Bureau

City/Town/Ville
TORONTO

Province, State/Province, État	Country/Pays	Postal Code/Code postal
ONTARIO	CANADA	M2B 3Z4

Director Information/Renseignements relatifs aux administrateurs

Resident Canadian/ Résident canadien   [X] YES/OUI   [ ] NO/NON   (Resident Canadian applies to directors of business corporations only.)/ (Résident canadien ne s'applique qu'aux administrateurs de personnes morales à but lucratif)

Date Elected/ Date d'élection Year/Année Month/Mois Day/Jour	Date Ceased/ Date de cessation Year/Année Month/Mois Day/Jour
1992 | 01 | 01	19

Officer Information/Renseignements relatifs aux dirigeants

	PRESIDENT/PRÉSIDENT Year/Année Month/Mois Day/Jour	SECRETARY/SECRÉTAIRE Year/Année Month/Mois Day/Jour	TREASURER/TRÉSORIER Year/Année Month/Mois Day/Jour	GENERAL MANAGER/ DIRECTEUR GÉNÉRAL Year/Année Month/Mois Day/Jour	OTHER/AUTRE Year/Année Month/Mois Day/Jour
Date Appointed/ Date de nomination	1992 | 01 | 01	19	19	19	19
Date Ceased/ Date de cessation	19	19	19	19	19

DIRECTOR / OFFICER INFORMATION - RENSEIGNEMENTS RELATIFS AUX ADMINISTRATEURS/DIRIGEANTS

Full Name and Residential Address/Nom et adresse personnelle au complet

Last Name/Nom de famille	First Name/Prénom	Middle Names/Autres prénoms
DOE	JOHN	

Street Number/Numéro civique
999

Street Name/Nom de la rue
86TH STREET

Street Name (cont'd)/Nom de la rue (suite)   Suite/Bureau

City/Town/Ville
TORONTO

Province, State/Province, État	Country/Pays	Postal Code/Code postal
ONTARIO	CANADA	M2B 3Z4

Director Information/Renseignements relatifs aux administrateurs

Resident Canadian/ Résident canadien   [X] YES/OUI   [ ] NO/NON   (Resident Canadian applies to directors of business corporations only.)/ (Résident canadien ne s'applique qu'aux administrateurs de personnes morales à but lucratif)

Date Elected/ Date d'élection Year/Année Month/mois Day/Jour	Date Ceased/ Date de cessation Year/Année Month/Mois Day/Jour
1992 | 01 | 01	19

Officer Information/Renseignements relatifs aux dirigeants

	PRESIDENT/PRÉSIDENT Year/Année Month/Mois Day/Jour	SECRETARY/SECRÉTAIRE Year/Année Month/Mois Day/Jour	TREASURER/TRÉSORIER Year/Année Month/Mois Day/Jour	GENERAL MANAGER/ DIRECTEUR GÉNÉRAL Year/Année Month/Mois Day/Jour	OTHER/AUTRE Year/Année Month/Mois Day/Jour
Date Appointed/ Date de nomination	19	1992 | 01 | 01	19	19	19
Date Ceased/ Date de cessation	19	19	19	19	19

For Ministry Use Only
À l'usage du ministère seulement

Initials/Paraphes
LI ___ QA ___
DE ___ VER ___

694

Form 1 - Ontario Corporation/Formule 1 - Personnes morales en Ontario
Schedule A/Annexe A

All information must be typewritten in block capital letters using black ink in 10 or 12 pitch.
Toute les renseignements doivent être dactylographiée en caractères d'imprimerie à l'encre noire, en 10 ou 12 points.

For Ministry Use Only
À l'usage du ministère seulement
Page/Page _____ of/de _____

For Ministry Use Only / À l'usage du ministère seulement	Ontario Corporation Number / Numéro matricule de la personne morale en Ontario	Date of Incorporation/Amalgamation or Continuation / Date de constitution, fusion ou prorogation	For Ministry Use Only / À l'usage du ministère seulement
	000000	Year/Année 1981 Month/Mois 04 Day/Jour 01	

DIRECTOR / OFFICER INFORMATION - RENSEIGNEMENTS RELATIFS AUX ADMINISTRATEURS/DIRIGEANTS

Full Name and Residential Address/Nom et adresse personnelle au complet

Last Name/Nom de famille	First Name/Prénom	Middle Names/Autres prénoms
BROWN	JUNE	

Street Number/Numéro civique: 2346

Street Name/Nom de la rue: ABC AVENUE

Street Name (cont'd)/Nom de la rue (suite): | Suite/Bureau:

City/Town/Ville: TORONTO

Province, State/Province, État: ONTARIO | Country/Pays: CANADA | Postal Code/Code postal: M4G 9Z8

Director Information/Renseignements relatifs aux administrateurs

Resident Canadian/Résident canadien: [X] YES/OUI [ ] NO/NON
(Resident Canadian applies to directors of business corporations only.)/
(Résident canadien ne s'applique qu'aux administrateurs de personnes morales à but lucratif)

Date Elected/Date d'élection: Year/Année 19 81 Month/Mois 04 Day/Jour 01
Date Ceased/Date de cessation: Year/Année 1992 Month/Mois 01 Day/Jour 01

Officer Information/Renseignements relatifs aux dirigeants

	PRESIDENT/PRÉSIDENT			SECRETARY/SECRÉTAIRE			TREASURER/TRÉSORIER			GENERAL MANAGER/DIRECTEUR GÉNÉRAL			OTHER/AUTRE		
	Year/Année	Month/Mois	Day/Jour	Year/Année	Month/Mois	Day/Jour	Year/Année	Month/Mois	Day/Jour	Year/Année	Month/Mois	Day/Jour	Year/Année	Month/Mois	Day/Jour
Date Appointed/Date de nomination	19 81	04	01	19			19			19			19		
Date Ceased/Date de cessation	19 92	01	01	19			19			19			19		

DIRECTOR / OFFICER INFORMATION - RENSEIGNEMENTS RELATIFS AUX ADMINISTRATEURS/DIRIGEANTS

Full Name and Residential Address/Nom et adresse personnelle au complet

Last Name/Nom de famille	First Name/Prénom	Middle Names/Autres prénoms
BROWN	JAMES	

Street Number/Numéro civique: 2346

Street Name/Nom de la rue: ABC AVENUE

Street Name (cont'd)/Nom de la rue (suite): | Suite/Bureau:

City/Town/Ville: TORONTO

Province, State/Province, État: ONTARIO | Country/Pays: CANADA | Postal Code/Code postal: M4G 9Z8

Director Information/Renseignements relatifs aux administrateurs

Resident Canadian/Résident canadien: [X] YES/OUI [ ] NO/NON
(Resident Canadian applies to directors of business corporations only.)/
(Résident canadien ne s'applique qu'aux administrateurs de personnes morales à but lucratif)

Date Elected/Date d'élection: Year/Année 1981 Month/Mois 04 Day/Jour 01
Date Ceased/Date de cessation: Year/Année 19 92 Month/Mois 01 Day/Jour 01

Officer Information/Renseignements relatifs aux dirigeants

	PRESIDENT/PRÉSIDENT			SECRETARY/SECRÉTAIRE			TREASURER/TRÉSORIER			GENERAL MANAGER/DIRECTEUR GÉNÉRAL			OTHER/AUTRE		
	Year/Année	Month/Mois	Day/Jour	Year/Année	Month/Mois	Day/Jour	Year/Année	Month/Mois	Day/Jour	Year/Année	Month/Mois	Day/Jour	Year/Année	Month/Mois	Day/Jour
Date Appointed/Date de nomination	19			1981	04	01	19			19			19		
Date Ceased/Date de cessation	19			1992	01	01	19			19			19		

For Ministry Use Only / À l'usage du ministère seulement

Initials/Paraphes
U _____ QA _____
DE _____ VER _____

9F101
RELEASE OF VENDOR SHAREHOLDER
TO TARGET COMPANY

[See Para. 9.620]

R E L E A S E

TO: SUBJECT CORPORATION
   ("the Corporation")

In consideration of the sum of One Dollar ($1.00) of lawful money of Canada and for other good and valuable consideration, the receipt of which is hereby acknowledged, the undersigned hereby remises, releases and forever discharges the Corporation of and from all actions, causes of action, suits, debts, duties, accounts, bonds, covenants, contracts, claims and demands whatsoever which the undersigned as sole shareholder of the Corporation now have or hereafter can, shall or may have for or by reason of or in any way arising out of any cause, matter or thing whatsoever existing up to the present time and in particular without in any way limiting the generality of the foregoing for or by reason of or in any way arising out of any and all claims for moneys advanced, dividends, bonuses, expenses, participation in profit or earnings or other remuneration whether authorized or provided by by-law, resolution, contract or otherwise.

The provisions hereof shall enure to the benefit of the successors and assigns of the Corporation, and shall be binding upon the successors and assigns of the undersigned.

IN WITNESS WHEREOF the proper signing officer of the Corporation has executed the same under corporate seal, the _____ day of (*month, year*).

VENDOR INC.

Per: _____

June Brown
President

9F102
INDEMNITY OF PURCHASER SHAREHOLDER TO NEW DIRECTOR

[See Para. 9.620]

[Note: To be completed for each Director]

TO: JANE DOE
        (the "Director")

WHEREAS the Director has at the request of Purchaser Limited (the "Shareholder") consented to act as a director of Subject Corporation (the "Corporation");

AND WHEREAS as a condition of agreeing to act as a director of the Corporation, the Director has required the Shareholder to provide and the Shareholder has agreed to provide an indemnity in her favour;

NOW THEREFORE THIS INDEMNITY WITNESSETH that:

1. The Director is hereby relieved and saved harmless by the Shareholder from all duties and liabilities to which a director of the Corporation may be subject, including any liabilities under section 131 of the Ontario Business Corporations Act (the "Act").

2. The Director and her heirs and legal representatives, respectively, are hereby indemnified and saved harmless by the Shareholder from and against all costs, charges and expenses, including all amounts paid to settle any action or satisfy any judgment reasonably incurred by or on behalf of the Director in respect of any civil, criminal or administrative action or proceeding to which the Director is a party (or any such proceeding which might be threatened and in respect of which the Director is threatened to be made a party) by reason of her being or having been a director of the Corporation, or by reason of any breach by the Shareholder of the rights, powers, duties and liabilities expressed herein to be assumed by the Shareholder.

3. The indemnity may not be amended without the prior written consent of the Director, and shall terminate at such time as the Director resigns as a director of the Corporation and such resignation becomes effective in accordance with the Act and the by-laws of the Corporation. The

termination of this indemnity shall not affect any obligation to indemnify the Director, by reason of any matter which has arisen or any circumstances which have occurred prior to such termination.

4.   This indemnity shall enure to the benefit of the Director and her heirs and legal representatives and shall be governed in accordance with the laws of the Province of Ontario and the laws of Canada applicable thereto.

The foregoing indemnity is hereby signed by the sole shareholder of the Corporation.

DATED the _____ day of (*month, year*).

PURCHASER LIMITED

Per: _____

Jane Doe
President

9F103
DECLARATION OF PURCHASER SHAREHOLDER TO NEW DIRECTORS RE: UNANIMOUS SHAREHOLDER AGREEMENT

[See Para. 9.620]

[Note: To be completed for each Director]

TO: JANE DOE
(the "Director")

WHEREAS Subject Corporation (the "Corporation") is a corporation to which the Ontario Business Corporation Act and amendments (together being the "Act") apply;

AND WHEREAS Purchaser Limited (the "Shareholder") is the registered and beneficial owner of all of the issued and outstanding shares of the Corporation;

AND WHEREAS the Shareholder, under the authority contained in the Act, wishes to enter into this Declaration so as to restrict the rights, powers and discretion of the directors of the Corporation to manage the business and affairs of the Corporation and to provide that the Shareholder shall assume the rights, powers and duties of such directors and thereby relieve such directors of their duties and liabilities to the fullest extent permitted by the Act;

AND WHEREAS it is intended that this Declaration shall be deemed to be a unanimous shareholder agreement pursuant to subsection 108(3) of the Act;

AND WHEREAS the Director has at the request of the Shareholder consented to act as a director of the Corporation, upon the condition that the Shareholder shall provide and the Shareholder hereby provides an indemnity in the Director's favour;

NOW THEREFORE THIS DECLARATION WITNESSETH that:

1. The powers of the directors of the Corporation to manage the business and affairs of the Corporation, whether such powers arise from the Act, the articles or the by-laws of the Corporation or otherwise, are hereby restricted to the fullest extent permitted by law.

2. In accordance with the Act and this Declaration, the Shareholder shall have, enjoy, exercise and perform all the rights, powers and duties of the directors of the Corporation to manage the business and affairs of the Corporation.

3. In exercising the rights, powers and duties granted and transferred hereby, the Shareholder shall be subject to the same duties and liabilities to which the directors of the Corporation would have been subject in the exercise of such rights and powers had this Declaration not been made.

4. The rights, powers and duties granted or transferred hereby to the Shareholder shall be exercised or performed to the extent appropriate by instrument in writing executed by the Shareholder and any transferee of any shares of the Corporation registered in the name of the Shareholder. Subject to the Act, any such transferee shall be deemed to be a party to this Declaration and shall be governed hereby in the same manner and to the same extent as the Shareholder. The shareholder shall cause a reference to this Declaration to be noted conspicuously on any share certificate issued by the Corporation.

5. In consideration hereof, the Shareholder hereby indemnifies and saves harmless the Director and her heirs and legal representatives,

respectively, from and against all costs, charges and expenses, including all amounts paid to settle any action or satisfy any judgment reasonably incurred by or on behalf of the Director in respect of any civil, criminal or administrative action or proceeding to which the Director is a party (or any such proceeding which might be threatened and in respect of which the Director is threatened to be made a party) by reason of her being or having been a director of the Corporation, or by reason of any breach by the Shareholder of the rights, powers, duties and liabilities expressed herein to be assumed by the Shareholder.

6. The Declaration shall continue in full force and effect until terminated by notice in writing given by the Shareholder to the Director, provided that such termination shall not affect any obligation of the Shareholder arising prior to the date of such termination, including any obligation to indemnify by reason of any matter which has arisen or any circumstances which have occurred prior to the termination.

7. This Declaration and the indemnity contained herein shall enure to the benefit of the Director and her heirs and legal representatives and shall be governed in accordance with the laws of the Province of _____ and the laws of Canada applicable thereto.

The foregoing Declaration is hereby signed by the sole shareholder of the Corporation.

DATED the _____ day of (*month, year*).

PURCHASER LIMITED

Per: _____

Jane Doe
President

9F104
RESOLUTION OF NEW DIRECTORS
RE CHANGING AUDITORS

[See Para. 9.620]

RESOLUTIONS OF THE SHAREHOLDER
OF
TARGET LIMITED

ACCEPTANCE OF RESIGNATION OF ACCOUNTANTS

BE IT RESOLVED that the resignation by Apple & Co. as accountant of the corporation is received and accepted in accordance with its terms.

APPOINTMENT OF AUDITOR

BE IT RESOLVED THAT White & Co. be appointed as the auditor of the Corporation to hold office until replaced by the Board or the shareholder, and to serve at a remuneration to be fixed by the directors of the Corporation, the directors being authorized to fix such remuneration from time to time.

The undersigned, being the sole shareholder of the Corporation entitled to vote, hereby signs the foregoing ordinary resolutions in accordance with the provisions of the *Business Corporations Act* (Ontario).

DATED the _____, 19_____.

PURCHASER INC.

Per: _____

9F105
INDEMNITY RE SHAREHOLDER'S SPOUSAL CLAIMS

[See Para. 9.620]

TO: Purchaser Inc.

WHEREAS, the undersigned is a party to an Option Agreement among June Brown and James Brown (the "Principals"), Target Limited (the "Company"), and Purchaser Inc. (hereinafter called "Purchaser") respecting the granting of an option on all of the undersigned's shares (hereinafter called "Shares") in the capital stock of the Company to the Purchaser;

AND WHEREAS, the undersigned is a shareholder of the Company;

AND WHEREAS, pursuant to paragraph (k) of article 9.01 of the Option Agreement, each of the Principals is required to provide an acknowledgement and waiver of his or her spouse confirming the representation and warranty, to the effect that no order has been made under the Family Law Act which would or does affect the said Shares in any manner whatsoever, nor is any application threatened or pending under the said Act by the spouse of the undersigned;

IN CONSIDERATION of the premises, other good and valuable consideration, the receipt and sufficiency of which is hereby acknowledged, the Purchaser entering into the Option Agreement, the undersigned shall indemnify and keep indemnified the Purchaser, its successors and assigns fully harmless from and against any liabilities for losses, damages, costs, charges and expenses of whatever kind or nature, including legal fees and disbursements, and against any liabilities, losses, damages, costs, charges, and expenses, including legal fees and disbursements the Purchaser may incur in connection with any one or more of the following events or circumstances:

1. the existence as of any order of a competent Court made pursuant to the Family Law Act or any domestic contract between the undersigned and her spouse which would or does affect the Shares of the Company held by the undersigned; or

2. the existence of any threatened or pending application by the spouse of the undersigned under the Family Law Act which affects the Shares held by the undersigned to the detriment of the Purchaser.

IN WITNESS WHEREOF the undersigned has executed and delivered this indemnity and has hereunto set his hand and seal this _____ day _____, 19____.

SIGNED, SEALED AND
DELIVERED in the presence of:

               }   _____
                                 June Brown

_____

9F106
Release and Indemity from Beneficiaries

[See Para. 9.624]

RELEASE AND INDEMNITY

WHEREAS MARY JANE SMITH, DECEASED, late of the City of Toronto, in the Municipality of Metropolitan Toronto died on or about the 31st day of January, 1992;

AND WHEREAS Letters Probate [*Certificate of Appointment of Estate Trustee With a Will*] were granted to Bob Jones (the "Executor"), of the City of Toronto, in the Municipality of Metropolitan Toronto, by the Ontario Court (General Division) on March 31, 1992;

AND WHEREAS pursuant to the terms of the Last Will and Testament of the late Mary Jane Smith, the Executor is authorized to sell the Subject Corporation (the "Corporation") in the administration of the estate of Mary Jane Smith;

AND WHEREAS pursuant to an Agreement dated July 31, 1992 the Executor agreed to the Corporation to the Purchaser for good and valuable consideration.

I DO BY THESE PRESENTS, release, quit, claim and forever discharge the Executor, his heirs, executors, administrators, successors and assigns of and from all actions, suits, payments, accounts, reckonings, claims and demands whatsoever in law or equity which I may now or hereafter have, arising in any manner out of the sale of the Corporation to the Purchaser, and I hereby declare that this Release and Discharge shall be binding on my heirs, executors, administrators and assigns.

I HEREBY COVENANT AND AGREE to indemnify and hold harmless the Executor to the extent of my beneficial interest in the said estate, in respect of any liability incurred by him in respect of all causes of action, suits, debts, duties, accounts, bonds, covenants, contracts, and demands whatsoever that any of the beneficiaries of the said estate now has or hereafter can, shall or may have for or by reason of or in any way arising out of the sale of the Corporation to the Purchaser by Bob Jones while he acted as Executor.

DATED this _____ day of _____, 19____.

SIGNED IN THE PRESENCE of:

_____   }   _____ (Seal)
Witness   Beneficiary

9F107
FAMILY LAW ACT WAIVER FROM SPOUSE

[See Para. 9.624]

WAIVER AND RELEASE

The Husband hereby releases, disclaims and waives:

(a)   any and all claims and rights that he may have, have had or may hereafter acquire with respect to all rights, if any, in or to the corporation held in the estate of the Wife or in any proprety of the corporation deemed to pass upon the death of the Wife, or by way of statutory allowance or otherwise and all rights under the laws of Ontario with respect to the corporation and in particular, without limiting the generality of the foregoing, Part V of the Succession Law Reform Act, R.S.O. 1990, c. S.26 or any successor or similar legislation in force from time to time in the province of Ontario;

(b)   all present or future rights, if any, with respect to the corporation held in the estate of the Wife under the Family Law Act, or any successor or similar legislation including, without limiting the generality of the foregoing, the right to receive any amount upon the death of the Wife from or by the corporation pursuant to the Family Law Act, or any successor or similar legislation in force from time to time in any jurisdiction; and

(c)   all rights to and interest in the corporation owned by the Wife and held in the estate of the Wife that she had under the laws of any jurisdiction, including all rights and claims involving possession of property, legal ownership of property, beneficial ownership of property, including where one party is alleged to hold property for the other as trustee on a resulting, implied or constructive trust including a constructive trust based on the doctrine of unjust enrichment.

SIGNED in the presence of:

_____   _____ (Seal)

A Commissioner etc. . .   Spouse

9F108
REPRESENTATIONS AS TO PROBATE TO BE INCLUDED IN PURCHASE AND SALE AGREEMENT

[See Para. 9.624]

The estate covenants, represents and warrants to and in favour of the purchaser as follows and acknowledges that the purchaser is relying upon such covenants, representations and warranties in connection with the purchase by the purchaser of the purchased shares [*or the purchased assets*]:

(a) the letters probate dated the 31st day of March, 1992 [*Certificate of Appointment of Estate Trustee With a Will dated (insert date)*] were issued by the Ontario Court (General Division) at Toronto in the estate of Mary Jane Smith, deceased, of the Last Will and Testament of said deceased, to Bob Jones as executor, which provides full authority for said executor under said Will to execute this agreement for and on behalf of the estate hereunder, and when this agreement is so executed by the said executor of and on behalf of the estate, this agreement constitutes valid and binding obligations of the estate enforceable against it in accordance with its terms;

(b) a true copy of such letters probate [*notarial copy of the Certificate of Appointment of Estate Trustee With a Will*] are attached hereto as Schedule.

9F109
Certificate of Estate as to Representations

[See Para. 9.624]

CERTIFICATE

TO: [_____] (the "Purchaser")

RE : Agreement made _____, 19___ between The Estate of Mary Jane Smith and the Purchaser (the "Agreement")

I, Bob Jones, the Executor of the estate of Mary Jane Smith (the "estate"), make reference to the agreement and in particular section ____ thereof and hereby certify that:

1. each of the representations and warranties of the Estate to the Purchaser as set out in the agreement are true and correct as of the time of delivery of this certificate on the date hereof, with the same force and effect as if such representations and warranties were made at and as of the time of delivery of this certificate; and

2. The estate has fulfilled each of the covenants required to be fulfilled by them under the agreement.

DATED at Toronto, Ontario, this _____ day of _____, 19___.

ESTATE OF MARY JANE SMITH

_____   By: _____
Witness   Bob Jones, Executor

9F110
Release by Estate in Favour of Purchaser

[See Para. 9.624]

RELEASE

TO: _____ (the "Corporation")

In consideration of the sum of ten dollars ($10.00) in lawful money of Canada now paid by the corporation to the undersigned (the receipt of which is hereby acknowledged) and for other good and valuable consideration, the undersigned hereby remises, releases and forever discharges the corporation of and from all actions, causes of action, suits, debts, dues, accounts, bonds, covenants, contracts, claims and demands whatsoever, which the undersigned or Mary Jane Smith as an officer, employee, director or shareholder of the corporation or otherwise had, now has or hereafter can, shall or may have for, or by reason of, or in any way arising out of any cause, matter or thing whatsoever existing up to the present time and in particular, without in any way limiting the generality of the foregoing, for, or by reason of, or in any way arising out of any and all claims for moneys advanced, salary, wages, bonus, expenses, retirement or pension allowances, directors' fees, profits or earnings or other remuneration whether authorized or provided for by by-law, resolution, contract or otherwise and for, or by reason of, or in any way arising out of the ending of the employment of Mary Jane Smith with the corporation; provided, however, that the foregoing release shall not affect the corporation's obligations arising under an agreement made July 31, 1992 between the purchaser and the corporation or any agreements, documents or instruments executed pursuant to the terms thereof.

The provisions hereof shall enure to the benefit of the successors and assigns of the corporation and shall be binding upon the heirs, executors, administrators, successors and assigns of the undersigned.

IN WITNESS WHEREOF the hand and seal of the undersigned has hereunto been affixed the _____ day of _____, 19____.

Signed, Sealed and Delivered
in the presence of:

ESTATE OF MARY JANE SMITH

By: _____

Bob Jones, Executor

9F111
Declaration of Receiver on Ability to Sell

[See Para. 9.650]

STATUTORY DECLARATION

IN THE MATTER OF a sale by Receiver Limited ("Receiver") in its capacity as receiver and manager of Debtor Inc. ("Debtor") on behalf of _____ Bank (the "Bank") to Purchaser Inc. ("Purchaser") pursuant to a bill a sale dated _____, 19____I, John Jones in the Town of Richmond Hill in the Regional Municipality of York, province of Ontario do solemnly declare that:

1. I am a Vice President of Receiver and as such have personal knowledge of the matters hereinafter deposed to or have been advised and do believe the matters hereinafter deposed to.

2. Attached hereto are true and complete copies of the security held by the Bank in respect of the liabilities of the Debtor being the following:
    (a) general security agreement in favour of the Bank dated _____, 19_____, a copy of which is attached hereto as Schedule A;
    (b) general assignment of accounts in favour of the Bank dated _____, 19_____, a copy of which is attached hereto as Schedule B; and
    (c) chattel mortgage in favour of the Bank dated _____, 19_____, a copy of which is attached hereto as Schedule C.

3. Attached hereto as Schedules D, E and F are copies of the three financing statements registered pursuant to the Personal Property Security Act by which the Bank perfected its aforesaid security agreements.

4. Receiver was appointed receiver and manager of the Debtor by the Bank by appointment letter dated _____, 19_____, a copy of which is attached hereto as Schedule G, and the said appointment has not been revoked as of the date hereof.

5. Notice of sale pursuant to Section 63 of the Personal Property Security Act was issued on behalf of the Bank on _____, 19_____, a copy of which is annexed hereto as Schedule H and sent by registered mail to the persons listed in Schedule I. Since the issuance of this notice, Receiver and the Bank have received no notice of intention to redeem in respect of the assets of the Debtor, or been served with any proceeding by a third party seeking to enjoin this sale.

6. I believe that each of the Bank and Receiver is not a non-resident within the meaning of Section 116 of the Income Tax Act (Canada) and will not be such a non-resident at the time of completion of this transaction.

And I make this solemn declaration conscientiously believing it to be true and knowing that it is of the same force and effect as if made under oath.

DECLARED BEFORE ME at the
City of Toronto, in the
Municipality of Metropolitan
Toronto, this _____ day of
_____, 19_____

A Commissioner, etc.

_____
John Jones

9F112
Receivership Bill of Sale

[See Para. 9.650]

BILL OF SALE

THIS INDENTURE made as of the _____ day of _____, 19_____

BETWEEN:

> _____ LIMITED, in its capacity as Receiver and Manager of the undertaking and property and assets of DEBTOR LTD., and as agent of _____ Bank, having a place of business as _____ King Street West, Toronto, Ontario,

> (hereinafter called the "Grantor")

OF THE FIRST PART

- and -

> PURCHASER LTD., a corporation incorporated under the laws of Canada, and having a place of business at 1 Dixie Road, Mississauga, Ontario,

> (hereinafter called the "Grantee")

OF THE SECOND PART

WHEREAS by a debenture (the "Debenture") dated August 21, 1981 issued by the Debtor Ltd. ("Debtor") in favour of _____ Bank, the Debtor mortgaged and charged all its undertaking and property and assets to and in favour of the Bank as more fully set out in the Debenture;

AND WHEREAS by a Security Agreement dated October 14, 1982 and numerous chattel mortgages (collectively, the "Security"), the Debtor charged its vehicles in favour of the Bank;

AND WHEREAS pursuant to the powers conferred by the Debenture, the Bank appointed the Grantor receiver and manager of the undertaking and the property and assets of the Debtor, and as agent of the Bank under the Security, both on _____, 19_____;

AND WHEREAS the Grantor has agreed to sell and the Grantee has agreed to purchase all the assets owned by the Debtor other than (i) any accounts receivable or book debts due or accruing to the Debtor as of _____, 19____ (save and except the customer parts and service accounts receivables which are included in this sale), (ii) all 19_____ model year vehicles, and (iii) inventories of parts which have been returned by the Debtor to Supplier Ltd. (collectively referred to herein as the "Excluded Assets");

NOW THEREFORE THIS INDENTURE WITNESSES that in consideration of the sum of _____ Dollars ($_____) of lawful money of Canada and other good and valuable consideration now paid by the Grantee to the Grantor (the receipt whereof is hereby acknowledged) the Grantor doth hereby grant, sell, convey, assign, transfer and set over unto the Grantee, its successors and assigns, on an "as is where is basis" all right, title and interest of the Debtor and the Grantor in and to all the assets of the Debtor and, in particular, without limiting the generality of the foregoing, the assets described in Schedule "A" hereto (hereinafter collectively referred to as the "Assets") provided always that the Assets shall not include the Excluded Assets.

TO HOLD the Assets and all other right, title and interest of the Debtor and/or Grantor therein and thereto, unto and to the use of the Grantee.

The Grantor covenants with the Grantee that it has the right to sell, and that it has done no act to encumber the Assets.

The Grantor shall and will from time to time upon every reasonable request of the Grantee, but at the cost, charge and expense of the Grantee, take or cause to be taken such action, and execute and deliver or cause to be executed and delivered such documents and further assurances for the more effectually selling and assigning of the Assets to the Grantee according to the true intent and meaning of this indenture.

Save as aforesaid, nothing herein shall be deemed to be a representation, warranty, guarantee or covenant, expressed or implied, on the part of the Grantor for any cause, matter or thing whatsoever and for greater certainty, the Grantor does not warrant the accuracy or completeness of Schedule "A" hereto.

IN WITNESS WHEREOF this indenture has been executed as of the day and year first above written.

SIGNED, SEALED AND
DELIVERED

_____ LIMITED in its capacity
as Receiver and manager of
DEBTOR LTD. and as agent of
_____ BANK and not in its
personal capacity

In the presence of:

_____

By: _____

By: _____

SCHEDULE A

The following Assets of the Debtor located at 123 Dixie Road, Mississauga, Ontario:

1.   Customer Accounts for Receivables, Parts and Service

2.   Company Vehicles and Current Model Demos

3.   Used Vehicles

4.   Remaining Parts Inventory not returned to Supplier Ltd.

5.   Miscellaneous Service and Parts Inventories (including tires, gasoline, oil, grease, paint and body supplies, shop supplies, janitor supplies, remanufactured parts and work in process)

6.   Prepaid Expenses

7.   Fixed Assets (excluding land, buildings and building fixtures)

8.   Leased Vehicles

9F113
PPSA Notice of Sale

[See Para. 9.650]

REGISTERED MAIL

NOTICE PURSUANT TO SECTION 63 OF
THE PERSONAL PROPERTY SECURITY ACT (ONTARIO)

To : [debtor, all guarantors, all PPSA creditors and anyone else with an interest in the collateral of whom you are aware]

Attn:

And to:

Attn:

TAKE NOTICE that pursuant to a _____ dated _____, 199_____ and a _____ dated _____, 199___ (collectively the "Security") all made between carrying on business as _____ (the "Company") and _____ Bank (the "Secured Party") intends to dispose of the collateral thereby secured unless the collateral is redeemed.

1. The collateral consists of all personal property of the Company, including the personal property of the Company used in connection with or generated by its operation of the _____ located at _____.

2. The principal amount required to satisfy the obligation of the Company secured by the Security as at the _____ day of the _____, 199_____ is $_____, together with interest from _____, 199_____ to and including _____, 19_____ of $_____ and interest thereon from and including _____, 199_____ until payment in full at the rate per annum of _____%.

3. The Secured Party's address where payment should be made is:

_____ Bank
1 Queen Street West
Toronto, Ontario
M5H 2N2
Attention:

Tel:

4. The estimated expenses of the Secured Party pursuant to Section 63(1) of the said Act are _____ Dollars ($_____).

5. Upon payment of the amounts due as above described, you may redeem the said collateral. Upon payment, the payor will be credited with any rebates or allowances to which the Company is entitled by law or under any agreement with the Security Party.

6. Unless the amounts due as above described are paid by the _____ [1] day of _____, 19_____, the said collateral will be disposed of and the Company will be liable for any deficiency.

7. Unless payment of the amounts due as above-described is receiver on or before the _____ day of _____, 199_____, there will be a private sale, public tender or public auction of the said collateral.

DATED at Toronto this _____ day of _____, 199_____.

_____BANK
By its solicitors:

Per: _____

---

1.   Allow 10 days for deemed receipt by registered mail plus 15 days thereafter.

9F114
PPSA Notice to Remove Fixtures

[See Para. 9.650 and 9.178]

REGISTERED MAIL

NOTICE PURSUANT TO SECTION 34(5) OF
THE PERSONAL PROPERTY SECURITY ACT (ONTARIO)

To : [debtor, all guarantors, all PPSA creditors and anyone else with an interest in the collateral of whom you are aware]

Attn:

And to:

Attn:

TAKE NOTICE that pursuant to a _____ dated _____, 199_____ and a _____ dated _____, 199_____ (collectively the "Security") all made between   _____ carrying on business as _____ (the "Company") and _____ Bank (the "Secured Party"), the Secured Party intends to remove fixtures charged by the Security from the real property occupied by the Company described herein unless the obligations of the Company to the Secured party are satisfied.

1. The principal amount required to satisfy the obligation of the Company secured by the Security as at the _____ day of _____, 199_____ is $_____, together with interest thereon from _____, 199_____ to and including _____, 199_____ of $_____ and interest thereon from and including _____, 199_____ until payment in full at the rate per annum of _____%.

3. The real property to which the fixturs are affixed is municipally known as _____, Ontario and the legal description of the said real property is as follows:

4. The Secured Party's address where payment should be made is:

> _____ Bank
> 1 Queen Street West
> Toronto, Ontario
> M5H 2N2
>
> Attention:
>
> Tel:

5. Unless the amounts due as above described are paid by the _____[1] day of _____, 199_____, the said fixtures will be removed from the real property herein described.

DATED at Toronto this _____ day of _____, 19_____.

> _____BANK
> By its solicitors:
>
> Per: _____

---

1.   Allow 10 days for deemed receipt by registered mail and 10 days thereafter.

9F115
PPSA Notice of Removal of Accessions

[See Para. 9.650]

REGISTERED MAIL

NOTICE PURSUANT TO SECTION 35(4) OF
THE PERSONAL PROPERTY SECURITY ACT (ONTARIO)

To: [debtor, all guarantors, all PPSA creditors registered against either debtor or VIN of subject "motor vehicles", and any other person of whom you know to have an interest in the goods"motor vehicles" as defined in the Regulations]

Attn:

And to:

Attn:

TAKE NOTICE that pursuant to a _____ dated _____, 199_____ and a dated _____, 199_____ (collectively the "Security") all made between _____ carrying on business as _____ (the "Company") and _____ Bank (the "Secured Party"), the Secured Party intends to remove the accessions charged to the Secured Party under the Security unless the said accessions are redeemed.

1. The accessions charged in favour of the Secured Party are described as follows:

2. The goods from which the said accessions will be removed are described as follows:

3. The principal amount required to satisfy the obligation of the Company secured by the Security as at the _____ day of _____, 19_____ is $_____, together with interest thereon from _____,19_____ to and including _____, 19_____ of $_____ and interest thereon from and including _____, 19_____ until payment in full at the rate per annum of _____%.

4. The Secured Party's address where payment should be made is:

> _____ Bank
> 1 Queen Street West
> Toronto, Ontario
> M5H 2N2
>
> Attn:
>
> Tel:

5. Unless the amounts due as above described are paid by the _____[1] day of _____, 19_____, the said accessions will be removed from the goods described above.

DATED at Toronto this _____ day of _____, 19_____.

> _____BANK
> By its solicitors:
>
> Per: _____

_____

1. give 10 days for deemed receipt by registered mail plus 10 days thereafter.

9F116

AGREEMENT OF PURCHASE AND SALE

[See Para. 9.651]

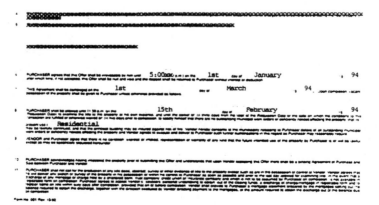

Toronto Real Estate Board

FOR USE IN THE PROVINCE OF ONTARIO

AGREEMENT OF PURCHASE AND SALE

PURCHASER   John Smith

VENDOR   XYZ Bank (under power of sale)

AGENT   ABC Realco   ABC Realco

LISTING BROKER   CO-OPERATING BROKER

PROPERTY having on the south side of Main Street   City   Somewhere

having a frontage of 100 feet   more or less by a depth of 200 feet   more or less and described as

Lot 10, Concession 1, City of Somewhere, Regional Municipality of Oz

at the PURCHASE PRICE of

THREE HUNDRED THOUSAND——————————————— CANADIAN DOLLARS (CDN) $ 300,000.00——————

PURCHASER submits with the Offer TWENTY-FIVE THOUSAND   CANADIAN DOLLARS (CDN) $ 25,000.00——

payable by cash cheque to the Listing Broker as a deposit to be held by him in trust pending completion of other termination of this Agreement and to be credited on account of the purchase price on completion.

Purchaser agrees to pay the balance of the purchase price to the vendor on closing in cash or by certified cheque, subject to the usual adjustments.

CONTINUED ON SCHEDULE "A" ATTACHED WHICH FORMS PART OF THIS AGREEMENT OF PURCHASE AND SALE.

PURCHASER agrees that this Offer shall be irrevocable by him until 5:00 p.m. on the 1st day of January , 94 after which time, if not accepted, this Offer shall be null and void and the deposit shall be returned to Purchaser without interest or deduction.

This Agreement shall be completed on the 1st day of March , 94 upon completion vacant possession of the property shall be given to Purchaser unless otherwise provided as follows:

PURCHASER shall be allowed until 11:59 p.m. on the 15th day of February , 94

present use: Residential

VENDOR and Purchaser agree that there is no condition, warranty, representation or collateral agreement

PURCHASER acknowledges having inspected the property prior to submitting this Offer

PURCHASER shall not call for the production of any title deed

Form No. 501 Rev 10-92

12　PROVIDED that the title to the property is good and free from all registered restrictions, charges, liens, and encumbrances except as otherwise specifically provided in this Agreement and save and except for (a) any registered restrictions or covenants that run with the land providing that such are complied with; (b) any registered municipal agreements and registered agreements with public utilities or regulated unless providing such have been complied with, or security has been posted to ensure compliance and completion, as evidenced by a letter from the relevant municipality or regulated utility; (c) any minor easements for the supply of domestic utility or telephone services to the property or adjacent properties, and (d) any easements for drainage, storm or sanitary sewers, public utility lines, telephone lines, cable television lines or other services which do not materially affect the present use of the property...

13　IF Vendor's spouse has not joined in this Agreement or executed Spousal Clause below, Vendor covenants on consent of Vendor's spouse to this transaction on or before completion...

14　ALL buildings on property and all other things being purchased shall be and remain until completion at the risk of Vendor. Pending completion, Vendor shall hold all insurance policies, if any, and the proceeds thereof in trust for the parties as their interest may appear...

15　PROVIDED that this Agreement shall be effective to create an interest in the property only if the subdivision control provisions of the Planning Act are complied with by Vendor on or before completion.

16　PURCHASER shall be credited towards the Purchase Price with the amount, if any, which it shall be necessary for Purchaser to pay to the Receiver General of Canada in order to satisfy Purchaser's liability in respect of tax payable by Vendor under the non-residency provisions of the Income Tax Act by reason of this sale. Purchaser shall not claim such credit if Vendor delivers on completion the prescribed certificate or his statutory declaration that he is not then a non-resident of Canada.

17　ANY rents, mortgage interest, realty taxes, local improvement charges, water and unmetered utility charges and the cost of fuel as applicable shall be apportioned and allowed to the day of completion (the day itself to be apportioned to Purchaser).

18　THE Transfer/Deed shall, save for the Land Transfer Tax Affidavits, be prepared in registrable form at the expense of Vendor and the Mortgage at the expense of Purchaser...

19　TIME shall in all respects be of the essence hereof provided that the time for doing or completing of any matter provided for herein may be extended or abridged by an agreement in writing signed by Vendor and Purchaser or by their respective solicitors who are hereby expressly appointed in this regard.

20　ANY tender of documents or money hereunder may be made upon Vendor or Purchaser or their respective solicitors on the day for completion of this Agreement. Money may be tendered by bank draft or cheque certified by a chartered bank, trust company or Province of Ontario Savings Office.

21　THIS Agreement including any schedules attached hereto shall constitute the entire agreement between the Purchaser and Vendor. There is no representation, warranty, collateral agreement or condition whether direct or collateral or express or implied which induced any party hereto to enter into this Agreement or on which reliance is placed by any such party, or which affects this Agreement or the property or supported hereby other than as expressed herein. This Agreement shall be read with all changes of gender or number required by the context. In the event of conflict between any provision written or typed in this Agreement and any provision in the printed portion hereof the written or typed provision shall supersede the printed provisions to the extent of such conflict.

22　NO insurance shall be transferred on completion. If Vendor is taking back a mortgage, or Purchaser is assuming a mortgage, Purchaser shall supply Vendor with reasonable evidence of adequate insurance to protect the Vendor's interests on completion.

23　IF this Agreement of Purchase and Sale contains a direction for the deposit to be placed in an interest bearing account or term deposit, the Purchaser and/or Vendor are to provide their Social Insurance Number to the Agent and failing which the agent may retain the interest in the interest bearing account or term deposit and not make payment of interest to any party until such information is provided as to the party or parties to whom payment is to be made.

DATED AT　**City of Somewhere**　　this　**28th**　day of　**December**　　　19 **93**

SIGNED, SEALED AND DELIVERED
in the presence of　　　　　　　　　IN WITNESS whereof I have hereunto set my hand and seal

　　　　　　　　　　　　　　　　(Purchaser)　　　　　(Affix Seal)　　　　(Date)

　John Smith

　　　　　　　　　　　　　　　　(Purchaser)　　　　　(Affix Seal)　　　　(Date)

THE UNDERSIGNED accepts the above Offer and agrees with the Listing Broker above named in consideration for services in procuring the said Offer, to pay him on completion a commission as provided on the Listing Agreement, plus applicable federal goods and services tax on such commission, which commission and taxes shall be deducted from the deposit. If said deposit is insufficient, the undersigned hereby irrevocably instructs my/our solicitor to pay direct to the Listing Broker any unpaid balance of commission and such taxes from the proceeds of the sale prior to any payment to the undersigned on completion, as advised by the Listing Broker to my/our solicitor.

DATED AT　　　　　　　　　　　this　　　　day of　　　　　　　　　19

SIGNED, SEALED AND DELIVERED
in the presence of　　　　　　　　　IN WITNESS whereof I have hereunto set my hand and seal

　　　　　　　　　　　　　　　XYZ BANK

　Per:

　　　　　　　　　　　　　　　　(Vendor)　　　　　(Affix Seal)　　　　(Date)

　I have authority to bind XYZ Bank.

　　　　　　　　　　　　　　　　(Vendor)　　　　　(Affix Seal)　　　　(Date)

SPOUSAL CLAUSE
In consideration of the sum of One ($1.00) Dollar (receipt of which is hereby acknowledged) and the entering into of this Agreement by the Purchaser, the undersigned spouse of the Vendor hereby consents to the disposition evidenced hereby pursuant to the Family Law Act, 1986 and agrees to execute any and all necessary or incidental documents to give full force and effect to such sale.

　(Witness)　　　　　　　　　　(Spouse)　　　　　　　　　　(Dated)

COMMISSION TRUST AGREEMENT

The Listing Broker in consideration of the preparation and submission of this agreement, hereby declares that the right to commission, and all amounts payable or paid thereunder are held in trust by the Listing Broker for and on behalf of the Listing Broker and Co-Operating Broker as their interests may be.

　(Listing Broker or Sales Representative)　　　　　　　(Co-Operating Broker or Sales Representative)

ACKNOWLEDGEMENT

I/We acknowledge receipt of a signed copy of this accepted Agreement of Purchase and Sale and authorize a copy to be forwarded to my/our solicitor

I/We acknowledge receipt of a signed copy of this accepted Agreement of Purchase and Sale and authorize a copy to be forwarded to my/our solicitor

(Vendor)	(Date)	(Purchaser)	(Date)
(Vendor)	(Date)	(Purchaser)	(Date)

Vendor's Address　　　　　　　　　　　　Purchaser's Address

　　　　　　　Telephone No　　　　　　　　　　　　　　　Telephone No

Vendor's Solicitor　　　　　　　　　　　Purchaser's Solicitor

Solicitor's Address　　　　　　　　　　　Solicitor's Address

　　　　　　　Telephone No　　　　　　　　　　　　　　　Telephone No

Form No. 301 Rev. 10/92

SCHEDULE "A"

To an agreement of purchase and sale made between XYZ Bank under power of sale) as Vendor and John Smith as Purchaser.

The following terms and conditions shall apply to and shall form part of any agreement of purchase and sale ("the Agreement") to which this Schedule is attached, notwithstanding any provision to contrary:

1. The Vendor and the Purchaser expressly acknowledge and agree that where there is any conflict or discrepancy between the terms and conditions in this Schedule, and the terms and conditions in the Agreement attached hereto, the terms and conditions in this Schedule shall supersede and shall apply in place of such other conflicting terms and conditions.

2. The Purchaser acknowledges that the Vendor is making the within sale pursuant to its power of sale contained in the mortgage registered in favour of the Vendor against the title to the property, and agrees that it will accept title pursuant to the exercise thereof and pursuant to the applicable provisions of the *Mortgages Act* of Ontario. Purchaser agrees that the transfer/deed shall not contain any covenants except that the Vendor has done no act to encumber the property.

3. The Vendor warrants that, on the date of acceptance of the Agreement, there is default under the Vendor's mortgage which entitles the Vendor to enforce its power of sale remedy. The only evidence of default which the Purchaser may require from the Vendor shall be a statutory declaration made by the Vendor (or a representative thereof) setting forth the facts entitling the Vendor to sell under power of sale, including the particulars of the notice of exercising the power of sale, the names of the persons upon whom service of the notice was effected, and declaring that the default under the mortgage entitling the Vendor to exercise the power of sale has continued up to and including the date of acceptance of this Agreement.

4. The Purchaser agrees that the Vendor shall only be required to deliver a discharge, release or re-assignment of any mortgage, assignment, lien or other encumbrance now registered against the title to the property which is in priority to the Vendor's mortgage. Purchaser agrees to accept Vendor's Solicitors' undertaking to provide such discharge, release or re-assignment subsequent to closing should same not be available on or before closing.

5.   Notwithstanding anything to the contrary set out in this Agreement, if
        the Vendor's mortgage is brought into good standing or paid off prior
        to the completion of the within sale, or if a certificate of pending
        litigation or caution is registered against the property, or if the
        Purchaser submits a valid title requisition which the Vendor is unable
        or unwilling to satisfy prior to closing, or if the sale of the property is
        restrained by a court of competent jurisdiction (whether or not such
        court order is under appeal by any party to the court proceedings), or
        if the exercise of the power of sale of the property by the Vendor is in
        any way placed in issue, or if the consent to assumption of any prior
        mortgage is required and has not been obtained, then the Vendor may,
        at its option, elect by written notice to the Purchaser to:

        (a)   terminate this Agreement, whereupon the deposit will be
                returned to the Purchaser with interest earned thereon (if any),
                and neither party will have any further rights or liabilities
                hereunder; or

        (b)   extend the date of closing otherwise established pursuant to this
                Agreement for a period (i) up to sixty (60) days from the date
                originally set for closing; or (ii) 15 days following conclusion of
                the judicial proceedings preventing or restraining the sale of the
                property, whichever period is longer, to enable the Vendor to
                obtain an order vacating such restraining order or such certificate
                or to satisfy such title requisition   or to take appropriate steps to
                resolve the issue raised, as the case may be.
                Notwithstanding the foregoing, the Vendor at its sole option
                shall have the further right to extend the closing date beyond the
                sixty (60) day period referred to above for a further period of one
                (1) year, pending determination of court proceedings, by notice
                in writing delivered to the Purchaser or its solicitors at any time
                on or before any   extended closing date.

6.   The Purchaser acknowledges that no representations or warranties
        have been made by the Vendor, or anyone acting on its behalf, to the
        Purchaser as to the condition of the property or any buildings located
        thereon, or as to the performance of any parts thereof or as to the
        permitted use(s) thereof. The Purchaser acknowledges that the
        property is sold on an "as is, where is" basis including, without
        limitation, status of possession, outstanding work orders, deficiency
        notices, directives and zoning and building code violations. The
        Purchaser shall complete the purchase and take possession of the
        property as it exists on the date of closing. Purchaser agrees that it will
        accept the property on closing subject to any judicial, municipal or
        other governmental by-laws, agreements, restrictions or orders
        affecting or regarding its use or condition, as well as subject to any

registered restrictions, agreements, easements, rights-of-way or covenants which run with the land.

7. Notwithstanding any other provision of this Agreement, the Purchaser acknowledges that the Purchase Price does not include any chattels, and that the following fixtures may be installed on a rental basis: hot water heater, water softener, water filter, gas heater (and all appurtenant attachments), cable television and any type of heating or cooling system. All fixtures and chattels are transferred on an "as is, where is" basis and no representation, warranty or condition is expressed nor can be implied as to description, fitness for purpose, merchantability, quantity, condition or quality thereof or in respect of any matter or thing whatsoever and the Purchaser shall be deemed to have relied entirely on his own investigation and inspection. Without limiting the generality of the foregoing, it is expressly acknowledged and agreed by the Purchaser that any and all representations, conditions or warranties, express or implied pursuant to the *Sale of Goods Act* of Ontario do not apply hereto and have been waived by the Purchaser. The Vendor will deliver possession only of such fixtures and chattels as found on the property on closing without bill of sale, warranty or other title documentation and shall make no adjustment in the Purchase Price with respect thereto. The Vendor will not be responsible for the removal of any chattels found on the property prior to or on the date of closing.

8. All improvements on the property, and all other things being purchased, shall be and remain until closing at the risk of the Vendor. In the event of substantial damage, the Vendor may, at its option, terminate this Agreement and, if the Vendor elects to terminate this Agreement, the agent shall return the deposit, together with interest thereon (if any), to the Purchaser.

9. Vendor agrees to deliver all keys to the property to the Purchaser on the date of closing.

10. Purchaser agrees that the transaction contemplated hereunder is a "taxable supply" under the Excise Tax Act of Canada (the "Act") and is therefore subject to goods and services tax ("GST") pursuant to the Act, that GST is not included in the purchase price and that the Purchaser is obligated to pay GST on the purchase price to the Vendor on the closing date for remittance by the Vendor to the Receiver General (Canada). If the Purchaser is a registrant under the Act and wishes to self-assess and remit GST to the Receiver General (Canada) directly,

then the Purchaser shall provide the Vendor evidence (such evidence to be satisfactory to the Vendor in its sole discretion) that it is registered under the Act and that its registration has not been cancelled. The Purchaser shall indemnify the Vendor in respect of any loss, cost, damage and/or liability which the Vendor may suffer, incur, be charged with or be assessed with as a result of the Purchaser not being registered under the Act.

OR

Purchaser agrees that the transaction contemplated hereunder may be a "taxable supply" under the Excise Tax Act of Canada (the "Act") and may therefore be subject to goods and services tax ("GST") pursuant to the Act, that GST is not included in the purchase price and that the Purchaser is obligated to pay to the Vendor on the closing date, for remittance by the Vendor to the Receiver General (Canada), any GST payable with respect to the transaction.

11. In the event that vacant possession cannot be provided by the closing date, the Vendor may, at its sole option, extend the closing date by written notice to the Purchaser for any period or periods not exceeding in total sixty (60) days. Should the closing date be extended by the Vendor as aforesaid, and should the Vendor be unable to provide vacant possession by the expiration of the extension period or periods, the Purchaser shall have the option of accepting the property with the existing occupants. Should the Purchaser not be willing to accept the property with the existing occupants the Vendor may terminate this Agreement, whereupon the deposit will be returned to the Purchaser with interest earned thereon (if any), and neither party will have any further rights or liabilities hereunder. By executing this Agreement the Purchaser acknowledges that the occupation of this property is required by himself, herself, his or her spouse or a child or a parent of hers or of his. Should the Purchaser decide to accept the property with the existing occupants it is acknowledged by the Purchaser that the Vendor shall not be responsible to account or adjust for any prepaid rent and shall not be required to provide any documentation signed by any occupant confirming the status of a tenancy.

12. This Agreement may be negotiated via telefax and shall be firm and binding at the time an acceptance is fax by the accepting party. The parties agree to execute an original of this Agreement containing the identical terms of a faxed version of this Agreement, forthwith upon acceptance of the faxed version of this Agreement.

13. The Vendor covenants that it has done no act to encumber the property as at the date hereof and the Vendor covenants that it shall do not act to encumber the property from the date of acceptance hereof to the date of closing. The Vendor shall not sell or dispose of the property between the date hereof and the date of closing. The Vendor shall not be required to furnish or produce any survey, plan, abstract, deed, declaration or other document or evidence of title, except those in its possession.

14. Any termination right provided for in this Agreement shall be by written notice delivered to the address set out below or by confirmed telefax to the other party or his/her solicitor whereupon the Agreement shall be at an end and the deposit shall be returned to the Purchaser with interest earned thereon (if any):

Vendor   —   XYZ Bank, 100 Bay Street, Suite 1000,
                      Toronto, Ontario (telefax no. 222-2222)

Purchaser   —   John Smith, 14 King Street,
                      Somewhere, Ontario (telefax no. 778-8787)

15. Without limiting paragraph 6, the Vendor has no knowledge and makes no representation whatsoever with respect to the property as to the existence or non-existence of urea formaldehyde foam insulation, asbestos, PCB's, radium, radon or any other substances, liquids or materials which may be hazardous or toxic.

16. Any real estate commission payable in connection with this transaction shall be paid only upon successful completion of the sale of the property.

17. Purchaser will not register the within Agreement or any notice or assignment thereof or any caution (any such registration being deemed to be a breach by Purchaser of the within Agreement and entitling Vendor to cancel the same in addition to any other remedy Vendor may have). This Agreement is personal to Purchaser and neither this Agreement nor any monies paid hereunder create any interest in the property or any part thereof in favour of Purchaser. Purchaser may not assign or encumber the within Agreement without Vendor's prior written approval.

18. Default in any amount payable pursuant to this Agreement on the date or within the time specified, shall constitute substantial default hereunder, and the Vendor shall have the right to terminate this Agreement, in which case all deposit moneys paid by the Purchaser

shall be forfeited in full. Without prejudice to the Vendor's rights as to forfeiture of deposit moneys as aforesaid, and in addition thereto, the Vendor shall have the right to recover from the Purchaser all additional costs, losses and damages arising out of default on the part of the Purchaser pursuant to any provision contained in this Agreement.

19. The description of the property set out herein is believed by the Vendor to be correct, but if any nonmaterial misstatement, error or omission shall be found to or in the particulars thereof, the same shall not annul the sale or enable the Purchaser to be relieved of any obligation hereunder, nor shall any compensation be allowed to either the Vendor or the Purchaser in respect thereof.

20. The Purchaser agrees to accept the property as shown on the survey attached to this Agreement as Schedule "B" and acknowledges that the Vendor shall not be required to provide any other survey in connection with this transaction.

21. The Purchaser agrees that it will accept possession of the property on closing subject to all existing tenancies, that it will assume all existing tenancies in accordance with the terms thereof and that it will not require the Vendor to obtain vacant possession of all or any part of the property. It is acknowledged by the Purchaser that the Vendor shall not be responsible to account or adjust for any current or prepaid rents or to make any other adjustments in favour of the Purchaser, other than for rent actually received by the Vendor. [**compare with paragraph 11 and use appropriate one**]

22. The Vendor shall not be responsible for the payment of, and there shall be no adjustment for, development levies, imposts or charges, local improvement charges, sewer charges or for any utility arrears or current utility accounts affecting the property to and including closing (and the Purchaser agrees to accept the property and to complete the purchase thereof subject to any such outstanding development levies, imposts or charges, local improvement charges, sewer charges or utility arrears or current unpaid utility accounts).

9F117
NOTICE OF SALE UNDER CHARGE/MORTGAGE

[See Para. 9.151]

TO: [chargor/mortgagor]

AND TO: The Parties shown on Schedule "A" attached hereto.

TAKE NOTICE that default has been made in payment of the moneys due under a certain charge/mortgage dated the _____ day of _____, _____ made

BETWEEN:

—[chargor/mortgagor]—

Chargor/Mortgagor

- and -

—[chargee/mortgagee]—

Chargee/Mortgagee

- and –

_____

Guarantor

- and -

_____

Consenting Spouse

on the security of ALL AND SINGULAR that certain parcel or tract of land and premises situate, lying and being in the _____ [city] _____ of _____ [municipality] _____ and being comprised of _____ [legal description] _____ registered in the _____ [registry office] _____ (No. _____) which charge/mortgage was registered on the day of _____, _____ in the _____ [registry office] _____ (No. _____) as Instrument No. _____ (the "Charge/Mortgage").

AND _____ [chargee/mortgagee] _____ hereby gives you notice that the amounts now due on the Charge/Mortgage for principal money, interest and costs, respectively, are as follows:

Principal money	_____	Interest as of
[date]	_____	
Cost of these	_____	
proceedings		
TOTAL	$_____	

AND UNLESS the said sums, together with interest thereon at the rate of _____% per annum calculated _____ and any further costs and disbursements incurred in these proceedings, are paid on or before the _____ day of _____, _____, [chargee/mortgagee] shall sell the property covered by the said Charge/Mortgage under the provisions contained in it.

THIS NOTICE is given to you as you appear to have an interest in the charged/mortgaged property and may be entitled to redeem the same.

DATED at _____, this _____ day of _____, _____.

—[chargee/mortgagee]—

By its solicitor and authorized agent
Joe Solicitor,
100 Bay Street, Suite 2000,
Toronto, Ontario

Per:_____
[solicitor for chargee/mortgagee]

9F118
STATUTORY DECLARATION OF CHARGEE (LAND TITLES ACT)

[See Para. 9.651]

IN THE MATTER OF _____ (legal description) _____.

AND IN THE MATTER OF a sale thereof under power of sale contained in Charge No. _____, made by _____ (chargor) to _____ (chargee), dated the _____ day of _____,_____ , and registered in the _____ (No. _____) on _____, _____.

I, _____, of the _____, in the _____, do solemnly declare that:

1. I am a _____, with _____ (chargee), the registered owner of Charge No. and, as such, have personal knowledge of the facts hereafter declared.

2. To the best of my knowledge and belief, money or moneys worth was actually advanced or supplied under the said Charge without _____ (chargee) having actual notice of any encumbrance registered or filed subsequent to the Charge.

3. To the best of my knowledge and belief, subsections 78(2) and 78(5) of the Construction Lien Act, R.S.O. 1990, c. C.30 do not give priority to any lien under the Act over Charge No. _____.

4. Default entitling _____ (chargee) to sell the land was made in respect of payment of Charge No. _____ on _____, _____ and the said Charge remained in default at the time of a sale under the said Charge was made.

5. The Charge remains in default as of the date hereof.

6. The Charge has priority over the following subsequent encumbrances affecting the same lands:
    (a) _____
    (b) _____ AND I MAKE this solemn declaration conscientiously believing it to be true and knowing that it is of the same force and effect as if made under oath.

DECLARED before me at the

_____ , in the _____, this

_____ day of _____, _____.

Per: _____

A Commissioner, etc.

9F119
STATUTORY DECLARATION OF SOLICITOR
(LAND TITLES ACT)

[See Para. 9.651]

IN THE MATTER OF _____ .

AND IN THE MATTER OF a sale thereof under power of sale contained in Charge No._____ , made by _____ (chargor) to _____ (chargee), dated the _____ day of _____ , _____ , and registered in the _____ (No. _____) on _____ , _____ .

    I, _____ (solicitor), of the City of Toronto, in the Municipality of Metropolitan Toronto, solicitor, do solemnly declare that:

1.   I am the solicitor herein for (chargee) the registered owner of Charge No. _____ , and as such have personal knowledge of the facts herein deposed to.

2.   _____ (chargee) has agreed to sell the property comprised in the Charge to _____ (purchaser).

3.   I have made or caused to be made a thorough search in the _____ (No. _____) and found no persons entitled to notice of exercising the power of sale other than the following who were served with notice as required by the Mortgages Act.

    (a)   _____

    (b)   _____

4.   In my opinion, the sale proceedings carried out by _____ , in exercise of the power of sale contained in said Charge No. _____ , are in compliance with Part III of the Mortgages Act, R.S.O. 1990, c. M.40, the terms of the Charge, the Farm Debt Review Act, and other relevant requirements of law.

    AND I MAKE this solemn declaration conscientiously believing it to be true and knowing that it is of the same force and effect as if made under oath.

DECLARED before me at the
_____ (city), this _____ day
of _____, _____.

A Commissioner, etc.

_____

9F120
STATUTORY DECLARATION AS TO SERVICE OF NOTICE OF SALE UNDER CHARGE (LAND TITLES ACT)

[See Para. 9.651]

IN THE MATTER OF title to _____, in the _____ of _____, in the _____ of _____.

AND IN THE MATTER OF a sale thereof under power of sale contained in the Charge No. _____ , made by _____ [mortgagor] to _____ [mortgagee] dated the day of _____, _____, and registered in the _____ (No. _____) of _____ [date], _____.

I,_____ , of the _____ of _____, in the _____ of _____, do solemnly declare that:

1. I did, on the _____ day of _____, _____ serve those parties set out on Schedule 1 hereto with a Notice of Sale under Charge, a true copy of which is annexed hereto and marked as Exhibit "A" by sending the same by registered mail in accordance with section 33 of the Mortgages Act, R.S.O. 1990, c. M.40.

2. The original Certificate of Post Office Registration in support thereof is hereto attached and marked as Exhibit "B".

_____ [If, for some reason spouse was not included with the parties served, include this paragraph]

3. I did, on the _____ day of _____, _____, personally serve _____, _____ [wife/husband] of the chargor, with a Notice of Sale under Charge, a true copy of which is annexed hereto and marked as Exhibit "A" by delivering to ad leaving the

same with the said _____ in accordance with section 33 of the Mortgages Act, R.S.O. 1990, c. M.40.

AND I MAKE this solemn declaration conscientiously believing it to be true and knowing that it is of the same force and effect as if made under oath.

DECLARED before me at the
_____ [city] of _____,in the
_____, [municipality] of
_____, this   day of
_____, _____.

_____

A Commissioner, etc.

9F121
DECLARATION OF MORTGAGEE

[See Para. 9.651]

CANADA

PROVINCE OF ONTARIO

JUDICIAL DISTRICT OF YORK

TO WIT:

IN THE MATTER OF title to (legal description) _____
AND IN THE MATTER OF a sale thereof under power of sale contained in a mortgage dated the _____ day of _____, _____, made by_____ , as mortgagor, _____, as mortgagee, registered in the _____ (No. _____) as Instrument No. _____.
AND IN THE MATTER OF a sale of the above-mentioned lands and premises by _____ (mortgagee).

I, _____ (mortgagee), of the _____, in the _____, do solemnly declare that:

1. I am _____ (position) with _____ (mortgagee) (the "Mortgagee") and, as such, have knowledge of the matters hereinafter declared.

2. Pursuant to the mortgage dated the _____ day of _____, _____, and registered in the _____ (No. ____) on the _____ day of _____, _____ as Instrument No. _____ (the "Mortgage") _____ (mortgagor) mortgaged the above referred to lands and premises to the Mortgagee.

3. The Mortgage has been in default since the _____ day of _____, _____, and has remained in default to the date hereof.

4. The Mortgage remained in default at the time when the Mortgagee entered into the agreement of purchase and sale of the above referred to lands and premises to _____ (purchaser).

5. There is presently owing on the Mortgage for principal money, interest, taxes, insurance premiums, appraisal fees and costs in excess of the sum of $_____, together with the costs and expenses of the above-mentioned sale.

6. The Mortgagee has not, nor has any person or persons on its behalf or as agent, received the moneys referred to in paragraph 5 hereof, or any security for the same, other than the Mortgage.

7. So far as I am aware, the Mortgagee has not received any written notice of any statutory lien against the above referred to lands and premises in favour of the Crown or any other public authority, nor, so far as I am aware, the Mortgagee has not received actual notice in writing of any other interest in the above referred to lands and premises other than those served with the notice of sale herein.

8. No action for foreclosure of the Mortgage has been commenced by the Mortgagee.

AND I MAKE this solemn declaration conscientiously believing it to be true and knowing that it is of the same force and effect as if made under oath and by virtue of the Canada Evidence Act.

DECLARED before me at the
_____ , in the _____, this
_____ day of _____, _____.

_____

A Commissioner, etc.

9F122
DECLARATION OF SOLICITOR
(REGISTRY)

[See. Para. 9.651]

IN THE MATTER OF title to (legal description) _____

CANADA

PROVINCE OF ONTARIO

JUDICIAL DISTRICT OF YORK

TO WIT:

AND IN THE MATTER OF a sale thereof under power of sale contained in a mortgage dated the _____ day of _____, _____, made by_____ , as mortgagor, and _____, as mortgagee, and registered in the _____ (No. _____) as Instrument No. _____.

AND IN THE MATTER OF a sale of the above-mentioned lands and premises by _____ (mortgagee).

I, (solicitor) _____, of the _____, in the _____, solicitor, do solemnly declare that:

1. I am the solicitor herein for (mortgagor) _____ and, as such, have knowledge of the matters herein declared.

2. Pursuant to the mortgage dated the _____ day of _____, _____, and registered in the _____ (No. _____) on the _____ day of _____, as Instrument No. _____ (the "Mortgage") (mortgagor) _____ mortgaged the above referred to lands and premises to (mortgagee) _____.

3. I have read over the material in connection with the sale of the above referred to lands and premises under the power of sale contained in the Mortgage and I am of the opinion that it complies with Part III of the Mortgages Act, R.S.O. 1990, c. M.40, and this statutory declaration is delivered pursuant to section 35 of the said Act.

AND I MAKE this solemn declaration conscientiously believing it to be true and knowing that it is of the same force and effect as if made under oath and by virtue of the Canada Evidence Act.

DECLARED before me at the
_____ , in the _____ , this
_____ day of _____ , _____ .

_____

A Commissioner, etc.

9F123
DECLARATION AS TO SERVICE

[See Para. 9.651]

CANADA

PROVINCE OF ONTARIO

JUDICIAL DISTRICT OF YORK

TO WIT:

IN THE MATTER OF title to
_____ , in the _____ of
_____ , in the _____ of
_____ .

AND IN THE MATTER OF a sale thereof under power of sale contained in a mortgage dated the _____ day of _____ , _____ , made by_____ , as mortgagor, and _____ , as mortgagee, and registered in the _____ (No. _____) as Instrument No. _____ .

AND IN THE MATTER OF a sale of the above-mentioned lands and premises by [mortgagee]._____ .

I, _____ , of the _____ of _____ , in the _____ of _____ , do solemnly declare that:

1.   I am [a secretary, a messenger] _____ in the employ of [law firm – Solicitor] _____, solicitors for [mortgagee] _____, and as such, have knowledge of the matters herein declared.

2.   I did, on the _____ day of ,_____ , _____ personally deposit in Her Majesty's Post Office, at [post office address] _____, of [number of envelopes sent by registered mail] _____ (_____) true copies of the Notice of Sale under Mortgage herein annexed as Exhibit "A" to this my declaration, the same being enclosed in fully prepaid registered envelopes addressed to the persons set out in Exhibit "B" hereto.

3.   Exhibit "B" to this my declaration is a photocopy of the Certificate of Post Office Registration for the said [number of envelopes sent by registered mail] _____ [8] _____ envelopes.

     AND I MAKE this solemn declaration conscientiously believing it to be true and knowing that it is of the same force and effect as if made under oath and by virtue of the Canada Evidence Act.

DECLARED before me at the
[city] _____ of _____, in the
[municipality] _____ of
_____ this   day of
_____, _____.

                                                    _____
                                                    [secretary/messenger]

A Commissioner, etc.

9F124
VENDOR'S DIRECTION RE: PAYMENT OF BALANCE DUE ON CLOSING

[See Para. 9.651]

DIRECTION

TO: John Smith

AND TO: Jane Counsel
           His solicitor herein

RE: XYZ Bank Sale to Smith -
         Parcel 10-1, Section 1-1,
         being Lot 10, Concession 1, City of Somewhere -
         123 Main Street, Somewhere

The undersigned hereby authorizes and directs you to make the balance of the money due on closing payable to its solicitor, _name of solicitor, in trust, or as he may otherwise in writing direct and this shall be your good and sufficient authority for so doing.

DATED at Toronto, this _____ day of _____, 1991.

XYZ BANK

Per:_____
Name:
Position:

Per:_____
Name:
Position:

9F125
VENDOR'S STATEMENT RE: SECTION 116 OF INCOME TAX ACT

[See Paras. 9.651 and 9.010]

TO: John Smith

AND TO: Jane Counsel
             His solicitor herein

RE: XYZ Bank Sale to Smith -
         Parcel 10-1, Section 1-1,
         being Lot 10, Concession 1, City of Somewhere -
         123 Main Street, Somewhere

SECTION 116 STATEMENT

The undersigned is not now, and will not be at the time of closing, a non-resident of Canada within the meaning of the Income Tax Act of Canada.

DATED at Toronto this   day of   , 1991.

XYZ BANK

Per:_____
Name:
Position:

Per:_____
Name:
Position:

9F126
VENDOR'S GENERAL UNDERTAKING

[See Para. 9.651]

TO: John Smith

AND TO: Jane Counsel
         His solicitor herein

RE:
PURCHASER	:	John Smith
VENDOR	:	XYZ BANK
ADDRESS	:	123 Main Street, Somewhere
DESCRIPTION	:	Lot 10, Concession 1
MUNICIPALITY	:	City of Somewhere
CLOSING DATE	:	June 1, 1991
FILE NUMBER	:	000-456

UNDERTAKING

In consideration of the closing of the above transaction, THE UNDERSIGNED undertakes and covenants as follows:

(a) To deliver vacant possession on closing (except if otherwise specified under the agreement of purchase and sale).

(b) To pay public utility rates, including hydro, water and gas accounts, if any, up to the date of closing.

(c) to pay all realty taxes in accordance with the statement of adjustments, and to re-adjust the statement of adjustments forthwith upon demand.

(d) To provide keys on closing.

DATED at   the   day of   , 1991.

           XYZ BANK

           Per:_____

           Name:

           Position:

Per:_____
Name:
Position:

9F127
VENDOR'S SOLICITOR'S REDIRECTION RE: PAYMENT OF BALANCE DUE ON CLOSING

[See Para. 9.651]

DIRECTION

TO: John Smith

AND TO: Jane Counsel
           His solicitor herein

RE: XYZ Bank Sale to Smith -
           Parcel 10-1, Section 1-1,
           being Lot 10, Concession 1, City of Somewhere -
           123 Main Street, Somewhere

_____

   The undersigned hereby authorizes and directs you to make the balance of the money due on closing payable as follows:

_____	=	$_____
_____	=	$_____
_____	=	$_____
_____	=	$_____

This shall be your good and sufficient authority for so doing.

DATED at Toronto, this   day of   , 1991.

_____
Joe Solicitor

9F128
PURCHASER'S UNDERTAKING TO READJUST

[See Para. 9.651]

UNDERTAKING

TO: XYZ BANK

AND TO: Joe Solicitor
His solicitor herein

RE: XYZ Bank Sale to Smith -
Parcel 10-1, Section 1-1,
being Lot 10, Concession 1, City of Somewhere -
123 Main Street, Somewhere

In consideration of the closing of the above-mentioned transaction and the receipt from you of a valid and registrable conveyance of the subject lands, the undersigned hereby undertakes as follows:

To re-adjust municipal taxes and other items in the Statement of Adjustments, if necessary.

DATED at   , this   day of   , 1991.

_____
John Smith

9F129
TRANSFER/DEED OF LAND (LAND TITLES SYSTEM)

[See Para. 9.651]

Transfer/Deed of Land

Form 1 — Land Registration Reform Act, 1984

A

(1) Registry ☐ Land Titles ☒	(2) Page 1 of ___ pages

(3) Property Identifier(s) Block ___ Property ___ — Additional See Schedule ☐

(4) Consideration

THREE HUNDRED THOUSAND -- 00/100 Dollars $ 300,000.00

(5) Description This is a Property Division ☐ Property Consolidation ☐

Parcel 10-1, Section 1-1,
City of Somewhere,
Municipality of Metropolitan Toronto.

New Property Identifiers — Additional See Schedule ☐

Executions — Additional See Schedule ☐

(6) This Document Contains	(a) Redescription New Easement Plan/Sketch ☐	(b) Schedule for Description ☐ Additional Parties ☐ Other ☒	(7) Interest/Estate Transferred Fee Simple

(8) Transferor(s) The transferor hereby transfers the land to the transferee and certifies that the transferor is at least eighteen years old and that:

This transfer is made pursuant to the power of sale contained in Charge/Mortgage No. LT22222 under Part III of the Mortgages Act.

Name(s)	Signature(s)	Date of Signature Y M D
	Per: Name: Position:	1991
We have authority to bind the Bank.	Per: Name: Position:	1991

(9) Spouse(s) of Transferor(s) I hereby consent to this transaction

Name(s)	Signature(s)	Date of Signature Y M D

(10) Transferor(s) Address for Service King & Bay, Toronto, Ontario

(11) Transferee(s)

	Date of Birth Y M D
SMITH, John	1950 01 01

(12) Transferee(s) Address for Service 321 Pleasant Avenue, Somewhere, Ontario

(13) Transferor(s) The transferor verifies that to the best of the transferor's knowledge and belief, this transfer does not contravene section 49 of the Planning Act, 1983.

Signature ___ Date of Signature Y M D ___ Signature ___ Date of Signature Y M D ___

Solicitor for Transferor(s) I have explained the effect of section 49 of the Planning Act, 1983 to the transferor and I have made inquiries of the transferor to determine that this transfer does not contravene that section and based on the information supplied by the transferor, to the best of my knowledge and belief, this transfer does not contravene that section. I am an Ontario solicitor in good standing.

Name and Address of Solicitor ___ Signature ___ Date of Signature Y M D ___

(14) Solicitor for Transferee(s) I have investigated the title to this land and to abutting land where relevant and I am satisfied that the title records reveal no contravention as set out in subclause 49 (21a) (c) (ii) of the Planning Act, 1983 and that to the best of my knowledge and belief this transfer does not contravene section 49 of the Planning Act 1983. I act independently of the solicitor for the transferor(s) and I am an Ontario solicitor in good standing.

Name and Address of Solicitor ___ Signature ___ Date of Signature Y M D ___

(15) Assessment Roll Number of Property	Cty 12	Mun 34	Map 567	Sub 890	Par 12340	Fees and Tax	
						Registration Fee	
(16) Municipal Address of Property 123 Main Street Somewhere, Ontario			**(17) Document Prepared by:** Joe Solicitor 100 Bay Street Suite 2000 Toronto, Ontario			Land Transfer Tax	
						Total	

* Form and Schedule reprinted with permission of Dye & Durham Co. Ltd.

SCHEDULE "A"

This transfer shall be deemed to include none of those implied covenants contained in Subsection 5(1) of the Land Registration Reform Act, R.S.O., 1990 c. L.4, but shall include only those covenants as are expressly set out as follows:

The transferor hereby covenants to and with the transferee and persons deriving title under the transferee that the transferor has not done anything whereby the land is or may be encumbered, except as the records of the land registry office disclose.

9F130
TRANSFER/DEED OF LAND (REGISTRY SYSTEM)

[See Para. 9.651]

Province of Ontario

Transfer/Deed of Land
Form 1 — Land Registration Reform Act, 1984

A

(1) Registry ☒ Land Titles ☐	(2) Page 1 of	pages

(3) Property Identifier(s)   Block   Property   Additional See Schedule ☐

(4) Consideration   THREE HUNDRED THOUSAND -------------- ------------------ 00/100 Dollars $ 300,000.00

(5) Description   This is a: Property Division ☐   Property Consolidation ☐

Lot 10, Concession 1,
City of Somewhere,
Municipality of Metropolitan Toronto.

New Property Identifiers   Additional See Schedule ☐

Executions   Additional See Schedule ☐

(6) This Document Contains   (a) Redescription New Easement Plan/Sketch ☐   (b) Schedule for Description ☐ Parties ☐ Other ☐   (7) Interest/Estate Transferred Fee Simple

(8) Transferor(s) The transferor hereby transfers the land to the transferee and certifies that the transferor is at least eighteen years old and that
This transfer is made pursuant to the power of sale contained in Charge/

Mortgage No. CA22222 under Part III of the Mortgages Act.

Name(s)	Signature(s)	Date of Signature Y M D
XYZ BANK	Per:	1991
	Name:	
	Position:	
	Per:	1991
We have authority	Name:	
to bind the Bank.	Position:	

(9) Spouse(s) of Transferor(s) I hereby consent to this transaction
Name(s)   Signature(s)   Date of Signature Y M D

(10) Transferor(s) Address for Service   King & Bay, Toronto, Ontario

(11) Transferee(s)   Date of Birth Y M D

SMITH, John   1950 01 01

(12) Transferee(s) Address for Service   321 Pleasant Avenue, Somewhere, Ontario

(15) Assessment Roll Number of Property   Cty 12 Mun 34 Map 567 Sub 890 Par 12340   Fees and Tax

(16) Municipal Address of Property	(17) Document Prepared by:		
123 Main Street Somewhere, Ontario	Joe Solicitor 100 Bay Street Suite 2000 Toronto, Ontario	Registration Fee	
		Land Transfer Tax	
		Total	

* Form and Schedules reprinted with permission of Dye & Durham Co. Ltd.

Schedule "A"
Land Registration Reform Act, 1984
Recitals for Deed Under Power of Sale (Registry)
(*Attach to Form 1*)

Province of Ontario

Schedule "A"
Land Registration Reform Act, 1984
Recitals for Deed Under Power of Sale (Registry)
(Attach to Form 1)

Page of

S

WHEREAS:

1. By a Mortgage dated the 2nd day of April 19 90 and registered in the Land Registry Office for the Registry Division of Toronto Boroughs (No. 64) as Instrument No. CA22222 on the 3rd day of April 19 90.

   Acme Inc.

   as Mortgagor

   did mortgage the lands herein to

   XYZ Bank

   as Mortgagee

   for securing payment of the sum of Two Hundred and Fifty Thousand ---------------- ----------------------- ($250,000.00) -------------------- 00/100 DOLLARS

   and interest as therein mentioned.

2. The Mortgagee, on default of payment under the said Mortgage for fifteen (15) days is entitled on thirty-five (35) days notice to sell the said lands.

3. Such default has been made in payment of the principal and interest secured by the said Mortgage and notice of exercising the power to sell the said lands has been duly given by the Mortgagee to all persons entitled thereto.

4. Such default has not been remedied and the time set forth in the notice of sale has expired.

5. Statutory Declarations setting forth the particulars of such default, the service of notice of sale and the sale proceedings have been deposited and registered in the said Land Registry Office as Instrument No. CA33333.

AND THEREFORE under and by virtue of the powers of sale contained in the said Mortgage, the said lands were sold to the Transferee.

In construing this document, the words "Mortgagor", "Mortgagee" and "Transferee" and all personal pronouns shall be read as the number and gender of the party or parties referred to herein requires and all necessary grammatical changes, as the content requires, shall be deemed to be made

FOR OFFICE USE ONLY

APRIL 1985

745

SCHEDULE "B"

This transfer shall be deemed to include none of those implied covenants contained in Subsection 5(1) of the Land Registration Reform Act, R.S.O., 1990 c. L.4, but shall include only those covenants as are expressly set out as follows:

The transferor hereby covenants to and with the transferee and persons deriving title under the transferee that the transferor has not done anything whereby the land is or may be encumbered, except as the records of the land registry office disclose.

9F131
DOCUMENT GENERAL RE-DEPOSIT (SECTION 99(1) REGISTRY ACT)

[See Para. 9.651]

* Form reprinted with permission of Dye & Durham Co. Ltd.

9F132
ACKNOWLEDGMENT OF JOINT REPRESENTATION

[See Para. 9.675]

ACKNOWLEDGMENT

The undersigned hereby acknowledge that they agreed to have the law firm of _____ represent all of them with respect to the negotiation and completion of the $1,800,000 loan being made by _____ Bank to _____ Inc., guaranteed by Jane Doe.

The undersigned further acknowledge that no information received by _____ in connection with this matter from any of them can be treated as confidential so far as the others are concerned and that if a conflict develops which cannot be resolved, _____ cannot continue to act for all of them and may have to withdraw completely.

DATED at Toronto this _____ day of _____, 19____.

_____ BANK

Per: _____

Per: _____

_____ INC.

Per: _____
Jane Doe, President

Signed in the presence of:

_____   _____
                                 Jane Doe

9F133
DEMAND PROMISSORY NOTE—FIXED RATE

[See Para. 9.687]

Amount: $_____   Dated: _____, 19____

FOR VALUE RECEIVED, the undersigned, _____ Inc. acknowledges itself indebted and promises to pay on demand to or to the order of _____ Bank and its successors and assigns (the "Lender") at the offices of the Lender at _____. Ontario or at such other place as the Lender shall in writing direct, the sum of _____ dollars ($_____) of lawful money of Canada, together with interest thereon at the rate of _____% per annum. Interest hereunder shall be calculated daily and payable monthly in arrears from the date hereof until payment in full, both before and after default and judgment, with interest on overdue interest at the same rate.

For the purposes of this Note, whenever interest is calculated on the basis of a year of 365 or 366 days, each rate of interest determined pursuant to such calculation expressed as an annual rate for the purposes of the Interest Act (Canada) is equivalent to such rate so determined, multiplied by the number of days in the calendar year with respect to which the same is to be ascertained and divided by 365 or 366, as the case may be. The parties further agree that for the purposes of the Interest Act (Canada), (i) the principle of deemed reinvestment of interest shall not apply to any interest calculation under this promissory note, and (ii) the rates of interest stipulated in this promissory note are intended to be nominal rates and not effective rates or yields.

Until demand payments of principal and interest hereunder shall be payable in blended payments in the following amounts on the following dates:

Number of Payments	Amounts	Frequency	Payment Initial	Final
23	$_____	Monthly	__ 15, 19____	__ 15, 19____
1	$_____	Once	__ 15, 19____	

Interest at the aforesaid rate shall be paid on the 15th day of each and every month in each and every year starting on _____15, 19____

Default in the payment of any principal or interest on the date when due hereunder shall at the option of the Lender, cause all amounts due hereunder to become immediately due and payable.

This promissory note evidences borrowing under and is collateral and subject to the terms of a Loan Agreement dated _____, 19____ made among the undersigned, the Lender and other third party Guarantors.

The undersigned hereby waives demand and presentment for payment, and notice of non-payment and notice of protest and dishonour of this note.

EXECUTED at _____ this _____ day of _____, 19____.

_____ INC.

Per: _____

c/s

Per: _____

9F134
DEMAND PROMISSORY NOTE—FLOATING RATE

[See Para. 9.687]

Amount: $ _____   Dated:_____, 19____

FOR VALUE RECEIVED, the undersigned, _____ Inc. acknowledges itself indebted and promises to pay on demand to or to the order of _____ Bank and its successors and assigns (the "Lender") at the offices of the Lender at _____, Toronto, Ontario or at such other place as the Lender shall in writing direct, the sum of _____ Dollars ($_____) of lawful money of Canada, together with interest thereon at the rate per annum equal to the Lender's Prime Rate plus two percent (2.0%). "Prime Rate" means at any time the prime lending rate of interest expressed as a rate per annum which the Lender establishes at its head office in Toronto, Ontario, as the reference rate of interest it will charge at such time for demand loans in Canadian dollars to its Canadian customers and which it refers to as its "prime rate". Interest hereunder shall be calculated daily and payable monthly in arrears from the date hereof until payment in full, both before and after default and judgment, with interest on overdue interest at the same rate.

For the purposes of this Note, whenever interest is calculated on the basis of a year of 365 or 366 days, each rate of interest determined pursuant to such calculation expressed as an annual rate for the purposes of the Interest Act (Canada) is equivalent to such rate so determined, multiplied by the number of days in the calendar year with respect to which the same is to be ascertained and divided by 365 or 366, as the case may be. The parties further agree that for the purposes of the Interest Act (Canada), (i) the principle of deemed reinvestment of interest shall not apply to any interest calculation under this promissory note, and (ii) the rates of interest stipulated in this promissory note are intended to be nominal rates and not effective rates of yields.

Until demand payments of principal and interest hereunder shall be payable in blended payments in the following amounts on the following dates:

Number of Payments	Amounts	Frequency	Payment Initial	Final
23	$_____	Monthly	__ 15, 19____	__ 15, 19____
1	$_____	Once	__ 15, 19____	

Interest at the aforesaid rate shall be paid on the 15th day of each and every month in each and every year starting on _____15, 19____

Default in the payment of any principal or interest on the date when due hereunder shall at the option of the Lender, cause all amounts due hereunder to become immediately due and payable.

This promissory note evidences borrowing under and is collateral and subject to the terms of a Loan Agreement dated _____, 19____ made among the undersigned, the Lender and other third party Guarantors.

The undersigned hereby waives demand and presentment for payment, and notice of non-payment and notice of protest and dishonour of this note.

EXECUTED at _____ this _____ day of _____, 19_____.

_____ INC.

per: _____

c/s

per: _____

9F135
GENERAL SECURITY AGREEMENT

[See Para. 9.688]

THIS AGREEMENT made as of the _____ day of _____, 19____

B E T W E E N:

_____ BANK, a Canadian chartered bank

(hereinafter called the "Bank")

OF THE FIRST PART

and

PURCHASER INC., a corporation incorporated under the laws of the Province of Ontario

(herein called the "Borrower")

OF THE SECOND PART

THIS AGREEMENT WITNESSES that, in consideration of the premises and other good and valuable consideration, the Borrower agrees with the Bank as follows:

ARTICLE 1
INTERPRETATION

1.1 Defined Terms. In this agreement, unless there is something in the context or subject matter inconsistent therewith,

"Accounts" means all debts, amounts, claims and moneys which now are, or which may at any time hereafter be, due or owing to or owed by the Borrower, whether or not earned by performance excluding, to the extent that an assignment in favour of the Bank is restricted by law, any such debts, amounts, claims and moneys due from the Government of Canada or any department or agency thereof or any Crown corporation; all securities, mortgages, bills, notes and other documents now held or owned, or which may be hereafter taken, held or owned, by or on behalf of the Borrower, in respect of the said debts, amounts, claims and moneys or any part thereof; and all books, documents and papers recording, evidencing or relating to the said debts, amounts, claims and moneys or any part thereof;

"Banking Day" means any day other than a Saturday or a Sunday on which banks generally are open for business in Toronto, Ontario;

"Chattel Paper" means all present and future agreements made between the Borrower as secured party and others which evidence both a monetary obligation and a security interest in or a lease of specific goods;

"Collateral" means all undertaking, property and assets of the Borrower, now owned or hereafter acquired and any proceeds from the sale or other disposition thereof, all of which is further described, without limitation, all Accounts, Inventory, Equipment, Intangibles, Documents of Title, Money, Chattel Paper, Instruments, Securities, Documents, Proceeds, and Leaseholds;

"Credit Agreement" means the agreement made as of _____, 19____ between the Borrower, _____, and the Bank, as the same may be amended, modified, supplemented or replaced from time to time, and pursuant to which the Bank established certain credit facilities in favour of the Borrower;

"Documents" means all documents, including, without limitation, all books, invoices, letters, papers and other records, in any form evidencing or relating to the Collateral, all of which are herein called the "Documents";

"Documents of Title" means any writing now or hereafter owned by the Borrower that purports to be issued by or addressed to a bailee and purports to cover such goods and chattels in the bailee's possession as are identified or fungible portions of an identified mass, whether such goods and chattels are Inventory or Equipment, and which writing is treated in the ordinary course of business as establishing that the person in possession of such writing is entitled to receive, hold and dispose of the said writing and the goods and chattels it covers, and further, whether such writing is negotiable in form or otherwise, including bills of lading and warehouse receipts;

"Equipment" means all equipment now owned or hereafter acquired by the Borrower, including, without limitation, all machinery, fixtures, plant, tools, furniture, chattels, vehicles of any kind or description including, without limitation, motor vehicles, parts, accessories installed in or affixed or attached to any of the foregoing, all drawings, specifications, plans and manuals relating thereto, and any other tangible personal property which is not Inventory and all items described in Schedule "A" hereto;

"Event of Default" shall have the meaning ascribed thereto in Section 5 hereof and in the Credit Agreement;

"Instruments" means all present and future bills, notes and cheques (as such are defined pursuant to the Bills of Exchange Act (Canada)) of the Borrower, and all other writings of the Borrower that evidence a right to the payment of money and are of a type that in the ordinary course of business are transferred by delivery without any necessary endorsement or assignment, and all letters of credit and advices of credit of the Borrower provided that such letters of credit and advices of credit state that they must be surrendered upon claiming payment thereunder;

"Inventory" means all goods or chattels now or hereinafter forming the inventory of the Borrower including, without limitation, the goods, merchandise, raw materials, work in process, finished goods, goods held for sale or resale or lease or that have been leased or that are to be, or have been, furnished under a contract of service, and goods used in or procured for packing or packaging;

"Intangibles" means all intangible property now owned or hereafter acquired by the Borrower and which is not Accounts including, without limitation, all contractual rights, goodwill, patents, trademarks, trade names, copyrights and other intellectual property of the Borrower and all other choses in action of the Borrower of every kind, whether due or owing at the present time or hereafter to become due or owing;

"Leaseholds" subject to Section 2.3, all leases, now owned or hereafter acquired by the Borrower as tenant (whether oral or written) or any agreement therefor;

"Money" means all money now or hereafter owned by the Borrower, whether such money is authorized or adopted by the Parliament of Canada as part of its currency or by any foreign government as part of its currency;

"Obligations" means the aggregate of all indebtedness, obligations and liabilities of the Borrower to the Bank, whether incurred prior to, at the time of, or subsequent to the execution hereof, including extensions and renewals, and including, without limitation: advances to the Borrower; letters of credit and letters of guarantee issued by the Bank on behalf of the Borrower, whether or not drawn upon; bankers' acceptances of the Borrower which have been accepted by the Bank; tender cheques certified by the Bank on behalf of the Borrower, whether or not negotiated; obligations or liabilities of the Borrower to third parties financed or guaranteed by the Bank; all interest payable by the Borrower to the Bank; obligations or liabilities of the

Borrower under any present or future guarantee by the Borrower of the payment or performance or both of the debts, obligations or liabilities of a third party to the Bank; and debts, obligations or liabilities of the Borrower under any agreement with the Bank including, without limitation, this agreement, the Credit Agreement and any promissory note, debt obligation or any other agreement whatsoever, whether it or they be in writing;

"PPSA" means the Personal Property Security Act (Ontario), as amended from time to time, and any regulations thereto;

"Prime Rate" means the rate of interest per annum charged by the Bank to its customers in Toronto, Ontario for loans of Canadian dollars, as the same is adjusted from time to time.

Proceeds" means all property in any form derived directly or indirectly from any dealing with the Collateral including, without limitation, property that indemnifies or compensates for the expropriation, destruction, or damage of the Collateral or the proceeds therefrom and all proceeds of proceeds;

"Securities" means all present and future securities held by the Borrower, including shares, options, rights, warrants, joint venture interests in limited partnerships, trust units, bonds, debentures and al other documents which constitute evidence of a share, participation or other interest of the Borrower in property or in an enterprise or which constitute evidence of an obligation of the issuer; including, without limitation, an uncertificated security within the meaning of Part VI (Investment Securities) of the Business Corporation Act (Ontario) and all substitutions therefor and dividends and income derived therefrom;

1.2 Other Usages. References to "this agreement", "hereof", "herein", "hereto" and like references refer to this General Security Agreement and not to any particular Article, Section or other subdivision of this agreement.

1.3 Plural and Singular. Where the context so requires, the words importing the singular number shall include the plural and vice versa.

1.4 Headings. The division of this agreement into Articles and Sections and the insertion of headings in this agreement are for convenience of reference only and shall not affect the construction or interpretation of this agreement.

1.5 Currency. Unless otherwise specified herein, all statements of or references to dollar amounts in this agreement shall mean lawful money of Canada.

1.6 Applicable Law. This agreement and all documents delivered pursuant hereto shall be governed by and construed and interpreted in accordance with the laws of the Province of Ontario and the laws of Canada applicable therein and the parties hereto do hereby attorn to the exclusive jurisdiction of the courts of the Province of Ontario.

1.7 Prohibited Provisions. In the event that any provision or any part of any provision hereof is deemed to be invalid by reason of the operation of any law or by reason of the interpretation placed thereon by a court, this agreement shall be construed as not containing such provision or such part of such provision and the invalidity of such provision or such part shall not affect the validity of any other provision or the remainder of such provision hereof, and all other provisions hereof which are otherwise lawful and valid shall remain in full force and effect.

1.8 Time of the Essence. Time shall in all respects be of the essence of this agreement.

1.9 Schedules. Each and every one of the schedules which is referred to in this agreement and attached to this agreement shall form a part of this agreement.

ARTICLE 2
SECURITY INTEREST

2.1 Grant of Security Interest. As general and continuing security for the payment and performance of all Obligations, the Borrower hereby:

(a)   grants to the Bank a security interest in the Collateral excluding the Accounts; and

(b)   assigns, transfers and sets over the Bank all Accounts.

Whenever used elsewhere in this agreement, the expression "security interest" refers to the security interest created in (a) above and/or the assignment created in (b) above, as the context may require or permit.

2.2 Attachment of Security Interest. The parties hereby agree that they intend the security interest to attach to the Collateral upon execution of this agreement.

2.3 Exception re: Leaseholds and Contractual Rights. The last day of the term of any lease, sublease or agreement therefor is specifically excepted from the security interest created by this agreement, but the Borrower agrees to stand possessed of such last day in trust for such person as the Bank may direct and the Borrower shall assign and dispose thereof in accordance with such direction. To the extent that the security interest created by this agreement in any contractual rights (other than Accounts) would constitute a breach or cause the acceleration of such contract, to which the Borrower is a party, said security interest shall not be granted hereunder but the Borrower shall hold its interest therein in trust for the Bank, and shall grant a security interest in such contractual rights to the Bank forthwith upon obtaining the appropriate consents to the attachment of said security interest.

ARTICLE 3
COVENANTS OF THE BORROWER

3.1 Covenants. The Borrower hereby covenants and agrees with the Bank as follows:

(a)　The Borrower agrees to promptly notify the Bank in writing of the acquisition by the Borrower of any personal property which is not of the nature or type described by the definition of Collateral, and the Borrower agrees to execute and deliver at its own expense from time to time amendments to this agreement or additional security agreements as may be reasonably required by the Bank, in order that a security interest shall be granted and shall attach to such personal property.

(b)　The Borrower shall prevent the Collateral from becoming an accession to any personal property not subject to the security interest created by this agreement, or becoming affixed to any real property.

(c)　The Borrower shall deliver to the Bank from time to time as the same are acquired by the Borrower all items of Collateral comprising Chattel Paper, Instruments, Securities and those Document of Title which are negotiable.

(d)　The Borrower shall use its best efforts to obtain a written agreement from each landlord of the Borrower in favour of the Bank and in form and substance satisfactory to the Bank, whereby such landlord:

(i)　agrees to give notice to the Bank of any default by the Borrower under the lease and a reasonable opportunity to cure such default prior to the exercise of any remedies by the landlord; and

(ii)　acknowledges the security interest created by this agreement and the right of the Bank to enforce the security interest created by this agreement in priority of any claim of such landlord.

3.2 Performance of Covenants by the Bank. The Bank may, in its sole discretion and upon notice to the Borrower, perform any covenant of the Borrower under this agreement that the Borrower fails to perform and that the Bank is capable of performing, including any covenant the performance of which requires the payment of money, provided that the Bank will not be obligated to perform any such covenant on behalf of the Borrower and no such performance by the Bank will require the Bank further to perform the Borrower's covenants nor operate as a derogation of the rights and remedies of the Bank under this agreement.

ARTICLE 4
DEALING WITH COLLATERAL

4.1 General Restrictions. Except as specifically permitted herein or in the Credit Agreement, the Borrower shall not, without the prior written consent of the Bank:

(a)   sell, lease or otherwise dispose of the Collateral or any part thereof;

(b)   release, surrender or abandon possession of the Collateral or any part thereof;

(c)   move or transfer the Collateral or any part thereof from its present location as specified in Schedule "B" hereto; or

(d)   enter into or grant, create, assume or suffer to exist any mortgage, charge, hypothec, assignment, pledge, lien or other security interest or encumbrance affecting any of the Collateral.

4.2 Release by the Bank. The Bank, may at its discretion, at any time release from the security interest created by this agreement any part or parts of the Collateral or any other security or any surety for the Obligations either with or without sufficient consideration therefor without thereby releasing any other part of the Collateral or any person from this agreement.

4.3 Proceeds Held in Trust. All Proceeds that are monies collected or received by the Borrower will be received by the Borrower in trust for the Bank and will be forthwith paid to the Bank. The Bank shall not exercise its rights under this Section, and the Borrower's trust obligations under this Section need not be complied with, unless such Proceeds arise from a disposition of Collateral which is not permitted hereunder or unless and until the security hereby constituted becomes enforceable.

ARTICLE 5
DEFAULT AND ENFORCEMENT

5.1 Enforceability of Security. The security hereby constituted shall become enforceable in each and every one of the following events:

(a) if the Borrower defaults (subject to applicable grace periods) in payment or performance of any of the Obligations; or

(b) if an Event of Default occurs as specified in the Credit Agreement; or

(c) if the Borrower ceases to carry on business, makes a sale in bulk of its assets, is adjudged bankrupt, makes an assignment in bankruptcy, makes a proposal or plan of arrangement with its creditors, or if any of its creditors seize its assets; or

(d) there is a change in control of the voting stock of the Borrower from that now held on the Borrower amalgamates without the prior written consent of the Lender; or the Borrower is in default of its obligation to any of its other creditors; or

(e) if the Bank in good faith believes and has commercially reasonable grounds to believe that the prospect of payment or performance of the Obligations is or is about to be impaired or that the Collateral is or is about to be placed in jeopardy.

5.2 Remedies. At any time after the happening of any event by which the security hereby constituted becomes enforceable, the Bank shall have the following rights, powers and remedies:

(a) to appoint any person to be an agent or any person to be a receiver, manager or receiver and manager (herein called the "Receiver") of the Collateral and to remove any Receiver so appointed and to appoint another if the Bank so desires; it being agreed that any Receiver appointed pursuant to the provisions of this agreement shall have all of the powers of the Bank hereunder, and in addition, shall have the power to carry on the business of the Borrower;

(b) to make payments to parties having prior charges or encumbrances on the Collateral;

(c) to enter onto any premises where the Collateral may be located;

(d) to take possession of all or any part of the Collateral and any premises where such Collateral is located with power to exclude the Borrower, its agents and its servants from such Collateral and such premises;

(e) to preserve, protect and maintain the Collateral and make such repairs to, replacements thereof and additions thereto as the Bank shall deem advisable;

(f) to enjoy and exercise all powers necessary or incidental to the performance of all functions provided for in this agreement including, without limitation, the power to purchase on credit, the power to borrow in the Borrower's name or in the name of the Receiver and to advance its own money to the Borrower at such rates of interest as it may deem reasonable, provided that the Receiver shall borrow money only with the prior consent of the Bank, and to grant security interests in the Collateral in priority to the security interest created by this agreement, as security for the money so borrowed;

(g) to sell, lease or dispose of all or any part of the Collateral whether by public or private sale or lease or otherwise and on any terms, so long as every aspect of the disposition is commercially reasonable, including without limitation, terms that provide time for payment on credit; provided that

   (i) the Bank or the Receiver will not be required to sell, lease or dispose of the Collateral, but may peaceably and quietly take, hold, use, occupy, possess and enjoy the Collateral without molestation, eviction, hindrance or interruption by the Borrower or any other person or persons whomever, for such period of time as is commercially reasonable;

   (ii) the Bank or the Receiver may convey, transfer and assign to a purchaser or purchasers the title to any of the Collateral so sold; and

   (iii) subject to Section 5.8, the Borrower will be entitled to be credited with the actual proceeds of any such sale, lease or other disposition only when such proceeds are received by the Bank or the Receiver in cash;

(h) to enjoy and exercise all of the rights and remedies of a secured party under the PPSA;

(i) to dispose of all or any part of the Collateral in the condition in which it was on the date possession of it was taken, or after any commercially reasonable repair, processing or preparation for disposition;

(j) to sell or otherwise dispose of any part of the Collateral without giving any notice whatsoever where:

   (i) the Collateral is perishable;

   (ii) the Bank or the Receiver believes on reasonable grounds that the Collateral will decline speedily in value;

(iii) the Collateral is of a type customarily sold on a recognized market;

(iv) the cost of care and storage of the Collateral is disproportionately large relative to its value;

(v) every person entitled by law to receive a notice of disposition consents in writing to the immediate disposition of the Collateral; or

(vi) the Receiver disposes of the Collateral in the course of the Borrower's business;

(k) to notify the account debtors or obligors under any Accounts of the assignment of such Accounts to the Bank and to direct such account debtors or obligors to make payment of all amounts due or to become due to the Borrower thereunder directly to the Bank, and to give valid and binding receipts and discharges therefor and in respect thereof and, upon such notification and at the expense of the Borrower, to enforce collection of any such Accounts, and to adjust, settle or compromise the amount or payment thereof, in the same manner and to the same extent as the Borrower might have done;

(l) to commence, continue or defend proceedings in any court of competent jurisdiction in the name of the Bank, the Receiver or the Borrower for the purpose of exercising any of the rights, powers and remedies set out in this Section, including the institution of proceedings for the appointment of a receiver, manager or receiver and manager of the Collateral; and

(m) at the sole option of the Bank, provided notice is given in the manner required by the PPSA to the Borrower and to any other person to whom the PPSA requires notice to be given, to elect to retain all or any part of the Collateral in satisfaction of the Obligations.

5.3 Special Rules re Accounts. After the security hereby constituted becomes enforceable,

(a) all Money or other form of payment received by the Borrower in respect of the Accounts shall be received in trust for the benefit of the Bank hereunder, shall be segregated from other funds of the Borrower and shall be forthwith paid over to the Bank in the same form as so received (with any necessary endorsement) to be held as cash collateral and applied as provided by Section 5.8; and

(b) the Borrower shall not adjust, settle or compromise the amount or payment of any Accounts, or release wholly or partly any account debtor or obligor thereof, or allow any credit or discount thereon.

5.4 Receiver as Agent. The Receiver shall be deemed to be the agent of the Borrower for the purpose of establishing liability for the acts or omissions of the Receiver and the Bank shall not be liable for such acts or omissions and, without restricting the generality of the foregoing, the Borrower hereby irrevocably authorizes the Bank to give instructions to the Receiver relating to the performance of its duties as set out herein.

5.5 Expenses of Enforcement. The Borrower shall pay to the Receiver the remuneration of the Receiver and all costs and expenses (including, without limitation, legal fees and disbursements on a solicitor and his own client basis) properly incurred by the Receiver pursuant to its appointment and the exercise of its powers hereunder, and shall pay to the Bank and the Receiver as required all amounts of money (including interest thereon) borrowed or advanced by either of them pursuant to the powers set out herein, and the obligations of the Borrower to the Bank and the Receiver pursuant to this Section 5.5 shall be payable on demand and shall bear interest at an annual rate equal to the Prime Rate plus three percent (3%), which interest shall be calculated and compounded monthly and payable on demand.

5.6 Indulgences and Releases. Either the Bank or the Receiver may grant extensions of time and other indulgences, take and give up securities, accept compositions, grant releases and discharges, release any part of the Collateral to third parties and otherwise deal with the Borrower, debtors of the Borrower, sureties and others and with the Collateral and other security as the Bank or the Receiver may see fit without prejudice to the Obligations or the right of the Bank and the Receiver to repossess, hold, collect and realize the Collateral.

5.7 No Liability for Failure to Exercise Remedies. The Bank and the Receiver shall not be liable or accountable to the Borrower or to any other person for any failure to exercise any of the rights, powers and remedies set out in Section 5.2, and shall not be bound to commence, continue or defend proceedings for the purpose of preserving or protecting any rights of the Bank, the Receiver, the Borrower or any other party in respect of the same.

5.8 Proceeds of Disposition. Subject to the claims, if any, of the prior secured creditors of the Borrower, all moneys received by the Bank or by the Receiver pursuant to Section 5.2 shall be applied as follows:

    (a)   first, in payment of all costs and expenses incurred by the Bank in the exercise of all or any of the powers granted to it under this agreement and in payment of all of the remuneration of the Receiver and all costs and expenses properly incurred by the Receiver in the exercise of all or any of the powers granted to it under this agreement, including, without limitation, the remuneration, costs and expenses referred to in Section 5.5;

(b) second, in payment of all amounts of money borrowed or advanced by either of the Bank or the Receiver pursuant to the powers set out in this agreement and any interest thereon;

(c) third, in payment of the Obligations, provided that if there are not sufficient moneys to pay all of the Obligations, the Bank may apply the moneys available to such part or parts thereof as the Bank, in its sole discretion, may determine; and

(d) fourth, in payment of any surplus in accordance with applicable law.

5.9 Borrower Liable for Deficiency. If the monies received by the Bank or the Receiver pursuant to Section 5.2 are not sufficient to pay the claims set out in Section 5.8, the Borrower shall immediately pay the Bank the amount of such deficiency.

5.10 Restriction on Borrower. Upon the Bank taking possession of the collateral or the appointment of a Receiver, all the powers, functions, rights and privileges of the Borrower or any officer, director, servant or agent of the Borrower with respect to the Collateral shall, to the extent permitted by law, be suspended unless specifically continued by the written consent of the Bank; however, all other powers, functions, rights and privileges of the Borrower or any officer, director, servant or agent of the Borrower shall be unaffected by such events.

5.11 Rights Cumulative. All rights and remedies of the Bank set out in this agreement shall be cumulative and no right or remedy contained herein is intended to be exclusive but each shall be in addition to every other right or remedy contained herein or in any existing or future security document or now or hereafter existing at law or in equity or by statute. The taking of a judgment or judgments with respect to any of the Obligations shall not operate as a merger of any of the covenants contained in this agreement.

5.12 Care by the Bank. The Bank shall be deemed to have exercised reasonable care in the custody and preservation of any of the Collateral in the Bank's possession if it takes such action for that purpose as the Borrower requests in writing, but failure of the Bank to comply with any such request shall not be deemed to be (or to be evidence of) a failure to exercise reasonable care, and no failure of the Bank to preserve or protect any rights with respect to such Collateral against prior parties, or to do any act with respect to the preservation of such Collateral not so requested by the Borrower, shall be deemed a failure to exercise reasonable care in the custody or preservation of such Collateral.

5.13 Standards of Sale. Without prejudice to the ability of the Bank to dispose of the Collateral in any manner which is commercially reasonable, the Borrower acknowledges that a disposition of Collateral by the Bank which takes place substantially in accordance with the following provisions shall be deemed to be commercially reasonable:

    (a)   Collateral may be disposed of in whole or in part;

    (b)   the purchaser or lessee of such Collateral may be a customer of the Bank;

    (c)   the disposition may be for cash or credit, or part cash and part credit; and

    (d)   the Bank may establish a reserve bid in respect of all or any portion of the Collateral.

5.14 Application by Borrower re: Receiver. The Borrower hereby irrevocably waives its right to make an application to any court with respect to the appointment, powers or remuneration of the Receiver.

ARTICLE 6
GENERAL

6.1 Waiver. Any breach by the Borrower of any of the provisions contained in this agreement or any default by the Borrower in the observance or performance of any covenant or condition required to be observed or performed by the Borrower hereunder, may only be waived by the Bank in writing, provided that no such waiver by the Bank shall extend to or be taken in any manner to affect any subsequent breach or default or the rights resulting therefrom.

6.2 The Bank as Attorney. The Borrower hereby irrevocably appoints the Bank and any person further designated by the Bank to be the attorney of the Borrower for and in the name of the Borrower to execute and do any deeds, documents, transfers, demands, assignments, assurances, consents and things which the Borrower is obliged to sign, execute or do hereunder and, after the happening of any event by which the security hereby constituted becomes enforceable, to commence, continue and defend any proceedings authorized to be taken hereunder and generally to use the name of the Borrower in the exercise of all or any of the powers hereby conferred on the Bank.

6.3 Further Assurances. The Borrower shall do, execute, acknowledge and deliver or cause to be done, executed, acknowledged and delivered, such further acts, deeds, mortgages, transfers and assurances as the Bank shall reasonably require for the better assuring, charging, assigning and conferring unto the Bank a security interest in the Collateral or property intended to be charged hereunder, or which the Borrower may hereafter become bound to charge in favour of the Bank, for the purpose of accomplishing and effecting the intention of this agreement.

6.4 Continuing Security. The security interest constituted hereby shall be deemed to be a continuing security for the Obligations until all of the Obligations from time to time are paid and performed in full and any and all commitments of the Bank in favour of the Borrower have been cancelled under the Credit Agreement and otherwise.

6.5 No Obligation to Advance. Neither the execution nor delivery of this agreement shall obligate the Bank to advance any moneys to the Borrower.

6.6 Consumer Goods. Notwithstanding any other clause in this agreement, in no event shall goods that are used or acquired for use primarily for personal, family or household purposes form part of the Collateral.

6.7 Notices. All notices and other communications provided for herein shall be in writing and shall be personally delivered to an officer or other responsible employee of the addressee or sent by facsimile, charges prepaid, at or to the applicable address or telefacsimile number, as the case may be, of the party set opposite its name below or at or to such other address or addresses or telefacsimile number or numbers as either party may from time to time designate to the other party in such manner. Any communication which is personally delivered as aforesaid shall be deemed to have been validly and effectively given on the date of such delivery if such date is a Banking Day and such delivery was made during normal business hours of the recipient; otherwise, it should be deemed to have been validly and effectively given on the Banking Day next following such date of delivery. Any communication which is transmitted by telefacsimile as aforesaid shall be deemed to have been validly and effectively given on the date of transmission if such date is a Banking Day and such transmission was made during normal business hours of the recipient; otherwise, it shall be deemed to have been validly and effectively given on the Banking Day next following such date of transmission.

In the case of the Borrower:

_____

_____

_____

In the case of the Bank:

_____

_____

_____

6.8 Assignment. The Bank may assign or transfer this agreement, any of its rights hereunder or any part thereof.

6.9 Successors and Assigns. This agreement shall enure to the benefit of the Bank and its successors and assigns and shall be binding upon the Borrower and its successors and assigns.

6.10 Entire Agreement. This agreement and the agreements referred to herein and any document, agreement or instrument delivered pursuant to such agreements constitute the entire agreement between the parties hereto and supersede any prior agreements, undertakings, declarations, representations and undertakings, both written and verbal, in respect of the subject matter hereof.

6.11 Receipt of Copy of Agreement. The Borrower hereby acknowledges receipt of an executed copy of this agreement.

IN WITNESS WHEREOF the Borrower has executed this agreement.

_____ BANK

per: _____

per: _____ c/s

PURCHASER INC.

per: _____

per: _____ c/s

SCHEDULE "A"
LIST OF EQUIPMENT

NB: Section 11 of the PPSA regarding attachment and sufficient descriptions.

Schedule B"
LOCATIONS OF COLLATERAL

9F136
SAMPLE P.P.S.A. REGISTRATION FOR G.S.A.

[See Para. 9.688]

9F136:1
ELECTRONICALLY PRODUCED DRAFT AND
VERIFICATION STATEMENT

OPPSR MANAGEMENT SYSTEM (MT01)	1c00001713-01
May 7, 1997 at 11:21AM	DRAFTED

F I N A N C I N G   S T A T E M E N T

REGISTRATION ACT	REGISTRATION PERIOD	CAUTION FILING
PPSA	5 Year(s)	[ ]

DEBTORS

Business
Purchaser Inc.   Corp No. :
123 Main Street
Toronto   ON
M5H 3S1

SECURED PARTIES

Big Bank
123 Main   Street
Toronto   ON
M4C 1S9

COLLATERAL

CONSUMER GOODS	INVENTORY	EQUIPMENT	ACCOUNTS	OTHER	VEHICLES INCLUDED
[ ]	[√]	[√]	[√]	[√]	[√]

PRINCIPAL AMOUNT SECURED   MATURITY DATE

* * * * * END OF FINANCING STATEMENT * * * * *

SUMMARY OF FINANCE STATEMENT
State : DRAFTED

Statement Was Set To Drafted : MAY 7,1997 at 11:21AM by BABE

Your Reference Number   : 1234 - 003   JEB
Charge Customer   : NO
Bill Secured Party   : YES   1046   Big Bank

POST REGISTRATION SEARCH
will be performed on the following:

BUSINESS Debtor Name   : Purchaser Inc.

Approved By : _____

Financing Statement   . . . Last Page . . .   Page 1

```
OPPSR MANAGEMENT SYSTEM (MT01)                          1c00001713-01
May 8, 1997 at 11:41AM                                  REGISTERED
```

F I N A N C I N G   S T A T E M E N T

REGISTRATION NUMBER	FILE NUMBER	EXPIRY DATE
970507184115294238	830615472	PPR: May 7, 2002
		OPPSR: May 7, 2002

	REGISTRATION ACT	REGISTRATION PERIOD	CAUTION FILING
1c·01·01	PPSA	5 Year(s)	[ ]

DEBTORS

```
Business
1c·01·03 Purchaser Inc.                        Corp No. :
1c·01·04 123 Main Street
         Toronto          ON
         M5H 3S1
```

SECURED PARTIES

```
1c·01·08 Big Bank
1c·01·09 123 Main     Street
         Toronto          ON
         M4C 1S9
```

COLLATERAL

	CONSUMER GOODS	INVENTORY	EQUIPMENT	ACCOUNTS	OTHER	VEHICLES INCLUDED
1c·01·10	[ ]	[√]	[√]	[√]	[√]	[√]

PRINCIPAL AMOUNT SECURED	MATURITY DATE

* * * * * END OF FINANCING STATEMENT * * * * *

SUMMARY OF FINANCE STATEMENT
State : REGISTERED

```
Statement Was Transmitted    : MAY  7,1997 at  6:41PM by BELINDA

Your Reference Number        : 1234 - 003    JEB
Charge Customer              : NO
Bill Secured Party           : YES   1046    Big Bank
Registration Billing Amount  : $45.70
```

```
Financing Statement         . . . Last Page . . .           Page  1
```

VERIFICATION STATEMENT/ETAT DE VERIFICATION

REG UNDER/T. ENREG	REG PERIOD/PERIODE	CAUTION FILING/AVERTIS
Personal Property Security Act	5	[ ]
REG NUM/NO ENREGIST	REF FILE NUM/NO DE REFERENCE	EXPIRY DATE/DATE D'EXPIRATION
9705071841152942388	830615472	7 MAY 2002

Correcting: REG NUM/NO ENREGIST 970507184115294238

DEBTORS/DEBITEUR
CORPORATION NUMBER

Purchaser Inc.
123 Main Street
Toronto ON M5H 3S1

SECURED PARTIES/CREANCIER GARANTI

Big Bank
123 Main   Street
Toronto ON M4C 1S9

COLLATERAL/BIENS GREVES

CONS GOODS/BIENS CONS	INVTRY/STOCK	EQUIP/MATER	ACCTS/COMPT	OTHER/AUTRE	MV INCL/VA INCLUS
[ ]	[√]	[√]	[√]	[√]	[√]

AMOUNT/MONTANT   DATE OF MATURITY/DATE ECHEANCE

AGENT/AGENT

Miller Thomson
20 Queen Street West, Box 27, Suite 2500
Toronto, ON M5H 3S1

```
*  *  *  *  *  END OF VERIFICATION STATEMENT  *  *  *  *  *
*  *  *  *  *  FIN DE L'ETAT DE VERIFICATION  *  *  *  *  *
```

Verification Statement
Etat De Verification

Last Page . . .
Derniere Page . . .   Page   1

9F137
PPSA NOTICE TO DEBTOR OF REGISTRATION

[See Para. 9.688]

[Date]

<u>REGISTERED MAIL</u>

[To Debtor address]

Attention: _____

Dear : _____ :

Re: _____Bank (the "Bank")

We have acted on behalf of the Bank with respect to   registration pursuant to the Personal Property Act (the "PPSA") which we effected on behalf of the Bank against you.

Please find enclosed a copy of the registration which we made on _____, 199____ against you with respect to the security agreement you issued to the Bank as security for repayment of your loans.

A copy of this registration is forwarded to you in accordance with the requirements of the PPSA.

Yours very truly,

_____

Encl.

9F138
PMSI NOTICE

[See Para. 9.689]

REGISTERED MAIL

[to prior registered PPSA creditors and s. 427 secured Banks[1] and anyone else with an interest in Debtor's collateral]

Dear Sirs:

Re:_____ (the "Debtor")

TAKE NOTICE that the undersigned has acquired and expects to acquire from time to time, pursuant to the Personal Property Security Act (Ontario), a purchase-money security interest in inventory supplied to the Debtor, which inventory is more particularly described as follows:

> all of the products described in Schedule "A" hereto supplied to the Debtor and financed by the undersigned and all parts, supplies and accessories, and all products derived therefrom and proceeds thereof.

THIS NOTICE is given to you in accordance with the Personal Property Security Act.

_____ BANK

By its solicitors:

Per: _____

---

1. Non-PPSA creditors should sign a specific postponement as a PMSI notice is only effective to other PPSA creditors.

9F139
P.P.S.A. FIXTURES FILINGS
[See Para. 9.688]

Document General
Form 4 — Land Registration Reform Act, 1984

D

(1) Registry ☐   Land Titles ☐   (2) Page 1 of 2 pages

(3) Property Identifier(s)   Block   Property   Additional See Schedule ☐

(4) Nature of Document
NOTICE OF SECURITY INTEREST UNDER THE PERSONAL PROPERTY SECURITY ACT

(5) Consideration   Dollars $

(6) Description
Part Lot 8,
Concession 3
Township of York (now City of Toronto),
being parts 1, 2 and 3 on Plan 51R-1234

New Property Identifiers   Additional See Schedule ☐

Executions   Additional See Schedule ☐

(7) This Document Contains: (a) Redescription New Easement Plan/Sketch ☐   (b) Schedule for: Description ☐ Additional Parties ☐ Other ☐

(8) This Document provides as follows:

NOTICE IS HEREBY GIVEN THAT:

1. By a security agreement made between * Inc. of the address set out in Section 11 below as debtor and * Bank as creditor, a security interest has been created in the collateral described in the Schedule "A" attached hereto.

2. The description of the land upon which such collateral is located or is affixed or is to be affixed, is set out in Section 6 above.

3. The address of the secured party for service is set out in Section 13 below.

Continued on Schedule ☐

(9) This Document relates to instrument number(s)

(10) Party(ies) (Set out Status or Interest)
Name(s)   Signature(s)   Date of Signature Y M D

* Inc.
(Debtor & Tenant)   I/We have authority to bind the Corporation

Investments Ltd.
(Owner & Landlord)   I/We have authority to bind the Corporation

(11) Address for Service

(12) Party(ies) (Set out Status or Interest)
Name(s)   Signature(s)   Date of Signature Y M D

* Bank   (Creditor)
by its solicitors   Per:

(13) Address for Service

(14) Municipal Address of Property
123 White St.
Toronto, Ontario

(15) Document Prepared by:
20 Queen Street West
27th Floor
Toronto, Ontario
M5H 3S1

Fees and Tax
Registration Fee
Total

9F140
ASSIGNMENT OF BOOK DEBTS

[See Para. 9.690]

TO: _____ Bank

    (hereinafter called "Lender")

    THE UNDERSIGNED _____ Inc., (hereinafter called the "Assignor") for good and valuable consideration hereby assigns, transfers, and sets over unto Lender all debts, accounts, choses in action, claims, demands, and moneys now due and owing or accruing due or which may hereafter become due or owing to the Assignor, including (without limiting the foregoing) moneys which may become payable under any policy of insurance in respect of any loss by fire or other cause which has been or may be incurred by the Assignor, together with all contracts, securities, bills, notes, lien notes, judgments, chattel mortgages and all other rights, benefits and documents now or hereafter taken, vested in or held by the Assignor in respect of or as security for such debts, accounts, choses in action, claims, demands, and moneys hereby assigned or intended so to be or any part thereof and the full benefit and advantage thereof, and all rights of action, claim, or demand which the Assignor now has or may at any time hereafter have against any person or persons, firm or corporation in respect thereof.

    AND THE ASSIGNOR hereby nominates, constitutes, and appoints Lender to be the true and lawful attorney of the Assignor in the name of the Assignor to ask, demand, and receive of and from any and all debtors of the Assignor the debts severally owing or which may become owing from them, and on non-payment of the same or any part thereof to commence and prosecute any action or proceeding for the recovery of the same and to use all other lawful remedies which the Assignor could or might have used for such recovery, and on receipt or recovery to sign and give good and effectual receipt or receipts for the same with full power from time to time to appoint a substitute or substitutes for all or any of the purposes aforesaid, and in case of any difficulty or dispute with any debtor of the Assignor to submit such difficulty or dispute to arbitration in such manner as Lender shall see fit and to compound, compromise, and accept part in satisfaction for payment of the whole of any debt hereby assigned or to grant an extension of time for payment thereof either with or without security; all as Lender in his absolute discretion shall deem expedient, and the Assignor hereby agrees to ratify whatsoever Lender shall lawfully do or cause to be done in the premises and to indemnify Lender of and from all loss, costs, charges, and expenses by reason of any such proceeding.

THE ASSIGNOR hereby further assigns, transfers, and sets over unto Lender each and all the book or books of record and otherwise, together with all papers, documents, and writings whatsoever which shall at any time during the continuance of this Indenture be in the possession, power, custody, or control of the Assignor relating or referring to the said book debts, claims and rights hereby assigned or intended so to be or in any way representing or evidencing same.

THE ASSIGNOR further hereby covenants, promises and agrees to and with Lender to well and truly execute or cause to be executed all or any such further or other document or documents as shall or may be required by Lender to more completely or fully vest in Lender the said book debts, claims, and rights hereby assigned or intended so to be and the right to receive the said moneys or to enable the said Lender to recover same and will from time to time prepare and deliver to Lender all deeds, books, vouchers, promissory notes, bills of exchange, accounts, letters, invoices, papers, and all other documents in any way relating to the said book debts, claims, and rights hereby assigned.

PROVIDED and it is hereby distinctly understood and agreed that these presents are and shall be a continuing collateral security to Lender for the general balance due at any time by the Assignor to Lender and all indebtedness for which the Assignor now is or are or may hereafter be liable to Lender and all renewals thereof, and substitutions therefor and all bills of exchange, promissory notes, cheques, and other instruments whatsoever in any wise representing or securing the same and all future bills, notes, or other instruments which may at any time hereafter be given or taken in renewal of or in substitution therefor either in whole or in part or as in any wise representing the said indebtedness or any part thereof together with all costs, charges, and expenses to which Lender shall be put in connection therewith or in connection with the collection or recovery of any of the book debts, claims, or rights hereby assigned, notwithstanding any change in the nature or form of said indebtedness or in the bills, notes, or other obligations representing the same or any part thereof or in the names or the parties to such bills, notes, or other obligations so held as collateral thereto.

PROVIDED ALWAYS and it is hereby distinctly agreed that these presents are and shall be continuing and collateral security to the present and any future indebtedness of the Assignor to Lender and shall not create any merger of the said indebtedness in respect of any sum or sums so owing or which may hereafter become owing or any bill of exchange, promissory note, or other security given for the same or any parts or parts thereof or of any contract in respect thereof and shall not operate as a release to the Assignor or suspend, impair, or otherwise affect the rights and remedies of Lender from time to time in respect of any such indebtedness and further shall not in any way operate as a release to or affect the rights of the Lender as against any third party or parties liable for such indebtedness or any part or parts thereof or upon any bill of exchange, promissory note, or other security or contract representing the same upon any bill of exchange, promissory note, or other security or contract representing the same or any part thereof or which may be taken as security therefor or for any part thereof.

IT IS FURTHER UNDERSTOOD AND AGREED that the agreement between the parties is that the existing indebtedness of the Assignor to Lender as well as all future indebtedness, no matter how secured, shall be treated as secured hereby and that the said existing indebtedness shall be treated as continuing notwithstanding new transactions with the Assignor, the intention of the parties being that this present existing indebtedness may remain undischarged, except as to any amount by which the total indebtedness of the Assignor to Lender may be actually reduced below the present amount of same.

IT IS HEREBY DECLARED AND AGREED by and between the parties hereto that the word "Lender" wherever used throughout this Agreement shall extend to and include the legal representatives, successors and assigns of "Lender" and the word "Assignor" wherever used throughout this Agreement shall extend to and include the successors and assigns of the Assignor.

THIS INSTRUMENT shall be governed and construed in accordance with the laws of the Province of Ontario, and the Assignor expressly attorns to the courts and laws of the said Province.

The parties expressly request that this Agreement as well as all documents relating thereto be drawn up in English. Les parties ont expressément exigé que cette convention ainsi que tous les documents s'y rattachant soient rédiges en Anglais.

IN WITNESS WHEREOF the undersigned has hereunto set its corporate seal under the hands of its duly authorized officer(s) this _____ day of _____, 19____.

_____ INC.

by:_____

c/s

by:_____

9F141
P.P.S.A. REGISTRATION FOR ASSIGNMENT OF BOOK DEBTS

[See Paras. 9.690 and 9.501]

778

9F141:1
ELECTRONICALLY PRODUCED DRAFT
AND VERIFICATION STATEMENT

OPPSR MANAGEMENT SYSTEM (MT01)   1c00001714-01
May 7, 1997 at 11:22AM   **DRAFTED**

F I N A N C I N G   S T A T E M E N T

REGISTRATION ACT	REGISTRATION PERIOD	CAUTION FILING
PPSA	5 Year(s)	[ ]

DEBTORS

Business   Purchaser Inc.   Corp No. :
         123 Ian Street
         Toronto   ON
         M5H 3S1

SECURED PARTIES

         Big Bank
         123 Main   Street
         Toronto   ON
         M4C 1S9

COLLATERAL

CONSUMER GOODS	INVENTORY	EQUIPMENT	ACCOUNTS	OTHER	VEHICLES INCLUDED
[ ]	[ ]	[ ]	[✓]	[✓]	[ ]

PRINCIPAL AMOUNT SECURED   MATURITY DATE

* * * * * END OF FINANCING STATEMENT * * * * *

SUMMARY OF FINANCE STATEMENT
State : DRAFTED

Statement Was Set To Drafted : MAY 7,1997 at 11:22AM by BABE

Your Reference Number   : 1234 - 003 JEB
Charge Customer   : NO
Bill Secured Party   : YES 1046 Big Bank

POST REGISTRATION SEARCH
will be performed on the following:

BUSINESS Debtor Name   : Purchaser Inc.

Approved By: _____

Financing Statement   . . . Last Page . . .   Page 1

OPPSR MANAGEMENT SYSTEM (MT01)
May 8, 1997 at 11:41AM

1c00001714-01
REGISTERED

F I N A N C I N G   S T A T E M E N T

REGISTRATION NUMBER	FILE NUMBER	EXPIRY DATE
970507184115294239	830615481	PPR: May 7, 2002
		OPPSR: May 7, 2002

	REGISTRATION ACT	REGISTRATION PERIOD	CAUTION FILING
1c·01·01	PPSA	5 Year(s)	[ ]

DEBTORS

Business
1c·01·03 Purchaser Inc.
1c·01·04 123 Ian Street   Corp No. :
        Toronto   ON
        M5H 3S1

SECURED PARTIES

1c·01·08 Big Bank
1c·01·09 123 Main   Street
        Toronto   ON
        M4C 1S9

COLLATERAL

	CONSUMER GOODS	INVENTORY	EQUIPMENT	ACCOUNTS	OTHER	VEHICLES INCLUDED
1c·01·10	[ ]	[ ]	[ ]	[√]	[√]	[ ]

PRINCIPAL AMOUNT SECURED   MATURITY DATE

* * * * * END OF FINANCING STATEMENT * * * * *

SUMMARY OF FINANCE STATEMENT
State : REGISTERED

Statement Was Transmitted   : MAY 7,1997 at 6:41PM by BELINDA

Your Reference Number   : 1234 - 003   JEB
Charge Customer   : NO
Bill Secured Party   : YES   1046   Big Bank
Registration Billing Amount : $45.70

VERIFICATION STATEMENT/ETAT DE VERIFICATION

REG UNDER/T. ENREG
Personal Property Security Act

REG PERIOD/PERIODE
5

CAUTION FILING/AVERTIS
[ ]

REG NUM/NO ENREGIST
9705071841152 94239

REF FILE NUM/NO DE REFERENCE
830615481

EXPIRY DATE/DATE D'EXPIRATION
7 MAY 2002

DEBTORS/DEBITEUR

CORPORATION NUMBER

Purchaser Inc.
123 Ian Street
Toronto ON M5H 3S1

SECURED PARTIES/CREANCIER GARANTI

Big Bank
123 Main Street
Toronto ON M4C 1S9

COLLATERAL/BIENS GREVES

CONS GOODS/BIENS CONS	INVTRY/STOCK	EQUIP/MATER	ACCTS/COMPT	OTHER/AUTRE	MV INCL/VA INCLUS
[ ]	[ ]	[ ]	[√]	[√]	[ ]

AMOUNT/MONTANT

DATE OF MATURITY/DATE ECHEANCE

AGENT/AGENT

Miller Thomson
20 Queen Street West, Box 27, Suite 2500
Toronto, ON M5H 3S1

```
*  *  *  *  *  END OF VERIFICATION STATEMENT  *  *  *  *  *
*  *  *  *  *  FIN DE L'ETAT DE VERIFICATION  *  *  *  *  *
```

Verification Statement
Etat De Verification

Last Page . . .
Derniere Page . . .   Page   1

9F142
HYPOTHECATION AND PLEDGE AGREEMENT

[See Para. 9.693]

THE UNDERSIGNED, hereby deposits with and transfers to _____ Bank (the "Bank") or to any nominee or nominees of the Bank, listed hereunder, the following:

Number of Shares	Security	Class of Stock
10	_____ Inc.	Common

IN CONSIDERATION of the sum of one dollar (the receipt whereof is hereby acknowledged) made by the Bank to the undersigned; "Security") shall be held by the Bank as continuing security for the performance of the debts, obligations and liabilities of the undersigned to the Bank (the "Liabilities").

The Bank is hereby authorized on default, or without default and without demand of payment if in the opinion of the Bank the Security is depreciated or liable to be depreciated, or on the insolvency of the undersigned, and without notice to the undersigned and as an when and if the Bank shall think proper to sell the Security or any part thereof and without prejudice to their claim for any deficiency. At any such sale, the Bank may purchase the whole or any part of the Security sold free from any right of redemption on the part of the undersigned which is hereby waived and released, the undersigned hereby expressly waiving all and every formality prescribed by law in relation to any such sale and authorizing the Bank or any nominee or nominees of the Bank as attorney irrevocable with power of substitution for and in the name of the undersigned to sign and seal all documents and to fill in all blanks in signed powers of attorney and transfers necessary in order to complete the transfer of the Security to the Bank, or any nominee or nominees of the Bank or any purchaser. This hypothecation shall entitle the Bank, or any nominee or nominees of the Bank, either before or after default of payment of the Liabilities and without notice or demand of any kind, to cause any or all such Security to be transferred on the books of the Company to the Bank, or any nominee or nominees of the Bank, and shall entitle it, him or them at its, his or their option, to represent the same at any meeting of the Company and vote thereon.

DATED at Toronto this _____ day of _____, 19__.

SIGNED IN THE PRESENCE OF

_____

                                   _____
                                               Jane Doe

9F143
POWER OF ATTORNEY TO TRANSFER SHARES

[See Para. 9.693]

FOR VALUE RECEIVED, the undersigned hereby sells, assigns and transfers unto _____ of _____ 10 Common shares in the capital of _____ Inc. (the "Corporation") standing in the name of the undersigned on the books of the Corporation represented by Certificate No. _____ and hereby irrevocably constitutes and appoints _____ the attorney of the undersigned, to transfer the said share(s) on the books of the said Corporation with full power of substitution in the premises.

DATED at Toronto, this _____ day of _____, 19____.

SIGNED in the presence of:

_____

                                     _____
                                               Jane Doe

9F144
SUBSTITUTION AGREEMENT

[See Para. 9.693]

To: _____ BANK (the "Bank")

Notwithstanding the certain Hypothecation and Pledge Agreement executed by the undersigned in favour of the Bank and dated the _____ day of _____, 19____, whereby certain securities listed therein are specifically hypothecated by the undersigned to the Bank, it is anticipated by the undersigned that such or other securities heretofore and hereafter lodged or delivered to the Bank in substitution therefor and/or as additional security, and the undersigned therefore in consideration of advances heretofore, now or hereafter made by the Bank to the undersigned hereby confirms and agrees that any and all securities heretofore or hereafter received by the Bank for the account of the undersigned which may or may not be listed on the said Hypothecation and Pledge Agreement abovementioned are and shall be held by the Bank as continuing security for the undersigned's indebtedness and liability to the Bank whether heretofore, now or hereafter contracted and incurred in accordance with the provisions of the aforementioned Hypothecation and Pledge Agreement.

DATED at Toronto, Ontario this _____ day of _____, 19____.

SIGNED in the presence of:

_____   _____
                                        Jane Doe

9F145
CERTIFIED COPY OF THE
RESOLUTIONS OF THE BOARD OF DIRECTORS
OF
* INC.

[See Para. 9.693]

TRANSFER OF SHARES:

WE, the undersigned, being all the directors of * Inc. (hereinafter referred to as the "Corporation"), hereby consent to the adoption of each and every one of the following resolutions this _____ day of _____, 19____.

WHEREAS Jane Doe has agreed to hypothecate and pledge the * Bank ("Bank") her shares of the Corporation as security for her indebtedness to the Bank;

NOW THEREFORE BE IT RESOLVED THAT:

1.   the following transfers of the Shares be and are hereby approved and consented to:
     (i)   the transfer at any time or from time to time of any or all of the Shares from Jane Doe to the Bank or any transferee or transferees from time to time designated by the Bank; and
     (ii)   the transfer at any time or from time to time of any or all of the Shares from the Bank or to any transferee or transferees from time to time designated by the Bank.

2.   any officer of the Corporation be and he is hereby authorized and directed to register any such transfer or transfers of the Shares upon presentation to the Corporation of share certificates representing such Shares duly endorsed.

CERTIFIED to be a true copy of a resolution of the Board of Directors of _____ Inc. passed the _____ day of _____, 19____, which resolution is in full force and effect, unamended as of the date hereof.

DATED this _____ day of _____, 19____.

_____
Secretary

9F146
GUARANTEE

[See Para. 9.695]

THIS GUARANTEE dated as of the _____ day of _____, 19____ is made by Jane Doe, a businesswoman, of _____, Ontario _____ (herein referred to as the "Guarantor") in favour of * Bank (herein referred to as the "Lender").

WHEREAS:

A.   * Inc., a corporation duly incorporated pursuant to the laws of the Province of Ontario and having a place of business at _____, Ontario _____ (herein referred to as the "Borrower"), has issued in favour of the Lender a note of even date (such note as it may hereafter be amended, modified, supplemented, renewed, substituted or replaced from time to time is herein referred to as the "note") pursuant to which the Borrower has agreed to repay its indebtedness to the Lender.

B.   The Guarantor wishes the Borrower, which is wholly owned by the Guarantor, to repay the indebtedness in accordance with the terms set out in the Note in favour of the Lender and, therefore, is willing to execute and deliver this Guarantee to the Lender.

NOW THEREFORE in consideration of the Lender accepting repayment of the indebtedness in accordance with the note and for other good and valuable consideration, the receipt and sufficiency of which is hereby acknowledged by the Guarantor, the Guarantor agrees as follows:

1.   Interpretation. All terms defined in the note and not otherwise defined herein and used in this Guarantee shall have the meanings ascribed thereto in the note.

2.   Guarantee. The Guarantor hereby unconditionally and irrevocably guarantees, as a continuing obligation, payment to the Lender forthwith after demand therefor of all present and future indebtedness, obligations and liabilities of any kind whatsoever which the Bor-rower has incurred or may incur or be under to the Lender arising under or in connection with the note (herein collectively referred to as the "obligations"). All amounts payable by the Guarantor hereunder shall

be paid to the Lender at his address as aforesaid or as otherwise directed by the Lender. For greater certainty, this shall be a continuing guarantee and shall cover all of the obligations now or hereafter existing and shall apply to and secure any ultimate balance due or remaining due to the Lender.

3.   Dealings With Borrower. The Lender may make advances, grant accommodations, make payments, grant extensions of time, renewals or indulgences, take and give up securities including other guarantees, abstain from taking securities or from perfecting securities, cease or refrain from giving credit or making loans or advances, accept compositions, grant releases and discharges and otherwise deal with the Borrower and with other parties and securities as the Lender sees fit, and apply all monies received from the Borrower or others or from security upon such part of the obligations as he, in his absolute discretion, may think best, without the consent of, or notice to, the Guarantor and without prejudice to, or in any way limiting or lessening, the liability of the Guarantor hereunder. Without limiting the generality of the foregoing, the Guarantor hereby authorizes and empowers the Lender, in his sole and unfettered discretion, without any notice to the Guarantor or any other person, to exercise any right or remedy which the Lender may have against the Borrower or with respect to any security, whether real, personal or intangible, for the obligations, including judicial and non-judicial foreclosure, without affecting in any way the liability of the Guarantor hereunder and the Guarantor shall be liable to the Lender for any deficiency resulting from the exercise by the Lender of any such right or remedy, even though any rights or remedies which the Guarantor may have against the Borrower or any other person may have been altered or diminished by the exercise of any such right or remedy.

4.   Recourse Against Borrower. The Lender shall not be bound to exercise all or any of his rights and remedies or to exhaust his recourse against the Borrower or others or any security before being entitled to payment from the Guarantor under this Guarantee.

5.   Loss of Securities. Any loss of, or neglect or omission with respect to any security held by the Lender, whether occasioned through the fault of the Lender or otherwise, shall not discharge in whole or in part, or limit or lessen the liability of the Guarantor hereunder.

6.   Settlement of Accounts. Any account settled or stated between the Lender and the Borrower or admitted by or on behalf of the Borrower shall be accepted by the Guarantor as conclusive evidence that the amount thereby appearing due by the Borrower to the Lender is so due.

7.   Change in Composition of Borrower. Neither change in the name, objects, capital structure or constitution, membership, ownership or control of the Borrower nor any other circumstance including, without limitation, the amalgamation of the Borrower with another corporation, any defect in, omission from, failure to file or register or defective filings or registrations of any instrument under which the Lender has taken any security or collateral for payment of any of the Obligations or the performance or observance of any obligation of the Guarantor to the Lender or any circumstance affecting the Borrower or the Guarantor, which might otherwise afford a legal or equitable defence to the Guarantor or a discharge of the Guarantee shall affect or in any way limit or lessen the liability of the Guarantor hereunder.

8.   Waiver. No delay on the part of the Lender in exercising any of his options, powers or rights, or partial or single exercise thereof, shall constitute a waiver thereof. No waiver of any of his rights hereunder, and no modification or amendment of this Guarantee, shall be deemed to be made by the Lender unless the same shall be in writing, duly signed on behalf of the Lender, and each such waiver, if any, shall apply with respect to the specific   instance involved, and shall in no way impair the rights of the Lender or the obligations of the Guarantor to the Lender in any other respect at any other time.

9.   Guarantee of All Monies Borrowed. All monies, advances, renewals and credits in fact borrowed or obtained by the Borrower from the Lender under or in connection with the note shall be deemed to form part of the obligations notwithstanding any incapacity, disability or lack of limitation of status or power of the Borrower or of the directors, officers, employees, partners or agents thereof, or that the Borrower may not be a legal or suable entity, or any irregularity, defect or informality in the borrowing or obtaining of such monies, advances, renewals or credits, whether known to the Lender or not. The Lender shall not be obliged to enquire into the powers of the Borrower or its directors, partners or agents acting or

purporting to act on its behalf, and monies, advances, renewals or credits in fact borrowed or obtained from the Lender in the professed exercise of any power of the Borrower or its directors, partners or agents shall be deemed to form part of the obligations hereby guaranteed even though the incurring of such monies, advances, renewals or credits was irregular, fraudulent, defective or informally effected or exceeded the powers of the Borrower or its directors, partneres, or agents. Any part of the obligations which may not be recoverable from the Guarantor by the Lender on the basis of a guarantee shall be recoverable by the Lender from the Guarantor as principal debtor in respect thereof and shall be paid to the Lender forthwith after demand therefor as herein provided.

10. Assignment by Lender. The Lender may from time to time and without notice to, or the consent of the Guarantor assign or transfer all or any of the obligations or any interest therein to any person and, notwithstanding any such assignment or transfer or any subsequent assignment or transfer thereof, any such obligation or part thereof so transferred or assigned shall be and shall remain an "obligation" for the purpose of this Guarantee and any immediate and successive assignee or transferee of any obligation or any interest therein shall, to the extent of the interest so assigned or transferred, be entitled to the benefit of, and the right to enforce this Guarantee to the same extent as if such person were the Lender. In the event of any such assignment or transfer, the Lender shall retain the right to enforce this Guarantee for his own benefit as to any obligation which has not been so assigned or transferred.

11. Revival of Indebtedness. The Guarantor agrees that, if at any time all or any part of any payment previously applied by the Lender to any obligation is or must be rescinded or returned by the Lender for any reason whatsoever (including, without limitation, the insolvency, bankruptcy or reorganization of the Borrower), such obligation shall, for the purpose of this Guarantee, to the extent that such payment is or must be rescinded or returned, be deemed to have continued in existence, notwithstanding such application by the Lender, and this Guarantee shall continue to be effective or be reinstated, as the case may be, as to such Obligation, all as though such application by the Lender had not been made.

12. Postponement. If the Lender receives from the Guarantor a payment or payments in full or on account of the liability of the

Guarantor hereunder, then the Guarantor shall not be entitled to claim repayment against the Borrower or the Borrower's estate until the Lender's claims against the Borrower have been paid in full. In case of liquidation, winding-up or bankruptcy of the Borrower (whether voluntary or involuntary) or if the Borrower shall make a bulk sale of any of its assets within the bulk transfer provisions of any applicable legislation or any composition with creditors or scheme of arrangement, the Lender shall have the right to rank for his full claim and receive all dividends or other payments in respect thereof in priority to the Guarantor until the Lender's claim has been paid in full, and the Guarantor shall continue to be liable hereunder up to the amount guaranteed, less any payments made by the Guarantor, for any balance which may be owing the Lender by the Borrower. In the event of the valuation by the Lender of any of his security and/or the retention thereof by the Lender, such valuation and/or retention shall not, as between the Lender and the Guarantor, be considered as a purchase of such security or as payment or satisfaction or reduction of the obligations or any part thereof. Any and all rights the Guarantor may have as surety, whether at law, in equity or otherwise, that are inconsistent with any of the provisions contained in this Guarantee are hereby waived. The foregoing provisions of this paragraph shall not in any way limit or lessen the liability of the Guarantor under any other paragraph of this Guarantee.

13. Legal Expenses. The Guarantor shall from time to time upon demand by the Lender forthwith pay to the Lender all expenses (including legal fees) incurred by the Lender in the preparation of this Guarantee and the preservation or enforcement of any of his rights hereunder.

14. Additional Security. This Guarantee is in addition to, and not in substitution for, and without prejudice to, any security of any kind (including, without limitation, other guarantees) now or hereafter held by the Lender and any other rights or remedies that the Lender might have.

15. Taxes and Set-off. All payments to be made by the Guarantor hereunder shall be made without set-off or counterclaim and without deduction for any taxes, levies, duties, fees, deductions, withholdings, restrictions or conditions or any nature whatsoever. If, at any time, any applicable law, regulation or international agreement

requires the Guarantor to make any such deduction or withholding from any such payment, the sum due from the Guarantor in respect of such payment shall be increased to the extent necessary to ensure that, after the making of such deduction or withholding, the Lender receives a net sum equal to the sum which he would have received had no deduction or withholding been required.

16. Interest. The Guarantor shall pay to the Lender in respect to any amount payable hereunder (including interest) that is not paid when due, interest from the due date thereof, until paid and after demand, default and judgment at a rate of interest per annum equal to ____%, such interest to be paid monthly on the last day of each calendar month and calculated annually, not in advance.

17. Demand for Payment. A demand for payment shall be deemed to have been given where a notice in writing containing such a demand is sent by registered and receipted mail or prepaid courier to the Guarantor at the address of the Guarantor as aforesaid or at such other address as the Guarantor may subsequently specify by written notice received by the Lender. Any such notice shall be deemed to have been received on the date of delivery.

18. Responsibility to Keep Informed. So long as any of the obligations remain unpaid or outstanding, the Guarantor assumes all responsibility for being and keeping herself informed of the financial condition of the Borrower and of all circumstances bearing upon the nature, scope and extent of the risk which the Guarantor assumes and incurs under this Guarantee.

19. No Escrow. Possession of this Guarantee by the Lender shall be conclusive evidence against the Guarantor that this Guarantee was not delivered in escrow or pursuant to any agreement that it should not be effective until any conditions precedent or subsequent have been complied with unless, at the time or receipt of this Guarantee by the Lender, the Guarantor obtains from the Lender a letter setting out the terms and conditions under which this Guarantee was delivered and the conditions, if any, to be observed before it becomes effective.

20. Governing Law and Submission to Jurisdiction. This Guarantee shall be governed by and construed in accordance with the laws of

the province of Ontario and the laws of Canada applicable therein and the Guarantor hereby accepts and irrevocably submits to the jurisdiction of the courts of the province of Ontario and acknowledges their competence and agrees to be bound by any judgment thereof except that nothing herein shall limit the Lender's right to bring proceedings against the Guarantor elsewhere.

21. Successors and Assigns. This Guarantee shall extend and enure to the benefit of the Lender and his heirs, executors, administrators, successors and assigns and shall be binding upon the Guarantor and the heirs, executors, administrators successors and permitted assigns of the Guarantor. If there is more than one Guarantor referred to herein, then their obligations shall be joint and several.

22. Time. Time is of the essence with respect to the terms and provisions of this Guarantee and the time for performance of the obligations of the Guarantor under this Guarantee are to be strictly construed.

IN WITNESS WHEREOF, this Guarantee has been made and delivered as of the date first above written.

_____   _____
Witness   Jane Doe

9F147
RESOLUTION OF THE BOARD OF DIRECTORS
OF XYZ HOLDINGS LIMITED
(the "Corporation")

[See Para. 9.695]

GUARANTEE OF LOAN OF DEBTOR INC. ("Debtor")
TO BIG BANK (the "Bank")

WHEREAS:

A.   The Bank has agreed to extend a credit facility to Debtor as evidenced by a demand operating facility agreement dated June 21, 2003 between the Bank and Debtor (the "Commitment").

B.   The Corporation has agreed to enter into a limited guarantee of up to $1,000,000 (the "Guarantee") of the present and future obligations of Debtor to the Bank.

C.   The Corporation has also agreed to issue to the Bank a general security agreement to secure the Guarantee (the "GSA").

D.   The Corporation has agreed to give the foregoing financial assistance to Debtor, more particularly described in the Notice of Disclosure to Shareholders (the "Notice") attached hereto as Schedule 1.

E.   Pursuant to Section 20 of the Business Corporations Act (Ontario) the Corporation is required to disclose to its shareholders all material financial assistance.

NOW THEREFORE BE IT RESOLVED THAT:

1.   The acceptance, execution and delivery by the Corporation of the Commitment as guarantor is hereby ratified, approved and confirmed and the Corporation agrees to be bound by the terms and conditions therein set out.

2.   The Corporation shall provide the Guarantee and the GSA as contemplated in the Commitment.

3.   The Corporation be and it is hereby authorized and directed to execute and deliver all documents and instruments as may be required by the Bank, including without limitation:
     (a)   the Guarantee and cause the issuance of the GSA; and
     (b)   all other documents as may be necessary to support the Guarantee and the GSA granting security over the assets of the Corporation
     the foregoing documents being collectively referred to as the "Documents".

4.   Any officer or director of the Corporation ("Authorized Officer") be and each of them is hereby authorized and directed for and on behalf of the Corporation whether under corporate seal or otherwise, to execute and deliver the Documents, substantially in the form of the draft Documents presented to and approved by the directors of the Corporation, subject to such alterations, amendments or additions to which the Authorized Officer executing and delivering the Documents may agree, the execution

by such Authorized Officer to be conclusive proof of his or her agreement to any amendments, alterations or additions incorporated therein and the Corporation shall be bound thereby.

5.   Any Authorized Officer by and is hereby authorized on behalf of the Corporation to take such further action and to sign such further documents as may be required to give full force and effect to the terms and provisions of the Commitment and the documents and transactions contemplated or as otherwise may be required to give fully effect to these resolutions.

6.   The execution and delivery of any other agreements, instruments or documents described above which may have been executed or delivered prior to the adoption of these resolutions regardless of by which officer, director or other employee such agreement, instrument or document was executed and delivered, and regardless of any informality in such execution or delivery, be and the same hereby are ratified, approved and confirmed in all respects.

THE UNDERSIGNED, being all the directors of the Corporation, pass the foregoing resolutions pursuant to the provisions of the Business Corporations Act (Ontario). This resolution may be executed in several counterparts, each of which when so executed, shall be deemed to be an original and such counterparts together shall constitute one and the same instrument which shall be sufficiently evidenced by any such original counterpart and facsimile copies of signatures shall be treated as originals for all purposes.

DATED the   day of July, 2003.

THE UNDERSIGNED, being all of the shareholders of the Corporation, confirm the foregoing resolutions and receipt of the section 20 notice of financial assistance, as evidenced by their respective signatures. This resolution may be executed in several counterparts, each of which when so executed, shall be deemed to be an original and such counterparts together shall constitute one and the same instrument which shall be sufficiently evidenced by any such original counterpart and facsimile copies of signatures shall be treated as originals for all purposes.

DATED the   day of   , 2003.

123 ONTARIO INC.   **456 ONTARIO INC.**

By: _____   By: _____

Schedule 1

NOTICE OF DISCLOSURE TO SHAREHOLDERS
**Pursuant to subsections 20(2) and (4) of the Business Corporations Act
(Ontario)**

TO: 123 Ontario Inc.
         456 Ontario Inc.
         (the "Shareholders")

FROM: XYZ HOLDINGS LIMITED (the "Corporation")

Pursuant to Section 20 of the *Business Corporations Act* (Ontario), the Corporation hereby gives notice to its shareholders of the following financial assistance that the Corporation has given in the amounts, on the dates and the terms set out below.

Debtor	Brief Description of Financial Assistance	Date financial assistance given
XYZ Holdings Limited	Guarantee of Indebtedness of Debtor Inc in favour of Big Bank limited to $1,000,000 and a general security agreement over all of its present and future personal property to secure such guarantee	July , 2003

DATED the   day of July, 2003.

XYZ HOLDINGS LIMITED

By: _____

, President

9F148
CERTIFICATE OF INDEPENDENT LEGAL ADVICE

[See Para. 9.696]

TO: * BANK

    I refer to a guarantee dated the _____ day of _____, 19____ signed by Jane Doe, together with her husband, John Doe, to and in favour of * Bank, guaranteeing payment of all present and future indebtedness and liability of * Inc. (the "Borrower") to * Bank and interest thereon after demand (the "Guarantee"), and Postponement Agreement dated the _____ day of _____, 19____ signed by Jane Doe to and in favour of * Bank subordinating certain payments due to her by the Borrower (the "Subordination"), and an Assignment of Life Insurance Policy dated the _____ day of _____, 19____ made by John Doe as insured, the Borrower and Jane Doe as beneficiary, assigning the proceeds of the life insurance policy therein described to * Bank (the "Assignment").

    I examined the said Jane Doe separately and apart from her husband and explained to her the nature and effect of the Guarantee, the Subordination and the Assignment. She appeared to understand my explanation and she then acknowledged and declared to me that she fully understood the nature and effect of the Guarantee, the Subordination and the Assignment, as and for her own act, freely and voluntarily and without fear, threat or compulsion of, from or by her husband.

    I do not act for her husband, * Bank or the Borrower in this matter.

    DATED this _____ day of _____, 19____.

_____
Jane Doe's Solicitor
(please print name & address below)

_____

_____

_____

ACKNOWLEDGMENT BY CLIENT

I, the undersigned, hereby acknowledge and declare that all the statements made in the foregoing Certificate of Independent Legal Advice are true and correct, that the Bank or any agents of the Bank has not used any compulsion or made any threat or exercised any undue influence to induce me to execute the _____ referred to in the said Certificate of Independent Legal Advice and that my solicitor, in advising me as stated therein, was consulted by me as my personal solicitor and in my interest only.

_____
Jane Doe

_____
Signature of solicitor as witness

9F149
CERTIFICATE OF NON-RESTRICTION OF CORPORATE POWERS

[See Para. 9.700]

To: * Bank
         (the "Lender")

I, the undersigned, Secretary of * Inc. (the "Corporation"), hereby certify that there are no provisions in the articles or by-laws of the Corporation or in any unanimous shareholder agreement which restrict, limit or regulate in any way the powers of the Corporation to borrow monies upon the credit of the Corporation and to issue, reissue, sell or pledge debt obligations of the Corporation, and to give a guarantee on behalf of the Corporation to secure performance of an obligation of any person and to create security interests by way of mortgage, hypothecation, pledge or otherwise covering all or any of the property and assets of the Corporation present and future as security for all or any monies borrowed by the Corporation from the Lender or any other liability of the Corporation to the Lender.

This certificate shall remain in force and be binding upon the Corporation as regards the Lender until a certificate repealing or replacing this certificate shall have been received by the Lender.

DATED at Toronto, Ontario the _____ day of _____, 19____.

_____
Secretary

9F150
AUTHORIZING RESOLUTION

[See Para. 9.700]

CERTIFIED COPY OF
RESOLUTION OF THE BOARD OF DIRECTORS
OF
* INC.
(the "Corporation")

BORROWING FROM * BANK

WHEREAS the Corporation has applied to borrow from * Bank (the "Bank") the principal sum of $_____ (the "Principal Sum");

AND WHEREAS the Bank has agreed to lend to the Corporation the Principal Sum under such terms and conditions as more particularly set forth in the commitment letter from the Bank to the Corporation dated the _____ day of _____, 19____ (the "Commitment Letter") and accepted by the Corporation on the _____ day of _____, 19____;

AND WHEREAS the Bank requires that the Principal Sum be secured by promissory notes, an assignment of book debts, a security over inven-tory agreement, a fixed and floating charge debenture, a pledge of the debenture, and an assignment of the insurance policies covering the assets owned by the Corporation;

AND WHEREAS the Corporation has agreed to grant to the Bank such promissory notes, assignment of book debts, a security over inventory agreement, debenture, pledge of debenture and assignment of insurance to secure repayment of the said Principal Sum;

NOW THEREFORE BE IT RESOLVED that:

1. the Corporation is authorized and directed to borrow from the Bank the Principal Sum under such terms and conditions as more particularly set forth in the Commitment Letter;

2. the execution and delivery of the Commitment Letter is hereby confirmed, ratified, sanctioned, approved and authorized;

3. the execution and delivery of the Bank's forms of General Assignment of Book Debts and Security over Inventory Agreements, both dated _____, 19____ are hereby confirmed, ratified, sanctioned and approved and authorized;

4. the Corporation is authorized and directed to grant to the Lender promissory notes to evidence its borrowings from the Bank, to issue to the Bank its form of debenture in the amount of $_____ creating fixed and floating charges on the assets of the Corporation specified therein (the "Debenture"), to pledge such Debenture to the Bank and to assign to the Bank the insurance policies covering the assets owned by the Corporation; and

5. any director or officer of the Corporation is hereby authorized to sign execute all documents and instruments and to do all things necessary or desirable to effect such borrowing, including the execution and delivery to the Lender of promissory notes to evidence the borrowing, the Debenture, a pledge of the Debenture and an assignment of the insurance covering the assets owned by the Corporation to secure repayment of the said Principal Sum.

The undersigned, being the Secretary of * Inc. hereby certifies the foregoing to be a true and correct copy of resolutions of the board of directors of the Corporation made the _____ day of _____, 19____ and that the foregoing is in full force and effect unamended as of the date hereof.

DATED the _____ day of _____, 19____.

_____ c/s

Secretary

9F151
CERTIFICATE RE: REPRESENTATIONS AND EVENTS OF DEFAULT

[See Para. 9.700]

To: * BANK

The undersigned hereby certifies that as of the date hereof, the undersigned is not in breach of any representation, covenant or condition contained in the commitment letter issued by * Bank dated _____, 19____ and accepted by the undersigned on _____, 19____ or any event of default as specified or defined in any of the security documents given by the undersigned to * Bank with respect to the loans and advances contemplated in such commitment letter.

DATED at Toronto this _____ day of _____, 19____.

Signed in the presence of:

_____

_____
Jane Doe

9F152
ACKNOWLEDGMENT RE: TERMS SURVIVING ADVANCE

[See Para. 9.700]

To: * BANK

The undersigned hereby acknowledges that all representations, covenants and conditions contained in the commitment letter issued by * Bank dated _____, 19____ and accepted by the undersigned on _____, 19____ survive the advance of funds contemplated in such commitment letter until the indebtedness of the undersigned has been repaid to * Bank in full.

DATED at Toronto this _____ day of _____, 19____.

Signed in the presence of:

_____   _____
                                  Jane Doe

9F153
OPINION OF BORROWER'S COUNSEL

[See Para. 9.701]

[LETTERHEAD OF BORROWER'S COUNSEL]

_____, 19____

*   Bank

_____ branch

_____

_____

Attention: *

*   Solicitor

_____ (address)

_____

_____

Attention: *

Dear Sirs:

Re: * Inc.

We have acted on behalf of * Inc. (the "Company") in connection with the loan referred to in the * Bank (the "Bank") commitment letter dated _____, 19____ (the "Commitment") and accepted by the Company on _____, 19____.

A. Documents

In acting as such counsel, we have participated in the preparation of and have examined executed copies of the following documents:

1.   the Commitment;

2.   Demand Debenture dated _____, 19____ made by the Company in favour of the Bank, given as security for all present and future indebtedness and liability of the Company to the Bank (the "Debenture") in the principal amount of $_____ containing fixed and floating charges on the property, assets and undertaking of the Company;

3.   agreement dated _____, 19____ (the "Pledge") pursuant to which the Company pledged the Debenture to the Bank;

4.   security over inventory agreement dated _____, 19____ made by the Company in favour of the Bank creating security interests in its inventories and the proceeds thereof; and

5.   general assignment of book debts dated _____, 19____ executed by the Company.

The instruments referred to in paragraphs 2 to 5 above are sometimes referred to collectively as the "Security".

In addition, we examined the following documents:

(i)   Certificate of Status issued for the Company dated _____, 19____ issued by the Ontario Ministry of Consumer and Commercial Relations;

(ii)   Certificate of the Company dated _____, 19____ to which certificate is attached a certified copy of the resolution of the board of directors of the Company respecting this transaction;

(iii) Notarial copies of the constating documents of the Company in force as of _____, 19____;

(iv)   Notarial copies of all the by-laws of the Company in force as of _____, 19____;

(v)   Certificate of Officer of the Company dated _____, 19____ respecting non-restriction of its borrowing powers; and

(vi)   Certificate of the President of the Company dated _____, 19____, a copy of which certificate is annexed hereto.

B. Opinions

In connection with the opinions hereinafter expressed, we have considered such questions of law and we have examined such statutes and regulations, corporate records, certificates and other documents as we have deemed relevant and necessary as the basis for the opinions hereinafter set forth. We have assumed the genuineness of all signatures and the authenticity of all documents submitted to us as originals, other than the Security, and the conformity to originals of all documents submitted to us as certified or photostat (or similarly reproduced copies).

Based upon and subject to the foregoing, and the qualifications hereafter expressed, we are of the opinion that:

1. The Company is a corporation duly incorporated, organized and validly subsisting under the laws of the Province of Ontario, with full corporate right, power and authority to own its properties and assets, and to carry on its business in the province of Ontario, as now conducted and to enter into and perform each of the Commitment and the Security.

2. The Commitment and the Security have been duly authorized, executed and delivered to the Bank by the Company and constitute valid and binding obligations of the Company enforceable against the Company in accordance with their respective terms.

3. Neither the execution and delivery nor the consummation by the Company of the transactions contemplated in the Commitment and the Security (i) contravene (A) its statute of incorporation, certificate and articles of amalgamation or by-laws; or (B) to the best of our knowledge, any contractual restriction binding or affecting the Company; (ii) violate any law, rule, regulation having the force or law or, to the best ouf our knowledge, any judgment, injunction, determination or award which is binding on the Company; or (iii) to the best of our knowledge, result in, or require, the creation or imposition of any lien upon or security interest in or with respect to any of the properties now owned or hereafter acquired by the Company under any contractual provision binding on or affecting the Company, other than in favour of the Bank.

4. No consent, authorization, license, franchise, permit, approval or order of any court, regulator, body or governmental agency is

required for the execution and delivery of each of the Commitment and the Security and the consummation by the Company of the transactions therein contemplated.

5.   To the best of our knowledge, after due enquiry with members of this firm and appropriate senior officers of the Company, there is no pending or threatened action or proceeding affecting the Company before any court, governmental agency or arbitrator, which may materially adversely affect the financial condition or operations of the Company or which purports to affect the legality, validity or enforceability of any of the Commitment and the Security or the mortgages, pledges, charges or other security interests granted by the Company thereunder.

The opinions expressed herein are subject to the following qualifications:

1.   The opinions expressed above are limited to the laws of the province of Ontario and the laws of Canada applicable therein force on the date hereof.

2.   The enforceability of the obligations of the Company are subject to bankruptcy, insolvency, moratorium and other legislation affecting creditors rights generally, including the Personal Property Security Act, and no opinion is expressed herein as to the availability of any equitable remedy, and to due registration of the Security in all places where registration may be necessary or advisable.

Your very truly,

TO: [YOUR LAW FIRM]

The undersigned, the President of * Inc. (the "Company") hereby certifies to you as follows on behalf of the Company, knowing the same is being relied upon for your letter of opinion of * Bank and its counsel of even date herewith. Capitalized words used herein shall have the same meaning as in the aforesaid letter of opinion:

1.   Neither the execution and delivery nor the consummation by the Company of the transactions contemplated in the Commitment and the Security (i) contravene any contractual restriction binding or affecting the Company; (ii) judgment, injunction, determination or award which is binding on the Company; or (iii) result in, or require, the creation or imposition of any lien upon or security

interest in or with respect to any of the properties now owned or hereafter acquired by the Company under any contractual provision binding on or affecting the Company other than   in favour of the Bank.

2. No consent, authorization, license, franchise, permit, approval or order of any court regulator, body or governmental agency is required for the execution and delivery of each of the Commitment and Security and the consummation by the Company of the transactions therein contemplated.

3. There is no pending or threatened action or proceeding affecting the Company before any court, governmental agency or arbitrator, which may materially adversely affect the financial condition or operations of the Company or which purports to affect the legality, validity or enforceability of any of the Commitment and the Security or the mortgages, pledges, charges or other security interests granted by the Company thereunder.

DATED at Toronto this _____ day of _____, 19____.

_____
Jane Doe

9F153:1
CBA-O ILLUSTRATIVE OPINION LETTER

The Personal Property Security Opinion Report

Written by: *R. John Cameron*
              David L. Denomme
              Michael Disney
              Wilfred M. Estey
              Brian C. Keith
              Kenneth C. Morlock

The 180 page report is a piece of excellent scholarship and an invaluable analysis of the components of an opinion for secured transactions. It may be purchased from:

> Canadian Bar Association – Ontario
> 865 Carling St, 5th Floor
> Ottawa, ON K1S 5S8
> Contact: Publications Coordinator
> Bus. Ph: (613) 237-2925
>   (800) 267-8860
> Fax: (613) 237-0185
> Email: info@cba.org

I hope the attached Illustrative Opinion becomes the standard to save our clients time and money in needless opinion negotiation.

Canadian Bar Association – Ontario
Illustrative Opinion
(see prior page for full service reference)

OPINION TEXT:

(Date)

(Name and Address of Secured Party)

(Name and Address of Secured Party's Counsel)

Dear Sirs/Mesdames:

Credit Agreement made between *(the Debtor)* and *(the Secured Party)*

1.   SCOPE OF OPINION

Introduction

1.1 We have acted as counsel for _____ (the "Debtor") [*and its subsidiary,* _____ *(the "Subsidiary"),*] in connection with a credit agreement dated _____ (the "Credit Agreement") made between the Debtor and _____ (the "Secured Party"), and in connection with the security documents contemplated by the Credit Agreement.

1.2   This opinion is given to you pursuant to section _____ of the Credit Agreement. [*Capitalized terms used but not defined in this opinion have the respective meanings attributed to those terms in the Credit Agreement.*] Except as otherwise defined in this opinion, "Collateral" means all of the property defined as such in any Security Document.

Examination of Documents

1.3   We have participated in the preparation of and examined an executed copy of each of the following:

1.3.1   the Credit Agreement;

1.3.2   a general security agreement dated _____ (the 'GSA') made between the Debtor and the Secured Party; and

1.3.3   a share pledge agreement dated _____ (the "Share Pledge Agreement") made between the Debtor and the Secured

Party pledging the shares of the Subsidiary to the Secured Party.

The GSA and the Share Pledge Agreement are sometimes collectively referred to as the "Security Documents".

1.4 We have also made such investigations and examined originals or copies, certified or otherwise identified to our satisfaction, of such certificates of public officials and of such other certificates, documents and records as we considered necessary or relevant for purposes of the opinions expressed below, including:

1.4.1   the articles and by-laws of the Debtor and the Subsidiary;

1.4.2   a resolution of the board of directors of the Debtor authorizing, among other things, the execution, delivery and performance of the Credit Agreement and each of the Security Documents;

[1.4.3   a resolution of the [board of directors/shareholders] of the Subsidiary approving the transfer of the Pledged Shares (as defined in paragraph 1.7 below) from the Debtor to [the Secured Party]/[__, a nominee for the Secured Party (the "Nominee")], and the transfer of the Pledged Shares by the [Secured Party]/[Nominee] to a third party in connection with and disposition of the Pledged shares by the [Secured Party]/[Nominee];

1.4.4   a certificate of status dated __ issued in respect of [each of] the Debtor [and the Subsidiary] pursuant to the *Business Corporations Act* (Ontario) (the "OBCA");

1.4.5   a certificate of the ___[identify officer(s) by title] of [each of] the Debtor [and the Subsidiary] with respect to certain factual matters, a copy of [each of] which has been delivered to you; and

[1.4.6   the agreements (the "Material Agreements") specified in Schedule __ to [each of] the certificate[s] described in paragraph 1.4.5 above.]

Searches and Registrations

1.5   We have conducted, or have caused to be conducted, the searches identified in Schedule "A" (the "Searches") for filings or registrations made in those offices of public record, in each case as of the dates set forth in Schedule "A". The Searches were conducted in respect of the current name [and all former names] of the Debtor [and of its predecessors by amalgamation or arrangement], except for the bankruptcy searches described in paragraph (c) of Schedule "A", which were conducted only against the current name of the Debtor. The results of the Searches are also set out in Schedule "A". {s.s. 1.4.4 and 5.3}

1.6   [We have registered a financing statement]/[A financing statement has been registered] on behalf of the Secured Party under the *Personal Property Security Act* (Ontario) (the "PPSA") on __, 199__, as registration no. __, reference file no. __ (the "Financing Statement") for a period of __ years [(as requested by counsel for the Secured Party)]. {s.s. 1.4.3}

[1.7   The certificate[s] representing __ [common] shares of the Subsidiary (the "Pledged Shares") [was]/[were] delivered to [counsel for] the Secured Party on __, 199__. The [Secured Party]/[Nominee] has been registered as the owner of the Pledged Shares in the share transfer register of the Subsidiary. A new share certificate in the name of the [Secured Party]/[Nominee} has been issued and delivered to [counsel for] the Secured Party.]

Assumptions

1.8   We have made the following assumptions:

    1.8.1   with respect to all documents examined by us, the genuineness of all signatures, the legal capacity of individuals signing any documents, the authenticity of all documents submitted to us as originals and the conformity to authentic original documents of all documents submitted to us as certified, conformed, telecopied or photocopied copies;

    1.8.2   the certificate[s] of status with respect to the Debtor [and the Subsidiary] referred to in paragraph 1.4.4. above continue[s]] to be accurate as of the date of this opinion as if issued on that date;

1.8.3   the Credit Agreement and each of the Security Documents have been duly authorized, executed and delivered by the Secured Party and constitute legal, valid and binding obligations of the Secured Party, enforceable against it in accordance with their terms; and

1.8.4   the Collateral does not include consumer goods (as defined in the PPSA).

Laws Addressed

1.9   This opinion is limited to the laws of the Province of Ontario and the federal laws of Canada applicable in Ontario. Without limiting the generality of the immediately preceding sentence, we express no opinion with respect to the laws of any other jurisdiction to the extent that those laws may govern the validity, perfection, effect of perfection or non-perfection or enforcement of the security interests created by the Security Documents as a result of the application of Ontario conflict of laws rules, including without limitation sections 5 to 8 of the PPSA. In addition, we express no opinion whether, pursuant to those conflict of laws rules, Ontario laws would govern the validity, perfection, effect of perfection or non-perfection or enforcement of those security interests. {s.s. 7.7.2.2}

2.   OPINIONS

Based upon and subject to the foregoing, and to the qualifications expressed below, we are of the opinion that:

Corporate Opinions

2.1   [Each of] the Debtor [and the Subsidiary] is incorporated and existing under the OBCA.

2.2   The Debtor has the corporate power and capacity to carry on [its] business [as presently conducted], to own [its] properties and assets, and to execute, deliver and perform its obligations under the Credit Agreement and each of the Security Documents.

2.3   the Debtor has taken all necessary corporate action to authorize the execution, delivery and performance by it of the Credit Agreement and each of the Security Documents, and the Debtor has duly executed and delivered the Credit Agreement and each of the Security Documents.

[2.4   All necessary corporate action has been taken by the Subsidiary [and its shareholders] to authorize the transfer of the Pledged shares contemplated by the Share Pledge Agreement, including the registration, on the share transfer register of the Subsidiary, of the transfer of the Pledged shares to the [Secured Party]/[Nominee] and any subsequent transfer of the Pledged Shares by the [Secured Party]/[Nominee] in connection with any disposition of the Pledged Shares by the [Secured party]/[Nominee].

Non-contravention and No Breach Opinion

2.5   The execution, delivery and performance of the Credit Agreement and each of the Security Documents by the Debtor do not:

    2.5.1   breach or result in a default under:

        2.5.1.1   the articles or by-laws of the Debtor,

        2.5.1.2   any law, statute, rule or regulation to which the Debtor is subject [, or

        2.5.1.3   any Material Agreement; or

    2.5.2   according to the terms of any Material Agreement:

        2.5.2.1   result in the creation of any security interest, lien or encumbrance on any of the Debtor's property other than the security interest in favour of the Secured Party created by the Security Documents,

        2.5.2.2   require the Debtor to create any security interest, lien or encumbrance on any of its property, or

        2.5.2.3   result in the forfeiture of any of the Debtor's property.]

Regulatory Approval Opinion

2.6   No authorization, consent, permit or approval of, or other action, by or filing with or notice to,, any governmental agency or authority, regulatory body, court, tribunal or other similar entity having jurisdiction is required [at this time] in connection with the execution, delivery and performance of the Credit

Agreement or any of the Security Documents by the Debtor other than registration of the Financing Statement under the PPSA, which has been effected as described in paragraph 1.6 above [, and __].

Share Capital Opinions

[2.7   The authorized capital of the Subsidiary consists of ___ common shares.]

[2.8   the Pledged Shares have been duly and validly issued and are outstanding as fully paid and non-assessable shares.]

[2.9   The Debtor is the registered owner of the Pledged Shares.]

Enforceability Opinion

2.10   The Credit Agreement and each of the Security Documents constitute legal, valid and binding obligations of the Debtor, enforceable against it in accordance with their terms. {s.s. 2.1}

Creation of Security Interest

2.11   Each of the Security Documents creates a valid security interest in favour of the Secured Party in any Collateral (as defined therein) in which the Debtor now has rights, and is sufficient to create a valid security interest in favour of the Secured Party in any Collateral (as defined therein) in which the Debtor hereafter acquires rights when those rights are acquired by the Debtor, in each case to secure payment and performance of the [obligations described therein as being secured thereby]/[the Obligations [(as defined in the Credit Agreement)]]. {s.s. 3.2.2.4(b) and 4.3.2}

Registration of Security Interest

2.12   Registration has been made in all public offices provided for under the laws of Ontario or the federal laws of Canada where such registration is necessary or desirable to preserve, protect or perfect the security interests created by each Security Document in favour of the Secured Party in the Collateral (as defined therein.) {s.s. 4.2.1.3 and 4.2.1.5}

Search Review Opinion

2.13   The Searches disclosed no writ of seizure and sale, other writ or bankruptcy filing in respect of the Debtor or its property. {s.s. 5.3}

2.14 The Searches disclosed no registration which is sufficient to perfect a security or other interest in any Collateral [(a "Potentially Conflicting Filing"), other than:]

[2.14.1 the registrations identified in Part I of Schedule "B", each of which may perfect security or other interest ranking prior to the security interests created by the Security Documents;]

[2.14.2 the registrations identified in Part II of Schedule "B", in respect of each of which a subordination agreement in favour of the Secured Party has been obtained [, in a form approved by counsel to the Secured Party];]

[2.14.3 the registrations identified in Part III of Schedule "B", in respect of each of which an acknowledgment addressed to the Secured Party has been obtained, [in a form approved by counsel to the Secured Party,] which states that:

2.14.3.1 the Potentially Conflicting Filing is limited to collateral described in a security agreement or other document attached to the acknowledgment, and

2.14.3.2 any additional security or other interest which may be perfected by that Potentially Conflicting Filing will be subordinate to the security interest of the Secured party;]

[2.14.4 the registrations identified in Part IV of Schedule "B", none of which is sufficient to perfect security or other interests in the Collateral except to the extent they perfect a security interest in proceeds;] {Paragraph 2.14.4 is inappropriate where the Collateral consists of all present and future personal property of the Debtor, such as would be the case under the GSA, but paragraph 2.14.4 is included in this Illustrative Opinion for reference in other situations.}

[2.14.5 the registrations under the PPSA identified in Part V of Schedule "B", each of which was registered after registration of the Financing Statement but which may perfect security or other interests ranking prior to the security interests created by the Security Documents in limited circumstances (such as certain purchase-money security interest in Collateral) as set forth in the PPSA;] [and]

[2.14.6 other registrations in respect of each of which a discharge has been obtained.] {s.s. 5.3}

[2.15 Each of the security or other interests perfected by the Potentially Conflicting Filings constitutes a Permitted Lien [as defined in the Credit Agreement)] [or has been discharged. {s.s. 5.3}

Good Faith Purchaser Opinion

2.16   Provided that the Secured Party is acting in good faith and has no notice of any adverse claim affecting the Pledged Shares, the security interest of the Secured Party in the Pledged Shares has priority over any other security interest in the Pledged Shares perfected by registration or temporarily perfected under the PPSA, and the Secured Party has acquired the Pledged Shares free of any adverse claim. {s.s. 5.6}

Pending Litigation Opinion

2.17 We have not been retained to represent the Debtor in respect of any:

2.17.1   court, administrative, regulatory or similar proceeding (whether civil, quasi-criminal or criminal),

2.17.2   arbitration or other dispute settlement procedure, or

2.17.3   investigation or inquiry by any governmental, administrative, regulatory or other similar body,

that, if determined adversely to the Debtor, would:

2.17.4   prohibit the Debtor from executing, delivering or performing any of its obligations under the Credit Agreement or the Security Documents,

2.17.5   result in the creation of any security interest, lien or encumbrance on any of the Debtor's property other than security interests in favour of the Secured Party created by the Security Documents,

2.17.6   require the Debtor to create any security interest, lien or encumbrance on any of its property, or

2.17.7   result in the forfeiture of any of the Debtor's property (other than the levying of execution against such property to obtain payment of a judgment against the Debtor),

[other than __].

3.   QUALIFICATIONS

The foregoing opinions are subject to the following qualifications:

3.1   The enforceability of the Credit Agreement and of each of the Security Documents is subject to bankruptcy, insolvency, reorganization, arrangement, winding-up, moratorium and other similar laws of general application affecting the enforcement of creditors' rights generally [("Insolvency Laws")].

3.2   The enforceability of the Credit Agreement and of each of the Security Documents is subject to [general equitable principles, including] the fact that the availability of equitable remedies, such as injunctive relief and specific performance, is in the discretion of a court.

3.3   The PPSA imposes certain obligations on secured creditors which cannot be varied by contract. The PPSA may also affect the enforcement of certain rights and remedies contained in the Security Documents to the extent that those rights and remedies are inconsistent with or contrary to the PPSA including, without limitation, sections 16, 17 and 39 and Part V of the PPSA. {s.s. 2.3.1.1.}

3.4   The Secured Party may be required to give the Debtor a reasonable time to repay following a demand for payment prior to taking any action to enforce its right of repayment or before exercising any of the rights and remedies expressed to be exercisable by the Secured Party in the Credit Agreement or in any of the Security Documents. {s.s. 2.3.3.}

[3.5   We express no opinion as to the due authorization, execution or delivery of the subordination agreement (s) and acknowledgment(s) referred to in paragraphs 2.14.2 and 2.14.3 above [nor as to the enforceability of such agreement(s) or acknowledgment(s)].] {s.s. 5.3}

Validity of Security Interests

[3.6 We have taken no steps to provide the notices or to obtain the acknowledgments prescribed in Part VII of the Financial Administration Act (Canada) relating to the assignment of federal Crown debts. An assignment of federal Crown debts which does not comply with that Act is ineffective as between the assignor and the assignee and as against the Crown . Consequently, the Secured Party would not have a valid security interest in federal Crown debts unless that Act is complied with.] {s.s. 6.2.2.4.}

[3.7 We express no opinion as to whether a security interest may be created in:

3.7.1   property consisting of a receivable, licence, approval, privilege, franchise, permit, lease or agreement (collectively, "Special Property") to the extent that the terms of the Special Property or any applicable law prohibit its assignment or require a consent, approval or other authorization or registration which has not been made or given, or {s.s. 6.2.2.1}

3.7.2   permits, quotas or licences which are held by or issued to the Debtor. {s.s. 6.2.1}

[However, none of the Material Agreements, the rights of the Debtor under the Material Agreements or __ constitute Special Property.]]

[3.8 It is unclear whether the Secured Party can obtain a valid security interest in the Debtor's deposit accounts with the Secured Party as provided for in the Security Documents. However, [this would not affect any rights of set-off available to the Secured Party under the Security Documents or otherwise.]/[the rights of set-off in the GSA and under applicable law and the restrictions in the GSA on the Debtor's ability to withdraw or obtain payment of amounts in those deposit accounts:

3.8.1   would be effective against an assignee of the Debtor's rights and against a person, such as an execution creditor, claiming through the Debtor, and

3.8.2   would be effective notwithstanding the application of any Insolvency Laws, except that the Secured Party's rights of set-off may be stayed temporarily in connection with proceedings under Insolvency Laws.]] {s.s. 6.2.3}

3.9   We express no opinion as to any security interest created by the Security Documents with respect to any property of the Debtor that is transformed in such a way that it is not identifiable or traceable or any proceeds or property of the Debtor that are not identifiable or traceable. {s.s. 3.2.2.2(b) and 4.3.3}

Registrations

[3.10 We have not registered [the GSA]/[any of the Security Documents] or notice thereof in any land registry office or under any land registry statutes even though the [GSA]/[Security Documents] may create a security interest [in the Debtor's real property or leases of real property or] in property which is now or may hereafter become a fixture or a right to payment under a lease, mortgage or charge of real property.] {s.s. 4.3.4 and 6.3.1}

[3.11 No registrations have been made:

> 3.11.1   under the *Patent Act* (Canada), *the Trade-marks Act* (Canada), the *Industrial Designs Act* (Canada) , the *Integrated Circuit Topography Act* (Canada), *the Copyright Act* (Canada) or the *Plant Breeders' Rights Act* (Canada),
>
> 3.11.2   under the *Canada Shipping Act* in respect of any vessel which is registered or recorded under that Act, or
>
> 3.11.3   under the *Canada Transportation Act* or the *Railways Act* (Ontario) in respect of any rolling stock to which the provisions of either of those Acts may apply.] {s.s. 6.4.1, 6.4.3 and 6.4.4}

No Title or Priority Opinion

3.12   Except for the opinion(s) expressed in paragraph [s. 2.9 and] 2.16 above, we express no opinion as to whether the Debtor has title to or any rights in the Collateral, nor as to the priority of any security interest created by the Security Documents. {s.s. 3.2.2.4(a)}

4.   INFORMATION ABOUT MAINTAINING PERFECTION AND OTHER MATTERS

Maintaining Perfection of Security Interests

4.1   The following actions are required in order to maintain perfection of the security interests created by the Security Documents:

[4.1.1   The registration period of the Financing Statement will expire, and the security interest perfected thereby will become unperfected, on __ unless the registration period is extended prior to that time by registration under the PPSA of a financing change statement designated as a renewal. We assume no responsibility for registering this financing change statement or for reminding you of the date by which it must be registered.] {s.s. 4.3.1}

4.1.2   Any change in the name of the Debtor and any transfer by the Debtor of any or all of the Collateral will require the filing of a financing change statement under the PPSA:

4.1.2.1   within 15 days of the Secured Party consenting to the transfer of Collateral, or

4.1.2.2   within 30 days of the Secured Party learning of the transfer of Collateral or change of name, as the case may be, and the information necessary to register the financing change statement.

We assume no responsibility for making this type of registration nor for notifying you if circumstances arise which necessitate this type of registration. {s.s. 4.3.1}

4.1.3   Additional registrations may be required in other jurisdictions if any of the Collateral is removed from Ontario or if the Debtor moves its [sole place of business]/[chief executive office] from Ontario. {s.s. 7.5.1}

Other Matters

4.2   You should also be aware of the following matters:

[4.2.1   Perfection of the security interest in the Pledged Shares by possession of the Pledged Shares continues only so long as the Secured Party or a person on its behalf other than the Debtor or its agent continues to hold the Pledged Shares as collateral.] {s.s. 4.3.1}

[4.2.2   The board of directors of the Subsidiary has passed a resolution approving the transfer of the Pledged Shares to the [Secured Party]/[Nominee] and also approving any transfer of the Pledged Shares by the [Secured Party]/[Nominee]. There is some doubt about the directors' power to irrevocably bind themselves to the approval of any such transfer of the Pledged Shares by the [Secured Party]/[Nominee].] {s.s.6.5}

4.2.3   Notwithstanding that the security interest created by the Security Documents have been perfected by registration of the Financing Statement, a security interest in instruments, securities, chattel paper, goods, money and negotiable documents of title (each as defined in the PPSA) perfected by registration will be defeated by certain claimants obtaining possession of the property in the circumstances described in the PPSA. {s.s. 4.3.5 and 5.2.(d)}

4.2.4   If the Collateral includes a motor vehicle (as defined in the Regulation under the PPSA) which is classified as equipment of the Debtor and which is sold by the Debtor out of the ordinary course of business, the buyer of that motor vehicle will take it free and clear of the security interests created in the Security Documents unless:

4.2.4.1   the vehicle identification number is set out in the Financing Statement, or

4.2.4.2   the buyer knew that the sale constituted a breach of the Security Documents.

As to paragraph 4.2.4.1 above, no vehicle identification number is set out in the Financing Statement {s.s. 5.4.2(g)}

[4.2.5   An assignment of a debt or account will not be binding on the obligor to the extent that such debt or account is paid or otherwise discharged before notice of the assignment is given to the obligor, together with a direction to pay the same to the Secured Party.] {s.s. 4.2.1.2 and 4.2.1.4}

5.   RELIANCE

This opinion may be relied upon only by the Secured Party, [its permitted assigns and other participants in the [Credit Facility (as defined in the Credit Agreement)] and counsel to the Secured Party, for the purposes of the transaction contemplated by this opinion. It may not be relied upon by any other person or for any other purpose, nor may it be quoted in whole or in part or otherwise referred to, without prior written consent.

Yours very truly,

APPENDIX "A"

ADDITIONAL PARAGRAPHS

INTRODUCTORY NOTE:

The additional paragraphs in this Appendix are included for reference purposes only. Each of these paragraphs may be necessary or appropriate in particular opinions but will not be required in others. The paragraphs in Part I of this Appendix pertain directly to personal property security opinions. Most of these paragraphs are discussed in the Commentary. The paragraphs in Part II of this Appendix, some of which are also discussed in the Commentary, pertain to financing opinions generally.

PART I

PARAGRAPHS DIRECTLY RELATING TO PERSONAL PROPERTY SECURITY OPINIONS

Searches and Registrations

1.5A The Searches constitute all searches which are customarily conducted under the laws of Ontario and the federal laws of Canada applicable therein for security and other interests in personal property of a kind similar to the Collateral as of the applicable date[s] identified in Schedule "A". For your information, our searches did not include searches

    1.5A.1   in any land registry office for security and other interests in or affecting real property,

    1.5A.2   under the *Patent Act* (Canada), the *Trade-marks Act* (Canada), the *Industrial Designs Act* (Canada) the *Integrated Circuit topography Act* (Canada), the *Plant Breeders' Rights Act* (Canada) for security and other interests affecting intellectual property governed by those statues,

1.5A.3   under the *Canada Shipping Act* for security and other interests affecting any vessel which is registered or recorded under that Act,

1.5A.4   under the *Canada Transportation Act*, the *Railway Act* (Canada) or the *Railways Act* (Ontario) for security and other interests affecting rolling stock, or

1.5A.5   for writs of seizure and sale and other writs filed outside the [Judicial District of York] which we have been informed is the jurisdiction in which the [sole place of business]/[chief executive office] of the Debtor is located. {s.s. 5.2}

Assumptions

1.8.5   the description of [the items] of Collateral specified in [Schedule __ to] the GSA is accurate; {s.s. 3.2.2.2(a)}

1.8.6   the parties to the Security Documents have not agreed orally or in any written agreement (other than the Security Documents, which do not postpone attachment) to postpone the time for attachment of the security interest contemplated in the Security Documents; {s.s. 3.2.2.5}

1.8.7   the Secured Party or a person on its behalf other than the Debtor or its agent has possession of the Pledged Shares; {s.s. 1.4.6.3, 4.2.2 and 7.9}

1.8.8   the information referred to in paragraph [1.8A] below {under "Instructions and Information" - see immediately below} is accurate. {s.s.1.4.3 and 1.4.6.2}

Instructions and Information

1.8A You [or the Debtor, as indicated below] have provided us with the following instructions and information:

1.8A.1   the current name [and all former names] of the Debtor [and of its predecessors by amalgamation or arrangement][, in each case including both the English and French versions,] [(as provided by the Debtor)]; {s.s. 1.4.3}

1.8A.2   the names of any previous owners of the Collateral [(as provided by the Debtor)]; {s.s. 1.4.3}

1.8A.3   the [sole place of business]/[chief executive office] of the Debtor [(as provided by the Debtor)]; {s.s. 1.4.3}

1.8A.4   instructions [(as provided by counsel to the Secured Party)] that no registrations or filings were to be made, other than the registration of the Financing Statement under the PPSA; and {s.s. 1.4.3}

1.8A.5   confirmation that the motor vehicle identification numbers, if any, [(as provided by the Debtor)] have been correctly set out on the Financing Statement. {s.s. 1.4.6.2}

OPINIONS

Registration of Security Interest

2.12.A   The only registrations necessary to maintain the perfection of the security interests created by the Security Documents in favour of the Secured Party are referred to in paragraphs [s 4.1.1 and] 4.1.2 below. {s.s. 4.2.1.5 and 4.3.1}

Potentially Conflicting Filings and Status as a Good Faith Purchaser

2.16A   The Searches disclosed no registration which is sufficient to perfect a security or other interest in any Collateral described in the Share Pledge Agreement [(a "Potentially Conflicting Filing"), other than:]

[2.16A.1   the registrations identified in Part I of Schedule "C", in respect of each of which an acknowledgement addressed to the Secured Party has been obtained, [in a form approved by counsel to the Secured Party,] which states that:

2.16A.2.1   the Potentially Conflicting Filing is limited to collateral described in a security agreement or other document attached to the acknowledgement, which we have reviewed and we confirm does not include the Collateral described in the Share Pledge Agreement, and

2.16A.2.2   the secured creditor or other claimant on whose behalf the acknowledgment is delivered does not presently have a security interest or other adverse claim to the Collateral described in the Share Pledge Agreement;] and

[2.16A.3   the registrations identified in Part III of Schedule "C", in respect of which the certificate described in paragraph 1.4.5 above indicates that those registrations do not relate to security interests or other adverse claims affecting the Collateral described in the Share Pledge Agreement.] {s.s. 5.6.2.4(c)}

2.16B   Provided that the Secured Party is acting in good faith and has no notice of any adverse claim affecting the Pledged Shares other than the information described in this opinion relating to Potentially conflicting Filings:

2.16B.1   the security interest of the Secured Party in the Pledged Shares has priority over any other security interest in the Pledged Shares perfected by regis-tration or temporarily perfected under the PPSA, and

2.16B.2   the Secured Party has acquired the Pledged Shares free of any adverse claim,

including without limitation in either case any security interest or other adverse claim now or hereafter perfected by the Potentially Conflicting Filings. {s.s. 5.6.2.4(c)}

QUALIFICATIONS

General Enforceability

3.3A   The PPSA imposes certain obligations on secured creditors which cannot be varied by contract. The PPSA may also affect the enforcement of certain rights and remedies contained in the Security Documents to the extent that those rights and remedies are inconsistent with or contrary to the PPSA including, without limitation, sections 16, 17 and 39 and Part V of the PPSA. However, the PPSA does not render any of the Security Documents invalid as a whole, and there exist, in each Security Document or pursuant to applicable law, legally adequate remedies for realization of the principal benefits of the Collateral (as defined in that Security Document) purported to be provided by that Security Document {s.s. 2.3.1.2}

3.4A We express no opinion as to the enforceability of any provision of the Security Documents which is inconsistent with or contrary to any provision of the Credit Agreement. {s.s. 2.3.10}

3.4B We express no opinion as to the enforceability of any provision of the security Documents or the Credit Agreement which purports to suspend, in the circumstances prescribed therein, the powers of the board of directors of the Debtor. {s.s. 2.3.9}

3.4C A receiver or receiver and manager appointed pursuant to [the Credit Agreement or] any of the Security Documents may, for certain purposes, be treated as the agent of the Secured Party and not solely the agent of the Debtor notwithstanding any provision in such documents to the contrary. {s.s. 2.3.2}

Licences for Enforcement

3.5A We express no opinion as to any licences, permits or approvals that may be required in connection with the enforcement of the Security Documents by the Secured Party or by a person on its behalf, whether such enforcement involves the operation of the business of the Debtor or a sale, transfer or disposition of its property and assets. {s.s. 2.3.7 and 7.10.2}

PART II

PARAGRAPHS RELATING GENERALLY TO FINANCING OPINIONS

QUALIFICATIONS

General Enforceability

3.5B We express no opinion as to the enforceability of section __ of the Credit Agreement, which may be characterized by a court as an unenforceable penalty and not as a genuine pre-estimate of damages. {s.s. 2.3.11}

3.5C Pursuant to the provisions of section 8 of the *Interest Act* (Canada), no fine, penalty or rate of interest may be exacted on any arrears of principal or interest secured by a mortgage on real property that has the effect of increasing the charge on the arrears beyond the rate of interest payable on principal money not in arrears. {s.s. 2.3.11}

3.5D The provisions for payment of interest under the Credit Agreement may not be enforceable if those provisions provide for the receipt of interest by the Secured party at a "criminal rate" within the meaning of section 347 of the *Criminal Code* (Canada) [a copy of which is attached hereto.] {s.s. 2.3.11}

3.5E Notwithstanding section___ of the Credit Agreement [, section ___ of the GSA or section ___ of the Share Pledge Agreement], any certificate or determination provided for therein may be subject to challenge in a court on the grounds of fraud, collusion, mistake on the face of the certificate, or mistake on the basis that the certificate differed in a material respect from the certificate contemplated in such provision. {s.s. 2.3.8}

3.5F We express no opinion as to the enforceability of any provision of the Credit Agreement or Security Documents:

> 3.5F.1   which purports to waive all defences which might be available to, or constitute a discharge of the liability of the Debtor;

> 3.5F.2   to the extent is purports to exculpate the Secured Party or its agents from liability in respect of acts or omissions which may be illegal, fraudulent or involve wilful misconduct; {s.s. 2.3.2}

> 3.5F.3   which states that amendments or waivers of or with respect to the Credit Agreement or the Security Documents that are not in writing will not be effective. {s.s. 2.3.11}

3.5G Provisions contained in the Credit Agreement and each Security Document which purport to sever from the Credit Agreement or that Security Document any provision which is prohibited or unenforceable under applicable law without affecting the enforceability or validity of the remainder of the Credit Agreement or that Security Document may be enforced only in the discretion of a court {s.s. 2.3.11}

3.5H The enforceability of the indemnity contained in section ___ of the Credit Agreement [, section ___ of the GSA or section ___ of the Share Pledge Agreement] may be limited by applicable law to the extent it directly or indirectly relates to liabilities imposed on the Secured Party by law for which it would be contrary to public policy to require the Debtor to indemnify the Secured Party.

3.5I   We express no opinion as to the enforceability of any provision of the Credit Agreement or Security Documents which requires the Debtor to pay, or to indemnify the Secured Party for, the costs and expenses of the Secured Party in connection with judicial proceedings, since those provisions may derogate from a court's discretion to determine by whom and to what extent those costs should be paid. {s.s. 2.3.4}

3.5J   A judgment of an Ontario court may only be awarded in Canadian currency. [That judgment may be based on a rate of exchange determined in accordance with section 121 of the *Courts of Justice Act* (Ontario), which rate of exchange may be the rate in existence on a day other than the day of payment of such judgment.]/[However, the Credit Agreement contains a provision with respect to currency conversion which will be given effect by the courts in the Province of Ontario]. {s.s. 2.3.5}

SCHEDULE "A"

SEARCHES AND RESULTS OF SEARCHES

We have made searches or inquiries for:

(a) security or other interest in the personal property of the Debtor registered under the PPSA as of __, 19__;

- Result: [Clear]/__ [; see also Schedule "B" below] /[A copy of the PPSA search results have been delivered to you[;see also Schedule "B" below.]

(b) notices of intention of the Debtor to give security under section 427 of the *Bank Act* (Canada) registered with the Bank of Canada at [Toronto, Ontario] as of __, 19__;

- Result: [Clear]/[__ [; see also Schedule "B" below]]/[or A copy of the certificate received has been delivered to you [; see also Schedule "B" below.]]

(c) proceedings under the *Bankruptcy and Insolvency Act* (Canada) in respect of the Debtor as of __, 19__ recorded in the Ontario Court of Justice (General Division) (in Bankruptcy), as of __, 19__ recorded in the [Official Receiver's Office for the Municipality of Metropolitan Toronto] and as of __, 19__ recorded in the Office of the Superintendent of Bankruptcy;

- Result: [Clear]/[__]/[a copy of the certificate(s) received has been delivered to you].

(d) writs of seizure and sale and other writs filed under the *Execution Act* (Ontario) in the [Judicial District of York] in respect of the property of the Debtor as of __, 19__;

- Result: [Clear]/[__]/[a copy of the certificate(s) received has been delivered to you.

All searches described in paragraphs (a), (b) and (d) above were conducted against the current name [and all former names] of the Debtor [and of its predecessors by amalgamation or arrangement] [, in each case including both the English and French versions]. The bankruptcy searches described in paragraph (c) above were conducted against only the current name of the Debtor [including both the English and French versions].

[The searches described in paragraphs (a) and (b) above revealed Potentially Conflicting Filings (as defined in paragraph 2.14 of the opinion). Schedule "B" addresses the manner in which [some of] those Potentially Conflicting Filings have been dealt with.]

9F154
OPINION OF LENDER'S COUNSEL

[See Paras. 9.079.4 and 9.701]

LETTERHEAD OF LENDER'S COUNSEL

(*Date*)

_____Bank

Attention: ____

Dear Sirs:

Re: ____ Limited

We have acted on behalf of Big Bank (the "Bank") in connection with the loan referred to in the Bank's commitment letter dated ____, (the "Commitment") and accepted by ____ Limited (the "Company") on ____ ,

A. Document

In acting as such counsel, we have participated in the preparation of those documents which do not constitute the Bank's preprinted forms and have examined executed copies of the following documents:

1. the Commitment;

2. demand debenture dated _____, made by the Company in favour of the Bank, on the Bank's form no. _____ given as security for all present and future indebtedness and liability of the Company to the Bank (the "Debenture") in the principal amount of $_____;

3. agreement dated _____, (the "Pledge") pursuant to which the Company pledged the Debenture to the Bank;

4. an assignment of book debts dated _____ (the "Assignment") issued by the Company to the Bank on the Bank's preprinted form no. _____;

5. a general security agreement dated _____ (the "GSA") issued by the Company to the Bank on the Bank's preprinted form no. _____; and

6. a pledge dated _____ (the "Pledge") of the _____ common shares owned by the Company in the capital stock of Canadian Subco (the "Shares") made in favour of the Bank on the Bank's preprinted form no. _____.

The instruments referred to in paragraphs 2 to 6 above are sometimes referred to collectively as the "Security").

In addition we examined the following documents:

(i) Certificate of Status issued for the Company dated _____, issued by the Ontario Ministry of Consumer and Commercial Relations;

(ii) Certificate of the Company dated _____, to which certificate is attached a certified copy of the resolution of the board of directors of the Company respecting this transaction;

(iii) Notarial copies of the constating documents of the Company as of _____;

(iv) Notarial copies of all the by-laws of the Company in force as of _____;

(v) Certificate of officer of the Company dated _____, respecting non-restriction of its borrowing powers;

(vi) the opinion letter of Messers. _____ dated _____, (the "Opinion") given as counsel for the Company for this transaction;

(vii) the letter of the Bank dated _____ accepting certain security granted by the Company as prior permitted encumbrances;

(viii) a certified copy of the resolution of the directors of Canadian Subco dated _____, authorizing the transfer of the Shares pursuant to the Pledge; and

(ix) certificate no. _____ representing the Shares issued in the name of the Bank.

B. Searches

We conducted searches on _____, in the Province of Ontario against the Company under the following statutes or in the following offices:

1. the Personal Property Security Act (the "PPSA");

2. the Executions Act for the Judicial Districts of York and Peel;

3. the Bulk Sales Act for the Judicial District of York and Peel;

4. the Bank Act for registrations with the Toronto Agency of the Bank of Canada;

5. the Toronto office of the Registrar for the Supreme Court of Ontario in Bankruptcy; and

6. the Ottawa offices of the Official Receiver in Bankruptcy.

The above searches disclosed only the registrations against the Company referred to in Schedule "A" appended to this letter.

C. Instructions

We confirm your instructions for this transaction as follows:

(a) the PPSA registration for the Security was to be made for a period of ten (10) years;

(b)   the Bank would make its own delivery to the Company of a copy of the verification statement issued by the Ministry for the registration made by us for the Security;

(c)   the certificate representing the Shares was to be delivered to Mr. John Jones of the Bank, which delivery we effected personally at closing on *;

(d)   the Bank will obtain such promissory note(s) as it requires from the Company to evidence advances of funds;

(e)   the Bank did not require any consent and acknowledgement of the landlord and/or mortgagees of the real property occupied by the Company as tenant or registration of a fixtures notice against title to such real property;

(f)   the Bank accepted as prior permitted encumbrances the four PPSA registrations made against the Company listed in Schedule "C" to the Debenture and as Schedule "A" to this opinion; and

(g)   the Bank undertook to effect its own registrations for the Assignment in the provinces of British Columbia, Alberta, Saskatchewan and Manitoba, where the customers of the Company are located.

D. Registrations

We registered a financing statement/claim for lien for the Security pursuant to the PPSA in respect of the Company of July 1, 1993 as registration number 930701 1510 0043 1234.

E. Opinions

In connection with the opinions hereinafter expressed, we have considered such questions of law and we have examined such statutes and regulations, corporate records, certificates and other documents as we have deemed relevant and necessary as the basis for the opinions hereinafter set forth. We have assumed the genuineness of all signatures and the authenticity of all documents submitted to us as originals, other than the Security, and the conformity to originals of all documents submitted to us as certified or photostat (or similarly reproduced copies).

We are not and have not been corporated counsel for the Company. With respect to the opinions set forth in paragraphs 1 to 5 below, we have relied upon the Opinion. We have reviewed the Opinion and believe you are entitled to rely thereon.

Based upon and subject to the foregoing, and the qualifications hereafter expressed, we are of the opinion that:

1. The Company is a corporation duly incorporated, organized and validly subsisting under the laws of the province of Ontario, with full corporate right, power and authority to own its properties and assets, and to carry on its business in the province of Ontario, as now conducted and to enter into and perform each of the Commitment and the Security.

2. The Commitment and the Security have been duly authorized, executed and delivered to the Bank by the Company and constitute valid and binding obligations of the Company enforceable against the Company in accordance with their respective terms.

3. Neither the execution and delivery nor the consummation by the Company of the transactions contemplated in the Commitment and the Security:

    (i)   contravene (a) its statute of incorporation, certificate and articles of amalgamation or by-laws; or (B) to the best of our knowledge, any contractual restriction binding or affecting the Company;

    (ii)   violate any law, rule, regulation having the force or law or, to the best of our knowledge, any judgment, injunction, determination or award which is binding on the Company; or

    (iii) to the best of our knowledge, result in, or require, the creation or imposition of any lien upon or security interest in or with respect to any of the properties now owned or hereafter acquired by the Company under any contractual provision binding on or affecting the Company, other than in favour of the Bank.

4. No consent, authorization, licence, franchise, permit, approval or order of any court, regulator, body or governmental agency is required for the   execution and delivery of each of the Commitment and the Security and the Consummation by the Company of the transactions therein contemplated.

5. To the best of our knowledge, after due enquiry with members of this firm and appropriate senior officers of the Company, there is no pending or threatened action or proceeding affecting the Company before any court, governmental agency or arbitrator, which may materially adversely affect the financial condition or

operations of the Company or which purports to affect the legality, validity or enforceability of any of the Commitment and the Security or the mortgages, pledges, charges or other security interests granted by the Company thereunder.

6. Except with respect to the interests in the real property occupied by the Company as tenant, the Security has been registered or filed in all offices in the Province of Ontario where such registration or filing is necessary or desirable, to register the security interests therein granted or constituted in favour of the Lender.

The opinions expressed herein are subject to the following qualifications:

1. The opinions expressed above are limited to the laws of the Province of Ontario and the laws of Canada applicable therein in force on the date hereof.

2. The enforceability of the obligations of the Company are subject to:
    (i)   bankruptcy, insolvency, moratorium and other legislation affecting creditors rights generally;
    (ii)   the provisions of the PPSA;
    (iii)   no opinion is expressed herein as to the availability of any equitable remedy;
    (iv)   the Bank, or an agent on behalf of the Bank, retaining possession of the Shares for as long as the obligations of the Company remain outstanding; and
    (v)   the security interests perfected by the prior PPSA registrations listed in Schedule "A" hereto.

3. The Province of Ontario does not have title registry for personal property and we are therefore unable to express any opinion as to the title of the Borrower to its personal property, nor have we made any searches, investigations or enquiries in that regard. We have assumed that the Company has rights in the collateral described in the Security.

4. We are unable to determine by search (i) any lien given by statute where registration is not required or by rule of law; or (ii) any registrations or filings against the Company or its property which did not appear in the register searched because of delays in

recording registrations or because of the failure of departmental officials to record a registration or an instrument created by the Company where registration thereof has not yet been effected.

5. Registration under the PPSA is only effective for a ten (10) year period from the date of registration and must be renewed prior to the expiration of each such period. In addition, further registrations will be required if the Bank learns that the Company has changed its name or has transferred all or part of its interest in the assets for which such registration was made. Failure to make such registrations may leave the Bank subsequent in priority to third parties. The obligation to effect such registrations is upon the Bank and we do not maintain a reminder system for such purposes.

6. [Recite additional qualifications set forth in the Opinion.]

Yours very truly,

SCHEDULE "A"

SUMMARY OF SEARCHES IN ONTARIO ON:

* LIMITED

As of:	*, 19___ (*, 19___ for the PPSA)
From:	June 1, 1987
Addresses:	1. *, Toronto (York)
	2. *, Mississauga (Peel)

1. CORPORATE

Jurisdiction:	Ontario
Created:	Articles of Incorporation; June 1, 1987
Original Name :	123456 Ontario Inc.
Changed:	January 1, 1989
To:	* Limited
Reg'd Office:	*, Toronto
Directors:	1. Jane Doe
	2. John Doe
Last Filing:	July 27, 1992
Business Style:	Widgets Co., filed July 25, 1987

Searches therefore conducted on:

1. 123456 Ontario Inc.

2. Canadian Opco

3. Widgets Co.

2. BANKRUPTCY (as of *, 19____)

— clear for Toronto offices of the Supreme Court of Ontario and the Ottawa office of the Official Receiver

3. SECTION 427, BANK ACT SECURITY OVER INVENTORY

— clear for Toronto Agency of Bank of Canada

4. EXECUTIONS

— clear for Judicial Districts of York and Peel

5. BILLS OF SALE

— clear for Judicial Districts of York and Peel

6. BULK SALES

— clear for Judicial Districts of York and Peel

7. PERSONAL PROPERTY SECURITY ACT

Note: 1. Registrations filed before October 10, 1989 expire in 3 years; registrations filed on or after that date expire when indicated; registrations under the CSRA do not expire until discharged.
2. CSRA filings (if any) have been entered in chronological order, but this does not determine priority.

i) 891004 1510 43 1234
Secured: The Supply House Inc.
* Street, Toronto
Collateral: Inventory, Order
Description: security over inventory and the proceeds thereof

ii)   891102   0130   43   2345
      Secured: Jane Doe
                                *, Toronto
      Collateral: Book Debts, Order
      Description: and the proceeds thereof

iii) 900201   1310   43   3456
      Secured: Acme Leasing Corporation
                                * Street, Toronto
      Collateral: Equipment
      Description: 1 photocopier

iv)   900630   1010   43   4567
      Secured: Acme Leasing Corporation
                                * Road, Willowdale
      Collateral: Equipment
      Description: 1 cellular telephone and the proceeds thereof

v)   930701   1510   0043   1234
      File #:   123456789
      Reg. Length: 10 years
      Secured: * Bank
                                * , Toronto
      Collateral: Inventory, Equipment, Accounts, Other,
                                Motor Vehicle

9F155
Closing Agenda

* BANK ("Bank")
$_____ LOAN TO
* INC. ("Borrower")

<u>CLOSING AGENDA</u>

Date: _____ , 19____
Time: 10:00 a.m. EST
Place: Offices of [solicitor]
Parties Present: 1.   On behalf of Bank
                               —

                     2.   On behalf of Borrower
                               — Jane Doe
                     3.   On behalf of [solicitor]
                               —

                     4.   On behalf of Black & White, counsel to
                               the Borrower
                               —

                               —

Escrow: All deliveries, payments and the proceedings called for at
          closing shall be in escrow until all items on the closing agenda
          have been completed and all persons tendering or receiving
          documents at the closing acknowledge satisfaction with the
          same, at which time the escrow may be taken up by the
          respective parties described below and the proceedings will
          thereupon be effective.

A. Documents Already Completed

1.	Commitment letter dated _____ , 19____	done by Bank
2.	General Assignment of Book Debts	done by Bank
3.	Security over Inventory Agreement	done by Bank
4.	Guarantee of Jane Doe limited to $_____	done by Bank
5.	Guarantee of John Doe limited to $_____	done by Bank

B. Documents to be Delivered

No.	Document Description	Party Tabling	No. of Copies
1.	Certificate of Status for Borrower	Borrower	4
2.	Notarial copy of charter of Borrower	Borrower	4
3.	Notarial copy of by-laws of Borrower	Borrower	4
4.	Certificate of officer with certified copy of resolution of directors of Borrower authorizing the loan and the Security attached	Borrower	4
5.	Certificate of non-restriction on borrower	Borrower	4
6.	(a) General Security Agreement of Borrower to Bank	Borrower	4
	(b) PPSA financing statement	Bank	1+3P
	(c) Debtor's acknowledgement of copy of registration	Bank	4
7.	(a) Pledge of Shares in Borrower owned by Jane Doe	Borrower	4
	(b) Delivery of certificate no. _____ for 10 common shares, issued in name of Bank		1+3P
	(c) Certified copy of resolution of directors of Borrower authorizing the transfer for Jane Doe to Bank		4
8.	(a) Certified copy of Borrower's insurance policy naming Bank as loss payee	Borrower	1+3P
	(b) Letter of agent advising premiums paid		
9.	Evidence of Equity Injection of $_____	Borrower	4
10.	(a) Letter Bank accepting permitted emcumbrances	Bank	4
	(b) Letter of Bank waiving consent of Landlord	Bank	4
11.	Opinion letter of Black & White	Borrower	4
12.	Opinion letter of (solicitor) for this transaction	Bank	4

INDEX

Note: References are to paragraph number (i.e., 9470), form number (i.e., **9F32**), or checklist number (i.e., 9C9).

INDEX

C

Canada Revenue Agency
consent and authorization, **9F29**
search letter for, **9F28**
Canadian Human Rights Commission, 9.230
consent and authorization, **9F15**
search letter, **9F14**
Collective Agreement, 9.242
Competition Act
sale of a business, and 9.060 - 9.063
Confidentiality
solicitor-client privilege clause, **9F34**
Criminal Code
sale of a business, and, 9.290.1

E

Employer Health Tax
consent to release of information, **9F31**
sale of a business, and, 9.330
search letter, **9F30**
Employment Contracts
sale of a business, and, 9.310, 9.672
Employment Equity
sale of a business, and
federal, 9.230
search letter
federal, **9F16**
Employment Standards Act
sale of a business, and, 9.250
search letter, **9F4**, **9F19**
Environment
access and testing, alternative clauses, **9F35:2**
audit and cleanup
alternative clauses
extensive detailed, **9F35:4**
general, **9F35:3**
certificates of approval, 9.362
transfer, 9.363
checklist, 9C9, 9C9:1
considerations, 9.360-9.365
contractual arrangements, 9.365
contractual provisions, 9C9:1
due diligence, 9.364
liability, 9.361
limitations on vendor's obligations
alternative clauses, **9F35:8**
orders, clean up, 9.360
representations and warranties
extensive detailed, **9F35:6**
general, **9F35:5**
sale of property on 'as is' basis
alternative clauses, **9F35:1**
search letter, **9F17:14**

vendor's continuing responsibilities and indemnification
alternative clauses, **9F35:7**

Equipment
assignment of, **9F48**

F

Fixtures
sale of a business, and, 9.204

G

Goods and Service Tax (GST)
purchase and sale of a business
assets, 9.042, 9.043, 9.422
generally, 9.040, 9.420
shares, 9.041, 9.421
Grievances, 9.244

H

Human Rights Code (Ontario)
sale of a business, and, 9.270
Human Rights Commission (Ontario)
consent and authorization, **9F23**
search letter, **9F22**

I

Industrial Health and Safety
consent and authorization, **9F27**
request form, **9F26**
search letter, **9F25**

L

Labour Canada
contact list, 9.230
searches on sale of a business, 9.230
Labour Relations Board (Ontario)
sale of a business, and, 9.243
search letter, **9F17**
Land Transfer Tax
sale of a business, and, 9.075 - 9.078. *See also* Sale of a Business
Lease, 9F40
assignment of, **9F40**
landlord
certificate, **9F41**
consent to assignment, **9F42**
consent to mortgage, **9F43**
notice of, **9F39:2**
Letter
sale of a business, 9.100, **9F2**

INDEX

INDEX